OPERATION WORLD

OPERATION WORLD

A day-to-day guide to praying for the world

PATRICK JOHNSTONE

STL Books

WEC Publications

OPERATION WORLD

1st edition	Dorothea Mission	1974
2nd edition	STL	1978
revised	STL	1979
3rd edition	STL	1980
4th edition	(completely rewritten and enlarged) STL & WEC International	1986
Reprinted	STL & WEC International	1986
Reprinted	STL & WEC International	1987

British Library Cataloguing in Publication Data

Johnstone, P.J.

Operation world : a day-to-day guide to praying for the world.——4th ed.

1. Prayer

I. Title

264'.1 BV210.2

ISBN 1-85078-007-2

STL ISBN 1 85078 007 2

WEC ISBN 0 900828 42 0

STL Books are published by Send The Light
(Operation Mobilisation),
PO Box 48, Bromley, Kent, England
and PO Box 28, Waynesboro, GA 30830, USA.

Published jointly with WEC Publications,
Bulstrode, Gerrards Cross, Bucks. SL9 8SZ, England.

This book is also obtainable from WEC International as follows:
48 Woodside Avenue, Strathfield, NSW 2135, Australia.
37 Aberdeen Avenue, Hamilton, Ont. L8P 2N6, Canada.
PO Box 27264, Mt. Roskill, Auckland 4, New Zealand.
PO Box 47777, Greyville, 4023, Republic of South Africa.
Box 1707, Fort Washington, PA 19034, USA.

Cover designed by Gillard Bros. Graphics.

Typesetting and page make-up by WEC Press.

Production and printing by Nuprint Ltd, Harpenden, Herts AL5 4SE.

CONTENTS

INDEX

Key to Index

1. **BOLD CAPITALS** — Regions as defined in this book.
2. **Bold lower case** — states and territories included in the main body of the book.
3. Lower case — an alternative or commonly used name. The name used in the book follows in bold type.
4. *Lower case italics* — Either a name no longer used or a territory that has been absorbed by the state in brackets following.

Note:

1. Territories that have no page number are so small that they have not been described. These 10 territories have a total population of 15,000.

2. Some territories have, for brevity, been included **in** the state that rules them or **with** similar nearby territories.

3. There are 12 territories with no permanent inhabitants that have not been listed.

Specialized ministries are included in the prayer calendar for December.

The following have been selected from the many ministries and specific outreaches which operate worldwide.

PREFACE TO THE FOURTH EDITION

Operation World

As the fourth edition is published, it is appropriate to give a brief history of how such a book came to be written. This is partly a personal testimony and partly an expression of thanks to God and to the many who have made such a volume a reality.

This book is but one of a number of attempts throughout Christian history to give an account of the growth and status of Christianity. I owe a great debt to the remarkable ***World Christian Encyclopedia***, which has been published since the last edition of ***Operation World***, and to its editor, Dr David Barrett, for much encouragement and advice in the compilation of this edition.

This book is also one of a number of prayer surveys that have been published down the years. Perhaps an unusual feature in this volume is an attempt to bring facts and figures together with a spiritual burden and emphasis on prayer in a form that may touch and motivate Christians for world evangelization.

This is, therefore, NOT intended to be a complete reference book. I have not developed a comprehensive bibliography nor have I annotated sources. This would have greatly enlarged the book making it less suitable for its primary purpose.

The Origin of *Operation World*

1900 **Dr Andrew Murray**, that great man of God in South Africa, wrote a book entitled ***The Key to the Missionary Problem.*** Its subject matter is still so relevant that **CLC** published an edition in 1983 contemporized by Leona Choy. In this book Andrew Murray put out a challenge for Christians and churches to hold a **Week of Prayer for the World**. As far as I know that challenge was never really taken up over the following decades.

1943 God called **Hans von Staden** to preach the gospel in the rapidly developing urban slums of Southern Africa. The Dorothea Mission, under his leadership, became one of the early urban evangelistic agencies in that part of the world. Many people turned from sin and bondage to the liberty there is in Jesus Christ. Prayer was a major emphasis in the work. As a result, all of us who were workers of the Dorothea Mission received a wider vision for the world, and for this I will be eternally grateful.

1962 The Dorothea Mission arranged the first of what became a series of over 100 **Weeks of Prayer for the World**, which were convened in African and European countries. The author's first experience in his missionary career was to share in that first Week of Prayer.

1963 A small **Week of Prayer for the World** was arranged by Robert Footner and the author, in **Nairobi, Kenya**. The pressing need for prayer information, in written and visual form, impelled me to compile some sheets of world facts and figures for use during that time. This was the forerunner of the present volume!

1964 Hans von Staden encouraged me to write a booklet with prayer information on 30 needy countries for use in subsequent Weeks of Prayer for the world. He suggested the title ***Operation World***, which suitably expresses the vision of the book for spiritual warfare, active involvement and goal-oriented objectives we want to impart. That first publication was very simple and was produced on a Gestetner machine! It was later printed in West Germany.

1970 A new edition was proposed by Hans von Staden. I rashly said that any future edition would have to cover the world. I did not know what I was undertaking! The work began, using odd moments in a busy itinerant ministry of team evangelism and Bible translation in Zimbabwe (then Rhodesia). My office was the back of a van, or church vestries in dozens of towns and cities of that land. Two cardboard boxes served as a filing cabinet. There were frequent interruptions, mainly visits by African people seeking salvation or wanting to know more about the Christian life. My major problems were lack of any good missiological libraries and increasing postal isolation from the outside world. Rhodesia became ostracized by many countries around the world, and letters frequently had to be sent to informants via middle-men in other lands.

1974 The first full ***Operation World*** was lovingly and painstakingly typeset by the Dorothea Mission printer, **Kees Lugthart**. Unfortunately it was not possible to sell the 3-4,000 copies that were printed. Nevertheless copies of this book found their way around the world. **Dr Ralph Winter** in the USA arranged for a reprint in 1976, by the William Carey Library, in an adapted form and under the title "World Handbook for the World Christian".

1976 **Operation Mobilization** became involved. **George Verwer** pressed for an updated version of the book. This was completed in 1978 in Zimbabwe, and retyped and published by **STL Books** (**OM**) in Britain in 1978 with its present cover. The remarkable tie-up between the title of the book and that of the new publishers must have been planned by the Lord. It was certainly not premeditated.

1977 **Dave Hicks**, of **OM**, then director of the M.V.Logos, was moved to condense the information from the 1974 edition to produce prayer cards on 52 needy nations. This has expanded into a ministry of challenge to Christians in about 20 languages, which continues to this day; the number of prayer cards has increased to 72.

1978 The multiplication of ***Operation World*** versions in other languages began. Editions have now appeared in German, French, Portuguese, Spanish and half the book in Korean. Several revised editions in English were printed in 1979 and 1980.

1979 My wife, Jill, and I, received an invitation to become International Research Secretaries of WEC International. We were graciously released by the Dorothea Mission for this wider ministry which we assumed in 1980. But before taking up the post, we responded to an invitation from **OM** to participate in their work on the ship M.V.Logos for a year. That time spent in Asia and the Pacific was a thrilling and stimulating experience, and a valuable introduction to a wider public ministry of communicating the challenge for world evangelization. It was also an unusual way to return from Africa to our homeland in the UK, and an unforgettable, formative experience for our children Peter, Timothy and Ruth.

1983 Information gathering and writing began on the present edition. The pressures of combining this with a full ministry in **WEC**, and being involved in exciting new advances to unreached peoples, areas and cities by our mission, have not been easy. Learning to use a new technology in processing a vastly increased flow of information has been valuable, but it has taken time. It has taken three years, thousands of letters, hundreds of thousands of pages of reading, and months of typing, checking, and editing to prepare the manuscript for typesetting. The generosity of **MARC (World Vision)** and **OC Ministries** helped towards the purchase of computer equipment. Without the voracious reading and information culling of my wife, Jill, and the efficient typing of the manuscript into a computer by Diane Pfotzer, of the USA, and Violet Edson of WEC, UK, and the painstaking processing and checking of the statistics by Ian Case, this edition would never have been ready. The thousands of informants, correctors, advisers and checkers cannot all be named. May their reward one day be great, and their ministry enhanced and blessed through prayer stimulated by this volume!

1986 As this edition goes for publication, we send it out with fervent prayer that the Lord Jesus Christ may be glorified, the Church mobilized and world evangelization furthered. To Him be all the praise, for it is only by His grace that the spiritual battles to bring this book to completion have been won.

Patrick Johnstone
WEC International
Gerrards Cross
Bucks. SL9 8SZ
England.

THE ETHOS OF OPERATION WORLD

There are certain fundamental assumptions I have made in compiling this book. I realize that I cannot satisfy all readers, but I trust that in this edition I have been more appreciative of other theological and political points of view. However, my own perspectives inevitably influence the selection of material and opinions expressed, and for these I must accept responsibility.

All views here expressed are my own and not necessarily those of the publishers or of any organization mentioned in this book. I value constructive advice for future revisions. However, I have made the following decisions:

1. **Readership**. I am writing for those who can be broadly classified as evangelical Christians, i.e., those who believe the whole Bible to be the Word of God.

2. **Theology**. As an evangelical believer, I have sought to take a middle position in more controversial issues that perplex Evangelicals, such as church government, baptism, the sovereignty of God, the work of the Holy Spirit, social involvement, etc. The perceptive reader will, no doubt, see an unintended bias that reflects the author's own views!

3. **Politics**. Inevitably I have been more negative about regimes and political ideologies that put pressure on Christians *because* they are Christian, and have said less about those who still give Christians freedom to witness, but may manifest some most unpleasant traits in discrimination, use of money, oppression, etc. Occasionally, I have refrained from saying too much about some of the latter because it could have a negative effect on present Christian work in those countries.

4. **Time validity**. The text has been written with a view to validity for 1986-1990. Some minor revisions can be expected in future reprints before 1990. The fact that the statistics and text are computerized will facilitate future revisions and updates.

5. **A greater emphasis on the Church**. Earlier editions were rightly criticized for over-emphasizing mission agencies and the contribution of missionaries. I have sought to rectify this; but it is important to realize that it is often these very agencies that are the most efficient communicators of prayer information, hence the present system of highlighting mission initials. The churches planted by missions are often identified by the letters of that mission, but this does not signify continued colonial control!.

6. **The selection of agencies** mentioned is not intended to be an expression of favour or disfavour. I have sought to draw attention to some of international and interdenominational interest to English-speaking readers. Hopefully, the other language versions will give greater place to agencies based in their own language areas.

7. **The burden.** My longing is that the book will be seen as a tool for prayer. The spiritual tone and vision that expresses the heart of our heavenly Father is what should be in the forefront. All other issues **must** be secondary.

PRAYER [illegible]

AND WORLD EVANGELISATION

How often [illegible] place [illegible] the [illegible] in [illegible] [illegible] this [illegible] [illegible] and [illegible]

[illegible] whatever [illegible] the mind [illegible] [illegible] we [illegible] [illegible] of [illegible] make [illegible] God [illegible]

Prayer [illegible] the Kingdom of God. [illegible] Prayer [illegible] from [illegible] works, [illegible] the Lord [illegible] God [illegible] Scriptures [illegible]

[illegible]

1. [illegible] God. [illegible] [illegible] He had [illegible]

2. [illegible] God [illegible] could [illegible] as [illegible]

[illegible] that pray [illegible] [illegible] Gospel [illegible] and [illegible] to [illegible] most [illegible] and [illegible] prayer [illegible]

PRAYER
AND WORLD EVANGELIZATION

How often have you seen a wall-plaque with the words "Prayer Changes Things"? All believers readily give mental and verbal assent to this, but do we really believe it? What a difference there would be in our personal and corporate prayer life if we did. What a difference in the world too!

There is some confusion among believers about prayer. Is prayer just an act of obedience to a Sovereign God, or do we change His mind as did the importunate widow pleading her cause to the unjust judge? Unless we are utterly convinced of its essentiality and efficacy, we will never make prayer our central ministry as God intended.

Prayer is fundamental in the Kingdom of God. It is not an optional extra, nor is it a last resort when all other methods have failed. Prayerlessness is a sin (1 Sam. 12:23); without prayer God's plån for the world cannot be achieved. We do not just pray **for** the work, prayer **is** the work! Prayer lifts Christian activities from the realm of human effort to the divine. Someone made the statement "When man works, **man** works; when man prays, **God** works." Through prayer we become co-workers with the Lord God Almighty. We move from time into eternity, sharing in the eternal counsels of God. Would that we could grasp the significance of the ministry of intercession! Some unusual Scriptures can help us:

In Revelation 5:1-8:5 there is the magnificent mystery of the opening of the seven seals. Whether their primary application is future, past or present, is not relevant here, but certain principles are of abiding significance and can be applied today.

1. **Only the Lamb could open the seals**. All the earth-shaking, awesome forces unleashed on the world are released by the Lord Jesus Christ. He reigns today. He is in the control room of the universe. He is the only Ultimate Cause; all the sins of man and machinations of Satan ultimately have to enhance the glory and kingdom of our Saviour. This is true of our world today — in wars, famines, earthquakes, or the evil that apparently has the ascendancy. All God's actions are just and loving. We have become too enemy-conscious, and can over-do the spiritual warfare aspect of intercession. We need to be more God-conscious, so that we can laugh the laugh of faith **knowing** that we have power over all the power of the enemy (Luke 10:19). He has already lost control because of Calvary where the Lamb was slain. What confidence and rest of heart this gives us as we face a world in turmoil and in such spiritual need.

2. **Only through the prayers of the saints** will God's purposes be carried out (Rev. 5:8 and 8:1-5). The seventh seal, the final one, is unusual! Why was there silence in heaven for half-an-hour? It was not just for dramatic effect, or the silence before the storm. It was because God would not act until His people prayed. Once their prayers had risen to the throne, God poured out the fire from the altar upon the earth. The fire of the Spirit comes in answer to prayer (Acts 1:4, 14; Acts 2:1-8), but so does the fire of judgement! James and John wanted to call down fire from heaven on the Samaritans (Luke 9:54), but in rebuking them Jesus did not **deny** they could! How the Saviour longed to kindle that fire (Luke 12:49). We now have that awesome authority as we pray in the Spirit! Let us use it.

The implications are immense. Do you realise that prayer may have brought about the Soviet invasion of Afghanistan? This was judgement on a nation that had resisted Christianity and killed those who responded to the gospel message; and it was also redemptive, for never before have Afghans been so exposed and open to the gospel as today. Is it possible that mighty intercessions for China stirred up Communism and the Cultural Revolution to turn an unresponsive nation into one of the most astonishing areas of Christian expansion the world has ever seen? Can it be that the Sahelian famines and Latin American revolutions may be the means of gospel breakthroughs long prayed for? It is a solemn thing to intercede for the nations of the world!

Let us mobilize prayer! We can tip the scales of history. Christians can be the controlling factor in the unfolding drama of today's world — let us not allow ourselves to be chased around by the enemy, but let us go up at once and take the kingdoms of this world for Jesus (Num. 13:30; Dan. 7:18) — He is delighted to give them to us (Dan. 7:22 and 27; Luke 12:32).

In practical terms, may these truths make our prayer lives as individuals, and in prayer meetings, outward-looking, Satan-shaking, captive-releasing, kingdom-taking, revival-giving, Christ-glorifying power channels for God!

Operation World is written to provide fuel for such prayer meetings. May fire from the altar fall on every place and people named in this volume!

How to use OPERATION WORLD

The whole book has been restructured for use together with a prayer diary. Various Christian agencies produce such diaries every year. To name two:

1. **World Wide Publications (Billy Graham Assoc.** and **YWAM)**
   1303 Hennepin Avenue, Minneapolis, Minnesota 55403, USA.
2. **Chinese Coordination Centre of World Evangelism (CCCOWE)**
   Prayer Diary edited by Thomas Wang
   P.O. Box 98435, Tsim Sha Tsui, Hong Kong.

You may find it useful to order one.

Many have made valuable suggestions for using *Operation World.* The wealth of information could otherwise be rather overwhelming. Here are a few simple and practical ideas:

1. **In the home**
   a) **Pray through the book** using the running calendar.
   b) **Pray more specifically for one of the eight regions.** You will find an index of the states and territories in each region between pages 42 and 82. The region is indicated in the upper box above the calendar date. The index includes a suggested monthly prayer cycle for each region, and some other useful information.
   c) **Pray for a different area of the world each day of the week** by selecting one or two items from one country at a time in that region, e.g.,

Africa	Sunday
Asia	Monday
Eastern Europe	Tuesday
Latin America	Wednesday
Middle East	Thursday
Pacific & Caribbean	Friday
The West	Saturday

   Some practical points:
   a) **News items** — turn them into prayer after reading about the spiritual needs of the lands mentioned.
   b) **Prayer letters and missionary magazines** can become more meaningful once the background is known.
   c) **Loose-leaf copies of *Operation World*** have been requested by some. The technical and marketing problems involved would make it a very expensive production. Why not do it yourself? A printer would quickly cut off the binding for you!

2. **In local churches**
Missions should be at the heart of every church fellowship. Sadly this is often not the case, because information is not readily available. Use ***Operation World*** to inform and challenge believers to prayer.
   a) **Church services**. Use the church bulletin to quote relevant excerpts for prayer. This will bring world vision to the fore in the heart of the congregation.
   b) **Prayer meetings**. Background information in ***Operation World*** can be used to stimulate more informed prayer for the ministry and goals of missionaries with whom the fellowship is linked.
   c) **Magazines** and church periodicals may be effective means for disseminating prayer needs to a wider Christian readership. Please obtain the publishers' permission for reprinting substantial portions for wider distribution; we may have more up-to-date information to help you further.

3. **In teaching on missions**. Many Bible schools, seminaries and training programmes have made use of earlier editions for teaching purposes. This stimulates an interest and concern for world evangelization, and challenges students to consider commitment to missionary service.

4. **Prayer Days, Prayer Conferences and Concerts of Prayer**. The original purpose of this book was to provide prayer fuel for weeks of prayer for the world. Here are a few guidelines for prayer session leaders:

a) **Be brief**. The people are gathered to *pray*, and not to be impressed by the amount of information presented! Only a quarter to one-third of the time should be set aside for reporting on the need.

b) **Be personal**. We have deliberately refrained from mentioning individuals, but rather to give the overall situation in a given country. Personal information on individual workers, etc., may be added by the leader.

c) **Be selective**. Too many facts will not be retained unless they are written down. Rather select those items for prayer that will challenge and burden believers long after the meeting.

d) **Beware of statistics:** too many figures make any report very dull! This is why the statistical sections are in a smaller type. Only choose those statistics that specifically apply to the prayer items you mention. The many figures are given so that you may have the facts available.

e) **Be dependent** on the leading of the Holy Spirit. The burdens imparted by Him will inspire others to pray in the Spirit, and move them into God's will for their lives. This could mean commitment in intercession, financial giving, or even going to a particular area or people for which prayer has been made.

EXPLANATION OF THE STATISTICS

Please read this chapter before using the statistics given.

Every regional and country section is divided into two parts:

1. The two columns of statistical background information.
2. The specific items for prayer.

The statistics are included as background to the prayer information, hence the difference in type size!

A brief explanation of their significance is given below. A fuller explanation of the sources and how these figures were handled is given in appendices 5 and 6.

Availability, consistency and accuracy of secular, religious and Christian statistics vary enormously from country to country and among denominations. Inadequate sources, varying dates of publication and my further editing and compiling of the statistics all add to the margin of error. I have used the most recent and reliable information available to me. I therefore plead for the sympathy of the reader in any errors or discrepancies! Any more recent surveys, or statistics that could improve the accuracy of future editions would be most gratefully received by the author at the address at the end of the Preface.

I trust that these figures are sufficient to give a reasonably balanced and objective evangelical perspective of the world today. It is encouraging to see what God *is* doing!

All statistics apply to June 1985 unless otherwise stated in the text. In many cases this has meant that I have had to project from earlier known statistics according to estimated growth rates prevailing at that time.

Area in square kilometres. This is rounded to the nearest 1,000 sq.km. in all but the smaller territories. The area given does not imply approval or disapproval of the status quo in 1985, but is a reflection of the actual situation. Disputed territories, such as the West Bank of Jordan (Palestine) and the Falkland Islands (Malvinas) are in this category but are respectively included under Israel, and as a British colony.

Population: Rounded to the nearest 100,000 people in the larger nations.

Peoples: The ethnic diversity is listed in a manner considered to be the most helpful for the reader. Major groupings of peoples are given as a **percentage** of the total population. The larger ethnic groups within those groupings are given in **absolute numbers**, and are valid for June 1985. Smaller ethnic groups are not mentioned by name, but are included in the total, as are all identifiable groups of refugees and migrants from other lands. The world and regional totals, therefore, represent the sum total of all the identifiable **ethno-linguistic people groups within a nation**, i.e. the Indian Tamil may be included 13-14 times as a separate identity because identifiable groups exist in that number of states.

Literacy: The highest publicized figure is given. **Functional** literacy may be much lower!

Official languages were those known to be recognized as such in June 1985.

All languages: This represents the total of all indigenous languages spoken within each nation. The figure is quoted from the Ethnologue (**SIL**) unless fuller information was available elsewhere. The regional and world totals are simply an addition of the figures for each country, i.e. English and French, as world languages, are enumerated many times in the regional totals.

Bible translations: The number of languages in which there is a full Bible (Bi), or only a New Testament (NT), or just portions (por) is given. Comparing these three totals with the number of languages in the country will give a rough guide as to the extent of need for Bible translation work. Further information is given in the points for prayer.

Capitals and cities: Populations are UN estimates for 1985 for **conurbations**, and not just the population that may live within specific municipal boundaries. The figures given are often significantly higher than those officially quoted. Most world class cities are mentioned by name, i.e. those with populations that exceed 1,000,000.

Economy: The "income/person" is the total Gross National Product in US dollars divided by the total population. The sum derived is compared to the average income per person in the USA. It is an approximate guide to the relative living standards of the different nations of the world.

Politics: The brief comments are intended to be aids to prayer, and not a full political assessment. It is hopefully not too biassed by the author's own viewpoint!

Religion

1. **Non-Christian religions** are listed in order of numerical importance.

2. **Six ecclesiological types of Christians** have been used: Roman Catholics, Other Catholics, Orthodox, Indigenous marginal groups, Foreign marginal groups and Protestants. The Protestants are always placed last in the list.

3. **The percentage of Christians** represents the total number who are claimed to be Christian, either by individuals themselves in a government census, or by the churches to which they are affiliated; whichever percentage is the larger being the figure used.

4. Where the official percentage of Christians is significantly higher than that claimed by the churches, additional figures for nominal and affiliated Christians are given.

5. All subsequent percentages for the various ecclesiastical families add up to the **affiliated** figure and *not* the total figure, which also includes nominal Christians.

6. In countries where many Christians have double affiliation, or have joined other churches or religions without severing links with their original group, the official figures of larger denominations have been adjusted accordingly. This is an attempt to simplify the methodology used in the ***World Christian Encyclopedia.***

7. Practising or churchgoing percentages are given where known. These are percentages of the total number of adherents.

8. Two figures are given for each ecclesiastical type: first, adherents (a); second, adult or communicant members (m).

9. Where useful, the larger denominations are listed in order of numerical size of adherents or adult members. I have not been able to be consistent in using adherents or adult members because of the great diversity in understanding of the term "members" by different denominations. I have used the one which most nearly reflects the majority of statistics gathered.

10. All figures are projections to June 1985, but these have frequently been derived from much earlier and sometimes unreliable figures. Where there is much uncertainty I have used "approx", "est." or "(?)". Many churches do not keep statistics, so hopefully these estimates are helpful.

11. **Evangelical** percentages are carefully derived according to the methodology described in Appendix 5. However, the degree of accuracy is reduced in lands where there are large traditional denominations to which the majority of the population belongs. The assessment of the evangelical percentage becomes more subjective!

12. **Missionary statistics.** These are hard to obtain — especially for Third World countries. I suspect that in some lands many cross-cultural missionaries have not been included. All known missionaries serving longer than one year are included in the figures.

a) **Missionaries TO a country** represent foreigners who enter the land for ministry. The ratio of missionaries to population is a means of comparing the relative concentrations of foreign missionaries in different lands.

b) **Missionaries FROM WITHIN a country** represent all those known to minister across **cultural** barriers either within or outside their own nation; or those serving in itinerant or executive leadership positions based in their homelands. This avoids the more artificial distinction that crossing a **national** boundary defines who is, and who is not, a missionary! The ratio of missionaries to Protestant adherents gives a measure of the missionary involvement of the Protestant Church in each country.

ABBREVIATIONS

A full list of **organizational** abbreviations in **bold** type is given in Appendix 2 together with contact addresses.

A full list of other **abbreviations** is given in Appendix 3.

Some important **definitions** of concepts and words such as church, people group, unreached people group, evangelical, revival, missionary, etc., are given in Appendix 4.

A few important abbreviations essential for understanding the following pages are given below:

1. **a & m** are frequently used in Christian statistics.

   a = affiliated Christians or **a**dherents, and represents the wider Christian community associated with a church or group of churches. It includes the children of believers, regular church attenders and any who could be considered part of the wider fellowship of that church.

   m = adult or communicant **m**embers.

2. **approx.**; **est.**; **(?)** have been used to express uncertainty about the accuracy of the statistics to which they apply.

3. **Bi**; **NT**; **por** refer to the number of languages into which **Bi**bles, **N**ew **T**estaments and Scripture **por**tions have been translated and *not* the number of translations available in a national language.

4. **The graphs**. We have included two small but simple graphs with every country, where useful, to show the change of religious affiliations over this century, and to show the growth or decline of Evangelicals as a percentage of the total population. A brief explanation of their meaning is given below (in reverse order).

The meaning of Graph 2.

The growth of evangelical Christian adherents as a percentage of the total population is shown.

The dotted line represents the position in 1985.

The time scale is *different* to the previous graph and only covers 1950-2000, the period of the most dramatic change for Evangelicals in history.

The percentage of the population indicated *varies* between countries. So carefully note the scale on the right hand side before comparisons are made.

Occasionally the evangelical growth is compared with that of another religious group over the same period. In that case it can be identified by the letter beside the line, and compared with the line for the Evangelicals, which is marked as 'E'.

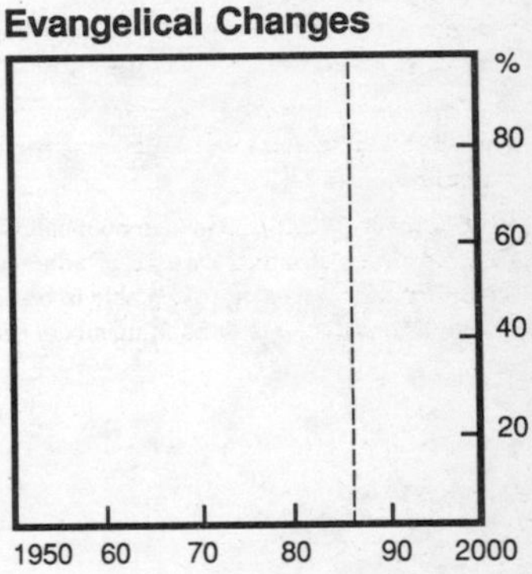

The meaning of graph 1

The purpose of the graph is to show the growth of the missionary religions over this century.

The non-Christian religions and ideologies are shown from the **top downwards.**

The major Christian traditions are shown from the **bottom upwards.** Where the number of Christians is very small only the total Christian population is given.

Usually the population from where most converts are being drawn is indicated in the middle.

The small unshaded portions in between indicate the total of either non-Christian or Christian religions or traditions too small in percentage to be of significance here. Please refer to the accompanying statistics for that country to identify them.

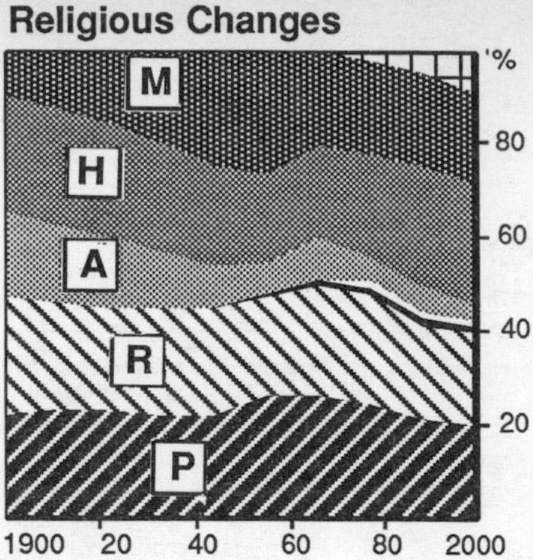

Key to the figures

The time scale on the bottom line is 1900-2000.

1985 is the year for which the statistics in this book are valid. 1985-2000 represents projections through that period.

The right hand vertical scale allows the proportions of the major religious groups to be seen in comparison with each other, and as a percentage of the country's total population.

Key to shading

Non-Christian

- N **Non-religious/ Atheist**
- M **Muslim**
- H **Hindu**
- B **Buddhist/Chinese/ Japanese religions**
- J **Jews**
- A **Traditional religions/Animist/ Spiritist**/etc.
- **Various. Other.**

Christian

- S **Marginal, Sects**
- O **Orthodox**
- R **Roman Catholic**
- P **Protestant**
- **Christian** (general)

The letter on the graph will help identify the religion without referring constantly to this key. It is usually the **first** letter of the religion listed under the **Religion** section. Only the more significant religions are shaded and labelled.

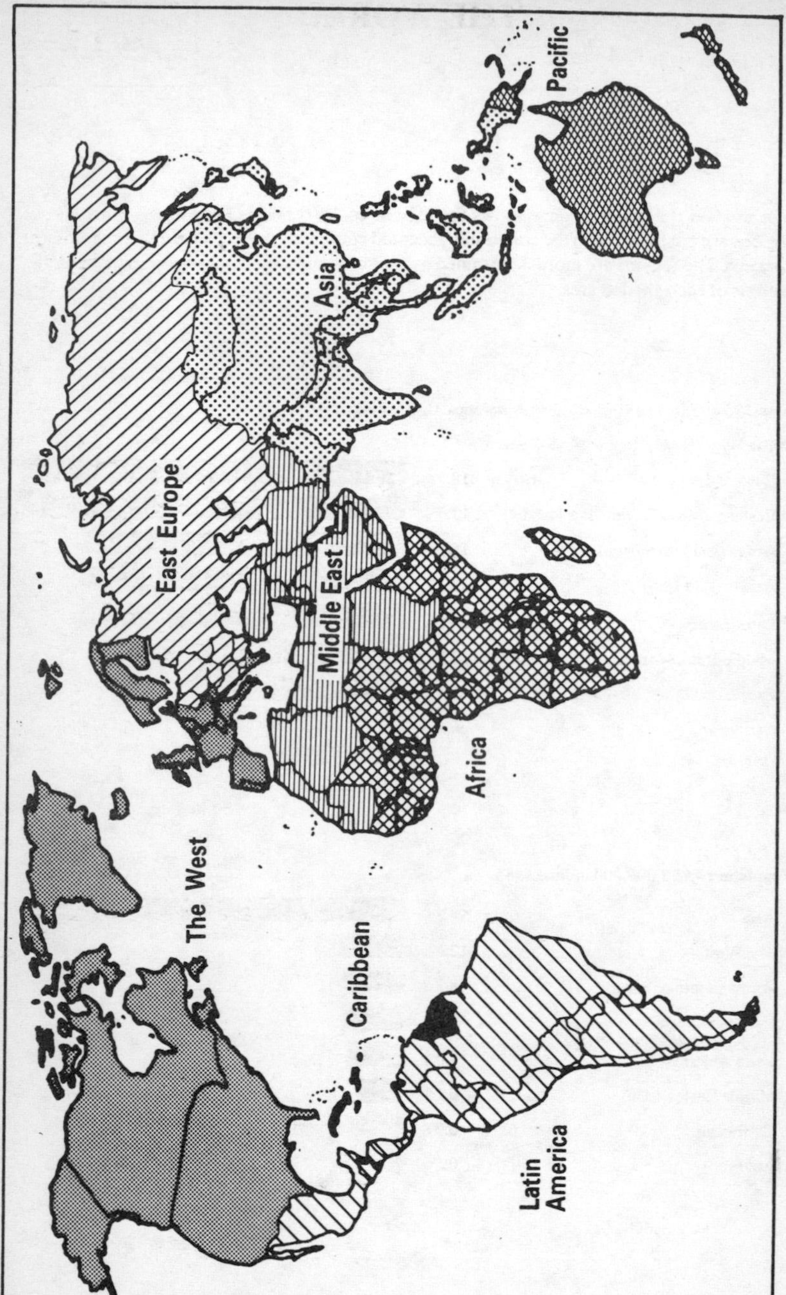
East Europe
Asia
Pacific
Middle East
Africa
The West
Caribbean
Latin America

THE WORLD

Jan 1-5

The map on the opposite page shows the regions of the world as used in this book. These regions are not identical to the commonly accepted continents, which is a purely geographical concept. The regions are more determined by the socio-political commonalities that link the nations of each shaded area.

Area 135,695,000 sq.km. excluding Antarctica. Divided in this survey into:

The West (North America and Western Europe)	18.5%
Eastern Europe (including all USSR)	17.5%
Africa (south of Sahara)	15.4%
Asia (east of Iran)	15.2%
Latin America	14.6%
Middle East (Morocco to Afghanistan)	12.0%
Pacific (including Australia)	6.3%
Caribbean	0.5%

Population 4,825,000,000 in June 1985.

Asia	54.7%
The West	12.8%
Africa (South of Sahara)	8.7%
Eastern Europe	8.6%
Latin America	7.8%
Middle East	6.2%
Caribbean	0.7%
Pacific	0.5%

Annual growth 1.7%. The rate increased rapidly this century, but is now gradually slowing. Annual growth rates in regions:

Africa	2.9%
Middle East	2.8%
Latin America	2.4%
Caribbean	1.8%
Asia	1.7%
The Pacific	1.2%
Eastern Europe	0.8%
The West	0.4%

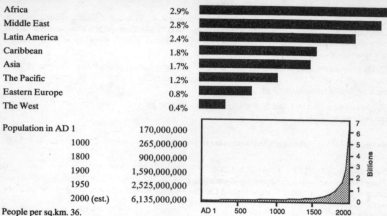

Population in AD	1	170,000,000
	1000	265,000,000
	1800	900,000,000
	1900	1,590,000,000
	1950	2,525,000,000
	2000 (est.)	6,135,000,000

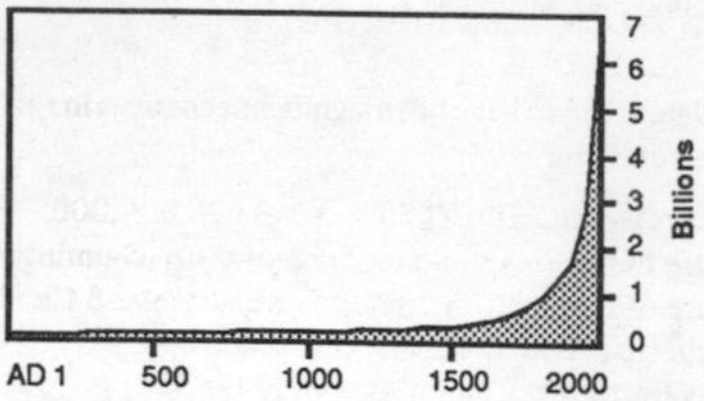

People per sq.km. 36.

Peoples: There are various ways of dividing up the world's population:

a) Nations and territories with over 1,000 people: 218.

b) All languages in the world (excluding dialects): 5,455 (**SIL** figure).

c) All languages as a sum of total spoken in each nation or territory: 8,287 (i.e. English, French and Spanish are counted many times since they are so widely spoken).

d) All distinct ethno-linguistic groups with a sufficient distinctiveness within each nation for which church planting may be necessary: 12,017. It is probable that nearly 9,000 of these already have a viable church within the culture, and therefore are at least minimally reached. There remain over 3,000 for which cross-cultural church planting ministries have either been inititiated, or will need to be, if all races, tribes, peoples and tongues (Rev. 7:9-10) are to be represented before the throne of the Lamb.

Cities: World class cities are defined as those of over one million inhabitants. There are 305 of these. This survey uses the (generally) higher figure for conurbations (i.e. satellite cities and suburbs) rather than the more strictly defined metropolitan areas. **Urbanization** 41%.

Economy: Major trends are discernible.

1. **The unequal distribution of the world's wealth.**
The more industrial northern nations have become richer and the less developed south poorer. Some small states with large oil reserves became very wealthy. Income/person in more developed countries: $9,380 (66% of USA) and in less developed countries $700 (5% of USA).

2. **The oil price rises of 1974 and 1978** radically altered the world's economy, trade patterns, and development programmes. Economic growth slowed or stopped. Many nations slid into debt on a massive scale. The poorer nations suffered particularly severely because of the decline in the value of agricultural and other mineral exports and the misuse of public funds. It remains to be seen whether the collapse of high oil prices in 1985/6 will reverse these trends.

3. **The lack of effective long-term development programmes for the Third World.** High population growth and human abuse of natural resources are changing weather patterns, causing famines of ever greater severity and enormous socio-political stresses.

4. **The shift of economic power** from the north Atlantic to the Pacific nations. All these have significant implications for the spread of the gospel.

Politics: Some major features of the past 40 years that vitally influence the world today:

1. **The post-World War II break-up of the old colonial empires.** Since 1943 there have been 96 nations that have gained their freedom from colonial rule. This independence has not brought spiritual freedom.

2. **The rise of two major power blocs.** The so-called First World (predominantly Western nations and Japan) is being challenged by the expansion of Soviet-led Second World Communist nations. The vast military expenditure of wealth on expensive weapons of terrifying destructiveness has increased the potential for military disasters too horrible to contemplate. The widespread and indiscriminate export of such weapons has multiplied and prolonged localized wars. The resulting fear and insecurity have opened hearts and minds to the Prince of peace.

3. **The multiplication of ethnic nationalist movements**. Ethnic minorities all over the world have been pressing for cultural and social identity, self-rule or independence. This has increased tensions, guerrilla warfare and international terrorism all over the world.

4. **The development of communications** has shrunk the world. Rapid air travel, satellite communications, computers, photocopiers, etc., have broken down age-old cultural and geographical barriers, and turned our world into a global village. An event in one part of the world can provoke almost immediate reaction in other continents.

5. **The vast movements of population** have led to the cultural and religious diversification of many countries. The reasons for these movements are many — migration for better jobs, refugees from persecution, famine and war, etc.

The factors described in 4. and 5. give unprecedented opportunities for evangelism among hitherto unreached peoples.

Religion: There have been significant changes in religious affiliation this century. The graphs below indicate some of them.

Non-religious/Atheist 20%. Total 970,000,000.
There has been a rapid increase of those claiming no religious affiliation. This has largely been at the expense of nominal Christianity in Europe and Chinese religions in Asia. There are about 20 states in the world that claim to be Marxist-Leninist.

Muslim 18.4%. Total 890,000,000.
Most live in the great belt of territory stretching from West Africa to Central and South East Asia. It is the majority religion in 37 nations and a significant minority of over 1% in 44 others. Growth this century has been steady; predominantly through an above-average birthrate, and also through conversions in parts of Africa, India and Indonesia. The Muslim world is undoubtedly the hardest field for Christian mission work and Islam the most vigorous of the non-Christian missionary religions.

Hindu 13.1%. Total 630,000,000.
The majority religion of three nations, and a significant minority in 11 other lands. Hinduism has made notable missionary inroads among young people in the West.

Buddhist/Chinese/Japanese, folk religions 11.5%. Total 556,000,000.
Buddhism is the state religion of five nations in Asia, the majority in a further four, and a significant minority in yet another 11. Of this total about 196,000,000 are followers of the mixture of Chinese religions Taoism, Confucianism and Buddhism. The various religious systems are so intermingled that a clear differentiation is hard to make.

Jews 0.32%. Total 15,350,000.
About 52% of these are in the West, 23% in Communist lands and only 19% in their national homeland, Israel.

Animist/traditional religions 2.8%. Only about 135,000,000, and the percentage is steadily falling.

Other 1.4%. Numerous other smaller religious groups: Sikh 16,000,000; Various new religions 12,000,000; Spiritist 6,708,000; Baha'i 4,440,000; Jain 3,349,000; Parsee 172,000, etc.

Christian 32.4%. Total 1,563,000,000. Nominal 3.4%. Affiliated 29%. 1,398,000,000a.
The serious decline in Europe has been offset by the thrilling growth elsewhere, but the overall percentage change has been small this century. Christianity is the majority religion of five of the eight areas into which the world has been divided in this book. Of the 215 states and territories described only 20 have a resident population that is less than 1% Christian. Christianity has truly become a **world** religion in this century. Only a small proportion of this number would actually be born-again Christians; but God alone knows how many! The Lamb's book of life would make fascinating reading!

Roman Catholic 17.5%. Total 846,000,000. Affiliated 16.4%. 793,000,000a.
Catholics are in the majority in 58 states and territories, and a significant minority of over 1% in 106 more. The largest numbers are to be found in Latin America, Europe, parts of Africa and the Philippines. The Vatican II Council brought radical changes to the Church. For a time, the charismatic movement had a deep impact, but this has somewhat diminished in the 1980s. Pope John-Paul II has reduced the degree of theological diversity within the Church by emphasizing a more conservative position.

Orthodox 3.2%. Total 155,000,000. Affiliated 2.5%. 120,300,000a.
Orthodox Christians are in the majority in four lands and compose more than 1% of the population in a further 19. The majority of Orthodox Christians live in Eastern Europe, Ethiopia, or are diverse minority groups in the Middle East.

Marginal groups 1.2%. Total 57,000,000. Affiliated 1%. 49,400,000a.
Diverse Western and "Third World" marginal groups are included. Worldwide movements of Western origin, such as the Mormons and Jehovah's Witnesses, and syncretic African groups are the largest.

Protestant 10.4%. Total 501,000,000. Affiliated 8.8%. 426,000,000a.

The 51,000,000 Anglicans are included in this total. Protestants are in the majority in 35 states and compose over 1% of the resident population in 111 more. The majority live in North America, Northern Europe, the Pacific and parts of Africa, and a growing number in Asia (particularly China). Those Protestants who could be classified as Evangelicals (see definitions in Appendix 4) number approximately 245,451,000, or 5.1%, of the world's population. Nearly half of these would be adult or communicant members of these churches and denominations. The growth of Evangelicals as a percentage of the world's population is shown in graph 2. The bar graph below compares the regional concentrations of Evangelicals.

Region	Number of Evangelicals	% of region's population
The West	72.2 mn.	11.7%
Asia	71.5 mn.	2.7%
Africa	47.8 mn.	11.4%
Latin America	34.3 mn.	9.1%
Eastern Europe	11.5 mn.	2.8%
Pacific	4.3 mn.	17.6%
Caribbean	2.6 mn.	7.9%
Middle East	0.8 mn.	0.3%
Total	245.0 mn.	5.1%

Missionaries to the world 81,000 in approximately 1,800 Protestant missionary sending agencies. Of these about 650 agencies are based in North America, 500 in Europe and an increasing number in other parts of the world. The number of missionaries serving the Lord is given according to regional origin. I have made a distinction between Western and non-Western missionaries to indicate the thrilling growth from lands that have not traditionally sent out missionaries. Truly, we are seeing a healthy world mobilization of missionary workers that we should encourage in prayer!

Religious Changes

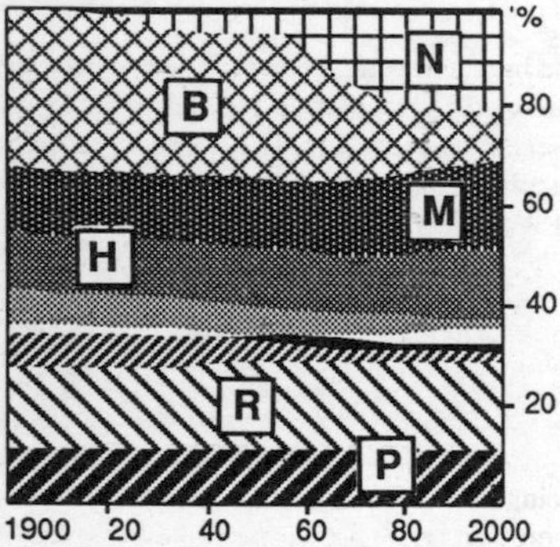

Evangelical Changes

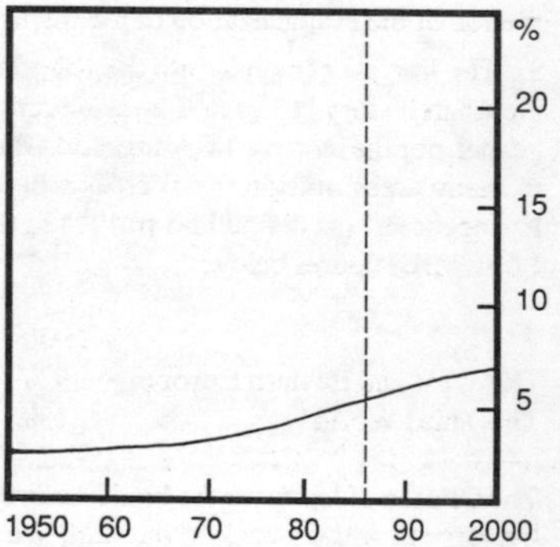

	Westerners		Non-Westerners	
from	Number	Percentage of total	Number	Percentage of total
North America	49,000	60.5	—	—
Europe	16,047	19.8	—	—
Pacific	4,250	5.3	343	0.4
Africa	960	1.2	1,755	2.2
Asia	—	—	7,107	8.8
Latin America	—	—	1,314	1.6
Caribbean	—	—	121	0.1
Middle East	—	—	111	0.1
TOTALS	70,257	86.7%	10,751	13.3%
In 1978 the total figures were estimated to be:				
	56,600	90%	6,600	10%

Of the 81,000 world total of Protestant missionaries, an estimated 51,750 have moved from their homeland to reside in a foreign land. The breakdown by region:

To		Ratio missionaries to population
Asia	12,806	1 : 206,000
Africa	12,661	1 : 33,100
Latin America	11,262	1 : 33,500
The West	7,328	1 : 84,500
Pacific	3,735	1 : 6,540
Caribbean	1,948	1 : 16,400
Middle East	1,564	1 : 190,200
Eastern Europe	440	1 : 950,000

The worldwide advance of the gospel

An immense unseen battle rages in the heavenlies between the armies of the Lord Jesus Christ and the hosts of darkness. To us on earth the outcome may appear to be in doubt, yet it is not, for Christ has already won the victory. Even from an earthly viewpoint there is already much to encourage God's people as they participate in this warfare by prayer. In subsequent pages there are many praise items given, but here are a few of global importance for which praise should be given to our Living God. May these praise points lead on to prayer for the completion of the evangelization of the world!

1. **The harvest of people into the Kingdom of God in recent years has been unprecedented.** Never in history has such a high percentage of the world's population been exposed to the gospel, nor the increase of evangelical Christians been so encouraging. The rate of ingathering in many areas outside the West has been spectacular. The share of the percentage of "all Evangelicals" (as defined on p. 496) in the Third World has steadily increased this century. Look at the figures below:

	1800	1900	1960	1970	1980	1985
The West and Eastern Europe	99%	91%	68%	64%	50%	34%
The Third World	1%	9%	32%	36%	50%	66%

The Church of Jesus may be battle-scarred and facing serious internal and external problems, but it is not with its back to the wall! We are moving forward — let us speed the progress by prayer.

2. **The growth of evangelical believers in the Third World** has accelerated dramatically since World War II, with 1975-85 seeing the fastest growth. During that period Evangelicals in the West and Eastern Europe increased by 1.3% annually. The total number was 75 million in 1975 and nearly 86 million in 1985. In the Third World (omitting China) the increase was 6.7% annually, and the total number grew from 68 million to 130 million.

3. **The dramatic breakthrough in China** since 1975 is hard to quantify. Reliable estimates are that 45-50 million people may have come to faith in Christ since then. This increase, if substantiated, would mean that evangelical believers have increased in the Third World from 74 million to 174 million, or an average annual increase of 9%.

4. **The greatest growth** has occurred in some Asian lands, Latin America, and in Africa's Bible belts. Parts of South Asia, the Middle East and parts of Africa are a sobering contrast. These latter are the major pioneering areas for missionaries in the last part of this century. Please see the regional descriptions for more detail.

5. **The Muslim world is a major challenge**, but the last 10 years have been more encouraging than ever before. Despite the rise of Islamic fundamentalism Muslims have been more exposed to the gospel, and been more responsive to it, than ever before. It is still "the day of small things" (Zech. 4:10), but the number of converts out of Islam has increased, and for the first time churches have come into being in a number of Muslim cities and nations. The cracks in the seemingly impenetrable wall of Islam can be widened by prayer!

6. **Communist territorial gains have not been an ideological success**. On the contrary, Communist-instigated revolutions, wars and takeovers have opened up new opportunities for the Word of God to enter the hearts of hitherto unreached peoples that were once hardened to the gospel — both within those countries and among refugees from them. Yet the persecution and suffering of the Church in these lands is often acute, and the burden carried by the believers is heavy. Believers around the world must share it with them.

7. **The extent of the unfinished task is enormous**, but we are making progress! Never before have we had such a clear picture of what remains to be done. We have a task which can be achieved! The Great Commission has two major goals:

i) **To preach the gospel to every creature** (Mark 16:15). This is the challenge to evangelism. It is estimated that possibly 60-77% of the world's population has had some exposure to the claims of Christ (depending on one's definition of what degree of exposure and understanding is needed). This means that there may be between one and two billion who have never been evangelized in such a way that they can respond to the gospel, and those numbers are steadily dropping, despite world population growth.

ii) **To make disciples of all peoples** (i.e., biblical nations) (Matthew 28:18-20). All the distinct races, tribes, peoples and tongues of the world must be so discipled that there are *at a minimum* some representatives of every one of them among the redeemed before the Throne of the Lamb (Rev. 7:9-10). The measurable minimum, or goal, is for us to see at least one or two viable, witnessing fellowships of believers or churches in every one of these peoples. In this survey we have estimated the total number of ethno-linguistic people groups within the nations of the world to be 12,017. We also estimate that there may be viable churches in around 8,000-9,000 of these, but there are possibly 3,000-4,000 peoples without any Christian witness — some are very small minorities within a nation, others are quite large. Many are praying that we may achieve our goal by AD 2000.

The Church

The whole of God's plan of redemption centres round the Church of His beloved Son. This is why He called Abraham (Gen. 12:3; Gal. 3:8). It is for the Church that Christ died (Eph. 2:16), and as its Head He lives (Eph. 1:22). As part of His Body, our longing should be for its upbuilding and perfection (Col. 1:24). One day soon the Bride of Christ, the Church, will be complete and perfect (Eph. 5:27; Rev. 7:9-10)!

The Church on earth is only an imperfect manifestation of the one, true and invisible Church of the Lord Jesus Christ, yet we are promised by Jesus that the gates of hell will not prevail against it. In some lands there are hundreds of thousands of congregations and in others may be only one or two. The wheat and the tares are mixed, the divisions and weaknesses are all too plain and obvious, yet the Holy Spirit is working in and through the Church in all its diversity of doctrines, denominations, languages and personalities. It is through the Church that God wants redemption to be proclaimed to mankind. Prayer points through the book major on the needs of the Church. Here are a few suggested items of wider application:

1. **The effective functioning of local congregations**. Each should be an organism, a body. Each member has gifts to contribute to the upbuilding of the whole, yet rarely do congregations function in this way. This emphasis on "body life" has come into prominence in the past two decades. May every congregation be an effective body through which the Holy Spirit can work!

2. **Leadership is the key**. Pastors, ministers and elders need constant upholding in prayer. There is a worldwide lack of men and women truly called of God and deeply taught in the Scriptures to lead the churches — people willing to suffer scorn, poverty and the shame of the Cross for the sake of the Saviour who redeemed them. Those who accurately and effectively expound the Scriptures are few, especially in areas where the churches are growing rapidly. May all leaders be an example to their flocks in holy living, evangelism and missionary concern for a lost world!

3. **Spiritual depth is rare** in many congregations. Superficiality, an inadequate devotional life and worldliness are common. This highlights the need for effective teaching of the content, doctrines, and applicability to life and witness, of the Word of God in the mother tongue.

4. **Victorious optimism** is rare where evangelical believers are a small and despised minority. These believers are often introspective and timid, and hardly a mighty force for the pulling down of the fortifications of the devil. Believers need prayer that they may witness boldly and effectively.

5. **Purity of doctrine**. Too often believers' thoughts, prejudices and fears are moulded more by the prevailing culture, philosophies, superstitions and religions of the society around them than by the Bible. Humanism in the West, Hinduism in India, etc., are examples. All such can rob Christians of their assurance, power and joy in the face of a hostile world, and sidetrack believers into secondary or irrelevant issues.

6. **Young people** in this modern age are often lost to the church and become worldly, even after a Christian upbringing, because of a growing generation gap. Every new generation needs to be evangelized afresh, or the churches soon become nominal. Young people need prayer as never before.

7. **Revival** has occurred in various parts of the world this century (see Regions), but not on the scale, nor with the effect, for which believers long in this critical and momentous time of history.

8. **Missionary vision**. An Acts 1:8 strategy is needed for every church and denomination. Amazing results have been achieved by a dedicated few. How speedily the world would be evangelized if all believers and every congregation obeyed the commands of Jesus in Acts 1, and believed His promises for the enablement through the Holy Spirit. Pray for the awakening and growth of missionary concern. Pray for effective and practical missionary involvement in praying, giving and going.

The Harvest Force

The Church is God's means for evangelizing the world, but from New Testament times men and women as individuals and teams have been set apart and sent out with the apostolic task of preaching the gospel beyond the reach of local congregations. Those members of the Church who move out in this way constitute the missionary force of the world.

1. Mission agencies

There has been a multiplication of Protestant missionary sending and support agencies over the past two centuries; this has become a worldwide phenomenon of great significance. Pray for:

a) **Effective strategies** to evangelize the world and plant churches among its diverse peoples. Lack of such can lead to misuse of resources and frustration of personnel.

b) **Adaptability** in a rapidly changing world. Few agencies are easily able to change structures and strategies to cope with the new and challenging demands of such a changing world.

c) **Leadership** in mission agencies. These leaders need: wisdom in setting clear objectives, guidance in the selection and placing of workers, ability to give pastoral care and to maintain good relationships with secular authorities, etc.

d) **Harmonious cooperation and fellowship with missionary sending and missionary receiving churches.** The growing emphasis on local church responsibility for world evangelism can lead to tensions and misunderstandings, unless mutual responsibilities and relationships are clearly understood. The local churches and missionary agencies need each other. Neither can do the job alone.

e) **Effective cooperation** rather than competitiveness between missionary agencies over finances, personnel, and areas of ministry, is needed. There is often unnecessary duplication of effort, and a lack of corporate planning together about ways to get the job done.

2. **Missionaries**

The old type of individualistic missionary of the colonial era is no longer acceptable. Team work and an ability to work with, and under, leaders of other nationalities make great demands. The modern missionary must be a self-effacing spiritual giant! The missionary's personal walk with God is vital. The harsh realities of the modern world soon dispel the imagined glamour of pioneer missionary work. Pray for:

a) **Vital, supportive home fellowships of believers** who are willing to pray the missionary out to the field and keep him there through his or her years of greatest effectiveness.

b) **The supply of his/her financial need.** Missionary ministries are more expensive to maintain than those at home. Many live sacrificially for Christ, yet their living standards may appear sumptuous to local people, and a wise balance is needed. The problems of exchange control, export of currency, inflation, artificial exchange rates, endemic bribery, etc., are constant points of concern.

c) **Adequate preparation for missionary work.** This is arduous and long — theological training, ministry experience, language learning, and adaptation to a new land may take years before an effective ministry can be exercised. Those years can be traumatic and discouraging for both single workers and young married couples.

d) **Cultural adjustment.** Culture shock is the subject of much humour, but is very real. Many prospective missionaries cannot make the adjustment to new foods, life styles, languages, value systems and attitudes. Some return home disillusioned and with a sense of failure, others react wrongly on the field and hinder their fellowship and witness; yet others go too far in their adaptation and compromise their health and sometimes their faith. Balance and objectivity are needed.

e) **Protection from Satan's attacks.** In many areas Satan's kingdom has never been challenged before. The powers of darkness are real. Missionaries need discernment and authority to resist attacks he makes through health, the mind, opponents of the gospel and even Christian workers. They need the victorious faith that will "bind the strong man and spoil his goods".

f) **Family life.** For some, especially single lady missionaries, the missionary call may mean foregoing marriage for the sake of the gospel. The loneliness of single workers can be a heavy burden to bear. For others, family life may be made difficult by living conditions, inadequate amenities, lack of finance or be disrupted by long separations, many visitors and overmuch work. Missionaries' children may have to be separated from their parents for long periods because of education, and can become resentful or rebellious in their teens. Pray that missionary families may be an effective witness and example of all that a Christian family should be.

g) **Commitment to God's will.** The assurance that God has guided to a particular ministry is the only anchor to retain workers in difficult situations, misunderstandings, broken relationships and 'impossible' crises. Pray that none may leave a place of calling for a negative reason, but only because of a positive leading from God.

h) **Fruitfulness.** All workers need the anointing of God on their lives, and an effective ministry that bears eternal fruit. For this they need clear objectives and time to achieve them. Too much time can be spent on survival and handling trivial interruptions, and too little on the real reason for being there. Only the Holy Spirit can give a worker that constraining love of Christ for sinners — human pity and love are inadequate.

i) **A sense of urgency**. Expulsions, or enforced departure from the field could suddenly terminate a ministry. The missionary needs to work hard to train his successors and help local believers to maturity.

j) **Homecoming** for furlough, or for home ministry, which can be traumatic. Returning missionaries need the continued support of God's people for overcoming re-entry shock and establishment of an effective rapport with churches at home, and of an effective ministry.

The leaders of the nations of this world

The Scriptures clearly command that prayer be made for kings and all in authority (1 Tim. 2:1-2).

As we pray for the rulers of this world remember that all authority ***has*** been given to the Lord Jesus Christ, the King of kings and Lord of lords. (Ps. 2:1-12; Math. 28:18-20; Rev. 17:14.) In fact, all who rule can only do so because God placed them in their position of authority, whether they know it or not. He can just as easily remove them. (Rom. 13:1-7).

We live in a chaotic world; many rulers are self-seeking sinners, some are blatantly evil. Like Hezekiah (2 Kings 19:8-34), we can intercede when wicked rulers defy our God, and when they oppose the spread of the gospel. His prayer changed the course of history. Ours can too! We have the authority in Jesus to change the hearts and minds of world leaders, and even to remove them.

We ought to pray for . . .

1. **Those who give just and godly leadership, many of whom are committed Christians**. They need upholding in prayer. They have to make difficult decisions. Pray that they may continually stand firm for what is good, moral, and just for the nations they rule and not give way to numerous pressure groups who would wish to gain advantage for vested interests, or push for the relaxation of laws that forbid what the Bible names as sin.

2. **Those governments that impose ethnic discrimination as official policy**. Such policies cause distress and tensions in those societies, and acute ethical, social and financial stresses for Christian leaders and all believers. There are at least nine states in Africa (South Africa is not the only case, but is the most well known), five in the Middle East, three in Eastern Europe and one in the Pacific where this is so. Sadly, sometimes authorities who claim to be Christian are the ones responsible. There are many more states all over the world where there is unofficial but painful social and legal discrimination against social, caste, and ethnic minorities — both indigenous and migrant.

3. **The one-man dictatorships and one-party states** that exist in numerous countries. Most maintain a facade of democracy, but all too often these systems exist for the protection and enrichment of a privileged elite. Frequently the only way open, humanly speaking, for government change is through coups or revolutions. The economic impoverishment of the majority and the widespread development of corruption in such states greatly complicates the life and ministry of churches and missions. Great wisdom is needed for Christian leaders that they may not succumb to the temptation of using corrupt methods themselves (perpetuating the situation), or condone injustice and support violence, hatred and revolution. Believers need to be in the world, but not of it, and learn the efficacy of prayer to change situations.

4. **The leaders of lands where there are great difficulties in obtaining visas** for expatriate Christian workers, but where some can enter and work and — in certain areas — churches do exist. It is in these countries (listed below) where large numbers of totally unreached people groups live:

Africa:	Benin, Congo, Ethiopia, Madagascar, Mauritius, Seychelles.
Asia:	Bangladesh, Burma, China, India, Laos, Malaysia, Nepal, Sri Lanka, Vietnam.
Europe:	Cyprus, Greece, Malta.
Middle East:	Jordan, Kuwait, Oman, Sudan, Syria, UAE.
The Americas:	Cuba.

5. **Leaders who actively persecute Christians, to restrict the gospel and the Church.** The persecution they promote can bring spiritual benefits — the purification of the Church, the stimulation of earnest prayer, an outpouring of the Spirit of God, and a more rapid spread of the gospel. Yet the people of God suffer under their cruelty or discrimination. Countries where such leadership exists are:

Africa:	Angola, Burundi, Ethiopia.
Asia:	North Korea, Kampuchea.
Eastern Europe:	Albania, Bulgaria, Romania, USSR.
Middle East:	Algeria, Iraq and Morocco.
The Americas:	Cuba.

6. **Leaders who oppose the entry and spread of the gospel.** Pray that the opposition may be used to actively prepare the hearts of those they rule for the coming of the gospel, or that their attitude may change, or that they be replaced by leaders more sympathetic to the gospel. In the last 20 years this has happened in such countries as Indonesia (1965), China (1976-9) and Benin.

Countries closed to the entry or open proclamation of the gospel, and also without a viable indigenous church, are:

Africa:	Comores, Somalia.
Asia:	Bhutan, North Korea, Mongolia, Kampuchea, Maldives.
Eastern Europe:	Albania.
Middle East:	Afghanistan, Algeria, Iran, Iraq, Libya, Mauritania, Morocco, Qatar, Saudi Arabia, Tunisia, Turkey, Yemen (North), Yemen (South).

In Appendix 1 on page 464 is a list of the decision-making rulers of the nations and territories of the world. You may wish to pray for some by name. Keep the list up to date as leadership changes occur.

Jan 6-8

AFRICA

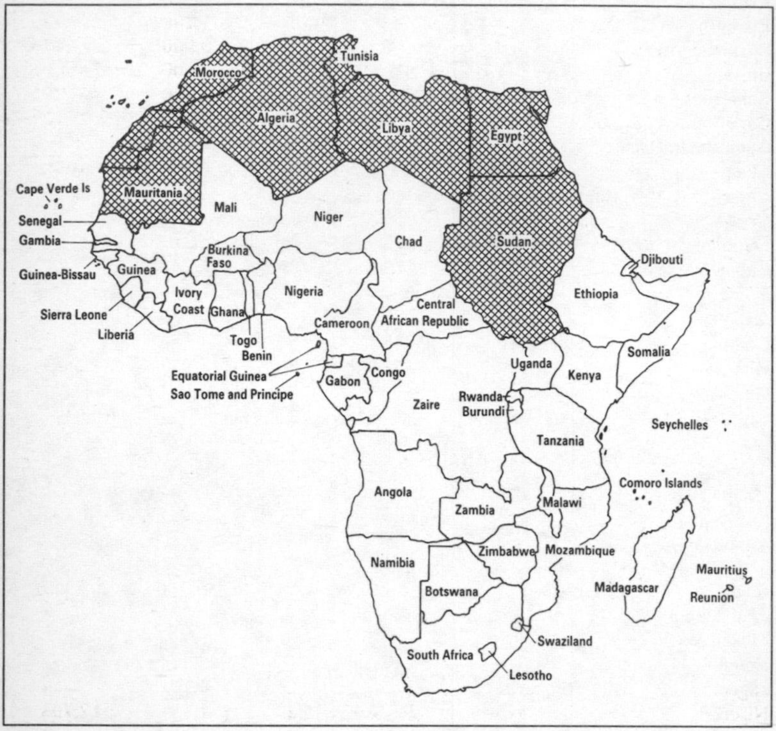

Area 30,000,000 sq.km. However, in this book we are including the seven majority Arabic-speaking lands of North Africa in the Middle East, to which they culturally belong. The Sahara Desert separates the Arab North from the African South.

Africa south of the Sahara has an area of 20,865,000 sq.km. (15.4% of the earth's surface). The countries included and described in this area are listed on the opposite page.

Country	Page No.	Prayer Calendar day	month	Population in thousands	Evangelicals in thousands
Angola	88	1-3	1	7,900	608
Benin	105	4-5	1	4,000	48
Botswana	110	6	1	1,100	13
Burkina Faso	119	7-8	1	6,900	97
Burundi	124	9-10	1	4,600	437
Cameroon	126	11-13	1	9,700	388
Cape Verde	130	14	1	351	10
Central Afr. Rep.	131	15-16	1	2,700	756
Chad	133	17-18	1	5,200	572
Comoros & Mayotte	147	19	1	412	—
Congo	149	20	1	1,700	255
Djibouti	159	21	1	340	—
Equat. Guinea	168	22	1	411	11
Ethiopia	169	23-26	1	35,631	3,421
Gabon	182	27	1	820	47
Gambia	183	28	1	724	1
Ghana	190	29-1	2	12,700	1,143
Guinea	202	2-4	2	6,100	25
Guinea-Bissau	203	5	2	848	6
Ivory Coast	252	6-7	2	10,100	374
Kenya	265	8-10	2	20,200	5,353
Lesotho	276	11	2	1,520	41
Liberia	278	12-13	2	2,200	156
Madagascar	283	14-15	2	10,037	180
Malawi	285	16-17	2	7,100	1,050
Mali	291	18-19	2	7,700	45
Mauritius	295	20	2	993	4
Mozambique	306	21-23	2	13,900	626
Namibia	308	24	2	1,128	192
Niger	321	25	2	6,500	4
Nigeria	323	26-30	2	91,200	12,768
Reunion	355	1	3	535	3
Rwanda	358	2-3	3	6,300	1,008
Sao Tomé & Principe	363	4	3	120	5
Senegal	366	5-7	3	6,700	3
Seychelles	368	8	3	72	1
Sierra Leone	370	9-10	3	3,600	54
Somalia	375	11-12	3	6,500	1
South Africa	377	13-16	3	32,100	4,815
Swaziland	394	17	3	647	123
Tanzania	402	18-19	3	21,700	1,953
Togo	409	20-21	3	3,000	36
Uganda	418	22-23	3	14,700	3,660
Zaire	454	24-26	3	33,100	5,826
Zambia	458	27-28	3	6,800	496
Zimbabwe	461	29-30	3	8,600	602
Others	—	—	—	7	0

Two small island territories, St Helena and British Indian Ocean Territory, are so small that they have not been included.
Ceuta and Melilla on the north African coast are included with Spain.
Sahara (Western Sahara) is included with Morocco.

Population 419,200,000. 8.7% of the world's population. Annual growth 2.9%. The continent with the highest growth rate, and also highest death rate. People per sq.km. 20.

Peoples: An estimated 2,988 ethno-linguistic people groups.

Indigenous African 97.4%. Almost entirely Negroid peoples of three major types — West African, Sudanic and Bantu. There are remnants of the pre-negroid peoples: **Pygmies** in the rain forests of Central Africa (332,000), **Khoi-khoi** in Southern Africa (283,000).

European 1.3%. Nearly all in South Africa; significant minorities in most lands.

Mixed race 0.8%. Mainly South Africa, Reunion and Mauritius.

Asian 0.45%. Predominantly Indians in Mauritius, and Natal in South Africa. Significant minorities in East and Central Africa.

Berber/Arab 0.3%. Mainly Tuareg (1,000,000) and Maures in Western Sahelian nations, and Arabs along the east coast of Africa.

Languages: Over 1,730 known languages are spoken; 32% of the world's total.

Official languages: The increasing use of French (22 countries), English (18 countries), Portuguese (4) and Spanish (1) is often at the expense of indigenous languages. In only six nations is an African language officially used as the main means of conducting the nation's business.

Bible translation: Africa has the largest number of languages and Bible translation needs, apart from India. Translations completed: 97Bi 152NT 226por. There are 307 languages that are likely to need translation work, and a possible total of 964.

Cities: There are 30 world class cities of over one million inhabitants. Urbanization 28%, but increasing rapidly. The urban poor will be a very significant and explosive factor by 2000.

Economy: No other continent has suffered such a series of natural, political and economic disasters over the past 25 years. Food production has declined in a time of rapid population growth. In 1985, it was estimated that 145,000,000 Africans had a precarious food supply, 21,000,000 were dependent on foreign aid and 2,500,000 were still refugees because of famine. The worst hit areas have been the Sahel extending from Senegal in the west to Ethiopia and Somalia in the east, and parts of southern Africa. The Sahara is extending southwards on average at 45 km. every year, worsening the ecological disaster. The reasons for this sad state of affairs:

1. Uncontrolled population growth, with rapid de-afforestation.
2. Maladministration, and the favouring of the educated elite and the more politically active urban population.
3. Low investment in agriculture and development of viable methods of food production, distribution and sale.

The possibility of marked improvement in more than a handful of countries is slight. There are about 18 nations whose economies have effectually collapsed.

Politics — Black Africa's isolation from the rest of the world ended in the 'Scramble for Africa' by the European colonial powers in the last century. For all its faults, the 100 years of colonial rule brought peace, education, better health services and some economic development. In the short space of 23 years since 1957, independence under Black African government has come to all but Namibia (South West Africa), South Africa, Mayotte (Comoros) and Réunion.

Independence has brought many problems — let us bear these in mind as we pray for the evangelization of this great continent.

1. **Colonially drawn frontiers** cut across racial, cultural and tribal boundaries, making some countries ungovernable or economically unviable. Many of the tensions in the continent today are due to this factor — Somali belligerence; Zairois instability; Chad, Sudanese, Nigerian and Ethiopian civil wars; the fighting over the former Spanish Sahara, etc. Tribalism is a hard fact of life in Africa, and makes a multi-party democracy a rare luxury, and one-party and military regimes the norm. Unfortunately no adequate mechanism for peaceful governmental change has been devised, so military coups and revolutions have been all-too frequent.

2. **Economic weaknesses** lead to 'neo-colonialism' (economic dominance and exploitation by industrial nations), and also to resentments against foreign trading interests of Greeks, Lebanese and Indians, etc. The very unequal distribution of wealth in independent countries has stirred up social unrest and led to leftist revolutionary takeovers in many lands.

3. **Nationalism**, and frustration over the unresolved racial divisions in South Africa, have sometimes led to the rejection of much of Western culture and a search for an African identity. This has led to the rejection of Christianity by some governments and the persecution of believers, such as occurred in Zaire, Chad and Equatorial Guinea.

4. **The political importance of Africa.** The massive African vote in the United Nations (out of all proportion to its population size or economic power) leads to the wooing of these states by the contending power blocs of the world. This has also led to military interventions by France in Chad, the USSR and Cuba in Angola, Ethiopia, etc.

Religion: The major ideological clash is between Christianity and Islam and both have made considerable advances in this century, as the graph opposite shows.

Traditional religions 20%. 84,000,000. The marked numerical decline belies the continuing hold of witchcraft, fear of spirits, fetishism and ancestor worship. Only four countries in Black Africa still have a majority of those following traditional religions — Benin, Guinea-Bissau, Mozambique and Sierra Leone.

Muslim 25%. Of the estimated 220,000,000 Muslims in Africa, 105,000,000 live south of the Sahara in Black Africa. The rest are Arabs and Berbers of North Africa and are included in the Middle East. There are only nine African states with a Muslim majority, though Muslims ***claim*** more than this. These are **Comoros** (and Mayotte), Djibouti, Gambia, Guinea, Mali, Niger, Senegal, **Somalia**. Only the two highlighted are closed for conventional missionary work.

Hindu 0.14%. 580,000. Almost entirely in the Indian communities of southern and eastern Africa, and in a majority in Mauritius.

Christian 53.6%. 225,000,000. Nominal 10%. Affiliated 43.5%. 182,000,000a. The eight million Christians in Black Africa (three million Orthodox in Ethiopia) in 1900 have grown to 225 million today. There are 26 nations in Africa that are majority Christian.

Roman Catholic 15.8%. 66,300,000a. Rapid growth through a large infusion of resources and manpower, and widespread institutional work. Nominalism and a serious lack of African priests and leaders are key problems.

African Independent Churches 5.9%. 24,900,000a. Possibly over 7,000 denominations and groups predominantly in Anglophone countries and Zaire. Some are fairly biblical in theology, but the majority are more or less syncretistic with little understanding of the way of salvation. Some are breakaways from mission-founded denominations, others have risen in protest against the impact of Western Christianity on African culture. The growth of these churches is significant and large.

Orthodox 3.6%. 15,100,000a. Almost entirely in Ethiopia where there have been centuries of stagnation and spiritual decline. The advent of Marxism has shaken the Church out of lethargy. There is a small evangelical wing. There are some Orthodox in East and South Africa.

Foreign marginal groups 0.4%. 1,600,000a.

Protestant 17.8%. 74,400,000a. Rapid growth over the past two decades in nearly every non-Muslim country. There are two remarkable "Bible Belts" across Africa, one extends from Nigeria through Chad, Central Africa Republic, North Zaire, Rwanda and Uganda to Kenya with millions of evangelical believers (see list of evangelical numbers on the previous page). The other spans an arc of territory from Angola through Zambia, southern Zaire and Malawi to the Lomwe people in northern Mozambique.

Evangelical 11.4% of population. 47,800,000a.
Missionaries to Africa 12,660 (1: 33,100 people).
Missionaries from within Africa 2,715 (1:27,400 Protestants).

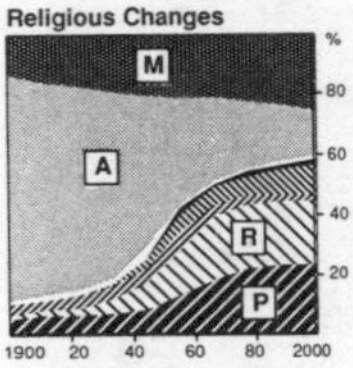

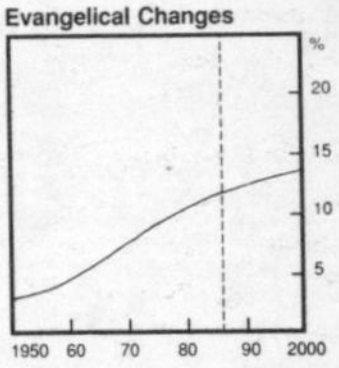

1. **Praise items:**

a) **The exciting harvest**. The dramatic ingathering into the churches is unique in history. Africa is the first continent to become majority Christian within a single century. Note the graph above.

b) **The spiritual hunger** has grown in the backlash of post-independence disillusionment because of the insecurity, economic stress and political ineptitude. The bad news of Africa has dominated the world's media, but the good news of church growth has not.

c) **The vigour and vitality of many younger churches**. Some of the older churches have stagnated, and growth in some of the more recent evangelical denominations is slowing down, but the third wave of advance has begun in many long-Christianized areas of East and West Africa, and parts of Southern Africa. Much of this is a more indigenous, and authentically evangelical, African expression of the gospel and often more pentecostal in flavour.

d) **Revivals in Africa** this century have had worldwide impact — the East African Revival being one such. There is revival enthusiasm in Uganda, Ghana and several areas in southern Africa.

e) **The impact of the gospel on educated young people** in English speaking countries has been extraordinary. The work of **SU** and PAFES(**IFES**) among secondary and university students in a number of countries is likely to prove decisive for the leadership of the churches in the 1990s.

f) **The resilience of African Christians** under persecution has been an example to the Church worldwide. In recent years Christians have suffered for their faith in Zaire, Sudan, Chad, Mozambique and Angola. Persecution is a present reality in Ethiopia and Burundi.

2. **The African Church in crisis**. Prayer and effort will have to be made to conserve the fruit of growth and prevent spiritual tragedy on a massive scale.

a) Much church growth has been without a deep repentance from sin and the works of darkness. In many churches there are still people bound by the fear of witchcraft. The decisive confrontation with Satan's forces has yet to be made in many areas.

b) Many have come to faith, but lack teaching. Syncretism is widespread because the Word of God is not adequately taught and understood.

c) The critical lack of trained leadership is crippling growth. The poverty of most churches makes it hard to support those in training or in the ministry.

d) There have been few Christians prepared to speak out for moral uprightness and ethical standards in societies riddled with corruption, greed and favouritism. Often church leaders have become, themselves, part of the problem.

e) Denominational confusion and barriers are more often caused by personalities and tribalism than doctrine. Spiritual unity across denominational barriers is too rare.

3. **The challenge of the "isms"**:

a) **Islam** is the strongest ideological contender for the hearts of Africans. Muslim advances since 1960 have been meagre in all except in western Sahelian Africa. It is only in some of those lands that conversions to Islam have exceeded those to Christianity. Many gains were only temporary — through force in Sudan and Amin's Uganda, political intrigue in Nigeria and Cameroon, and financial encouragements in many impoverished states. Yet there is a growing sophistication in Muslim missionary activities in Zaire, South Africa and elsewhere. Nevertheless one of the major needs for pioneer missionary advance in Africa today, is among the millions of uncommitted followers of traditional religions who live in a belt across the continent from Senegal to Ethiopia. Pray that uncommitted peoples may be evangelized before they turn to Islam. Pray also for a greater sensitivity and awareness among African Christians of the spiritual need of Muslims — the most unreached section of the population in Black Africa. Praise the Lord for increased conversions to Christ out of Islam in Nigeria and other lands, but may the trickle of new believers become a flood!

b) **Revolutionary socialism**, often openly claiming to be Marxist-Leninist, has shaken up many countries. Over 20 nations have had, or still have, revolutionary regimes, but Communism has not generally been attractive to Africans. Christians have suffered restrictions and even severe persecution under some regimes, but only a few are openly repressive to Christians in 1986 for ideological reasons. Pray that believers in lands with revolutionary governments may be both wise towards the authorities, and firm in their faith. Pray that restrictions on worship and witness in Burundi and Ethiopia may be lifted and imprisoned Christians freed. Pray also that the barrenness of atheist ideology may create a greater earnestness for fellowship with the living God.

c) **Syncretism** is a major problem for both Muslims and Christian churches. The majority have entered the new religions without leaving the old ways. There needs to be clear teaching and decisive power encounters in many areas before lasting breakthroughs are achieved. Pray that missionaries may understand the real issues, and that Christian leaders may make a clear stand for biblical truth and make no compromise with the enemy of souls.

4. **The lack of trained leadership** has reached crisis proportions. Leadership at every level is needed — for village congregations, for the urban educated, for theological training. Pray for:

a) **Institutions**. There are over 20 post-secondary and numerous primary and secondary level theological institutions in Africa. **AEAM** has an effective accreditation scheme, but it is difficult for many institutions to reach the required level.

b) **A relevant curriculum** that is biblical yet Africa-oriented. Too much teaching is Western-oriented.

c) **Harmony among staff**. Tensions among missionaries and between missionary and national staff have sometimes not been a spiritual example to the students they teach.

d) **Selection of students**. Discernment to know who are anointed of the Spirit for future leadership and who apply for baser motives of prestige, desire for education, etc.

e) **Funds**. The poverty of the Church and lack of understanding among those who could give, hampers the development of Bible training institutions. The needs for buildings, libraries, student grants and travel, are endless. Western churches need to give as freely for providing spiritual food to the starving Christians as they have done to provide for Africa's famines.

f) **TEE programmes** are vital for training lay leadership. Over 100 programmes are in operation, but some are less than successful. Funding, difficulties in travel, low motivation and the failure to involve the real leaders have all been problems.

5. **The theological vacuum must be filled.** A truly indigenous evangelical African theology has been slow to develop. A clear stand by African theologians to expound the universal and unchangeable truths of Scripture is needed which will also counteract:

a) **Western liberal theology** which never really took root in Africa, but the deadening influence of missionaries who were affected by it are evident in many mainline denominations where nominal orthodoxy, compromise, and power struggles for leadership have sapped away spiritual life.

b) **African theology.** The term used to describe attempts to find God in the pre-Christian religions of Africa rather than in the Bible. Syncretism (mixing Christianity with non-Christian religions) and universalism (all will ultimately be saved) are widespread.

c) **Black theology.** The Marxist-influenced Black Power expression of "liberation theology" which equates political liberation with salvation.

6. **The need for expatriate missionaries** from Africa and other continents is just as great. The appeal for a "moratorium of missions" (the total withdrawal of all missions in order to help the Church to maturity) has validity if paternalistic attitudes are maintained, but is not Scriptural or wise. The need for missionaries of all types is enormous.

a) **Pioneer areas still abound** (see below), but a far higher degree of commitment and sacrifice will be required to reach present pioneer areas where conditions are sometimes very hard.

b) **Church support missionaries** for teaching, youth work, etc., are needed as never before. Yet the willingness to work under African leadership and as part of the Church in Africa is essential.

c) **Specialists** for Bible translation, education, agriculture, health etc., are constantly requested by African Christians. In many countries the secular authorities have been unable to satisfy the basic human needs, and much has had to be taken up again by churches who do not have the resources to provide them.

7. The Unreached of Africa:

a) **The most spiritually needy countries of Africa.** There are 11 nations in Africa with evangelical believers constituting less than 1% of the population: Comoros, Djibouti, Gambia, Guinea, Guinea-Bissau, Mali, Niger, Réunion, Senegal, Seychelles and Somalia. A further five have less than 2% evangelical believers: Benin, Burkina Faso, Madagascar, Sierra Leone and Togo.

b) **Unreached peoples.** Many peoples in the Sahel, parts of West and Central Africa, Ethiopia, Mozambique, etc., are still without a viable church within their culture. Only an estimation of that number can be made at this stage — but probably about 700 of the 2,364 ethno-linguistic people groups in Africa are in this category.

c) **Over 300 languages** definitely need Bible translation teams. The actual number may be much higher.

8. **The missionary vision of the Church in Africa.** Few realize how much of the pioneer missionary work in Africa has actually been done by humble, dedicated African missionaries who have crossed cultural and national boundaries to evangelize peoples not their own. Pray for:

a) **Churches to see the importance of the missionary task.** Most Africans think missionary work to be the job for Europeans.

b) **Funds to be made available** to train and send out missionaries. Exchange controls and poverty prevent the vision, many churches have, from being realized to the full.

c) **Adequate training facilities** for cross-cultural missionaries. Beginnings have been made in Nigeria, South Africa, Kenya, Zaire and Ghana.

Jan 9-12

ASIA

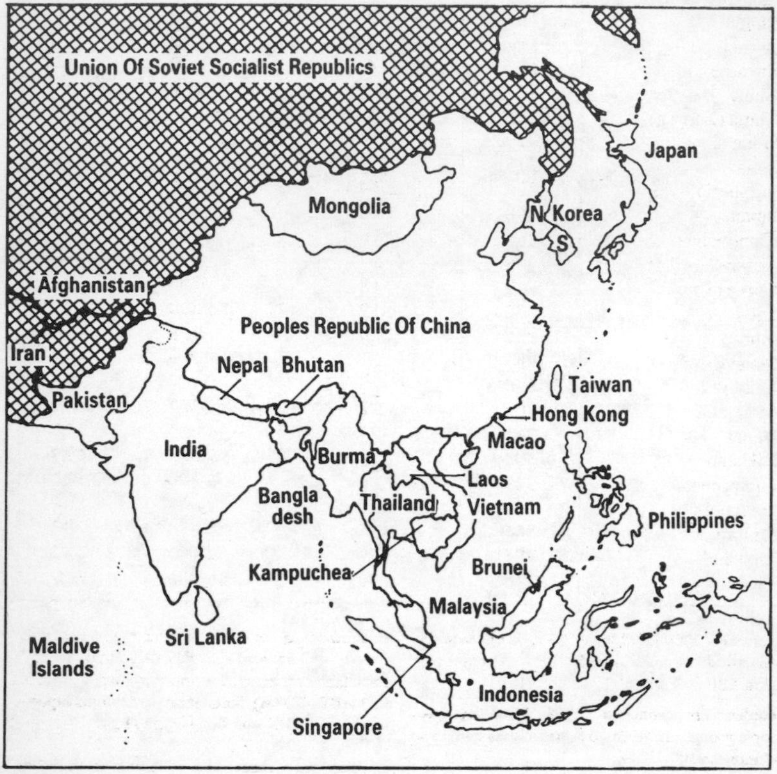

Area 20,657,000 sq.km., 15.2% of the land area of the world. However, in this book we have included Siberia (USSR east of the Ural Mountains) in Eastern Europe, and Western Asia (including Afghanistan) in the Middle East. The whole of Asia is actually 29% of the land area of the world.

Country	Page No.	Prayer Calendar day of month	Population in thousands	Evangelicals in thousands
Bangladesh	99	1	101,500	100
Bhutan	107	2	1,400	1
Brunei	116	3	279	1
Burma	122	4	36,900	1,144
China	137	5-7	1,042,000	45,000
China (Taiwan)	142	8	19,200	480
Hong Kong	210	9	5,400	280
India	215	10-11	748,000	5,236
Indonesia	229	12-13	168,400	7,241
Japan	258	14-15	120,800	278
Kampuchea	263	16	6,200	2
Korea (North)	268	17	20,082	100
Korea (South)	269	18	42,700	7,685
Laos	272	19	3,800	46
Macao	282	20	415	4
Malaysia	287	21	15,700	188
Maldives	290	22	177	—
Mongolia	302	23	1,800	—
Nepal	311	24	16,000	26
Pakistan	332	25	99,200	198
Philippines	345	26	56,800	3,522
Singapore	372	27	2,600	104
Sri Lanka	386	28	16,400	33
Thailand	405	29	52,700	105
Vietnam	446	30	60,500	303

Population 2,640,000,000, 54.7% of the world's population. Annual growth 1.8%. People per sq.km. 130.

Peoples: An estimated 3,868 ethno-linguistic people groups, of which 46% are in India and 23% in Indonesia.

Languages: Over 1,480 known languages are spoken, or 27% of the world's total. There are probably many more Indian languages not included in this **SIL** figure.

Bible translations completed 50Bi 102NT 199por. There are 209 languages that are likely to need translation work, but this figure may be as high as 1,000.

Cities: There are 93 world class cities of over one million inhabitants. Urbanization 27%, i.e. despite the rapid growth of great cities in Asia nearly three-quarters of the population is still rural.

Economy: All but a few nations have weathered the oil price rise storms remarkably well. The contrast between the wealth and economic growth of the Pacific Rim nations, Japan, South Korea, Taiwan, Hong Kong, Malaysia and Singapore, and the abject poverty of parts of South Asia and Philippines is marked. Though the two giant nations, India and China, have begun a radical transformation and improvement of their economies, possibilities for real improvements in the coming decade in Bangladesh, Nepal, Indochina and Pakistan look small. Income/person for Asia is $834 (6% of USA), but of the major nations Japan's figure is $10,100 and Bangladesh $130.

Politics: Out of the ferment of the past 80 years has emerged a younger, stronger and more vigorous group of nations. A number of major factors have been formative:

a) **The political dominance of Western nations has ended.** In 1945 only four nations were not under some form of foreign rule. The last two remaining territories, Hong Kong and Macao will soon revert to Chinese rule.

b) **Independence has renewed ancient rivalries and hostilities** — between Muslims and Hindus in the Indian subcontinent, between China and India, Korea and Japan, Muslims and Christians in the Philippines, etc.

c) **Modern political frontiers enclose national minorities** who resent central government control, and become a source of strife and instability — Nagas in India, Baluchis and Pathans in Pakistan, Muslims and tribal groups in Burma, Moros in the Philippines, Malays in Thailand, etc.

d) **Immigrant minorities** help the economies of their host nations through their business skills and initiative, but they can become an economic and potential political threat. **The Chinese** all over Southeast Asia form one such group; **the Indians** in Malaysia, and the many **Vietnamese, Laotian and Cambodian** refugees are other significant and often resented minorities.

e) **The post World War II expansion of Communism** gravely disturbed the political balance in the region between 1945 and 1975. During that period, China, North Korea and the four nations of Indochina became Communist. The poverty of Vietnam after 30 years of war and the new moderation of China's leaders since that time appear to have reduced the threat of further major expansion, except where ethnic tensions (Burma, Pakistan) or abuse of political power (Philippines) give Marxists a lever for provoking guerrilla wars.

f) **The growing economic and political power of China** and the extraordinary industrial power of Japan are major factors in the emerging Asia of today.

Religion: Independence gave a boost to the Muslim, Buddhist and Hindu religions, and often increased their missionary endeavours to win back Christians and convert those of minority religions.

Non-religious/Atheist 27.4%. 723,000,000. An estimated figure, representing mostly Chinese. There are six Communist States: China, North Korea, Mongolia, Laos, Kampuchea and Vietnam. There are varying degrees of persecution of religious faith among them; from the relative freedom of Laos to the harshness of North Korea.

Hindu 23.8%. 627,000,000. The majority in India, Nepal and Bali (Indonesia), and a significant minority in four other lands.

Buddhist/Chinese religions/Shintoist, etc., 21%. 554,000,000, including all religions new and old that are intermingled with Buddhism. Buddhist majority lands are: Bhutan, Burma, Kampuchea, Laos, Sri Lanka, Thailand and Vietnam. Japan is a mixture of Shintoism, Buddhism and new religions.

Muslim 16.9%. 445,500,000. Islam is the majority religion of six nations: Bangladesh, Brunei, Indonesia, Malaysia, Maldives and Pakistan. It is a significant minority in 14 others.

Animist 1.3%. 34,600,000. Predominantly among ethnic and tribal minorities scattered throughout Asia. Hinduism and Buddhism are much influenced by an animistic world view.

Sikhs 0.6%. 16,000,000. **Other** 1.9%.

Christian 7.3%. 193,000,000. Nominal 0.5%. Affiliated 6.8%. 178,500,000a. The majority religion in only the Philippines, but a rapidly growing minority in Korea, China, Indonesia and Singapore.

Roman Catholic 2.6%. 68,800,000a.
The majority in the Philippines, and large minorities in Vietnam, Sri Lanka and India.

Orthodox 0.07%. 1,820,000a.
Almost entirely Syrian Churches in Southwest India.

Marginal groups 0.24%. 6,340,000a.

Protestant 3.7%. 96,200,000a. Korea is likely to be the first major Protestant majority country in Asia.

Evangelical 2.7% of population. 71,500,000a.

Missionaries to Asia (both Western and Asian, etc.) 12,806 (1:206,000 people).

Missionaries from within Asia 7,100 (1:13,500 Protestants). The majority are cross-cultural missionaries in India.

Religious Changes

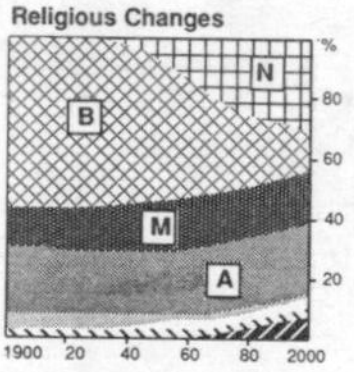

Evangelical Changes

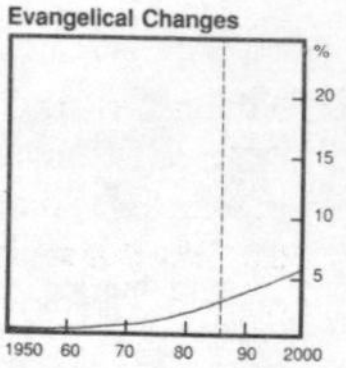

1. **Praise God for the gospel advances in Asia over the last 200 years.**

a) **The gospel has been preached in nearly every country in Asia.** Only in the Maldives and Mongolia is there no organized indigenous Church. In 19 of the 25 nations over 1% of the population is Christian; in seven it is over 10%. Just 200 years ago there were only a few Protestant churches in the whole of Asia.

b) **The most dramatic gospel advances have occurred over the past 20 years.** Notable is the growth of the Church in South Korea, China and Indonesia. Over the last 10 years maybe nearly 50 million have believed in Christ in China alone. Over the past 10 years the number of Protestants (including Chinese house churches) has increased by 9.8% annually.

c) **The maturing of churches in Asia** has been remarkable, with rapidly rising educational standards among pastors. There are probably more seminary students in South Korea than in all Europe!

d) **Revival has deeply influenced some areas** — notably West Timor in Indonesia in 1965, Nagaland in India in 1976 and more recently in many areas of China. Many other areas of most rapid church growth *need* revival, for the two are not the same!

e) **The rapidly growing missionary movement** in Asian churches is encouraging. Many young people in Korea, Indonesia, Philippines, Japan, and among overseas Chinese in many lands, are enthused with a vision for a lost world. The multiplication of Indian missionary agencies and missionaries has been remarkable.

2. **The needs of the Church** are great. Not all is positive and encouraging.
   a) **The Church, as a whole**, is stagnant or even losing ground in Sri Lanka, parts of India, Bangladesh, Taiwan and, to an extent, even Hong Kong, though in each land the more evangelistic bodies are growing. There is much nominalism that needs to be replaced by a living, vibrant faith.
   b) **The Church is under pressure** from, or discriminated against by, non-Christian religious majorities. Muslims have sought to limit or stop all outreach where they have the political power to do so. The social and family pressures in Hindu and Buddhist societies make conversion hard, and Christians are too frequently hedged in to a single section of the community. Believers under such pressure need a new boldness. In some countries, almost the entire Christian community is drawn from the more isolated, or despised sections of society, e.g. Hindu sweeper castes in Pakistan, tribal peoples in Bangladesh, lower caste and untouchables in India, Chinese and Indians in Malaya, etc. Only the Holy Spirit can sweep away barriers erected by man, which stop the flow of life to other communities in these lands. The breakthrough must yet come.
   c) **Persecution is very real in Communist states.** Despite the greater degree of freedom for Christians in China, there are believers in prison for their faith. The Church, where it exists, only does so illegally in North Korea, Mongolia and Kampuchea. In Vietnam, Christians are under constant surveillance and pressure.

3. **The unfinished task is enormous**:
   a) **Vast areas in Central Asia**: Tibet, Kashmir, Northwest China and the Himalaya region have never been effectively evangelized.
   b) **The Muslim bloc** is almost untouched. Apart from Javanese Muslims in Indonesia, few have heard the gospel and even fewer have believed. There has, until now, only been a trickle of converts to Christ from Muslim Malays, Indians, Bengalis, Pakistanis, etc. Very few national or expatriate workers are even engaged in seeking to win them.
   c) **The Hindus** have only been marginally evangelized. Some reckon that only 1-2% of all Christians in India are first generation converts out of Hinduism. The higher castes and the millions of North India, are some of the least reached groups of Asia. A new and concerted effort must be made to win Hindus to the Saviour. Much of present Indian cross-cultural outreach is to the tribal peoples. More should be done for the Hindus.
   d) **The Buddhists**, in Buddhist majority lands, are largely unreached. Missionary outreach has had meagre results and church growth has been slow among Buddhist peoples. Only among the weakly Buddhist Chinese, and then among the Vietnamese and Cambodians in the early '70s has there been more fruit. The churches in Thailand are, however, growing more than for many years.
   e) **Numerous unreached peoples** are unreachable by the present Christian work force. There are many barriers to overcome — closed lands, visa problems and the rigidity of the social and religious bonds that hold them.
   f) **In 14 lands out of the 25, the percentage of Evangelicals is less than 1%**, and in five it is less than 0.1%, the latter being Bangladesh, Bhutan, Kampuchea, Maldives and Mongolia. Of these only Bangladesh is reasonably open for missionary activity. There may still be over 1.2 billion men, women and children in Asia who have never heard anything of the gospel message.

4. **Missionaries are needed**, but it is increasingly difficult to obtain precious missionary visas. Although more unevangelized people live in Asia than in the other continents, and there are more unreached people groups, they often cannot be reached by present means. Pray for:
   a) **Restrictions on the entrance of missionaries to be relaxed.** Such restrictions can be just as severe for Asian missionaries moving to other lands in the region.
   b) **The most effective use of the present missionary force** for pioneer work and to train national believers to pioneer among unreached peoples.
   c) **Greater mobilization of indigenous churches and agencies** who can send cross-cultural missionaries within their own country. In India the growth in numbers of Indian

missionaries has more or less balanced the steady decline of the expatriate missionary force.

d) **Innovative methods of communicating the gospel**; other ways of entry for Christians, use of media, literature, etc. The job ***must*** be done!

5. **The missionary vision of the Asian Church** has grown in a spectacular way. There are many expressions of that vision:

a) Outreach to neighbouring ethnic or tribal groups. This has frequently occurred in Burma, India, Malaysia, Indonesia, Philippines, etc.

b) Outreach to people of the same ethnic groups in other lands (Chinese, Korean and Japanese missionary work was, until recently, more of this type).

c) In partnership with Western and international agencies. Many missions such as **OM**, **OMF**, **SIM**, **WEC** and others are becoming a channel to send Asian missionaries internationally. Chinese, Filipino and Korean missionaries are using this means.

d) The emergence of a growing number of Asian sending agencies. There may now be 300-400 such.

Pray for:

a) **Effective church support** for missionary outreach. Few realize the cost in prayer, personnel and finances or the implications of long-term missionary involvement.

b) **Adequate cross-cultural training** which is rarely available, and there is a real danger that Asian missionaries will repeat the cultural mistakes that Western missionaries have made. Close international cooperation is the best strategy.

c) **Useful cooperation on the field**. In most lands Asian and Western missionaries need to learn to work together and value each other's gifts. This is not easy.

d) **Retention of Asian missionaries** who are serving cross-culturally, will be a big long-term problem unless issues such as the education of missionaries' children, retirement, etc., are tackled.

Jan 13

THE CARIBBEAN AREA

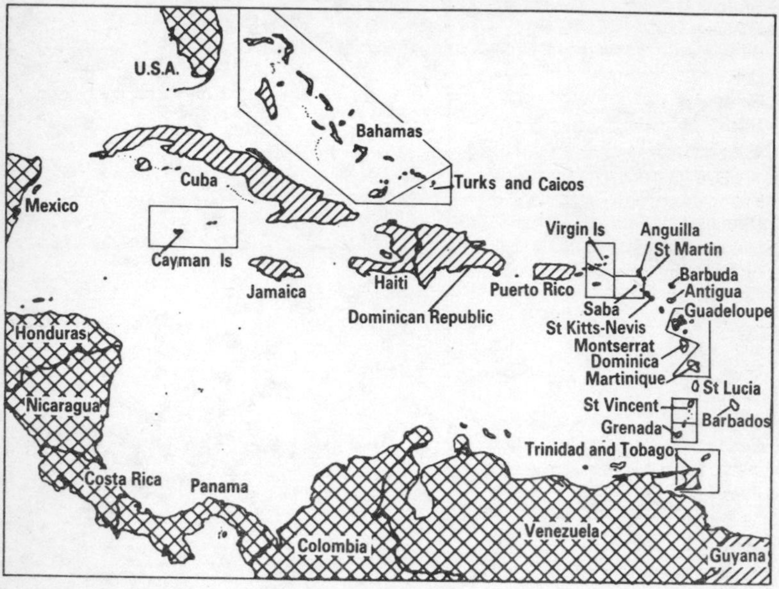

Area 730,000 sq.km. 0.5% of the land surface of the world.

Here the Caribbean is being defined as:

1. All the islands of the Caribbean and Bermuda.
2. The four non-Spanish speaking enclaves on the Latin American mainland; namely Belize, French Guiana, Guyana and Suriname. The Guyanas are shown more clearly on the map of Latin America on p. 63.

Country	Page No.	Prayer Calendar day of month	Population in thousands	Evangelicals in thousands
Anguilla	115	1	7	See Br. Antilles
Antigua	90	2	80	8
Bahamas	97	3	256	77
Barbados	101	4	300	56
Belize	104	5	184	22
Bermuda	115	6	69	See Br. Antilles
British Antilles	115	—	(130)	21
British Virgin Is	115	7	15	See Br. Antilles
Cayman Is.	115	8	18	See Br. Antilles
Cuba	153	9-11	10,100	212
Dominica	160	12	87	5
Dominican Rep.	161	13	6,200	291
French Guiana	180	14	68	3
Grenada	197	15	118	12
Guadeloupe	198	16	334	See Martinique
Guyana	205	17	979	85
Haiti	207	18-19	5,800	713
Jamaica	255	20	2,358	330
Martinique	198	21	328	19
Montserrat	115	22	12	See Br. Antilles
Netherlands Antilles	315	23	270	7
Puerto Rico	353	24	3,350	697
St. Kitts-Nevis	359	25	45	10
St. Lucia	360	26	127	6
St. Vincent	361	27	118	15
Suriname	392	28	393	12
Trinidad and Tobago	412	29	1,252	138
Turks and Caicos Is.	115	30	9	See Br. Antilles
US Virgin Is.	439	31	123	17

The six small territories still under British rule are grouped together under the British Antilles. This is not a single political entity, but is used for convenience here.

Population 33,000,000. 0.7% of the world's population. Annual growth 1.8%. People per sq.km. 45; great disparities:

1) Mainland territories	1,624,000	People per sq.km.	3
2) Greater Antilles	27,808,000	People per sq.km.	132
3) Lesser Antilles	3,568,000	People per sq.km.	132

Peoples

Amerindians 0.37%, the original inhabitants, have been virtually wiped out through disease and ill treatment: 60,000 in 10 tribes in the Guianas and 61,000 in three tribes in Belize.

Europeans 30%, largely Spanish (96%), some British, French, Dutch, etc. The majority originally came as sugar planters. The European component is a majority only in Cuba.

Negroes 35%, introduced as slave labour for the sugar plantations. These, together with the mixed blood **Creoles** or **Mulattos** 30%, form the majority in all territories except Cuba, Guyana and Suriname.

Asians 3.7% — brought in by the British and Dutch from India and Java (Indonesia) to Trinidad, Guyana and Suriname. There are about 91,000 Chinese in these three lands and Cuba. Asians are in the majority in Guyana and Suriname.

Cities: There are only four world class cities of over one million. Urbanization 44%.

Economy: The mainland states are underdeveloped and underpopulated, with great economic potential if the political determination were there. Most islands are overpopulated, with limited possibilities for development; hence much poverty and emigration to North America and Europe. There is overdependence on sugar growing and tourism. The economy is further held back by poor communications between the many and scattered islands, and the collapse of the oil refining industry.

Politics: But for Puerto Rico, all the larger territories are independent. Britain, United States, France and the Netherlands still rule a number of the smaller and less viable islands and territories. Hopes of greater political unity are limited because of:

a) **Language divisions** — due to the haphazard acquisition of colonial possessions by the European powers. The Caribbean population is linguistically divided thus: Spanish 59%, French 21%, English 17%, Dutch 3%.

b) **The insularity of the island peoples.** Each island has its own character and is resentful of outside influence and control. There are 27 political entities in the region.

c) **Communism** which has been assiduously propagated by Cuba in the Caribbean, Latin America and Africa since 1960, but with relatively little long-term success. Several other states, Grenada, Jamaica, Guyana and Suriname have temporarily sought to apply Marxism since then, but with disastrous consequences. Only the latter two still have dictatorial and leftist regimes in power. The economic instability and political pressures will continue to give opportunity for destabilization and subversion. The escalation of the violence in Central America is watched with concern.

Religion has been much determined by the original colonizing power.

Non-Christian religions 6.6%. Hindus 780,000. Muslims 260,000. Mostly East Indians and Javanese. Animists 750,000. Large numbers of nominal Catholics are practising spiritists or followers of Voodooism in Haiti and, to a lesser extent, elsewhere.

Non-religious/Atheist 18.4%. 6,050,000a. Almost entirely in Cuba.

Christian 75%. 24,800,000. Nominal 9%. Affiliated 66%. 21,800,000a.

Roman Catholic 50.6%. 16,700,000a. Originally brought by the Spanish conquerors. All the Spanish and French-speaking lands — Netherlands Antilles, Dominica and St. Lucia — are predominantly Catholic, but all have a growing Protestant minority.

Marginal groups 1.1%. 364,000a.

Protestant 14.4%. 4,750,000a. Almost all the English-speaking territories are predominantly Protestant, but nominalism is common.

Evangelical 7.9% of population, but strongest in Bahamas, Barbados, Puerto Rico and Jamaica. 2,600,000a.

Missionaries to Caribbean lands 1,948 (1:16,940 people).

Missionaries from Caribbean lands 121 (1: 39,300 Protestants).

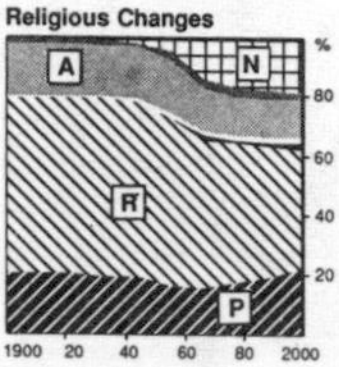

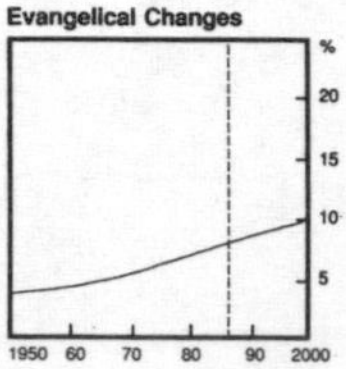

1. **The relative stagnation of the Church** in the Caribbean is cause for deep concern. Once Caribbean missionaries played a major role in evangelizing West Africa. Why not again? In many churches there is much enthusiasm, but less depth and little outreach. There is much religion without personal faith in Christ, and various cults are making rapid inroads.

2. **The Church is under great pressure** in Cuba and, to an extent, in Guyana because of the atheistic position of the government. Pray for believers in these lands that their faith may be strong and their spiritual cutting edge maintained. Believers need adequate preparation for the possibility of persecution in territories where there is now religious freedom.

3. **The difficult economic situation** in most islands is a great challenge. Limited financial resources cripple church development and outreach. There are simply not the personnel with the training to cope with the serious moral slide and breakdown in family life. In some islands 85% of children are born out of wedlock. Often Christian leaders are part of the problem. Pray for revival.

4. **Young people** are poorly provided for in most churches. High unemployment and limited prospects for economic advancement in many islands could drive many to seek revolutionary solutions. Pray for adequate and effective youth and children's programmes to be developed and implemented in the churches.

See Jamaica on p. 255 for other items of prayer for the Caribbean.

Jan 14-16

EASTERN EUROPE

For the purpose of this survey, all the Communist states of Europe and the whole of the USSR (including Siberia) are grouped together. See Asia map for Siberia.

Country	Page No.	Prayer Calendar day of month	Population in thousands	Evangelicals in thousands
Albania	84	1-2	3,000	—
Bulgaria	117	3-4	8,900	48
Czechoslovakia	156	5-6	15,500	326
East Germany	185	7-8	16,700	1,837
Hungary	212	9-10	10,748	398
Poland	349	11-13	37,300	186
Romania	356	14-16	22,800	2,508
USSR	420	17-27	278,000	8,060
Yugoslavia	451	28-30	23,100	40

Area 23,676,600 sq.km. 17.5% of the land surface of the world.

Population 416,048,000. 8.6% of the world's population. Annual growth 0.8%. People per sq.km. 18.

Peoples: Over 238 distinct ethno-linguistic people groups.
Slavic 66%. Predominantly Russian, Ukrainian, Polish, etc.
Other Indo-European and Caucasian 15%. A large variety of peoples ranging from German, Armenian, Kirghiz, etc.
Turkic-Altaic 12%. Predominantly in Central Asia and Siberia.
Other 6.2% including Finnish, Hungarian, etc.

Languages: An estimated 200 languages are in use.

Cities: There are 37 world class cities of over one million inhabitants. Urbanization 63%.

Economy: Centralized bureaucratic control of Eastern European economies and the emphasis on military spending, public ownership and heavy industry has kept living standards down, stunted initiative, and hindered healthy development. The serious economic failures of both industry and agriculture in the USSR and other Communist states are making Communism a less attractive alternative to other nations of the world.

Politics: The stated aim of the rulers of the USSR is the replacement of all other politico-economic systems with Communism. That aim has been pursued worldwide with tenacity through propaganda, subversion, promotion of local revolutions, guerrilla wars and military occupation. The pursuit of world conquest has been aided by the build-up of an enormous military machine of considerable sophistication. The expansion of Communism since 1917 has been dramatic and costly in terms of human suffering. There are approximately 17 nations in the world with commitment to Marxist-Leninist dogma, and possibly 15-20 other regimes that claim to be such with varying degrees of enthusiasm. The occupation of Afghanistan in 1979 may ultimately prove to be the peak of USSR expansionism. The divisions within the Communist bloc (the Russian-Chinese confrontations, nationalistic Marxism in Yugoslavia, Albania, Ethiopia, etc.) and the restiveness of subject minorities within the USSR and satellite states of Eastern Europe highlight the potential for future problems for the leaders of the USSR.

Religion: Marxism-Leninism is the official state ideology in each nation of the region. Atheism is an inseparable part of that ideology. All constitutions except that of Albania proclaim the freedom of citizens to believe in a religion, but the extent of that freedom varies widely from state to state, and even within each state. In all states the free practice of religion and its proclamation are controlled or forbidden. All statistics are estimates.
Non-religious/Atheist 38.7%. 161,040,000. A large and growing minority who profess no religious affiliation. Membership of the various Communist and allied Parties is about 29,000,000 or 7% of the total population. The latter is a privileged elite that has become the upper class of a "classless" society.
Muslim 13%. 54,100,000. Predominantly in Soviet Central Asia, the majority of Turkic ethnic origin.
Jews 0.46%. 1,903,000. Rapid decline over the past 50 years due to Nazi exterminations, Communist persecutions and emigration. Only numerically significant today in the USSR, Romania and Hungary.
Other 0.2%. Buddhists, Shamanists, etc.
Christian 47.7%. 199,000,000. Nominal 8.1%. Affiliated 39.6%. 165,000,000a. Drastic decline in professing Christians under Communism, though the quality and dynamism of Christian commitment has increased. Protestant Christians have grown numerically in most countries.

Roman Catholic 16.4%. 68,100,000a.
The majority in Poland, Czechoslovakia and Hungary.

Orthodox 18.2%. 75,700,000a.
The majority of Christians in Romania, Bulgaria, USSR and Yugoslavia.

Protestant 4.8%. 19,850,000a.
The majority of Christians only in East Germany, but a significantly growing minority in Romania and USSR.

Evangelical 2.8% of total population. 11,500,000a.

Religious Changes

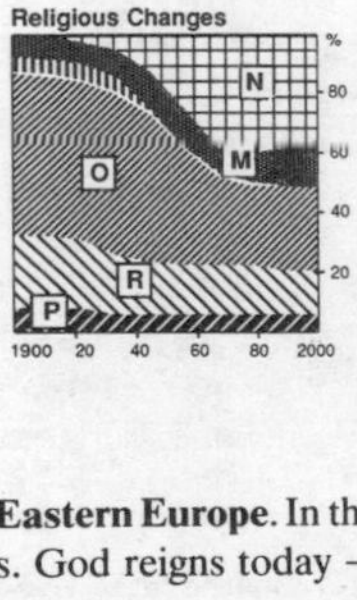

Evangelical Changes

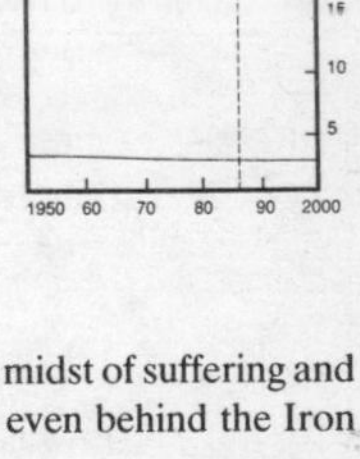

1. **Praise God for the growth of the Church in Eastern Europe.** In the midst of suffering and trials, the Holy Spirit is working in many areas. God reigns today — even behind the Iron Curtain!

a) **Evangelical believers have ultimately increased** in every country of the region since the coming of Communism, with the possible exception of Albania and Bulgaria.

b) **Young people** are turning to Christ in large numbers in parts of the USSR, Poland and Romania despite years of constant atheistic indoctrination, and the very real threat this brings to their future prospects for further education and employment.

c) **The infamous "Gulags" or prison camps** have been places of intense suffering and martyrdom for many believers; but through them prisoners have been won to Christ and large areas of Siberia evangelized. Pray for this form of prison evangelism.

d) **The thrilling growth of the Church in Romania and parts of the USSR** has been with touches of revival too. In both lands the pressure of the authorities on the churches has been particularly severe.

e) **The widespread impact of Christian radio programmes** has been remarkable. One well-known radio preacher has an estimated audience of four million or more every time he speaks!

2. **The confrontation between Christianity and atheism.** The two are incompatible. Christianity is the only ideology with mass appeal that has been able to stand up to Communism and even expand under its, sometimes, extreme efforts to eradicate religious belief. Pray for the triumph of the Cross in this spiritual conflict.

a) **Marx predicted that religion would wither away with the advent of Communism.** Hence the bitter hatred of atheists for the gospel which upsets their theory. Pray that the active efforts of atheist teachers, discriminatory laws, secret police and prisons to speed the demise of Christianity may not only fail, but that the Church may emerge victorious.

b) **In 1985 the new leader of the Soviet Union, Mikhail Gorbachev** vowed he would achieve what his predecessors failed to achieve — the elimination of religious belief in the USSR. Pray that his failure may be abundantly demonstrated in coming years!

c) **The massive propaganda machine for atheism** pours out an endless stream of vilification and scorn on any who have a religion. Pray that the emptiness and hopelessness of this godless creed may create a great hunger for the living God. Materialist Communism can never satisfy the deepest needs of the human heart. Pray also that true believers may shine as lights for the Lord Jesus and draw many to Him by their exemplary life style and witness.

d) **The major target of atheist activity** is to prevent the emergence of new leaders for the churches. The few trained pastors are stretched to their limits. Pray for all means used to provide effective educated leadership for the future, despite the efforts of the authorities to hinder this. Pastoral discipleship programmes, and TEE are used by the churches to train leaders, and also, in some cases, residential schools and seminaries. A number of agencies in the West are seeking to help in this ministry.

3. **Persecution is a present reality** despite propaganda to the contrary and despite the 1975 Helsinki Agreement signed by the Communist powers, in which guarantees of religious freedom were given. Conditions vary widely. Pray for:

a) **Lands where no organized churches are permitted. Albania** has proudly claimed to be the world's first atheist state. Can this situation be pleasingto our heavenly Father?

b) **Lands with strict control of registered churches**. The authorities attempt to manipulate, intimidate and control the leadership so that any effective growth and outreach is prevented. In some cases pastors and leaders are chosen or appointed by the atheist authorities. The result is compromise on the part of some leaders and the multiplication of unregistered or underground churches. Such is the case in **Bulgaria, Romania** and **USSR**. The unregistered believers, and registered churches that refuse harsh government controls, are vigorously persecuted. Persecution takes many forms — exile, imprisonment, commitment to mental hospitals, deprivation of parental rights, and loss of employment. The level of persecution has been stepped up in these three lands since 1975.

c) **Lands with restrictions on Christian activities.** In **Czechoslovakia, East Germany** and **Hungary** the churches have a measure of freedom within limits. Christians rarely suffer imprisonment for their faith, but discrimination in employment and education can occur, and atheist propaganda is just as unremitting.

d) **Lands with considerable freedom for Christian worship and witness.** Both Poland and Yugoslavia permit a wide range of Christian activities, and even the printing of literature and training of Christian workers. Yet it is in these two lands that the evangelical witness is the weakest in Eastern Europe (with the obvious exception of Albania).

4. **Assistance from the Free World.** Much can be done to encourage our brethren and equip them with the tools to grow and reach out to the lost around them. Pray for the following ministries:

a) **Prayer.** Vital intercession is what believers request most frequently in these lands.

b) **Publicity** helps believers who are being pressurized or unfairly imprisoned. Pray for believers' organizations behind the Iron Curtain, and agencies in the Free World, which seek to bring such needs to public notice. Pray that the authorities may become more sensitive to the adverse publicity their activities provoke.

c) **The provision of literature** is of prime importance, but difficult to obtain. The importation of Bibles and Christian literature is forbidden on the grounds that it is subversive, despite constitutional guarantees of religious freedom. Many organizations are involved in preparing scripts, printing and distributing Bibles and literature. Pray for all involved in this hazardous ministry.

d) **Christian radio** has been a potent means for evangelism, church planting and teaching Christians. Some estimate that as many as one to two million in the region may have come to faith in Christ, mainly through this ministry. The Communist Bloc is surrounded — by radio stations! Agencies with a major input being **HCJB** (Ecuador), **TWR, FEBC, FEBA, IBRA.**

e) **Agencies based in the Free World** who have a specific service ministry to these lands. There are many areas to be covered in prayer — confidentiality, protection of contacts, avoidance of unnecessary duplication of effort, fruitful cooperation among agencies, safety for those travelling, supernatural deliverances in difficult situations, etc.

5. **The unreached**

a) **Albania** is one of the least evangelized countries in the world. There is no known evangelical witness.

b) **Large areas of Yugoslavia** and **Poland** are without an evangelical congregation.

c) **Numerous East European minorities** remain largely unreached — the Jews, Muslims and most ethnic groups in Yugoslavia.

d) **Numerous peoples in the USSR** are without a known Christian witness. This is especially true for Central Asian Muslim peoples and Siberian minorities.

6. **Missionary outreach.** The Great Commission is just as valid for Eastern Europe. The ways and means of obeying His command may have to be unusual. Pray for:

a) **An increase in missionary vision among believers in these lands.** Survival rather than cross-cultural outreach has been more prominent in the past. Many students from unreached ethnic groups and closed lands study in the cities of Eastern Europe. Numerous ethnic minorities in the USSR and Eastern Europe can only be reached by local believers, but few have the understanding or experience for such ministry.

b) **An increase in dedicated workers from the Free World** committed to the evangelization of this vast region, and effective means of deploying them in vital ministries.

c) **An effective long-term strategy** to evangelize, plant churches and provide the Scriptures for every unreached people group, area, city and country in Eastern Europe.

For further prayer information contact:

i) Keston College, Heathfield Road, Keston, Kent BR2 6BA, UK.

ii) Licht im Osten, Postfach 1340, 7015 Korntal-Münchingen 1, West Germany.

iii) **ECM; OD; SGA,** please see Appendix 2.

Jan 17-18

LATIN AMERICA

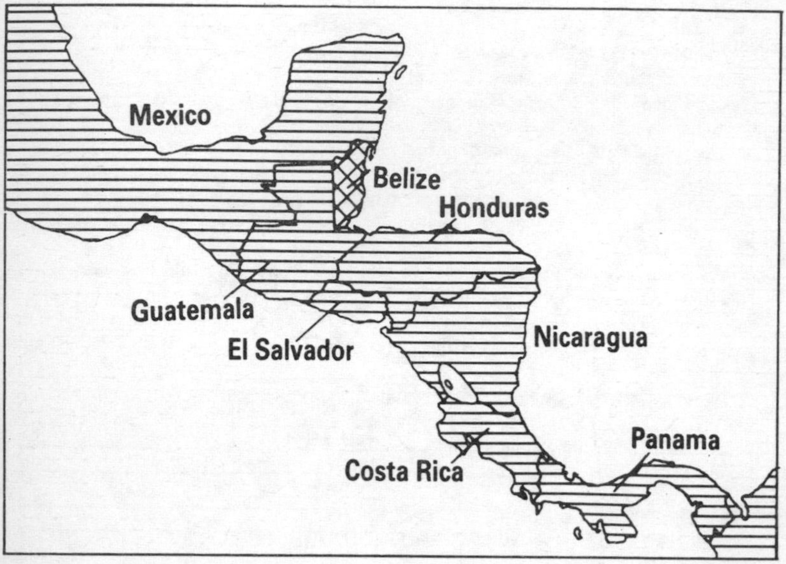

Country	Page No.	Prayer Calendar day of month	Population in thousands	Evangelicals in thousands
Argentina	91	1-2	30,600	1,438
Bolivia	108	3-4	6,200	403
Brazil	112	5-7	138,400	22,144
Chile	135	8-9	12,000	2,592
Colombia	145	10-11	29,400	706
Costa Rica	151	12	2,600	169
Ecuador	162	13-14	9,400	301
El Salvador	166	15-16	5,500	704
Falkland Islands	172	17-18	3	—
Guatemala	200	17-18	8,403	1,597
Honduras	209	19	4,372	385
Mexico	297	20-21	80,484	2,495
Nicaragua	319	22-23	3,218	203
Panama	335	24	2,140	210
Paraguay	340	25	3,600	90
Peru	342	26-27	19,500	585
Uruguay	440	28	3,036	58
Venezuela	443	29-30	17,300	363

Guyana
Venezuela
Suriname
French Guiana
Colombia
Ecuador
Brazil
Peru
Bolivia
Paraguay
Chile
Argentina
Uruguay
Falklands

Area 19,841,000 sq.km., 14.6% of the world's surface. Here we are defining Latin America as all the Spanish and Portuguese-speaking mainland states of Central and South America. The disputed Falkland Islands/Islas Malvinas are also included, but the other mainland states (Belize, French Guiana, Guyana and Suriname) are included in the Caribbean Region.

Population 376,156,000. 7.8% of the world's population. Annual growth 2.3%. People per sq.km. 19.

Peoples. The racial intermingling has been on such a scale that a rigid breakdown of ethnic groups is impossible. There is more class consciousness than colour consciousness in most countries. There are five main components to the population:

Amerindians 11%. The original inhabitants. A majority in Guatemala and Bolivia and nearly half the population in Peru and Ecuador. Two major types:

Highland nations 9.7%, whose empires were crushed by the Spanish in the 16th century. The major peoples being the Quechua 16,700,000 and Aymara 3,100,000 of Peru, Bolivia, etc., and the Aztec 5,100,000 and Maya 6,700,000 of Central America — all with numerous ethnic and language subdivisions.

Lowland tribes and smaller peoples 1.3%. Estimates as to the number of people groups vary between 800 and 1,400. Most are very small indeed.

Europeans 41.4%.

In Spanish-speaking lands 56%.

In Portuguese-speaking Brazil 44%.

Large minorities of Italians, Germans, Ukrainians, Poles, etc., are being rapidly absorbed into the two major language groups, but many linguistic 'islands' of a variety of languages are found all over the continent. The European element is a majority in Argentina, Brazil, Chile, Costa Rica and Uruguay.

Blacks 6.9%. Descendants of slaves brought from Africa. Most live in Brazil, but many live along the Caribbean and Pacific coasts of Venezuela, Colombia and Ecuador.

Mixed Race 39.8%. A majority in eight nations.

Mestizos (in South America) and **Ladinos** (in Central America) are mixed European and Amerindian. Many Amerindians become Mestizos simply by adopting Spanish as their language.

Mulattos are mixed European, Amerindian and Black.

Asians 0.8%. Considerable Japanese and Korean emigration to Brazil, and Chinese to all parts of the continent.

Cities: There are 35 world class cities of over one million inhabitants, which include two of the world's largest cities, Sao Paulo in Brazil and Mexico City. Urbanization 67%.

Economy: Rapid population growth, corrupt despotic regimes and mounting international debt since 1978 have provoked major economic crises in the 1980s. Mexico, Brazil, Argentina, Bolivia and Peru have particularly serious international debt problems. In some lands violent changes could be precipitated by the lowering of living standards, increased poverty and only a meagre hope of any rapid improvement. The yawning gap between the rich elite and the poor is one that must be narrowed if peaceful change is to occur.

Politics. There are a number of major trends in the region:

a) **Increasing democratization over the past decade.** In 1986 only Chile and Paraguay had military dictatorships. Mexico and Nicaragua have rightist and leftist regimes respectively; neither have much time for truly democratic elections or a democratic opposition.

b) **Marxist revolutionary forces** control Nicaragua and contest El Salvador, but bitter warfare continues with detrimental effects on surrounding nations.

c) **Communist guerrilla activity** in Peru, Colombia and Guatemala is a further destabilizing factor in the region, threatening those fragile democracies that strive to rectify past mistakes.

d) **The emergence of powerful narcotics empires** in many states is a danger to the credibility and stability of national governments. The problem is particularly acute in Colombia, Bolivia, Peru and Mexico.

Religion: In 1900 almost the entire population was considered Catholic. The changes since then have been dramatic — from a narrow traditionalism, with strong opposition to Protestant missionary activity, to freedom of religion and a rapid growth of Evangelicals.

Non-religious/Atheist 2.2%. 8,200,000. Many young urban intellectuals have become secularists and Marxists.

Animist 2.1%. 7,800,000. Much Christo-paganism is evident in areas where there is a concentration of Amerindians, and in Brazil spiritism, with African roots, has a strong hold especially among nominal Catholics.

Jews 0.28%. 1,070,000. The majority living in Argentina, Uruguay and Brazil.

Muslim 0.11%. 424,000. Most are of Middle Eastern origin.

Christian 94.9%. 357,000,000. Affiliated 94.2%. 354,000,000a.

Roman Catholic 82.2%. 309,100,000a. Practising Catholics: the percentage varies from 10% in Uruguay to 20% in Costa Rica.

The forced conversion of the Amerindian population by the invading Spanish led to a weak, syncretic church very dependent on foreign personnel.

Other Catholic 0.8%. 2,900,000a.

Marginal groups 0.9%. 3,450,000a.

Orthodox 0.13%. 483,000a.

Protestant 10.2%. 38,300,000a. About 75% of all Protestants (or Evangélicos as they are known in Latin America) are Pentecostal believers.

Evangelical 9.1% of population. 34,300,000a. Missionaries to Latin America 11,262 (1:33,400 people).
Missionaries from within Latin America 1,314 (1:29,100 Protestants).

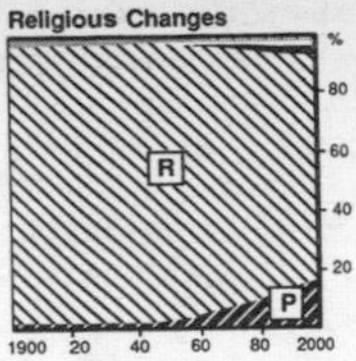

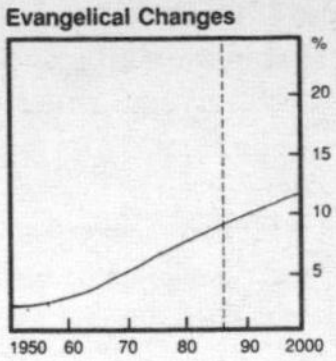

1. **Praise the Lord for the powerful work of the Holy Spirit in Latin America this century.** This has been one of the great success stories of modern missionary endeavour in times of persecution and severe economic stress.

a) **Evangelicals have grown** from an estimated 200-300,000 in 1900 to 34,300,000 in 1985. This will increase to 80,000,000 by the end of the century, if present growth rates continue.

b) **Nearly 10% of the population is evangelical Christian**, with the highest percentage for Chile (21%), followed by Guatemala (19%) and Brazil (16%). There are, in fact, more evangelical Christians in Brazil than in the whole of Europe, excluding the USSR!

c) **The regular churchgoing population** of Evangelicals in most countries now exceeds that of the Catholics.

d) **Pentecostalism has had astonishing success** in Brazil, Chile, etc., yet enthusiastic rejoicing over this growth must be tempered by sadness because of the divisiveness that, in many lands, has afflicted Pentecostal Churches.

e) **Stresses and turmoil in the region have stimulated faster church growth.** The number of Evangelicals in Central America tripled between 1967 and 1978, and since then the growth rate has accelerated in strife-torn El Salvador and Guatemala.

f) **The impact of the Scriptures on Catholics** has opened the hearts of millions to a personal encounter with the Lord Jesus. Many have become fervent evangelical believers, both within the Catholic Church and, increasingly, outside it.

g) **People movements are growing among the Amerindians** who have been long resistant or indifferent to the gospel. The present growth of Quechua and Aymara churches in the Andes, and Mayan peoples in Central America is exciting.

h) **The value of Bible translation.** The pioneer work of **SIL** in providing NTs in indigenous languages, has sparked off ingatherings of peoples into churches across the continent. In some lands the work of translation has been virtually completed. Praise the Lord for a task well done!

i) **The missionary vision has been spreading rapidly** in Latin American churches. Brazilians especially are moving out in increasing numbers to all continents, including Europe.

j) **The effective use of radio and TV for the gospel.** There are over 3,000 Christian radio programmes transmitted to 22 Spanish-speaking countries each month.

2. **The Roman Catholic Church** has passed through 30 years of tumultuous change. The traditional monolithic structure that once dominated the continent has gone for ever. The impact of the Vatican II Council, theological diversity, emphasis on Bible reading, and the influence of the charismatic movement, have been enormous. Pope John Paul II has pulled the Church back from political and doctrinal extremes to a more traditional Catholicism. Various powerful movements are discernible:

a) **Concern for the poor and social justice**. Some priests have become revolutionaries espousing liberation theology. Over 200,000 Base Communities have brought lay leadership and social involvement to the fore all over the continent.

b) **The charismatic movement** grew rapidly during the '70s, but is not growing at the same pace now. Millions have been involved, some joined evangelical churches, but others remained inside the Catholic Church with its unchanged dogma and sacramentalism.

c) **The traditional Catholics** have re-emerged as a strong force again. This may lead to a cooling of relationships with Evangelicals. Popular, and often syncretic, Catholicism is still widespread. Pray for Catholics to come to a personal faith in Christ. Millions still strive to earn their entrance into heaven by their pilgrimages, works, and ceremonies.

3. **The major challenges facing Evangelicals today**:
   a) **Growth has made the Evangelicals a potent political force**. Political power can divert Christians from the primacy of evangelism. Believers must uphold righteousness and not blatant corruption or partisan politics.
   b) **Social and economic injustices** have to be faced realistically. Some try to ignore them, others accommodate too much with liberation theology — a system based on Marxist presuppositions. The prophetic role of the Church must not be lost.
   c) **Economic changes** are inevitable. Believers need to be ready for them, whether they be gradual or explosive.
   d) **Persecution** from bigoted Catholics is largely a thing of the past, but a present reality from Marxist guerrillas. Gradually, increasing pressures are being applied to Christians in Nicaragua. The killing of Christians and pastors, and destruction of churches have occurred in Guatemala, El Salvador, Peru and Colombia in the last few years. Christians need to be prepared to suffer for their Saviour.
   e) **Provision of trained leadership**. The response to the gospel has been too fast for adequate teaching and discipling of new converts. The potential for error, over-emphases and second generation nominalism is high. Many congregations are led by lay leaders who have insufficient Bible training for the ministry they exercise.
   f) **Denominationalism** has been a major problem; much being imported. Even more serious are the divisions over personalities and doctrine.
   g) **The development of a truly biblical, yet Latin American theology** is needed to counter the influence of liberation theology, secularism and Marxism.
   h) **The integration of Amerindian churches** into the main stream of Christianity in their countries.

4. **The unfinished task**. Many people groups and sections of the population are either unreached or only marginally so. Here are a few general pointers to such:
   a) **Upper and upper middle classes**. More missionary input is needed. Much evangelical outreach has been to the less wealthy. The great cities where most live are a major challenge.
   b) **Students** in the universities. Only a small minority are Evangelicals, usually far smaller than the national average. **IFES** has a well established work in over 12 countries, with younger movements in others. Pray for all agencies concentrating on this strategic sector of the community. Social ethics are a major issue, and Marxist thinking is strong in faculty and on campuses. A clear, radiant evangelical student witness is a key target for every university.
   c) **Several countries have been less affected by Evangelicals**. The Church has been slow to grow in Paraguay, Uruguay and Venezuela and, in all, the percentage of Evangelicals is below 2%.
   d) **Amerindian peoples**. In most of the smaller tribes there are Bible translation and church planting ministries. However, among some tribes in Colombia, Venezuela, and parts of Brazil and Mexico various factors have prevented the effective establishment of an ongoing work. These are: geographical inaccessibility, government restrictions, the assiduous activities of anti-Christian anthropologists and, increasingly, narcotics gangs who have taken over whole areas and terrorized local people to further their evil activities. The total population of unreached is relatively small, probably not exceeding one million, but found in numerous small tribes. Other Amerindian peoples have still remained unresponsive and breakthroughs for the gospel are awaited.
   e) **Immigrant communities** from all over the world are often unreached. The **Chinese** in Central America (100,000) and Peru (60,000) are two such. **Japanese** in Brazil have been more influenced by Catholics than Evangelicals. **Muslims** are increasing in nearly all countries; their numbers are small, but significant, most being from the Middle East, and especially Lebanon.

f) **The Jews** of the southern part of the continent are one of the least evangelized major concentrations of their people in the world.

5. **The missionary vision of Latin American churches** has been growing:

   a) **Many international and regional conferences** have reinforced the challenge of the Great Commission.

   b) **Various international and indigenous agencies are actively recruiting,** training and sending out missionaries. This is especially true of Brazil, but also true of Argentina and El Salvador. There are over 60 indigenous sending agencies reported in Latin America today.

   c) **Finance is a major limitation** and lack of it will prevent the present trickle of cross-cultural missionaries from becoming a flood.

   d) **Churches need to learn the privileges and responsibilities** of supporting cross-cultural outreach within their own lands and abroad.

Jan 19-20

MIDDLE EAST

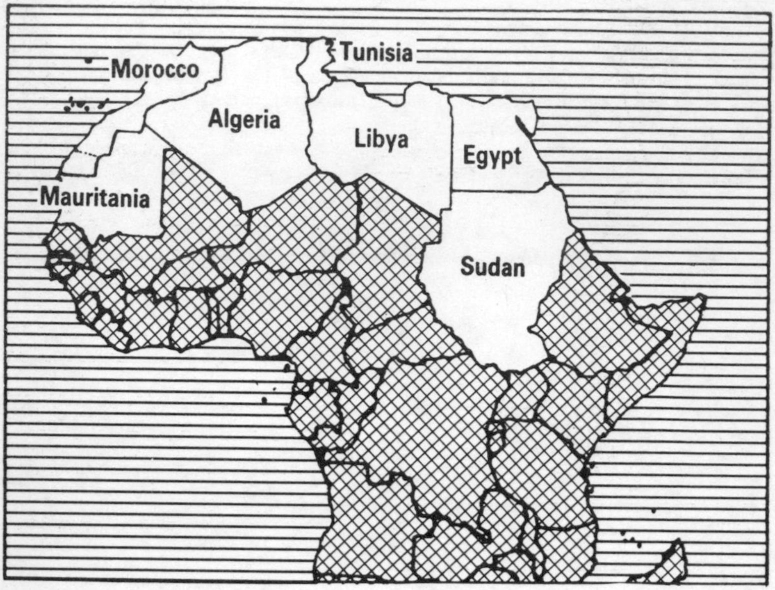

In this survey the Middle East is defined as the Arab lands of North Africa, and all lands of Southwest Asia to the west of Pakistan.

Country	Page No.	Prayer Calendar day of month	Population in thousands	Evangelicals in thousands
Afghanistan	83	1	10,000	—
Algeria	85	2	22,475	1
Bahrain	98	3	400	6
Egypt	164	4-5	48,300	333
Iran	240	6-7	45,100	80
Iraq	242	8	15,475	2
Israel	246	9-10	4,300	10
Jordan	261	11	3,600	10
Kuwait	271	12	1,900	4
Lebanon	274	13	2,600	15
Libya	280	14	4,000	6
Mauritania	294	15	1,890	—

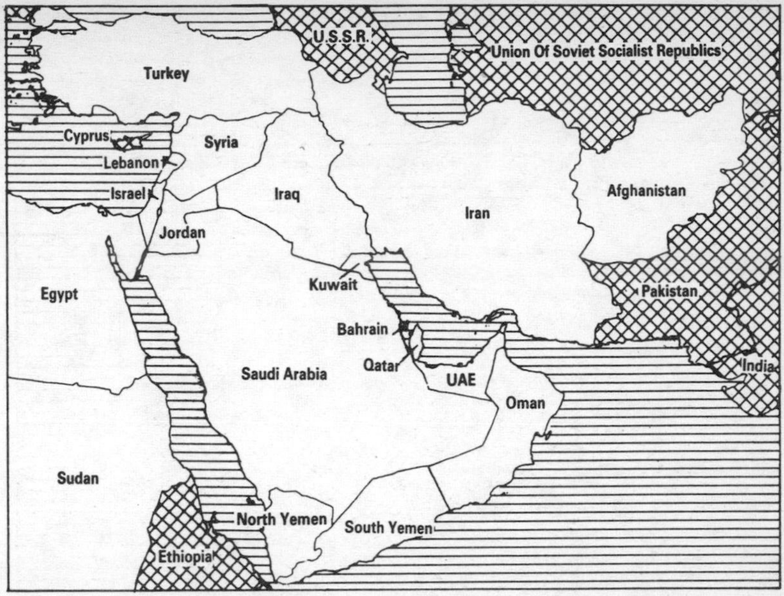

Country	Page No.	Prayer Calendar day of month	Population in thousands	Evangelicals in thousands
Morocco	303	16-17	24,300	1
Oman	330	18	1,200	1
Qatar	354	19	285	4
Saudi Arabia	364	20	11,200	34
Sudan	389	21-22	21,800	654
Syria	400	23	10,600	24
Tunisia	413	24	7,156	—
Turkey	414	25-26	51,420	1
United Arab Emirates	427	27	1,300	30
Western Sahara see Morocco	303	28	—	—
Yemen (North)	449	29	6,100	—
Yemen (South)	450	30	2,116	—

Note: In many of the countries where the evangelical population is small, the majority of the evangelicals are foreigners.

Area 16,278,000 sq.km., 12% of the land surface of the world. Only 5% of the land in the Middle East has sufficient water for cultivation.

Population 297,517,000. 6.2% of the world's population. Annual growth 2.8%. People per sq.km. 18.

Peoples: There are seven major groupings of peoples:

Arabs 51.5%. The Arabs conquered the entire region, except Asia Minor (today's Turkey), in the seventh and eighth centuries, Arabizing the Egyptians and Arameans (Syrians).

Indo-Iranian peoples 19.5%. The major peoples are the Farsi, Iranis and the Kurds. There are about 130 smaller ethnic groups.

Turkic peoples 17.8%. For centuries the Ottoman Turks ruled most of the countries in the Middle East and North Africa until the turn of this century. Only 45% of Turkic peoples live in the Middle East, the majority live in Central Asia.

Berber peoples 4.7%. Many Berbers have become Arabic-speaking, but 14 million across North Africa still adhere to their ancient customs and languages. There are possibly 38 distinct Berber languages spoken.
African peoples 4.3%. The great majority live in the Sudan, and culturally belong to Africa south of the Sahara, but are included in the Middle East. Other African peoples live in Egypt (Nubians), Libya and southern Mauritania.
Jews 1%. Almost entirely in the State of Israel.
Immigrant minorities 1.3%. Westerners, Asians, etc., predominantly in the oil producing states of the Arabian/Persian Gulf and Libya.

Cities: There are 24 of the world class cities of over one million people. Urbanization 46%.

Economy: Two Middle Eastern wars have had a radical effect on the world economy: the 1973 Yom Kippur War between Israel and the Arab states, and the 1978 Iran revolution and subsequent war with Iraq. These both provoked massive rises in the price of oil, causing a major redistribution of the world's wealth to the lands of the Middle East which then produced 70% of the world's oil. Some states in the region became fabulously wealthy, while others remained in great poverty. The average income/person in North Yemen is $510 and in the United Arab Emirates it is $21,340. The collapse of the high oil prices in 1985-86 is bringing yet further major adjustments to the region.

Politics: The strategic geographic position of the Middle East and the enormous reserves of oil ensure its continued importance to the world. It is a recognized source of contention between the two superpowers. There are many causes for tension and confrontation, and even potential for sparking off a world war:

a) The festering political sore of the existence of Israel and the unresolved Palestinian problem, with the endless round of international terrorism it has provoked.

b) The confrontation between the Arab and non-Arab peoples with its present focus on the long-drawn-out Iran-Iraq War.

c) The tensions between two very different branches of Islam — the Sunni and Shi'a; a strong contributory factor to the agony of Lebanon.

d) The ideological tensions which mirror the tensions between the West and the Communist Bloc. The USSR invasion of Afghanistan and the divisions among the Arab nations are examples of this.

e) The restiveness of ethnic minorities in the region — the Southern Sudanese, the Kurds and the Berbers.

Religion: Three major world religions had their beginnings in the region: Judaism, Christianity and Islam, all claiming a spiritual descent from Abraham. Jerusalem is a holy city to all three, and so a focal point for political and religious concerns today.
Muslim 92.3%. 274,600,000. Two major branches of Islam being Sunni and Shi'a, with further numerous subdivisions and break-away groups. 31% of the world's Muslims live in the region.
Traditional religions 1.1%. 3,270,000. Almost entirely among the peoples of south Sudan.
Non-religious/Atheist 0.5%. 1,390,000. Mainly intellectuals and in South Yemen, the only Marxist state in the region.
Jews 1%. 2,980,000. About 19% of the world's Jews live in Israel.
Christian 4.8%. 14,300,000. Affiliated 4.5%. 13,500,000a. A slow, but steady decline through emigration, a lower birthrate and unremitting pressures on Christian minorities by Muslim authorities.

Orthodox 3.1%. 9,300,000a. Numerous groups divided by ethnic origin and doctrine. They are direct descendants of the early churches and have survived through the centuries of Muslim domination and discrimination.

Roman Catholic 1%. 2,860,000a. Most are non-Latin Uniate Churches which broke away from various Eastern Orthodox Churches (after the schism between the Eastern and Western [Catholic] churches in the eleventh century), and acknowledged the authority of the Pope while retaining their own rites and traditions.

Protestant 0.44%. 1,320,000a.
The actual distribution of Protestants is very uneven, ethnically and geographically. The majority are foreign residents and southern Sudanese. Other larger groups are among ethnic minorities — Assyrians, Armenians, etc. Those who are of a Muslim background may not exceed 10,000. The major indigenous Arab Protestant groups are in Egypt and Lebanon.

Evangelical 0.28% of the population. 820,000a.

Missionaries involved in Middle Eastern ministries est. 1,564 (1:190,000 people). There are possibly a further 300-400 missionaries around the world ministering to immigrant communities from the Middle East.
Missionaries from within the Middle East est. 111.

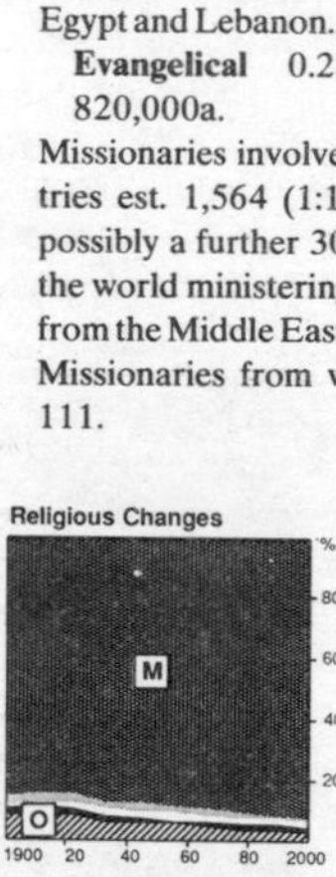

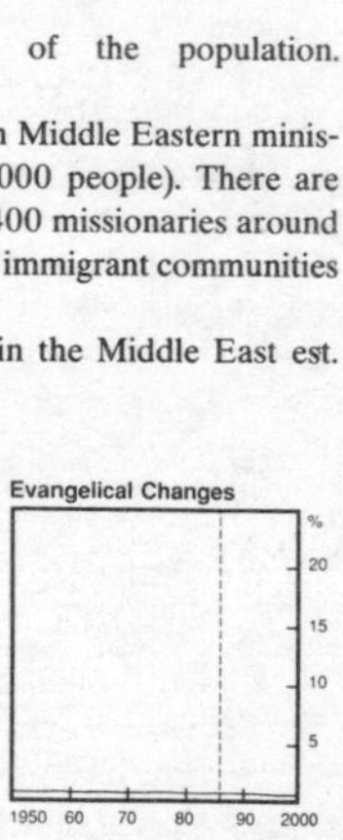

1. **The home of the early Church is now the most needy mission field in the world.** Spiritual decline and the Muslim conquests between the seventh and fifteenth centuries have steadily

reduced the percentage of Christians in the region. Centuries of discriminatory legislation and taxation and, at times, outright persecution have led to many nominal Christians converting to Islam. Emigration and, occasionally, massacres have further reduced numbers.

a) The indigenous Church disappeared in North Africa and Central Asia, and in more recent times has almost done so in Turkey and Iran. Pray for the rebirth of lively churches in these areas.

b) The ancient churches of Egypt, Jordan, Syria and Lebanon are still a significant minority, but are continually under pressure. Pray not only for their survival, but also for spiritual renewal to replace dead formalism, and a survival mentality, and to produce a vigorous new life and effective outreach to the Muslim majority. This has happened in parts of the large, and key, Egyptian Coptic Church.

Pray that the Great Commission might be so obeyed that the area evangelized in the first century will be effectively covered with the gospel again before Jesus returns.

2. **Islam has become the greatest missionary challenge to the Christian Church.**

a) **Muslims are convinced that Christianity is divided, decadent and in decline,** and that their religion is the answer to mankind's problems. Pray that their eyes may be opened to see who the Lord Jesus really is, and that they may be drawn to the gospel of grace.

b) **The new confidence** that independence and oil wealth has given Muslim nations, is giving greater incentive to spread the message of Islam to the world and thwart all Christian missionary efforts where they can. Pray that such plans may be confounded.

c) **Islamic fundamentalism** has brought revolution to Iran and tensions right through the Muslim world. A return to traditional Islam is seen as the answer to Western secularism and culture which has so influenced Muslim nations. Pray that the harshness and extremism often manifested may cause many Muslims to consider the claims of Christ.

3. **Praise can be given to God for much that is positive**:

a) **More Muslims in the Middle East are hearing and responding to the gospel** than ever before, but their numbers are still only few. There may be no more than 10,000 Christians from a Muslim background in the region, but even that number is a miracle.

b) **Islamic fundamentalism** is dividing and confusing Muslims with its extremism and harshness. Many fear the imposition of Islamic law in their nations. More and more are seriously reconsidering their allegiance to Islam.

c) **The political disarray** over attitudes towards Israel, and the Iran-Iraq conflict are exploding the myth of Islamic brotherhood. There are cracks in the wall of Islam!

d) **The increasingly effective use of the media**, such as video tapes, cassettes and radio, is exposing many more Muslims to the gospel — with good results.

e) **The growing concern for and commitment of Christians** to Muslim evangelism in the Middle East and to immigrant communities in other lands. The multiplying of prayer groups that concentrate on the spiritual need of Muslims is encouraging.

f) **The increasing number of volunteers** for service among Middle Eastern peoples. Both long-term and short-term Christians are moving out as tentmaker missionaries and witnesses.

4. **Believers from a Muslim background** are few and often scattered. Pressures on them are usually acute, from relatives, in employment and from the authorities. For many, emigration is the only way out of impossible situations. Pray for:

a) **All who have come to Christ out of Islam.** They need fellowship, but often cannot find it with Christians from a different background. They need to study the Word and become established, but rarely have the time or facilities. They need courage in the face of intimidation, threats, ostracism and even physical danger.

b) **The witness of believers.** They need deliverance from fear, a commendable life style, and inspiration to witness wisely, and to expect fruit from their witness.

c) **Christian homes.** These are few. Unequal marriages between Christians and Muslims are a major cause of backsliding. The Muslim world needs to see the beauty of a Christian home.

d) **Church planting.** Too few congregations of former Muslims exist.

e) **Trained leaders** are rare; some migrate to other lands for ministry. There are only two evangelical Arabic Bible schools in the world. TEE is being developed in some areas.

f) **Cultivation of a missionary vision.** Arab missionaries are more acceptable than Westerners in many lands. There are now about 70 Middle Eastern missionaries — from Egypt, Jordan, Sudan and Syria, who are serving the Lord in other Middle Eastern countries. Some Middle Eastern Christians work in lands closed to normal mission work, in Libya, Arabia, etc. This vision needs to be encouraged. Pray for the excellent work done in this respect by **OM** and **YWAM** in mobilizing and training young people in Jordan, Sudan and Egypt.

5. **Effective means of reaching Muslims** must be exploited to the full:

a) **Medical work**: This opens up countries and hearts to the gospel, and is the only way in which missionary work can be done in some states, especially in famine-stricken areas. Pray for this ministry, that it may create opportunities for a witness to Muslims. There are openings for medical workers with Christian agencies, and in government hospitals.

b) **Personal witness** by nationals and expatriates is the most effective way, but this needs a high degree of self-giving, much love and patience, and great faith.

c) **Literature.** Good evangelistic literature for Muslims, and teaching literature in Arabic for Christians is being produced in increasing quality and quantity by such groups as the Carmel Mission, **MECO**, etc. Pray for ex-Muslims engaged in writing these materials, for publishers, bookstores, and all who seek to get this literature into the hands of those who need it. **OM** has distributed much literature in various Middle Eastern countries in recent years. Pray for fruit.

d) **Radio** is the most effective (and sometimes the only) means of witnessing to Muslims in many areas. There are studios for the production of programmes in Spain (**GMU**), France (**NAM**), Lebanon (**FEBA**) for broadcasting by **TWR** in Monaco and Cyprus, ELWA (**SIM**) in Liberia, and **FEBA** in Seychelles. The response has been good and very effective when follow up is possible by BCCs and personal contacts with Christians.

e) **Bible correspondence courses**, in combination with Christian radio, have been used of the Lord to win more Muslims to Christ than any other means. This is especially true of North Africa, Turkey and Iran. Pray for missions involved in this ministry: **GMU**, **NAM**, **IFES**, etc. This witness is subject to much opposition by Muslim authorities — postal censorship and harassment of students, etc. Pray for these students, that they may be won for Christ and brought into living fellowships of believers.

f) **Gospel recordings, and audio and video cassette tapes** are proving ideal tools for evangelism and Christian teaching in areas that can never be visited by missionaries.

g) **Muslims in other lands** are more accessible. Pray for all involved in ministry to students and workers in Europe and North America. Pray that converts from this ministry may become effective witnesses when they return home.

6. **The unreached**. So many could be named:

a) **Countless villages and towns** where the gospel has never been proclaimed.

b) **University students**: only in Egypt is there an established evangelical student work.

c) **The lands closed to the gospel and without a single known indigenous evangelical church**: Mauritania, Libya, Saudia Arabia, Qatar, Kuwait, UAE, North Yemen. In each of these lands there are, however, groups of expatriate believers.

d) **The 15 lands where indigenous evangelical believers number less than 1,000**. In addition to the above: Afghanistan, Algeria, Bahrain, Morocco, Oman, Tunisia, Turkey, South Yemen.

e) **The numerous ethnic minorities** without a single known believer or portion of God's Word in their own language.

f) **Muslim women** who are virtually inaccessible in their prison-like seclusion in many lands.

g) **The nomadic tribes** of North Africa, Arabia, Iran and Afghanistan.

Pray that ways and means, as well as manpower, may be provided to reach them.

Further prayer information

For security reasons, little has been indicated in this book of specific Christian agencies in the nations of the region. There are many who would use such information to hinder, or stop work now being done. If the Lord leads you we suggest you contact:

a) **FFM**, a prayer fellowship of Christians worldwide which provides good prayer information covering the Muslim world. See Appendix 2 for address.

b) The agencies listed in Appendix 2: **BMMF, Fron., MECO, NAM, OM, WEC, YWAM**, who all have a deep concern for, and involvement in, the area.

c) MEM: Middle East Media, P.O. Box 1845, Limassol, Cyprus.

d) MMEC: Ministry to Middle East Christians, P.O. Box 1081, Limassol, Cyprus.

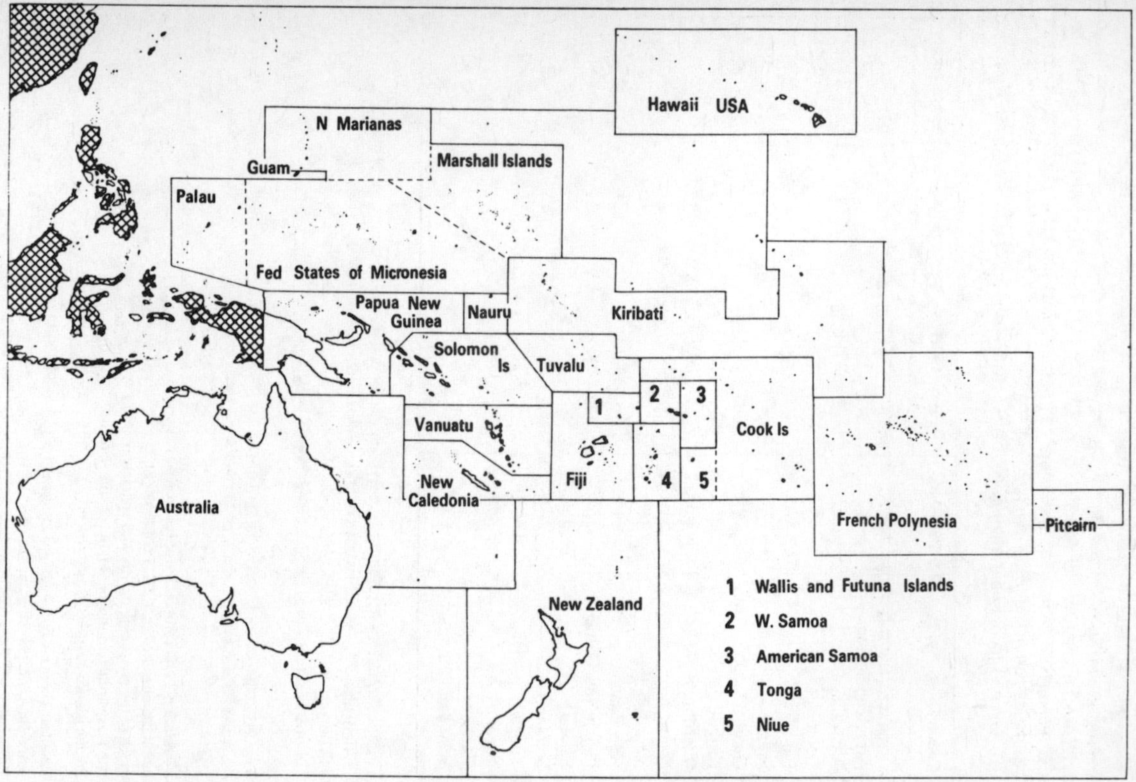
Hawaii USA
N Marianas
Marshall Islands
Guam
Palau
Fed States of Micronesia
Papua New Guinea
Nauru
Kiribati
Solomon Is
Tuvalu
1
2
3
Vanuatu
Cook Is
New Caledonia
Fiji
4
5
Australia
French Polynesia
Pitcairn
New Zealand
1 Wallis and Futuna Islands
2 W. Samoa
3 American Samoa
4 Tonga
5 Niue

PACIFIC

Jan 21

The region consists of:

1. Australia and New Zealand.
2. Papua New Guinea i.e., the eastern half of the island of New Guinea, the western half being part of Indonesia (see p. 229).
3. Over 30 major island archipelagos of several thousand inhabited islands in the Pacific.

Country	**Page No.**	**Prayer Calendar** day of month	**Population** in thousands	**Evangelicals** in thousands
American Samoa	87	1	34	6
Australia	93	2-7	15,800	2,212
Cook Is.	150	8	23	1
Fiji	173	9-10	684	55
French Polynesia	181	11	164	6
Guam	199	12	110	8
Kiribati	267	13	62	4
Micronesia	300	14-15	155	24
Nauru	310	16	8	—
New Caledonia	316	17	157	13
New Zealand	317	18-20	3,210	536
Papua New Guinea	337	21-25	3,300	693
Samoa	362	26	164	15
Solomon Islands	374	27	273	88
Tonga	411	28	108	8
Tuvalu	See Kiribati	—	8	—
Vanuatu	442	29	138	28
Wallis and Futuna	448	30	13	0

The small territories not mentioned above are included in:

Australia — Christmas Island, Cocos Islands, Norfolk Is.
Micronesia — Canton and Enderbury Is., Johnston Is., Wake Is.
Cook Islands — Niue, Pitcairn Is. and Tokelau.

Area 8,500,000 sq.km. (6.3% of the land surface of the world). Spread over a vast area of the Pacific Ocean.

Population 24,411,000. 0.5% of the world's population. Annual growth 1.2%. People per sq.km. 3; much of the area being the dry and sparsely populated Australian outback. Many of the smaller Pacific islands are densely populated.

Peoples: There are five major groupings and 1,500 ethno-linguistic people groups.
European 75%. The majority in Australia and New Zealand, where most are of British descent. Large French minority in New Caledonia.
Melanesian 18% (Melanesia means 'black islands'). The majority of indigenous inhabitants in New Guinea, Solomon Islands, New Caledonia and Fiji. A significant minority in Australia. Melanesians are unique for the variety of languages spoken.
Polynesian 4% (Polynesia means 'many islands'). The majority of indigenous inhabitants of New Zealand and islands of the central Pacific. The Polynesians are one of the most remarkable seafaring races in the world.
Micronesian 1% (Micronesia means 'small islands'). The majority in island groups on, or north of, the equator.
Asian 2%. Indian majority in Fiji, and smaller communities in Australia and New Zealand. Chinese communities in many territories throughout the region.

Languages 934 (**SIL** total). **Bible translations** 14Bi 82NT 176por. There are between 176 and 600 languages in which Bible translation work may still be needed, most being spoken by a very small number of people.

Cities: There are six world class cities in the region. Urbanization 71%.

Economy: The affluence and development of Australia and New Zealand is in contrast to the subsistence economies of most of the other territories. Overpopulation and lack of work opportunities have stimulated large inter-island migrations to the wealthier areas. Average income/person $8,570.

Politics: All but a handful of the smaller territories are either independent or have internal self-government.

Religion: In every state and territory except Fiji the great majority of people are Christian.
Non-religious/Atheist 17.5%. 4,270,000. Mostly in Australia.
Hindu 1.2%. 283,000 and **Muslim** 1.2%. 300,000. Mainly Fijian Indians.
Jews 0.3%. 66,000. Mainly in Australia and New Zealand.
Animists 0.8%. 182,000. Pockets of peoples in New Guinea and a few in Solomon Islands.
Other 0.75%.
Christian 78.3%. 19,100,000. Affiliated 73.8%. 18,000,000a.
Roman Catholic 25%. 6,100,000a.
Marginal groups 1.8%. 440,000a.
Orthodox 2%. 500,000a.
Protestant 44.9%. 10,960,000a.
Evangelical 17.6% of population. 4,300,000a.
Missionaries to the Pacific 3,735 (1:6,540 people). Majority in Papua New Guinea.
Missionaries from within the Pacific 4,593 (1:2,390 Protestants).

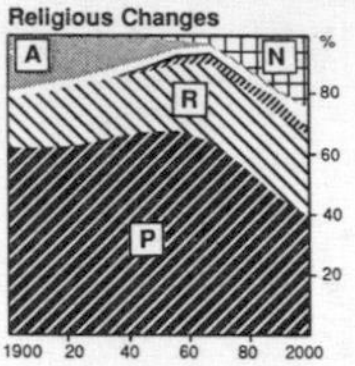

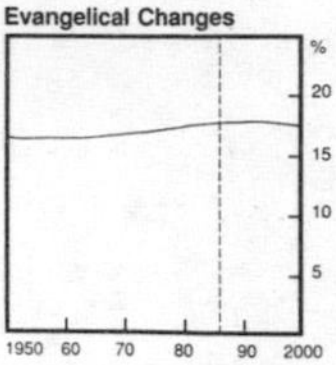

1. **Praise God for His workings in the Pacific!**
 a) **The Pacific was one of the first areas to be evangelized in the modern Protestant missionary movement.** Few areas of the world have claimed more missionary lives through disease, violent death and cannibalism. Praise God for the sacrificial labours of those early LMS, Methodist and Anglican missionaries.
 b) **Great people movements** over the past 200 years have brought whole peoples and islands into Christianity. Some of the most strongly Protestant Christian nations in the world are in this region. The Solomon Islands have the remarkable distinction of being possibly the nation with the highest percentage of Evangelical believers in the world. These people movements continue to this day in Papua New Guinea.
 c) **The missionary movement of Pacific islanders** is a dramatic and thrilling story. Many of the island groups were actually pioneered for Christ by these intrepid islanders in the last century.
 d) **Recent revivals** and movings of the Holy Spirit have stirred the churches in both the Solomon Islands and in New Zealand.
2. **The present spiritual need of the Church.** Decline in commitment, church attendance and spirituality is sadly the norm in most areas.
 a) **Secularism and materialism** in Australia and New Caledonia, and dead formalism elsewhere are sapping away the spiritual life of the churches. The need is for revival.
 b) **Inadequate teaching** on true repentance, personal faith and a daily walk with the Lord in the island churches has led to a widespread misunderstanding of the true nature of the gospel, syncretic beliefs and, in Melanesia, strange cults that are partly pagan.
 c) **The waning of missionary concern.** The Pacific islanders have lost much of their burden for world evangelization. Only in New Zealand has this burden been maintained. Pray that the flagging zeal of Christians for the extension of God's Kingdom may be reawakened.
3. **Unreached peoples** are few; pray for:
 a) **Remaining unevangelized and unoccupied tribes** in New Guinea's interior — a few such still exist. Many more are only superficially evangelized.
 b) **There are few evangelical believers** in parts of New Caledonia, French Polynesia, and on many of the nominally Christian island groups. Some areas need to be re-evangelized.
 c) **The Indians of Fiji** are the largest unreached people in the Pacific. Pray for the effective evangelization of these Muslims and Hindus.
 d) **Bible translation** is a major necessity. What remains to be done is being researched, but many hundreds of smaller language groups may still need translators.

[illegible]

[illegible]

[illegible]

[illegible]

Jan 22-24

THE WEST

Country	Page No.	Prayer Calendar day	month	Population in thousands	Evangelicals in thousands
Andorra	87	1	1	41	—
Austria	95	2-3	1	7,600	47
Belgium	102	4-5	1	9,866	39
Canada	128	6-9	1	25,400	1,651
Cyprus	155	10	1	692	2
Denmark	158	11-12	1	5,140	308
Finland	175	13-14	1	4,900	784
France	177	15-19	1	54,556	343
Germany, West	187	20-23	1	60,900	4,263
Gibralter	193	24	1	31	1
Greece	194	25-26	1	10,010	14
Greenland	196	27	1	54	2
Iceland	214	28	1	237	7
Ireland	244	29-30	1	3,600	22

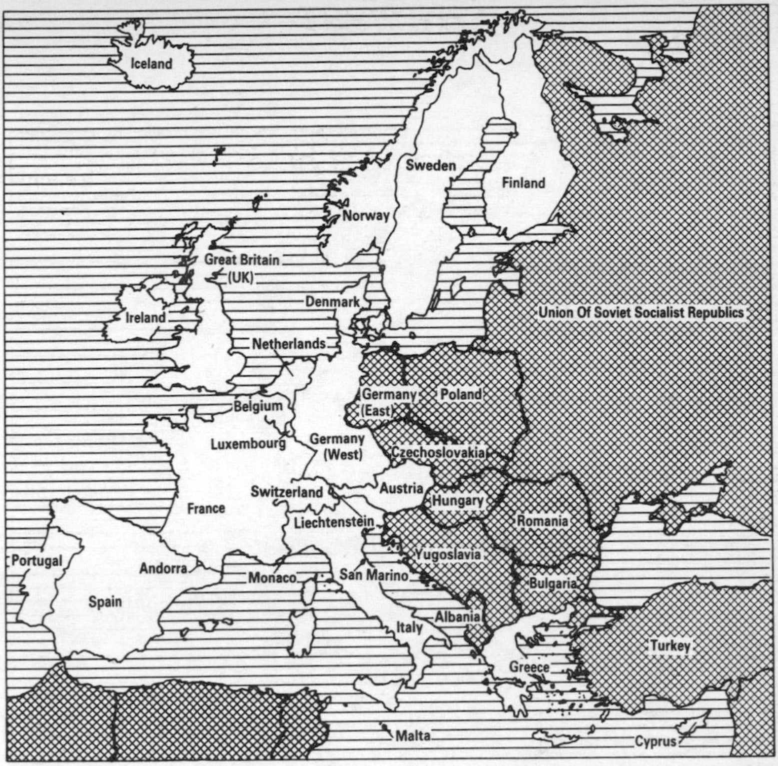

Country	Page No.	Prayer Calendar day	month	Population in thousands	Evangelicals in thousands
Italy	249	1-4	2	57,400	344
Liechtenstein	281	5	2	28	—
Luxemburg	281	6	2	366	—
Malta	293	7	2	365	—
Monaco	301	8	2	27	—
Netherlands	313	9-10	2	14,500	1,160
Norway	329	10	2	4,200	840
Portugal	351	11-12	2	10,300	62
San Marino	363	13	2	23	—
St. Pierre & Miquelon	360	14	2	6	—
Spain	383	15-17	2	38,700	131
Sweden	396	18-19	2	8,300	465
Switzerland	398	20-21	2	6,500	260
UK of GB & NI	428	22-25	2	56,600	5,046
USA	434	26-30	2	238,900	66,852

The following territories are included in:
Denmark — Faeroe Islands
Italy — The Vatican
Norway — Jan Mayen and Svalbard Islands
United Kingdom — Channel Islands, Isle of Man.

Area 25,141,000 sq.km., of which North America (four states and territories) is 21,529,000 sq.km., and Western/Southern Europe (25 states and territories) is 3,612,000 sq.km. This is 18.5% of the world's land surface.

Population 619,242,000. 12.8% of the world's population. Annual growth 0.4%. People per sq.km. 25.

Peoples: A total of 1,070 ethno-linguistic people groups.
European origin 92%.
African origin 4.6%. In North America 27,000,000; in Europe 1,300,000.
Asian origin 1.3%. The majority being in the USA.
Middle Eastern origin 1.2%. The majority being in Europe.
Other 1%.
Migrant labour is a major phenomenon in the southwest of the USA (Hispanics) and Western Europe (Southern Europe, Middle East). Their numbers at any one time may be as high as 20 million.

Languages 460, 419 of these being indigenous languages of North America. Bible translations 37Bi 78NT 127por. Bible translation work may still be necessary in 38-70 languages in North America.

Cities: There are 76 world class cities of over one million inhabitants, 40 of these being in North America. Urbanization 76%.

Economy: The West's control of sea trade, and the industrial revolution of the 19th century, enriched the north Atlantic nations and helped to create the present imbalance of wealth between the 'north' and the 'south' nations. The West's mastery of information technology in the post-industrial age ensures its continued economic and cultural dominance in world affairs.

Politics: The nations of the West have dominated the political, cultural and economic life of the world for 500 years. Dramatic changes have taken place since the end of World War II.

a) **Colonial powers granted independence to 96 nations** between 1943 and 1984. The political influence of these newly independent nations is significant.

b) **The rise of the military power of the USSR** and the expansion of its sphere of influence and military might, has resulted in varying degrees of tension and confrontation, globally and locally, between the superpowers and their allies.

c) **The impact of the 1974-84 oil price rises**, and their subsequent reduction, are having immense, but still little understood, repercussions. International relationships, power blocs and economic, industrial and trade patterns are affected.

Religion: After the Muslim invasions of the eighth century, Christianity was virtually wiped out in the lands of the Middle East where the early Church first took root. For nearly 1,000 years the countries of the West became the last major refuge for Christianity. The encircling Muslim lands effectively prevented any missionary outreach to Africa and Asia. It was not until the Reformation in the 16th century that the Church was revitalized to eventually become a force for world evangelization. The last 250 years have been years of worldwide advance for the gospel. Yet in this time, a deadening secular humanism has effectually become the dominating force in society. This philosophy has corrupted every part of its culture — art, music, social values, morality and theology. The decline in churchgoing and Christian profession this century is clearly shown below in graph 1.
Non-religious/Atheist 10%. 62,200,000. The majority of Europeans, and a large minority of North Americans, maintain no real link with any church.
Muslim 1.6%. 9,800,000. About 90% of these are from immigrant communities. Only in the US Black community have there been conversions on any scale among resident ethnic groups.
Jews 1.5%. 9,200,000. About 53% of the world's Jews live in the West.
Christian 86.5%. 536,000,000. Nominal 11.5%. Affiliated 75%. 465,000,000a. Actual churchgoing is far higher in the USA than elsewhere:
- **Roman Catholic** 41.2%. 255,000,000a. A Christian majority in 15 states and territories.
- **Marginal groups** 1.9%. 11,900,000a. The majority being in North America.
- **Orthodox** 2.8%. 17,400,000a. Minorities in most countries, majority in Greece and Cyprus.
- **Protestant** 29%. 180,000,000a. A Christian majority in 9 states.
  - **Evangelicals** 11.7% of the population. 72,200,000a.

Missionaries to the West 7,328.
Missionaries from the West 65,027 (1:2,700 Protestants).

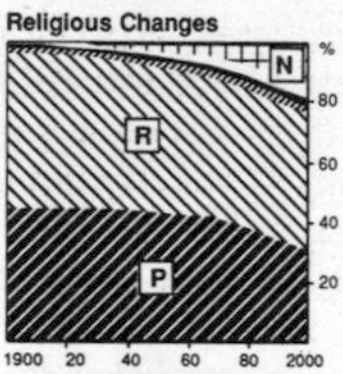

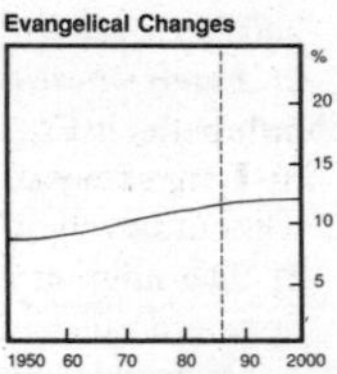

1. **Encouraging signs of spiritual awakening** are evident in the West. The overall decline in church affiliation and church attendance can obscure the positive developments:

a) **Past revivals** have left a legacy of dynamism and spiritual wealth — the Puritan, Pietist, Methodist and 19th century awakenings ultimately led to blessing for the world in the 200-

year old modern missionary movement. It can happen again! Never before has the potential for the West to speedily and deeply affect the world been as great as now. In recent years there have been localized revivals in Scotland, Finland, Canada and the USA.

b) **The steady growth in numbers, confidence and influence of Evangelicals** in both North America and Europe is encouraging (see graph 2 on p. 80). This growth is not only in younger evangelical and Pentecostal denominations, but also in mainline churches where some denominations are returning to their biblical roots, and an ever increasing proportion of pastors are Evangelicals. Liberal theology that helped to empty many churches is being eclipsed, and the decline in Protestant church attendances appears to be ending.

c) **The multiplication of youth, service and missionary agencies** with a strong emphasis on evangelism, discipleship and world evangelization. The youth of today are often showing far more concern for spiritual reality than their parents of the World War II generation.

d) **The renewal movement** has deeply affected nearly every denomination in most countries. This has brought a new emphasis on the work of the Holy Spirit, and an interest in the Scriptures. Many nominal congregations have been transformed.

e) **The remarkable turning to Christ** of many thousands of the world's 6,000,000 **Gypsies** in parts of Europe. The Gypsy churches in Spain have become the largest evangelical fellowship of churches in that land.

f) **The rapid growth of evangelical churches** in once strongly traditional **Catholic Quebec**, in Canada, is cause for rejoicing.

2. **The spiritual need of the West**:

a) **A godless materialism** has become the formative philosophy of the majority – particularly in Europe. To term Europe today as 'post-Christian' or as going through a process of 'de-Christianization' is a sad partial truth. Pray that this trend may be reversed by an intervention of God, and that empty churches and chapels may once more be filled with people praising God.

b) **In many countries an increasing percentage of the population has had no meaningful contact with biblical Christianity for generations.** Parts of Europe, especially, are now some of the most spiritually dark areas in the world; southern Europe is, possibly, after the Muslim Middle East, the hardest mission field on earth. Many Westerners live in the afterglow of a great Christian heritage which is being eroded by rampant secularism and an indifference to anything to do with God. This new generation must be evangelized.

c) **The individualism and selfish spirit of acquisition** has impaired the commitment even of Christians to any cause that might involve sacrifice. The dedication of many Communists and Muslims is a sobering contrast. Pray for the deepening of spiritual life and dedication to the Lord in the churches of the West.

3. **The less reached of the West**. An increasing worldwide emphasis on missionary work in the West is discernible, but such cross-cultural work is not easy and response has been slow. The missionary casualty rate is high. Pray for effective outreach to:

a) **The 15 states and territories** where less than 1% of the population is evangelical Christian.

b) **The mini-states** of Andorra, Liechtenstein, St. Pierre and Miquelon, Malta, Monaco and San Marino where there are no viable indigenous evangelical congregations.

c) **Lands where the evangelical witness is very small**; Luxemburg, Greece and Spain. It is little better in France, Belgium, Portugal and Italy.

d) **Large areas** of many West European nations, both Catholic and Protestant, which are without a strong, clear gospel witness.

e) **The migrant workers** who need the gospel. Most are from unevangelized areas of Southern Europe and the Middle East.

f) **Overseas students**. These number about 500,000 at any one time – especially in the USA, Canada, Britain and France. Many come from lands closed to conventional missionary work.

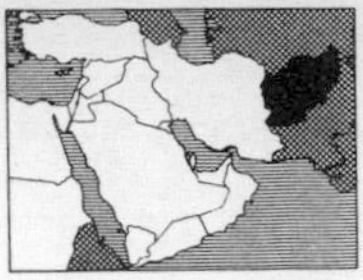

AFGHANISTAN

(Democratic Republic of Afghanistan)

Middle East

Jan 25-26

Area 647,000 sq.km. Dry and mountainous, but with fertile valleys. This strategic land has been called the "Crossroads of Central Asia".

Population 10,000,000. Growth rate −3.7%; decline due to the continuing war. People per sq.km. 15.

Peoples
Pushtun (related to Pakistani Pathans) 55%.
Tajik (speaking Dari, a Persian dialect) 27%.
Uzbek 5.3%, **Hazara** 2.7%, **Turkoman** 2%.
Smaller groups (45) 8%.
Russian 1%. Over 150,000 troops.

Literacy 6%. **Official languages:** Pushtun, Dari. **All languages** 47. **Bible translations** 3Bi 2NT 7por.

Economy: Very poor with increasing famine. Many areas have been devastated by the scorched earth policy of the Russians to quell resistance. Income/person $160 (1% of USA).

Politics: Autocratic monarchy overthrown in 1973. Republican rule ended in a pro-Marxist coup in 1978. Growing Muslim opposition to the government provoked the Russian invasion and partial subjugation of the country.

Capital: Kabul 1,500,000; the majority being refugees. Urbanization 16%. Nomadic population 15%.

Religion: Avowed support of Islam in efforts to lessen Muslim hatred of the Russians and suspicion of the new government.
Muslim 99%. Sunni 90%, Shi'a 10%.
Hindu 0.6%, **Sikh** 2,000.
Christian — number unknown, but increasing since 1979.

1. **The Russian invasion of 1979-80** has caused immense suffering. More than half of the nation's schools and much farmland have been deliberately destroyed. An estimated 600,000 have lost their lives and over 5,000,000 have fled to Pakistan and Iran in the subsequent fighting with the invaders. Pray that this tragic situation may be the means by which many hearts are opened to the gospel.

2. **Afghanistan is virtually unevangelized.** Pray that this land may be fully opened to the preaching of the gospel. Officially there has been religious freedom since 1964, but proselytization is forbidden. The Marxist government has not opposed any religious activity at this stage because of its unpopularity in this staunchly Muslim nation.

3. **Unreached peoples — none can be considered reached with the gospel.** Pray especially for the **Uzbeks** in the north; the **Hazaras** in the centre; the many **Nuristani tribes** north and east of Kabul, only recently Islamized; the nomadic Pushtun tribes of the west and the **Baluchis** in the south.

4. **There are still foreign Christians serving the Lord** in the land as doctors, teachers, etc. Pray that their lives may commend the Saviour to the people to whom they minister and earn opportunities to testify to them. Pray that they may be able to minister there in the midst of difficult and dangerous conditions for as long as the Lord wills.

5. **Afghan believers are few** and mostly Dari-speaking; but since the invasion, they have become bolder for their Lord, and more Afghans are coming to Christ than ever before. Pray for their protection in persecution, and growth in numbers and grace. Pray that living churches may be planted all over the country.

6. **The few Bibles and NTs in the country, in Pushtun and Kabuli Farsi,** are not easily understood; however, the Dari New Testament has just been completed. Pray for the wise and effective distribution of God's Word. Pray for the translation of the Scriptures into other languages too; work is in progress in six, but at least five other languages definitely need translators.

7. **Afghans outside the country.** Pray for those who witness to Afghan students and refugees in the West, in hospitals and in the growing number of refugee settlements over the border in Pakistan. Pray for open doors and hearts among these suffering and sorrowing people.

8. **There is a lack of suitable gospel cassette tapes and records. GRI** has produced recordings in 59 languages and dialects; distribution is the problem. Pray for all seeking to use these media for reaching out to the Afghans. Pray for the daily half-hour Farsi and 15-minute Dari and Pushtun broadcasts from **FEBA** in the Seychelles.

Eastern Europe
Jan 27-28

ALBANIA
(The People's Socialist Republic of Albania)

Area 28,700 sq.km. A mountainous Balkan state on the Adriatic Sea.

Population 3,000,000. Annual growth 2.2%. People per sq.km. 105.

Peoples
Albanian 91%. Two dialects — Gheg in the north, Tosk in the south. Descended from the ancient Illyrians to whom Paul preached.
Greek 6%. **Gypsy** 2.4%.

Literacy 71%. **Official language:** Tosk Albanian. **All languages** 5. **Bible translations** 1Bi 1NT 3por.

Capital: Tirana 220,000. Urbanization 40%.

Economy: Europe's poorest and least developed country. Income/person $1,300 (9% of USA).

Politics: Became a Communist Republic in 1945. The most harsh and ruthless Communist regime in Europe. The land has become progressively isolated from other lands — from the West in 1945, from USSR in 1961 and from China in 1976.

Religion: Albania proudly claimed to be the world's first atheist state. The land's extreme isolation from the outside world enabled the rulers to eradicate all organized religion in a "cultural revolution" in 1967 modelled on that of China. All 2,196 mosques, churches and religious buildings were destroyed or converted to secular use. All those known to have religious beliefs are now killed, imprisoned or in hiding.
Since all organized religious activity is suppressed, we can only estimate the present situation. In brackets are the figures for 1945:

Non-religious/Atheist 75%.
Muslim 20%. (69%) Mainly Sunni, some Shi'ite.
Christian 5%. (31%).
- **Orthodox** 3%. (19.2%) Mainly Tosk.
- **Roman Catholic** 2%. (11.8%) Mainly Gheg.
- **Protestant** — a handful (?).

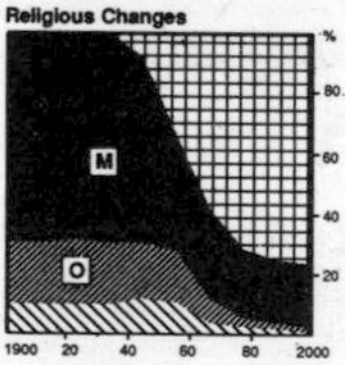

1. **Albania is Europe's most closed and least evangelized land.** Only for a brief period before World War II were there some evangelical missionaries in the country. The death of Hoxha, the long-ruling dictator, in 1985 could lead to change. Pray this land open!

2. **Albania was Europe's only Muslim state.** Marxism has suppressed Islam too. The people live in fear and in a state little better than slavery. Pray that the liberating gospel may be proclaimed freely to them.

3. **There are still believers meeting together in secret** — despite the claim that all religious superstitions have been eradicated. The Albanian press complained in 1975 that there was a remarkable increase in the public and secret practice of religion! A wave of arrests of Christians was reported in 1981.

4. **Albanians outside the country are more accessible:**
   a) **In Yugoslavia** 1,800,000, where there is a small group of believers; the only such in the world.
   b) **In Italy** 260,000, where centuries-old Albanian communities and new refugees live.

c) **In n.w. Greece** 12,000 living in villages near the border.
d) **In w. Europe** where Albanian guest workers from Yugoslavia have sought employment.

Pray for these to be evangelized. There are less than 50 known ethnic Albanian evangelical believers in the world.

5. **The New Testament was printed in 1937 in Gheg.** A revised New Testament in modern Albanian was printed in 1981. Pray for its effective distribution and impact on lives.

6. **Christian literature in Albanian** has been almost totally lacking since World War II. A number of books and booklets have been produced recently, mainly for the Albanians living outside Albania. Pray that some of this literature may find its way over virtually sealed borders with Greece and Yugoslavia. Pray for those who receive such literature — possession of which may lead to a death sentence. It is almost impossible for the few well-guarded tourists to distribute any literature inside the country. Pray that the slight thaw in relations with the West may result in more openings.

7. **The Greek minority** has been heavily persecuted, and a large proportion are in prisons and labour camps. Pray for them.

8. **Christian radio broadcasts** are the only way, at present, to get the gospel into the land. Pray for the raising up of more believers in the West who are fluent in Albanian who can help **ECM** and **OD** prepare programmes for transmission by **TWR** from Monaco and **IBRA** from Lisbon. There are now six programmes beamed into Albania every week. Pray that the news of these broadcasts may reach those who need the message of the gospel. Pray for good reception in Albania, where radio receivers are few and of poor quality, and where the government frequently jams incoming broadcasts.

ALGERIA

(The People's Democratic Republic of Algeria)

Middle East
Jan 29-30

Area 2,382,000 sq.km. Agriculturalized on the Mediterranean coast, in the Atlas mountains and oases. 80% is Sahara Desert.

Population 22,475,000. Annual growth 3.3%. People per sq.km. 9; 90% near the coast. About 1.7 million Algerians are migrants in Europe.

Peoples
Arab-Berber 79%. Speaking Arabic.
Berber (8 groups) 20%. Kabyle 2,700,000; Shawiya 1,100,000; Mzab (5 groups) 100,000; Tuareg 15,000.
European 0.8%. French 120,000; Russian 10,000, etc.

Literacy 38%. **Official language:** Arabic. French and, increasingly, English widely used. 25% speak one of the Berber dialects. **All languages** 15. **Bible translations** 1Bi 2NT 5por.

Capital: Algiers 1,650,000. Urbanization 52%.

Economy: Heavily dependent on oil exports. Over 50% of work force is in agriculture, but its potential has not been effectively exploited. Income/person $2,400 (17% of USA). Inflation 9%.

Politics: French colony for 132 years. Independence in 1962 after a bitter war of liberation. A one-party socialist republic with a military-civilian government.

Religion: Since independence, the government has actively encouraged the development of an Islamic Arab socialist state. Proselytism is not allowed.
Muslim 99.5%. Increasing tendency to a more orthodox and radical expression of Ibadi Islam.
Christian 0.3%. Nominal 0.05%. Affiliated 0.25%.
  Roman Catholic 0.24%. 53,000a.
  Orthodox 0.01%. 2,400a.
  Protestant 0.01%. 2,900a; 1,100m. 70% are expatriates.
  Cross-cultural Christians witnessing in Algeria 30 (1:750,000) in 5 agencies.

1. **Opposition to the gospel is intense.** A hundred years of tearful sowing the seed by a tenacious succession of missionaries has yet to bear fruit. Satan's forces must be overcome in the heavenlies. Muslims have a long and bitter memory of "Christian" conquests, colonialism and atrocities, so miracles are needed to overcome the centuries of prejudice.

2. **Independence failed to provide the prosperity and progress expected.** Young people are frustrated and dissatisfied. Many seek solutions in fundamentalist Islam and Berber nationalism but rarely in the gospel, for few have heard it. Pray for ways and means of reaching out to them.

3. **Berber nationalism** is a potent force among the younger generation who resent Arabic political, religious and cultural domination and increased efforts to Arabize them. Pray that this may bring many back to the faith of their ancestors. The majority of Algerian Christians are Kabyle.

4. **The unreached** — really the whole nation.
   a) **The growing cities** — the educated elite, the middle classes, and the teeming slums.
   b) **The Kabyle in the Djurdjura Atlas Region.** There are no longer any missionaries in the country speaking the language, and any efforts to evangelize them in their own language is a politically sensitive issue. Many live in France.
   c) **The Shawiya** — no known believers.
   d) **The Tuareg** 1-2 believers known. No continuing work in Algeria.
   e) **The Mzab** oasis towns in the Sahara. No known Christians and no specific effort ever launched to evangelize them in their tight-knit communities.

5. **The Algerians outside the country are more accessible to the gospel,** and more so since travel restrictions abroad were eased. **NAM**, **GMU**, and others have ministry among them in France and Belgium. Pray for effective outreach to tourists and residents in Europe. Pray for churches to be planted that also have a vision to evangelize in their native land.

6. **The tiny Church is growing,** even more so since 1981. Yet threats and intimidation by family, friends, employers and police are commonplace. Most believers are young, and the girls are often forced into marriage to Muslims. Fear frequently leads to isolation from fellowship, compromise and backsliding. Pray for perseverance, stickability, willingness to suffer where necessary and boldness to witness. Pray for the conversion of the families of believers. There are now about five indigenous church fellowships.

7. **Mature leadership is scarce.** Praise God for the precious few! Everything militates against the development of shepherds for the flock — the social pressures, the lack of Christian homes and families, disunity and the lack of teaching and teaching materials. The low-key TEE programme in use is a vital aid. Pray that new leaders will be raised up and preserved. An easy way out for many Christians is emigration. Praise God for a greater maturity and willingness to accept responsibility at all levels by national brothers. Pray for them.

8. **The active mission force** has steadily declined since 1970 with a number of expulsions. Missionaries are severely restricted in their activities. All use secular jobs for residency and as a platform for witnessing. Personal witness and discipleship, camps and Bible Study groups are the main opportunities for service. What wisdom, tact, courage and faith these servants of God need in the midst of frequent discouragements and insecurity! What sensitivity they need in tactfully helping the few groups of believers to maturity without dominating them!

9. **Literature in Arabic and especially Kabyle may not be imported.** The one Christian bookshop (**UBS**) may only sell literature in other languages. Pray for an end to restrictions and the wide dissemination of Christian literature, gospel cassettes and Bibles. Pray for those writing, printing and distributing literature among North Africans in Europe, and that some of this literature may be taken or sent to Algeria.

10. **Radio programmes** prepared by **GMU** in Spain and **NAM** in France and transmitted by **TWR** in Monaco have proved the most widespread and effective means of evangelism and teaching of isolated believers. Possibly thousands have been converted in North Africa. Pray for the follow up through Radio School of the Bible (**NAM**), visitation, BCCs and literature. Pray that literature may not be intercepted in the post and that those receiving correspondence for Christians may be free from harassment. A BCC in Kabyle is an urgent need. The Kabyle radio programmes are particularly effective.

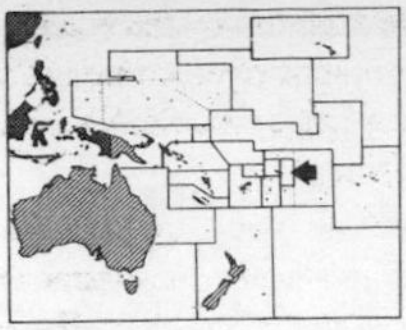

AMERICAN SAMOA
(The US Territory of American Samoa)

Pacific

Jan 31

Area 200 sq.km. Six small volcanic islands in the Samoan Archipelago.

Population 33,500. Many now living in California. Annual growth 1.1%. People per sq.km. 167.

Peoples: Samoan 89%; **Euronesian** (mixed) 10%; **US white** 1%.

Literacy 98%. **Official languages:** Samoan, English. **All languages** 2. **Bible translations** 2Bi.

Capital: Pago Pago 14,000.

Economy: Tourism, fishing, canning. Income/person $7,000 (50% of USA).

Politics: US territory since 1900.

Religion
Christian 99%. Affiliated 93.3%.
Roman Catholic 16.6%. Practising 75%. 5,600a; 2,560m.

Marginal groups (3) 12.5%. 4,200a. Mormons 2,800a.
Protestant 63.9%. 21,400a; 12,700m. Denominations 9. Largest (adult members):

Congregational Chr. Ch. (LMS)	7,800
Assemblies of God	3,100

Evangelical 17.8% of population.
Missionaries to American Samoa 10 (1:3,400 people) in 3 agencies.
Missionaries from American Samoa 2 (1:10,700 Protestants).

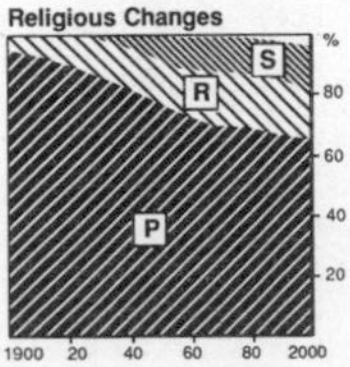

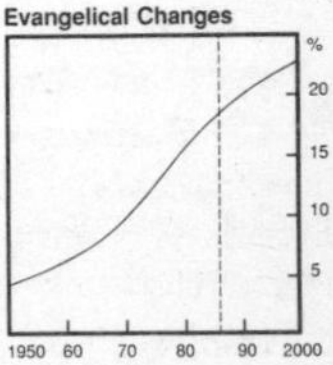

Points for prayer: See Samoa on p.362.

ANDORRA
(The Co-Principality of Andorra)

The West

Feb 1

Area 453 sq.km. In the heart of the Pyrenean Mountains between Spain and France.

Population 41,000. Annual growth 4.9%. People per sq.km. 90.

Peoples
Andorran 18%.
Foreigners 82%. Spanish 19,500; French 3,000; 30 other nationalities represented.

Literacy 92%. **Official language:** Catalan (Spanish).

Capital: Andorra la Vella 16,000. Urbanization 39%.

Economy: Wealthy through tourism and duty-free trading.

Politics: Self-governing co-principality since 1278; nominally ruled by the President of France and Spanish Bishop of Urgel.

Religion: Officially Catholic.
Christian 99%. Nominal 10.3%. Affiliated 88.7%.
Roman Catholic 87.8%. 36,000a.
Marginal groups 0.7%. Jehovah's Witnesses 300a.
Protestant 0.2%. 80a.
Missionaries to Andorra 0.

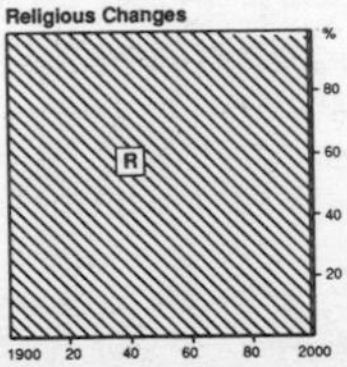

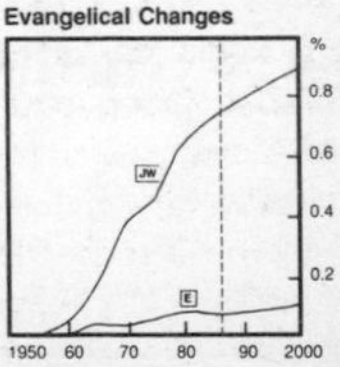

1. **There is not one known Andorrano evangelical believer.** Pray that a strong witness for the gospel may soon be established in this materialistic and cosmopolitan society.

2. **The only Evangelicals** who regularly meet together are 10 Spanish and a further five Filipino sisters. **WEF** maintains regular contact with these two groups. Pray for their witness to local and foreign residents.

3. **Christian literature** has been distributed throughout the country on several occasions in the '70s by both the Pocket Testament League and **ECM.** Pray for lasting fruit.

Africa
Feb 2-3

ANGOLA
(The People's Republic of Angola)

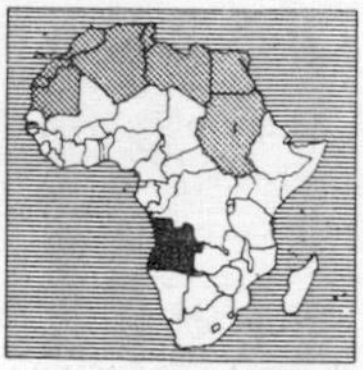

Area 1,247,000 sq.km. Coastal state that dominates Zaire's and Zambia's trade routes to the Atlantic.

Population 7,900,000. Annual growth 2.5%. People per sq.km. 6.3.

Peoples
Indigenous (34 peoples) 99%. Ovimbundu 2,500,000; Mbunda 1,700,000; Kongo 730,000; Chokwe 580,000; Luchazi 580,000; Nyaneka 290,000; Kwanyama 140,000; Lunda 70,000; Herero 56,000; Bushmen 15,000.
Minorities 1%. Portuguese/mixed race 30,000; Cuban 25,000.
Refugees — to Zambia 100,000; Zaire 70,000; Namibia 50,000.

Literacy 15%. **Official language:** Portuguese. **All languages** 30. **Bible translations** 6Bi 4NT 8por.

Capital: Luanda 950,000. Many refugees from the interior. Urbanization 24%.

Economy: Potentially wealthy, but the economy is in a state of collapse as a result of the post-independence flight of skilled personnel and 25 years of continual war. Income/person $670 (5% of USA).

Politics: A Portuguese colony for 450 years. Independence was won in 1975 after 15 years of warfare. The Marxist-oriented MPLA gained control of the central government with Cuban aid. This rule is contested by the UNITA nationalist movement (which controls 25%, and infiltrates 75% of the country) and weakened further by military incursions of South African forces.

Religion: The former President vowed to eradicate Christianity within 20 years, but the present instability has led to some freedom for Christians in government-controlled areas despite continued atheistic propaganda, intimidation and localized persecution.
Non-religious/Atheist 4%.
African Traditionalist 16%.
Christian 80%. Nominal 24.6%. Affiliated 55.4%.
Roman Catholic 41%. 3,240,000a; 1,800,000m. Many baptized, but low church attendance and commitment.
Indigenous marginal groups (12) 1.8%. 142,000a.
Protestant 11.7%. 924,000a; 473,000m. Denominations 24. Largest (adult members):

Church of God	app. 100,000
Seventh Day Adventist Ch.	78,000
Methodist Church	75,000
United Church	70,000
Brethren Assemblies	64,000
Baptist Church (**BMS**)	33,000
Ev. Ch. in S.W. Angola (**AME**)	29,000
Un. of Ev. Chs. in S.A. (**AEF**)	20,000

Evangelical 7.7% of population.
Missionaries to Angola 46 (1:172,000 people) in 8 agencies.

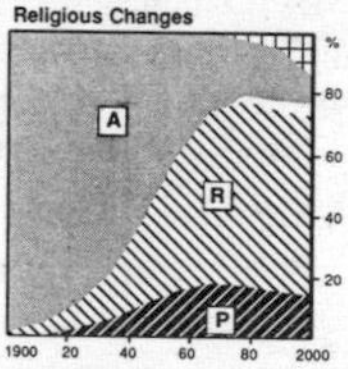

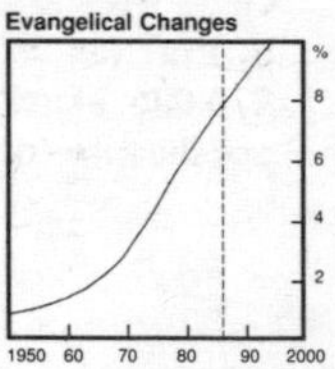

1. **Pray for the peace of this unhappy land.** Many areas of the centre and south are scenes of both bitter civil war and confrontation with South African forces from Namibia.

There have been enormous casualties through fighting and famine. Many have fled to surrounding lands. Pray for freedom for the gospel and a government that honours God. Praise the Lord for thrilling accounts of full and growing churches in most areas!

2. **Many refugees have fled to Zambia, Zaire and Namibia.** Pray for the Christian workers ministering to their spiritual needs in Namibia; most of these refugees are being evangelized for the first time. Efforts are being made for the evangelization of the refugees in Zambia (**AEF**-Ev. Ch. of Zambia and **Brethren**); there are over 50 assemblies of Chokwe refugees among them!

3. **There has been an increase in witchcraft in many areas** since independence. Many believers have suffered persecution as a result. Pray for such a manifestation of the power of God that many of Satan's captives may be freed.

4. **The Church in the government-controlled areas** nearer the coast was more nominal in the past. Suffering is purifying many but causing bitterness, hatred, and a tribalistic spirit among others. Over 53 congregations of Christian refugees have been formed in the area. The Church is under considerable pressure, and some leaders have compromised with Marxism. There are limitations on youth work and the building of new churches. Pray for the witness of the Christians in times of much intimidation and persecution. The Evangelical Fellowship of Angola was formed in 1974, and provides a means of fellowship among believers and a channel of communication to the authorities.

5. **The churches in the war-ravaged centre and south** continue to meet together. Many have to function in incredibly difficult situations — famine, destruction, loss of believers who "disappear" to fight, lack of leaders, lack of money to buy Bibles, etc. A few Bible schools still manage to carry on.

6. **Leadership training.** The beginnings of an evangelical seminary have been made in Lubango. There are also several new Bible schools in the country. Pray for adequate biblical teaching for the rising generation of leaders in the churches.

7. **Some missionaries of AEF, AME and the Brethren** still work in the country, but often with restrictions on their ministry. In some areas they may not preach; in others they face danger in travelling in war zones, shortages and many trials. Pray for them, and pray for reinforcements and the issuing of necessary visas. The number of workers needed will greatly increase should peace come to the land. The **SBC** are renewing their ministry in the land, and the Lutherans are commencing a new work.

8. **Praise the Lord for the commencement of evangelical student groups (IFES).** There are three groups in universities with one staff worker.

9. **Literature and Bibles are scarce** and in great demand. Pray for the supplies entering from Namibia, Canada, Portugal and Brazil, that these books and Bibles may reach those who need them. Many Spanish Bibles have also been taken in for distribution among the Cubans.

10. **Radio broadcasts reach the land in three languages from TWR** in Swaziland.

11. **Unreached peoples:**
    a) **A number of peoples in this land have never been evangelized** because of the difficulties missionaries experience in entering or moving around the country. There is nothing of God's Word in many of the languages.
    b) **Pray for the largely unevangelized** Huila 200,000; Mbwela 140,000; Kwangali 270,000; Macubai; Bushmen 15,000, and Mbukushu 11,000 in the south (**AEF** area); and the tribes of the northeast including the Mbangala in the **Brethren** area.

Caribbean

ANGUILLA
(The Colony of Anguilla)

See British Antilles p. 115

Caribbean
Feb 4

ANTIGUA
(The State of Antigua and Barbuda)

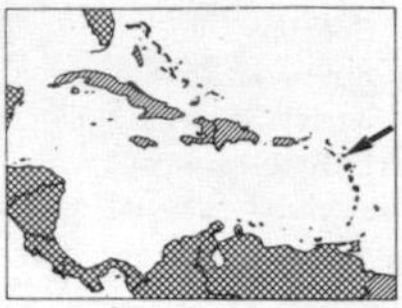

Area 443 sq.km. Three islands; Antigua volcanic, Barbuda coralline.

Population 80,000. Annual growth 1%. People per sq.km. 181.

Peoples: African/Eurafrican 96%; **European** 1.3%; **East Indian** 0.2%.

Literacy 89%. **Languages:** English, English Creole.

Capital: St. John's 29,000.

Economy: Dependent on tourism, vegetables and foreign aid. Income/person $1,730 (12% of USA). Inflation 12.5%.

Politics: British colony for 349 years; independence 1981.

Religion
Spiritist 2%, **Baha'i** 0.7%, **Muslim** 0.4%.
Christian 96.9%. Nominal 30.6%. Affiliated 66.3%.
Roman Catholic 8.7%. 7,000a; 4,800m.

Marginal groups 0.7%. Mainly Jehovah's Witnesses.

Protestant 57%. 45,600a; 21,700m. Denominations 15. Largest (adult members):

Anglican Church	11,500
Moravian Church	2,800
Methodist Church	2,200
Wesleyan Church	1,000

Evangelical 9.7% of population.

Missionaries to Antigua 10 (1:8,000 people) in 4 agencies.

Missionaries from Antigua 0.

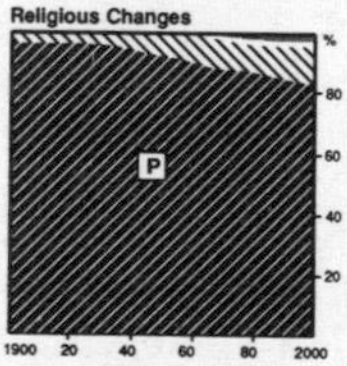

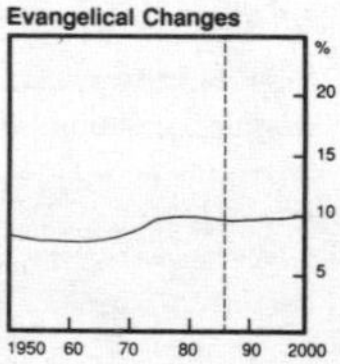

Points for Prayer: See Jamaica on p. 255.

ARGENTINA
(The Argentine Republic)

Latin America

Feb 5-7

Area 2,777,000 sq.km. Latin America's second largest country with a great range of climate, rainfall and topography.

Population 30,600,000. Annual growth 1.6%. People per sq.km. 11.

Peoples

European 87%. A fusion of many nationalities, but largely Spanish, Italian and other East and West Europeans. Many minorities have retained a considerable degree of national identity.

Mestizo 10%. Largely Paraguayan, Bolivian and Chilean.

Amerindian 1.9%. Quechua 300,000; Mapuche 50,000; Lowland peoples (9) 208,000, mostly in the Chaco in the far north and Patagonia in the far south.

Literacy 93%. **Official language:** Spanish. **All languages** 21. **Bible translations** 1Bi 4NT 6por.

Capital: Buenos Aires 11,400,000. Other major cities: Cordoba 1,140,000; Rosario 1,000,000. Urbanization 82%.

Economy: Largely based on agriculture but increasingly industrialized. The relatively high standard of living and the economy have been badly affected by runaway inflation (700% in 1984). High unemployment. Income/person $2,030 (14% of USA).

Politics: Independent from Spain in 1816. Peronist misrule, inflation and increasing leftist urban terrorism provoked the 1976 military takeover. The military government's incompetence, military adventurism and bad record on human rights led to the restoration of democratic rule in 1983. The new government is courageously facing up to the crises assailing the land.

Religion: Roman Catholicism is the official religion, but the new government has declared total freedom of conscience.

Non-religious/Atheist 1.8%.

Jews 2%. The fifth largest group of Jews in the world.

Muslim 0.2%. Mainly Palestinian and Lebanese.

Christian 95.5%. Affiliated 93.6%.

Roman Catholic 86.5%. Practising 63%. 26,500,000a; 17,200,000m. There are over 1.7 mill. baptized Catholics who have joined evangelical or other groups. After years of declining attendances and influence, there has been a reversal of this trend and much activity to win the youth.

Orthodox (6 groups) 0.5%.

Marginal groups 1.1%. Largest adherents:

Mormons	63,500
Jehovah's Witnesses	56,500
New Apostolic	38,000

Protestant 5.5%. 1,680,000a; 603,700m. Denominations approximately 150; Largest (adult members):

Seventh Day Adventists		53,600
Assemblies of God		50,000
Visión de Futuro	(?)	50,000
Brethren		40,000
Baptist Convention (**SBC**)		36,500
Christian Assemblies		36,000
Anglican (**SAMS**)		19,000

Evangelical 4.7% of population.

Missionaries to Argentina 590 (1:52,000 people) in 58 agencies.

Missionaries from Argentina est. 50.

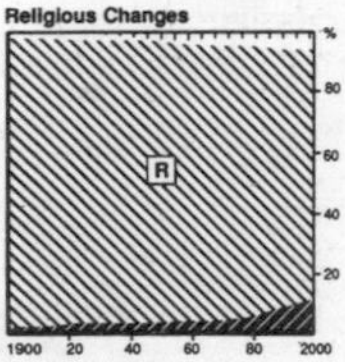

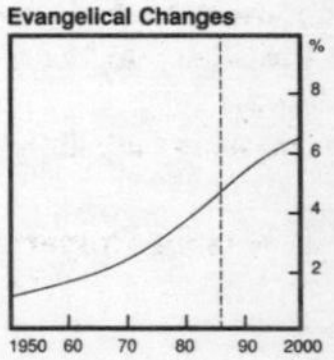

1. **A feeling of helpless despair swept through the nation due to the political and economic upheavals of the last decade.** This helped to open the hearts of many to the gospel. Pray that many may turn from superstition, witchcraft and sin to a living hope in Jesus. Pray for the young people and their salvation, as many have turned to immorality and drugs. Praise for the new air of excitement and expectation among Evangelicals for future advance!

2. **There is still prejudice against Protestants,** which is heightened by the activities of fast-growing sectarian groups such as the Mormons and Jehovah's Witnesses. Pray for a fervent evangelistic spirit among the believers and a willingness to witness to the Roman Catholic majority.

3. **There have been many conversions in the land since 1976,** but this has not resulted in the expected growth in the churches. The rate of backsliding is high. Pray for revival to stir the churches into new life. The dramatic impact in imaginative evangelism and church growth by "Visión de Futuro" is cause for much praise. Many believe that Argentina is on the threshold of great church growth; pray it into being.

4. **Areas of weakness in the Protestant churches are shared for prayerful concern.**
   a) Superficiality in conversions and inadequate follow up of those who profess faith in Christ.
   b) Divisiveness over personalities and doctrine — especially the charismatic issue.
   c) Insufficient leaders for the churches to be able both to teach the believers and mobilize them for evangelism.
   d) The high loss rate of believers' children to the world.

5. **The "Allianza Cristiana de las Iglesias Evangélicas" (ACIERA)** was formed in 1982 as a rallying point for Evangelicals. Its purpose is to promote evangelism and give a united stand for biblical truth nationally and internationally. Pray for a unity of believers that will speed the evangelization of Argentina and the world.

6. **The immigrant minority Churches** make up approx. 20% of the Protestants. They have attended to the spiritual needs of their own communities (such as the Italian, Danish, Dutch, Welsh, etc.) but have not evangelized the Spanish-speaking majority; though some, such as the Italian, Russian and Chilean believers, have evangelized their own groups. They are in decline, partly because their Spanish-speaking children do not feel at home in the churches.

7. **Leadership training** — there is a need for godly theologians and pastors who will stand for the truth in the Argentinian context. Many theological colleges emphasize humanism, liberation theology and social action rather than the preaching of the Word. The Protestant Church is largely evangelical, but could be influenced by such teaching.

8. **Missions.** The greatest need is for mature missionaries able to assist the Church in Bible teaching, church planting and imparting a missionary vision. Pray for the church planting and support work of missionaries linked with **SBC** (64), **Brethren** (43), **CMA** (21), **GMU** (12), etc.

9. **The less evangelized peoples and areas:**
   a) The sparsely inhabited Patagonia in the south, and the north and west of Argentina.
   b) The 500,000 Jews, most of whom live in the environs of Buenos Aires.
   c) The urban slum areas.

10. **The Amerindians of the Chaco in the north have been responding to the gospel.** Most of the Mataco (13,000) and Choroti (800 in the **SAMS** area), nearly all the Toba (20,000, **Pentecostals**) and many of the Chiriguano (23,000, **Baptists**) are committed Christians. Pockets of animism remain. Pray for Bible translation work in nine of the 21 Indian languages **(UBS)**. Pray for effective integration of these Christians into national life. **GRI** has recordings in all nine languages.

11. **The missionary vision of the Argentinian Church is small but growing.** A number of evangelical and Pentecostal churches support missionaries in Argentina and abroad. Pray for this vision to grow despite the economic difficulties in the land.

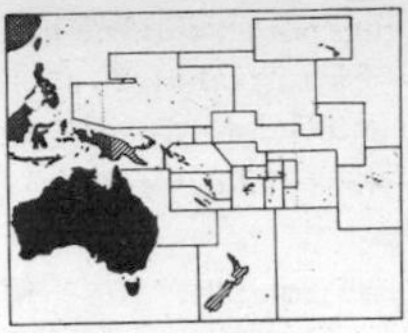

AUSTRALIA
(The Commonwealth of Australia)

Pacific

Feb 8-9

Area 7,687,000 sq.km. This island continent is largely grassland and desert in the interior but better watered in the east, southeast and southwest coastal regions, where most live in highly concentrated urban areas.

Population 15,800,000. Annual growth 1.1%. Immigration 0.3%. People per sq.km. 2.

Peoples
British origin 82.6%.
Other European 13%.
Middle Eastern 2%. Arab-speaking 250,000.
Asian 1.3%. Chinese, Vietnamese, Indian.
Australian Aborigine 1.1%. 172,000. (In 1780 approx. 300,000 speaking 260 languages.) About 50,000 are still nomadic.

Literacy 99%. **Official language:** English. Nearly 10% of the population do not use English as their first language. **All indigenous living languages** 121. **Bible translations** 1Bi 2NT 28por.

Capital: Canberra 260,000. Other cities: Sydney 3,500,000; Melbourne 3,000,000; Brisbane 1,160,000; Adelaide 1,000,000; Perth 980,000. Urbanization 86%.

Economy: Wealthy mixed economy based on industry, agriculture and mining, but world recession and severe droughts slowed the economy in the '80s. Income/person $10,780 (77% of USA). Inflation 10.4%.

Politics: Parliamentary democracy, independent of Britain in 1901.

Religion: A secular state with freedom of religion.
Non-religious/Atheist, etc. 21.8%.
Muslim 1.5%. Predominantly Turks, Arabs and Yugoslavs.
Jews 0.4%. **Chinese religions** 0.3%.
Christian 76%. Affiliated 73.1%. Weekly church attendance is nearer 12% of the population.

Roman Catholic 26.7%. 4,100,000a; 2,860,000m. High proportion of continental European nationalities.
Orthodox 3.1%. Over 28 denominations mainly from Eastern Europe and Middle East.
Marginal groups 1.1%. 182,000a; 99,000m. Over 54 cults. Largest (adherents):

Jehovah's Witnesses	79,000
Mormons	47,000

Protestant 42%. A further 10% nominal Protestants. 6,630,000a; 1,890,000m. Denominations 150. Largest (adherents):

Anglican Church	3,860,000
Uniting Church	1,460,000
Presbyterian Ch. (continuing)	213,000
Baptist Union	204,000
Lutheran Church	114,050
Churches of Christ	92,000
Salvation Army	75,000
Methodist Church (continuing)	67,000
Seventh Day Adventist Church	54,000
Assemblies of God	35,500
Congregational Union	25,000
Brethren	22,000

Evangelical 17% of population.
Missionaries to Australia (cross-cultural) approx. 600 (1:26,000 people).
Missionaries from within Australia 2,690 (1:2,460 Protestants) in 62 agencies.

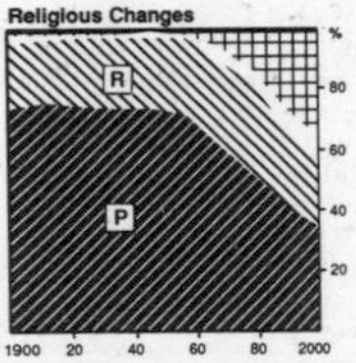

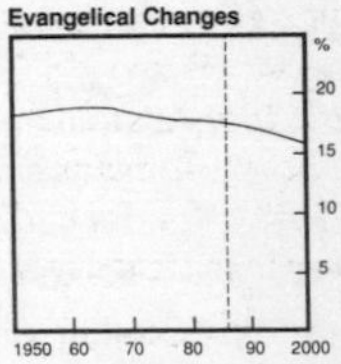

1. **Australia has become a very secular society**, and the same materialism, permissiveness and rejection of traditional authority characteristic of the whole Western World is just as discernible here. There has been a greater openness to the gospel since 1977, when Christians began taking the trouble to reach people on *their* ground.

2. **The decline in church attendance is causing deep concern** (1966 35%, 1976 18%). This decline is most noticeable in some of the larger and more traditional churches, but there is some growth in the more evangelical denominations, particularly in the various Pentecostal and charismatic churches and groups. Pray for revival.

3. **The Evangelicals are strong in the Sydney Anglican diocese,** and in the mainline churches, several have evangelical majorities while all of the rest have significant and active

minorities. Pray that overall there might be a greater return to biblical truth and emphasis on evangelism and missions in the churches.

4. **The missionary vision of many Australians has been encouraging.** Pray that this vision may be shared so that missionary concern becomes a normal part of church life. Pray for the well-filled Bible schools and theological colleges which are training many for the mission field. Pray also for those who have gone out that all, whether in home or mission ministries, may have a heart for world evangelization.

5. **Unreached peoples** — both among the indigenous inhabitants and the four million non-British post-war immigrants and their families. Pray for those local churches with an active ministry to such communities and also for the work of **ECM** among the European minorities.

a) **Aborigine tribes** — only a few isolated groups have failed to respond to the very considerable missionary effort now being made all over the country.

b) **Many people in the working-class urban areas** and in isolated mining and farming communities in the vast interior, n.w. and north have had no contact with the true gospel.

c) **Muslims** — around 300,000, with 200,000 living in the Sydney area. The majority of this very diverse community is Arab-speaking; 200,000 from Lebanon, Egypt, etc.; others are Turkish (30,000), Yugoslav, etc. Small beginnings are being made to reach these peoples, and there are Arabic and Turkish-speaking groups of believers.

d) **Chinese** 160,000 (30,000 being refugees from Vietnam). About 20% of the Chinese are Christian in name, others are secular or adhere to the various Chinese traditional religions. There are lively groups of believers in the cities and among overseas Chinese students in universities. Pray for the complete evangelization of the non-Christians and the newly-arrived refugees.

e) **Vietnamese** 28,000. Mostly refugees recently arrived. There are a few Christian congregations. **AsEF** is expanding a ministry to meet the spiritual needs of Asian communities in each state.

f) **The Yugoslavs** are ethnically diverse, and most still retain the use of their mother tongue; Croatian 70,000; Serbian 35,000; Macedonian 70,000; etc. They originate from one of Europe's least evangelized countries. There are very few believers among them.

g) **Jews** (78,000) — half live in Melbourne, but relatively few have become Christian.

h) **Southern Europeans.** Many second and third generation settlers have assimilated into English-speaking Australian society. Many, however, still use their original languages: Italian 450,000; Greek 230,000; Polish 90,000; Spanish 60,000; Maltese 60,000. These represent strategic minorities that, if evangelized and motivated, could make a decisive impact for God on their lands of origin.

6. **The 166,000 indigenous Aborigines** have suffered much in their contacts with Western culture, and their political and land rights have become a major political issue. Some have adapted and have been absorbed into the life of the nation, but many have sunk into moral and spiritual degradation, and others have retreated into the more inaccessible and inhospitable parts of the country. Yet in the last eight years an indigenous revival movement in the north has spread through parts of the west and centre of the country with thousands being soundly converted.

a) Pray for the **Aboriginal Evangelical Fellowship**, a key coordinating body of Aboriginal Christians, as it encourages leadership development through its training college, outreach and church planting in every Aboriginal community.

b) Pray for the nearly 500 missionaries in 26 denominational and interdenominational societies working among these people (such as the **Aborigine Inland Mission, United Aborigine Mission,** etc.).

c) Bible translation is in progress in 33 of these small language groups (through the 50 **SIL** and **UBS** workers); 16 languages have a portion of the NT. Ten still need translators.

d) The use of **GRI** records and cassettes in 81 languages is a vital contribution to evangelizing, with the great linguistic variety among the Aborigines.

7. **The witness among the 332,000 tertiary students in the 79 universities and colleges.** Various groups are active — **AFES(IFES), Student Life, Navigators,** etc., and few colleges

are without witnessing fellowships. Pray for these key ministries. Pray for witness among overseas students; one of the most active is the Overseas Chinese Fellowship.

8. **Young people.** The Inter-Schools Christian Fellowship has a valuable ministry in secondary schools. Many groups, such as Youth For Christ, God Squad, etc., are now evangelizing among young people.

9. **Christian radio and television** could be more effectively utilized by Evangelicals through the national and local broadcasting networks, who are required, by law, to give a percentage of time weekly to religious broadcasts.

AUSTRIA
(The Republic of Austria)

The West

Feb 10-11

Area 84,000 sq.km. A landlocked central European state.

Population 7,600,000. Annual growth 0%. People per sq.km. 90.

Peoples
German-speaking 95.5%.
Minorities: Slovene 0.3%, Croatian 0.3%.
Migrant labourers: Yugoslav (Slovene, Serbo-Croat, Albanian, etc.) 160,000; Turk 25,000; Greek 12,000.

Capital: Vienna 1,770,000 (nearly one quarter of the population). Urbanization 54%.

Literacy 99%. **Official language:** German.

Economy: Stable and with relatively little unemployment. Income/person $9,210 (65% of USA).

Politics: Once part of the great Austro-Hungarian Empire but now a stable, neutral buffer state between the Communist Bloc and the West but whose sympathies lie with the latter.

Religion: Freedom of religion guaranteed by constitution.
Non-religious/Atheist 4%.
Muslim 1.3%. Turks, Iranians, Yugoslavs.
Jews 0.1%. 8,000 (2.8% in 1934).
Christian 94.7%. Affiliated 90.4%.
Roman Catholic 83%. Practising 40%. 6,300,000a; 4,900,000m.
Old Catholics 0.3%.
Orthodox 0.8%.
Marginal groups 0.6%. Mormons 2,847a; Jehovah's Witnesses 26,500a.
Protestant 5.6%. 425,000a. Denominations 32. Largest (adherents):

Lutheran Church	379,000
Reformed Church	15,400
Baptist Churches (2)	1,900
Methodist Church	1,700
Assemblies of God	1,200
Brethren	500
Volksmission	300

Evangelical 0.62% of population.
Missionaries to Austria 395 (1:19,200 people) in 60 agencies.
Missionaries from Austria 24 (1:17,700 Protestants).

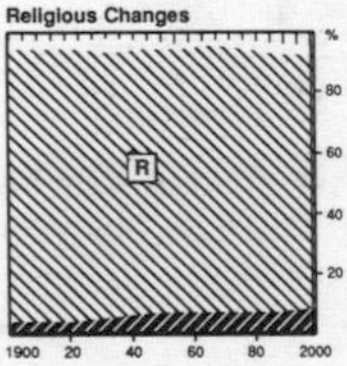

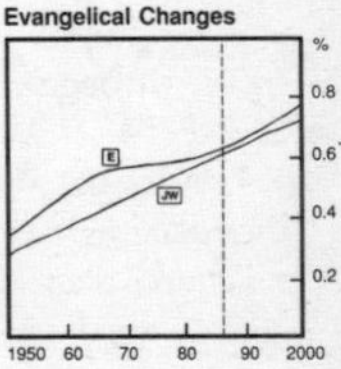

1. **Austria is a mission field with only a small evangelical witness.** No more than 20% of the people are estimated to have ever had contact with the gospel. Many have had dealings with the occult, and the illegitimacy and suicide rates are among the highest in Europe.

2. **Many areas are without a permanent witness**, though this lack is beginning to be met. It is reckoned that only about 160 of the 4,000 towns and villages have a group of believers that regularly meets together. There are still about 55 towns of over 5,000 people with no permanent witness. Most of the believers are found in the cities. Pray for a great harvest of souls.

Pray especially for the 300,000 people in the easternmost province of Vorarlberg, reputedly the "hardest" area in the land.

3. **The land is nominally Roman Catholic**, but there is a marked drift away from the church in the cities. Nevertheless, people still fear to have too much contact with Evangelicals thinking them to be a sect. Pray that the barriers to the entry of the gospel into their hearts may be broken down.

4. **There is much formality and lifelessness in the Evangelical Lutheran and Reformed Churches**, and they are losing 2,300 people annually. There are a number of Bible-believing pastors, and their number is now being increased by graduates (15 in 1982) of the Free Evangelical Seminary in Basel, Switzerland. Pray for the Pastors' Prayer Fellowship, an evangelical fellowship within the Lutheran Church. Pray for a move of the Spirit of God in these churches that will make them a force for the evangelization of the land.

5. **The evangelical witness is small but growing.** There are about 200 Bible study or church groups meeting regularly — most being very new. There are now possibly 10-15,000 born-again believers in the country. Pray for the growth of this church planting ministry. The first Austrian evangelical, interdenominational Bible school at Ampflwang opened in 1984; graduates from this school could be a decisive factor for church growth in coming years.

6. **The believers need prayer** — for there is not sufficient concern for the evangelization of the lost, and they are too conscious of being a small and despised minority within the Roman Catholic majority. There are too few young Austrian believers coming forward for full-time service. The Lutheran and the free churches worked together for a special year of evangelism in Austria in 1985.

7. **The cults are aggressive and growing in numbers.** There are more active followers of the Jehovah's Witnesses and Mormons than committed evangelical believers. Their pervasive influence complicates any evangelistic outreach. Many young people are led astray by modern Eastern and Western youth cults.

8. **There is a growing missionary force.** Pray that these missionaries may adapt well to the Austrian situation. Most missionaries are involved in evangelism and church planting. There are a number of German-speaking missions with over 56 missionaries as well as **TEAM** (25), **CBFMS** (21), **SBC** (19), **GEM** (16), **ECM** (14), **GMU** (12), **BCU** (4), etc. Pray also for the witness of **OM** in mobilizing locals and tourists in aggressive evangelism.

9. **The witness among students** is one of the most fruitful in the land today. There are strong groups in the seven universities, and the groups are growing in depth and outreach. Pray that these young Christians may have an impact on the land and its churches. Pray for the ministries of **OSB(IFES)**, **CCC** and **Navigators** on the campuses of Austria. Both **CEF** and **SU** have an appreciated ministry to school-age children.

10. **The Austrians are keen readers, so literature is a vital means of witness.** Pray for the Scripture distribution of the Bible Society and the literature ministries of Austrian Bible Mission and **CLC**.

11. **Migrant labourers** — little has yet been done for the Muslim Turks. There is one small Yugoslav church in Vienna, but most of this large community has yet to be evangelized. They could prove strategic for the evangelizing of Yugoslavia.

BAHAMAS

(Commonwealth of the Bahamas)

Caribbean

Feb 12

Area 14,000 sq.km. An archipelago of 700 coral islands between Florida and Cuba. Forty are inhabited.

Population 256,000. Annual growth 1.9%. People per sq.km. 18.

Peoples: African 73%; **Eurafrican** 14%; **European** 12.5%. **Other minorities:** Jews 700, Chinese 500. **Foreign-born** (Haitian, USA, etc.) 16%.

Literacy 93%. **Official language:** English.

Capital: Nassau 136,000. Urbanization 54%.

Economy: Prosperous through tourism, oil refining, finance and illegal drug traffic. Income/person $4,060 (29% of USA). Inflation 7.6%.

Politics: Independent from Britain in 1973 as a parliamentary monarchy. Stable government since independence.

Religion

Non-religious/Atheist 3.8%. **Spiritist** 1%. **Jews** 0.3%.

Christian 94.7%. Nominal 24.1%. Affiliated 70.6%.

Roman Catholic 12.7% Practising 70%. 32,500a; 19,400m.

Orthodox 0.4%. Mainly Greeks.

Marginal groups (5) 1.1%. Jehovah's Witnesses 654m.

Protestant 56.4%. 144,000a; 71,400m. Denominations 30. Largest (adult members):

Baptist Union	20,500
Anglican Church	10,000
Seventh Day Adventist Church	9,500
Methodist Church	7,200
Church of God of Prophecy	3,300
Brethren	2,800
Church of God (Cleveland)	2,416

Evangelical 30% of population.

Missionaries to Bahamas 112 (1:2,300 people) in 14 agencies.

Missionaries from Bahamas 0 (?).

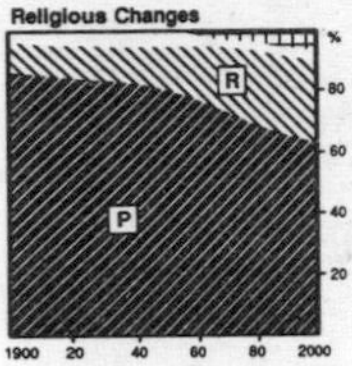

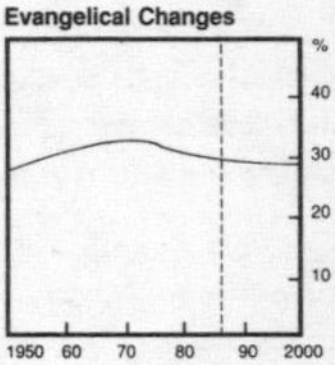

Points for prayer: See Jamaica on p. 255.

B

Middle East

Feb 13

BAHRAIN
(The State of Bahrain)

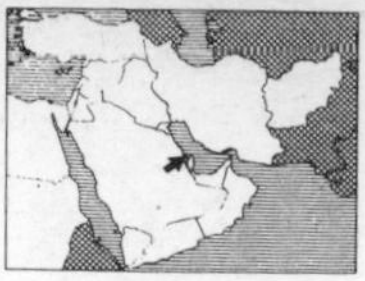

Area 622 sq.km. Eleven islands in the Arabian Gulf between the Qatar peninsula and Saudi Arabian mainland.

Population 400,000. Natural growth 2.7%. Immigration growth 0.6%. People per sq.km. 643.

Peoples
Arab 79%. Indigenous 69%, immigrant 10%.
Iranian 12%. **Indian** 3%. **Pakistani** 3%.
Western (British, US) 3%.

Literacy 40%. **Official language:** Arabic.

Capital: Manama 121,000. Urbanization 78%.

Economy: Diversifying from oil production to become a major Gulf industrial and banking centre. Income/person $10,360 (73% of USA).

Politics: British protection until 1971. Absolute monarchy since 1975.

Religion: Islam is the official religion, and all Bahrainis are considered Muslim. No evangelism among them is permitted. Christian expatriate churches have been favourably welcomed.
Muslim 90.8%. Sunni 40% (largely urban), Shi'a 55% (rural and Iranians).
Hindu 2.2%.
Christian 7%. Nominal 3.2%. Affiliated 3.8%.
Roman Catholic 1.7%. 6,800a. (Indians, Lebanese, Westerners).
Orthodox 0.1%. 500a. (Indians, Lebanese).
Protestant 2%. 8,000a; 3,280m. Denominations 12. Largest (adult members):

Anglican Church	1,740
National Evangelical Church	550

(5 congregations using different languages); a number of Indian groups.
Evangelical 1% of population.
Missionaries to Bahrain 16 (1:25,000).

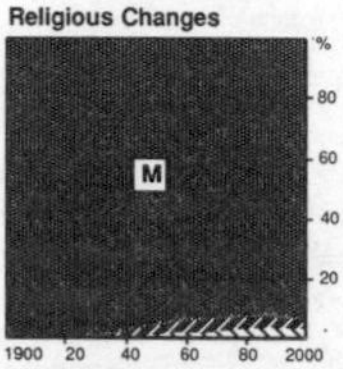

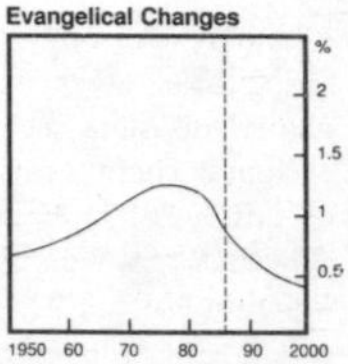

1. **Bahrain has provided a good base for Christian witness** since the beginning of this century. Pray for continued freedom for the tactful witness through expatriate Christians. Pray especially for the one Arab-speaking congregation of around 150 (40% Bahraini) and their witness to the many Muslims who have never been exposed to the gospel.

2. **There are a number of avenues for tactful witness** to the Arab majority.
   a) The expatriate Christians employed there — meeting in churches and house fellowships.
   b) The Christian missionaries serving in the country.
   c) The well-known American Mission Hospital which has a good reputation.
   d) The Christian bookstore with a high annual sale of Christian literature.

3. **Half the labour force of 200,000 is foreign**, and includes people from 45 nations. Pray for Christians within some of these national groups, that in the prevailing concern for material things they may win people for Christ. Pray especially for the Iranians, Muslim Pakistanis, also Hindu and Muslim Indians from South India.

4. **FEBA Radio from the Seychelles is well received.** Pray for the financing and producing of Arabic broadcasts suitable for breaking down Islamic misconceptions of the gospel.

BANGLADESH
(The People's Republic of Bangladesh)

Asia

Feb 14-17

Area 144,000 sq.km. Occupying the delta and floodplains of the Ganges and Brahmaputra Rivers, with high rainfall and frequent flooding.

Population 101,500,000. Annual growth 2.8%. People per sq.km. 704.

Peoples
Bengali 98%.
Bihari 1%. Mostly in refugee camps.
Tribal peoples 0.7%. 640,000 people in 28 tribes. Largest: Chakma 300,000.

Capital: Dhaka 4,017,000. Chittagong 1,700,000. Urbanization 13.5%.

Literacy 25%. **Official languages:** Bengali; English used widely. **All languages** 33. **Bible translations** 13Bi 3NT 8por.

Economy: One of the world's poorest nations, suffering from gross overpopulation and periodic natural disasters such as devastating floods and cyclones. There seems little hope that the poverty of this unhappy land will ever be substantially alleviated. Income/person $130 (1% of USA). Inflation 12%.

Politics: Formerly East Pakistan; independent in 1971 after bitter civil war and defeat of Pakistan by Indian and Bangladesh forces. Corruption, instability, assassinations and 18 coups have marred the years since then. The military took over the government in 1982 but is unable to cope with the serious problems the country faces.

Religion: A secular state since 1971 despite the large Muslim majority. The present military government is taking the country closer to the Islamic bloc; this is opening up tensions between the Muslim conservatives and progressives and could provoke stricter limitations on Christian work.

Muslim 87%. Almost all are Sunni, a few Shi'a.
Hindu 11.7%. Decreasing through emigration and lower fertility.
Buddhist 0.6%. Mainly among the Chakma, Magh and Mru peoples.
Tribal religions 0.1%. Among the Garo, Santal, etc.
Christian 0.38%.

Roman Catholic 0.18%. Practising 59%. 190,000a.

Protestant 0.18%. 188,000a; 72,600m. Denominations 25. Largest (adult members):

Baptist Union of B.(**BMS**)	11,500
Garo Baptist Union	10,000
Bawm Evangelical Chr. Church	9,600
All One in Christ Fellowship	7,100
Evang. Lutheran Church	5,000
Ch. of B. (Ang.-Presby.)	4,400
Seventh Day Adventist Church	4,200
Assemblies of God	2,400
Bangl. Bapt. Union	1,790

Evangelical 0.10% of population.

Missionaries to Bangladesh 440 (1:230,000 people) in 30 agencies.

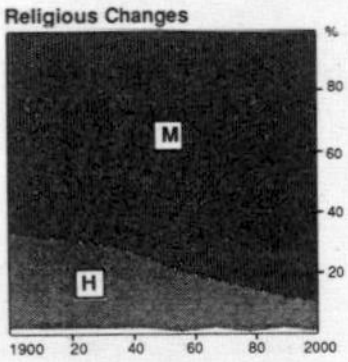

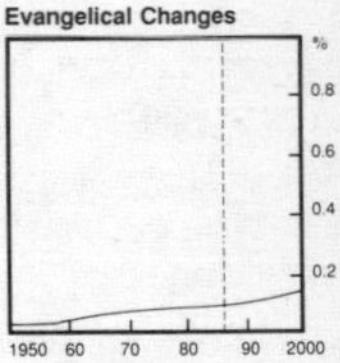

1. **Bangladesh has been a hard field for the gospel.** Revulsion at the cruelty of Pakistan's repression in the name of Islam in the 1971 civil war temporarily weakened Bangladeshi loyalty to Islam. These influences are now lessening, and many obstacles are being raised to hinder the entry and activities of missionaries. Yet the vast majority of the population has never once heard the gospel. Pray for the hold of the powers of darkness on the land to be loosed. Pray for a stable, moderate government.

2. **There are signs of an abundant harvest to be reaped. Pray it in!**

   a) There are many aid programmes through Christian relief organizations. The inter-mission "HEED" Bangladesh, **WV, TEAR Fund,** etc. have opened hearts to the Christian message. Pray for all involved in decision making and implementing these programmes. Pray for eternal fruit among tribals, Hindus and Muslims. These programmes have been under increasing attack by enemies of the gospel.

   b) **The openness of Muslims** in some areas to innovative methods of evangelism is encouraging. Pray for strong witnessing churches to be planted and for protection in persecution of all who follow Christ.

c) **There are several Hindu castes that have shown marked response to the gospel** — the Namasudra, and now the Muchi (S. Baptists), but only four of the 29 lower castes have shown any significant response.

d) **The people movements among certain tribal peoples.** Pankho, Bawm (100%), Garo (70%), Oraon (60%), Khasi (50%) and Mahili (50%) are now majority Christian. The turning to the Lord continues among the Santals (25%) and Munda (15%). Pray for the work of various Baptist groups, Presbyterians, Lutherans, etc. among them — that strong, missionary-minded churches may soon be a reality.

3. **Unreached peoples:**

a) **Hindus** — All the higher castes are unreached; of the 29 lower castes, there are four which have shown some response to the gospel (over 2% Christian), in six others there are a few Christians; but in the other 11 there are hardly any. Pray that Hindus may be won in large numbers — they feel insecure as a minority in a Muslim country.

b) **The Muslim majority** has hardly been touched by the gospel, most evangelism is being directed to the religious minorities. Only 25 full-time Christian workers are giving the major part of their time to evangelize these **82 million** people.

c) **The Biharis** are Muslims who are unwelcome in Bangladesh but are not allowed to return to India or go to Pakistan. They live in large refugee camps. Pray that their dilemma may bring an openness to the gospel.

d) **The Rohingya Muslims** (250,000) (refugees from Burma in 1978) have never been evangelized.

e) **The tribal peoples** — some have resisted the gospel, or have not had adequate opportunity to hear: the Animist Mru (some are Baptists), the Buddhist Chakma (some are Baptists), Magh and Khyang.

f) **The students** — only a small witness (**IFES**, and several denominations) among the 272,000 tertiary students. Pray for strong witnessing groups in the six universities.

4. **The Church in Bengal has been plagued by nominalism,** spiritual shallowness, introspective inferiority (almost all are from low caste Hinduism or minority tribal peoples), and dependence on missionary aid and initiative. There are too many unfortunate divisions between different sections of the Church. Pray for revival and maturity to make these churches a power for evangelism for all peoples in the country.

5. **Praise God for growth in some churches** — significant people movement ingatherings by Lutherans and Baptists among the tribals. There is a rising confidence that there are going to be breakthroughs soon. Outreach by some churches is leading to growth — the Bangladesh Baptist Union aims to plant 200 churches in the '80s. Pray for these and other plans for growth in numbers and spirituality to be realized. The Church is growing now at twice the population rate.

6. **The training of leadership for the churches** is very inadequate, yet it was here in this land that the modern missionary movement began nearly 200 years ago!

a) The TEE courses are run by several groups, one being linked with the **College of Christian Theology**, which is a short-term residential school.

b) **The Discipleship Training Centre** is the only long-term Bengali-speaking residential Bible school in the country. There are 18 graduates serving the Lord.

c) The **AoG** and other churches run short-term Bible schools.

7. **Missions** have been welcomed for their social uplift programmes, hence the emphasis on institutions and aid programmes. Since 1980, increased limitations have been placed on missionaries with all projects, plans, and finances needing government approval and strict quota ceilings for the number of missionaries allowed. Yet reinforcements are needed. Pray for visas, patience with red tape, and strategic usefulness for the small missionary force in a pressurized situation. Some agencies are: **BMS** (70+), Assoc. of Baptists for World Evangelization (54), **CCC** (48), **ICF** (27), **BMMF** (24), **SBC** (20).

8. **Christian literature is in great demand because of:**

a) Mass distribution by **Young Christian Workers, EHC, UBS,** etc.

b) **Bible Correspondence Courses** run by **ICF** and others; the former with a staff of 30 in six centres processing over 12,000 papers a month. Pray for these and all efforts to follow up contacts, and for many to be added to the churches. Pray for the presses of the **AoG** and Assoc. of Baptists for World Evangelization.

c) A great yearning in the hearts of many for viable spiritual answers.

9. **The Scriptures** — distribution of portions and sales of Bibles has risen year by year. Pray specifically for:

a) The Bible Society and its extensive ministry of production and distribution of Scriptures. The Bible is in 13 languages and the NT in three.

b) The 20 full-time Bible colporteurs. Only 1,800 Bibles were distributed in 1983; Bibles are in short supply due to import restrictions.

c) The wise distribution of the NT for Muslims — 60,000 distributed since 1981. It is well received by Muslims, but there is opposition from many churches. Pray for either permission to import more, or for the printing of a new edition in Bangladesh. Pray for the translation of the OT now in progress.

d) The translation of the Bible into tribal languages — at least six, and possibly nine, translations are needed; work is in progress in three of these.

10. **Media for outreach.** Radio programmes from **FEBC** Manila are broadcast twice daily in Bengali. Pray for strategic programming that will enable churches to be planted. A cassette ministry for both the Scriptures and messages could be expanded with great effect in this predominantly illiterate population. **GRI** has recordings in 16 languages.

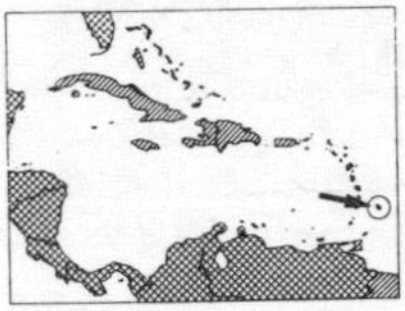

BARBADOS
(The Dominion of Barbados)

Caribbean

Feb 18

Area 430 sq.km. Most easterly of the Windward Islands.

Population 300,000. Annual growth 0.4%. People per sq.km. 698.

Peoples: African 89%; **Eurafrican** 6%; **European** 4.3%; **Asian** 0.3%.

Literacy 99%. **Official language:** English.

Capital: Bridgetown 108,000. Urbanization 65%.

Economy: Tourism and sugar are the mainstays of the economy. Income/person $3,930 (28% of USA). Inflation 14.2%.

Politics: Independent from Britain as a parliamentary democracy in 1966. Stable government since then.

Religion
Non-religious 7%. **Baha'i** 0.6%. **Muslim** 0.2%.
Christian 92%. Nominal 26.2%. Affiliated 65.8%.
Roman Catholic 4.1%. 12,300a; 6,900m.
Marginal groups (8) 2.5%. Jehovah's Witnesses 1,545m.
Protestant 59.3%. 178,000a; 66,800m. Denominations 37. Largest (adult members):

Anglican Church	32,560
Seventh Day Adventists	6,600
Methodist Church	6,300
NT Church of God	4,710

Evangelical 18.7% of population.
Missionaries to Barbados 43 (1:7,000 people) in 12 agencies.
Missionaries from Barbados 3 (?).

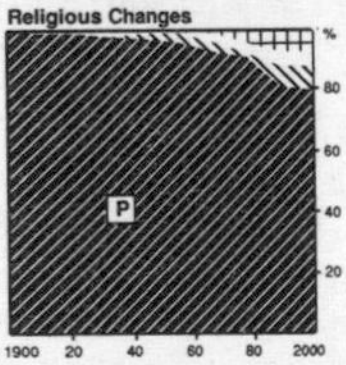

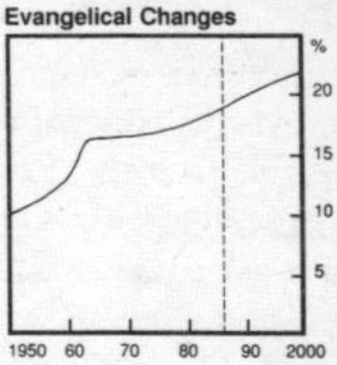

Points for prayer: See Jamaica on p. 255.

The West
Feb 19-20

BELGIUM
(Kingdom of Belgium)

Area 30,500 sq.km. One of the Low Countries, often called "The Crossroads of Europe".

Population 9,866,000. Annual growth 0.1%. Densely populated. People per sq.km. 323

Peoples
Flemish (Dutch-speaking) 57.3%. Largely in north and west.
Walloon (French-speaking) 33.4%. Largely in south and east.
German 0.65%. **Jews** 0.4%.
Other EEC citizens 5%.
Other immigrant workers 3.2%. North African 200,000; Spanish 70,000; Turk 65,000.

Literacy 98%. **Official languages:** Flemish, French and German. **All indigenous languages** 4. **Bible translations** 3Bi.

Capital: Brussels 1,100,000 — HQ for the EEC and NATO. Urbanization 95%.

Economy: Highly industrialized and wealthy, but economy faltering due to weak governments and world recession. Income/person $9,160 (65% of USA). Inflation 7.5%.

Politics: Constitutional monarchy since 1830. Political stability harmed by disagreements between the Walloons and Flemings since the mid-1960s with fragmentation of most political parties along linguistic and regional lines.

Religion
Non-religious/Atheist 7.7%.
Muslim 2.9%. Mainly North African and Turk.
Jews 0.4%. Half the pre-war number.
Christian 89%.
Roman Catholic 85.8%. Practising 30%. 8,500,000a; 6,400,000m.
Orthodox (3) 0.55%. 55,000a.
Marginal groups (14) 0.7%. 69,000a; Jehovah's Witnesses 40,000; Mormons 3,600.
Protestant 1%. 94,000a; 45,900m. Denominations 29. Largest (adult members):

United Protestant Church	17,100
Union of Ev. Free Chs.(**BEM**)	6,800
Anglican Church	3,840
Brethren	3,000
Assemblies of God	2,200

Evangelical 0.4% of population.
Missionaries to Belgium approx. 350 (1:28,000 people) in over 30 agencies.
Missionaries from within Belgium approx. 40.

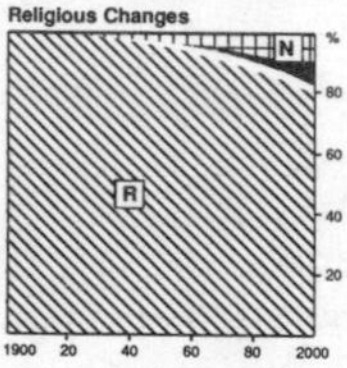

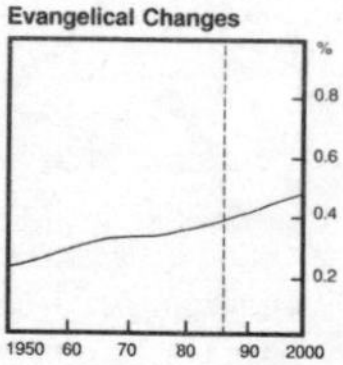

1. **Belgium is one of the less evangelized lands of the world.** Only 60 km. from the coast of England it is a land that is as much a mission field as India, for the proportion of Evangelicals to the population is about the same. The former colony, the Belgian Congo (now Zaire), has nearly 200 times as many evangelical believers as Belgium itself.

2. **The majority of the people are Roman Catholic,** though few are ardent. The Roman Catholic Church is losing much of its influence — dramatically illustrated when the **GEM** acquired one of the largest Jesuit colleges in Europe as a new and larger base for the Belgian Bible Institute. Vatican II and the theological turmoil within the RC Church have brought a new spirit of enquiry to the people, but all too often the sects gain attention with their offer of salvation by works.

3. **The Protestant witness is very small.** The largest Protestant body, a recent union of three denominations, is very much influenced by liberal theology and is not growing. The more evangelical wing is being blessed by increased growth over the last eight years. The UEELB (**BEM**) churches plan to increase their 60 churches by 50 during the '80s. The **Brethren** have planted seven assemblies over the past eight years.

4. **Freedom for evangelism has never been greater,** but it is hard to present the gospel to individuals and families. Pray for the literature and door-to-door evangelism of **OM** teams. Pray for the work by **OM, IFES, CCC** in the relatively more receptive student population. There

are nine evangelical groups among the 80,000 university students. Pray for all involved in evangelism and church planting; they need special courage and perseverance in this hard land.

5. **Bible training** — pray for the enlarged Belgian Bible Institute (**GEM**) with 164 students (most are from Holland) and also for the **AoG** Continental Bible School in Brussels with 60 students. There are very few Belgian young people coming forward for the Lord's work. Pray that this lack may be remedied.

6. **Missions. BEM** is the largest mission. The 103 workers make good use of summer campaigns, year teams and long-term church planters to strengthen existing groups and also plant new churches where no evangelical witness exists. Some other missions being **GEM** (27), **SBC** (18), **GMU** (16), **AoG** (14), Biblical Literature Fellowship (12).

7. **Literature** is being produced and used by many groups including **Biblical Literature Fellowship** (with five bookstores in Belgium and a large printing, publishing and distribution operation in Belgium and beyond), **SU, AoG**, and **OM. OM** handed out a piece of literature to every home in the country in 1972, and now has 40 workers in outreach teams. The **BEM** has its own press at Genk and operates five Christian bookshops. Pray for fruit from all this literature evangelism.

8. **Operation Mobilisation** has its HQ for Europe in Zaventem, where 47 workers administer the large operation necessary to train and send out young people for the summer and year programmes all over the needy areas of Europe, the Middle East and South Asia. Pray for these many young people as they go out distributing literature and evangelizing. Pray that many may be called into full-time service as a result of this short-term ministry.

9. **Unreached areas of Belgium**

a) Of the 2,500 administrative districts in Belgium, 2,200 have no gospel witness.
b) There are 140 towns of over 6,000 people without an evangelical congregation.
c) In Flanders (5,000,000 people) there are only 2,000 known Protestant families.
d) Antwerp (660,000) has but eight small Protestant churches.
e) Luxemburg province (250,000) has six small groups with about 30 believers.

10. **Unreached peoples in Belgium.**

a) **The North Africans** (Moroccans 105,000; Algerians 11,000; Tunisians 7,000) are almost entirely Muslim, and present a unique and urgent challenge for prayer and evangelism. Three **GMU** couples work among these people. "Good News by Telephone" in a number of languages has proved a fruitful method of witness; pray for this and the prospective ministry of "Radio Good News".

b) **The Turks** (64,000) have proved unresponsive to all efforts to evangelize them.

c) **Diplomats, EEC bureaucrats and businessmen in Brussels** are often from lands where the gospel is little known. There is little being done specifically for these people.

Caribbean

Feb 21

BELIZE
(The Colony of Belize)

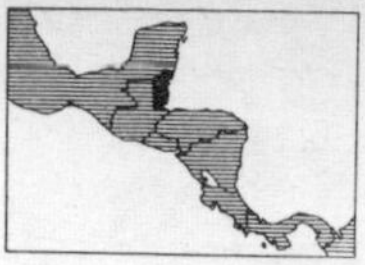

Area 23,000 sq.km. A low-lying, swampy enclave to the east of Guatemala on the Central American mainland.

Population 184,000. Annual growth 2.5% Emigration rate 1.8%. People per sq.km. 8.

Capital: Belmopan 5,500. Largest town: Belize 45,000. Urbanization 49%.

Peoples
African/Eurafrican 45%. Mainly English-speaking.
Amerindian 25%. Mayan tribes speaking three distinct languages.
Mestizo/Ladino 19%. Many Spanish-speaking Guatemalans and Hondurans.
Black Carib 8%. Descendants of African slaves and Arawakan Indians.
East Indian 2.2%, **Other** 1%. Chinese 200, Syrian 170, German (Mennonites), British.

Literacy 90%. **Official language:** English; Spanish widely used. **All languages** 9. **Bible translations** 2Bi 4NT 0por.

Economy: Underdeveloped yet relatively prosperous. Income/person $870 (6% of USA).

Politics: Independence from Britain in 1981. British forces remain to prevent annexation by neighbouring Guatemala.

Religion: A secular state with freedom of religion.
Baha'i 1%. **Spiritist/Animist** 3%. **Jews** 0.5%.

Christian 95.5%. Nominal 13.8%. Affiliated 81.7%.
Roman Catholic 53.8%. Practising 35%. 99,000a.
Marginal groups 2%. 3,700a; Jehovah's Witnesses 3,100a.
Protestant 25.8%. Mainly among English-speaking coastal people. 47,500a; 24,000m. Denominations 20. Largest (adult members):

Seventh Day Adventist Church	7,600
Anglican Church	4,590
Mennonite Church	2,200
Methodist Church	1,600
Nazarene Church	1,400
Baptist Church (**SBC**)	800
Assemblies of God	800
AECB (**GMU**)	400

Evangelical 12% of population.
Missionaries to Belize 80 (1:23,000 people) in 21 agencies.
Missionaries from within Belize 0.

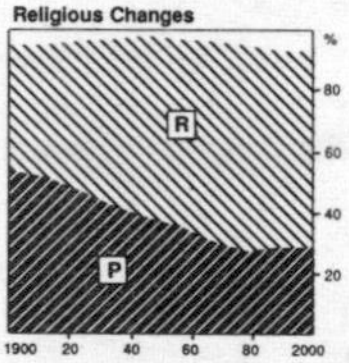

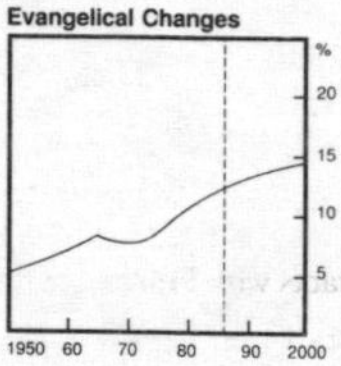

1. **This tiny land has quite a strong evangelical witness** through the Baptists, **Brethren**, Mennonites, **Nazarenes** and Pentecostals, as well as the **GMU**. There are growing churches with evangelistic vision that use both Spanish and English.

2. **Most Belizeans are very nominal** in their adherence to Christianity, with much underlying animism among the Mayas and black magic among the Black Caribs. Pray for a moving of God's Spirit among them.

3. Of the **mission groups** the largest are **GMU** (13), and Mennonites (12). Pray for their witness to the various peoples in a difficult climate. Pray for the many new churches that have been planted. Pray for the witness and growth in grace and maturity.

4. **Unreached peoples of Belize.** In only *one* group, the **Mayan Kekchi**, has there been a recent breakthrough with over 800 coming to the Lord. Pray for the same to happen among:
   a) **The Mayan Mapan** (5,500) — only a handful of isolated Nazarene and Mennonite believers.
   b) **The Mayan Yucatec** — about 120 believers (Presbyterian).
   c) **The Black Caribs** — although nominally Christian, most are still animists and retain their own language. There are some Nazarene and Brethren believers.
   d) **The East Indians** (3,000) — few believers known.
   e) **The Chinese** (200) — no active work among them.

BENIN

(The People's Republic of Benin)

Africa

Feb 22-23

Area 113,000 sq.km. A long, narrow country wedged between Nigeria and Togo.

Population 4,000,000. Annual growth 2.8%. People per sq.km. 35, denser at the coast.

Peoples

African tribes (42) 99.5%. Major groups: Fon 975,000; Yoruba (Egba, Nago) 490,000; Gun 470,000; Adja-Watchi 400,000; Bariba 400,000; Mina-Ewe 270,000; Fulani 230,000; Somba 220,000; Aizo 176,000; Dompago 175,000; Kotokoli 150,000; Songhai 78,000; Busa (Boko) 60,000; Gurma 40,000, etc.

Literacy 38%. **Official language:** French. **All languages** 51. **Bible translations** 4Bi 8NT 2por.

Capitals: Porto Novo 132,000 and Cotonou 800,000. Urbanization 30%.

Economy: Poor and underdeveloped with most people engaged in subsistence farming. Many of the more skilled are emigrating to Niger, etc. Income/person $290 (2% of USA).

Politics: Independent from France in 1960. The seventh coup since independence in 1974 brought the present military government to power. It has espoused Marxism-Leninism as the country's guide, but since 1982 it has renewed strong contacts with France.

Religion: Earlier ideological pressures and limitations upon churches and missions are now somewhat relaxed, with less hostility being shown to Muslims and Christians. Atheism is openly taught in the education system, but practical application of Marxism in daily life has been less than vigorous! In 1985 the government offered radio time for religious broadcasts to Muslims and Christians.

Tribal religions 59%. Strong among the Fon, Dompago, Boko, Bariba and Egba.

Muslim 16.8%. Predominant among Nago in south, Dompago, Fulani, Songhai (Dendi) in north, spreading in other tribes — Gun, Bariba, etc.

Christian 24%. Affiliated 21.3%.

Roman Catholic 16%. 640,000a; 370,000m.

Foreign marginal groups 0.2%. 7,000a.

Indigenous marginal groups (20) 1.9%. 77,600a.

Protestant 3.2%. 128,000a; 61,000m. Denominations 9. Largest (adult members):

Protestant Methodist Church	40,000
Assemblies of God	5,000
Un. des Eglises Evangeliques (**SIM**)	4,000
Baptist Convention (**SBC**)	520

Evangelical 0.9% of population.

Missionaries to Benin 94 (1:42,500 people) in 8 agencies.

Religious Changes

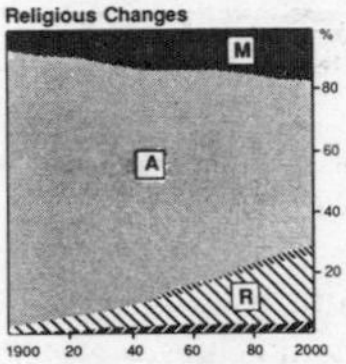

Evangelical Changes

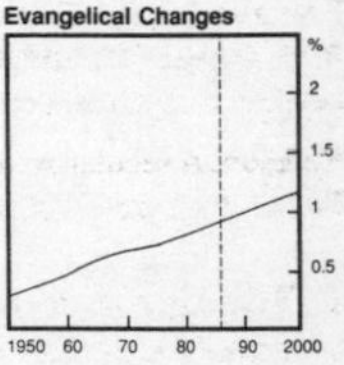

1. **This land has been tragically ignored by missions.** The entry of missionaries was almost stopped several years ago, but now some expansion of the work is possible. Pray for the calling and entry of missionaries — pioneer workers, church planters, doctors, agriculturalists, translators, youth workers, etc.

2. **Unreached peoples.** There is not one tribe in Benin with a thriving, witnessing church that is vitally evangelizing its own people. This is the least evangelized of all the non-Muslim countries of Africa. It is a race against time as both Islam and atheism spread their influence. Pray specifically for:

a) **The Fon** — a strategic, well-educated and powerful people but in bondage to a fetishism that has remained unchallenged by the gospel despite the fact that 20% of the tribe is nominally Christian. Both **AoG** and **SIM** now have a small work among them.

b) **Other southern ethnic groups** are largely fetishist or superficially Christian and only minimally reached, such as the Mina-Ewe, Busa and many smaller peoples.

c) **The central peoples** are being much influenced by Islam, as well as being fetishists such as the Egba/Yoruba (**SIM** now have 11 churches in this big tribe). Among the 50,000 Pila-Pila Christians are few; many are turning to Islam.

d) **The northern peoples. AoG** work among the Somba, Soruba 6,000, Bariba and eight other smaller groups and the **SIM** among these and the Busa, Dompago, Nyantruki 6,000, and Monkole 9,000. The Evangelical Baptists have recently moved workers into the area. The percentage of believers is still small and the influence of Islam growing.

e) **The Muslim people groups** present a great challenge. The proportion of Muslims in most peoples is growing, but very little effort has been directed to their evangelization. Only among the less strongly Muslim Fulani has there been a response to the gospel; there are 360 believers in six churches (UEEB-**SIM**). There is no work among the Kotokoli and the Songhai and no known Christians.

3. **Missions.** For years the Methodists have had a localized witness among the Gun, Mina and Yoruba in the south, but this work is rather stagnant and little has been done to reach out to other tribes. Since 1946 **SIM** (64 missionaries among 10 peoples) and Assemblies of God have made a great effort in the north and centre of the country. **SIM** runs the only evangelical mission hospital in Benin and has a useful ministry of rural development. Pray that the small body of workers may be reinforced, strategically located and divinely inspired for the evangelization of Benin. There are signs of a breakthrough in several areas.
4. **The churches** are strongest among the Dompago, Bariba and Kilinga and growing fast among the Busa. Pray for wisdom for the leaders in these days of difficult decisions of principle when confronted by an atheistic system. Christian workers are too few. There are three small Bible schools; one is for the Fulani, the first of its kind in all West Africa. Pray for a greater evangelistic concern and outreach to other tribes. Believers have a good testimony because of their high economic, agricultural and family standards.
5. **New Life For All** has proved a valuable stimulus to evangelism among the Fulani Christians. Now the programme has been launched among the Bariba and Dompago. Pray for a significant ingathering of souls.
6. **It is only in the last few years that an evangelical work has begun in the key coastal cities.** Many people of different tribes from all over the country have migrated to these cities seeking work. Pray for the work of the **SBC**, **AoG** and **SIM.** Of the million inhabitants of these cities, there are less than 1,000 believers associated with evangelical congregations.
7. **Young people are open to the gospel** but are under much pressure from atheistic propaganda. Outreach to youth has been limited by lack of committed workers. Several churches run youth centres. **SU** is still small but growing in size, and there are two GBU(**IFES**) groups in Cotonou.
8. **Bible translation** is a great need. There are 28 languages without a NT. **SIM** translation teams are working in seven others. The teams aim to complete these projects by 1990; pray them through. The people need the Scriptures, but time could be short. **GRI** has made recordings in 28 languages.

Caribbean

BERMUDA

(Colony of Bermuda)

See British Antilles on p. 115.

BHUTAN
(Kingdom of Bhutan — Druk Yul)

Asia

Feb 24

Area 47,000 sq.km. A small kingdom in the eastern Himalaya mountains.

Population 1,400,000. Annual growth 2%. People per sq.km. 25 (mostly living in the rich central valleys).

Peoples
Drukpa 67%. Two groups. Those related to the Tibetans speak Dzongkha. The other major language is Sharchopa in the east with 11 different dialects.
Nepali 20%. Mainly Gurung, Rai and Limba. A rather despised, immigrant community.
Assamese, **Sikkimese** and **Arunachal peoples** 13%. Loba 66,000; Kirati 22,000; Lepcha 22,000; Santali 10,000, etc.
Tibetan refugees 1,000 (once 7,000).

Literacy 5%. **Official language:** Dzongkha. **All languages** 15. **Bible translations** 2Bi 2por.

Capital: Thimpu 81,000. Urbanization 6%.

Economy: Undeveloped subsistence economy but with development potential. Income/person $85 (0.6% of USA).

Politics: Moving from feudalism to a constitutional monarchy. Isolated from the outside world until the trade and cultural links with Tibet were severed after the Chinese Communist invasion. India plays a dominant role in foreign affairs of Bhutan and also in its development.

Religion: Unity and independence of the country under state religion of Buddhism. All public worship, evangelism and proselytization by any other religion is illegal.
Lamaistic Buddhist 69.6%. With a strong element of animism.
Hindu 24.6%. Largely Nepali and Assamese.
Muslim 5%. All Indian.
Christian 0.1%. Bhutanese Nepali and Santali.
Roman Catholic about 330 Indians.
Protestant about 1,200 meeting in house groups. Mainly Nepalis, Indians.
Missionaries to Bhutan 25 (1:56,000 people) in 5 agencies.

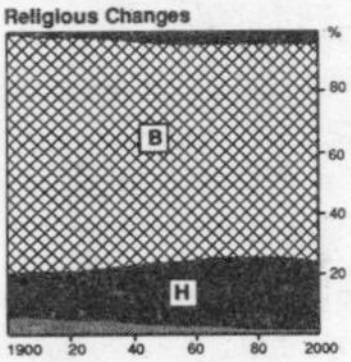

1. **Totally closed and all groups unreached until 1965,** but now there is a small Christian witness. Pray for the full opening of this land for the gospel. Pray for the salvation of government leaders.

2. **There are only about 10 known believers among the Drukpa majority** and none at all in many of the smaller people groups.

3. **The number of believers** among the Bhutanese Nepali has grown dramatically since 1970 through the fervent witness of believers inside Bhutan and on the Indian side of the border. Believers meet in about 20 places but mainly along the southern border. It is not easy for foreign Christians to fellowship with them. Pray for these believers who face considerable pressure from the authorities.

4. **Missions** have been welcomed to operate several small leprosy hospitals and run various agricultural and educational programmes. Pray for the silent witness of workers of the Leprosy Mission, **BMMF**, Norwegian Santal Mission and the Danish Mission to Lepers. These missions were asked to give an undertaking not to proselytize. The German Christoffel Mission is planning a blind school. Pray for a relaxation of limitations on witnessing.

5. **Christians in government service** — mostly Indians and some Westerners — have good opportunities to witness all over the country. Pray for Christians who have to work in such frustrating and lonely situations.

6. **Indian believers** are active in the border region in evangelism and literature distribution among visitors from Bhutan. Pray for conversions among many of the Bhutanese who visit the

churches over the border in India. Pray also for Bhutanese students in India and lands around the world that there they may hear the gospel.

7. **Literature distribution** is possible in Bhutan in a limited way, through personal contacts and the mail. Pray for fruit from the literature now spreading through the land.

8. **Bible translation** — only the gospel of Mark is available in Dzongkha, but this needs to be revised. Pray for the translation of the Scriptures and other Christian literature into the two major languages of the Drukpas.

9. **Radio programmes** in local languages have not yet been made.

Latin America

Feb 25-26

BOLIVIA
(The Republic of Bolivia)

Area 1,099,000 sq.km. Landlocked Andean State. High plateau in southwest, tropical lowlands in north and east.

Population 6,200,000. Annual growth 2.7%. People per sq.km. 6.

Peoples
European 10%. Mainly of Spanish descent; dominating the political and economic life of the country.
Mestizo 25%. Mixed race, Spanish-speaking, predominantly urban.
Amerindian 64%.
Highland peoples 62%. Quechua 2,200,000, Aymara 1,660,000, mixed Aymara-Quechua 130,000.
Lowland peoples (33 groups) 2%. Chiquitano 40,000; Guarani 22,000; Baure, Guarayu, Ignaciano all 10,000; Ayore, Carinena, Chipaya all about 2,000. Many other smaller groups.
Asian 0.48%. Japanese, Chinese. **Foreign** 0.5%.

Literacy 68%. **Official language:** Spanish. **All languages** 46. **Bible translations** 1Bi 12NT 12por.

Capital: La Paz 1,084,000. Urbanization 40%.

Economy: South America's poorest country. Two centuries of corrupt, unstable government together with the world recession, uncontrolled international borrowing and drought have brought this potentially wealthy country to its knees. Bolivia was the first nation to publically renounce its foreign debt. The land has vast reserves of minerals and unused agricultural land. The major exports are cocaine (illegal), tin and oil. Income/person $510 (4% of USA). Inflation 2,700% in 1984; paper money is the third-largest import.

Politics: Independence from Spain 1825. Chronic instability since then. In 160 years there have been over 200 successful coups or revolutions. The elected government has virtually lost control, and the country slides into violence, chaos and despair.

Religion: The Catholic Church is recognized as the State Church, but relationships between church and state have frequently been less than cordial. There is freedom for other religions and churches to operate.
Non-religious/Atheist 1.5%.
Animist 1% officially; over 50% of the population is baptized but are practising animists or Christo-pagan.
Baha'i 3%. Rapid growth among highland Amerindians.
Christian 94.4%. Affiliated 91.4%.
Roman Catholic 83% (officially 91%, but 8% have become Protestants or Baha'i). Practising 12%. 5,150,000a; 3,300,000m.
Foreign marginal groups (2) 0.7%. 44,900a; 18,000m. Mormons 14,200m.
Protestant 7.6%. 471,000a; 234,000m. Denominations 106. Largest (adult members):

Seventh Day Adventist Ch.	44,000
Assemblies of God	30,000
Evang. Ch. Union (**AEM-SIM**)	20,000
Baptist Union (**CBOMB**)	17,000
Friends (Quakers)	11,000
Bolivian Church of God	7,500
Mennonite Church	7,000
Brethren Assemblies	6,600
Church of the Nazarene	6,400

Evangelical 6.5% of population.
Missionaries to Bolivia 650 (1:9,500 people) in 50 agencies.
Missionaries from within Bolivia 4 (1:120,000 Protestants).

Religious Changes

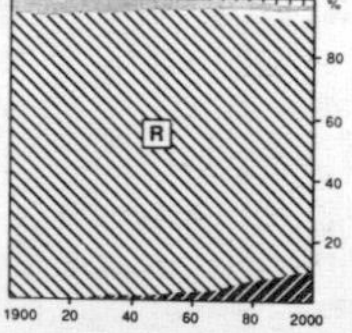

Evangelical Changes

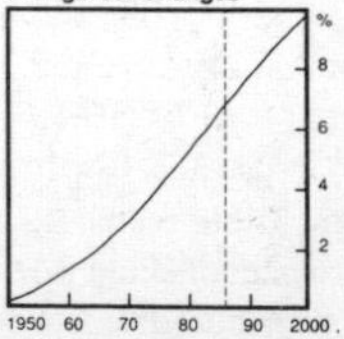

1. **The great responsiveness of Bolivians to the gospel is cause for praise to God.** There is widespread hunger in nearly all levels of society due to economic and political disasters in the '80s. The growth of Evangelicals is most noticeable among:

a) **The Aymara.** A people movement since 1930 with 17% growth per year has resulted in nearly 20% of these animistic people becoming Evangelicals (Baptist, **AoG**, Friends, Methodist and **AEM**-related churches).

b) **The mining communities and urban areas** with many conversions through evangelistic outreach and campaigns among the mestizos.

c) **The 130,000 lowland Amerindian tribes.** Their evangelization is nearly complete.

2. **Protestant churches in Bolivia are growing at about 10% per year** (see graph). The Evangelism-in-Depth campaign together with wide use of home Bible studies, mass rallies and the media has reaped an abundant harvest.

3. **There are basic weaknesses** that warrant prayer. Evangelicals have had relatively little impact on politics, the military, and the economic life of the country. Illiteracy, apathy, lack of Bible knowledge, denominational rivalries, and fear of witnessing are widespread. There is a widening generation gap with few young people being adequately helped in the churches. Cross-cultural missionary outreach is hardly ever preached. Pray for the effective implementation of the **NLFA** programme in mobilizing churches and congregations for witnessing in 1986 and beyond.

4. **The unreached.** About 65% of the population is unchurched; many of these live in areas with limited opportunity to hear the gospel. Churches need a vision for such areas and the initiative to send out church planting teams. Of note are:

a) **The upper classes** that for long have controlled the politics and economy but are now shocked by the economic collapse. Initiatives by **AEM-SIM, CMA, USCWM,** Anglicans and others are bearing fruit, and new congregations are being formed.

b) **The students in the nine universities**, disillusioned with traditional Catholicism, often secular, leftist in political views and discouraged by interrupted courses and bleak future prospects. Long neglected but now open to the gospel. There are about 500 students in eight universities linked with the CCU**(IFES)**, others are linked with the ministry of **CCC** in several universities.

c) **The Quechua** in the high Andes and lowland farming colonies are largely Christo-pagans and have long resisted the gospel. By 1975 only 1.7% were evangelical. This has begun to change, but many areas yet remain to be evangelized.

5. **Leadership training** is vital for the many growing churches at their own levels — from jungle village tribal churches to sophisticated elite city congregations. There are over 25 Protestant seminaries and Bible schools as well as a number of TEE institutes and BCCs available. All these can never provide maturity and spiritual authority without the deep working of the Spirit of God. Men and women who know their God are needed!

6. **The Lowland tribes are numerous and small.** At great cost, and with considerable success, missions such as **NTM, AEM**, South American Mission, **WGM, GMU** and **UWM** have planted indigenous churches in all but one or two small tribes. Prayer must be concentrated on the teaching of God's Word, maturation of indigenous leaders, integration of these believers into Bolivian life and the sound conversion of the second generation of Christians. Praise the Lord for a missionary task so well done!

7. **Foreign missions.** Early missionaries struggled long against hostility, persecution and harsh living conditions before the harvest ripened. The contribution of **AEM** has been unique in pioneering most of the major gospel advances and ministries in the country. The large missionary body needs to concentrate more on church planting among the Quechua and upper classes, and the discipling of the youth. It is for these ministries that new missionaries must be recruited. Major missions being **NTM** (131 missionaries), Mennonites (63), **SIL** (51), **AEM-SIM** (41), **WGM** (41), South America Mission (41), Canadian Baptists (35), **GMU** (35), **Brethren** (15), **AoG** (14).

8. **Bible translation and distribution.** The Bible Society has played a major role in every aspect of Bible work and now has its own press. Over one million New Testaments have been distributed in schools. The Aymara and Quechua Bibles are in great demand. **SIL** has

almost achieved the amazing objective of completing the Bible translation programme for all the Amerindian languages that warranted it. May God's Word become part of the life of the Bolivian nation.

9. **The media** have had a wide impact — through many TV and radio programmes on national and private stations, wide use of literature in publishing and distribution of tracts, teaching materials and books. Pray that these may help to establish a vibrant, witnessing, literate Church.

Africa

Feb 27

BOTSWANA

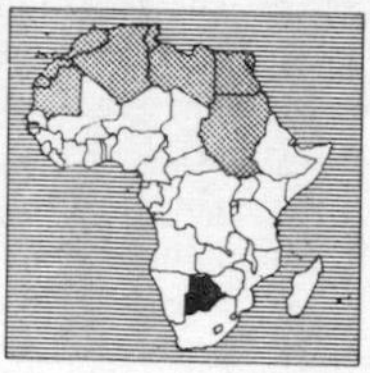

Area 600,000 sq.km. Very dry; Kalahari Desert occupies centre, east and south.

Population 1,100,000. Annual growth 3.7%. People per sq.km. 2.

Peoples

Tswana 70%. Eight main tribes. Majority along southeast border with South Africa.

Minority Bantu peoples 21%. Kalanga 105,000; Yeyi 25,000; Ndebele 15,000; Herero 12,000; Lozi 9,000; Subia 8,000.

San (Bushmen) 4.8% (50,000). Nomadic tribes in Kalahari, speaking at least 40 different languages and dialects.

European/Coloured 1%.

Refugees 3%. Angolan (Mbukushu 4,000), Zimbabwean (Ndebele, Shona), South African (Sotho, Pedi, Zulu, Xhosa), Namibian.

Literacy 40%. **Official languages:** English, Tswana. **All languages** 18. **Bible translations** 9Bi 3por.

Capital: Gaberone 175,000. Urbanization 37%.

Economy: Dependence on cattle and subsistence agriculture, but drought and famine are commonplace. Mining is increasingly important to the economy. Income/person $920 (6% of USA).

Politics: Independent of Britain in 1966. One of Africa's most stable governments, working hard to lessen dependence on South Africa for trade and employment of a large proportion of the work force.

Religion: Freedom of religion, though local chiefs have a powerful voice in all religious activities in their own areas.

Tribal religions 49%. Found among all tribes but especially Bushmen, Yeyi and Mbukushu.

Baha'i 0.6%. A syncretic Muslim sect.

Christian 50%. Nominal 25.6%. Affiliated 24.4%.

African indigenous churches 5.8% (over 55 groups). Mainly syncretic "Zionist" and healing churches. 63,000a.

Roman Catholic 3.6%. Practising 40%. 39,500a; 18,850m.

Protestant 14.7%. 162,000a; 58,500m. Denominations 25. Largest (adult members):

Un. Congregational Church (LMS)	12,000
Lutheran Church	8,840
Methodist Church	7,900
Seventh Day Adventist Church	6,700
Assemblies of God	3,800
Dutch Reformed Church (**NGK**)	3,640
Anglican Church	3,000

Evangelical 4% of population.

Missionaries to Botswana 160 (1:6,900 people) in 17 agencies.

Missionaries from within Botswana 8 (?).

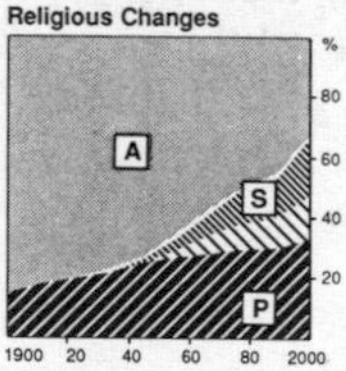

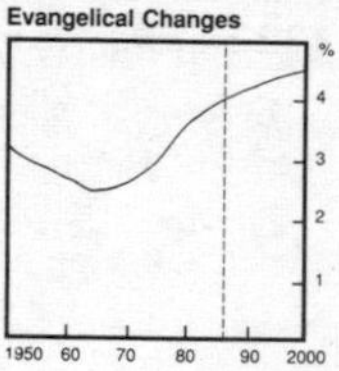

1. **The Tswana people** were the first Bantu people in southern Africa to respond to the gospel, and a great turning to God among several of the Tswana tribes occurred in the last century through the LMS from England. Modern theology among later missionaries stunted further development of the Church and little real spiritual life remains.

2. **The tragic decline continues in the older churches.** Only 11 ageing pastors remain in the UCCSA. The Tswana are Christian in name, but actually given over to immorality and drunkenness that is accentuated by the breakdown of family life and poverty. Other missions followed late in the last century, but nominalism is also a problem with these churches because each became virtually the "state church" of the tribe that welcomed that particular group. Pray for revival and a reversal of the moral collapse.

3. **Unreached peoples:**
   a) Many **Tswana** of this generation have never heard the true gospel.
   b) The **Kalanga.** Although some are members of churches, there is no Protestant Kalanga-speaking congregation in the country. They resent the cultural dominance of the Tswana.
   c) The **Yeyi** of the Okavango Swamp have only been exposed to nominal Christianity in the medium of the Tswana language.
   d) The **Mbukushu** and **Subia** in the north have never received a clear presentation of the gospel.
   e) The **Herero** are mostly nominal Lutherans or of the fire-worshipping "Oruuano" Church.
   f) The **San** are being reached by **AEF, NGK** and Lutherans. Pray for the evangelization of these elusive nomadic, and poverty-stricken settled Bushmen; also for the right strategy for church planting.

4. **The last 15 years have been a time of a new evangelical penetration.** The growing work of the Southern Baptists (22 missionaries), **AEF** (13), **AoG** (4), **Brethren** (2), etc., needs prayer. The spiritual and physical conditions are not easy. Pray for the planting of witnessing churches in which Christians exhibit true holiness and a love for the Scriptures. The impact of Christ For All Nations evangelistic crusades in Gaberone and Francistown since 1975 has been significant.

5. **The training and support of pastors and leaders** is a great need. There are few pastors, and the scattered and poor congregations are barely able to support them. Pray for the **AoG** Bible School, and the **AEF** Shashi Bible Training College. Pray for the raising up of men of God able to turn the nation back to Him.

6. **Young people** are a most needy section of the population. There are 23 secondary schools, some very atheistic indeed. Immorality, even among the very young, is so prevalent that it is very hard for a young person to follow the Lord. Pray for the witness of **SU** with groups in most of these schools and the lively **IFES** group in Gaberone.

7. **There is a lack of full-time workers** due to the poverty of the congregations, and a lack of training facilities. There are enormous difficulties for those who seek to evangelize such a semi-nomadic and scattered population. Pray for the calling of national and missionary workers to reach this land for Christ.

8. **Literature** for the rapidly increasing literate population is scarce and often expensive.

9. **Bible translation** in the minority languages is essential, but wisdom is needed in the choice of dialects that need the Scriptures — especially for the many and varied Bushmen dialects. **GRI** has made recordings in 19 languages.

Latin America
Feb 28- Mar 3

BRAZIL
(The Federal Republic of Brazil)

Area 8,512,000 sq.km. One half of the land surface and population of South America. The world's fifth largest country (36 times the size of the United Kingdom!).

Population 138,400,000. Annual growth 2.3%. People per sq.km. 16.

Peoples: Brazil is a "melting pot" of the nations, with much intermarriage, so percentages given below are not meant to indicate rigid categories.
European 54%. Portuguese 15%, Italian 11%, Spanish 10%, German 3%.
African 11%. Descendants of slaves brought from West Africa and Angola.
Mixed race 33%. Mestizo and Mulatto.
Asian 1.5%. Japanese 1,000,000; Chinese 60,000; Arab, etc.
Amerindian 0.1%. In 1900 there were 500,000 in 230 tribes, but now there are less than 100,000 in 140 tribes and still decreasing through the encroachments of civilization, loss of land and disease.

Literacy 78%. **Official language:** Portuguese. **All languages** 152. **Bible translations** 1Bi 18NT 38por.

Capital: Brasilia 1,332,000. Other major cities: Sao Paulo 16,412,000; Rio de Janeiro 12,525,000; Recife 2,900,000; Porto Alegre 3,073,000; Belo Horizonte 3,785,000; Curitiba 2,827,000; Salvador 2,000,000; Fortaleza 1,900,000. Urbanization 67%.

Economy: Vast economic potential in the developing hinterland of the north and west, rapid growth and industrialization in the '60s and '70s in the south made Brazil one of the leading industrial and trading nations in the world. Lack of oil reserves, rampant inflation and crippling international debt has blunted growth and brought economic hardship to many. Income/person $1,890 (13% of USA). Inflation 44.6%.

Politics: A republic with authoritarian military government since 1964. There was a return to a fully democratic government in 1985.

Religion: Complete freedom of religion.
Non-religious/Atheist 1.4%. Secularism is on the increase in the middle and upper classes.
Buddhist 0.3%. **Muslim** 0.1%.
Spiritist 30-35% (estimate). Probably 14% of all Brazilians are openly associated and more than 60% dabble in the various forms of spiritism of European, Amerindian and especially African origin while still claiming to be Christian.
Christian 93%.
Roman Catholic 73.1%. Practising 12%. 101,000,000a; 60,707,000m. There are 18 mill. baptized Catholics who have joined evangelical or other groups.
Other Catholic (2) 2%. 2,770,000a.
Marginal groups (58) 0.52%. 724,000a. Jehovah's Witnesses 474,000a; Mormons 161,800a.
Protestant 17.4%. 24,120,000a; 10,377,000m.
Denominations 350. Largest (adult members):

Assemblies of God	5,000,300
Christian Congregation	1,253,000
Baptist Convention (**SBC**)	602,000
Conference of Lutheran Chs.	580,000
Brazil for Christ	450,000
Seventh Day Adventist Church	403,000
Cruzada Nacional (ICFG)	250,000
Presbyterian Church	149,000
Evangelical Lutheran Church	128,000
Un. of Ev. Congreg. Chs (**EUSA**)	115,000
All other churches	1,445,000

Evangelical 16% of population.
Missionaries to Brazil 2,600 (1:53,000 people) in 139 agencies.
Missionaries from within Brazil 840 (1:28,700 Protestants) in about 35 agencies.

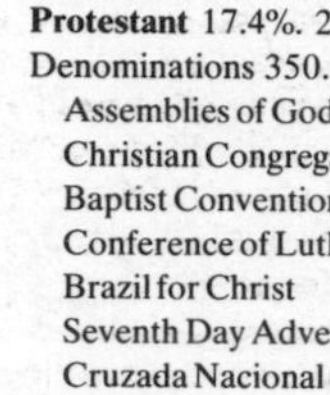

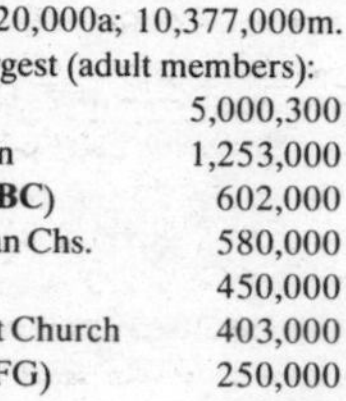

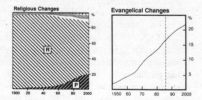

1. **Praise God for the astonishing growth of Evangelicals** (77% 1960-70 and 155% 1970-80). Vigorous evangelism and church planting among an exceptionally responsive people continues. Pray for the Brazilian church that it may mature and become a blessing to the nation and to the world.

2. **Successful growth from a few thousand evangelical believers in 1900** to a churchgoing population of nearly 24 million today brings a new form of pressure. The Evangelicals have

become a powerful influence in the land, which lays them open to the wooing of politicians. Pray for a spirit of humility, separation from worldliness, deliverance from power-seeking among Christian leaders, and, above all, for revival; present growth is not revival. Pray that Christian leaders may seek *first* the Kingdom of God.

3. **The Catholic Church is in serious trouble**, and faces a discouraging future. There is a dearth of priests, the majority being over the age of 50 and from abroad. Average Sunday attendances are lower than that for Evangelicals. The left wing of the church has espoused liberation theology, and has become a strong pressure group within the church through 80,000 "Base Communities" which initiate social actions that are often anti-government.

4. **The challenges facing Brazilian Evangelicals.**
a) **The Pentecostals** (around 75% of all Evangelicals) have grown fast, but sometimes at the expense of depth, adequate biblical teaching and provision of well-trained leaders. Hence superficiality, backsliding and openness to divisions and error are common.
b) **Non-Pentecostal Evangelicals** — formalism, lack of evangelistic concern, dominance of foreign missionary structures, and divisive arguments over the charismatic issue have frequently resulted in slower growth, denominational splits, and lack of cooperation between denominations.
c) **Liberation theology**, with its emphasis on political and social solutions to Brazil's many national woes, has gained a significant hearing in some churches and seminaries. Pray for the raising up of fine theologians that may equip the church to maintain loyalty to the Scriptures and balance in teaching its truths. Pray that world evangelization may be *the* priority in the churches.
d) **There is a dearth of local leadership** able to sustain church growth and retain the fruits of evangelism. Pray for the 80 seminaries, 50 Bible institutes training over 9,000 students and the many TEE programmes being run all over the country by many denominations. Pray that God may raise up labourers for the home and foreign mission fields.

5. **Spiritism is a dynamic force for evil in Brazil.** It appeals to the emotions and offers physical healing; both traits make it an attractive alternative to traditional Christianity. In 1975 there were at least 14,000 spiritist centres guided by 420,000 mediums. Pray both for the deliverance of many from the power of the occult and for Christians willing and spiritually equipped to minister to those bound by Satan.

6. **The challenge to reach the less evangelized people groups.**
a) **The squalid favelas (slums) are a blight in every major city**. One-third of the urban population live in such places where poverty, hopelessness, crime and disease make these people hard to reach.
b) **In the southern cities** live 400,000 abandoned children.
c) **The secularized, wealthy middle and upper classes.** These have been generally less responsive.
d) **Young people** are, on the whole, not well cared for in the churches. There is a need for more missionary and national youth workers — especially among the restive and often Marxist students. There are about 1,200,000 university students in over 44 universities. The **CCC** and **Navigators** are active, and the ABU(**IFES**) is having a significant impact with groups in most universities. They help students come to the Lord, build them up in the Word and encourage missionary vision. The ABU is also pioneering a ministry to Christian graduates.
e) **The one million Japanese** are over 60% RC and only 3% Protestant. There are 80 evangelical churches with 7,000 adult Japanese believers. Pray for the witness of the Japan Holiness Church (**OMSI**), Japan Evangelical Mission and **UFM**. Pray that these Japanese churches may enter into the main stream of Brazilian life.
f) **The 60,000 Chinese** live largely in Sao Paulo where there are 12 small evangelical congregations, but the percentage of Christians (1.7%) is low.
g) **The little settlements** along the many rivers in the vast Amazon jungle are poor and needy, physically and spiritually. The believers are few and often isolated. **UFM** is doing a pioneer work in the Upper Amazon region in planting little churches. These churches

need prayer — they constantly suffer the loss of key members to the towns and cities. Pray for those engaged in pioneer evangelism by means of river launches — a hard and dangerous ministry.

h) **The pioneer colonies** along the new roads being driven through the virgin jungles of the west and north — the Brazilian church is seeking to reach out to these rough settlements and plant churches.

i) **The Amerindian tribes yet to be reached.** Possibly about 40 small tribal groups totalling around 5,000 remain to be contacted with the gospel. About 52 tribes are "assimilated" into national life, and a further 45 marginally so. Up until 1978 a considerable witness in the majority of the tribes was seriously curtailed by the government. At that time **SIL** was working in 41 tribes, **NTM** in 20, **UFM** in five; but in a number of these a viable indigenous church had yet to be planted. Pray for the complete evangelization of these tribes.

7. **The missionary situation has been delicate for the last seven years.** Government restrictions in the late '70s virtually stopped the entry of new missionaries and limited the activities of missionaries among the tribal Amerindians. Numbers fell from 2,900 Protestant missionaries in 1970 to 2,500 in 1980. The largest are Southern Baptists (292), **NTM** (199), **SIL** (179). Pray for the wise and strategic deployment of the missionary force to the best advantage of the Brazilian Church, and the issuing of visas to new missionaries still needed. The issuing of visas has eased a little since 1980.

8. **The limitations on missionary activity among the Amerindian tribes** since 1978 was triggered by a combined assault of anti-Christian anthropologists, demands for Indian lands by development agencies and corrupt officials. Pray that this unholy alliance may be thwarted and that evangelism, Bible translation and church planting may continue. Pray that this situation may stimulate a deeper concern among Brazilian churches to send missionaries to work among them. Some Brazilians are serving in international missions in the area, and a Brazilian mission (ALEM) was formed in 1983 to carry on Bible translation programmes. Bible translation continues in 64 languages, but between eight and possibly 50 other languages may yet require translation teams.

9. **The missionary vision** of the Brazilian Church is rapidly "taking off"! Praise God for this. Pray that the full potential of the massive church may be realized through wise, Spirit-guided planning. Also pray for adequate training, channelling and pastoral care of missionaries who are leaving Brazil for all parts of the world. There are now over 30 Brazilian-based missions, of which 13 are denominational (largest, Baptist Convention — 370) and the rest interdenominational; some of these are Brazilian bases for international missions, such as **SIL, NTM, WEC**. Of the 720 missionaries in 1981, about 120 were serving in cross-cultural situations in Brazil, and about 160 had gone to other lands.

10. **Christian literature is in greater demand as literacy increases.** Many denominational and interdenominational publishing and distributing agencies are ministering in this field — most under the umbrella of the coordinating Evangelical Literature Committee of Brazil. We mention the ministries of **EUSA, CLC** and **IFES** in particular. There is a need for more Brazilian writers. Pray for the distribution of evangelistic literature, especially the ministry of **WEC** through *CEDO,* an evangelistic broadsheet with a large circulation. Pray for the Brazilian Bible Society to attain its bold distribution goals; in 1982, 70 million Scripture portions/Bibles were distributed.

11. **Christian radio and TV** have a significant impact. Pray for the many broadcasts through 85 evangelical TV/radio stations, Christian programmes on secular stations and through **TWR** Bonaire.

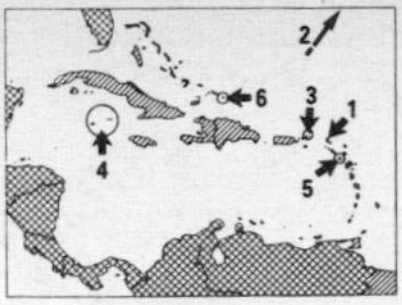

BRITISH ANTILLES

Caribbean

Mar 4

The six island groups in the Caribbean and the North Atlantic that have preferred to remain as British Colonies are grouped together.

	Area sq.km.	Population	Annual growth	People/ sq.km.	Capital	Income/person $ US ('79)
Anguilla	91	6,500	0%	71	The Valley	550
Bermuda	53	63,700	0.5%	1,200	Hamilton	7,600
British Virgin Is.	153	13,500	2.2%	88	Road Town	2,300
Cayman Is.	260	20,900	4.6%	80	George Town	5,300
Montserrat	102	11,700	0.2%	115	Plymouth	1,800
Turks & Caicos Is.	430	8,500	3.3%	20	Cockburn Town	1,300
TOTALS	1,089	124,800	1.5%	115		

Peoples
African 63%. **Eurafrican** 15%.
European 21.5%. Most on Bermuda and Cayman Islands.
Asian, etc. 0.5%.

Literacy varies between 82% (Anguilla) to 99% (Bermuda). **Official language:** English.

Economy: All island groups are small, isolated and poor unless there is tourism and tax-haven financing — as in Bermuda and Cayman Is.

Politics: British Colonial rule but with a high degree of local autonomy.

Religion: Statistics are difficult to obtain for these islands and the figures quoted are apporoximations only.
Non-Christian 3%. Non-religious, Baha'i, Muslim, etc.
Christian 97%. Nominal 18%. Affiliated 79%.
Roman Catholic 10%. 12,700a.
Marginal groups 1.7%. 2,100a.
Protestant 67%. 83,000a. Largest churches on each island group — in order of size:
Anguilla (80% Protestant): Anglican, Methodist.
Bermuda (66% Protestant): Anglican, Catholic, African Methodist Episcopal, Seventh Day Adventist Church.
British Virgins (61.1% Protestant): Methodist, Anglican, Catholic.
Cayman Is. (41% Protestant): United Church, SDA, Baptist.
Montserrat (65% Protestant): Anglican, Methodist, Catholic, SDA, Church of God of Prophecy.
Turks and Caicos (88% Protestant): Baptist, Methodist, Anglican, Church of God of Prophecy.
Evangelical 17%.
Missionaries to British Antilles 45 (1:2,800 people).

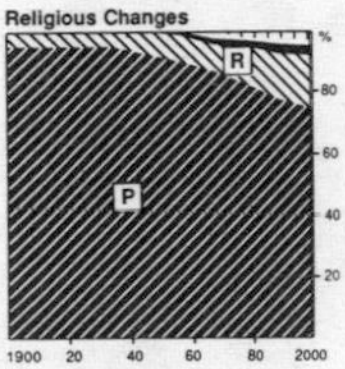

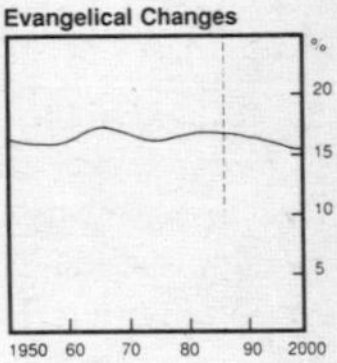

Points for prayer: See Jamaica, p. 255.

BRITISH VIRGIN ISLANDS

(Colony of British Virgin Islands)

See British Antilles above.

Asia

Mar 5

BRUNEI
(State of Brunei Darussalam)

Area 5,800 sq.km. Two small enclaves in Sarawak, East Malaysia on the island of Borneo.

Population 279,000. Annual growth 2.4%. People per sq.km. 48.

Peoples
Malay 40%. Dominant in government and civil service.
Chinese 26.7%. Control the trade and economy.
Expatriate 6.7%. Indian, European, Korean, Filipino.
Tribal peoples 27.3%. Kedayan 32,000; Dusun 16,000; Melanau 13,500; Murut 6,000; Iban; Kelabit; Punan.

Literacy 70%. **Official languages:** Malay, English. **All languages** 16. **Bible translations** 7Bi 3NT 1por.

Capital: Bandar Seri Begawan 100,000. Urbanization 76%.

Economy: Wealth and rapid development through large revenues from oil. Income/person $21,140 (150% of USA).

Politics: Refused to join the Malaysian Federation in 1963. A Protectorate of Britain until full independence in 1983.

Religion: Islam is the state religion. The free practice of other religions is guaranteed, but missions are not allowed to operate.
Muslim 64%. All Malays, some Melanau, Dusun and Kedayan.
Chinese Religions 19.6%
Animist 5%. **Hindu** 0.9%.
Christian 10%. Affiliated 4.4%.
Roman Catholic 1.8%. 5,100a; 70% Chinese.
Protestant 2.4%. 6,650a; 3,700m. Denominations 6. Largest (adult members):

Anglican Church	3,060
Evangelical Fellowships (3)	290
Seventh Day Adventist Church	270

Evangelical 0.41% of population.
Missionaries to Brunei 2 (1:140,000 people) in 1 agency.

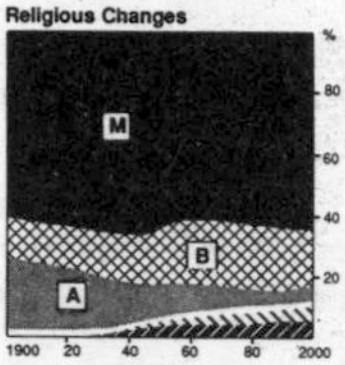

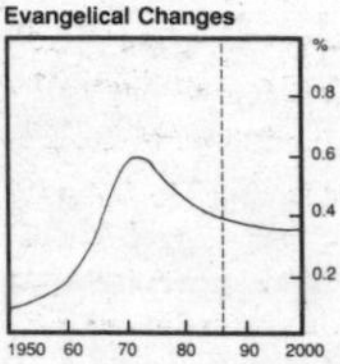

1. **No evangelism is permitted among the Muslims**, and there are no known believers who have come from this community. However there is a steady stream of conversions to Islam from among tribal and immigrant communities. Pray that through the pure lives of the Christians and the work of the Holy Spirit some may be saved.

2. **There is freedom for local Christians to evangelize non-Muslims.** The most significant response has been among the Chinese. About 15% of the Chinese are nominally Christian, but only about 600 attend Protestant churches regularly. Pray that material concerns may not keep the many unconverted Chinese from a full commitment to the Lord.

3. **The Bethel Mission and the Brunei Christian Fellowship** have a vigorous outreach by means of meetings, camps, literature, etc. among the Chinese, expatriates and tribal peoples. Pray for these live fellowships and their witness to all races.

4. **There are now some church groups among the tribal people** — Iban (Anglican), Kelabit (Bethel), Murut and other groups (BCF). Pray for every tribal group to be reached.

5. **The Expatriate churches** seek to meet the needs of the many national groups — English-speaking, Dutch, Korean, Filipino, etc. Pray that these expatriates may be a witness to the majority of their groups who are nominal or non-Christian.

BULGARIA

(Republic of Bulgaria)

Eastern Europe

Mar 6-7

Area 110,900 sq.km. One of the Balkan states.

Population 8,900,000. Annual growth 0.2%. People per sq.km. 80.

Peoples

Bulgarian 83%. A Slavic people.

Turk 8.5%. Turkey was the ruling power for 500 years.

Other minorities 8.5%. Gypsy 460,000; Macedonian 231,000; Armenian 30,000; Russian 25,000; Gagauz 16,000; Jew 7,000; Greek 7,000; Tatar 5,500.

Literacy 98%. **Official language:** Bulgarian (Slavic). **All languages** 9. **Bible translations** 3Bi 1NT 4por.

Capital: Sofia 1,200,000. Urbanization 60%.

Economy: Rapid industrialization and favourable trade agreements with USSR and less centralization of the economy have brought improvements in standards of living. Income/person $2,900(21% of USA). Inflation 1.9%.

Politics: Independent from Turkey in 1878. Communist rule since 1944. A hard line Marxist regime that is faithful to the USSR. Bulgaria is sometimes called "Little Russia".

Religion: Severe limitation and control of all organized religious groups. Church leaders are often government appointees.

Non-religious/Atheist 25.3%.

Muslim 10.4%. Turk, 30% of Gypsies, Pomak (Bulgar Muslims 300,000), Tatar.

Christian 64.2%.

Bulgarian Orthodox 61.7%. Practising 20%. 5,500,000a; 4,220,000m. The chief preserver of the national culture during the centuries of Turkish rule. Heavily infiltrated by Marxists.

Roman Catholic 0.7%. 66,000a; 51,000m. Severely persecuted at times.

Armenian Orthodox 0.25%.

Protestant 0.58%. 51,600a, 33,000m. Denominations 10. Largest (adult members):

Pentecostal Church	14,000
Congregational Church	4,700
Brethren Assemblies	est. 3,800
Seventh Day Adventist Church	3,400
Methodist Church	1,150
Baptist Church	720

Evangelical 0.54% of population.

Missionaries to Bulgaria 0.

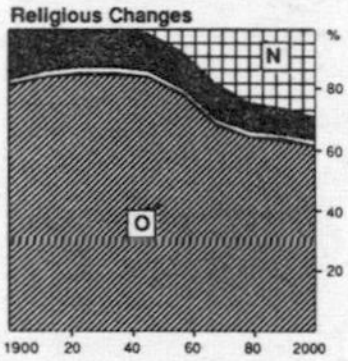

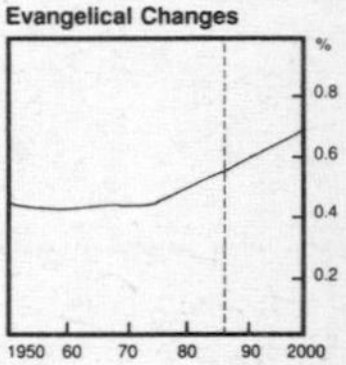

1. **Most Bulgarians have never had a chance to hear the true gospel;** their land is one of the more needy of Eastern Europe. Pray that they may hear of the Saviour.

2. **Minority groups are being forcibly integrated into the majority culture**, causing much grief and suffering.
   a) **The 800,000 Turkish Muslims** have suffered particularly, but no specific outreach to them is known.
   b) **The Gypsies** are partly Muslim and partly Orthodox, but, unlike elsewhere in Europe, there has not been a Pentecostal revival among them.
   c) **The Pomaks** were forcibly converted to Islam by the Turks. There has been no known outreach specifically directed to them.

3. **Propaganda against believers is extreme.** Pray that this continual assault on believers and the Bible may cause the many disillusioned Communists to seek for the Truth.

4. **The persecution of believers** has been very severe. Many Christian leaders suffered long terms of imprisonment and death in the early years of Communist rule. Since 1972 the level of persecution has again been stepped up, and many Christians are afraid to testify openly. Christian families and young people are subjected to much intimidation and discrimination. Some Pentecostal and Baptist churches were demolished in 1984.

5. **Pray for the leaders of the churches** who face constant harassment from the authorities and betrayal at the hands of informers who have infiltrated both official and underground groups. There are now about 40 Pentecostal and 23 Baptist pastors in the official churches, and others who live a hunted life ministering to the unofficial groups. It is impossible for those who desire to enter the ministry to obtain an adequate Bible training.

6. **The churches** are not restricted by law from holding meetings, but the long working hours and lack of Sunday rest greatly limit their activities. The limitation on registration of new churches forces many groups to meet illegally. Church growth has been negligible because of the fear, suspicion and jealousy even among believers. Pray for these believers that their faith may be strong and that their witness may win many to the Lord.

7. **Young people** are more receptive to the gospel despite their years of indoctrination in Marxism, but there is a strict restriction on their attendance at church services (except in the tourist season!). There is also a problem of a generation gap between the enthusiastic young believers and the older people in the churches.

8. **Christian literature:** none is allowed to be printed or distributed in the country. The famine of literature is so great that there is much hand copying of the Scriptures and good Christian books. The only literature for Christians is printed in the West. Pray for those who bring Bibles from the West to these believers and for safe distribution. The **UBS** supplied paper for the printing of 30,000 Bibles in the country in 1983, but these copies are not always reaching those who most desire them.

9. **Christian radio**: No programmes are produced at the present. Pray that broadcasts in Bulgarian may soon be recommenced.

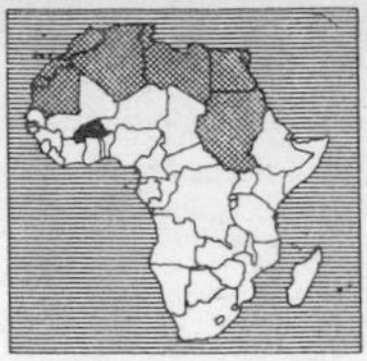

BURKINA FASO

Africa

Mar 8-9

Area 274,000 sq.km. A landlocked land of the Sahel. Prone to drought and famine.

Population 6,900,000. Annual growth 2.6%. People per sq.km. 25. Over 1,700,000 Burkinabé (people of Burkina Faso) have migrated to other lands; 80% to Ivory Coast, also to Niger, Mali and France.

Peoples: Over 60 distinct ethno-linguistic groups in five major language families.

Gur-Voltaic (35 groups) 80.5%.

Mossi-Gurma: Mossis 3,500,000, Gurma 400,000. Mossis are the dominant people in Burkina Faso.

Gurunsi: Dagari 150,000; Birifor 96,000; Lyele 75,000; Buli 65,000; Kusaale 55,000; Kassena 55,000; Nuna 48,000; Kurumba 30,000; Sissala 25,000; Ko 15,000; Puguli 11,000; Frafra 10,000; Nankana 5,000; Pana 5,000.

Senufo: Senufo 360,000; Karaboro 60,000; Tussian 25,000; Tyefo 10,000; Vige 6,000; Wara 4,000.

Lobi-Lobiri: Lobi 250,000; Gouin 50,000; Turka 12,000; Dyan 12,000; Dogosie 8,000; Komono 7,000; Gan 6,000.

Mande peoples (14) 10.8%. Bisa 270,000; Samo 250,000; Marka 140,000; Dioula 60,000; Samogho 15,000; Sambla 9,000.

Fulani (2) 6%. **Songhai** 2%. **Other** 2%; French and Westerners 3,500, Lebanese 400.

Literacy 12%. **Official language:** French; spoken by 10% of the population. **Trade languages:** Moré (the language of the Mossi), Dioula in south. **All languages** 50. **Bible translations** 2Bi 6NT 8por.

Capital: Ouagadougou 328,000. Urbanization 9%.

Economy: 83% of the population is dependent on subsistence agriculture and the intermittent rainfall. Much malnutrition and famine in the centre and north since early '70s. One of the poorest states in the world. Income/person $180 (1% of USA).

Politics: Independent of France in 1960. A series of economic disasters destabilized a succession of governments. Five coups since 1966; the last in 1983 leading to a revolutionary populist military regime with close links with Libya. The emphasis is on national self-reliance, collective ownership and socialism.

Religion: The attitude of the revolutionary government has not been clearly defined, and Christians could be placed under pressure.

Traditional religions 38%. Yet 99% of the population is animistic, irrespective of religion.

Muslim 46%. Growing rapidly in some areas. 10% of the country was Muslim in 1900.

Christian 16%. Affiliated 12.5%. Considerable growth since 1960.

Roman Catholic 10%. Practising 74%. 675,000a; 429,000m.

Indigenous marginal groups (4) 0.1%.

Protestant 1.5%. 104,000a; 40,000m. Denominations 14. Largest (adherents):

Assemblies of God	60,000
EAC (**CMA**)	11,000
Assoc. of Ev. Chs. (**SIM**)	9,000
Baptist Church (**SBC**)	4,000
Ev. Protestant Ch. (**WEC**)	2,000
Ev. Pentecostal Ch. (UVM)	2,000

Evangelical 1.4% of the population.

Missionaries to Burkina Faso 230 (1:30,000 people) in 14 agencies.

Missionaries from within Burkina Faso 6(?).

Religious Changes

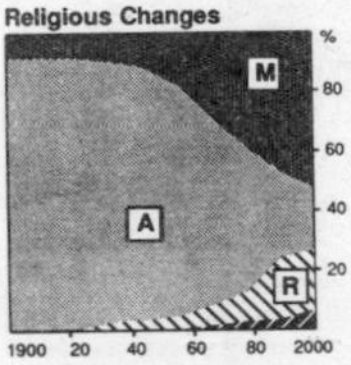

Evangelical Changes

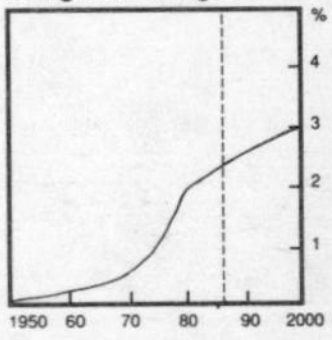

1. **Unreached peoples are numerous,** but there are few of them unoccupied by missions. The unreached:

a) The Muslim Soninké, Maninka, Tuareg, Songhai, Komono.

b) The many small pagan tribes in the south and west in the **CMA** and **WEC** areas.

c) The Lyele west of the capital.

d) Of the 7,000 rural villages, 5,000 have no Christian witness.

2. **Other peoples have been entered, but the response has generally been small** with only the Gurma and Bobo being more than 5% evangelical. The following missionary thrusts are worthy of prayer:

a) **CMA** to the Muslim Marka in the northwest.
b) The Mennonites to the Senufo groups and Syemou in the southwest.
c) **WEC** to the Birifor, Dagari, Gan, Dogosie, Puguli and Muslim Dioula.
d) **SIM** to Fulani in the north, Bisa in the northwest.
e) **AoG** to Fulse in the north and Gurunsi groups in the south.

3. **The power of the occult has yet to be decisively challenged and broken in many peoples of Burkina Faso.** Few countries in West Africa are more dominated by idolatry, fetishism and secret societies. Especially strong is that of the many Lobiri peoples in the southwest (**WEC** area), Gurma (**SIM**) in the east, Gurunsi (Canadian Pentecostals, **AoG**), Senufo and Bobo (**CMA**) in the west. Pray that the power of the risen Christ might be demonstrated for the saving of many.

4. **Islam is strong in the north** among the nomadic Fulani/Liptako, Songhai, Marka, Soninké and Tuareg, and in the urban areas among the trading Yarsi and Dioula. Most peoples have a growing minority of Muslims. Muslim Sufi brotherhoods are strong. It is only among the Fulani that several churches have emerged from those with a Muslim background (**SIM**, **AoG**). Too few missionaries are committed to the outreach. The political alliance with Libya is strengthening the hand of Muslims in the affairs of the country.

5. **The Catholics** have grown rapidly with 12,000 converts a year. 11% of the Mossis and most of the Dagari are Catholic, yet the strong heathenism within the hearts of the converts is unchallenged.

6. **Protestants were an insignificant minority before independence in 1960.** Church membership has increased ten-fold since then, with growth of **AoG** among the Mossi and Gurunsi, **SIM** among the Gurma and the beginnings of a breakthrough among the Lobi (**WEC**) and Bobo (**CMA**). Many of the peoples still need that breakthrough. Only the beginnings of a missionary concern for Muslims and for less evangelized peoples is evident among the believers.

7. **The Revolution of 1983 has dramatically changed the political and social structures of the country.** Committees for the Defence of the Revolution dominate local affairs. Christians are wary and sensitive to pressures exerted on them. Christian leaders need wisdom, humility, tact and firmness in the new situation; they must be upheld in prayer. A move of God's Spirit among the Christians is bringing a deeper understanding of the Word with a corresponding maturity in their lives, preparing them for whatever lies ahead.

8. **Leadership for the churches has been slow to develop** because of the prevailing poverty and illiteracy. Pray for the Bible schools run by the major churches and missions in local languages, and French language schools run by **SIM**, **CMA**, **AoG**, and Pentecostals. Pray for Christian leaders able to stand firm against the idolatrous practices of tribal society and against the demands of non-Christian national leaders.

9. **Young people** in the cities provided the energetic backing for the 1983 revolution. Christian young people now find it hard to stand out for the Lord. **SU** has a growing work in the relatively few high schools. There is one small GBU(**IFES**) group in the university.

10. **The massive emigration of Burkinabé to the cities and to Ivory Coast** is both a challenge and an opportunity for the gospel. The social upheavals, family breakdowns and economic stagnation caused by the emigration of most of the active men in the community are severe. The migrants have been neglected by Christian workers, and many are turning to Islam. The churches need to catch a vision for the cities, especially Ouagadougou and Abidjan (Ivory Coast). Pray for the calling out of evangelistic and church planting teams for the cities to which they have gone.

11. **Missionaries working in Burkina Faso** have a vital role in a land of so much physical and spiritual need. The work has been hard, and victories long in coming. Pray for their protection and encouragement. They need great sensitivity in these days of strident nationalism and suspicion of their motives. They need to know the Lord's priorities. Missionary reinforcements are needed in a wide range of ministries.

12. **Christian aid and relief** have been coordinated by the Federation of Evangelical Churches. Much is and has been done in alleviating suffering and staving off future disasters. Wisdom is needed by both missions and Christian leaders in the administration of this help. Massive internal migration, poor communications and the danger of distorting the fragile local economy all too easily result. Pray for the hearts of both Muslims and pagans to be opened to God's Word through such help.

13. **Bible translation is a ministry of major significance.** Only one indigenous language has the whole Bible — Moré. **SIL** (with 28 workers) is translating in 12 languages and surveying the needs of 28 others. Five other missions are involved in translation work in six languages. Present and future translators need prayer to complete the immense task. Literacy programmes are needed for many areas, so that Christians may read the new translations.

14. **The use of cassettes in evangelism and teaching has been little exploited** in a land of high illiteracy and little availability of literature. **GRI** has produced recordings in 40 languages and dialects.

BURMA
(The Socialist Republic of the Union of Burma)

Asia

Mar 10-11

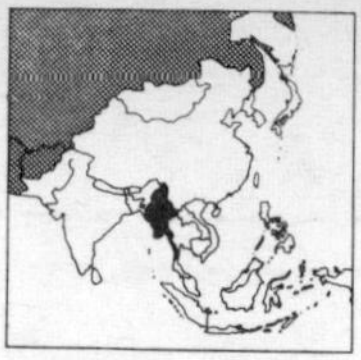

Area 678,000 sq.km. Isolated from India, China and Thailand by a ring of mountains.

Population 36,900,000. Annual growth 2.2%. People per sq.km. 54.

Peoples

Bhama 65.1% and related **Mogh** (Arakanese) 5%. The dominant people.

Ethnic minorities (with their own states within Union) 24.1%. Karen 4,000,000; Shan 2,660,000; Kachin 860,000; Mon 720,000; Chin 720,000; Kayah 190,000.

Other ethnic minorities 2.2%. Palaung 266,000; Lisu 200,000; Wa 150,000; Lahu 100,000; Akha 60,000; Lushai (Mizo) 40,000; Naga 30,000, etc.

Immigrant minorities 3.6%. Chinese 750,000; Bangladeshi/Indian 300,000.

Literacy 78%. **Official language:** Burmese. **All languages** 90. **Bible translations** 12Bi 10NT 16por.

Capital: Rangoon 2,674,000. Other major city: Mandalay 725,000. Urbanization 30%.

Economy: Very poor due to years of unrest, inefficient socialism and excessive isolationist policies of the government. Huge illegal trade in opium breeds corruption at every level in the country. Some economic relaxations since 1980. Income/person $180 (1% of USA). Inflation 9.2%.

Politics: The country has known little peace since the Japanese invasion in 1942. There has been much unrest and war since independence with constant ethnic and political revolts. One-party socialist republic since the 1962 military coup and almost total isolation of people and economy from international contacts.

Religion: There is freedom of religion. Buddhism is no longer the state religion, but it still has great influence in governmental affairs.

Buddhist 87%. Shot through with animist practices. Mainly Burmese, Shan, Mon and many Arakanese.

Animist 2%. Many Buddhists are more animist than Buddhist. Karen and many smaller tribes.

Muslim 3.6%. Bengali and Arakanese.

Hindu 0.9%. Indian.

Christian 5.9%. 95% from Animistic and 5% from Buddhist background; only 2% of Christians from Bhama majority.

Roman Catholic 1.2%. Practising 63%. 442,000a; 289,000m.

Protestant 4.7%. 1,730,000a; 668,000m.

Denominations 43. Largest (adult members):

Burma Baptist Convention	422,000
Assemblies of God	66,000
Church of Christ (ex CIM)	56,000
Anglican Church	20,000
Methodist Churches (2)	20,000
Presbyterian Church	11,900

Evangelical 3.1% of population.

Missionaries to Burma 2.

Missionaries from within Burma approx. 1,000 (1:1,700 Protestants).

Religious Changes

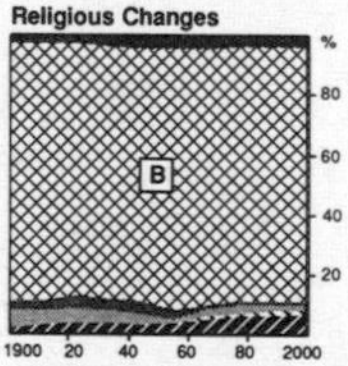

Evangelical Changes

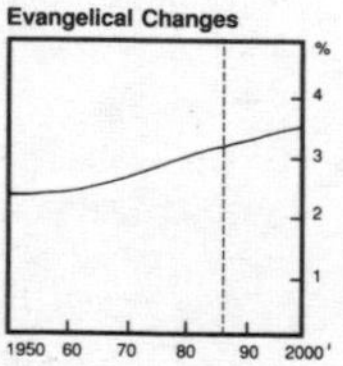

1. **Burma is a divided and troubled land** with private armies fighting for ethnic independence, Communism and protection of the lucrative opium trade. Pray that these trials may purify the church.

2. **Over the last few years the central government has given Christian workers and missionaries greater freedom to witness** — as a bulwark against Communism. Pray that opportunities may be used to the full.

3. **Missions** have done a good work, especially the American Baptist work pioneered by Adoniram Judson from 1813 onwards. So, when the government expelled all Protestant and most RC missionaries in 1966 (375 left the land), the Church was able to make the many painful adjustments speedily and carry on the ministry. Since that time, the believers have been almost completely isolated from contacts with Christians outside the country. Pray for the removal of restrictions.

4. **The churches have continued to grow steadily** at nearly 4% per year. The leadership in the churches gained in maturity and standing in the community after the expulsion of the missionaries. Christianity did not collapse, for it was rooted in the hearts of the people. Many Christians are well educated and are in positions of responsibility all over the country. Many young people have been converted in the churches and through various evangelical para-church groups. The Assemblies of God churches have shown marked growth.

5. **The most remarkable growth has taken place among the tribal people** and now the majority of the Kachin, Rawang, Lisu, Lahu, Lushai, 60% of the Chin, and 26% of the Karen are Christian. Pray that they may continue to evangelize every sub-group in their respective tribes and reach out to other unreached tribes and to the Bhama themselves.

6. **The challenges facing the Church in Burma:**

a) **Nominalism** among 3rd and 4th generation Christians. Pray for revival.

b) **Liberal theology** in some of the larger seminaries is creating a church leadership that scorns evangelicals and the message of new birth. Pray that the Bible may retain its rightful place in the affections of both leaders and church members. There are 35 seminaries and Bible colleges in Burma.

c) **Most Christians are from minority groups** which are embroiled in military actions against the central government. Pray that this may not cause bitterness, hatred of other peoples, or compromise of their faith.

d) **Economic hardship** is so great that many Christians in the "Golden Triangle" area are tempted to grow opium.

e) **Their isolation** from Christians in other countries needs to be ended and fellowship restored.

f) **There is a shortage of Bibles** and all forms of Christian literature in Burmese and minority languages because of strict import restrictions. For the first time some Burmese Bibles and NTs are being printed in Burma.

g) **Bible translation** is an unmet need with nothing of God's Word in 57 languages.

7. **The missionary burden of the Christians has been thrilling.** Right through the mountain areas missionaries have evangelized in one of Asia's most dramatic indigenous cross-cultural missionary outreaches. Teams of young people and pastors have made evangelistic tours in very difficult and dangerous conditions. There are now at least 1,000 Burmese missionaries — the largest: Burma Baptist Convention (890), Church of Christ (35), Presbyterian (33), Methodist (32). Pray for the growth of this enterprise and for a great harvest of souls to be won!

8. **Unreached peoples.**

a) **The Bhama people.** There are only 20,000 Protestants among them. It is not easy for the tribal believers to witness to them because of the years of mistrust. There is a new outreach by the Baptists in Rangoon. Pray for the conversion of Buddhists.

b) **Buddhist peoples** — especially the sophisticated, but resistant Shan (0.6% Christian), Mon (0.8% Christian), Mogh (handful), Palaung (few).

c) **The Animist peoples** — Moken (7,000 Sea Gypsies), Southern Chin, Dai, Tiddim, Nagas (now turning to Christianity through Lisu missionaries), the "wild" Wa, and many others.

d) **The Chinese** are only 2% Christian (75% of these being Protestant). Pray for the 8,000 Protestant Christians in 65 churches and their witness among the Chinese. The least reached groups are the Hakka and Cantonese-speaking Chinese. Many Chinese are being absorbed into the Burmese population.

e) **The 1,000,000 Muslim Rohingya and Kammas of Arakan** have been severely repressed by the central government. 250,000 Rohingya fled to Bangladesh in 1978. There are no known Christians among them.

Africa

Mar 12

BURUNDI
(Republic of Burundi)

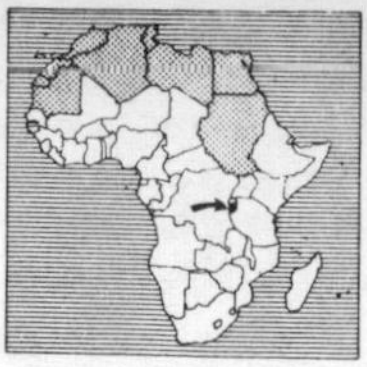

Area 27,800 sq.km. A mountainous country very similar to Rwanda to the north.

Population 4,600,000. Annual growth 2.7%. People per sq.km. 165.

Peoples
Tutsi 14%. The politically dominant minority.
Hutu 82%. A further 90,000 refugees now live in Tanzania.
Other 3.6%. Twa 50,000 (a pygmoid people); Rwandans 77,000; Zairois 40,000.

Literacy 25%. **Official languages:** Rundi, French. All speak Rundi. **Bible translations** 2Bi.

Capital: Bujumbura 178,000. Urbanization 4%.

Economy: One of the world's poorest states. Over-population and lack of natural resources make improvements hard to achieve. Income/person $240 (2% of USA).

Politics: The land gained independence from Belgium in 1962 as a constitutional monarchy. In 1966 the King was overthrown and was replaced by a military junta. An abortive Hutu revolt in 1972 was suppressed by the Tutsi army. In subsequent reprisals most Hutu leaders and intellectuals were killed or fled the country.

Religion: A secular state. Religious freedom is being steadily diminished. In 1984 all mid-week church meetings were banned. Some churches have been closed or had their ministry curtailed.

Muslim 1%. Gradual growth.
African traditional religions 12%.
Christian 86.6%. Nominal 24.8%. Affiliated 61.8%.
Roman Catholic 51%. Practising 74%. 2,350,000a; 1,406,000m.
Marginal groups 0.1%. 3,000a.
Protestant 10.6%. 486,000a; 234,700m.
Denominations 20. Largest (adult members):

Pentecostal Church (SFM)	122,000
Protestant Episcopal Ch.(CMS)	90,000
Un. Methodist Ch. (**WGM**-Free Meth)	26,600
Seventh Day Adventists	22,000
Ev. Brotherhood of Christ	6,700
Evangelical Friends (Quaker)	5,800
Union of Baptist Churches (**SBC**)	5,200
Emmanuel Church	3,000

Evangelical 9.5% of population.
Missionaries to Burundi 94(?) (1:49,000 people) in 16 agencies.
Missionaries from within Burundi 4(?).

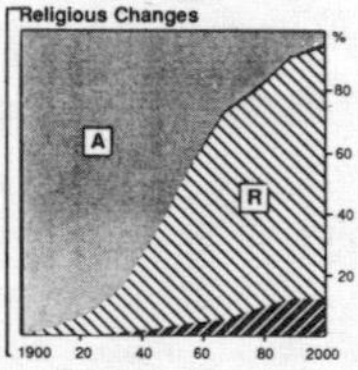

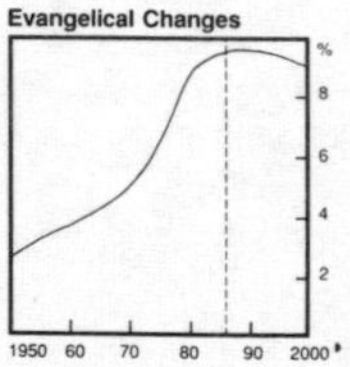

1. **The political situation is difficult** for Christians. Home meetings and mid-week gatherings may no longer be held. The work of some churches and missions has been banned and the entry of new missionaries is very difficult. Christians must live lives that commend the gospel to unbelieving leaders. Praise God that the gospel can still be preached. Pray that Christians may do so without fear or compromise.

2. **Ethnic divisions are still deep**, and the scars of the events of 1972 still not fully healed. Underlying tensions remain. Pray that believers may be channels of reconciliation and love.

3. **The East African revival stirred the Church in the '50s**, but liberalism and promiscuity has seriously damaged the credibility of many congregations. Pray for the Holy Spirit to be poured out afresh. Liberal theology has also made inroads. Praise the Lord for stirrings of new life in some areas and among young people in secondary schools and in the university (**IFES**). This movement has begun to deeply affect churches around the country.

4. **Leaders in the churches** have all too often become cold and set in their ways and more committed to structures than to preaching the gospel, yet there are those who remain faithful to their primary calling. Pray for the Mweya Theological Institute run by the Friends and United Methodists, and also the Bible School of the Pentecostal Church, and for staff and students. A new generation of leaders loyal to the Truth is needed.

5. **The missionary force has rapidly declined** due both to visa and relationship problems within the churches. Pray for sweet fellowship to prevail among national and expatriate personnel and also for new missionaries to be able to enter the land. There are many opportunities for Bible teachers, youth workers, literature and cassette specialists. Pray workers in despite the threat of expulsion for all missions.

6. **Areas of greater need:**

a) **The Twa** are relatively less evangelized, but integrate well into existing churches when converted.

b) A number of **towns** and **rural areas** are less evangelized and without a settled evangelical witness.

7. **The 90,000 refugees in Tanzania** have gradually put down roots in that land. There are thousands of Pentecostal believers and a further 3,000 Africa Gospel Church Christians (**WGM**) among these people. A number of Christian aid organizations are helping them (**WV**, AID, **TEAR Fund**).

8. **Literature** is scarce and costly, and Christian bookshops are few. There is very little available in Rundi.

9. **Pray for the newly formed IHCF**, and that there may be a strong Christian witness in all the medical centres.

10. **The government closed the Christian radio station "CORDAC" in 1977,** but a weekly evangelical programme is permitted every Saturday.

Africa

Mar 13-14

CAMEROON

(The Republic of Cameroon)

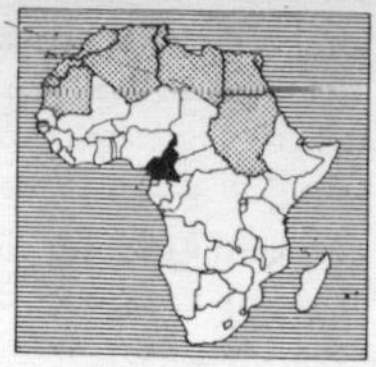

Area 475,000 sq.km. On the continental "hinge" between West and Central Africa. Semi-arid in the north, grasslands in the centre, rain-forest in the south.

Population 9,700,000. Annual growth 2.6%. People per sq.km. 20.

Peoples: Although there are over 200 languages only 40 have more than 50,000 speakers, and none more than 600,000. Major language groups are:
Bantu (121 groups) 59%. In the southern half of Cameroon.
Chadic Kirdi (55 groups) 16%. In the north.
Adamawa (34 groups) 9%. In the centre, including the Pygmy tribes.
Fulani 7%. In centre and north, where they are culturally dominant.
Other (10 groups) 9%. Including Nigerian-related peoples, Shuwa Arabs, Kanuri, Chadian refugees and French.

Literacy 50%. **Official languages:** French, English. **All languages** 233. **Bible translations** 13Bi 10NT 21por.

Capital: Yaoundé 474,000. Other city: Douala 719,000. Urbanization 34%.

Economy: A diversified agricultural economy. Development has been sure and steady. Income/person $800 (6% of USA).

Politics: Independent from France in 1960. Union with English-speaking W. Cameroon in 1961. A one-party republic. The former president, a Muslim, resigned in 1982. There have been a number of attempted coups since then. The present President is a Catholic. Potential for regional confrontations is high.

Religion: Secular state which guarantees religious freedom. Controls on Christian activities in the more Islamized north and promotion of Islam nation-wide until the recent change in leadership. Statistics are difficult to obtain and most figures are approximations.

Tribal religions 18%. Numerous among central and northern non-Muslim peoples and of considerable influence among Muslims and "Christians".
Muslim 23%. Strong among the Fulani, Mandara, Shua Arab, Kanuri, etc. in the north.
Baha'i 0.8%.
Christian 58%. Nominal 15%. Affiliated 43%. A large number of nominal Protestants and Catholics.
Roman Catholic 28%. Practising 38%. 2,700,000a; 1,600,000m.
Foreign marginal groups (2) 0.4%. 36,000a.
Indigenous marginal groups (22) 0.7%. 69,000a.
Protestant 14%. 1,360,000a; 751,000m.
Denominations 28. Largest (adult members):

All Presbyterians (5)	447,000
All Baptists (5)	145,000
All Lutherans (2)	44,500
Seventh Day Adventist Ch.	32,000
UEENC (**SUM**)	18,000

Evangelical 4% of population.
Missionaries to Cameroon 360 (1:27,000 people) in 30 agencies.
Missionaries from within Cameroon 36 (1:38,000 Protestants).

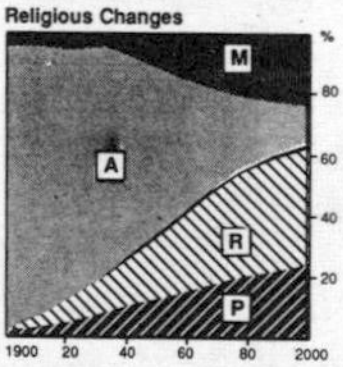

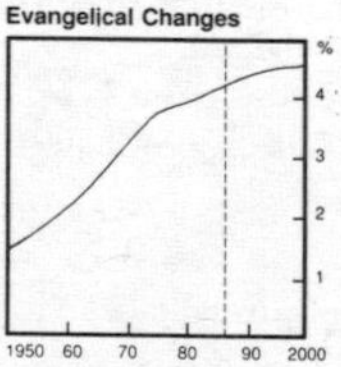

1. **Praise God for the steady growth of the Church** and present open doors for ministry. However, the land is only partially evangelized. Praise God for the touch of revival in the cities in 1978.

2. **Christians are most numerous in the south.** The Baptist, Presbyterian and Lutheran Churches are the largest groups. Inadequate pastoral care and clear teaching on biblical sanctification, together with liberalism in theological schools, have sapped the vitality and outreach of many churches in some denominations. To most, the Bible is a little-known book. Compromise with paganism, drunkenness, personality clashes, and divisions have been the bitter fruit. Pray for revival. Pray for the leaders of the denominations.

3. **The Christians in the centre and north are fewer in number**; 30% of the population is Muslim. Muslims were the traditional rulers of the area. Before 1982 there was some

localized harassment and persecution of believers; but since the more strict application of the secular state constitution, this has waned. The Lutheran Brethren, Union of Ev. Churches (**SUM**) and Baptists are the more significant bodies. Pray for a vigorous outreach by these believers to the pagan and Muslim peoples of the north.

C

4. **The theological colleges** are predominantly liberal in their theology. Pray for a decisive change in this sad state of affairs. Pray for born-again national and expatriate staff to be raised up for each school. Pray for more people to be called into full-time Christian work. The labourers are few.

5. **Bible translation** is the overwhelming challenge today. There are now 59 translation projects in hand — **UBS** with 18, **SIL** with 25. There are over 50 yet to be tackled. Pray for the present translation programme and for **SIL** workers in their ministry of translation and training of Cameroonian translators. The Fulani Bible is one of the latest and most strategic to be printed — 30 peoples use Fulani as their trade language.

6. **The missionary force.** The greatest contribution is from the USA, Norway, Switzerland, Netherlands and Germany. The largest agencies are **SIL** (70 workers), N. Amer. Baptists (47), **SUM** (33). Pioneer missionaries for unreached people and others willing to serve within the Cameroon Church in teaching, translation work, etc. are welcome. **RBMU** has recently entered three unreached people groups.

7. **Less reached peoples.** The need is insufficiently researched. Most peoples are at least marginally occupied, but over 25 do not have a viable, growing church within their culture.

a) **The Chadic Kirdi peoples** in the Mandara mountains, 30% Muslim, but mostly fetishists.

b) **The Giziga** 75,000; Mofu 50,000; Kapsiki 43,000, Gude 19,000, etc. (Luth. Brethren).

c) **The Adamawa peoples** have been less responsive — especially the Pygmy Baka 27,000 (Presbyterians and **RBMU**), Duru 50,000.

d) **The mountain peoples along the border with Nigeria,** Mambila 20,000, etc.

e) **Islam is dominant in eight peoples,** and Christians are very few. The powerful and numerous Fulani have done much to extend Islam. Pray for decisive gospel advances among Muslims — especially the Fulani 506,000, with only 10 known Christians; the Kanuri 56,000; Kotoko 45,000; Mandara 28,000; and also the Fali, Mbum, Bamum, Arab Shua, etc. The work of **SUM** and Lutheran Brethren missionaries has been hard, and only now are breakthroughs beginning.

f) **The 50,000 Chadian refugees**. Those from N'djamena are Muslim, but an increasing number of Christians from the south are fleeing persecution and violence from southern Chad.

Many other peoples have been only superficially or partially evangelized. Pray for the Cameroon Church to be roused to reach out cross-culturally.

8. **Supportive ministries.**

a) **Christian literature** is not used widely enough. There are only a handful of Christian distributors. Pray for the five **CLC** stores. More literature missionaries are needed.

b) **Cassette ministries** have been used by churches. **UBS** (Bible reading) and **GRI** with recordings available in 84 languages/dialects. A valuable tool in such a multilingual land.

c) **GBEEC(IFES)** and the witness among students is small but vibrant and growing.

The West

Mar 15-16

CANADA

(The Dominion of Canada)

Area 9,980,000 sq.km. The world's second largest country. Much is cold arctic tundra or sparsely populated forest.

Population 25,400,000. Annual growth 0.8%, largely through immigration. 80% of population live within 150 km. of the 7,000 km. US Border. People per sq.km. 2.6.

Peoples: A mosaic of many nations and peoples often retaining much of their original culture.
British 40%. Majority in east, centre and west.
French 29%. Majority in Quebec Province. Although Canada is officially bilingual with equal rights for all, the French minority includes a considerable separatist segment.
Other European 19.5%. German 1,500,000; Italian 800,000; Ukrainian 650,000; Dutch 490,000; Polish 366,000; Norwegian 195,000; Hungarian 146,000; Greek 140,000; Swedish 122,000; Yugoslav 122,000; Danish 98,000; Portuguese 98,000; Czech 73,000; Russian 70,000; Finnish 70,000; Belgian 50,000, etc.
Indigenous 5.4%. Amerindians (registered 340,000 in 61 tribes on reservations; non-registered 1,000,000), Eskimo 30,000.
Asian 3.3%. Indo-Pakistanis 350,000; Chinese 301,000; Vietnamese 90,000; Japanese 50,000; Korean 40,000.
Middle Eastern 1.1%. Mainly Arabic speaking.
African 0.8%. 200,000 North American, West Indian and African.
Latin American 0.8%. 200,000.

Literacy 99%. **Official languages:** English, French. **All indigenous languages** 70. **Bible translations** 2Bi 2NT 35por.

Capital: Ottawa 850,000. Major cities: Toronto 3,300,000; Montreal 3,300,000; Vancouver 1,350,000. Urbanization 76%.

Economy: One of the world's leading industrial nations. The USA is Canada's main trading partner. This interdependence moderates trends towards an economic nationalism. Income/person $12,000 (85% of USA). Inflation 8.6%.

Politics: Parliamentary and federal monarchy. Independent of Britain in 1867. Though the world's longest undefended border runs between Canada and the US, Canada's own cultural and political identity leads to an independent line in foreign affairs to its NATO ally.

Religion: Freedom of religion.
Non-religious/Atheist 7.5%.
Muslim 1.5%. Pakistani, Arab, etc.
Jews 1.4%. Some from N. Africa and USSR.
Hindu 0.5%. Mostly Indian.
Sikh 0.2%.
Baha'i 0.2%.
Animist 0.1%. Increasing again among Amerindians.
Christian 88%. Nominal 23.2%. Affiliated 64.8%.
Roman Catholic 39.6%. (A further 7% nominal.) Practising 40%. 10,060,000a. Majority of French, Spanish, Italian, Portuguese, etc.
Orthodox 2.4%. 612,000a. Denominations 31+. Mostly ethnic minorities of E. European, Greek and Middle Eastern origin.
Marginal groups 2.3%. Over 34 cults. Largest (adult members):

Mormons	90,000
Jehovah's Witnesses	77,003

Protestant 20.6%. (A further 15% nominal.) 5,220,000a; 2,880,000m. Denominations 180. Largest (adult members):

United Church	983,000
Anglican Church	588,000
Pentecostal (30 groups)	266,000
Lutheran (8 groups)	223,000
Presbyterian (5 groups)	210,000
Baptist (11 groups)	205,000
Mennonite (12 groups)	64,000

Evangelical 6.5% of population.
Missionaries to Canada approx. 300 (Mostly from the USA).
Missionaries from within Canada approx. 4,000 (1:1,300 Protestants) in over 50 agencies. Of these 420 serve in cross-cultural work in Canada.

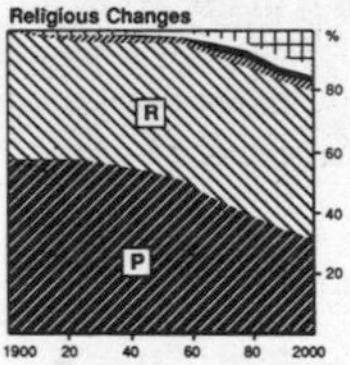

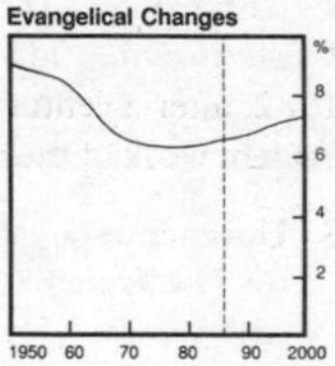

1. **Canada needs revival.** A localized revival in the Prairie provinces in 1972 brought blessing to many churches, but a wider and deeper work of God is needed. Praise God for evident blessing among French, native Canadians and some ethnic minorities since 1980.

2. **There is a drift away from the traditional churches** where nominalism, non-biblical theology and neglect of evangelism is common. Only about half of all Canadians have any real affiliation with a church. Pray that the Evangelicals within these denominations may be as salt and light.

3. **The evangelical witness is growing**, especially in Western Canada. Pray that it may become a mighty voice for God and righteousness in this materialistic society. The Pentecostal Assemblies of Canada is one of the fastest growing denominations. Among smaller evangelical denominations which are growing are the **CMA,** Association of Gospel Churches, Fellowship Baptists, **Nazarenes**, etc. Yet divisiveness among Evangelicals is often a sad reality. Pray for a greater concern for the evangelization of the many immigrant groups of Canada. The West Indian and Chinese evangelical churches are strong, and the latter growing fast.

4. **The large number of Bible institutes, colleges and theological seminaries** committed to the orthodox view of Scripture are fulfilling a major role in the growth of the evangelical witness. Most are concentrated in the western Prairie provinces. Pray for those in training and those teaching them, that world evangelization may have priority.

5. **The French Canadians** are, for the most part, nominally Catholic. There have been great changes in attitudes to the gospel since the '60s, and persecution of preachers and converts is a thing of the past. Through widespread evangelism many are coming to a personal faith. French-speaking evangelical churches increased from 150 in 1976 to nearly 400 in 1983, and in that time the number of evangelical believers has risen from 6,000 to nearly 40,000. Pray for all engaged in evangelism (**OM, YWAM**, etc.) and church planting (**Pentecostal Assemblies** (170 churches and groups), **Baptist** (75), **Brethren** (50), **CMA** (14), **BCU**, etc.). Work among young people has proved fruitful over the last three to four years, and many are showing interest in serving the Lord.

6. **The Amerindians** are largely Christian in name but active, evangelistic churches among them are in the minority.

a) **Pray for a moving of God's Spirit** to combat the effects of unintentionally paternalistic missionary work, the high incidence of social and economic problems, and the strident anti-White propaganda that draws many back into old heathen customs.

b) **Pray for the growth of strong, well-led churches** that are culturally Indian. In many parts of Canada a change came after 1981, and hardened communities have been responding to Christ in local revivals.

c) Pray for the considerable number of denominational (Anglican, United Church, **CMA**, **PAoG**, etc.) and interdenominational (**N. American Indian Mission, N. Canada Evang. Mission**, etc.) missions seeking to evangelize and plant churches — often in the inhospitable northern parts of the country.

d) Although only 25 languages are still actively used, **Bible translation or revision is needed.** Pray for the 22 **SIL** workers and others engaged in 22 language projects.

e) **The one million Amerindians living off reservations are neglected** and needy — especially in the cities.

7. **The Eskimos (or Inuit) in the Arctic** are mostly Anglican, but the impact of the worst of Western civilization has greatly altered and harmed the Eskimo way of life. However, since 1982, after a century of nominal Christianity, there has been a wave of conversions and an evident work of the Spirit across the Arctic.

8. **Unreached peoples:**

a) **The French Canadians** — many scores of towns and villages in Quebec have no known believers.

b) **Asian Indians** (220,000) — Hindus, Sikhs and Muslims — have rapidly increased through immigration from the UK, East Africa and South Asia. Most live in Toronto, Vancouver and Calgary. Only now is an active evangelistic ministry beginning among them (**CMA**, United Church, Mennonites, Baptists, etc.), although there are a number of indigenous Indian Christian groups.

c) **Arabic-speaking peoples** are mostly Muslim, but very little specific outreach to them has been undertaken. Most of the few believers are Lebanese.

d) **The East Indian community** is growing rapidly through immigration. In only two centres have churches been planted among these Hindus, Sikhs, and Muslims.

e) **The Greeks, Italians, and Portuguese** are needy communities with few churches.

9. **The missionary vision has been great,** but the number of missionaries has fallen of late. Pray for increased involvement by churches and individuals in the evangelization of the unreached in Canada and around the world. Pray for the stimulation of missionary concern in the many growing evangelical churches among the ethnic minorities; such a vision could be strategic for the evangelization of their lands of origin.

10. **Christian broadcasting.** There are a number of Christian stations and widely appreciated religious programmes on secular networks. **100 Huntley Street** is one such national programme. The air waves tend to be dominated by US networks, and there is need for a greater indigenization!

Africa

Mar 17

CAPE VERDE ISLANDS

(Republic of Cape Verde)

Area 4,033 sq.km. Fifteen dry, barren islands 600 km. off the West Coast of Africa.

Population 351,000. Annual growth 2.7%. People per sq.km. 87.

Peoples: Black 28% mainly from Guinea-Bissau. **Caboverdian Creole** (mixed race) 71%. **White** 1%.

Literacy 44%. **Official language:** Portuguese. **Trade language:** Portuguese Creole.

Capital: Praia 39,000.

Economy: Agricultural economy devastated by 15 years of drought. Heavily dependent on aid and remittances of migrants. Income/person $250 (2% of USA).

Politics: Independent of Portugal in 1974 as a one-party republic.

Religion: Secularization has accelerated since independence.

Non-religious/Atheist 1.2%.

Christian 98.8%. Nominal 4.4%. Affiliated 94.4%.

Roman Catholic 91%. 319,000a; 150,000m.

Marginal groups 0.22%. All Jehovah's Witnesses.

Protestant 3.3%. 11,700a; 3,500m. Denominations 2. Largest (adult members):

Church of the Nazarene	2,800
Seventh Day Adventist Ch.	700

Evangelical 3% of population.

Missionaries to Cape Verde 13 (1:27,000 people).

1. **The steady growth of the Evangelicals** has been primarily through the ministry of Nazarene missionaries. There are now churches on most islands with Caboverdian pastors, but the extreme poverty of the islands retards the maturing and growth of the churches.

2. **Caboverdians** live in large migrant communities in New England, USA; Senegal; Brazil; Guinea-Bissau and Angola. These are significant minorities which require specific evangelistic strategies.

CAYMAN ISLANDS

See British Antilles p. 115.

CENTRAL AFRICA REPUBLIC

Africa

Mar 18

Area 623,000 sq.km. A landlocked state in Africa's geographical centre. Variation from tropical forest in the southwest to semi-desert in the northeast.

Population 2,700,000. Annual growth 2.4%. People per sq.km. 4.

Peoples
Indigenous peoples 98%. Over 80 tribes. Main groups, each composed of a number of tribes: Banda 850,000; Gbaya 660,000; Mandja 175,000; Sara 170,000; Mbum 168,000; Ngbaka 160,000; Bantu (Sango, Ngundi, Kaka, Banziri, etc.) 100,000; Nzakara 90,000; Kare 50,000; Azande 40,000; Binga (Pygmies) 30-60,000 — many scattered groups.
Immigrant/Refugee 2%. Fulani, Hausa, Arab, French.

Literacy 20%. **Official language:** French. **National language:** Sango. **All languages** 54. **Bible translations** 4Bi 7NT 3por.

Capital: Bangui 380,000. Urbanization 41%.

Economy: Very poor and undeveloped due to the distance from the sea. Income/person $280 (2% of USA). Inflation 10.6%.

Politics: Independent from France in 1960. The flamboyant and tyrannical rule of "Emperor" Bokassa ended in a coup in 1979, when the former president ousted him. There has been a military government since September 1981.

Religion: There is freedom of religion.

Tribal religions 9%. Many "Christians" are actually still following the old ways.
Muslim 3.3%. In the far north, east along the Sudan border, some Fulani in the west and Arabs in towns and capital.
Christian 87.8%. Nominal 41.5%. Affiliated 46.4%.
Roman Catholic 17.4%. (A further 18.5% nominal Catholics.) 470,000a.
Marginal groups 0.6%. 15,000a.
Protestant 28.4%. (A further 23% nominal Protestant.) 767,000a; 302,000m. Denominations 12. Largest (adult members):

Grace Evangelical Brethren	113,600
Baptist Church (BMM)	80,000
Baptist Ch. of West (Örebro Miss.)	46,200
Eglise du Reveil (Elim)	14,800
Co-op Ev. Centrafricaine	12,300
Lutheran Church	8,580
Eglise Evang. Centrafricaine (**AIM**)	4,000

Evangelical 28% of population.
Missionaries to CAR 198 (1:13,600 people) in 11 agencies

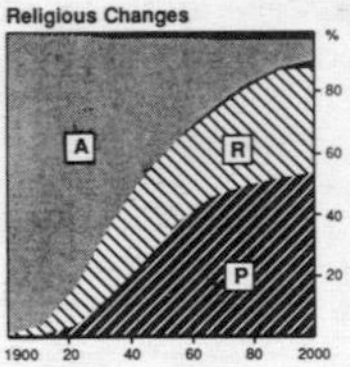

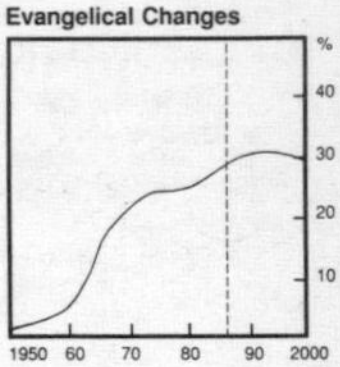

1. **Few countries have been better evangelized!** Praise God for the massive response to evangelism in the '60s and '70s that brought about great church growth. In the early '70s **New Life For All** was a vital ingredient in this ingathering. There are now evangelical churches in nearly every tribe and district.

2. **The growth has outstripped the ability of the churches to consolidate these gains effectively.** Many are nominally linked with Christianity, and few have more than a rudimentary grasp of the basic truths of the Bible. There is almost everywhere a desperate need for life-changing Bible teaching and trained men of God for this ministry.

3. **Many immature Christians are laid open to syncretic African and foreign sects** due to the low literacy rate, the lack of the Scriptures in local languages and the underlying, often unchallenged, powers of darkness. Pray for growth, stability and a rekindling of evangelistic zeal among the believers. Pray for revival.

4. **Leadership training.** There are a number of Bible schools run by the various churches for which there is the constant need for adequate national and expatriate staff. Pray that the right students may be called and that those trained may go out as spiritual and effective Christian workers. The large, underpopulated land makes TEE an essential tool for training local leaders, but much work must still be done to launch and maintain this programme all over the country.

5. **The missions** have played an important role in education and health as well as in planting churches, translating the Scriptures, etc. The largest are Baptist Mid-Missions (72 missionaries), Church of the Brethren Mission (54), Örebro (27), **AIM** (16). Pray for their health and spiritual keenness in an enervating climate. There are many opportunities for more missionary Bible teachers and those with special skills to help develop a strong indigenous church.

6. **There have been tragic divisions** between missions and missionaries and between missionaries and local church leaders that have not been a credit to the gospel. Pray for a deeper mutual understanding among the servants of the Lord. Pray for the healing of past wounds, and for cooperation in the building up of the Body of Christ. Pray also that the AEEC (Assoc. of C. African Evangelical Churches) may promote such.

7. **The Bangui Evangelical School of Theology** opened in 1977 as a result of the initiative of AEAM (Assoc. of Evangelicals of Africa and Madagascar). This is the first theological degree-level school for French-speaking Africa. After many birth pains, this school has now gained stability under African leadership. Pray for this institution and its spiritual impact throughout Africa. Pray for the provision of the right staff and resources. There are now 55 resident students, but it has the capacity to take in 120. The Grace Evang. Brethren also have a seminary at Bata.

8. **The development of secondary and university education** means that more must be done to meet the spiritual needs of students. Pray for the GBU(**IFES**) groups in Bangui, and for the Christian Unions now in most of the secondary schools. The Theological Training Secretary of **IFES** for Francophone Africa is based in Bangui. Churches are permitted to organize Bible teaching in school buildings after school hours. Pray that present opportunities may be well used.

9. **Bible translation** — only one language (the trade language, Sango) has the whole Bible. Pray for its revision. Over one million speak this language, and 200,000 use it as their home language. There are seven other languages in which Bible translation is now being undertaken, but up to 35 may need translators.

10. **Unreached peoples:**

There has been an influx of Muslims who present the greatest challenge at present — a task for which the local believers are not yet equipped.

a) **The Arabs** 20,000? Many have immigrated or fled from Sudan, and most live in the towns.

b) **The Hausa** 10,000? Strongly Muslim, nothing at present is being attempted.

c) **The Fulani** 15,000? are less strongly Muslim, and there is now some work by the Baptist Ch. of W. CAR and Swedish Örebro missionaries.

Other less evangelized indigenous groups. These include the many Pygmy tribes:

a) **The Pygmy Binga** 30,000? now being evangelized by French and local missionaries of Co-op. Ev. Centrafricaine.

b) **Sara** groups along the border with Chad are less evangelized. Some are Muslim.

c) The **Runga** 15,000 in the northern tip of the country are partly Muslim, and little has been done to reach this possibly key tribe which also lives in Chad and Sudan.

d) The **Fertit** on the Sudanese border.

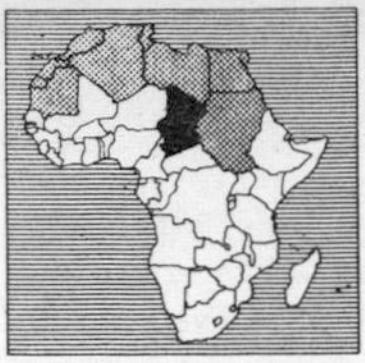

CHAD
(Republic of Chad)

Africa

Mar 19

Area 1,284,000 sq.km. Desert in the north, dry grassland in centre, thick bush in the south.

Population 5,200,000. Annual growth 2.1%. People per sq.km. 4. Most live in southwest.

Peoples: Tribal, cultural and regional differences have dominated the area for centuries. The ethnic and linguistic confusion defies a detailed breakdown!

Arab 14%. Most are nomadic and live interspersed among other peoples.

Northern peoples 5%. Predominantly Tubu (Teda, Daza) and Zaghawa-Bideyat. All are Muslim.

Central peoples of Sahel 30%. About 50 peoples; almost all are Muslim.

Southern peoples 51%. About 60 peoples. Predominantly Christian and animist.

Literacy 12%. **Official languages:** French (only spoken by the educated), Arabic (spoken by about 60% of the population). **All languages** 112. **Bible translations** 4Bi 12NT 5por.

Capital: N'djamena 300,000. Many are drought refugees. Urbanization 22%.

Economy: A subsistence economy due to the lack of rainfall, poor soil and distance from the sea. The dislocation caused by civil wars and the Sahel famines have made hundreds of thousands of central Chad people into refugees within the country and in surrounding lands. The famine was particularly severe in 1984.

Politics: Independent from France in 1960. The non-Muslim southerners were politically dominant until 1978, but since 1979 northern Muslim factions have fought between themselves for power. The northern desert is controlled by a faction armed by Libya, and the rest of the country is ruled by President Habré who has been supported by Sudan and France. There are several southern guerrilla armies opposing the control of the central government. The chances of sustained peace appear to be small.

Religion: The present president is Muslim, but promises have been made that freedom of religion will be maintained. There was much persecution of Christians between 1973 and 1975 by the then southerner President, and sporadic localized persecution since 1977.

Muslim 35%. All the Arabs and also the central and northern peoples.

Traditional religions 31%. Still strong in some southern peoples.

Christian 34%. Nominal 17%. Affiliated 17%. Most denominational statistics are approximations.

Roman Catholic 5.2%. Many more are nominally Catholic. 270,000a.

Marginal groups 0.6%. Some syncretic indigenous groups.

Protestant 11%. 560,000a; 175,000m. Denominations 8. Largest (adult members):

Christian Assemblies (Brethren)	(?)	80,000
EET (**TEAM, SUM, WEC**)		43,000
Baptist Church	(?)	20,000
Brethren Lutheran Church		14,500
Ev. Church of the Brethren		10,000
Church of God (Cleveland)		3,400

Evangelical 11% of population.

Missionaries to Chad approx. 110 (1:47,000 people) in 11 agencies; all evangelical.

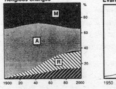

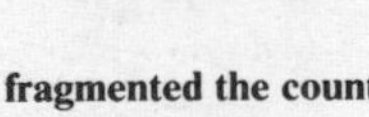

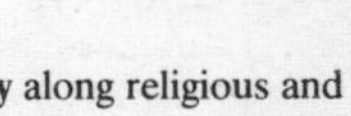

1. **The wars and fighting since independence fragmented the country** along religious and then ethnic lines. The memory of atrocities and suffering needs to be erased. Pray for reconciliation and peace, so that the message of the gospel may cross ethnic divisions to the many unreached peoples. Pray for a spirit of forgiveness and burden for the lost among the Christians.

2. **The church in the south grew fast in the '60s and '70s**. The work of **Brethren, TEAM,** Baptist and Lutheran missionaries was blessed of God. A period of refinement came in 1973. During the following two years the government persecuted the believers who refused to revert to heathen customs. Hundreds were martyred. Since 1977 marauding soldiers have made travel dangerous and brought suffering and destruction to various areas in the country. Pray for the believers in these testing years that their faith may not fail.

3. **The church needs much prayer:**

a) **Growth** has outstripped the availability of resources and trained personnel to disciple them. The lack of the Bible in many languages, and illiteracy, make this task the more urgent.

b) **The training of pastors and evangelists** has been hindered by war, evacuation of missionaries, and the lack of finances to support students in training. Pray for the three secondary level and 25 primary level schools in the south, and pray for the new generation of pastors that they may be men full of the Holy Spirit. Pray also for the refresher courses arranged for those already in the ministry.

c) **The spirit of tribalism and legalism is strong**. Pray for liberation in the Holy Spirit for every congregation. Revival is needed.

d) **There is a lack of concern and ability to communicate the gospel to Muslims.** Pray that southern Christians may become effective witnesses to Muslims moving into southern towns in large numbers, as well as sending out missionary workers to other areas.

4. **There are over 50 unreached peoples in Chad.** Almost all are Muslim:

a) **The Arab-speaking peoples** are largely nomadic and scattered through the country. They have frequent contact with southern Christians, but little is being done to evangelize them.

b) **The desert tribes of the north**, the Zaghawa, Tubu, Bideyat, etc., have never had a gospel witness.

c) **The tribes around Lake Chad.** A handful have responded to courageous attempts by Chadian and foreign missionaries (**TEAM**). Little is now being done for the Buduma, Kanembu, Fulani.

d) **The Bagirmi** (45,000) southeast of the capital have no known Christians. The first attempts are now being made to reach them (**WEC**).

e) **The 17 tribes of the Ouaddai** in the east central Chad: Tama 290,000; Massalit 250,000; Maba 200,000; Dadjo 110,000; Assungori 40,000; Massalat 25,000; Fur 5,000, etc. (French **SUM, WEC**). Only four Christians are known, all are Maba women.

f) The **Hadjerai** peoples (130,000), and Dadjo (100,000) of the central Guera region. There are a few isolated churches (**SUM**), but most are unreached.

g) **The capital** is reputed to be the most plundered in Africa. Many of its inhabitants have lived with war and destruction for years. Most of the congregations were scattered in 1979. Pray for the replanting of churches in this predominantly Muslim city.

5. **Missionary work continues despite the breakdown of the economy and administration.** In 1979 nearly all missionaries had to leave the country, but some are returning. The main missions are United Evangelical Mission (consisting of **TEAM** (26), **Baptist Mid-Mission** (17), **Lutheran Brethren Mission** (8), **Brethren** (7), **WEC** (6), **SUM** (5), Grace Brethren Church (2)). The need for new workers is obvious, but pray for those with the pioneer spirit and stickability to give years to language learning, necessary to contribute much to the unreached and to developing churches. Pray also for their daily provision and safety.

6. **Communications are poor and dangerous. MAF** work (with four workers and two planes) is vital for supplying those serving in outlying areas. Pray for safety; supply of needs; and secure, effective bases for this programme.

7. **Bible translation** is a pressing need because of the linguistic diversity. Some church services have to be conducted in three or four languages! The unrest and economic difficulties have slowed translation work now being done in 13 languages. Possibly 85 other languages are in need of NTs. The Bible Society is involved in eight projects, and **SIL** is surveying the need and sending in translation teams. Pray for wisdom, perseverance and safety for all involved.

CHILE

(The Republic of Chile)

Latin America

Mar 20

Area 757,000 sq.km. A 4,200-km.-long country wedged between the mountains of the Andes and the Pacific Ocean and averaging only 150 km. in width.

Population 12,000,000. Annual growth 1.8%. People per sq.km. 16.

Peoples: A relatively homogenous society.
Chilean 91.3%. European 20% (Spanish, Italian, French, British, German, etc.), Mestizo (mixed Spanish/Indian) 71.3%.
Amerindian 6.2%. Mapuche 550,000, Quechua 80,000, Aymara 57,000, six other small tribes.
Polynesian 0.02%. 2,500 on Easter Island, 4,500 km. to the west.
Other 1.5%. Mainly foreign residents.

Literacy 91%. **Official language:** Spanish. **All languages** 12. **Bible translations** 1Bi 1NT 1por.

Capital: Santiago 4,300,000. Urbanization 83%. 40% of the people live near the capital and 85% in the temperate central provinces. The northern desert, and wet, cold mountains in the south have few inhabitants.

Economy: Mining and export of minerals, especially copper, is the most important economic activity. Inflation, drought and the world recession hit the economy hard in 1982 and led to suffering and poverty for many. A gradual recovery is under way. Income/person $1,870 (13% of USA).

Politics: Republic independent from Spain in 1818. An elected minority leftist government was ousted in a military coup in 1973 after it had sought to seize full power unconstitutionally. The controversial rightist military government polarized both Protestants and Catholics and antagonized many other nations in the post-coup period by their disregard for human rights. Worsening economic conditions are hastening the gradual return to democratic civilian rule.

Religion: Freedom of religion. Both Catholics and Protestants have a strong influence.

Non-religious/Atheist 6.7%.
Animist 0.8%. Most open among a minority of Mapuche but permeating folk-Catholicism.
Christian 92%. Affiliated 88.2%.

Roman Catholic 63.4%. Many defections to Evangelicals and other ideologies. 7,610,000a; 5,860,000m. Regular attendance at mass 13% of communicants.

Orthodox 0.26%. Denominations 5. Russian, Greek, Armenian, Lebanese.

Marginal groups 2%. 245,000a. Largest (adherents):

Mormons	133,000
Jehovah's Witnesses	98,000

Protestant 22.5%. 2,710,000a; 1,190,000m. Denominations 85+. Some of the largest (adult members):

Pentecostal Methodist Church	300,000
Evang. Pentecostal Church	250,000
Pentecostal Church of God	129,000
Evang. Methodist Pentecostal	121,000
Seventh Day Adventist Church	56,000
Baptist Convention (**SBC**)	19,300
Christian Alliance (**CMA**)	10,000
Assemblies of God (**AoG**)	9,000
Int. Ch. of Foursq. Gospel	6,000
Lutheran Church in Chile	5,700
Anglican Church	3,000

Evangelical 21.6% of population.

Missionaries to Chile 440 (1:27,000 people) in 40 agencies.
Missionaries from Chile 100 (1:27,000 Protestants).

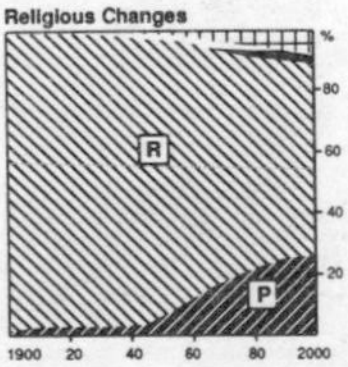

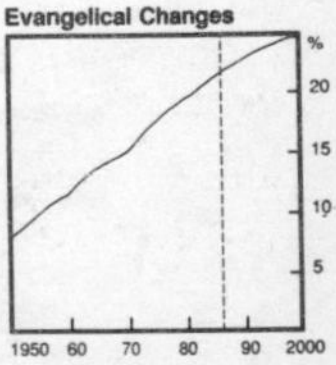

1. **Evangelical church growth has been dramatic**; a great ingathering of souls has been seen over the last 25 years. There are over 500 evangelical organizations in the country. Almost one-fifth of the population is now linked with a Pentecostal/evangelical Church. Praise God for this! The growth rate is tailing off because the gospel is having less impact on the younger generation, but opportunities for its proclamation have never been greater.

2. **The size of the evangelical community brings new responsibilities and dangers to the believers:**
   a) It is increasingly "respectable" to be an Evangelical. Pray for revival.

b) Political influence can be decisive, but also can be misused. Pray for a prophetic role in society for Christian leaders at this time of social unrest.

c) The rapid growth of Evangelicals has resulted in many zealous but poorly-taught believers. The lack of teaching lays many open to cults. Mormons are increasing.

3. **The complex political and economic crises since 1970 have divided Christians** and brought tensions in many churches. Pray that oneness in the Spirit among Christians may prevail, and that their example and witness may be redemptive in Chile's present agonies. Pray also that the country may have peace, justice and liberty.

4. **The Pentecostal churches** have a great evangelistic fervour, but are very often of little depth spiritually and doctrinally. The importance given to dominant personalities, and the neglect of Bible teaching, lead to frequent divisions. The Pentecostals have made a deep impact on the working class.

5. **The other evangelical churches** have had more success in the middle class; very often they do not have the power or the cultural adaptability necessary to reach all the social sectors. The Baptist churches and the churches of the **CMA** have satisfactory growth, but the Methodist and Presbyterian churches are stagnating.

6. **The Roman Catholic Church has been deeply affected** by two major forces.

a) **Social upheaval** and the response through "Liberation Theology" and the Basic Community movement.

b) **The widespread distribution and use of the Bible** and the growth of the charismatic movement, with a significant exodus of Catholics to the evangelical churches.

Both forces are being challenged by the conservative Pope John Paul II. Pray that many Catholics may find true liberation and peace through faith in Christ.

7. **Foreign missions in Chile.** The major agencies are Southern Baptists (72 missionaries), Gospel Mission of S. America (38), **CMA** (29), **CoN** (12). The major task for missionaries is to serve the large Chilean Church in teaching, developing Chilean leadership and encouraging a missionary vision. Pioneer work is limited to some peoples listed below and among the upper class and the urban slum dwellers. Pray that the missionaries' contribution may mature the Chilean Church and prove vital and invigorating.

8. **The growing Chilean missionary movement** needs prayer. Probably well over 100 Chileans (mainly Pentecostals) have initiated mission work in over 15 countries.

9. **Unreached Peoples**

a) **The Mapuche (Araucans)** are the largest and most fiercely independent of Chile's tribes. Many are now nominally Catholic (75%), but their old tribal religion is still strong. Some 4,000 are evangelical Anglicans. Pray for the **SAMS** missionaries working among them and also for the two **SIL** workers seeking to translate the NT into one of the four dialects.

b) **Rapa Nui** (Easter Islanders) are a largely Polynesian people. One **SIL** couple is learning the language in order to translate the NT into their language. Most are nominally Catholic.

c) **Remnants of five small tribes** in the south totalling less than 100 people.

10. **Literature** has played a vital role in bringing people into evangelical churches. Pray for the work of the **Bible Society**. Bookstores are run by **CLC** (eight workers) and many of the denominations.

11. **Student witness** in the 17 universities and among the 200,000 students is not strong. There are 10 GBU(**IFES**) groups, but only four are really viable. **CCC** (40 overseas workers) has a considerable impact on secondary schools and some universities. The most significant campus ministry is an indigenous ministry "Movimiento Revolución de Jesu-Cristo" which has grown rapidly and spread to 30 college and university campuses.

12. **Christian radio programmes** are widely available on national, commercial and Christian stations. **IBRA** radio has continuous transmission from 10 stations.

CHINA
(People's Republic of China)

Asia

Mar 21-27

Area 9,561,000 sq.km. The third largest state in the world. Taiwan, Hong Kong and Macao are not included here.

Population 1,042,000,000. By far the largest nation in the world; 21.8% of world's population. Most live in the better-watered central and eastern coastal provinces. Annual growth 1.1%. People per sq.km. 109.

Peoples
Chinese (Han) 93%. Eight major languages and 600 dialects but one written language common to all. Putunghua (Mandarin) 748 mill., Wu 90 mill., Yueh (Cantonese) 54 mill., Xiang (Hunanese) 53 mill., Hakka 43 mill., Minnan 32 mill., Gan 26 mill., Minpei 13 mill.
Ethnic minorities 7%. 55 minorities officially recognized. Largest: Zhuang 14 mill., Hui 7.6 mill., Uighur 6.3 mill., Yi 5.7 mill., Hmong (Miao) 5.3 mill., Manchu 4.5 mill., Tibetan 4 mill., Mongol 3.4 mill., Bouyei-Tai 3.2 mill., Tujia 3 mill., Korean 1.8 mill., Dong 1.5 mill., Bai 1.2 mill., Hani 1.1 mill. Many smaller minorities live in the mountainous south and southwest.

Literacy 76%. **Official language:** Putunghua (Mandarin Chinese); local languages in the five Autonomous Regions. **All languages** 115. **Bible translations** 13Bi 10NT 23por.

Capital: Beijing (Peking) 9.2 million. Other cities: Shanghai 11.9 mill., Tianjin 7.8 mill., Chongqing 6.5 mill., Guangzhou 5.6 mill., Shenyang 5.1 mill., Wuhan 4.2 mill., Nanjing 3.6 mill. Thirty-eight other cities of over one million inhabitants. Urbanization 21%.

Economy: Socialist, but since 1978 a more pragmatic economic policy has been pursued. The commune system has been dismantled and the peasants (80% of the population) allowed greater freedom to sell surplus crops. Some small-scale private enterprise (particularly in service industries) has been allowed in the cities. Overall living standards and personal incomes have risen. Income/person $290 (2% of USA).

Politics: This great and ancient nation has regained its place of importance in the world after nearly two centuries of decline and humiliation at the hands of the Western powers and Japan. Since the final conquest of mainland China in 1949, the Communist Party has remoulded the nation along Marxist lines. The Cultural Revolution (1966-76) was the culmination of this policy. It caused immeasurable suffering and economic chaos. Intellectuals and religious believers were cruelly persecuted. The loss of life was enormous. After the death of Mao in 1976 the radical leftists were discredited and removed from power. A more pragmatic leadership initiated a series of economic, political and cultural reforms and developed links with other nations, but all within definite limits. The Communist party still maintains strict control over every aspect of life. In the latter half of 1983 a series of campaigns were initiated against crime, leftists, and "spiritual" pollution to counter growing corruption, dissident Western influences and revivals of religion. However, since early 1984 the overall political climate has again relaxed, though in some provinces leftist influence still remains strong.

Religion: The elimination of all religious groups has always been the ultimate aim of the Marxist government. In the '50s the government engineered the infiltration, subversion and control of all organized Christianity. By 1958 this had been achieved through the Three Self Patriotic Movement among Protestants, and the Catholic Patriotic Association among Catholics. During the Cultural Revolution even these front structures were moribund, and all religious activity forced underground. In 1978 restrictions were eased and the TSPM and CPA resurrected as a means of regaining governmental control of the thousands of house churches. This has been only partially successful. Present government policy is to tolerate religious belief and allow worship under government supervision. Military personnel, Communist Party members and young people under 18 do not have that freedom.
All figures are estimates.
Atheist 12%. Communist Party members nearly 40 mill.
Non-religious 50%(?). The atheistic education system ensures that most young people have no religious knowledge.
Chinese religions (Taoism, Buddhism, Confucianism) 28%(?).
Animist 2%. Among tribal peoples of the south, etc.
Muslim 2.4%. Ten national minorities are Muslim.
Christian 5%(?). The official estimate for all Christians is 6 mill. House church and overseas researchers estimate 30 mill. to 50 mill.

Roman Catholic 0.6%. Divided between the official CPA and those remaining loyal to the Vatican (over 50%). 6,600,000a(?).

Marginal groups (3+) 0.1%. Various groups that are unitarian, "shouters", etc. 1,000,000a(?).

Protestant 4.3%. 45,000,000a, possibly subdivided thus:

Three Self Patriotic Movement	3,000,000a
TSPM related meeting points	9,000,000a
Home meetings	33,000,000a

Personnel in China-related ministries est. 600 but working from other lands.

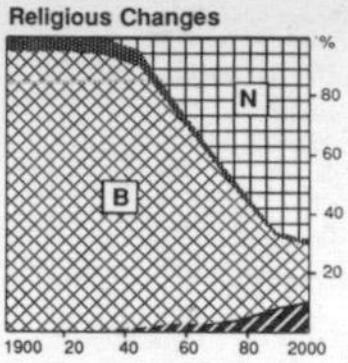

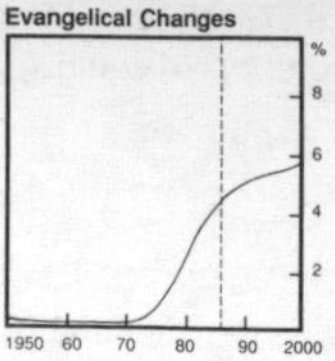

GENERAL

1. **God is being glorified in Communist China today**! Praise Him for:
   a) **The manifest bankruptcy of human ideologies in China.** Colossal blunders and changes in Party policy over 35 years have disillusioned the people. The fall of personality-cult leaders and the failure of promises for a better future have created a vacuum which only the gospel can fill. There may now be more Christians than Communist Party members.
   b) **The terrible persecutions** which have purified and indigenized the Chinese Church in a way which could never have otherwise been achieved.
   c) **The growth of the Church** through the radiant witness of Christians, miracles of the Holy Spirit and mighty revivals. Never in history have so many been converted over such a short time. Between 1977 and 1984 many millions have come to faith in Christ. There were about three million Catholics and one million Protestants in 1949.
   d) **The remarkable fruitfulness of Christian radio**, and the remarkable faith of those who broadcast into China with little visible evidence of a response. Some reckon that 50% of all conversions have been at least partly through radio ministry.
   e) **The thousands of believers who travailed in prayer** for a breakthrough over the last 150 years. The breakthrough *has* come in answer to prayer. Pray on!
   f) **For the 140 years of sacrificial missionary work** by thousands of missionaries. Their labour was not in vain, though many sowed without seeing the harvest. At one stage there were 8,500 Protestant missionaries, 1,000 of these being with CIM (**OMF**).

2. **The agonies suffered by the Chinese people during this century have removed many barriers to the gospel**. The hold of the old religions and culture, and the "foreignness" of Christianity, are no longer a major hindrance. Pray for the complete evangelization of China; possibly 500 million have yet to hear the gospel for the first time. 70% of the population have lived only under Communism.

3. **In order to cope with the problems of population growth, the integrity of the family has been imperilled by disregard for human rights** by the authorities, as well as enforced separations and harsh birth-control measures. The tragic social consequences have been divorce and abortion on a massive scale, female infanticide, violence and suicide. Pray for China's leaders — that they may rule with justice. Pray for Christian families to be a light and example to all around. Pray especially that the children of believers will follow in their parents' footsteps, despite mockery, discrimination and a constant barrage of atheistic propaganda.

THE CHURCH IN CHINA

1. **Revival has burst out in various provinces over the past 40 years**. The most recent outpourings of the Spirit have affected Henan, where there may be 10 million believers (if so, then over 20% Christian); Zhejiang, Anhui, Zhejiang and Fujian also have large Christian minorities. Shanghai may have one million believers. Some towns and villages and communes have a Christian majority. May the fire spread!

2. **The TSPM** is government-controlled and manipulated. It was resurrected from 13 years of oblivion as a means to regain the initiative from the home churches and control them. Some pastors and leaders are strongly political in their teaching and are more concerned about carrying out the government's religious policy than preaching the gospel. Pray for the thwarting

of these plans, and for wisdom for Christian leaders outside the TSPM in handling the threats and offers of compromise proffered them.

3. **Within the TSPM there are also many godly pastors, as well as large numbers of committed believers** in 4,000 reopened churches and 30,000 meeting points. Pray that they may fear God more than man and stand firm for the Truth. The young people are increasingly cut off from the official churches because of enforced compromises. Many home meetings have been coerced into links with the TSPM; pray that they may retain their zeal for God and His Kingdom.

4. **There are tens of thousands of home meetings** which are not directly linked with the TSPM. This is the heart of the true Church in China. Yet their rapid growth between 1978 and 1983 has been somewhat limited by pressures from the TSPM and persecution by the authorities since then. They desire to be free to preach Christ and His sacrificial death whatever the cost and without restriction so that all China may be evangelized. Pray that the evangelistic zeal of individuals and teams may continue unabated, and that outreach teams may penetrate to the far corners of the land.

5. **Persecution was very severe during the Cultural Revolution.** Most Bibles were destroyed, believers' homes looted, and believers humiliated. During that time many believers were imprisoned and even executed. In late 1983 a new wave of persecution began under the umbrella of the "anti-crime" and "spiritual pollution" campaigns. It has led to the arrest of hundreds of Christian leaders (especially in Henan), and the closure of "illegal" home meetings. Many have now been released, but pray for those in prison, scattered believers and for fugitive itinerant preachers who serve home meetings over wide areas.

6. **Leadership in the TSPM** will eventually pass into the hands of younger men and women trained in the Nanjing Seminary and six regional seminaries. In 1985 there were 231 students. Much of their course is Marxist-oriented and liberal in theology. Pray that students may retain a biblical faith and go out to faithfully serve God without compromise.

7. **The mushrooming growth of the home meetings strains leadership resources.** Pray for the ageing pastors trained before 1949, and their discipling of younger leaders. Pray for adequate training and spiritual maturity of new leaders in spite of no Bible schools and limited study materials and Bibles.

8. **The lack of sound Bible teaching** has caused some to be sidetracked into doctrinal error or emphasis of less important issues. Pray that the Church might keep to the centrality of the Cross and true to Scripture.

9. **The Catholics have been divided** through government interference. The CPA maintains a hostile stance to the leadership of the Vatican, but most Catholics remain loyal despite persecution. Their numbers have doubled since 1949.

SUPPORTIVE MINISTRIES

1. **Missionaries as such may not enter China.** Pray for Hong Kong Chinese and foreign believers who do — as students (5,000 long-term students by 1990), tourists (Hong Kong 2.5 mill., foreigners 400,000 in 1985), businessmen (five major special economic zones for foreign firms) and teachers. All need perseverance despite loneliness and restrictions, and they need zeal tempered by tact in order to have a vital ministry. There have been spiritual casualties among those who have gone to China in this way. Pray for fruitful contacts with Chinese for those who visit China.

2. **Bibles are still in short supply in many areas**; many were destroyed in the Cultural Revolution. 1.3 million Bibles and NTs have been printed legally in China, but distribution has been a problem. Hundreds of thousands of Bibles per year have been introduced into China by various means since 1978. Pray for those involved in printing and distributing Bibles from Hong Kong and within China. There are at least three new versions of the Bible available (**AO**, **UBS**, Living Bibles).

3. **There were over 10 million cassette players in China in 1984**. Pray for the wide use of Scripture, song and teaching tapes. Pray also for those who produce them both inside and outside mainland China.

4. **Christian radio programmes** have been used by the Lord for converting unbelievers and encouraging Christians. 80% of homes have a radio. Over 2,300 hours of broadcasting in five languages are beamed into China monthly. Pray especially for the extensive China-oriented broadcasting of **FEBC** (Manila, Saipan, Korea), **TWR** (Guam) and **FEBA** (Seychelles). There are many major programme producers such as **AO**, **OMF** and **CMA**. Pray for wisdom in programme selection and preparation that the message may meet the real needs of the people. There were over 50,000 letters received from listeners between 1979 and 1984. Pray for them and those who seek to help them.

5. **Christian literature** is hardly available, but in great demand. **Christian Communications Ltd**, **AO**, and many other publishing bodies are seeking to meet the insatiable demand for hymn books, Bible study and teaching materials, biographies, tracts, and apologetic materials to explain the gospel to students and intellectuals. Pray for all aspects of publication, entry into China and distribution.

CHINA'S UNREACHED

1. **There are many Chinese Christians**, but sectors of society are without an adequate witness. Pray for:

   a) **Communist Party members** 40 mill. Many being purged, many disillusioned.

   b) **Military personnel** 3.2 mill. Life is hard for the few believers.

   c) **Taoists, Buddhists and Confucianists**. Superstitious idolatry is on the increase in the post-Mao era. They need the freedom from bondage that the gospel can give them.

   d) **The 'lost generation' youth**. The education and future of millions of young people were jeopardized by the madness of the Cultural Revolution. Most are sick of Marxism but have no life philosophy except self-gratification. Many have turned to crime. 600 mill. have been born since 1949.

   e) **Students** are now a privileged elite. 1.2 mill. are studying in universities, but are strongly pressurized to avoid religion. Over 33,000 Chinese students have gone abroad for study since 1978; pray that Christians may befriend and win them to Christ. Many intellectuals have been reinstated after years of imprisonment. **OMF** and others are making a special effort to produce suitable literature to evangelize them.

2. **Many cities** have very few Christians; Liaoning, Tianjin and Beijing are the most prominent. The latter, being the capital, is particularly difficult with less freedom than elsewhere.

3. **The Northern and Western Provinces** are generally less evangelized than those of the south, though believers in Hunan province are still very restricted. Pray for:

   a) **Sichuan, Yunnan, and Xinjiang**.

   b) **Heilungkiang, Jilin Liaoning**, the old Manchuria.

   c) **Shaanxi, Gansu** and **Qinghai** south of Mongolia.

4. **Autonomous regions** created for areas with large proportions of ethnic minorities.

   a) **Tibet** (Xizang Zizhiqu) was conquered by the Red Army in 1950. Their independence was lost and their Lamaistic Buddhist religion virtually destroyed. Many died in the fighting, another 85,000 fled to India and beyond. This land has resisted the gospel for centuries, but among the refugees some churches have been planted in India **(TEAM)**. The gospel has hardly been preached in Tibet itself, though missionaries served among Tibetans in neighbouring provinces. There are believed to be several groups of believers. Pray Tibet open; it is opening for tourists!

   b) **Xinjiang Uygur Zizhiqu** (Sinkiang). The vast northwestern area of deserts, mountains and oases and, with Gansu Province, the home of nine Muslim peoples — the Uighur 6,300,000; Kazakh 950,000; Dongxiang 291,000; Kirghiz 118,000; Salar 72,000; Tadjik 27,000; Uzbek 14,000; and Bao. Only among the Uighur were there once a few churches,

but severe Muslim persecution ended their existence. In all these Turkic and Mongolian Muslim peoples there is only a handful of Christians. There are now 14,000 functioning mosques. 42% of the population is Han Chinese among whom there are a few thousand believers, mainly in the capital, Urumqi.

c) **Ningxia. The 7.6 mill. Chinese Muslim Hui** are scattered all over China, but the greatest concentration is in Ningxia. Nothing is known of any specific effort to reach these Muslims, and few have ever become Christian.

d) **Nei Monggol** (Inner Mongolia). The homeland of the Mongolian people, who now constitute but 10% of the total population. A few small groups of believers were formed through missionary work in the last century. There may be only a handful left. Several years ago there were reported to be several thousand Chinese believers, many being exiles for their faith. Recent news indicates that they may have multiplied to over one million believers! Pray that these believers may reach the hearts of the indigenous Buddhist people who cling to their culture.

e) **Guangxi Zhuang** in the south, the home of the 14 mill. Zhuang. They have had minimal contact with the gospel, and are one of the largest peoples in the world without even a book of the Bible in their language. Their religion is a mixture of Buddhism and animism.

5. **The smaller ethnic minorities.**

a) **Ethnic minority Christians** of Yunnan and south are numerous among the Yao 773,000; Lisu 500,000; Lahu 318,000; Wa 300,000; Akha 63,000 and, to a lesser extent, among the Yi 5,700,000, Hmong (Miao) 5,200,000, Jingpo 100,000. Christian groups have survived and grown, but the unavailability of Scriptures (even where translated) is serious. Pray for their growth in grace and vision to evangelize the totally unreached tribal groups all over the south and southwest of China, as well as the unreached of their own ethnic group. There are reports of unusual blessing in some of these peoples of late, and now 95% of the 350,000 Christians in Yunnan belong to minority groups.

b) **The 28 ethnic minorities in Yunnan**. Many are, as far as is known, unreached. Most are animistic: Hani 1,200,000; Nosu 581,000; Naxi 256,000; Punu 230,000, etc. Others are more influenced by Buddhism: Bouyei 2,200,000; Dai 877,000; Nung 105,000. All the latter are related to the Thai of Thailand.

c) **The Yi** 5.7 mill., who live all over the south. Only a handful of RCs among them.

d) **The Li** 850,000 animistic people on Hainan Island.

e) **The Tuchia** 3 mill., and **Dong** 1.5 mill., who live in Hunan and Guizhou. Very few known Christians.

f) **The Koreans** 1.8 mill., of Jilin and Liaoning, among whom the Lord is working and where there are 120 churches and 50,000 believers; the great majority remain unreached.

6. **Reaching the ethnic minorities** must be achieved through local believers or by indirect means. Pray for:

a) **Chinese and ethnic minority Christians** to be used in cross-cultural evangelism and church planting.

b) **Bible translation** to be initiated in the 80 languages that are without a NT. Miracles will be needed to achieve the goal of supplying all ethnic groups with God's Word.

c) **Better use of radio.** There are no programmes aired in any minority language.

d) **Better use of cassette messages** in minority languages.

Prayer Information on China

1. Asian Report (**AO**).
2. China and the Church Today (**CCRC**).
3. Chinese around the World (**CCCOWE**).
4. Pray for China Fellowship (**OMF**).
5. Watchman on the Great Wall (**Institute of Chinese Studies, USCWM**).
6. "Pray for China" (Christian Communications Ltd, Box 95364, Tsimshatsui, Hong Kong).

Asia

CHINA (Taiwan)

(The Republic of China)

Mar 28-29

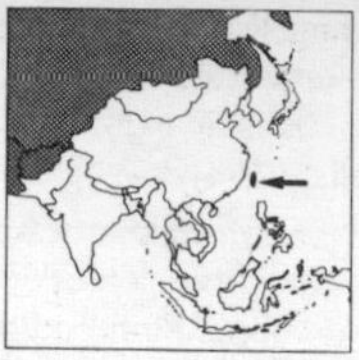

Area 36,000 sq.km. A mountainous island 300 km. off coast of mainland China.

Population 19,200,000. Annual growth 1.6%. People per sq.km. 533.

Peoples

Han Chinese 98% speaking three major languages.

Taiwanese (Hoklo, Minnan) 14,200,000. Over 300 years on Taiwan. Rural majority.

Hakka 2,100,000. About 200 years on Taiwan.

Mandarin 2.500,000. Refugees from Mainland China 1945-50. Predominantly urban.

Malayo-Polynesian mountain peoples (11) 1.7%. Largest: Ami 104,000; Paiwan 53,000; Tayal 46,000; Bunun 32,000; Sediq 20,000.

Literacy 90%. **Official language** and language of education: Mandarin. Hoklo is widely spoken. **All languages** 14. **Bible translations** 4Bi 5NT 1por.

Capital: Taipei 2,500,000. Major city: Kaoshiung 1,300,000. Urbanization 71%.

Economy: Rapid industrialization and economic growth to become one of the world's leading exporting states. Income/person $3,000 (21.3% of USA).

Politics: Under Japanese rule 1895-1945. After the fall of mainland China to the Communists in 1949, Taiwan became the refuge of the Nationalist Chinese government. A one-party republic dominated by mainlanders, but increasing Taiwanese participation in economic and political life is lessening communal tensions. International political isolation of Taiwan led to the loss of UN membership in 1971. Both Chinese governments seek reunification on their own terms.

Religion: Secular state with freedom of religion. The strong anti-communist stance of the government, and efforts to unify the country under one language, have placed it in conflict with some denominations — chiefly the large Presbyterian Church, whose membership is predominantly Taiwanese.

Non-religious/Atheist 20-30%. Many younger people are secular and abandon their family religions.

Chinese religions 60-70%. Blend of Confucianism, Taoism and Buddhism, with strong emphasis on veneration of ancestors.

Muslim 0.5%. Post-war immigrant Hui.

Tribal religions 0.5%. Minority of mountain peoples.

Christian 5%.

Roman Catholic 1.4%. Practising 50%. 275,000a; 151,000m.

Marginal groups 0.26%. 52,000a; 35,000m. Largest (adult members):

True Jesus Church	27,300
Mormons	6,100

Protestant 3.5%. 670,000a; 347,000m. Denominations 70, also numerous independent congregations. Largest (adult members):

Presbyterian Church of T.	95,000
Assembly Hall (W. Nee)	48,000
Baptist Conv. (**SBC**)	12,000
Seventh Day Adventist Church	6,078
T. Holiness Church (**OMS**)	4,495
Taiwan Lutheran Church	4,239
Free Methodist Church	3,800
Methodist Church	3,000
Assemblies of God	2,700
Chi. Evang. Luth. Church	2,000

Evangelical 2.5% of population.

Missionaries to Taiwan 863 (1:22,000 people) in over 80 agencies.

Missionaries from Taiwan 10 (1:67,000 Protestants). Many others have gone as "tentmaking" missionaries, or to pastor overseas Chinese congregations.

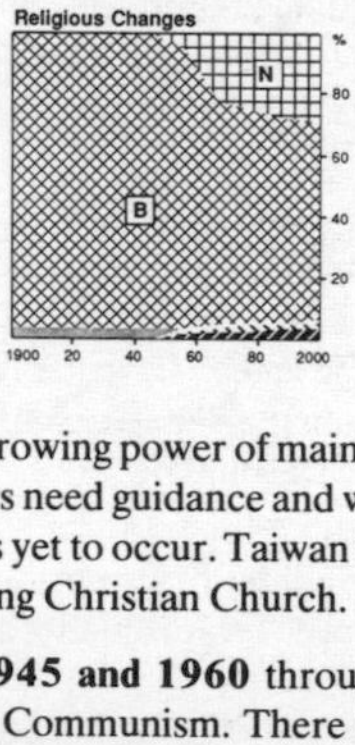

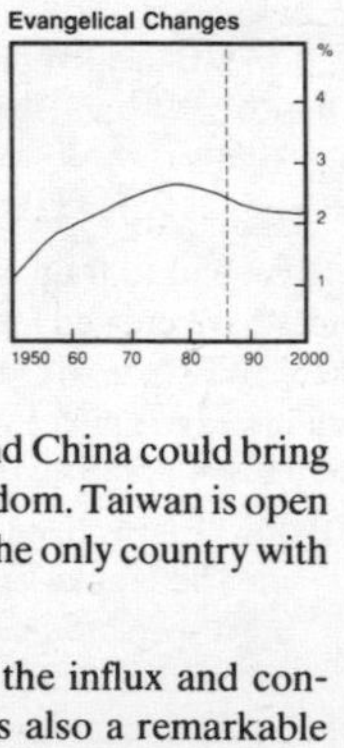

1. **Taiwan's political future is uncertain**. The growing power of mainland China could bring about changes. Chinese and international leaders need guidance and wisdom. Taiwan is open for the gospel, but the decisive breakthrough has yet to occur. Taiwan is the only country with a major Chinese population which has a shrinking Christian Church.

2. **The Church grew dramatically between 1945 and 1960** through the influx and conversion of Mandarin-speaking Chinese fleeing Communism. There was also a remarkable people movement in the mountain tribes. Stagnation has set in since then, despite major

evangelistic outreaches and investment of finance and manpower. There are many factors: the resurgent Chinese religions; entrenched veneration of ancestors; secularism; an alarmingly high level of backsliding; and the failure to mobilize Christians effectively for personal evangelism. Pray that change might come through the work of the Spirit.

3. **The Protestant Church** was dependent on foreign funds and personnel for too long. Nor has the profusion of denominations — many of foreign origin — encouraged a spirit of unity and cooperation. Indigenous groups and congregations have, therefore, fared better. Bible teaching, revival and effective outreach by a truly indigenized Chinese Church are the needs of the hour. There are encouraging signs of a new day for the gospel in the land.

4. **Protestants are unequally distributed among the different linguistic groups.** The majority of the mountain peoples are nominally Protestant (23% actively so) as are 4.6% of the Mandarin, 1% of the Hoklo and only 0.5% of the Hakka. Pray that the Hoklo (Taiwanese) and Hakka groups might open up for the gospel.

5. **There are 522 mountain churches** throughout the tribal areas. Most are Presbyterian, though an increasing number are of other denominations, as well as more sectarian groups such as True Jesus and Mormons. The breakdown of tribal life has been speeded by the drift of many to the cities, increased education of young people, and inability of parents to control and raise their children in a changing society. God gave revival to the Tayal in 1973 and Ami in 1983. Pray that these revivals may affect other areas to combat nominalism, spiritual decline, and inadequate Bible teaching. Poverty makes it hard for these little churches to support their pastors.

6. **The lack of pastors is becoming serious**. Of the 11,600 Protestant congregations of the plains, 200 are without pastors, and this may rise to 1,000 by the year 2000. Pray for the 20 seminaries and Bible schools in Taiwan, and pray for increased recruiting, effective training and a higher output of spiritual leaders. One such is the **China Evangelical Seminary**. More effective lay training programmes are also essential, so pray for TEE courses with over 800 studying in 60 centres.

7. **The witness among students**. The 300,000 students in 102 universities and colleges are one of the most open sections of the community. Many churches have well-used student centres. Both **CCC** and Campus Evangelical Fellowship (**IFES**) have an outreach to students, the latter with 40 full-time staff workers ministering also among secondary school students. Pray for vital growing groups and the integration of young believers into churches.

8. **Missions** — pioneered by the Presbyterians, but a great influx of new missions entered after their expulsion from mainland China in 1950. The majority concentrated on the Mandarin minority, and few went on to learn a second or third language. The Taiwanese and Hakka majority have been largely ignored until recently. There are many openings for missionaries in evangelism, church planting, Bible teaching and stimulating local congregations. Teaching English as a foreign language is a useful key for evangelism. In 1984 the government imposed a ceiling on the entry of missionary personnel. Pray in those called of God and willing to identify culturally in this day of opportunity. Some of the largest agencies are: **SBC** (111 missionaries), **TEAM** (70), **OMF** (62), **OMS** (33), **CCC** (32), **CBFMS** (27) and **SEND** (26).

9. **Missionary vision in Taiwan churches is growing.** Churches need help to cultivate this interest and to train and channel missionaries overseas. Student mission challenge conferences have created much interest (**IFES**). The Chinese edition of ***LOOK***, a missions broadsheet (**WEC**), is challenging many. Taiwanese missionaries are serving with denominational and interdenominational missions in five continents. Most have gone to minister to Chinese communities, but an increasing number are going to non-Chinese peoples.

10. **Less evangelized areas and peoples:**

a) **The Hakka communities** in the northeast and the southeast. Only about 20 missionaries speak the language. Several missions are commencing work among them (**TEAM**, **SEND Int.**, Presbyterians, etc.).

b) **The rural areas; mainly Hoklo.** Half of the 300 districts have few churches, 80 have only one church, 21 have none.

c) **The new industrial zones**. Many workers are new to the cities and more responsive. Pray for the Industrial Evangelical Fellowship which encourages an outreach to them, and for **OMF** missionaries who are also involved.

d) **The 60,000 Muslims**. There is no outreach to them.

e) **The Penghu Islanders** number 120,000. In 1964 there were 17 churches, but now two-thirds are closed. 10,000 Vietnam Chinese have been settled there.

11. **Help ministries.**

a) **Christian literature**. Much is now being published of both local and foreign origin. Pray for efforts by **CEF(IFES)** and others to sell Christian literature through the secular book market.

b) **Bible translation and distribution**. The Bible Society distributes a large number of Scriptures. Four tribal languages still need a NT; one is in the process of being translated.

c) **Radio**. Pray for fruit from extensive coverage by local broadcasters, and **FEBC** and **TWR** from abroad.

d) **Christian video tapes** are a key tool for evangelism. 50% of the population has access to a video recorder. Several Christian agencies are seeking to supply them.

COLOMBIA
(Republic of Colombia)

Latin America

Mar 30-31

Area 1,139,000 sq.km. NW corner of S. America. The fourth largest country in the continent. Mountains in west, plains and forests in east.

Population 29,400,000. Annual growth 2.1%. People per sq.km. 26. Only 3% live in the eastern half of the country.

Peoples
Spanish-speaking 97.4%. Approx. composition: Mestizo (Eurindian) 49%, Mulatto (Eurafrican) 21%, European 20%, African 7%.
Amerindians 1.6%. Approx. 100 tribes in about 10 language families. Largest: Guajiro 100,000; Paez 40,000; Catio 20,000; Guahibo 20,000.
Other 1%. Lebanese 120,000; Chinese 5,000, etc.

Literacy 84%. **Official language:** Spanish. **All languages** 75. **Bible translations** 1Bi 12NT 29por.

Capital: Bogotá 7 million. Other cities: Medellín 3,000,000, Cali 2,000,000, Barranquilla 1,500,000. Urbanization 67%.

Economy: Major export earners: coffee (legal) and cocaine (illegal). Income/person $1,890 (13% of USA). A great difference between incomes of rich and poor, but a growing middle class.

Politics: Independent from Spain in 1819. A democratic republic, but with several dictatorships and civil wars this century. The period of anarchy and civil war 1948-60 became known as "La Violencia", during which 300,000 died. The country is plagued by crime, Communist guerrilla movements, and narcotics terrorists.

Religion: The Roman Catholic Church is the state church, and is accorded a privileged position. Since 1974 there has been considerable freedom for Evangelicals to evangelize, though policy towards foreign missions has been somewhat restrictive.

Non-religious/Atheist 1.2%. **Tribal religions** 1.1%. **Muslim** 0.2%. **Baha'i** 0.1%.
Christian 97.4%.
Roman Catholic 93%. 27,250,000a; 14,000,000m.
Marginal groups (8) 1.1%. 330,000a; 114,000m.
Largest (adherents):

Unitarian Pentecostals	190,000
Jehovah's Witnesses	96,400
Mormons	39,500

Protestant 3.1%. 900,000a; 284,000m. Denominations 97+. Largest (adult members):

Seventh Day Adventist Church	76,000
Int. Ch. of Foursquare Gospel	35,000
Christian Crusade Church	21,000
Christian & Miss. Alliance	16,400
Panamerican Mission	15,000
Assemblies of God	11,500
Amerindian churches (**NTM**)	10,000
Baptist Convention (**SBC**)	9,300
Assoc. of Ev. Chs of East (**TEAM**)	9,000
Missionary Ev. Union (**GMU**)	7,900

Evangelical 2.4% of population.
Missionaries to Colombia 1,150 (1:25,500 people) in 70 agencies.
Missionaries from within Colombia approx. 40 (1:22,500 Protestants).

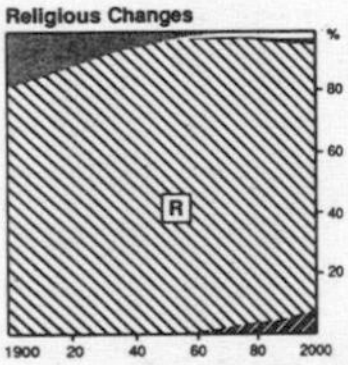

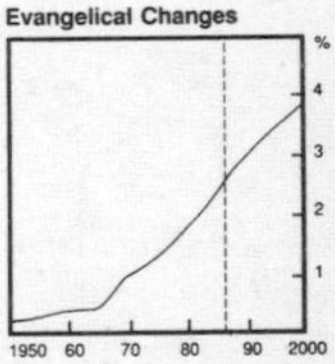

1. **Colombia has a reputation for being possibly one of the most violent countries in the world.** Six Communist guerrilla movements and the drug-trafficking "barons" dominate many areas of the country. Corruption, violence, assassination and murder have become commonplace. The government is losing credibility through compromises and inability to control the possible breakdown of society. Pray for the nation's leaders, for peace and for freedom for the gospel to be maintained.

2. **Evangelicals suffered considerable persecution until 1960.** During "La Violencia" a bigoted expression of Catholicism provoked destruction of churches and the robbery, rape and murder of believers. The last 25 years have been a time of freedom for ingathering among a receptive people. Praise God for growth. Pray also for the believers who face a renewed period of pressure during the '80s. A few pastors have been murdered, Christians intimidated and evangelism resisted by both terrorist groups and Catholic zealots.

3. **The Roman Catholic Church** has been radically affected by the changing political scene. Some priests have identified with leftist guerrillas, but the majority have become more conservative in the '80s. The charismatic movement is still widespread, but many Catholic charismatics have joined Pentecostal and other evangelical groups, or returned to the dogmas of Catholicism.

4. **Evangelical growth has been good.** In 1933 there were 15,000 Evangelicals; today there are about one million. The most rapid growth has been among Pentecostal and some interdenominational groups. Aggressive evangelism by congregations, open-air preaching, the 1968 Evangelism-in-Depth campaign, and successful mass evangelism efforts have spread the gospel far and wide. Yet growth has begun to slow down because of internal divisions, less receptivity among Catholics and the general intimidation and violence in the country. Pray for maturity and stability coupled with renewed growth among Evangelicals.

5. **The Evangelicals face serious problems that need solutions.** Pray about:

a) **The leadership crisis** has grown with the growth of the churches. There are too few deeply taught in the Word, too many personality clashes, and a tendency to autocratic leadership which has divided or diverted many congregations and denominations. There are about 20 theological institutions training pastors, one being the Biblical Seminary of Colombia of **OMS** with 51 students.

b) **The intimidation crisis** — should believers speak out or be silent in the face of the violence and fear gripping society?

c) **The divisions within the Body of Christ** have become a discredit to the name of the Lord and a poor witness to the government and people. Many denominations have been split over bitter personal rivalries, legal rights, properties, relationships between missionaries and Colombians, etc. CEDEC, the Evangelical Confederation of Colombia, is a body that links 46 evangelical denominations and coordinates the inter-church action. Pray for a decisive work of healing and spiritual unity.

d) **The ethical crisis.** Laxity in morals and finance has damaged the effectiveness of many Christian workers and groups. Pray for high standards of biblical holiness among the people of God.

6. **Missionaries are under great pressure.** Most missionaries are US citizens; one **SIL** missionary was killed in 1981, and many others have received death threats. Pray for courage and faithfulness to their calling in spite of the open hatred of the USA shown by leftists, guerrillas and narcotics gangs. Internal mission/church relationships have been a source of tension, division and grief. Great humility and sensitivity is required in the complex ecclesiastical scene in order to have a viable, fruitful ministry. Major mission agencies in Spanish-speaking work: **CCC** (291 workers), **SBC** (78), **CMA** (36), **TEAM** (30), **OMS** (29), **LAM** (24), **GMU** (21).

7. **Colombian missionary vision needs stimulation.** Many Amerindian peoples are closed to foreigners, but only a few Colombians have committed themselves to evangelize them. A handful of Colombians have gone to other lands, but church support is limited. The Spanish edition of ***Operation World*** is published in Colombia.

8. **Unreached peoples**, pray specifically for:

a) **Less evangelized cities and towns.** Medellín has only 53 evangelical churches for three million people. It is reputedly the nation's crime and narcotics capital.

b) **Nearly two million in Bogotá's slums.**

c) The thousands of **Gamines**, or homeless street urchins of the cities. **YWAM** has a ministry to them.

d) **The Syrian-Lebanese Muslim** community.

e) **Amerindian peoples** closed to evangelical church planters. Possibly 30-40 are in this category — e.g. Inga, Coreguaje, Cuiba, Desano, Epena, Huitoto, Saliba, Tucano, etc.

9. **Work among Amerindians has been a constant struggle** — travel and living conditions, indifference of the people, opposition of officials and anthropologists, inter-mission rivalry, and recently narcotics terrorists who force the Amerindians to grow cocaine and marijuana. In spite of it all, there has been some response with people movements to Christ. Pray for:

a) **Strong, viable, well-led churches**, able to cope with drug traffickers and modernization.
b) **Church planting ministries** of **NTM** (84 workers in 10 peoples), **SAM** in three northeastern peoples, **CMA** in two peoples, etc.
c) **Bible translation: SIL** has 248 workers committed to 40 translation projects; a number of NTs are nearing completion, eight languages await translators.
d) **GRI** recordings available in 58 languages.

10. **Supportive ministries.**
a) **Literature** is not sufficiently used; few churches have a vision for a literature ministry, yet it could be a major corrective for the lack of Bible teaching. **CLC** has two stores and a publishing house.
b) **Student work** has been slow and hard. Marxist ideology has dominated the campuses, yet UCU(**IFES**) groups have multiplied, with a vision to see an evangelical group witnessing on each campus.

COMORO ISLANDS

Africa

Apr 1

Four volcanic islands between Madagascar and Mozambique. The Republic declared itself independent from France in 1975, but one island, Mayotte, seceded to remain a French overseas territory. The Republic still claims Mayotte as part of its territory.

1. COMORES FEDERAL ISLAMIC REPUBLIC

Area 1,862 sq.km.

Population 360,000. Annual growth 3%. People per sq.km. 193.

Peoples
Comorian 98%. Mixed Arab, African and Malagasy ancestry.
Minorities — Makua 6,000; French 1,200; Malagasy 360.

Literacy 61%. **Official language:** Comorian (a Swahili dialect); Arabic and French used widely.

Capital: Moroni 25,000. Urbanization 19%.

Economy: Poor and dependent on the export of perfume oils and vanilla. Income/person $260. (2% of USA).

Politics: Much unrest in 1975-78 with coups and counter coups, but relative stability since.

Religion: An Islamic state, not in favour of open evangelism.
Muslim 99.7% (780 mosques).
Christian 0.2%.
Roman Catholic 0.1%. French, Malagasy and Reunionese. Total 300.
Protestant 0.1%. About 30 indigenous Comorians and 350 Malagasy.

1. **These islands were totally unevangelized until 1973.** In that year the first Comorian was converted. This man is the only national believer with Bible school training and is now the leader of the small group of Comorian believers. They have experienced much opposition and are not allowed to meet openly. Pray for their stability, growth in grace, boldness in testimony and increase in numbers.

2. **Mission work was permitted after independence.** After an initial period of considerable freedom to witness by the team of **AIM** missionaries, a revolutionary regime expelled them in 1978 as a result of some Muslims coming to Christ. A gradual re-entry of missionaries was permitted by the present government. Pray for the tactful low-key witness of 11 **AIM** missionaries serving the people through medical, veterinary, technical and teaching ministries on the three islands.

3. **Bible translation** may be needed for each of the four island dialects of Comorian. Pray for translation work in Shimaori, the dialect of Mayotte. The Gospel of Luke is in circulation, and a quarter of the NT translated.

2. THE (FRENCH) DEPARTMENT OF MAYOTTE

Area 376 sq.km.

Population 52,000. Annual growth 3.3%.

Peoples
Comorian (Mahorais) 86%.
Other 14%. Malagasy 4,500; French/Creole 2,800.

Literacy 63%. **Official language:** French; Shimaori and Malagasy widely used.

Capital: Dzaoudzi 7,000. Urbanization 3%.

Economy: French aid and expertise has made Mayotte more prosperous than the rest of the Comoros. Income/person $350 (2% of USA).

Religion: Freedom of religion.

Muslim 98.4%.

Christian 1.6%.

Roman Catholic 1.3%. Adherents 1,000. French, Malagasy, Creole.

Protestant 0.3%. Adherents 150. Malagasy, a handful of Comorians and French.

1. **Direct evangelism is permitted** but not necessarily well received by the Muslims. Pray for the witness among the Muslim Comorians and the nominally Christian Creole, French and Malagasy minorities. Pray for the right strategy for planting churches.

2. **The only organized Protestant churches** in the four islands are two evangelical groups among the Malagasy on Grand Comore (CFIR) and Mayotte, and isolated Christians elsewhere. Pray that their witness to other ethnic groups may be bold and effective.

CONGO
(The People's Republic of the Congo)

Africa

Apr 2

Area 342,000 sq.km. Northwest of Zaire and not to be confused with it.

Population 1,700,000. Annual growth 2.6%. People per sq.km. 5.

Peoples

African peoples 97.6%. 16 tribes, 75 sub-groups.

Major groups 77.5%. Kongo 720,000; Teke 310,000; Mbochi 171,000.

Minor groups 20.1%. Mbete 108,000; Eshira 62,000; Maka 47,000; Pygmy 20,000; Binga 16,000; Kota 7,000; Bongili 6,000.

Other 2.4%. French 20,000; Portuguese; Chinese; Greek; Cuban, etc.

Literacy 22%. **Official language:** French. **Trade languages:** Lingala, Kongo. **All languages** 55. **Bible translations** 5Bi 5NT 8por.

Capital: Brazzaville 450,000. Other city: Pointe Noire 200,000. Urbanization 48%.

Economy: Underdeveloped in the interior due to difficulties of travel, but rich oil and mineral deposits are bringing some wealth to the country. Income/person $1,230 (9% of USA). Inflation 9.5%.

Politics: Independent from France in 1960. Military coup in 1968 led to declaration of Africa's first "People's Republic". The Marxist government obtains aid from both Soviet Bloc and France. Its application of Marxist ideology has moderated since 1977.

Religion: After some years of intense Marxist propaganda, there is much more freedom under the present government. The ban on 18 church groups and expulsion of related missions in 1978 has now been lifted.

Tribal religions 20%: a pervasive and widespread force in syncretic indigenous churches and in the Catholic church that is regaining lost ground.

Muslim 2%.

Christian 77%. Nominal 10%. Affiliated 67%.

Roman Catholic 41%. 695,000a; 400,000m.

Indigenous marginal 9%. 150,000a. Over 17 groups. Largest:

Kimbanguists	56,000

Protestant 17%. 286,000a; 137,000m. Denominations 5. Largest (adult members):

Evang. Church of Congo	110,000
Salvation Army	18,000
Fundamental Christian Ch. (**UWM**)	2,000

Evangelical 15% of population.

Missionaries to Congo 55 (1:31,000 people).

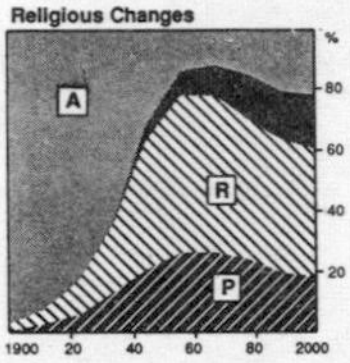

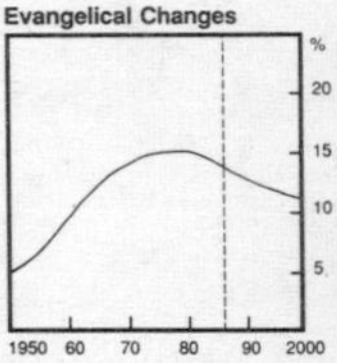

1. **Praise God that after some years of intense pressure on Christians,** there is a softening of official attitudes to Christian activities. Pray that this may continue. Pray for the government, and for committed Christians to be placed in positions of responsibility.

2. **Tribal religions have been encouraged by the government,** and churches are pressured to compromise with fetishism and ancestor worship. Indigenous prophetic-healing churches have greatly multiplied in numbers over the last 15 years. Pray for a deep work of God's Spirit in the hearts of those who bear the name of Christ, that all allegiance to the powers of darkness will be eradicated.

3. **Young people have been subjected to much ideological pressure.** All have to belong to the Union of Socialist Youth movement, but many are disillusioned with Marxist ideology. Youth activities in churches were curtailed for a time, but now there is freedom for churches to carry out their own youth programmes. Pray for many to turn to Christ.

4. **Dramatic church growth has strained the ability of the churches to disciple converts** and train adequate leadership. Two revivals (in the '20s and in 1947) have resulted in evangelical (and evangelistic) Protestant churches, that had mature leadership and spiritual resistance, standing up to a measure of persecution. Pray for the leadership — that all may have discernment in the face of pressures to compromise. Pray for the training of leaders in the two Bible schools. **UWM** has a four-year residential Bible training school as well as a TEE programme.

5. **The centre and north of the country** are thinly populated and many parts are difficult for travel. But there is a growing response to the gospel and a great need for those who can help establish strong, local churches. As a result of economic conditions, the churches generally are financially poor.

6. **Missions suffered much** with the expropriation of many institutions and expulsion of many agencies in 1978. The officially recognized churches are free to bring in their own missionary personnel. The majority of these are from Scandinavia, working with the Evangelical Church of Congo. However there are nine American **UWM** and **Global Outreach** missionaries in the northeast working with the Fundamental Christian Church, and 15 members of the **Salvation Army** from the continent of Europe working in the south. Pray that they may have wisdom and tact in the sensitive political situation. Pray that others may be able to enter the country again to complete the task of discipling the peoples of Congo.

7. **Unreached peoples**. The needs for evangelization and Bible translation must be better researched.

a) Parts of the large **Teke** tribe in the centre and north are unreached.

b) The **Pygmy** tribes (Bouraka, Garzi, Gundi, Monjombo) are semi-nomadic jungle groups who are hard to reach. Their numbers are unknown, but maybe over 20,000. There is no known outreach to them in their own languages.

c) **Other tribes** are believed to be unreached — Punu 46,000; Nzebi 45,000; Pol 30,000; Tsaangi 30,000; Pande 1,200 — but we have little information on any evangelism among them. Many live in the roadless jungles of the centre and north.

d) The **foreigners from Communist Bloc countries.** Pray that they may hear the gospel and take God's Word back to their homelands.

8. **Bible translation** — the two main languages of communication, Kongo and Lingala, have the complete Bible. One language has the New Testament, and there are plans to begin translation in several other languages in the near future. There are possibly 40 languages in which translation should be undertaken.

Pacific

Apr 3

COOK ISLANDS

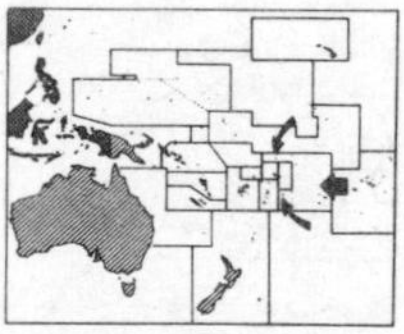

In this book, three island archipelagos associated with New Zealand are grouped together.

Area: Cook Is. 241 sq.km. Niue 263 sq.km. Tokelau 12.2 sq.km. Seventeen islands scattered over 2 mill. sq.km. of Pacific between Tonga and Tahiti.

Population: Cook Is. 18,000. Niue 3,500. Tokelau 1,550. Declining in all three territories due to emigration to New Zealand.

Peoples
Polynesians 84.4%. Seven languages including Cook Is. Maori (Rarotongan).
Other 15.6%. Euronesian 3,000; European 600.

Literacy 94%. **Official language:** English. **All languages** 8.

Economy: Dependent on agriculture and remittances from Islanders in New Zealand. Offshore banking in Cook Islands.

Politics: Cook and Niue Islands are self-governing states in free association with New Zealand. Tokelau is a New Zealand dependency.

Religion: Religious freedom with the majority in all three territories in the Congregational Church.
Baha'i 1.3%. **Other** 0.6%.
Christian 98%. Nominal 11%. Adherents 87%.
Roman Catholic 11%. Practising 45%. 2,600a; 1,300m.
Marginal groups 6%. 1,400a. Mainly Mormons.
Protestant 70%. 14,400a; 5,660m. Denominations 5. Largest (adherents):

Congregational Churches	12,000
Seventh Day Adventist Church	1,600

Evangelical 4.7% of population.
Missionaries to the Islands 10 (1:2,300 people).
Missionaries from the Islands 3 (1:5,300 Protestants, pastors in N.Z.)

1. **The Islanders have been Christian for 150 years,** but few have assurance of salvation. Pray for the evangelization of *this* generation.

2. **Many islands have no known evangelical witness,** and where it does exist it is limited to several **AoG** churches and small groups within the older churches. A new infusion of spiritual life must be prayed in.

3. **Migration to New Zealand** for employment has given another means of reaching the Islanders. 77% of Niue, 66% of Tokelau and 60% of Cook Islanders are now in New Zealand. Pray for the Island churches in Auckland, etc. Blessing there will affect the islands.

4. **Bible translation.** A revision of the Rarotongan Bible is needed **(UBS)**, and possibly translation into the smaller languages.

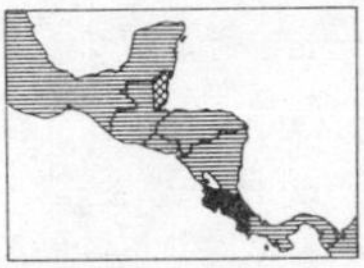

COSTA RICA
(Republic of Costa Rica)

Latin America

Apr 4

Area 51,000 sq.km. Rich agricultural land.

Population 2,600,000. Annual growth 2.7%. People per sq.km. 51.

Peoples
Spanish-speaking Costa Rican 95%. Spanish origin 87%, Mestizo/Mulatto 8%.
Amerindian 0.65%. Six peoples totalling 16,000.
Other minorities 3.3%. Nicaraguan 50,000; English-speaking Blacks 25,000; Chinese 7,000; Jews 2,000.

Literacy 90%. **Official language:** Spanish. **All languages** 9. **Bible translations** 2Bi 3por.

Capital: San Jose 875,000. Urbanization 48%.

Economy: Increasing tensions since 1979 due to the rapid deterioration of the economy. Income/person $1,100 (8% of USA). Inflation 18%.

Politics: Long one of the most stable and democratic Central American states, but the Nicaraguan conflict to the north is a destabilizing influence.

Religion: Roman Catholicism is the official religion, but there is freedom for other faiths. Legislation was being pressed in 1985 which would give preference to the Catholic Church and jeopardize some activities of Evangelicals.
Non-religious/Atheist 0.9%.
Other 0.9%. Jews, Baha'i, Tribal religions, etc.
Christian 98.2%. Affiliated 97.1%.
Roman Catholic 87%. Practising 20%. 2,270,000a; 1,185,000m.
Marginal groups (20) 2.2%. 57,000a.
Protestant 7.7%. 200,000a; 88,500m. Denominations 47. Largest (adult members):

Seventh Day Adventist Church	13,000
Church of God (Cleveland)	10,800
Assemblies of God	10,500
Ch. of the Foursquare Gospel	8,200
Assoc. of Bible Churches **(LAM)**	7,200
Assoc. of C.Amer. Chs. **(CAMI)**	3,500
Baptist Bible Fellowship	3,000

Evangelical 6.5% of population.
Missionaries to Costa Rica 330 (1:7,900 people) in 55 agencies.
Missionaries from Costa Rica 7 (?).

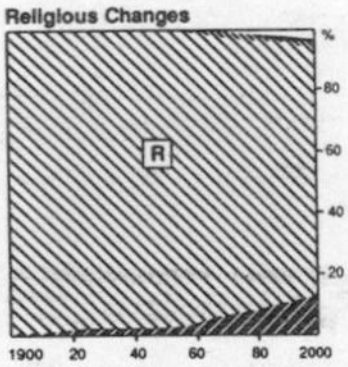

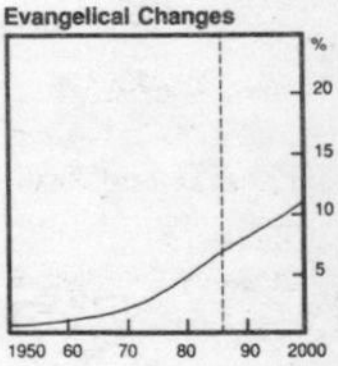

1. **The time of reaping in this receptive population has come.** The response is due to a moving of the Holy Spirit in the land, particularly through the effective witness of Evangelicals. Pray that this harvest may not be hampered by political unrest or dissension among believers.

2. **The Roman Catholic Church** was much influenced by charismatic renewal in the '70s. Many came to a living, personal faith in Christ for salvation. Now the leadership is re-emphasizing more conservative doctrines. Pray for the majority of Costa Ricans who are, at

best, nominally Catholic. Many are in great need — immorality, alcoholism and spiritism are rife.

3. **The Evangelical witness** grew three times as fast as the population in the '70s. Some of the Pentecostal, Baptist and **LAM**-related churches have grown fast, and more recently the **CAMI**-related churches have also grown well, but other denominations have stagnated or gone into decline. Pray for wise, Spirit-led leaders in the churches and for the effective discipling of converts and their deployment as witnesses for the gospel. There is a growing interest in setting up an indigenous, interdenominational, missionary-sending agency.

4. **Improved leadership training** has speeded growth. There are 20 Bible schools and seminaries, as well as an extensive TEE programme (1,070 students in 1978).

5. **Outreach to special groups.**

a) **Students** have proved less responsive to the gospel, and Christian student leadership has been weak in the past. There is a growing national student movement linked with ECU(**IFES**), **CCC** and ECO (a Pentecostal student work).

b) **Amerindian tribes.** All tribes are now being evangelized but most are either nominally Catholic or animist. **CAMI** among the Chirripo 3,500; Mennonites among the Bribri 4,500 and Talamanca 3,000; Assemblies of God among the Boruca 1,000 and Oritina. Bible portions are available in only three of these languages. **SIL** are commencing translation into Bribri.

c) **Chinese** — some have become Catholic and a few Evangelicals in four small groups. The Chinese Christian Mission started a work among them in 1985.

d) **Negroes** on the Caribbean coast are nominally Protestant, but few have a vital, life-changing faith in Christ.

6. **Missions**. The largest agencies are: **LAM** (59), S.Baptists (20), **Nazarene** (20), **CCC** (10). Pray for cooperation and close fellowship between them, for there is a frustrating duplication of effort and dominance of North Americans in many supportive agencies. Visas are becoming more difficult to obtain.

7. **Literature distribution** has been gravely affected by the nation's severe economic crisis. Pray for all engaged in this ministry in such circumstances.

8. **Christian radio. DIA** acts as a coordinating body for the production of radio programmes for all of the Spanish-speaking world. 5,000 programmes are now sent out by **DIA** to 500 radio stations in 21 countries. Pray for this ministry, that it may lead to conversions and church growth.

CUBA

(The Republic of Cuba)

Caribbean

Apr 5-6

Area 115,000 sq.km. The largest island in the Caribbean.

Population 10,100,000. Annual growth 1.1%. People per sq.km. 88.

Peoples
European origin 59%.
African/mixed origin 40%.
Other 1%. Chinese 35,000; Russian 20,000.

Literacy 96%. **Official language:** Spanish.

Capital: Havana 2,010,000. Urbanization 70%.

Economy: Poverty widespread since Communist takeover, and worsened by inefficient planning, loss of Western markets and fall in world sugar prices. Heavily dependent on USSR for trade, aid and defence. Income/person $1,400 (10% of USA).

Politics: Independent from Spain in 1898. Castro's revolution brought Communism to power in 1959. Since then, Cuba has sought to export revolution to Latin American and African countries.

Religion: There is a strict surveillance of all religious activities, and the gradual elimination of religious influence is being attempted.

Non-religious/Atheist 57%.
Spiritist 3%. Both of Afro-American and European origin.
Christian 40%.

Roman Catholic 38%. Practising 3%. 3,830,000a.

Protestant 2.4% (6% in 1957). 244,000a; 118,600m. Denominations 46. Largest (adult members) approx:

Iglesia Evang. Pentecostal	20,000
Assemblies of God	18,000
Baptist (3 groups)	17,300
Seventh Day Adventist Ch.	10,000
Assoc. Evangelical (**WT**)	10,000

Evangelical 2.1% of population.

Missionaries to Cuba 6.

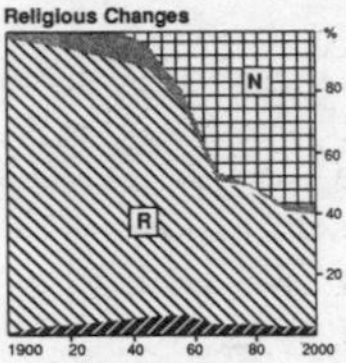

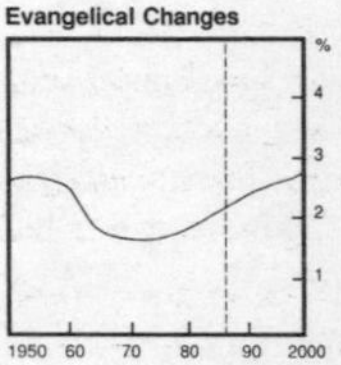

1. **Few Cubans have any meaningful contact with Christianity.** The identification of the Roman Catholic Church with Spanish colonial and subsequent repressive governments meant that the church was never strong in Cuban society. The church has therefore suffered catastrophically since the revolution. Nominal adherence dropped from 85% in 1957 to 38.5% in 1983, and less than 10% of these attend mass. The number of priests has dropped from 725 to 200 over the same period.

2. **The Protestant churches** were decimated by several emigrations of many believers to the USA, a move encouraged by the authorities to get rid of them. Growth and recovery has been slow, but the quality of spirituality has markedly increased. There are now over 1,000 functioning churches. The fastest growing are the Assemblies of God, SDAs and some Baptist churches — with reports of localized ingatherings of many hundreds into the Kingdom of God. Most of present growth is among unregistered churches.

3. **The churches face a severe leadership crisis** because so many pastors have left the country. Pray for adequately trained replacements and also for the six Bible schools/ seminaries still operating in Cuba. Pray for the 30 students in three Baptist seminaries, 10 in the Nazarene seminary, and others in the **WT**-founded seminary.

4. **Restrictions limit evangelism and growth of the churches**. No religious activities are allowed outside church buildings, and all church programmes and membership lists have to be submitted to the government. Pray for the believers to have boldness to witness and win the lost. Pray for vacation Bible schools and Christian camps (these are permitted by the government). Praise God that after many years the government has allowed building materials to be made available for repairing (and even enlarging!) church buildings.

5. **Persecution of believers** has moderated, but there is considerable discrimination of Christians in employment and education. Pray that believers may resist economic and social pressures to conform. A number of pastors and believers suffered much in earlier days.

6. **Help from outside the country.**

a) **Occasional pastoral visits by foreigners** — pray for all such and for their ministry in the churches. There are virtually no missionaries remaining in the country.

b) **Literature is in very short supply.** None is printed in the country, and very limited quantities are allowed to be imported. Pray for the provision of both Bibles and Christian literature. Some Bibles are legally imported through the **UBS**, but these may be distributed only through registered churches.

c) **Christian radio** is a vital and much appreciated ministry. Pray for all Spanish broadcasts from USA, **TWR** in Bonaire, Radio Lumiere (**WT**) in Haiti, etc.

d) **Cassette tapes** of teaching, preaching and music are widely used and valued.

7. **Unreached peoples**

a) **The majority of Cubans** have never really been exposed to a meaningful presentation of the gospel.

b) **Spiritists of African origin** are strong in some areas and need to know the delivering power of the gospel.

c) **The Chinese**, to a great extent, have been absorbed into the Cuban culture. There is no known specific outreach to them, though some are RCs and Anglicans.

d) **The Russians.** Few are likely to be Christian.

e) **African school children** from Marxist and leftist countries in that continent have been sent in their thousands for education and indoctrination. They are in schools on the Isle of Pines for later dissemination of Communism in their homelands. None have any opportunity of hearing the gospel.

8. **There are now about 1,000,000 Cuban refugees**, mostly from the white middle and upper classes, living in the USA. Pray for these uprooted people — they have many opportunities to trust in the Lord. It is estimated that 10% of these exiles are now Protestant. Pray that peace may come to their land again and permit their return.

CYPRUS
(Republic of Cyprus)

The West

Apr 7

Area 9,250 sq.km. An island republic in E. Mediterranean, but partitioned between Turkish-speaking North (36%) and Greek-speaking South (64%).

Population 692,000. People per sq.km. 73. (In North 145,000; people per sq.km. 43).

Peoples
Greek 75.5%. Only 9,000 in North.
Turk 18.5%. (Only 100 in South.) Including 20,000 Turkish troops and settlers.
Minorities 5%. (Nearly all in South.) Lebanese refugees 13,000; British and NATO military 11,000; Armenian 6,000.

Literacy 89%. **Official languages:** Greek in South, Turkish in North, with English widely used.

Capital: Nicosia 170,000. Urbanization 48%.

Economy: Severe disruption after 1974 partition. Rapid recovery in Greek South, but economic stagnation, unemployment and poverty in Turkish North. Income/person $3,043 (22% of USA). Inflation 8.0%.

Politics: After years of unrest by the Greek majority, independence from Britain was gained in 1960. Subsequent communal conflicts culminated in the 1974 abortive Greek coup and subsequent Turkish invasion and partition of the island. As a result, 200,000 people became refugees. All efforts to achieve a settlement have so far failed, and the country is, in reality, divided into two states. The Turkish zone declared itself an independent republic in 1983. Britain retains the use of two large "Sovereign Bases" in the Greek zone which are made available to NATO forces.

Religion: Open proselytizing is not allowed in either part of the country. In the Greek area the Orthodox Church is influential, and in the Turkish area Islam is dominant.
Muslim 18.5%. Turks in North and some Lebanese in South.
Non-religious/Atheist 2.4%. Most in the South.
Christian 79%.
Orthodox 75.2%. 520,000a.
Roman Catholic 1.4%. Maronite Lebanese, Greeks, etc.
Marginal groups 0.4%. Jehovah's Witnesses 3,000a.
Protestant 0.9%. Mostly British residents and military personnel. 6,370a; 2,600m. Largest (est. adult members):

British Protestants	2,000
Armenian Protestants	600
Greek Protestants	250

Evangelical 0.4% of population.
Missionaries in Cyprus est. 70 (almost all involved in international ministries).

1. **The Orthodox Church is very traditional,** and while individuals are free to change to another denomination, social pressures are so great that this rarely occurs. Pray for the gospel in its purity to be accepted by the many nominal Christians. The activity of Jehovah's Witnesses confuses the issue.

2. **Greek Evangelicals are few** and all are adherents of the Greek Evangelical Church or belong to several Pentecostal groups, numbering around 250, mostly in Limassol and Nicosia. There are only two or three missionaries who minister to the Greek majority in Greek, and they face much opposition from the Orthodox Church. Pray for the witness of Greek and non-Greek believers. Most of the Evangelicals are from the Armenian minority.

3. **The Logos bookstore (CLC)** is a vital distribution centre of books, tracts and BCCs. Pray for the effective use and distribution of this literature and also for the nationwide **EHC** tract distribution.

4. **Cyprus is a major base for Christian organizations ministering** to the surrounding Muslim and Jewish states. Pray for the stability of the country!
   a) **A number of missions** have HQs or regional centres in Cyprus (**MECO, CCC, YWAM, BMMF**, etc.).
   b) **Arabic literature** is both printed and stocked for distribution throughout the Middle East.
   c) **Christian radio** programmes are broadcast by several groups over Cyprus Radio in Arabic and Armenian, but not in Greek and Turkish.

Pray for all these operations in Cyprus, that they may be effective throughout the Middle East.

5. **The "Turkish Federated State of Cyprus"** is recognized only by Turkey and controlled by her armies. Because of centuries of hostility with Greek Christians, Christianity in any form is rejected. There are no known Turkish Christians in Cyprus and no direct outreach is possible at present. Pray for these barriers to be removed and a Turkish-speaking Church to become a reality.

6. **The 9,000 Greek Orthodox in the Turkish sector** are not able to hold Christian services. Pray for those who meet informally to study the Bible.

7. **The NATO forces** at the two large military bases are largely British. Pray for the witness of SASRA and the chaplains. Pray that a clear witness may be given by Christian servicemen to the Cypriots.

CZECHOSLOVAKIA

(Czechoslovak Socialist Republic)

Eastern Europe

Apr 8-9

Area 128,000 sq.km. Landlocked state in central Europe.

Population 15,500,000. Annual growth 0.3%. People per sq.km. 121.

Peoples
Czech 62.5%. In centre and west.
Slovak 29%. In east.
Other minorities 8.5%. Magyar (Hungarian) 620,000; Gypsy 385,000; Polish 80,000; German 77,000.
USSR forces, etc. 110,000.

Literacy 99%. **Official languages:** Czech, Slovak. **All languages** 8. **Bible translations** 6Bi 1por.

Capital: Prague 1,300,000. Urbanization 74%.

Economy: Highly industrialized and efficient before the Communist takeover. Now economy tied to that of Russia by disadvantageous trade agreements. Income/person $5,800 (35% of USA).

Politics: A federal republic of two nations — Czechs (Bohemia, Moravia and parts of Silesia) in the west and Slovaks in the east. Although a minority party, the Communists seized power in 1948. The liberalizing policies of the Dubcek Government (1966-68) were ended by the Russian invasion of 1968. Pervasive Soviet control reinforces the hard line stance of the present regime.

Religion: The remarkable freedom of the "Prague Spring" of 1968 has been replaced by increasing repression and persecution of the churches to almost Stalinist proportions. Since 1984, the Catholic leadership has taken a much stronger stance against the repressive policies of the authorities.

Non-religious/Atheist 21.3%. The Communists *claim* this to have been increased to 64%.
Jews 0.1%. 4,000 left of the 360,000 in 1938.
Christian 78.6%.
Roman Catholic 68%. 10,540,000a. Only 1 million attend church regularly.
Other Catholic 3.2%. 501,000a. Mainly the Czech Hussite Church which broke away from Rome in 1920.
Orthodox 1.2%. 181,000a.
Protestant 6%. 935,000a; 570,000m. Denominations 16. Largest (adult members):

Slovak Evang. Lutheran Church		300,000
Slovak Reformed Church	est.	100,000
Evang. Church of Czech Brethren		78,200
United Methodist Church		10,000
Moravian Church		9,700
Seventh Day Adventist Church		7,800
Church of Brethren (Congreg.)		6,000
Brethren	est.	5,400
Pentecostal Church (**AoG**)		4,600
Baptist Church		4,100

Evangelical 2.1% of population.

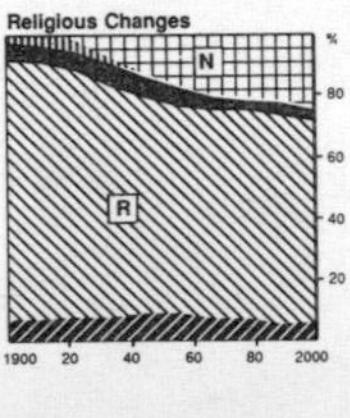

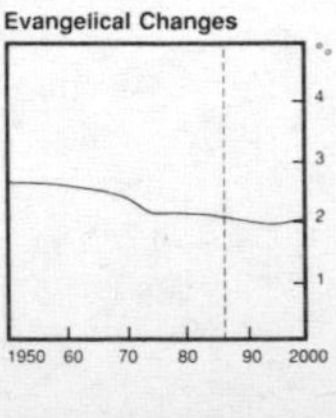

1. **The Czech Protestants** have been persecuted for nearly six centuries (since the martyrdom of the great early Reformer Huss in 1415). The Communist regime has followed a carefully stepped-up programme for the erosion of the Church's influence by forced compromise, control of leadership, intimidation and ultimate liquidation of the Church since 1973. This has been especially true of the Catholics and larger Protestant bodies. Teachers, civil servants and doctors lose their jobs, and Christian students have often been denied higher education if they engage in any religious activity. Persecution is more severe in Slovakia. Pray for our suffering brethren that they may stand firm and continue to win people for the Lord.

2. **The religious freedom of 1966-68 was a gift of God.** The rather discouraged Christian witness was revived by a move of the Spirit right across the country. It was especially marked in Slovakia where evangelical believers are relatively few. The churches were filled, many were converted and new churches built. The move was most evident among the young people. There has been a great deepening of spiritual life since the Russian invasion and the subsequent sufferings.

3. **Communism has been completely discredited** in the country by the Russian occupation of the land. Pray that this may lead to a great turning to the Lord in spite of the high cost of following the Saviour. There is a religious awakening in progress that disturbs the government, especially since it is largely underground.

4. **The dearth of trained leadership in the churches is critical.** Few desiring to serve the Lord have opportunity to study for their ministry.

5. **Pastors are subjected to severe pressures.** State approval and an oath of loyalty to the Marxist state has sometimes been enforced for the right to preach. The number and size of church gatherings have been severely cut, pastors are limited in the exercise of their ministry and much has to be done "illegally". Frequent harassment, arrests and imprisonments of pastors and leading Christians have increased since 1980. Pressures on the Catholic clergy and unregistered Protestant groups that refuse to conform to the government front organizations have been particularly severe.

6. **Unbiblical theology and formalism have entered the larger churches.** Yet there are several fast-growing Bible study and prayer groups, in which there are many young people, within both Protestant and Catholic churches. Pray for them.

7. **Bibles are in great demand, and the supplies are not sufficient to meet the need.** 120,000 Bibles were printed and distributed during 1969-73, and 100,000 copies of a new translation in Czech were printed in 1979. Pray for adequate supplies of Bibles to be made available, and for importation licences to continue to be granted to the Bible Society.

8. **Literature.** Christian literature from the West is banned, but it is in great demand as it meets the needs that the groups of young believers and the pastors have for biblical teaching. Pray for all who produce and distribute it – it is a sacrificial and dangerous occupation.

9. **Radio ministry.** Pray for those producing Czech and Slovak programmes both within the country and in the West. **HCJB** Ecuador broadcasts 67 hours/month and **TWR** Monaco 15 hours/month in Czech, and the latter nine hours/month in Slovak.

The West

Apr 10

DENMARK

(The Kingdom of Denmark)

Area 44,500 sq.km. The most southerly of the Scandinavian countries. The Faeroes (1,400 sq.km.) consist of 18 islands in the north Atlantic and are included with Denmark here.

Population 5,140,000. Annual growth −0.1%. People per sq.km. 118.

Peoples
Dane 95.4%. **German** 1.1%. **Faeroese** 0.9%.
Other European 1%.
Guestworkers, etc. 1.6%. Mainly Muslim Turks, and North Africans.

Literacy 99%.**Official language:** Danish, Faeroese.

Capital: Copenhagen 1,357,000. Urbanization 83%.

Economy: Based on agriculture and light industry. Wealthy welfare state. Income/person $11,490 (81% of USA).

Politics: Stable parliamentary democracy with a constitutional monarchy. A member of the European Economic Community (EEC). The Faeroe Islands are an overseas part of Denmark with a high degree of autonomy.

Religion: There is complete religious freedom, though the Lutheran Church is recognized as the national Church and is supported out of a state-levied church tax.
Non-religious/Atheist 6%. Many formerly linked with the national Church.
Muslim 1.3%. **Jews** 0.14%.
Christian 92.7%. The great majority no longer go to church.
Roman Catholic 0.5%. Practising 35%. 28,400a.
Marginal groups 0.6%. 31,000a. Largest (adherents):

Jehovah's Witnesses	30,000
Mormons	4,500

Protestant 91.5%. 4,700,000a; 3,400,000m.
Denominations 36. Largest (adult members):

National Church (Lutheran)	3,460,000
Apostolic Church	14,000
Baptist Church	6,450
Elim Church	5,700
Brethren (Faeroes)	4,700
Methodist Church	2,600
Mission Covenant Church	1,970

Evangelical 5-7% of population. On Faeroes it is 26%.
Missionaries from Denmark approx. 300 (1:15,700 Protestants).
Missionaries to Denmark approx. 18.

Religious Changes

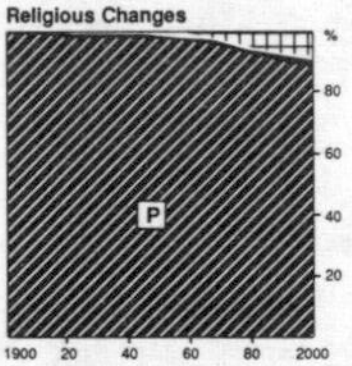

Evangelical Changes

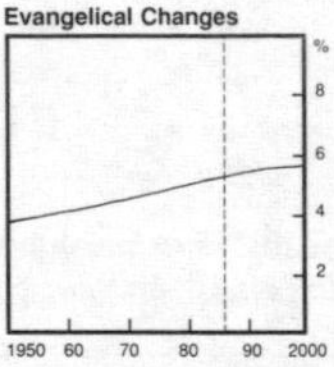

1. **Denmark needs a fresh visitation** from God. Although the vast majority still maintain formal links with the national church, church attendance in most parishes varies between 2% and 4%. Praise God for signs that the tide is turning against permissive secularism.

2. **Much of the Lutheran Church is formal**, and the fresh winds of the Holy Spirit must blow through this institution. An increasing number of pastors in the State Church have been touched by charismatic renewal and are exerting an influence for the gospel in some areas. Pray for all who preach the truth within the national church.

3. **The evangelical witness is small** both within and outside the State Church, so pray for all seeking to live for the Lord in this land that their testimony may lead many to a personal faith in the Lord. There has not been much active evangelism in the past, but the Lord is stirring up a number of groups around the country to win their countrymen to Christ. Pray for the raising up of many new evangelical congregations.

4. **Liberal theology has been strong in most Protestant denominations**. Pray for the Bible schools in the country — notably those of the Apostolic Bible School, the short-term School of Evangelism (**YWAM**), and a new evangelical Lutheran faculty in Aarhus. Pray for all graduates as they move out into the Lord's work at home and overseas.

5. **Young people** have been particularly affected by the negative effects of materialism around them, and have become more responsive to spiritual challenges. YFC and KFS(**IFES**) are finding more openings for ministry than ever before. Pray for evangelistic Bible studies run by KFS for both secular and theological(!) students at universities.

6. **The rapid growth of sects and eastern religions** is probably one factor that motivated the government to restrict the entry of any foreign missionaries. A number of North American missionaries have been affected.

7. **The missionary vision was once strong,** but it is now relatively weak. Most of the 300 Danish missionaries are evangelical. Pray for them and for a growth of interest in world evangelization in Denmark. There are unmet spiritual needs among guestworker Turks, Yugoslavs and Pakistanis as well as refugee Iranis and Iraqis.

8. **Literature.** The Danish Bible Society produced a new version of the NT in 1974, and work is in progress on the OT. Pray for the effective entry of God's Word into many homes and hearts. The capital city, Copenhagen, has only one Christian bookshop.

9. **The Faeroe Islands**, in the Atlantic between Iceland and Britain, is a self-governing overseas area of Denmark. Its population of 45,000 has a high proportion of evangelical believers, many being of the **Brethren** with 32 assemblies, and also of the Lutheran Church. Pray for Faeroese missionaries serving in a number of lands (Greenland, Iceland, etc.). Pray that Faeroese believers may share the gospel with the people on the Danish mainland. Over 10,000 Faeroese live in Denmark itself.

DJIBOUTI
(Republic of Djibouti)

Africa

Apr 11

Area 23,000 sq.km. A hot, dry, desert enclave in Ethiopia and Somalia.

Population 430,000. Annual growth 2.7%. People per sq.km. 19.

Peoples
Issa Somali 45% and **Afar** (Danakil) 40% are related to one another.
Minorities 5.2%. French 10,000; Arab 5,000; Yemeni; Ethiopian; Greek, etc.
Refugees 10.3%. From both Ethiopia and Somalia.

Capital: Djibouti 210,000. **Urbanization** 74%.

Literacy 36%. **Official languages:** French and Arabic (latter little used). **Trade languages:** Somali, Afar. **All languages** 4. **Bible translations** 2Bi 1por.

Economy: Unviable since the Somali-Ethiopian War which disrupted the traditional trade link between the Red Sea port of Djibouti and the railway to Addis Ababa. Now considerable aid is received in exchange for commitment to outside political and strategic interests. A notable effort is now being made to develop the economy — especially agriculture. Income/person $1,010 (7% of USA).

Politics: Independent from France in 1977, but French forces are still responsible for external defence and prevention of annexation by neighbouring Ethiopia and Somalia.

Religion: Considerable degree of religious freedom.
Muslim 96%. Almost all are Sunni.
Hindu 0.3%. **Non-religious/Atheist** 0.3%.
Christian 3.7%. Almost all French, a few Somalis and Afars.
Roman Catholic 3.2%. Adherents 11,000, of which a few are Somali.
Orthodox 0.42%. Ethiopians and some Greeks.
Protestant 0.06%. A single French Reformed expatriate group and a handful of Afar, Somali and Arab believers.

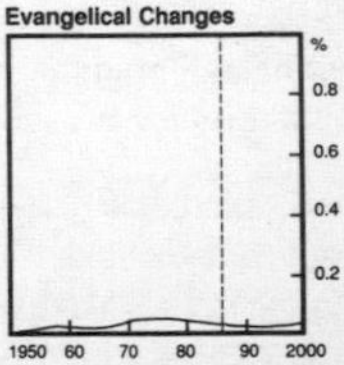

1. **The way opened for the first evangelical witness** in 1975. Praise God for this. Pray for the land to remain open so that a strong local church may be planted among the indigenous peoples.

2. **The only missionaries serving in the land are 13 workers of the RSMT**, though the French Mennonite Church is considering opening a ministry too. Pray for the missionaries serving in what is reputed to be the world's hottest country. Pray for reinforcements.

3. **Ministries have been established** in the realms of education, agriculture, literature, Bible translation and, lately, in public health, though opportunities abound for personal work. Much interest is shown in the Somali and Afar gospels. Pray that these ministries may lead to conversions.

4. **There is only a handful of scattered indigenous believers.** Pray for the planting of viable churches.

5. **Unreached peoples** are almost entirely Muslim.

a) **Afars** — whose main territory lies in Ethiopia. Pray for Bible translation work in progress as well as for Scripture portions and **GRI** gospel cassettes now in circulation. Pray also for the Afar radio broadcasts from Seychelles.

b) **Somalis** — little is now being done for this majority people — one of the few areas where Somalis may be openly evangelized.

c) **Arabs** — both the local and Yemeni Arabs need a specific approach directed to their spiritual needs.

d) **Refugees** — housed in camps on the borders — mainly Ethiopians.

Caribbean
Apr 12

DOMINICA
(The Commonwealth of Dominica)

Area 751 sq.km. Between the French islands of Guadeloupe and Martinique and ruled by France until 1759. This has determined much of its religious and cultural development.

Population 87,000. Annual growth 1.6%. People per sq.km. 115.

Peoples: African 89%, **Eurafrican** 7.3%, **European** 1%, **Asian** 1%, **Amerindian Caribs** 1.7%.

Literacy 80%. **Official language:** English, but 70% speak a French Creole. **All languages** 2. **Bible translations** 1Bi.

Capital: Roseau 12,000. Urbanization 30%.

Economy: Heavily dependent on export of bananas and coconuts. The 1978/80 hurricanes devastated the island, making this poor island even yet poorer. Income/person $970 ('81) (7% of USA). Inflation 4% ('84).

Politics: Independent from Britain in 1978. A republic with a short but stormy post-independence political history and a number of attempted coups.

Religion

Christian 99.8%. Nominal 12.6%. Affiliated 87.2%.

Roman Catholic 74.5%. 64,800a; 35,000m.

Marginal groups (2) 0.9%.

Protestant 11.8%. 10,300a; 5,680m. Denominations 18. Largest (adult members):

Seventh Day Adventist Church	1,800
Methodist Church	1,200
Churches of Christ in Chr. Union	820

Evangelical 5.8% of population.

Missionaries to Dominica 18 (1:4,800 people) in five agencies.

Missionaries from Dominica 0.

Points for Prayer: See Jamaica p. 255.

DOMINICAN REPUBLIC

Latin America

Apr 13

Area 49,000 sq.km. The eastern two-thirds of the island of Hispaniola, shared with Haiti.

Population 6,200,000. Annual growth 2.5%. People per sq.km. 126.

Peoples: Considerable mixing between races makes classification rather difficult.
Spanish descent 16%, **Eurafrican** (mixed race) 71%, **African** 10%.
Immigrant minorities 3%. European/N.American 1%; Haitian 1%; Jamaican 20,000; Chinese 4,500; Japanese.

Literacy 72%. **Official language:** Spanish. **All languages** 3. **Bible translations** 2Bi.

Capital: Santo Domingo 2,050,000. Urbanization 52%.

Economy: Fairly poor but good economic growth in early '70s. The recession and severe hurricanes in 1979 have severely affected the economy. Income/person $1,380 (10% of USA). Inflation 10%.

Politics: Independence four times — twice from Spain (1821/65), once from Haiti (1844) and once from the USA (1924)! Thirty years of repressive dictatorship ended in 1961, but instability and civil war prevailed until 1966. Relative stability with a fairly democratic government since.

Religion: Catholicism is the official religion, but there is freedom for other religions.

Spiritist 1%. Half the population probably have links with occult practices.
Non-religious/Atheist 0.9%.
Christian 98%. Nominal 14%. Affiliated 84%.
Roman Catholic 77%. Practising 11-16%. 4,790,000a.
Marginal groups 0.6%. 35,700a; 10,100m. Jehovah's Witnesses 31,282a.
Protestant 6.4%. 397,000a; 162,000m. Denominations 46. Largest (adult members):

Seventh Day Adventist Church	49,000
Assemblies of God	18,000
Church of God (Cleveland)	10,500
Ch. of God of Prophecy	7,400
Assembly of Chr. Churches	6,200
Free Methodist Church	6,100
Brethren Assemblies	5,800
Assoc. of Evang. Temples (**WT**)	1,100
Bible Christian Ch. (**UFM**)	1,050

Evangelical 4.7% of population.
Missionaries to the Dominican Republic 190 (1:32,600 people).

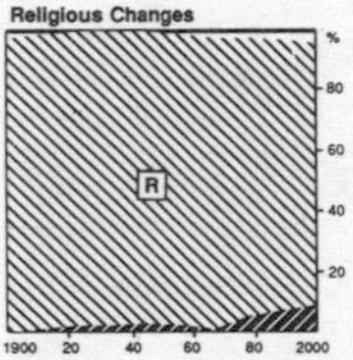

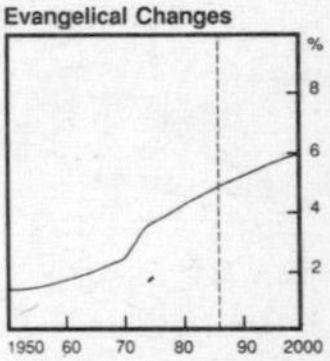

1. **Only since 1975 has there been significant growth in the Protestant Churches.** The Republic was one of the last of the Latin American countries to be entered by Evangelicals. Growth has largely been among the Pentecostal groups and the Seventh Day Adventists, but both the **Brethren** and Free Methodists have grown too. Pray for effective evangelization and the establishment of strong, well-led missionary-minded churches that have a vision to reach out in evangelism.

2. **There have been many leadership problems in the churches** — immaturity, mission/church relationships and lack of money to support pastors locally. Pray for the emergence of a strong and mature leadership. Pray for the Bible school ministry of many churches and missions — such as **WT** and **UFM**; there are now nine Bible schools or seminaries for Protestant churches.

3. **Missions** are involved in church planting, evangelistic and technical ministries. Some larger denominational and interdenominational agencies are **SBC** (20 workers), **WT** (18), **Brethren** (18), **UFM** (17), **CCC** (15). Reinforcements are needed — especially those already at home in a Latin American culture. This is a good potential field for Latin American missionaries.

4. **Unreached peoples.** Some sections of the population are less well reached by Evangelicals than others — especially the more staunchly Catholic upper classes, the Voodoo spiritists and the Haitian refugees. There are also many Hong Kong Chinese who have immigrated since 1983; there is no known work among them.

Latin America
Apr 14-15

ECUADOR
(The Republic of Ecuador)

E

Area 283,600 sq.km. Amazon jungle in east, high Andean Sierra in the centre, fertile coastal plain on Pacific Coast. Also the Galapagos Is. 1,000 km. to west.

Population 9,400,000. Annual growth 3.1%. People per sq.km. 33.

Peoples: Considerable racial mingling.
Spanish-speaking 57%. (Mestizo/Mulatto 41%, European 11%, African 5%).
Amerindian 42%. Quichua (9 dialects) 3,640,000 (predominantly in Sierra); Lowland tribes (8) 88,000 in east and north.
Other 1%. Including Chinese 7,000.

Literacy 84%. **Official language:** Spanish. **All languages** 22. **Bible translations** 1Bi 8NT 5por.

Capital: Quito 930,000. Other major city: Guayaquil 1,500,000. Urbanization 49%.

Economy: Unequal distribution of oil wealth worsened the lot of the poor majority, especially the Quichuas. The high birth rate together with a large foreign debt and currency devaluation are lowering living standards. Income/person $1,268 (9% of USA). Inflation 25%.

Politics: Military rule ended in 1979 with the re-institution of democracy. The 1984 elections brought a rightward shift in the government, with emphasis being made on economic recovery.

Religion: There is freedom of religion.
Non-religious/Atheist 0.7%.
Tribal religions 0.55%. **Baha'i** 0.34%.

Christian 98.1%. Affiliated 95.2%. A large proportion of the Quichua are more pagan than Christian.
Roman Catholic 91.0%. 8,500,000a; 4,400,000m. Weaker on the coast, stronger in the Sierra.
Marginal groups 0.9%. 87,300a; 40,000m. Main cults 3. Largest (adherents):

Mormons	45,000
Jehovah's Witnesses	36,200

Protestant 3.4%. 301,383a; 90,566m. Denominations 46. Largest (adult members):

Ev. Ind. Assoc. of Chim (**GMU**)	33,000
Christian Alliance Ch. (**CMA**)	9,400
Seventh Day Adventist Ch.	8,500
Church of Foursquare Gospel	6,521
Baptist Conv. (**SBC**)	5,700
Assemblies of God	3,995
Assoc. of **GMU** Churches (Span.)	3,156
Evang. Covenant Church	2,135
Independent Churches	12,800

Evangelical 3.2% of population.
Missionaries to Ecuador 822 (1:11,000 people) in 42 agencies.
Missionaries from within Ecuador est. 30 (1:9,000 Protestants).

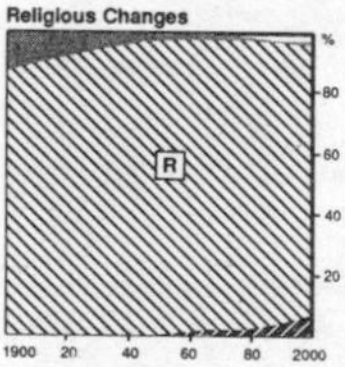

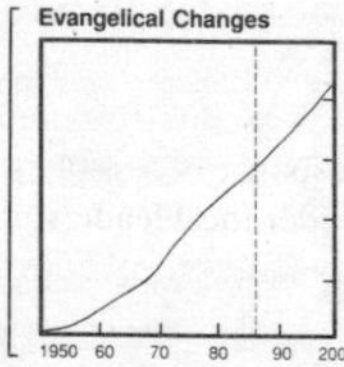

1. **The nation suffered severely in 1983** through both economic and climatic disasters, but this has further enhanced the receptivity of the people. Pray for the ripened spiritual harvest to be gathered in!

2. **Ecuador long held the record for the smallest percentage of evangelical believers in Latin America.** This was due to the strong opposition of the Roman Catholic Church in the past, divisions among believers and inefficient methods of outreach. Since 1960, there has been a sixfold increase of Evangelicals. Much of this growth has been through Pentecostal and **CMA** growth in the urban areas among the Spanish-speaking majority, and **GMU** among the Chimborazo Quichuas. Praise God for this; and pray for the unity of believers that transcends class, culture, personalities and denominational tags so that the Body of Christ may exert a decisive influence on the life of the nation.

3. **The most thrilling work of the Spirit of God is among the Quichuas** — with rapid church growth, moral uplift and the development of the latent talent and leadership gifts of these descendants of the ancient Incas. In 1967 there were but 120 believers among nearly 3,000,000 people, but now there are over 33,850 baptized believers and a community of

143,500! Almost 50% of Ecuador's Evangelicals are non-Spanish speaking. Pray for the **GMU, CMA** Covenant, Baptist, Lutheran and Pentecostal work among the various Quichua dialectic groups, and for the translation work on the OT in two major dialects. Pray for the Quichua leadership, especially for pastors and evangelists. Pray for wisdom for the Quichua church as various political groups try to woo the allegiance of the large evangelical community.

4. **The Quichua Church** has some fine leaders, but most lack training. **GMU** has a TEE programme with over 700 Quichua leaders studying the Word in 60 centres. Pray for the maturing of this church and also for its outreach to other provinces, the cities and even to Quichua in Colombia. The church needs Christian literature. Pray for the integration of the Quichua Church into national life and for the Spanish-speaking majority to be blessed by this fellowship.

E

5. **Pioneer work among the small jungle tribes** attracted worldwide attention in 1956 when five missionaries were killed by the primitive 500-strong Aucas. Through the work of **SIL** (translating in 12 languages), **GMU** (Shuara or Jivaro), **Brethren** (Waorani, Colorado), etc, few of these small tribes are without indigenous churches. Intense anti-missionary propaganda through humanist anthropologists, leftist agitators, materialist jungle exploiters and traders caused some curtailment of Bible translation and Christian work among these peoples. Pray that all the enemy's plans will be frustrated, and that isolated believers will mature spiritually, so that they may be able to stand firm in the midst of pressures of the modern world sweeping through their areas.

6. **Bible translation continues** despite the termination of government permission for **SIL** to continue after 1982. Pray for the completion of New Testaments in seven languages and for the commencement of translation into the four languages which are still without any portion of Scripture. Pray for the printing and distribution of God's Word through the Bible Society in the major Quichua languages as well as Spanish. The believers await the imminent publication of the complete Bible in Quichua.

7. **Missions.** The largest groups are **WRMF** (289 missionaries), **CMA** (76), **GMU** (62), **OMS** (47), **SBC** (38), **Brethren** (24). There are many opportunities for missionary recruits in supportive ministries, church planting and pioneer work in the groups mentioned below.

8. **The radio ministry of HCJB is known and appreciated both in Ecuador and worldwide.** The **World Radio Missionary Fellowship** prepares and transmits 500 programmes weekly in 12 languages internationally, as well as running a valuable coverage of Ecuador through both radio and television. Pray for this ministry and the extensive follow up work that the large response necessitates. Pray also for the two Quichua and one Shuara Christian radio stations, under local leadership but started by **GMU**, broadcasting to these indigenous groups. Both the Evangelical Covenant Church and Lutheran Church also run radio stations.

9. **Truly unreached peoples are very few,** but great needs remain.
   a) The large **urban slums** of Guyaquil and Quito, where economic deprivation and misery prevail.
   b) The **upper and middle classes** have been relatively unresponsive.
   c) **University and school students.** There are over eight agencies involved in campus ministries, including **CCC**, **IFES**, YFC, **LAM**, and four denominational groups. The work is small, but an impact is being made on the, often, radical university campuses.
   d) The 6,000 people living on the distant and barren **Galapagos Islands** with only one church which has two members and six adherents.
   e) The provinces of Carchi (130,000 people with eight churches) and Loja (361,000 people with only nine churches) are needy.

Middle East

Apr 16-18

EGYPT

(Arab Republic of Egypt)

Area 1,001,000 sq.km. 96% desert, and only 3% arable land along the banks of the Nile and around the Western Desert oases.

Population 48,300,000. Annual growth 2.7%. People per sq.km. 48; in fertile areas 1,600 people per sq.km.!

Peoples

Egyptian 86.4%. Speaking Arabic, but essentially the same people of ancient and biblical history.

Arab 6.3%. Lebanese, Sudanese, Yemeni, Palestinian, etc.

Nubian 3%. Mostly living in the southern part of the country.

Bedouin 2%. Many still nomadic in Sinai, etc.

Berber 2%. Most now Arabized, but a few still speaking a Berber dialect at the Siwa Oasis.

Other minorities 0.3%. Westerner, Armenian, Greek, etc.

Literacy 48%. **Official language:** Arabic. **All languages** 6. **Bible translations** 2Bi 1NT 2por.

Capital: Cairo 8,692,000 (unofficial figure nearer 12 million). Other major cities: Alexandria 3,162,000. Thirteen other cities with over 100,000 people. Rapid urbanization — now at 48%.

Economy: Poor; crippled by high birth rate and lack of agricultural land, but somewhat alleviated by US aid, and remittances from 1.8 million Egyptians resident abroad. Income/person $700 (5% of USA).

Politics: President Sadat's diplomacy (1970-81) ended the dominance of the USSR and won control of the valuable Suez Canal and Sinai oilfields from Israel as an outcome of the 1973 Yom Kippur War. The generally popular peace treaty with Israel in 1979 was bitterly opposed by many Arab nations and Muslim fundamentalists within the country and led to Egypt's isolation in the Middle East and Sadat's assassination. The present government of Pres. Mubarak is cautiously introducing political liberalizations and seeking rapprochement with other Arab states.

Religion: Islam is the state religion. Fundamentalist Muslims are pressing for the full Islamization of society. Christians are free to worship but not to openly evangelize Muslims. The 1981 clampdown on both Muslim fundamentalists and Christian leaders had its roots in tensions caused by enforced conversions to Islam and successful evangelism by Christians.

Muslim 82.4%. Cairo is the intellectual capital of Islam. Muslim fundamentalism has become a significant force over the last 10 years.

Non-religious/Atheist 0.4%.

Christian 17.2%. Though *officially* only 6%. Gradual erosion of this percentage through high emigration to the West (130,000 in N.America and Australia), lower birth rate, and pressures to convert to Islam.

Coptic Orthodox Church 15.7%. Practising 83%. 7,600,000a; 4,400,000m. One of the ancient churches that has survived 1,300 years of Muslim Arab persecution and discrimination.

Other Orthodox Churches (5) 0.34%.

Roman Catholic 0.33%. 155,000a; 89,000m. 7 groups and traditions.

Protestant 0.85%. 410,000a; 154,000m. Denominations 46. Largest (adult members):

Coptic Evangelical Church	88,000
Assemblies of God	13,000
Brethren (2 groups)	10,400
Free Methodist Church	9,000

Protestant Evangelical 0.69% of population, but possibly 3% if Orthodox included.

Missionaries to Egypt est.150 (1:322,000 people) in 27 agencies.

Missionaries from Egypt 25 (1:16,400 Protestants) in 3 agencies.

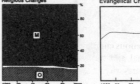

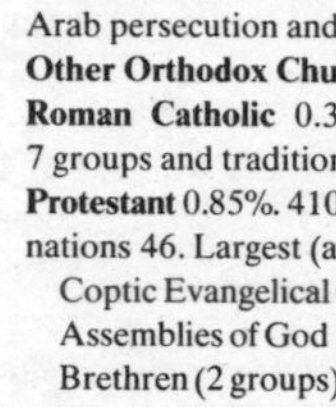

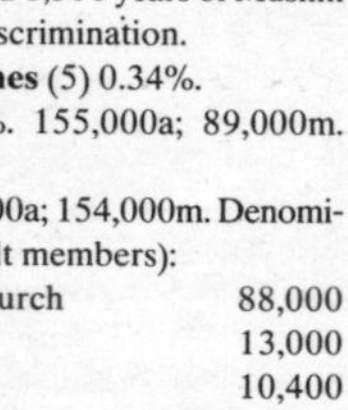

1. **Pray that the promise of Isaiah 19:19-22 for Egypt may be fulfilled.** In spite of legal difficulties and the increasing militancy of the Muslim Brotherhood, there is evident hunger for the Good News among Muslims, with several hundred Muslims turning to Christ every year. Pray that Egypt's economic trials and Islam's failure to meet man's deepest need may turn many to the Lord Jesus.

2. **Unreached peoples.** Few Muslims have ever heard a Christian testify. Pray that the Christians may win opportunities to speak through their Christ-like life. Specific prayer targets:

a) **The urban population** — many are uprooted peasants in squalid slums.

b) **The "fellaheen"** (peasants) in the rural villages of the Nile and oases.

c) **The Nubian people** who were largely converted from Christianity to Islam in the 17th century but are open to the gospel. Yet only portions of the Scriptures are available in one of the two languages still spoken by 10-15% of the Nubians.

d) **The desert dwellers** — Bedouin, Siwa Berber, etc. have had little contact with the gospel.

e) **Arab visitors** to Egypt come from many "closed" Muslim lands — especially during Ramadan to avoid the rigours of the Muslim fasting month!

3. **The Coptic Church** is by far the largest body of Christians in the Middle East and is a strategic key for the evangelization of the area. Pray that mounting pressures, communal tensions, detention of leaders and outright persecution by Muslim extremists since 1979 may strengthen and enliven the Church. There has been a marked increase in intercessory prayer as a result of these difficulties. The recent wave of persecution has brought together Orthodox and Protestant leaders as never before. Pray that all believers may give a united and effective witness to the majority Muslim community.

4. **A biblically based renewal movement in the Coptic Church** has steadily gained momentum since 1930, and its strong emphasis on Bible study and a warm personal faith has led to many becoming fervent witnesses for the Lord. Pray for the growth and effectiveness of this movement of the Spirit.

5. **The Protestant churches** sprang from the Orthodox minority, and for some decades had not seen significant growth. This is changing: there has been a growing renewal movement since 1973 and many young people are now coming to the Lord. Pray for new life to come to nominal Christians and for a consistent testimony before the Muslims. Pray that, despite the difficulties, Muslims may be reached *and* welcomed into the churches.

6. **The Christian witness among university students** is encouraging. There is a group in every faculty of Egypt's four big university complexes, even in the Al Azhar Muslim University where Muslim missionaries are trained. Pray that these believers may find open hearts among the 300,000 students and win them in the relatively open spirit of inquiry on the campuses. Pray that these believers may be built up in the Lord for future service through the witness of **IFES** and **CCC** workers. Work among children and young people is especially encouraging with many youth groups in churches and schools, summer conferences and camps.

7. **There is a dearth of volunteers for pastoral and missionary service.** Pray for the **YWAM** training courses run in Cyprus, which have been used of the Lord to give a vision to many young people. Pray for many such to give themselves for the Lord's work. Pray also for those in theological training at the Coptic Evangelical Church Seminary which had 50 students in 1985 (some from Sudan), the **AoG** and Free Methodist Bible schools, as well as in institutions abroad.

8. **There are more openings now for Christian service for expatriates than there have been for many years.** There are possibilities for ministry in expatriate community churches and with indigenous churches, as well as in service ministries such as literature, etc. and a variety of professional and business openings which provide opportunities for witness to the non-Christian majority. Pray for labourers!

9. **The missionary vision of the Egyptian church is growing,** but it is limited by lack of funds. Missionaries from Egypt would be more acceptable than Western missionaries in many Muslim lands. Pray that the many Egyptian Christians in the West and Middle Eastern oil states may catch the vision to support such a thrust.

10. **Christian literature** is freely printed and sold. Many Christian groups have moved their literature ministries from war-torn Lebanon to Egypt. Pray for:

a) **The many Christian bookstores** (10 in Cairo); for the effective use of this literature.

b) **The raising up of more local believers who are able to write** suitable evangelistic and teaching materials.

c) ***Magalla***, the mass-circulation magazine, has a Christian slant. Over 60,000 copies are sold per issue in 16 Middle Eastern lands. Pray for its continued publication despite opposition, and for its effectiveness in breaking down misconceptions about the gospel. Pray for all engaged in its publication. Pray also for the West European edition ***Magallati*** and its use among the 2,700,000 Arab speakers living in Europe as well as the numerous Arab tourists.

d) ***The Living New Testament***, recently published in Arabic, has stirred great interest among people of all religions — pray for eternal fruit.

11. **The film "Jesus" in Arabic is being widely shown**; pray that this vivid portrayal of the Saviour may open many hearts.

12. **Christian radio: TWR**'s Arabic medium-wave service is broadcast morning and evening. Pray for meaningful and effective programming fitted to the needs of this strategic nation.

Latin America

Apr 19-20

EL SALVADOR
(The Republic of El Salvador)

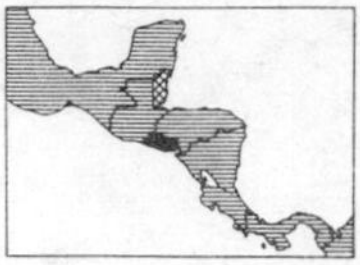

Area 21,400 sq.km. The smallest and most densely populated mainland state in the Americas.

Population 5,500,000. Annual growth 2.1%. People per sq.km. 259. 1,300,000 people are refugees, of whom 700,000 have fled the country (500,000 in USA; 35,000 in Honduras; others in Costa Rica, etc.).

Peoples
Spanish-speaking 99.4%. An amalgam of Ladino (Mestizo) 92.3%, Amerindian 5%, White 1.7%, Honduran 0.4%, etc. The use of the Indian languages Pipil, Lenca, etc. has virtually died out.
Other minorities 0.6%. N.American/European 5,000; Chinese 1,200; Jews 700.

Literacy 63%. **Official language:** Spanish. **All languages** 3.

Capital: San Salvador 515,000. Urbanization 45%.

Economy: Devastated by the five years of bitter civil war provoked by years of corrupt dictatorships and unequal distribution of land and wealth. Income/person $710 (5% of USA).

Politics: Sovereign independent state since 1841 but rarely with political stability or democratic freedoms. Many years of military-civilian rule ended with the election of a centrist civilian government in 1985. The government is under pressure to make the necessary social and economic changes in the face of popular/leftist guerrilla warfare. By early 1984 over 120,000 had been killed in the fighting or by murder squads of the contending forces.

Religion: Great freedom for evangelism although Catholicism is the state religion. There have been evident strains between the government and the Church since 1977, as the RC leadership began to speak up for the oppressed and the poor and promoted liberation theology.
Non-religious/Atheist 2% or more.
Other religions 0.6%.
Christian 97.2%. Affiliated 92.5%.
Roman Catholic 77.5%. Officially 94%. Many have joined other churches or ideologies. 4,260,000a; 2,300,000m.
Marginal groups 1.2%. 64,000a.
Protestant 14%. 766,000a; 256,000m. Denominations 49. Largest (adult members):

Assemblies of God	95,000
Seventh Day Adventist Church	31,600
Evangelical Chs. of CA (**CAMI**)	18,000
Baptists (5 groups)	16,500
All other Pentecostal (28 groups)	73,000

Evangelical 12.8% of population.
Missionaries to El Salvador 98 (1:56,000 people) in 16 agencies.
Missionaries from El Salvador 4 (1:192,000 Protestants).

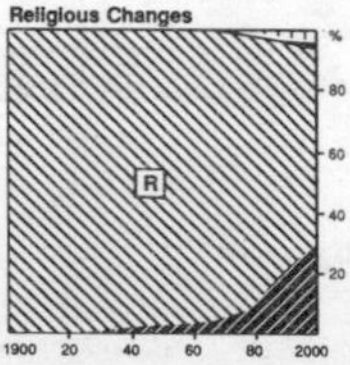

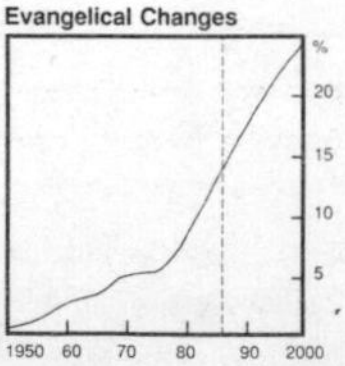

1. **An astonishing spiritual harvest is being gathered from all strata of society in the midst of the tragedy of war.** Between 1960 and 1970, 20,000 new members were added to evangelical churches; in the decade '70-'80, a further 100,000; but in the last five years 300,000 have come to Christ. The Assemblies of God and other Pentecostal Churches have grown most, but nearly all non-RC groups have also grown. Pray for the spiritual hunger of Salvadoreans to be met in Jesus ("*El Salvador*" is Spanish for "The Saviour").

2. **Christian leaders face agonizing pressures from both sides in the conflict.** Some have been murdered, and others have had to flee the country. Pray for all committed Christians who preach the truth in love and without compromise. It is the witness of the lives of converted people that has brought many to Christ. Pray also for growth in grace through adequate teaching for the many new Christians.

3. **Young people need special prayer** — their hopes of education and advancement have been ruined, and many are tempted to take up the gun in retaliation. Pray that many may take up the Cross to follow the Saviour whatever the cost. The university reopened in 1985 after being closed for five years. Pray for the 12,000 students, and for the MUC(**IFES**) groups being started.

4. **The training of leadership for the churches continues.** There are now 15 Bible schools, 3 seminaries and over 12 TEE programmes functioning! Pray for the provision of all material needs for staff and students in this time of economic stress.

5. **There are relatively few expatriate missionaries in the land.** All are engaged in church nurture ministries and in aid programmes for the 600,000 internally displaced refugees. They need prayer that they might be both wise and humble in the midst of many threats to their lives.

7. **Pray for the peace of this land,** and for a just settlement to the underlying causes of the present war that is increasingly involving the surrounding states and the superpowers. Pray also for the provision of the spiritual and physical needs of those living in refugee camps in surrounding lands, as well as for the many now illegally fleeing to the USA.

8. **The Church in El Salvador is being refined.** Pray that when peace comes, a surge of missionary endeavour may flow out of this land to other needy parts of the world.

Africa
Apr 21

EQUATORIAL GUINEA

(The Republic of Equatorial Guinea)

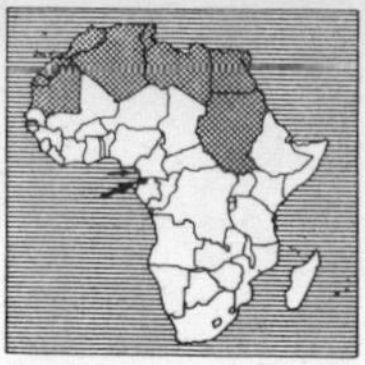

Area 28,000 sq.km. A small enclave, Rio Muni, on the African mainland; and several islands in the Gulf of Guinea: Bioko (2,000 sq.km.), Pagalu (10 sq.km.).

Population 411,000 (35% on Bioko). Annual growth 2.5%. People per sq.km. 14.7. The former ruler caused the deaths of about 60,000 people and the flight or expulsion of a further 140,000 between 1969 and 1978.

Peoples

Mainland tribes 91%. Ntum-Okak 320,000 (related to Fang in Gabon and Bulu in Cameroon); politically dominant; Combe 20,000; Seke 12,000; Ngumba 10,000; others (4) 5,300.

Island peoples 8%. Bubi 22,000; Pagalu 2,000; Creole 5,700.

Foreigners 1%. Spanish, Nigerian, Cameroonian, E. European.

Literacy 15%. **Official language:** Spanish. **All languages** 9. **Bible translations** 2Bi 2NT 3por.

Capital: Malabo 35,000. Urbanization 10%.

Economy: Total collapse by 1979 and very slow recovery under Spanish tutelage since. Income/person $140 (1% of USA).

Politics: Independence from Spain in 1968. A coup in 1969 brought Macias Nguema to power. This atheist dictator turned his country into a slave-labour camp with Soviet Bloc assistance. A coup in 1979 ousted him but, despite renewed links with Spain, instability continues.

Religion: After a decade of savage persecution, a cautious return to religious freedom.

Tribal religion 19%. Predominantly on mainland.

Non-religious/Atheist 3%.

Christian 77%.

Roman Catholic 70.5%. 283,000a; 189,600m. Most priests were expelled and some killed in the '70s.

Marginal groups 0.5%. Jehovah's Witnesses and several syncretic indigenous groups.

Protestant 6.2%. 25,500a; 8,400m. Denominations 6. Largest (adult members):

Reformed Ch. (Presby., **WEC**)	7,200
Methodist Ch. (on Bioko)	250

Evangelical 2.7% of population.

Missionaries to Equatorial Guinea 4 (1:103,000 people) in 3 agencies.

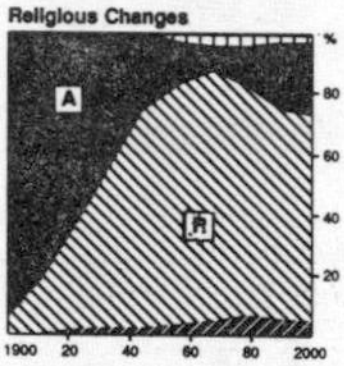

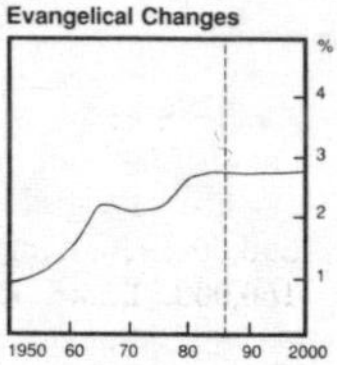

1. **This ravaged land will need years for recovery** from the effects of economic devastation, murder and exile of virtually all educated citizens. Political rivalries, corruption and attempted coups prolong the agony. Pray for stability and full freedom for the gospel.

2. **The persecuted Church has not emerged unscathed.** Church leaders were forced to compromise theologically or suffer. Tragically, many Protestant church leaders are living in sin and more interested in power politics than in the spiritual nurture of their flocks. Some vigorously resist any open preaching of the gospel. Pray both for repentance and revival.

3. **Theological education has been strongly influenced by liberal institutions in Cameroon.** Pray for adequate Bible training for a new generation of leaders, now woefully lacking.

4. **The return of missionaries has been hampered by the economic mess and church politics among the Protestants.** Pray for the **SBC** and **AoG** missionaries seeking to initiate work, and for the return of **WEC** missionaries to Rio Muni.

5. **Unreached peoples.** Much of the population has been baptized Catholic, but real understanding of the gospel is very limited; there are only a handful of evangelical congregations. Especially needy are the island peoples and the various tribes of central and northern Rio Muni.

ETHIOPIA

(Socialist Ethiopia)

Africa

Apr 22-24

Area 1,222,000 sq.km. Fertile mountain plateau surrounded by the deserts of the Red Sea coast, and the Somali, Kenya and Sudan borders.

Population 35,631,000. Annual growth 2.1%. People per sq.km. 29, but very unevenly distributed, with high densities in the highland valleys.

Peoples: There are over 200 major dialects spoken, but the 1974 revolution has stimulated a greater sense of national identity in this diversity.

Semitic origin 36%. Amharas (4 groups) 8,840,000 in C. & N. Highlands; Tigrinya 2,120,000 in C. Eritrea; Tigre 700,000 in N. Eritrea; and Gurage (4) 1,000,000 in S. Highlands. They originally came from Arabia, conquering and mixing with the local Hamitic peoples.

Cushitic 57%. Over 52 peoples in the east, centre and south.

Oromo 14,000,000 (Wolayta 3,400,000; Wallega 1,650,000; Arusi 1,050,000; Konso 400,000; and at least 14 other smaller groups.)

Somali 2,000,000 — but about 500,000 are refugees in Somalia.

Other significant peoples: Sidamo 1,000,000; Hadiya 950,000; Kambalfa 460,000; Gideo 390,000; Kafa 230,000; Afar 200,000; Awiya 160,000; Boran 150,000; Beja 90,000; Ari 60,000; She 50,000; Burji 30,000; Bako 25,000; Banna 25,000.

Nilotic-Sudanic 6%. Twenty-two peoples largely in south and west: Gumuz 250,000; Berta 140,000; Murle 140,000; Anuak 130,000; Ma'en 130,000; Nuer 130,000; Masengo 100,000; Nara 100,000; Tirma 50,000; Koma 43,000; Turkana 30,000; Mabaan 7,000; etc., and Kunama (Eritrea) 200,000.

Falasha Jew 15,000. Black Jews who still practise Old Testament animal sacrifices.

Foreign 0.8%. Arab 90,000; Eastern European; Westerner, etc.

Literacy 20%. **Official language:** Amharic, 65% of population are able to speak it. **All languages** over 100. **Bible translations** 5Bi 6NT 10por.

Capital: Addis Ababa 1,845,000. Other major city: Asmara 550,000. Urbanization 15%.

Economy: A semi-feudal society radically transformed by the changes and upheavals following the 1974 revolution. Agricultural reforms to improve acreage, quality and exports instituted, but anti-government resistance movements and serious droughts in '70s and '80s have hindered progress. Income/person $140 (1% of USA).

Politics: The government of Emperor Haile Selassie was overthrown in 1974 by the army, but the Provisional Military Administrative Council did not gain full political control until 1976. The Marxist-oriented government has had to contend with six separatist movements — the major ones being in the Ogaden in the east and Eritrea and Tigre Provinces in the north; bitter fighting still continues. Renewed nationalism and economic necessity is stimulating closer contacts with Western countries. The terrible famine of 1984/5 caused the death of one million people and was used by the authorities to control regional rebellions and impose collectivization of land by large resettlement campaigns.

Religion: Marxist-Leninism is the official doctrine of the government and therefore they are opposed to all religions and dedicated to their gradual elimination. However, persecution of Christians for their faith is generally local and sporadic rather than centrally organized, but pressure on believers is steadily on the increase. All statistics below are approximations.

Non-religious/Atheist 3%.

Tribal religions 10%. Mainly among the peoples of the south and west.

Muslim 35%. Strong in the north (Tigre), east (Afars), and southeast (Somalis and Oromo groups).

Christian 52%. Majority among Amharas, Tigre and many Oromo peoples of the Highlands.

Ethiopian Orthodox Church 41%. 14,600,000a; 8,600,000m.

Roman Catholic 0.7%. 242,000a; 140,000m.

Protestant 10%. 3,580,000a; 1,700,000m.

Denominations 36. Largest (adult members):

Kale Hiywot Church (KHC)	1,200,000
Mekane Yesu Church (ECMY)	560,000
Full Gosp. Believers' Church	100,000
Seventh Day Adventist Church	35,000
Assemblies of God	30,000
Mulu Wengel Church	19,000
Yihiywot Birhan Church	15,000
Meseret Kristos Church	6,000
Emmanuel Baptist Church	3,200
Evang. Church of Eritrea	2,500

Evangelical 9.6% of population. There are also Orthodox Christians who are evangelical.
Missionaries to Ethiopia approx. 400 (1:89,000 people).
Missionaries from within Ethiopia approx. 50 (1:71,600).

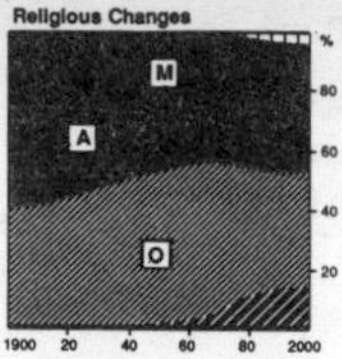

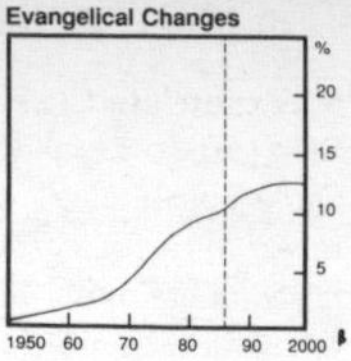

1. **Praise God for the thrilling growth of the evangelical witness in the new churches over the last 25 years** (from 241,000 adherents in 1960 to 3.5 million in 1985). Great vision, courageous evangelism, and vigorous leadership training have almost doubled the believers in the last 10 years of trial and hardship for the Church. All churches that are open are packed every Sunday.

2. **Pressures on Christians have been severe**, but defections have been few despite much suffering, imprisonment of leaders, confiscation of buildings and closure of churches in some areas. During 1985 over 700 churches in the province of Sidamo were closed. Pray for an unabated vision for the lost, courage if they are called upon to suffer for the name of Jesus, patience to love when they are misrepresented, and discernment to know the vital issues on which they need to stand firm. More specifically pray for the following:

a) **The KHC has grown in quality and quantity as a result of the last 10 stormy years.** Over 3,000 congregations (mainly in the south) are spread out over 13 of the country's 14 provinces though two-thirds of their buildings were closed down in 1985. Missionary outreach by national evangelists to unreached tribes continues — especially in the far south. Very little funding or missionary support comes from abroad, but there are still six **SIM** missionaries seconded to the KHC. Pray that the Lord may give local and national leadership, courage and vision for advance.

b) **The Mekane Yesu Church continues a vigorous and well-directed evangelistic outreach** despite great pressures in 1982 with the seizure of their central complex in Addis, closure of many churches in the west, and imprisonment of key leaders. A number of Lutheran missionaries are integrated into the ECMY.

c) **Various Pentecostal churches have grown dramatically of late**. The long-persecuted Mulu Wengel Church has greatly increased through urban house churches. Some Swedish and Finnish missionaries work in fellowship with several of these groups.

d) **Meseret Kristos Church (Mennonite), Emmanuel Baptist Church, and Brethren** have lost the use of many church buildings, but continue to quietly meet in house fellowships in the affected areas.

e) **The mushrooming illegal "house" churches** all over the country where church buildings have been closed.

f) **For those in prison for their faith.** Several hundred pastors and possibly 7,000 Christians were behind bars in 1985 at the very time Christians from around the world were pouring in famine aid. Pray for their witness and that their faith may be strengthened.

3. **The Orthodox Church is one of the ancient Eastern churches.** It is in a state of crisis due to its inability to adjust 19th century structures to today's revolutionary realities. Marxism has created many questions in people's minds which it is unable to answer, and this has helped many thousands of Orthodox Christians to a living faith in the Saviour. Churches are full and many new buildings constructed. Pray for those who love and serve the Lord within the Orthodox Church that through them blessing may come to the millions of nominal adherents.

4. **Vital programmes for the training of leaders continue despite the forcible closure or translocation of some institutions.** Pray for staff and students in the following:

a) The KHC seminary in Addis, the ECMY seminary, and the Orthodox St. Paul's seminary opened in 1982 with 20 students.

b) The Residential Bible schools of many denominations that continue to function under national leadership. The KHC has 3,500 students in 75 Bible schools.

c) The network of local evening and short-term Bible schools around the country of KHC, ECMY, etc.

d) The TEE programme run on an interdenominational basis from Addis Ababa.

5. **Expatriate Christian workers now number 400** (75% within newer churches), largest: **SIM** (50 workers), Lutheran, Pentecostals. Pray for tact, wisdom, strategic ministry openings, and a humble walk with God in a situation loaded with frustrations and tension points. No missionaries have been expelled since 1978 from Kafa Province, but restrictions on their movements limit itinerant ministries. Key ministries are predominantly supportive — linguistics, translation, literacy, medical, relief, and development; though there are openings in Bible teaching, etc. There are many openings for tentmaking missionaries (of which there are a number now), and their influence is making an impact in universities, medical facilities and aid organizations.

6. **Unreached peoples:**

a) **Eritrea.** About half the population is Orthodox Christian, but evangelical churches numbered only 27 in 1973. There are possibly 13,000 members in Eritrea or nearby Sudan; largely among the Tigrinya, and some among the Tigre and Kambalfa. Otherwise the Muslim Tigre, Beja, Barya, Afar, Arab, once Orthodox Marya and partly animistic Kambalfa are unreached. Pray for the continuing witness of Eritrean Christians in their strife-torn land. Over 500,000 refugees have fled to Sudan where some Eritrean and **MECO** workers seek to minister to them. Only in Djibouti are Afars now being reached **(RSMT).**

b) **The Northern provinces of Gojjam, Tigre, Begemidr** (95% Orthodox) **and Wallo** (65% Muslim, 35% Orthodox) had only 21 evangelical churches for 7,600,000 people in 1975. This area has been subjected to two terrible droughts and civil war in recent years. Few have heard the gospel among these Amhara, Tigrai and Oromo peoples who are largely nominally Orthodox and some of the latter Muslim.

c) **The Southeastern provinces** of Harar and Bale in the Ogaden are largely Muslim (Somali, Arusi Oromo, Boran), but with some animistic peoples too. Virtually no evangelical churches exist. 500,000 Somalis have fled to Somalia. Other Somalis are being reached in northeast Kenya through Kenyan, **SIM** and other missionaries. Somali literature and radio broadcasts are prepared in Nairobi.

d) **The unreached animistic peoples of south and west.** Although this is the area of highest concentration of evangelicals, and most successful cross-cultural evangelistic outreach by nationals to the many peoples of the area, a few peoples are still totally unreached: Ari; Dime; Anuak; Dasenach 22,000; Turkana; Bencho 7,000; Maji 22,000 and Suri 20,000.

e) **The Muslims** in all parts of the land have proved most resistant and out of 12 million possibly only a few hundred have come to faith in Christ. Pray that the Marxist plans to stir up Christian-Muslim antagonism may fail, and that the loving witness of Christians may break down barriers of history, prejudice and culture, and set many Muslims free through Jesus.

7. **Bible translation and distribution is an expanding ministry** despite pressures and limitations on distribution. Praise God that the revolutionary government reversed the old imperial government ban on publication of non-Amharic Scriptures. Pray specifically for:

a) **The Bible Society** involvement in 21 translation projects despite the expropriation of its HQ and many pressures on personnel.

b) **Translation work** on NT in Kambalfa, Hadiya, Kafa, Amaaro and Burji, and OT in Amharic, Oromo, Wolayta and Anuak continues. Pray for the translators and complex computer technology being used to speed the task. Pray for training schemes run for national translators — *at least* 30 languages need translators.

c) **Distribution** is permitted, but difficult. Importation of Scriptures is frequently delayed by the authorities. NTs in five languages have just been printed.

d) **The Key Scriptures Programme** in 15 languages has been of inestimable value in speeding the dissemination of 1,600 key verses of Scripture in booklet and cassette form.

e) **Scripture Union** could have a vital role to stimulate Scripture reading, but needs much prayer for an effective ministry to develop.

8. **Christian literature is in short supply.** The intensive government literacy campaign is creating millions of new readers hungry for *any* reading materials. The KHC press in Addis Ababa is working at full capacity producing teaching aids, books and commentaries, which are distributed without much restriction. However, no Christian magazine has been published since 1981. Pray that this ban may be lifted.

9. **Relief work** in drought and war-stricken areas is being undertaken by **SIMAid, World Vision** and over 40 other relief agencies, in association with the government. The assistance of **MAF** has facilitated distribution of food in some areas. Community development through the churches has been a major factor in moderating official pressures on Christians. Those involved in the outreach in rural areas need prayer for wisdom, patience and divine protection. Teams of Christian aid workers are also giving much encouragement to Christians in areas where churches have been closed, and also witnessing in previously unevangelized areas.

10. **The use of cassettes** for teaching of, as yet, unpublished Scriptures has been a vital tool for church growth. Pray for the provision of supplies and effective distribution.

11. **Radio.** Transmissions in Amharic and Somali are prepared in Nairobi for broadcast by **FEBA**, Seychelles. Pray for this programme to be widely received and expanded into other languages.

Latin America

Apr 25

FALKLAND ISLANDS

(Crown Colony of Falkland Islands or Islas Malvinas)

Area 16,300 sq.km. 200 islands in three groups: Falklands, South Georgia, S.Sandwich Is. in South Atlantic.

Population approx. 3,000. Indigenous growth 0.9%.

Peoples
Falkland islander (97% British) 68%.
British military forces, construction workers, etc. 21%.

Economy: Based on sheep products, but considerable potential for oil, fisheries, etc. Income/person $6,000 (43% of USA).

Capital: Stanley 1,500. Urbanization 50%.

Politics: Self-governing UK Colony. Argentinian claims as **Islas Malvinas** led to 1982 War of S. Atlantic.

Religion
Non-religious/Atheist 26.5%. Especially among military personnel.
Baha'i and **Other** 3.5%.
Christian 70%. Large majority non-practising.
Roman Catholic 10%. 300a; 180m.
Marginal 0.5%.
Protestant 60%. 1,800a; 300m.
Denominations 2.

1. **The traumatic Argentinian invasion** and their subsequent ejection by British forces in 1982, decisively affected the economic, political and spiritual life of the once complacent Falkland Islanders. Pray for a turning to God.

2. **There are only two small evangelical congregations** (Anglican and the Tabernacle United Free Church) and a handful of actively witnessing Christians.

3. **The British forces** based on the Islands face a lonely, thankless task — pray for openness to the gospel and to Christian witness by believers in the forces.

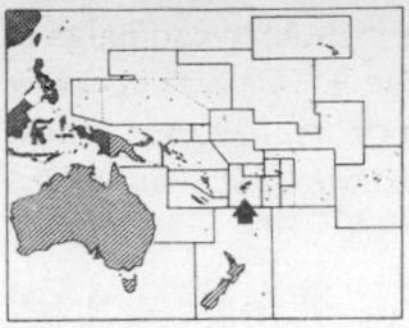

FIJI

(The Dominion of Fiji)

Area 18,000 sq.km. Two larger and 104 smaller inhabited islands.

Population 684,000. Annual growth 1.6%. People per sq.km. 37.

Peoples
Indian 50.8%. Mainly descendants of imported indentured labour (1879-1916) and subsequent immigration by Gujaratis and Sikhs.
Fijian 45.0%. The indigenous Polynesian-Melanesians speaking 22 dialects.
Pacific islander 1.3%. Samoan, Solomoni, Tongan.
Rotuman 1.2%. Polynesians on Rotuma Island.
Other minorities 1.9%. European 6,000; Chinese 5,500.

Literacy 88%. **Official language:** English. Commonly used: Hindustani, Bau Fijian.

Capital: Suva 136,000. Urbanization 46% (mainly Indians).

Economy: Rather dependent on the sugar industry and tourism. The Indian community dominates all commercial activities. Income/person $1,800 (13% of USA). Inflation 9.9%.

Politics: Independence from Britain in 1970 as a parliamentary democracy. There is a delicate balance of power towards the minority indigenous Fijians, but Indian resentments over the voting system and land tenure are contentious political issues.

Religion
Hindu 40.5%. 80% of all Indians.
Muslim 7.8%. 15% of all Indians. Sunni Islam and some Ammadiyah.
Sikh 0.7%. **Baha'i** 0.2%.
Non-religious/Atheist 0.8%.
Christian 50%.
Roman Catholic 8.1%. 55,500a; 28,800m.
Foreign marginal 1%. Largely Mormon, some Jehovah's Witnesses.
Indigenous marginal 0.3%. Three small groups.
Protestant 40%. 272,000a; 73,000m. Denominations 18. Largest (adult members):

Methodist	38,500
Seventh Day Adventist Ch.	8,900
Assemblies of God	6,000
Anglican	5,500
Anglican Orthodox	800
Brethren	600

Evangelical 8.1% of population.
Missionaries to Fiji 62 (1:11,000 people), mainly from Australia and USA.
Missionaries from Fiji 46 (1:5,000 Protestants), mainly Methodist, **CCC**.

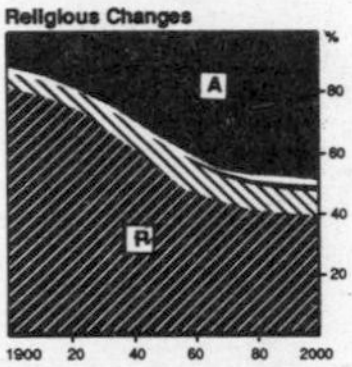

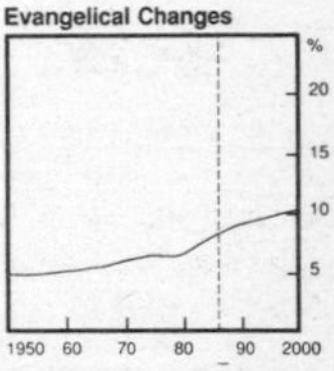

1. **The indigenous Fijians have been Christian for 100 years**, but the older churches are more cultural than spiritual; 90% of all Methodists are regular church attenders! Legalism, nominalism and lack of evangelism characterize the majority of churches. Yet there is an openness in the Methodist Church to biblical evangelism and teaching. Pray for a deep spiritual awakening. The newer evangelical churches and Mormons are growing quite rapidly. There are groups of charismatic believers that are growing in some sections of the Methodists, Anglicans and RCs.

2. **Tension between the two major communities** limits concern among Fijian Christians for the evangelization of the Indian majority. Pray that true believers may demonstrate that the Cross has broken down barriers to fellowship.

3. **Unreached peoples:**
   a) Alcoholism and broken homes are major social evils among Fijians. Pray for the **Salvation Army** and others seeking to reach out to such with counsel and the gospel.
   b) **Many outlying islands** are nominally Christian, but have been little exposed to genuine lived-out Christianity. Pray for those involved in boat ministry from island to island (**YWAM, UBS**-Daystar III).

c) **The large Hindu and Sikh community** is patchily evangelized and rather resistant to the gospel, but since 1951 there has been a steady stream of converts into Methodism, RC, **AoG, Brethren**, etc. However, less than 1% have become believers.

d) **The 53,000 Muslim community** is tightly knit and very resistant to the gospel. Little is being done to reach them, and the few converted to Christ have suffered considerable persecution.

4. **Leadership training for the churches.** Fiji plays an important role for the whole South Pacific. Pray for the Methodist Theological College, the **AoG** Bible School (65 students), and Ambassadors For Christ Bible School (11 students). Pray also for a stronger evangelical witness in the former.

5. **Missionary vision in the Fijian church is not as strong as it used to be**; pray for Fijians overseas and for a rekindling of enthusiasm for world evangelization. Over 270 Fijians have served as long-term missionaries over the last 120 years.

6. **Young people and students** are very responsive. Pray for the work of **CCC, YWAM**, Youth For Christ, **IFES, SU** and **CEF** through whom thousands are being evangelized. Pray for the integration of these young Christians in local congregations. Pray especially for the University of the South Pacific in Suva to which students from all over the Pacific come – often from islands where there is only nominal Christianity.

7. **The Bible Society of the South Pacific is based in Fiji.** Pray for their endeavours in undertaking surveys of translation needs (much needed in Fiji's dialects now), translation work, printing and distribution of God's Word throughout the Pacific.

FINLAND
(The Republic of Finland)

The West

Apr 27

Area 337,000 sq.km. This cold northern land is 70% forest and 10% lake.

Population 4,900,000. Annual growth 0.5%. People per sq.km. 15.

Peoples
Finn 93.2%. Speaking several Uralic languages (Finnish and Karelian) very different to the Indo-European languages.
Swedish 6.5%. Gradually being assimilated into the majority or emigrating.
Lapp 0.1%. 4,000 speaking three dialects.
Other minorities — Gypsy 8,000; Russian 4,000.

Literacy 100%. **Official languages:** Finnish, Swedish. **All languages** 7. **Bible translations** 2Bi 1NT 4por.

Capital: Helsinki 873,000. Urbanization 63%.

Economy: Strong, specialized, export-oriented economy based on wood products and industry. Income/person $10,440 (74% of USA).

Politics: Independent from Russia in 1917. Parliamentary democracy whose neutrality in the East-West confrontation is obligatory by treaty with USSR, its suspicious, giant neighbour.

Religion: The Lutheran Church is a People's Church with close links with the government. There is complete religious freedom.
Non-religious/Atheist 6.8%.
Jews 1,500. **Muslim** 1,000.
Christian 93%.
Roman Catholic 0.06%. 3,100a; 2,170m.
Orthodox 1%. 49,500a; 34,700m. Both Finnish and Russian.
Marginal groups 0.64%. 31,410a. Largest (adherents):

Jehovah's Witnesses	27,600
Mormons	3,790

Protestant 91.5%. 4,480,000a; 3,036,000m. Most Free Church members have not severed links with the People's Church. Denominations 26. Largest (adult members):

Evangelical Lutheran Church	2,959,000
Pentecostal Revival	38,000
Salvation Army	9,800
Free Church	7,000
Seventh Day Adventist Church	5,870
Baptist Churches (2)	2,500
Other Pentecostal Churches (6)	7,800

Evangelical approx. 16% of population.
Missionaries from Finland 700 (1:6,400 Protestants).
Missionaries to Finland 47.

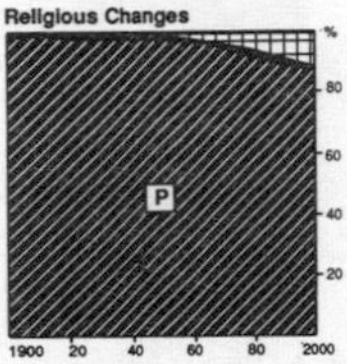

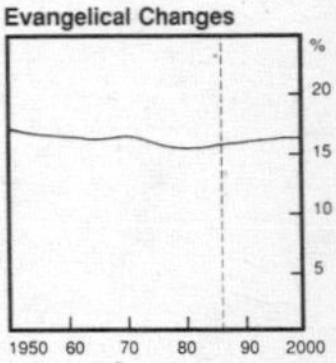

1. **Praise God for the awakenings and revivals over the past 200 years with a strong emphasis on prayer, repentance and confession.** The last revival occurred during the 1960s. Present interest in spiritual things could lead to revival again. May expectancy result in it happening — for the blessing of the world! There is a steady but slow increase in the number of active Christians.

2. **The Lutheran Church** is much more evangelical than most in Europe — a heritage of the revival movements that have deeply influenced its spirituality. This body is an umbrella for a large number of autonomous fellowships, revival and prayer groups and missions, where most committed Christians find their fellowship and platform for evangelism. About 15-20% of the population would regularly attend such meetings.

3. **The Free Churches, both Pentecostal and non-Pentecostal, are generally declining in numbers.** There is insufficient vision for evangelism and church growth, and far more could be done if there were a greater unity among believers.

4. **Few Christians are involved in direct evangelism.** Pray that Finns be freed from their natural reserve to be effective witnesses at home and overseas.

5. **Work among young people is** proving fruitful — through SEY(**IFES**), **CCC**, **Navs.**, etc. Pray for evangelistic outreach and discipling ministries among young people. 90% of Finnish young people attend confirmation camps!

6. **The Finnish Bible Society** has played a very significant role in promoting the translation, publication and distribution of the Scriptures. Translation is being undertaken into portions of Inari Lapp, but two other dialects, Utsjok and Koltta, are without any portions. The Karelian Finnish language needs a Bible translation — the majority live in the USSR.

7. **The missionary vision** has grown due to the revival in the '60s and early '70s. There are now about 700 missionaries (approx 320 Lutheran, 300 Pentecostal). Many young people have been stirred about the challenge of the unreached but face many obstacles: the high educational and professional requirements of the six recognized missionary societies within the Lutheran Church, the cultural isolation of Finland, and the limited vision among believers to support missionaries in interdenominational and international missions. Pray out many to the needy harvest fields!

8. **Less reached peoples:**

a) **Gypsies**, over half speaking Romany. Most are superficially Christian, but few are committed in their faith.

b) **The Swedish minority** is nominally Christian, but Evangelicals are proportionately fewer.

c) **The small immigrant Muslim** population.

d) **Russians.** Finnish neutrality puts the country in a unique relationship with the USSR. Many USSR citizens come as tourists to Finland, and many Finns have close business contacts with the USSR. Pray that these links may be sensitively and well used for the sake of the gospel.

FRANCE
(The French Republic)

The West

Apr 28-30

Area 551,000 sq.km. The largest country in Western Europe.

Population 54,556,000. Annual growth 0.4%. People per sq.km. 99.

Peoples

Indigenous 90.2%.

French 79%.

Minorities 10%. Alsatian 1,465,000; Breton 1,302,000; Flemish 380,000; Corsican 290,000; Basque 160,000.

Other minorities 2%. Jews 750,000; West Indian Antillean 230,000; Gypsy 160,000.

Foreign residents 9%.

North African/Middle Easterner 4%. Algerian 1,172,000; Moroccan 640,000; Tunisian 298,000; Turk 160,000; Irani 30,000.

European 3.2%. Portuguese 857,000; Italian 469,000; Spanish 430,000; Armenian 210,000; Polish 100,000; Yugoslavian 70,000.

Asian 1.2%. Vietnamese 250,000; Chinese 190,000; Laotian 100,000; Cambodian 70,000.

African 0.5%. Mostly from Francophone West Africa. Malian 20,000.

Literacy 98%. **Official language:** French.

Capital: Paris 10,413,000. The capital dominates the life of the country. Other major cities: Lyon 1,300,000; Marseille 1,230,000; Lille 1,100,000. Urbanization 79%.

Economy: Economic stability and growth gave the nation one of the highest standards of living in Europe. Oil price rises and world recession have bitten deep into those standards. Income/person $10,390 (74% of USA). Inflation 10%.

Politics: Democratic republic with strong executive presidency. A member of the EEC.

Religion: Secular state with freedom of religion.

Non-religious/Atheist 16.0%. Many were baptized as Christians.

Muslim 4.6%. North African, African, Turk, etc.

Jews 1.1%.

Christian 78%.

Roman Catholic 74%. Regular practising 6%. 40,500,000a; 29,800,000m.

Other Catholic 0.2%. Over 73 small groups.

Orthodox groups (17) 0.8%

Marginal groups 0.6%. Over 25 cults. Largest (adherents):

Jehovah's Witnesses	166,100
Mormons	13,100

Protestant 2%. 1,140,000a; 655,000m. Denominations 60 (also many independent congregations). Some of the largest (adult members):

Reformed Church	274,000
Lutheran Churches (3 groups)	145,000
Assemblies of God	75,000
Ref. Ch. of Alsace & Lorraine	47,000
Gypsy Pentecostal Church	15,600
Free Pentecostal Church	8,000
Federation of Baptist Churches	3,800
Brethren	3,200

Evangelical 0.63% of population.

Missionaries to France 905 (1:60,000 people) in 80 agencies.

Missionaries from France 373 (1:3,100 Protestants) in 32 agencies.

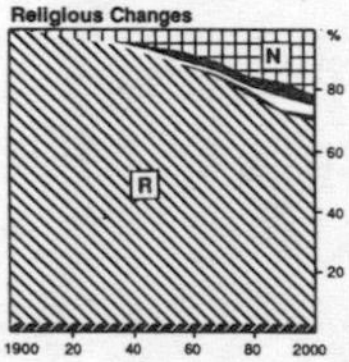

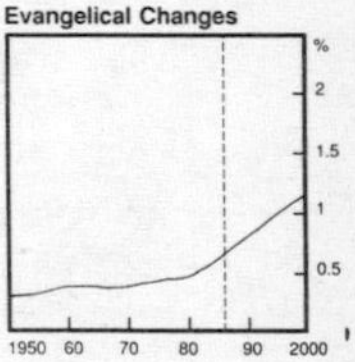

1. **France is a mission field.** This is the opinion both of Catholics and Evangelicals alike — though this suggestion would horrify most French. One of the world's most cultured and sophisticated nations is reaping the barren fruits of 200 years of secularization. Barriers to the gospel are many — intellectualism, rationalism, widespread involvement in the occult, individualism and a nodding acquaintance with institutional Catholicism. These must be broken down by fervent prayer. France is not only needy, but also hardened to the gospel.

2. **The unreached sectors of French society** are many:
   a) Over 43 million French people have no **real** link with a Christian church. Many more have a profound ignorance of the gospel.
   b) Large cities like Nancy, Nantes and Metz are spiritual deserts with four to five small evangelical churches in each.

c) Paris has one evangelical church for every 250,000 people.
d) Three of the 95 department capitals have no evangelical church.
e) Of the 38,000 *communes*, 36,000 have no resident evangelical witness.
f) The island of Corsica with 250,000 people has six small groups with 300 evangelical believers.
g) The Basques in the southwest are virtually without an evangelical witness in their language.
h) Many areas in central France and Brittany have few evangelical congregations.

3. **The unreached minorities:**
a) **The large Portuguese, Spanish and Italian communities** are more receptive than in their native lands. They have generally not adapted well to French society, but few believers evangelize them in their own language. There are but seven Portuguese or Spanish congregations for one million people.
b) **Jews.** France has the largest Jewish community in Europe with 400,000 in Paris alone. Sixteen workers in four missions labour among them (**MT**, **GMU** and the French TMPI). There are a few small groups of believers.
c) **The North Africans** number 2,200,000. They often congregate in urban ghettos. The vast majority are Muslims. Few have been evangelized, and many are antagonized by the racism of "Christians". Pray for the French and foreign organizations seeking to reach them. The largest of these, **NAM** with 74 missionaries, has an extensive ministry within France to them and also by means of radio and BCCs to France and North Africa; **Radio School of the Bible** has also had an impact. There are about 700 Christians converted from a Muslim background, but they and their small groups face much opposition.
d) **The Berbers** form a large minority of the North Africans, but no specific effort is being made to reach them in their own languages — Rif, Kabyle, etc.
e) **Black Africans** have come in large numbers as students, refugees and work-seekers from Muslim areas of Francophone Africa. There is little specific outreach to the Bambara; Wolof 30,000; Malinke 25,000; Soninke 5,000, etc. Many return to their homelands as leaders but influenced more by Marx and materialism than the gospel. Where are the workers?
f) **Indo-Chinese.** The flood of refugees generated by the tragic events in Vietnam is abating; the emotional and cultural shocks are not. They need the comfort that only Jesus can give. The present efforts by the few Laotian, Vietnamese, and Cambodian pastors and missionaries (**SAO**, **CMA**) cover the many scattered communities. A number have become Christians. There are four Chinese churches with three full-time workers, three Laotian, two Vietnamese and one Cambodian.
g) **The growing Turkish, Irani and Afghani** communities need to be evangelized.

4. **The influential Roman Catholic Church is in turmoil** with many tensions among the conservative traditionalists, liberals, modernists, radicals and the charismatic movement. The latter has opened the hearts of many to the truths of God's Word and the acceptance of the need to be born-again. Pray that many may be won to the Lord.

5. **The Protestants have had a long and glorious history.** At the height of the Reformation 48% of the population was Protestant. The persecution of these Huguenots in the 17th and 18th centuries reduced this to the present 2%. Protestants are more numerous in the southwest and in Alsace, but most are nominal and never attend church. Pastors in the Reformed Church are usually liberal in theology and some are radical in politics. Decline is the norm, but there are staunch evangelical believers in many congregations. Pray for a move of the Spirit in the large Reformed and Lutheran Churches. **OM** France has bold evangelistic plans for the nation entitled "Hope for the '80s". "Mission France" in 1986 is also a major evangelistic effort. Pray for these outreaches to make a lasting impact.

6. **The Evangelicals are few and scattered.** Growth has been slow but steady. There are about 1,300 evangelical congregations and a further 500 small groups in the whole country; most are very small. Many reckon that the number of truly born-again believers is but one per 1,000 people. There has been growth among the Assemblies of God, Baptists and a

number of smaller evangelical groups. The most responsive have been the Gypsies (with nearly half their total number now church-going as a result of a remarkable people movement) and the Antilleans (who form a large proportion of Parisian churches). Revival is the need — few Christians are delivered from spiritual bondages; fear of witnessing, indifference, marriage with unbelievers, and church divisions are the baleful results.

7. **There is a great need for Christian workers.** There are estimated to be 1,360 full-time French evangelical Christian workers in the country, i.e., one worker for every 40,000 people. Pray for the raising up of spiritual men of God for the ministry.

8. **The evangelical Bible schools and seminaries** are important for the whole French-speaking world. The significant ones — Lamorlaye Bible Institute (**GEM**) with 80 students from 20 countries, Nogent Bible Institute, Vaux Seminary for Free and Reformed Church students and Aix-en-Provence Seminary for Reformed students — are all evangelical and full. Many French believers also study at the Emmaus Bible School in Switzerland, and the Belgian Bible Institute in Heverlee, Belgium. Pray for the staff and students and for their influence through France and the French-speaking world.

9. **French Protestants are making a remarkable missionary contribution considering their small numbers.** This is strategically vital since Francophone lands include some of the neediest in the world. French missionaries serve in 34 lands in both French and international missions. The largest are the Reformed/Lutheran DEFAP (136 workers), Assemblies of God (76), Mission Biblique (41), CEM (34), Christian Action in Orient (17), **AME** (10). Pray for the French edition of ***Operation World*** and all other efforts to stimulate missionary vision.

10. **Young people are more receptive to the gospel.** Many groups and missions have specialized in this ministry — Youth for Christ, **CCC**, Young Life, Eau Vive, **ECM, TEAM** in running camps, clubs, coffee bars and ministering in secondary schools; Teen Challenge among drug addicts; **SU** in schools and through Bible reading notes. Pray for many young people to be saved and integrated into good evangelical churches — the latter step usually being much harder than the former!

11. **Foreign missions have a vital servant role to play in evangelism and church planting.** There are just not enough full-time French Christian workers to begin to meet the need. Missionaries find it hard to adapt and win acceptance, and all too often church planting has had limited effectiveness when foreign patterns are imported. Increasingly missionaries are finding a useful church planting ministry within indigenous structures (**SBC**, France Mission, Eau Vive, **BCU**, **ECM**, **WT**, **TEAM**, **UFM**, **GEM**, **GMU**, **WEC**, etc.) Fruit is hard-won, discouragements many, and the missionary dropout rate high. Pray for stickability, effectiveness, and spiritual power.

12. **Literature is a vital tool for evangelism and discipleship.** Literature campaigns by **EHC**, **CCC**, and **OM** have been useful to sow the seed widely. Pray for Christian publishing houses and bookstores (40; nine of which are **CLC**) who disseminate Christian literature.

13. **The Bible Society** published the *Good News Bible* in French in 1982. Pray for the impact of God's Word. Only 5% of the population owns a Bible and 80% have never even handled one.

14. **Radio and TV evangelism** has become a new tool since broadcasting licences were more easily obtained. Pray that Christians may cooperate to make effective use of these media. An association to promote this was started in 1982. Radio Evangile (French branch of **TWR**) is involved in training French believers for local broadcasting. The latter also has a significant radio ministry via **TWR** Monte Carlo (16 hours/month). **HCJB** broadcasts a further 77 hours/month to France from Ecuador.

15. **There are 68 universities and 800,000 students;** 100,000 of these are foreign students in Paris alone. Ministry to these students has national and worldwide implications! The evangelical witness has been slow to develop, but now there are 1,500 students linked with the 55 GBU(**IFES**) groups, though most are very small. Students are more open than ever, searching for reality in an ideological vacuum.

Caribbean

May 1

FRENCH GUIANA
(The Department of French Guiana)

Area 91,000 sq.km. Sparsely inhabited jungle territory in northeast South America.

Population 68,000. Annual growth 1.9%. People per sq.km. 0.8.

Peoples
Creole 54%. Mixed Black, White and Asian.
French 25%. 65% locally born.
Black 7.8%. Bush Negro.
Asian 5.2%. Chinese 2,200; Javanese 700; Hmong 600.
Amerindian 3.2%. 7 tribes.
Other minorities 4.8%. Brazilian 2,200, etc.

Literacy 78%. **Official language:** French. **All languages** 9. **Bible translations** 1Bi 2NT 2por.

Capital: Cayenne 40,000. Urbanization 79%.

Economy: For years infamous as a French penal colony. Undeveloped and dependent on French economic aid. Income/person $2,700 (19% of USA). Inflation 10.8%.

Politics: Overseas Department of France.

Religion: Situation as for Metropolitan France.
Non-religious/Atheist 5%.
Tribal/Animist 3.5%.
Chinese religions 1.3%. **Muslim** 1%. **Bahai** 0.7%.
Christian 88.3%. Nominal 13%. Affiliated 75.3%.
Roman Catholic 67.2%. Practising 25%. 45,700a; 24,000m.
Marginal groups 1.7%. 1,140a; 341m. All Jehovah's Witnesses.
Protestant 6.5%. 4,400a; 2,100m. Denominations 7. Largest (adult members):

Seventh Day Adventist Church	750
Assemblies of God	400
Reformed Church	350
Brethren	270

Evangelical 4.3% of population.
Missionaries to French Guiana 14 (1:4,900 people).

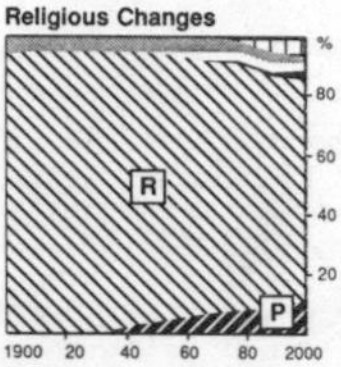

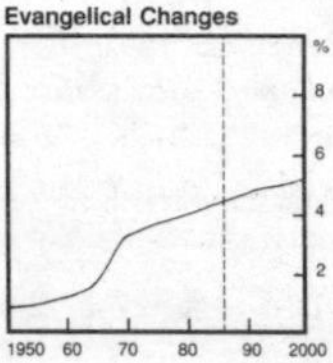

1. **This long-neglected land, with its diverse peoples, has only been partially evangelized by Evangelicals.** Among the many challenges are these peoples:
   a) **The Amerindian tribes** — never has any work been established among the inland tribes, but Christians of these tribes in Suriname and Brazil have made evangelistic forays. Pray for the Arawak 250, Emerillon 100, Oyapi 100, Palikur 120, and Wayana 250.
   b) The nominally Catholic **Caribs** 1,400.
   c) The inland settlements of largely animistic **Bush Negroes** 2,000.
   d) The **Chinese**. A small outreach by Suriname Chinese Christians has begun.

2. **The most effective church planting work** has been that of the **Assemblies of God** (among French-speaking) and **Brethren** (French, Hmong) along the coastal strip. The **Southern Baptists** commenced work in 1982.

3. **The Hmong refugees from Laos/Vietnam** are largely animistic but open to the gospel. There are now two little assemblies among them, but mature Hmong leadership is lacking.

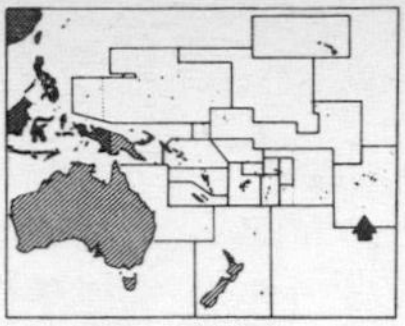

FRENCH POLYNESIA

(The Territory of French Polynesia)

Pacific

May 2

Area 4,000 sq.km. Five island archipelagos — (Society, Tuamotu, Marquesas, Austral and Gambier) in south-central Pacific. Tahiti is the largest island 1,042 sq.km.

Population 164,000. Annual growth 2.2%. People per sq.km. 41.

Peoples
Polynesian 75% (5 distinct languages). Tahitian 84,000; Tuamotuan 18,000; Marquesan 9,700; Tubuaian 9,500.
French and Euronesian (mixed) 16%.
Chinese 7%.

Literacy 95%. **Official language:** French. **All languages** 7. **Bible translations** 1Bi 2por.

Capital: Papeete 118,000. Urbanization 76%.

Economy: Prosperous through tourism, French military expenditure and aid. Income/person $8,190 (58% of USA). Inflation 10%.

Politics: French Overseas Territory, but with increasing agitation for independence.

Religion: Separation of Church and state, religious freedom.
Non-religious 12%. **Other** 1%.

Christian 87%. Nominal 11%. Affiliated 76%.
Roman Catholic 32.1%. Practising 20%. 52,700a; 27,400m.
Marginal groups (5) 7.4%. 12,000a; 6,600m. Largest (adherents):

Mormons	6,400
Sanito (indigenous)	3,900
Jehovah's Witnesses	1,600

Protestant 36.3%. 59,500a; 31,900m. Denominations 6. Largest (adherents):

Evang. Ch. of Polynesia (liberal)	28,250
Seventh Day Adventist Church	2,300
Pentecostal Church	840

Evangelical 3.9% of population.
Missionaries to French Polynesia 24 (1:6,800 people).
Missionaries from French Polynesia 0.

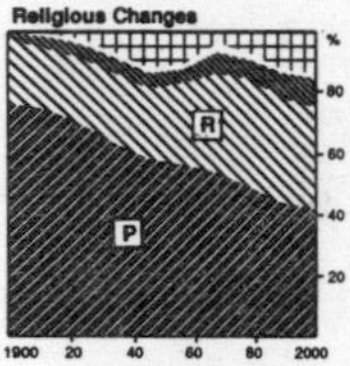

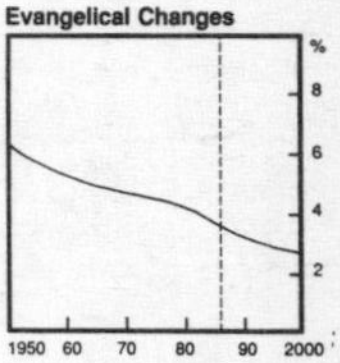

1. **Tahiti is a paradise gone tragically wrong.** Once a Christian nation, sending missionaries all over the Pacific, society is now collapsing through promiscuity, alcoholism, drug abuse and the breakdown of family life. Young people are frustrated and seeking answers in their confusion, but where are the fervent messengers of the gospel? No longer do Tahitian missionaries leave for other lands.

2. **Those with a vital personal faith are rare.** As a result, there is a reversion to the bondage of pagan occultism and a multiplication of syncretic and foreign sects — especially Mormons. Pray for a spiritual revolution to take place among the many nominal Catholic and Protestant Christians.

3. **There is only a handful of evangelical churches** (mainly on Tahiti) and very few evangelical pastors. Pray for those national and missionary workers who are preaching the gospel in very discouraging circumstances. There are several missionary workers of the **AoG**, Baptists and **YWAM**.

4. **Unreached peoples.** Almost all adhere to a form of Christianity, but many parts of these islands are without a clear gospel witness — especially the Mangarevans on the Gambier Islands and the Marquesans and Tuamotuans. Biblical Christianity is hardly known in these islands since they do not understand Tahitian, the only language with the Bible.

5. **Bible translation** is needed for at least two of the languages spoken in outlying island groups — Marquesas and Tuamotu. **SIL** is looking to God for two linguistic teams to start work.

Africa
May 3

GABON
(The Gabonese Republic)

Area 268,000 sq.km. 80% dense tropical rain forest.

Population 820,000. Annual growth 1.8%. People per sq.km. 3.

Peoples
Indigenous peoples 82%. About 40 distinct ethno-linguistic groups. Fang (5 groups) 272,000; Eshira-Punu (4) 136,000; Kota-Teke (9) 127,000; Ndjabi-Mbete (5) 102,000; Myene (6) 34,000; Okande and other smaller groups 37,000; Pygmies 5,000.
Other African peoples 12%. Refugees and migrant workers from Equatorial Guinea, Benin, etc.
French 6%.

Literacy 30%. **Official language:** French. **Trade language:** Fang. **All languages** 38. **Bible translations** 2Bi 4NT 8por.

Capital: Libreville 250,000. Urbanization 36%.

Economy: Country underpopulated, yet with immense resources of wood, oil and other minerals. One of Africa's most prosperous and stable economies. Income/person $4,250 (30% of USA).

Politics: Retains close economic and political links with France since independence in 1960. A one-party state.

Religion: There is freedom of religion for all.

African traditionalist 14%. In actual practice the predominant religious force.
Muslim 4%. Increasing fairly rapidly since 1973.
Christian 82%. A high rate of nominalism and superficiality.
Roman Catholic 55%. 450,000a; 297,000m.
Indigenous marginal groups (3+) 10%. 80,000a.
Foreign marginal groups (4) 0.6%. 5,300a.
Protestant 17%. 138,000a; 39,320m. Denominations 4. Largest (adult members):

Evang. Ch. of Gabon — Ang. (liberal)	22,300
Evang. Ch. of South Gabon (**CMA**)	10,800
Evang. Ch. of Gabon — Sima	4,000

Evangelical 5.7% of population.
Missionaries to Gabon 53 (1:15,500) in four agencies.

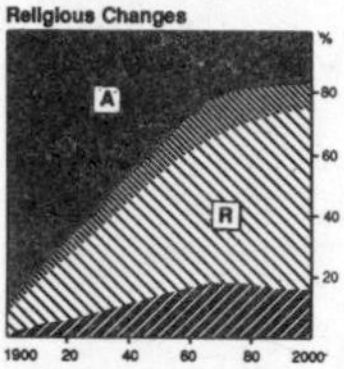

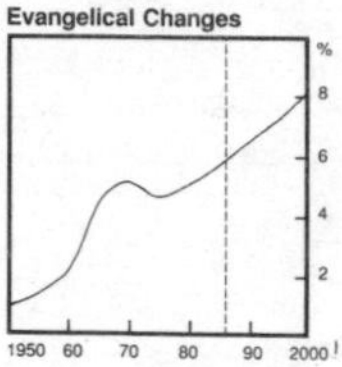

1. **Praise God for present freedom for the gospel,** but pray that the many years of neglect by evangelical missions may be made good. The great majority of the population has never been exposed to the life-changing gospel.

2. **Islam is the fastest growing religious group in the country.** The conversion of the President to Islam in 1973 initiated this growth. Many new mosques are now being built. Pray that the concern of believers at this development may stimulate vital and effective evangelism among Muslims and non-Muslims alike.

3. **Unreached peoples** are many, but the true situation is unclear and the spiritual needs inadequately surveyed. Over much of the country there is a nominal adherence to Catholicism; little culturally relevant evangelism or Bible translation work has been done. Much remains to be done in the capital, centre and north of the country. Pray for the following:

a) **In Libreville** less than 0.5% of the population are evangelical Christians, but the **CMA** Church is growing fast.

b) **The Fang** are the dominant people in Gabon, but many parts of their area have never been evangelized. Some areas in the east are closed to Protestant mission work. The strong Bwiti movement among the Fang is a mixture of paganism with Christian elements and has never been challenged by vigorous biblical evangelism.

c) **The Kota** (50,000) are unevangelized, with only *one* known born-again believer. Other groups such as the Kele (30,000), Wumbvu, Tsogo, Bakwele, Mbete and Seke are scarcely touched by the gospel.

d) **The various Pygmy tribes** are little known or understood and spiritually neglected.

e) **The refugees from Equatorial Guinea** are still numerous in the north. Very little evangelism has been directed to these people.

4. **The major Protestant denomination** is the fruit of French missionary work, but the legacy of liberal theology has been a stagnant, nominal daughter church with a leadership more concerned with social issues than evangelism. Pray for a move of God's Spirit.

5. **The evangelical witness** is limited to a Bible-based breakaway from the above body with some churches in Libreville and the north, and to the daughter church of **CMA** missionaries in the south. There are 42 **CMA** missionaries assisting in this body. Up to 1985 **CMA** was the *only* Protestant missionary agency in the country. God gave revival and a period of rapid growth in the south in 1968, but the last 10 years have been years of slower progress. **AEF** entered the north in 1985.

6. **Present opportunities in cities, mining communities, rural areas and schools are being lost because of the lack of workers.** There is only one small Bible school in the country (Ev. Ch. of S. Gabon), so pray for the calling of both pastors and cross-cultural workers for evangelism and church planting. Pray also for the TEE students, 175 of whom are in Libreville.

7. **Bible translation has been a neglected ministry**. Two languages have the whole Bible, four the New Testament, and eight more have just portions of the Scriptures (all-too-often archaic). There may be 27 languages for which NTs should be provided. Pray for adequate surveys of linguistic needs, and for translators to be raised up for peoples who need the Word of God in their own tongue. **GRI** has made recordings available in 25 Gabonese languages.

GAMBIA
(Republic of The Gambia)

Africa

May 4

Area 11,300 sq.km. A narrow enclave within Senegal and extending 400 km. along the Gambia River.

Population 724,000. Annual growth +2%. People per sq.km. 64.

Peoples: Over 11 ethnic groups. Largest: Mandingo 326,000; Fula 140,000; Wolof 105,000; Jola 51,000; Sarakole 47,000; Manjako 23,000; Aku 4,300, etc. The peoples are becoming very intermingled.

Literacy 10%. **Official language:** English. **Trade languages:** Mandingo, Wolof. **All languages** 12. **Bible translations** 1Bi 5por.

Capital: Banjul 167,000. Urbanization 25%.

Economy: Subsistence agriculture, and dependent on groundnut cultivation. Income/person $250 (2% of USA).

Politics: Independent from Britain in 1965. An attempted coup in 1981 was quelled with the aid of Senegalese forces. A confederation with Senegambia was launched in 1982. Some progress to integrating policies and economies of the countries has been made.

Religion: Islam has steadily grown in influence. Most Muslims are members of one of the three Sufi brotherhoods.

Islam 87%. Strongest among the Mandingo, Fula, Wolof, and other smaller groups.

Traditional religions 10%. Mainly among the Jola and Manjako, but many of these peoples are becoming Muslim.

Christian 2.9%.

Roman Catholic 2.1%. 15,500a.

Protestant 0.7%. 5,000a. Denominations 4. Largest (adherents):

Methodist Church	2,400
Anglican Church	1,200
Evangelical Fellowship (**WEC**)	100

Evangelical 0.12% of population.

Missionaries to the Gambia 56 (1:12,900 people) in 7 agencies.

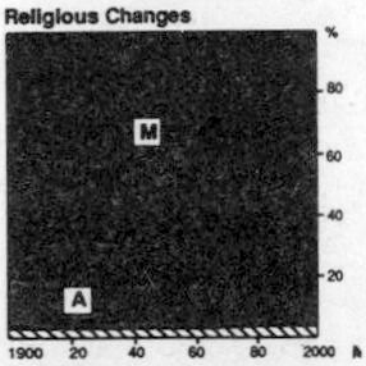

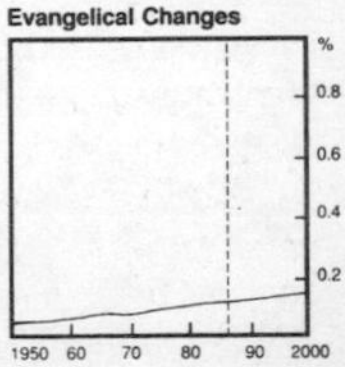

1. **Islam is dominant**, yet the land remains open for the gospel. Pray for both freedom to proclaim the gospel and openness of heart for Muslims to receive it. Little effort was ever directed by the older churches at reaching the Muslim majority; the key people being the Mandingo, a people made famous by Alex Haley's book ***Roots***. There is only a handful of believers among them.

2. **Islam is gradually gaining** ground in the few areas where there are pockets of uncommitted animist peoples. Pray for the evangelization of these peoples before the barriers of Islam further hinder the penetration of the gospel. There are many villages and towns up river where there has been little evangelism.

3. **Missionary work in the Gambia** was pioneered by the Anglicans and Methodists. Much of their work was confined to the Aku (Creole-speaking descendants of freed slaves in Banjul). The Catholics and Methodists have not seen significant advances among the other people groups. The Methodists have one rural Manjako and Malinke congregation. **WEC**, with 34 workers, has seen some small congregations emerge from Muslim backgrounds as a result of outreach through its medical and agricultural programme.

4. **The churches are largely nominal** and little credit to the gospel. Committed evangelical believers are very few indeed. Pray for a strong church to be raised up in the Gambia. There is only a handful of full-time Gambian Christian workers who preach the gospel.

5. **Young people** have flocked to Banjul suburban areas seeking work. Pray for ministries directed to them – **SU** in the secondary schools, and the youth work of **SBC**, **WEC** and YFC. Most youth work is in the capital and outlying area, though **WEC** has youth work inland as well.

GERMANY (EAST)
(German Democratic Republic)

Eastern Europe

May 5-6

Area 108,000 sq.km. The eastern 30% of the two Germanies.

Population 16,700,000. Annual growth -0.2%. Steadily decreasing since 1945 through emigration and low birth rates. People per sq.km. 154.

Peoples
German 95%.
Minority groups 2%. Slavic Sorbs, Wends, etc.
USSR military, etc. 3%. About 400,000 troops stationed in GDR.

Literacy 99%. **Official language:** German.

Capital: Berlin (East) 1,200,000. Urbanization 76%.

Economy: The GDR has become the most efficient and industrialized of the Communist satellite states in spite of post-war plunder by USSR occupation forces, the centralized bureaucratic economy, and unequal trade treaties. Income/person $6,000 (43% of USA).

Politics: Germany lost much of her eastern territories to the USSR and Poland at the end of World War II. The remaining third of the country was occupied by the Russians, who still maintain a large military presence. Although only theoretically independent, the world now recognizes it as a separate state. The German people showed their hatred of the Communist regime in an uprising in 1953, and by nearly three million fleeing to West Germany over the last 30 years. The infamous Wall surrounding the free enclave of West Berlin was built in 1961 to stop this flow. The whole frontier between the Germanies has since been similarly fortified. These are permanent reminders of the spiritual and moral failure of Communism.

Religion: Thirty years of subtle pressures on the powerful Protestant church have been replaced by a considerable relaxation since 1978 with greater internal freedoms for Christians.

Non-religious/Atheist 38.7%.

Christian 61.5%. Nominal 16.4%. Affiliated 45.1%.

Roman Catholic 7.4%. Practising 20%. 1,250,000a; 1,000,000m.

Marginal groups 0.87%. 147,000a. New Apostolic 105,000a., etc.

Protestant 36.7%. 6,200,000a; 4,910,000m. Denominations 19. Eight regional churches in two major groups (adherents):

EKU (Lutheran/Reformed)	3,000,000
VELK (Lutheran)	2,900,000

Free churches (adult members):

Methodist Church	35,000
Free Church Union (Baptist)	22,000
Seventh Day Adventist Church	10,000
Independent Lutheran	10,000
Reformed Church	8,400
Brethren	6,000

Evangelical 11% of population.

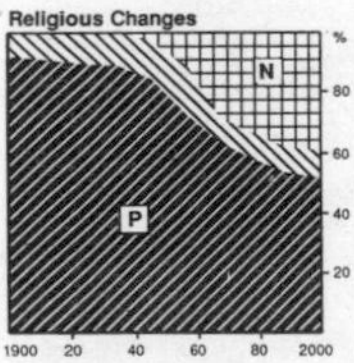

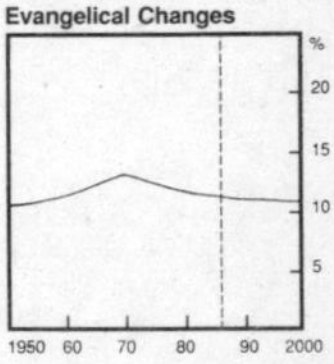

1. **Since 1978 there has been much more freedom for Christians** than in any other East European state. However, ceaseless and often subtle anti-religious propaganda has had an impact, and there has been a steady decline in membership of nearly all churches. Pray that believers may use present liberties to meet together and evangelize the many who have never entered a church. The rate of alcoholism (12% of the population) and the world's highest divorce rate demonstrate the spiritual need.

2. **East Germany is the only "Protestant" country in Eastern Europe.** Praise the Lord that the state authorities have been forced to come to terms with the strength of the Protestant presence — even to the extent of publically celebrating the 500-year commemoration of the birth of Luther! Yet the traumatic effects of the Church coming to terms with the new political realities have also brought a cleansing and healthy re-examination of structures. Pray for revival.

3. **The Decade of Mission was launched in 1980.** Pray that the churches may make evangelism their primary concern. Pray for the **Evangelical Alliance** which has become a focal point for the growing evangelical witness.

4. **Pastors are subjected to many pressures by the state.** Compromise is easy, but many have come to a personal commitment to the Lord. Many younger pastors seek to go to West Germany, and the government encourages this exodus. Pray for the pastors who remain that they may be stable and faithful to the Lord and their flocks. Pray for those pastors who fearlessly preach the gospel with great effect — there are an increasing number who do.

5. **The Church has gained the legal right to exist,** evangelize and administer its wide range of institutions after years of intense pressures. Pray that this hard-won battle may not be lost again through compromise with the state.

6. **Young people** have considerable freedom, but there is still some discrimination in education, and it is still very costly to follow Jesus in this atheistic state. The Communists provide alternative ceremonies as a substitute for baptism, confirmation and marriage that are not easy to refuse. There is a growing and enthusiastic response to the gospel, despite the danger such a response can bring to career advancement.

7. **Praise the Lord for many conversions** among people of all sections of the community. One of the main focuses for evangelism is actually Karl-Marx-Stadt! The charismatic movement has made considerable impact on church life.

8. **There are many nationalities represented** in the USSR military forces. Pray that some may be contacted and converted while in East Germany.

9. **Literature** is more freely available than in any other Communist land. 12% of all books produced are religious! Bibles and some Christian literature (censored) are sold in the shops, though there is a lack of good, new evangelical literature. Pray that this freedom may continue.

10. **The churches are still able to give theological training** to potential pastors. University theological faculties are dominated by Marxist staff, but the seminaries are still free of state interference. The Baptists and Methodists run their own seminaries. There is a serious shortage of suitable candidates for the ministry, and many congregations are without resident pastoral oversight.

11. **Christian radio.** The large and effective German branch of **TWR** in W.Germany produces a number of daily programmes for broadcasting to both Germanies. Weekly Christian programmes on radio and TV are permitted on state radio, but only for the State Churches which are largely liberal.

GERMANY (WEST)

(The Federal Republic of Germany)

The West

May 7-8

Area 248,000 sq.km. Nearly half of Germany's pre-World War II territory was lost to the USSR, Poland and Communist East Germany.

Population 60,900,000. Annual growth -0.27%. People per sq.km. 245. A further 16,700,000 Germans live in East Germany and 3,500,000 in E.Europe/USSR, and others in the Americas and South Africa/Namibia.

Peoples
German 92.6%. Danes 30,000.
Foreign 7.4%. Many immigrant workers and their families from:

S. Europe: Yugoslavs 613,000; Italians 565,000; Greeks 292,000; Spaniards 166,000; Portuguese 99,000.

Middle East/North Africa: Turks 1,552,000; Moroccans 44,000; Iranians 33,000; Tunisians 25,000, etc.

Asia: Chinese 40,000; Tamils from Sri Lanka 30,000; Vietnamese 26,000; Pakistanis and Indians 16,000; Koreans 14,000; Indonesians 9,000; Japanese 6,000.

Literacy 100%. **Official language:** German.

Capital: Bonn 515,000. Berlin 1,930,000, the former capital, is a divided city in the heart of East Germany. The western two-thirds is an island of liberty linked to the FRG, though not part of it. **Other major city complexes:** Ruhr Area 8,850,000; Hamburg 2,810,000; Stuttgart 2,790,000; Frankfurt 2,680,000; Munich 2,310,000. **Urbanization** 85%.

Economy: Highly industrialized, strong economy. The dramatic post-war recovery and growth has slowed and unemployment increased in the '80s. Income/person $11,420 (81% of USA).

Politics: After only 74 years as a united state, Germany was divided in 1945 into East (GDR) and West (FRG). The FRG became a sovereign federal democratic state with Länder in 1951. A member of EEC and NATO.

Religion: Religious freedom, but close cooperation between the government and the Roman Catholic Church and Protestant Established Churches (EKD) in religious education, radio, TV, church taxation through state channels, etc.

Non-religious/Atheist 5%.
Muslim 3%. Almost entirely immigrant minorities.
Jews 32,000 (564,000 in 1932 before the Nazi pogroms).
Christian 92%. Affiliated 86%. Only a minority of the population is involved in Christian activities.

Roman Catholic 42%. 25,600,000a; 19,700,000m. 70% hardly ever attend church.
Other Catholic groups (43) 0.1%.
Orthodox Churches (13) 0.8%. 485,000a. Greeks, E. Europeans.
Marginal groups (34) 1.5%. 892,000a; 515,000m. Largest (adherents):

New Apostolic Church	482,000
Jehovah's Witnesses (2 groups)	245,000
Mormons	27,500

Protestant (162 groups) 43%. 25,700,000a; 6,670,000m. Two major groupings:

Evangelische Kirche in Deutschland (EKD) 17 territorial or State Churches. 24,500,000a. Regular church attendance 1,400,000 (5.5% of those affiliated).

Free churches 1,200,000a; 420,000m. Total weekly church attendance 700,000. Denominations 150. Largest (adult members):

Baptists	60,000
Independent Lutheran Church	37,000
Methodist Church	33,500
Brethren	32,000
Seventh Day Adventist Church	25,000
Free Evangelical Churches	24,000
Assoc. of Free Pentecostal Chs	19,000
Mennonite Churches (2)	15,800

Conservative Evangelical 4.3% of population.

Missionaries to Germany 680.
Missionaries from Germany 2,686 (1:9,600 Protestants) in 62 agencies, including 311 short-term workers.

Religious Changes

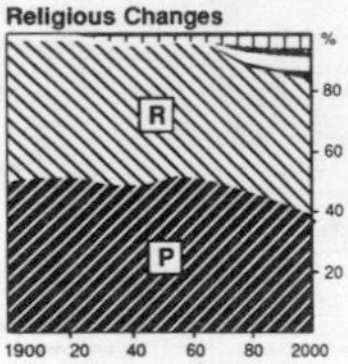

Evangelical Changes

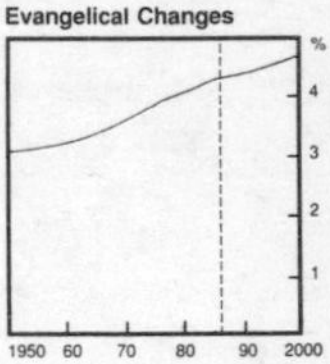

1. **Germany's spiritual restoration** — trust God for it! Humanism and destructive criticism of the Bible in the 19th century enfeebled the churches; compromise by many Christians during Hitler's Nazi tyranny and post-war paternalism and permissiveness has further eroded the witness of the Church in society. Widespread alcoholism (1.9 million alcoholics), divorce and

occultism (est. 6.8 million believe in witches) are symptoms of a sick and despairing society that has run out of viable solutions.

2. **The spiritual poverty** is highlighted by massive defections from organized Christianity (withdrawals from Protestant churches average about 113 annually). The only major growth in church attendances is in national and foreign sects. About one million Germans attend services run by such fringe groups. Whole areas of Germany are devoid of a clear gospel witness — partly due to the historic division of Germany between Protestants and Catholics and partly to the widespread effects of liberal theology. Especially poor in evangelical witness is predominantly Protestant north Germany and Berlin, and the urban areas.

3. **The Roman Catholics** are now more numerous than Protestants, but are likewise declining and divided. Many are seeking for a warm personal faith, but few Evangelicals are concerned to impart it.

4. **The EKD is a federation of Lutheran, Reformed and United State Churches**, but is deeply divided on political, moral and theological issues. The number of empty churches is a tragedy. Bible-believing pastors are in a small but growing minority. A new, dynamic moving of the Spirit of God is needed.

5. **The Free churches** are largely the outgrowth of the Pietist movement and to an extent from parent movements in the USA and UK. Evangelicals are proportionately stronger than in the EKD, and church attendance better, but growth in most churches has been minimal.

6. **An evangelical awakening is beginning to take place.** This is not only evident in the Free churches, but also in the far larger EKD:

a) **The Pietist movement** is a growing force within the EKD (especially in Wüttemberg in the south and in rural areas). There are many evangelical fellowships of the **Gnadau Union** within the EKD. Although there is general decline, the proportion of Evangelicals is rising markedly.

b) **The Confessional and "No Other Gospel" movements** of the '60s have gained good hearing and wide acceptance, and they are making a significant impact on theological thinking.

c) **The Evangelical Alliance** has become a rallying point for Evangelicals for social action, national weeks of prayer, evangelism and missionary information and outreach. Sadly, there is a major division between Pentecostals/charismatics and other Evangelicals. Pray for unity among God's people and that this may release rivers of life to the lost.

d) **New evangelical literature and books** covering a wide range of subjects have been a blessing to millions, and a decisive factor in the new evangelical awakening. 75% of all new Protestant book titles are now evangelical. Pray for writers, publishers and distributors of books. Pray for the impact of more than 150 evangelical magazines with a total circulation of 50 million.

7. **Theological education** has proved the major disaster area in the Protestant Church:

a) **The 13 universities that award theological degrees necessary** for acceptance into the EKD ministry have been the preserve of liberal, neo-orthodox and other non-biblical theologies for decades. Pray for more professors who openly proclaim the Truth to be raised up for these institutions. Students have emerged with their faith crippled and evangelistic concern stifled. Pray for evangelical students in these spiritual morgues, and pray for those who seek to help them stand true to the Scriptures through pre-university courses and the growing number of hostels that run parallel courses at university.

b) **German-speaking evangelical seminaries** are limited to Giessen (FTA) and Basel, Switzerland (FETA), and the seminaries of the Free churches; but graduates are only acceptable for pastoral ministry outside the EKD.

c) **Bible schools** are full, and a stream of young people are moving out to home and foreign fields — pray for such as Adelshofen, Brake, Liebenzell, Seeheim, Wiedenest, and for the College of Graduate Studies in Missiology established in 1984 in Korntal.

8. **West Berlin** is a 476 sq.km. enclave surrounded by the Communist-built "Wall of Shame". This sad and spiritually needy city is a challenge for evangelism. 12% of the population is now non-German, many being Turkish.

9. **Missionary vision has long been limited,** with proportionately one of the lowest missionary-sending figures for any country with such a large Protestant community. The total number of missionaries has remained constant for some years, but the proportion of Evangelicals has risen sharply to 80% of the total. Pray for a further increase. Pray for the Association of Evangelical Missions (**AEM**) with 51 members — a catalytic and vital stimulant for training, publicity and sending missionaries. One unique mission is the DMG (German Missionary Assoc.) with 180 missionaries serving with 25 international missions, but with no foreign fields of its own. Other significant German missions: Wiedenest (106 missionaries abroad), Liebenzell (142).

10. **Student work** is a vital ministry in the university world with its leftist leanings. Some work is done by both denominational and interdenominational groups, but this is inadequate in the face of the present receptiveness among young people. Pray for:

a) **SMD(IFES)** with 40 groups in universities (1,100,000 students) and 800 in secondary schools (3.5 million students but only 28 full-time staff workers).

b) **CCC** with 80 staff workers in six universities and in churches.

c) **Navigators** with 55 staff in university witness.

d) **Overseas Students** number 60,000, but little has been done to specifically meet their spiritual needs.

11. **Christian radio** — The German branch of **TWR** in West Germany, *Evangeliums-Rundfunk,* has made an impressive impact on the German-speaking world (including both Germanies) with 194 hours of programming every month. Programmes from Monaco may now be augmented through private radio stations and cable TV in Germany, Austria, Switzerland and Italy. Programmes are also provided for Italian, Greek, Spanish, Yugoslav and Turkish immigrant workers. Pray for the staff and their ministry.

12. **Unreached peoples — mainly immigrant guest workers and refugees.** The "AfA" is a fellowship of over 14 mission groups seeking to evangelize through a wide variety of ethnic ministries, with possibly 200 or so workers involved. A number of local congregations also seek to reach these people. Increasing rejection by Germans at work, in schools and in housing is stirring deep resentments and bitterness. Pray for Christians to have opportunity to share the gospel with them and a real loving concern. Pray for the planting of groups of believers that may ultimately affect their lands of origin. There are two main categories:

a) **Muslims** — challenging openings for reaching nearly two million: **Turks** (1,100,000) 4-5 agencies working among these hard, unresponsive people (Orientdienst, **WEC**, **OM**, **CBFMS**, etc). **Kurds** (400,000) from Turkey. Possibly 40-50 Christians among Turks and Kurds. Little direct Christian ministry in Kurmanji, the main dialect. **Irani** (33,000) and **Afghani refugees** (12,000) are now more open to the gospel. **North Africans** (83,000): little ministry to Arabs or Berbers. **Yugoslav Muslims** (130,000), mainly Albanian and Bosnian — a neglected group.

b) **Southern Europeans** — so many inadequately used opportunities among the nominal Catholic Italians, Spaniards and Portuguese and the Orthodox Greeks. Large areas in their homelands are devoid of an evangelical witness.

Africa

May 9-10

GHANA
(Republic of Ghana)

Area 238,500 sq.km. Grasslands in north, farmland and forest in south. Centre dominated by 520 km.-long Lake Volta.

Population 12,700,000. Annual growth 2.6%. People per sq.km. 52. Higher density in south.

Peoples: About 100 ethnic groups and 3 major language divisions.

Kwa 75%. 5 major sub-groups in centre and south.

- **Akan** (25 groups): Ashanti 1,900,000; Fante 1,700,000; Brong 708,000, etc., most speak dialects of Twi.
- **Ewe** (3) 1.9 mill. in southeast.
- **Ga-Adangme** (4) 1.3 mill. around Accra.
- **Guan** (13) 510,000 in centre and north.
- **C. Togo** (14) 125,000 on eastern border.

Gur 22%. 5 major sub-groups in north.

- **Mole-Dagbani** (13). Dagomba 460,000; Dagari-Birifor 420,000; Frafra 400,000; Kusasi 256,000.
- **Gurma** (5). Konkomba 450,000; Bimoba 68,000, etc.
- **Grusi** (5). Sisaala 300,000; Kasena 78,000, etc.

Mande 0.9%. 2 small groups.

Foreign 2%

Literacy 35%. **Official language:** English. **All languages** 60. **Bible translations** 4Bi 9NT 14por.

Capital: Accra 1,800,000. Other cities: Kumasi 800,000; Sekondi-Takoradi 255,000. Urbanization 32%.

Economy: Slowly recovering from almost total collapse in 1982. Earlier government overspending, mismanagement and corruption reduced this once prosperous land to poverty. Main exports are cocoa, gold and timber. Living standards were reduced by uncontrolled inflation, periods of drought and enforced repatriation of Ghanaians from Nigeria 1983-5. A slow recovery commenced in 1984. Inflation 750% (1983). Income/person $370 (3% of USA).

Politics: Independent from Britain in 1957. Nkrumah's "socialist" experiment was a disaster from which the nation will take years to recover. There have been five military regimes and three short-lived civilian governments since Nkrumah's overthrow in 1966. The government has had close links with Libya and retained power despite early unpopularity and harshness of leftist elements to political opponents. The government has become more relaxed and pragmatic in international relations since 1984.

Religion: Secular state with religious freedom, but some members of the military government are hostile to Christianity and have sought to hamper the spread of the gospel.

African traditional religions 31%. Mainly among peoples on the northern border.

Muslim 17%. Sunni 9%, Ahmaddiya 8%. The majority among the Dagomba, Gonja and Wali; growing minority among other northern peoples.

Christian 52%. Nominal 5%. Affiliated 47%. Note that figures are very tentative for some denominations.

Roman Catholic 11.3%. Practising 35%. 1,430,000a; 758,000m.

African marginal groups (700+) 12%. 1,500,000a.

Foreign marginal groups (14) 1.2%. 157,000a; 47,430m. Largest: Jehovah's Witnesses 27,730m.

Protestant 22.4%. Denominations 60+. 2,090,000a; 1,000,000m. Largest (adult members):

Methodist Church		186,966
Church of Pentecost		159,915
Presbyterian Church		132,860
Evangelical Presbyterian Ch.	(?)	76,400
Anglican Church	(?)	64,000
Seventh Day Adventist Church		56,000
Apostolic Church	(?)	32,000
Christ Apostolic Church	(?)	30,000
Assemblies of God		20,000
Baptist Convention (**SBC**)		19,000
African Methodist Episc. Zion		17,000

Evangelical 9% of population.

Missionaries to Ghana 380 (1:33,400 people) in 50 agencies.

Missionaries from within Ghana 25(?) (1:83,600 Protestants).

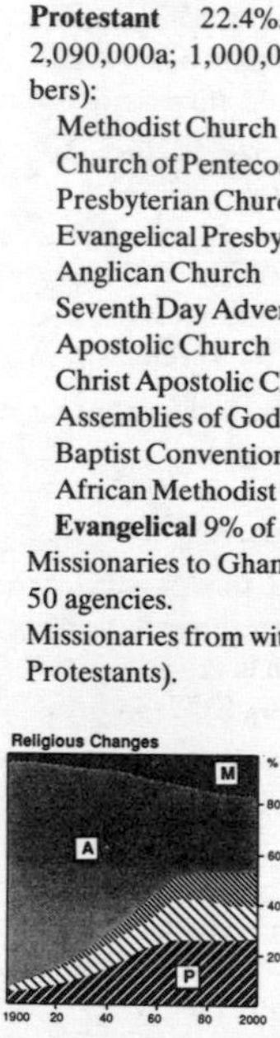

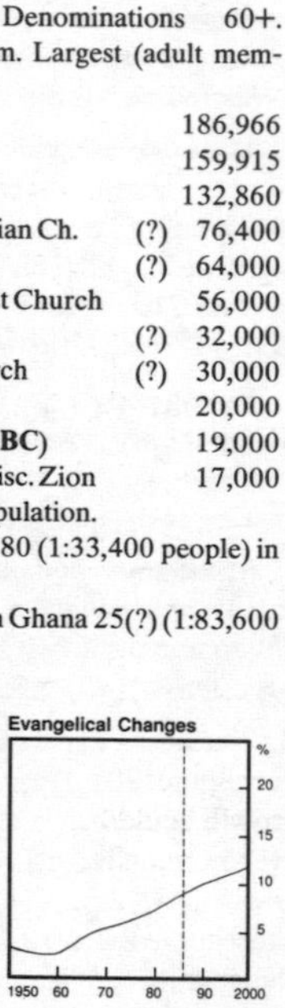

1. **The disasters that have befallen the land since independence can be seen as God's loving judgment.** Ghana's first president, Nkrumah, once said, "Seek ye the political kingdom and all these things will be added unto you." Instability, economic collapse and a series of natural and

social calamities reached a frightening climax in 1983/4. A wave of despair and a hunger after God has moved through the nation. Pray that Ghana may be blessed with a government that honours God and pursues righteousness.

2. **For years Christianity has had a large, nominal and traditional following in the more developed south.** Pagan world views and practices have gone hand in hand with Christian profession. The deadness and formality of many older churches have stimulated rapid growth of the African Independent Churches which offer excitement, involvement, and miracles, but not often salvation by faith. Some estimate that the number of these denominations exceeds 1,000! Pray that the true gospel may shine into the hearts of those who call themselves Christian but who are not born from above. Pray that a decisive break may be made from all fetishism and pagan bondages, and true liberty in Jesus be found.

3. **The present spiritual upsurge in Ghana** is in answer to prayer, and sacrificial service. The leavening work of literature, Scripture Union in the schools, the Ghana Evangelism Committee, and NLFA have brought many thousands to new life and invigorated many Presbyterian and Methodist churches. Numerous evangelical, charismatic and Pentecostal groups and fellowships have sprung up all over the south. In some of these denominations there has been rapid growth. Pray that a movement of the Spirit may spread to all churches and on to the unreached.

4. **Unity among believers is a prerequisite for advance.** This is being promoted by the Ghana Evangelism Committee through national conferences and sponsoring national evangelistic outreach. Most notable of the latter is NLFA, which has had a significant impact on a wide range of denominations since 1975 with many pastors and congregations coming into spiritual life.

5. **Mature Christian leaders** are in short supply in this time of rapid growth, economic stress and doctrinal confusion. Pray for lay-training schemes, the Maranatha Bible College **(SIM)** in Accra with 200 students, the 20 or so middle-level Bible schools, and the one degree-level seminary (with an increasingly evangelical student intake). Pray that the proportion of truly converted pastors in older denominations may continue to increase.

6. **The missionary vision of the Church** has been stunted by the national economic crisis and the reluctance of Ghanaians to go to the unevangelized peoples in the less developed north. **Christian Outreach Fellowship** (an indigenous Ghanaian interdenominational missionary organization) has placed a number of missionaries in northern Ghana and the Volta region of eastern Ghana. Pray for the Christian Service College in Kumasi and Maranatha Bible College, which both have the specific vision for training Ghanaian missionaries.

7. **Young people are in the forefront of the move of the Spirit.** Praise God for the impact of **SU** on the secondary schools and GHAFES(**IFES**), Navigators and CCC in the universities and colleges. Pray that the influence of converted young people may be decisive in church, mission and national affairs. May many hear God's call into full-time service.

8. **Missionary personnel** to serve with the Church as Bible teachers, translators, media experts and in pioneer outreach must be increased in this day of opportunity. Visas are hard to obtain and a quota system is in operation. Pray for missions serving the Lord in the land; the largest: **SBC** (48), **SIL** (46), **SIM** (44), **AoG** (30), **WEC** (20).

9. **The non-Christian peoples have never been so receptive.** A significant change occurred during the '80s. Pray out labourers to bring the ripened harvest in! Unprecedented church growth could be possible in the north. Among the 35 or so peoples in that area, only one is even nominally Christian — the Dagari (60% Catholic); in most, less than 2% are Christian of any variety, though only a handful of peoples are without a church in their midst. Most of the churches in the north have been small, weak, largely illiterate, and with a semiliterate leadership; but this is changing. Pray for NLFA plans to survey the needs of all Ghana with a view to planting a witnessing, growing church in every ethnic group, village and town.

10. **The unreached peoples of Ghana:**

a) **The fetishist peoples of the Upper Region** are beginning to respond; rapid church growth is possible among the Sisaala 125,000; Kasena 78,000; Builsa 133,000; Frafra

400,000; but response is slow among the Bimoba 60,000 (**SIM, AoG**); Kusasi 225,000; and Tampulma 10,000 (**AoG**). Other smaller groups are unoccupied by Christian workers. **SIM** is planning advances to other unreached peoples along the Togo border in the Volta Region.

b) **The fetishist peoples of the Northern Region**. A complex medley of small groups that are scarcely touched by the gospel; over 30 peoples are resident in the region, but there are viable evangelical churches in only 6-7 of these. **WEC** is planting churches in this area. Response is growing among the Birifor 45,000, and Konkomba 430,000, but there are not adequate labourers for the Nawuri, Nchumburu, Dega, Vagala, etc.

c) **The Islamized peoples of the north** have responded only minimally to the gospel, and more input is needed — the dominant Gonja 130,000 have less than 100 believers (**WEC**); Dagomba 480,000 (**AoG, SBC**); Wa 86,000 (Baptist Mid-Missions).

11. **Less evangelized sectors of society.**

a) **The cities** have grown by absorbing many ethnic groups. Those from the north in southern cities easily turn to Islam; little is being done by Christians to reach them. In Kumasi's 800,000 population, 40,000 are regular churchgoers, and possibly only 10% of these are born-again. Yet in that city are over 80 ethnic groups, 72 of which are unevangelized.

b) **The many pockets of fetishists** among the southern peoples; particularly the Ewe in the southeast; this is especially true among the Ewe sea and river fishermen all over Ghana.

12. **Bible translation** into all of Ghana's languages that warrant the input is an achievable goal. **UBS, SIL** and Ghanaian teams are working in 21 languages, but between 6 and 13 other languages are yet to be tackled.

13. **Supportive ministries.**

a) **Literature:** a chronic shortage due to lack of foreign exchange, or printing materials. Pray for the importation and economic distribution of Bibles (**UBS**) and Christian literature by such as Challenge Enterprises, an indigenous organization backed by **SIM. Africa Christian Press** publishes a range of good Christian books for distribution throughout Africa. Mature Christian authors are in short supply too. BCCs have been most successful (**SIM**, ISI/**AoG**).

b) **Christian films** have been used with great effect. The five mobile "cinevans" of Challenge Enterprises have a total audience of over 1.5 mill. annually.

c) **Christian cassettes** have only now become more widely used, but a dearth of workers, equipment and batteries limit the growth of what should be a key ministry. **GRI** has recordings in 50 languages.

GIBRALTAR

(Colony of Gibraltar)

The West
May 11

Area 6.5 sq.km. A famous rocky peninsula on the south coast of Spain.

Population 31,000. Annual growth 1.5%. People per sq.km. 4,770.

Peoples: Gibraltarian 63%, **Spanish** 14%, **British** 10%, **Moroccan** 9.5%.

Literacy 80%. **Official language**: English.

Economy: Seriously affected by Spanish border restrictions between 1968 and 1984 and the closure of the British naval dockyard. The border with Spain was reopened in 1985. Income/person $4,400 (31% of USA). Inflation 12.9%.

Politics: The British captured the Rock in 1704 and have long used it as a military base. The local population has steadfastly resisted Spanish pleas and economic pressures to return the Rock to Spain.

Religion: Religious freedom.
Muslim 9% (Moroccan), **Jews** 1.7%, **Hindu** 1.2%.
Christian 88%. Nominal 8%. Affiliated 80%.
- **Roman Catholic** 72%. Practising 30%. 21,000a; 12,000m.
- **Protestant** 8%. 2,500a; 1,200m. Mainly British Anglicans.
- Missionaries to Gibraltar 8 (1:3,900).

1. **The Protestant witness.** There are three English-speaking churches (Methodist, Presbyterian and Church of England) and two for the Spanish-speaking (Assemblies of God and Evangelical). The last two maintain a lively witness to the Gibraltarian majority.

2. **The witness to the Muslim Moroccans.** There are about 7,000 migrant labourers from Morocco. Pray that some of these may be won for the Lord. There is now a small group of Arab believers who meet regularly.

3. **CLC has a small bookshop** which maintains a witness to Arabs, Gibraltarians and tourists.

4. **Gibraltar could be a blessing to both Spain and North Africa.** Pray that its political future may make this possible.

The West

May 12-13

GREECE
(The Hellenic Republic)

Area 133,000 sq.km. Southernmost point of Balkan Peninsula in S. E. Europe and numerous islands in the Ionian, Aegean and Mediterranean Seas.

Population 10,010,000. Annual growth 0.6%. People per sq.km. 73.

Peoples

Greek 95%. The descendants of the ancient Greek civilization that has so enriched the world.

Indigenous minorities 4.5%. Macedonian 173,000; Turk 135,000; Albanian 58,000; Romanian 55,000; Bulgar 20,000; Armenian 15,000.

Immigrant Minorities 0.5%. Arab, etc. 30,000.

Literacy 88%. **Official language:** Greek.

Capital: Athens 4,200,000. Other major city: Thessalonika 1,000,000. Urbanization 65%.

Economy: The relative backwardness of the nation is rapidly changing through tourism, industrialization, trade and membership of the EEC. Income/person $4,540 (32% of USA). Inflation 15.6%.

Politics: Nearly four centuries of Turkish rule ended with independence in 1827. The last 45 years have been punctuated by World War II, two civil wars, two military dictatorships, and tensions with neighbouring Turkey over the issue of Cyprus. A Republic with a parliamentary democracy.

Religion: The Orthodox Church is recognized and legally protected by the state as the dominant and established religion. The new constitution of 1975 removed some of the very discriminatory legislation against non-Orthodox bodies, but there is not yet freedom of religion. There is now some discussion about the separation of Church and state.

Non-religious/Atheist 0.3%.

Muslim 1.5%. Mainly Turks, some Arabs.

Jews 3,900.

Christian 97.5%. Affiliated 95.8%.

Orthodox 94.8%. Church attendance 2-5%. 9,500,000a. Four regional and other breakaway and ethnic churches.

Roman Catholic 0.46%. 46,000a.

Marginal groups 0.4%. 39,000a; 22,170m. Largest (adult members): Jehovah's Witnesses 22,040.

Protestant 0.17%. 17,000a; 6,200m. Nearly half the Protestants are expatriates. Denominations 36. Largest (adult members):

Greek Evang. Ch. (Reformed)	1,650
Free Evangelical Church	990
Assemblies of God	900

Evangelical 0.14% of population.

Missionaries to Greece about 80 (1:125,000 people), but less than half use the Greek language.

1. **Europe's first country to be evangelized** (Acts 16:10), yet today it has the smallest evangelical community in the continent after Albania and Malta. Some reckon that there are only 10,000 Greek Evangelicals. A large minority of Evangelicals are expatriates in US forces, etc. The Macedonian call is just as valid today.

2. **The Orthodox Church dominates the cultural and religious life of the country.** Orthodoxy was the focal rallying point in the dark years of Turkish occupation, so, to many, to be a Greek is to be Orthodox. Pray that the bondage of traditionalism, idolatry and ignorance of the true gospel may be broken. There are some groups within the Orthodox fold that are coming to personal faith in Christ. An internal reformation or renewal is not impossible!

3. **The last decade has brought increasing liberty to preach the gospel**, and a decline in the hold of traditional Orthodoxy over the people, but in 1984 several evangelical leaders were sentenced to a period of imprisonment for "proselytization". Pray for complete cultural and legal equality for non-Orthodox believers concomitant with membership of the European Community.

4. **The Greek Protestants** are few, and there is little church growth. There are only three major groups and a number of small but growing Pentecostal Churches. The 130 churches are mostly in the Athens area, Thessalonika and Patros. The Pan Hellenic Evangelical Alliance was formed in 1977. It is extremely difficult to get permission to build churches. The believers are scattered and often hesitant to witness in a society that generally despises and occasionally persecutes them. Spirit-inspired outreach to sow the seed of the gospel must increase if Greece is to be evangelized.

5. **Widespread evangelism is the need!** Some groups are actively mobilizing young people (and older) to this end. Pray for **EHC**'s literature campaign now under way, and for the **Hellenic Missionary Union**'s bold new summer campaigns with personal and outdoor evangelism. HMU is an exciting, new Greek agency that desires to awaken Greek interest in world evangelization. **YWAM**'s influence through the long stay of the MV *Anastasis* has been significant.

6. **Theological training has been woefully lacking**, resulting in poorly taught pastors, leaders and believers who are open to doctrinal extremes and even error. In 1980 **GEM** opened a residential Bible institute with 11 students. The school has since expanded. It is the only Protestant school in the country.

7. **The unreached are many**; the great majority of Greeks have never heard a clear presentation of the gospel. More specifically:

a) **Many of the islands**, including Crete, Rhodes, etc.

b) **Most of the rural towns** and villages.

c) **The Turkish Muslims** in Thrace have no specific outreach to them.

d) **The many Yugoslav** holiday-makers in summer.

e) **The ethnic minorities** in the north are not officially recognized — the Slavic Macedonians and Bulgars and also the Albanians and Romanians.

f) **The university students** — there has been little established, lasting national student work, though attempts are being made by **IFES** and **CCC**. There is one strong group in Athens linked with **IFES**.

g) **Arab refugees** from Lebanon — no ministry among them. Greece is a key base for Middle Eastern outreach.

8. **Foreign missions** have made little impact due to visa restrictions. Most engaged in work among the Greeks are foreign-supported nationals or Greeks converted abroad. Significant missions are **GEM** (8 missionaries) in theological training, **AoG** (7), **OMS** (4) in church planting, **CCC** in student and professional evangelism, and AMG in hospital work. There are altogether 20 or so mission agencies. The possibility for entry of European missionaries from EEC countries is now high. Pray for labourers.

9. **Literature has been one of the most fruitful forms of evangelism.** Tracts are read! Pray for the vital, seed-sowing work of the Greek Bible Society in disseminating all or part of the Scriptures, **WLC** in their Every Home Crusade, **SU** in producing good Christian Bible Reading aids and the dozen or so itinerant Christian booksellers. There is so little variety in Christian literature available.

10. **Radio — TWR** and **IBRA** broadcast weekly to Greece. There has been a measure of response, but this ministry needs to be expanded for greater impact. At present there are only two hours of broadcasting per month.

11. **The Greek Diaspora is large** — USA 2,200,000; Germany 294,000; Australia 250,000; South Africa 60,000, etc. Believers in these lands should be more concerned for evangelization of the Greeks among them.

The West

May 14

GREENLAND

Area 2,176,000 sq.km. Large Arctic island, but only 15% ice-free for some of the year.

Population 54,000. Annual growth 0.8%. People per sq.km. 0.025; the world's lowest population density and largest island.

Peoples

Greenland Eskimo 79%, **Danish** 13%, **US military** 6%.

Literacy 93%. **Official languages:** Danish, Greenlandic.

Capital: Nuuk 9,500. Urbanization 85%.

Economy: Based on fishing and mining. Income/person $9,600 (69% of USA).

Politics: Overseas part of Denmark with home rule since 1979.

Religion: Lutheran Church monopoly until 1953.

Other 1.3%. Animists, Baha'i 300.

Christian 98.7%. Nominal 20.3%. Affiliated 78.3%.

Other 0.4%. Roman Catholics 70, Jehovah's Witnesses 170.

Protestant 77.9%. 42,000a; 31,000m. All Lutheran except for several small groups of Pentecostals and Brethren.

Evangelical 3.8% of population.

Missionaries to Greenland 4 (1:13,500 people).

1. **The Danish community** is largely Lutheran, but few know the Saviour in a personal way, and their lives are no witness to the Greenlander majority.

2. **Greenlanders** are nominally Christian, but the breakdown of their traditional culture has had devastating effects. Immorality, alcoholism, apathy, mental illness and poverty are the result. Pray that they may experience the work of the Life-giving Spirit. The archaic Greenlandic Bible is being revised.

3. **The evangelical witness is limited.** A few courageous servants of God from Scandinavia, the Faroes and the UK have won some to the Lord, and there are now a few groups of Pentecostal and Brethren believers. Travel conditions are harsh and difficult and the communities along the coasts isolated. Pray that "Greenland's icy mountains" may resound with the gospel message!

GRENADA

Caribbean

May 15

Area 344 sq.km. One larger island north of Trinidad and some of the Grenadine islets south of St. Vincent.

Population 118,000. Annual growth 1.2%. People per sq.km. 343.

Peoples: African 53%, **Eurafrican** 42%, **East Indian** 4.2%, **European** 0.8%.

Literacy 93%. **Official language:** English.

Capital: St. George's 12,000. Urbanization 15%.

Economy: Already poor and underdeveloped agricultural island at independence, but made poorer by the instability of the past decade and the emigration of the middle classes. Income/person $990 (7% of USA). Inflation 15% ('81). Unemployment 30%+.

Politics: Independent of Britain in 1974 as a parliamentary monarchy. Independence has proved stormy with bizarre dictatorships, repression, and two increasingly Marxist coups; the last of which provoked the US invasion of 1983 and ultimate restoration of a more democratic government.

Religion

Christian 99%. Nominal 5.2%. Affiliated 93.8%.

Roman Catholic 61%. 72,000a; 39,600m.

Marginal groups (4) 1.5%.

Protestant 31.3%. 37,000a; 15,100m. Denominations 27. Largest (adult members):

Anglican Church	6,300
Seventh Day Adventist Church	2,300
Methodist Church	940
Church of God (Cleveland)	850

Evangelical 10.5% of population.

Missionaries to Grenada 13 (1:9,000 people) in three agencies.

Missionaries from Grenada 2 (1:18,500 Protestants).

Points for Prayer: See Jamaica on p. 255.

Caribbean
May 16

GUADELOUPE and MARTINIQUE

(Overseas Departments of France)

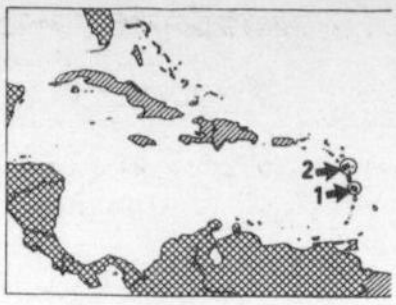

Area 2,881 sq.km. In the Leeward and Windward Islands. Martinique to the south is separated from the twin islands of Guadeloupe and its dependencies by Dominica.

Population 662,000, just under half in Martinique. Annual growth 1.2%. People per sq.km. 230, higher in Martinique.

Peoples: Eurafrican 91%, **African** 5%, **European** (mainly French) 2.1%, **East Indian** 1.4%.

Literacy 89%. **Official language:** French.

Capitals: Fort de France (Martinique) 181,000; Basse-Terre (Guadeloupe) 16,000. Urbanization 73%.

Economy: Large subsidies, secure markets for agricultural products and free emigration to France have made these islands relatively prosperous. Unemployment 40%. Income/person $4,270 (30% of USA). Inflation 11%.

Politics: French colonies since 1635. Overseas Departments of France since 1946.

Religion: Religious freedom, but with a strong secularist tendency.

Non-religious/Atheist 1.9%.

Muslim 0.4%. **Baha'i** 0.3%.

Christian 97.4%. Affiliated 93%.

Roman Catholic 82% (officially 90%). Practising 35%. 544,000a; 310,000m.

Marginal groups 2.2%. 14,470a; 5,150m. Largest (adult members):

Jehovah's Witnesses (Guadeloupe and Martinique) 5,100.

Protestant 8.4%. 55,560a; 22,700m. Denominations 11. Largest (adult members):

Seventh Day Adventist Ch. **(G & M)**	17,690
Assoc. of Ev. Chs. **(WT) (G)**	1,030
Assemblies of God **(G)**	990
Reformed Church **(G & M)**	810
Baptists **(SBC-G) (Ind-M)**	700
Brethren **(M)**	640
Church of God (Clevel.) **(G & M)**	260

Evangelical 2.8% of population.

Missionaries to Guadeloupe and Martinique 38 (1:17,400 people) in six agencies.

Missionaries from Guadeloupe and Martinique 0.

1. **The evident spiritual need is highlighted** by the breakdown in family life, widespread occultism, secular propaganda in schools and the marked growth of sects. Catholicism is a traditional veneer for most. There is a small but active independence movement encouraged by Cuba which brings an urgency to the need to evangelize these islands.

2. **Areas and peoples less reached with the gospel.**
   a) **The outlying dependencies** are less evangelized — St. Barthélemy, St. Martin and Marie Galante islands. Several missionaries of the Association of Evangelical Churches have recently moved to these islands.
   b) The **East Indians** number over 9,000. Most have become nominally Catholic, but retaining much of their Hindu beliefs. Little direct outreach has been directed to this community.

3. **There were hardly any born-again believers before 1946.** Since then, church growth has been significant despite persecution in earlier years. The most successful have been the SDA, **AoG** and **WT**-linked churches. The vital witness of believers, radio and TV evangelism and Christian literature have all played their part. **CLC** has a bookstore on Martinique, and **WT** one on Guadeloupe.

4. **Leadership training** for the growing churches is provided locally through **WT**'s TEE programme with 102 students and Discipling Center in Guadeloupe. Pray that mature Christian workers may be called for service at home and in the Francophone lands around the world.

5. **250,000 Antilleans have emigrated to France,** where they are known as *Antilleans.* They are a large minority in many Parisian evangelical churches. Pray for the witness of these believers. The great majority of Antilleans still need the Saviour. **WT** has established three churches amongst the Antilleans in the Paris area.

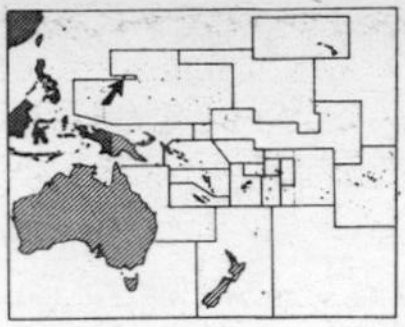

GUAM

(The U.S. Territory of Guam)

Pacific

May 17

Area 549 sq.km. One island; part of the Marianas Archipelago. Also included here are the three tiny US territories of Johnston Island, Midway Island, and Wake Island in the N. Pacific (14 sq.km.).

Population 110,000. Annual growth 1.5%. People per sq.km. 200. A further 1,000 military personnel on other islands.

Peoples
Chamorros (Micronesians mixed with Filipino, Spanish, Mexican) 48%.
US Citizens 21%. Almost entirely military personnel and their dependents.
Others 31%. Filipino 22,000; Korean 700; Micronesian 700.

Literacy 96%. **Official language:** English.

Capital: Agana 6,000 (Guam).

Economy: All islands are major US military bases, which are the mainstay of the Guam economy. Also tourism and light industry. Income/person $6,700 (48% of USA).

Politics: US territory since 1898. Commonwealth in association with USA since 1982.

Religion: Freedom of religion, though Roman Catholics numerically dominant since the days of Spanish rule which preceded that of the USA.

Non-religious/Atheist 0.9%. **Baha'i** 0.7%. **Other** 1.6%.

Christian 96.8%. Affiliated 91.2%.

Roman Catholic 78%. Practising 60%. 85,800a; 48,900m.

Marginal groups 1.2%. Two major cults. Largest (adherents):

Jehovah's Witnesses	690
Mormons	690

Protestant 12%. 13,100a; 5,300m. Denominations 20+. Largest (adult members):

Seventh Day Adventist Church	1,400
General Baptist Church	600
Assemblies of God	540
Baptist Convention (**SBC**)	500

Evangelical 7.6% of population.

Missionaries to Guam 110 (1:1,000 people) in 14 agencies.

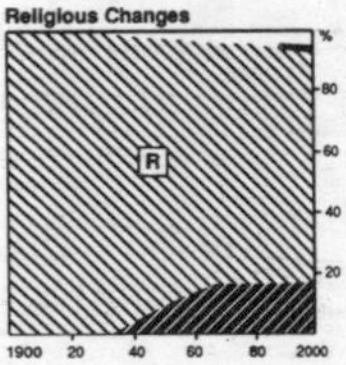

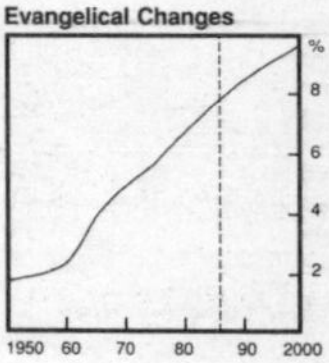

1. **The Chamorro people** are almost entirely Catholic. Only now is the New Testament about to be printed. Pray that the Scriptures may bring this indigenous people to faith in Christ.

2. **Immigrant minorities** are relatively less evangelized. Pray for the Filipinos, Koreans and Chinese.

3. **Most Protestants are among US military and their dependents.** There is a wide variety of denominations; many are evangelical. Pray for deeper spiritual life among believers and a sensitive witness to indigenous and immigrant peoples.

4. **Missions.** The majority of workers are committed to ministry among US personnel or for specialized ministries such as youth (**CCC**, **CEF**) or radio (**TWR**).

5. **Christian radio. TWR** has a powerful broadcasting station for reaching E. Asia, as well as local peoples in the Pacific. This is a key installation for the gospel to which 28 workers are committed.

Latin America

May 18-19

GUATEMALA

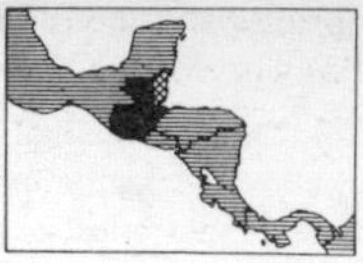

Area 109,000 sq.km. A land of lakes and volcanoes. Mexico's southern neighbour. Guatemala has a long-standing claim on English-speaking Belize to the east.

Population 8,403,000. Annual growth 3.5%. People per sq.km. 77. Many thousands of refugees in S. Mexico.

Peoples

Spanish-speaking 56%. Almost all mixed-race Ladinos.

English-speaking 2%. Blacks on the Caribbean coast.

Amerindian peoples 42%. Descendants of the Mayan civilization. Nineteen peoples speaking 40 languages. Main groups: Quiche 866,000; Yucatec Maya 688,000; Mam 643,000; Cakchiquel 522,000; Kekchi 376,000; Kanjobal 115,000; Pocomam 96,000; Chorti 85,000; Tzutujil 80,000; Ixil 72,000; Pocomchi 70,000; Achi 67,000; Chuj 48,000; Jacaltec 29,000.

Other minorities: Chinese 12,000; Black Carib 5,800.

Literacy 48%. **Official language:** Spanish. **All languages** 57. **Bible translations** 1Bi 16NT 23por.

Capital: Guatemala City 1,196,000. Urbanization 41%.

Economy: Underdeveloped but potentially rich. Unjust and inequitable land use has kept the majority in abject poverty. Guerrilla warfare has devastated large areas. Income/person $1,160 (8% of USA). Inflation 8.9%.

Politics: A series of dictatorships and military governments since 1840. The poor (largely Amerindian) have suffered years of indignity and deprivation. Officially sanctioned death squads murdered and plundered in response to guerrilla insurgency. Guatemala's shocking human rights record has gradually moderated since the 1981 coup, and the country slowly moves towards a more broad-based democratic system.

Religion: Official separation of Church and state with freedom of religion, but the Catholic Church has great influence. The erosion of that influence was a contributing factor to the coup which ousted the evangelical President Rios Montt in 1983.

Non-religious/Atheist 1%.

Animist/Spiritist 0.3%. Christo-paganism very strong among the Amerindians.

Christian 98.7%. Nominal 11.7%. Affiliated 87%. 7,320,000a; 3,680,000m.

Roman Catholic 66% (officially 78%, but with many losses to Evangelicals). 6,544,000a; 3,000,000m.

Marginal groups 0.7%. 60,600a; 26,400m. Largest (adherents):

Mormons	30,200
Jehovah's Witnesses	25,200

Protestant 20.4%. 1,720,000a; 659,000m. Denominations 220. Largest (adult members):

Assemblies of God	98,000
Prince of Peace	92,000
Ev. Church of C.America (**CAMI**)	70,000
Church of God (Cleveland)	55,000
Elim Pentecostal Church	30,000
Brethren	29,000
Church of the Nazarene	24,000
Presbyterian Church	19,300

Evangelical 19% of population.

Missionaries to Guatemala 457 (1:18,400 people) in 58 agencies, almost all North Americans.

Missionaries from Guatemala 9 (1:190,000 Protestants).

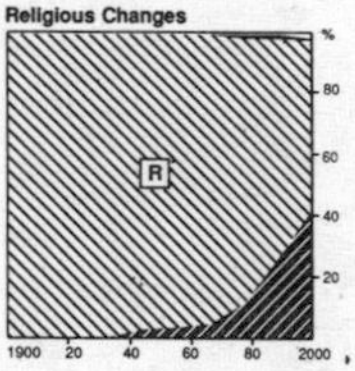

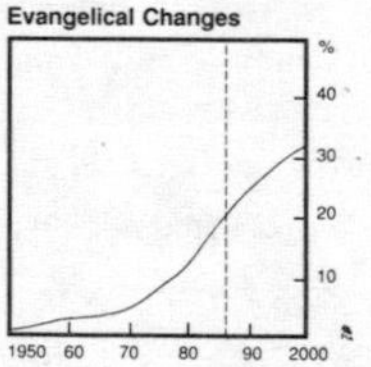

1. **Nearly one-fourth of the population may now be Evangelicals.** Dramatic growth has followed enormous missionary input, political instability, the devastating 1976 earthquake and violent guerrilla war. The harvest has been reaped in all sections of society. Praise God!

2. **The Evangelicals have now become a major component in society** — even to the extent of an evangelical President between 1981 and 1983. Pray that Christians may decisively change their selfish, corrupt, racialist and violent society.

3. **The Catholic Church** has suffered great decline in influence and numbers. Defection to the Evangelicals has been massive and resented. Espousal of liberation theology by some

priests and the disciplining of the large charismatic renewal movement has hastened the decline. Many Catholics are nominal or even animist at heart.

4. **The Evangelicals have grown**; but the multiplication of denominations, divisions among believers, rivalry and bitterness are hardly glorifying the Lord Jesus. Pray for true spiritual unity that transcends secondary issues and personalities. Pray also for spiritual energies to be channelled into the evangelization of the lost at home and abroad.

5. **Evangelistic outreach continues** through a multitude of avenues — wide use of Christian and commercial radio stations, mass evangelism campaigns (such as Luis Palau's 1982 campaign — with 700,000 attending one meeting!), large distribution of Christian literature and tracts (40 Christian bookshops), etc. Pray for the conservation of the fruit and the maturing of the believers as well as the winning of the new generation for Christ. Pray also for the "DAWN" programme launched by evangelical church leaders and **OCM** with the strategy of planting a witnessing church in every community in the country.

6. **Leadership training is well provided for** with six seminaries, 23 Bible schools and six TEE programmes (TEE was pioneered here by Presbyterians in the '60s and has now spread worldwide). Pray for the raising up of humble and effective leaders for the Body of Christ who will rise above the pettiness, divisions and carnality now all too common.

7. **The Amerindians** have begun to respond in large numbers to the gospel. Missions have reached out into every tribe. The most notable in church planting are **CAMI**, **Nazarenes** and **UWM. SIL** and others have contributed to the near completion of Bible translation for the 40 languages needing the Scriptures. The present guerrilla war has brought suffering to the people — with deaths and a massive refugee problem (many fleeing to Mexico, USA and to urban areas). The rural Christians have suffered considerably for their faith during this conflict.

8. **Foreign missions** have lavished a great deal of attention on the land. The hard battles in faith of the pioneers sowed today's harvest. Special note must be made of the Presbyterians, **CAMI,** Brethren and Nazarene pioneers. The large foreign input needs to be phased out and Guatemalan leadership and missionary outreach to other lands encouraged. There is only a small beginning being made by Guatemalans for missionary work.

9. **The unreached** — a relative term in well-evangelized Guatemala. A few minorities such as the Chinese and Black Caribs as well as the Pocomam, Pocomchi, Ixil, Jacaltec, and Upsantec tribes have shown less response to the gospel; yet there are active, growing churches among them. Pray for the 26,000 Guatemalan refugees known to be in Mexico.

Africa
May 20-21

GUINEA
(The Republic of Guinea)

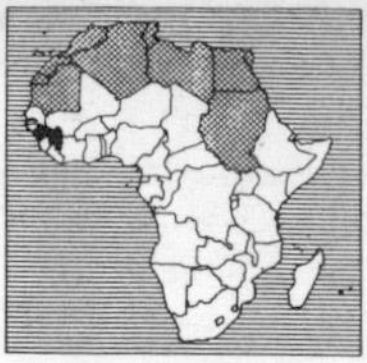

Area 246,000 sq.km. On Africa's west coast and between Guinea-Bissau and Sierra Leone.

Population 6,100,000. Annual growth 2.4%. People per sq.km. 25. 1-1.5 million political and economic refugees fled to other lands between 1958-83; only some have returned.

Peoples: Over 40 ethnic groups.
Mande 46% (13). Malinke 1,700,000; Soso 900,000; Yalunka 180,000; Kuranko 115,000; Konyanke 115,000; Wassulunka 63,000; Jakanke 11,000; Nalu 10,000; Lele 9,000; Mikifore 3,000.
Fula 34% (4 groups). **Mande-Fu** 11% (5). Kpelle 275,000; Toma 184,000; Vai 63,000; Mano 30,000; Loko 20,000.
Kissi 6%.
Other 3% (14). Baga 28,000; Landuma 13,000; Konyagi 12,000; Bassari 7,000; Badyaranke 5,000.

Literacy 11%. **Official language:** French. **Eight national languages:** Fula, Manding, Soso, Kissi, Kpelle, Toma, Konyagi, Bassari. **All languages** 20. **Bible translations** 1Bi 8NT 2por.

Capital: Conakry 1,032,000. Urbanization 22%.

Economy: Potentially the richest state of former French West Africa with abundant land, fertile soil, water and minerals. Reduced to subsistence and destitution by the foolishness and corruption of the former regime. Income/person $300 (2% of USA).

Politics: French colony until independence in 1958. President Sékou Touré led the unfortunate country into a disastrous flirtation with Marxism. The cruel, repressive regime was swept away in a military coup in 1983. Basic freedoms have been restored, but intertribal tensions could mar the prospects of long-term stability.

Religion: The former government leaders espoused Marxist rhetoric and a pro-Islamic stance. Christians, especially Catholics, suffered considerably at the hands of the authorities. The new regime has openly proclaimed religious liberty and invited missionary activity.
Muslim 70%. Strong among the dominant Malinke, Soso and Fula.
Tribal religions 28%. Predominantly among the forest peoples of the southeast and a few small coastal peoples.
Christian 1.4%. Affiliated 1.3%.
Roman Catholic 0.87%. 53,000a; 29,000m.
Protestant 0.46%. 28,100a; 10,900m. Denominations 5. Largest (adult members):

Eglise Evang. Protestante (**CMA**)	8,400
Anglican	1,000

Evangelical 0.41% of population.
Missionaries to Guinea 27 (1:226,000 people) in five agencies.

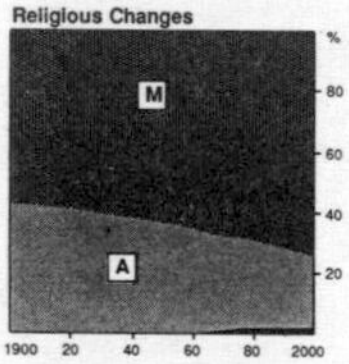

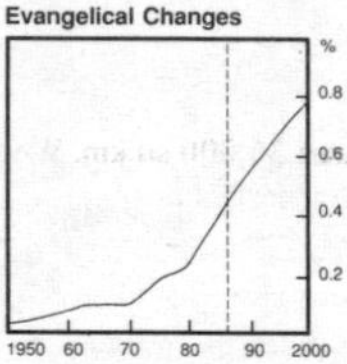

1. **Black Africa's least evangelized country is now open for the gospel.** Pray for the government, for stability and for religious liberty to be maintained.

2. **In only six peoples are there evangelical churches.** All the other peoples are almost completely unevangelized. Pray especially for the:
   a) **Malinke**, who are dominant and fairly strongly Muslim. **SIM** and **AME** plan outreach to them.
   b) **Fula** who were much oppressed by the former regime. Only one **CMA** missionary couple work among them.
   c) **Soso**, most of whom have become Muslim this century and are the major people in the coastal area. There are no churches, just a handful of Christians. **WEC/CAPRO** plan outreach to them.

3. **The Evangelical Church has matured and grown** steadily among the Kissi, Toma and, to an extent, among the Kpelle. Even in this area only 2.6% of the people are linked with the 120 organized churches. The great majority are animists and have yet to respond to the gospel. The southern Christians have had little vision for and less impact on the Muslim areas and majority. Pray for a strong, missionary-minded Church. Several pastors have gone to witness among the Malinke.

4. **In the Muslim majority** areas there is just a handful of isolated believers. The Anglican Church among the Soso and Baga has been in decline, and many adherents have been lost to Islam. Pray for a radiant witness in every part of the country.

5. **The Christians need Bible teaching and more pastors able to provide it.** Pray for the only Bible school in the country at Telekoro (**CMA**). Pray also for the launching of a proposed TEE programme.

6. **Missionaries have fought a long and lonely battle with relatively little fruit.** All RC and most Protestant missionaries were expelled in 1967. Only 11 **CMA** missionaries remained to man the base in Conakry and the Bible Institute in Telekoro until the arrival of **AME** in 1981. Pray for all present and future missionaries and their ministry in a land of harsh living conditions and poor communications.

7. **Missionaries of high calibre** are needed for the newly opened doors. Pray for wise strategies and warm cooperation among evangelical groups seeking to enter the country.

8. **Radio programmes** from ELWA (**SIM**) in Liberia have a large audience and considerable acceptance among the Muslim Fula and Malinke. Pray for interest to become earnest desire and for church planting to result.

9. **Literature** is in short supply; there is only one Christian bookstore in the country, but literacy is low. **A cassette ministry** in this predominantly Muslim and multilingual land could be vital. **GRI** has recordings in 20 languages.

10. **Bible translation**. A translation programme and translators are required, for much remains to be done.

GUINEA-BISSAU

(The Republic of Guinea-Bissau)

Africa

May 22

Area 36,000 sq.km. Wedged between Senegal and Guinea-Conakry.

Population 848,000. Annual growth 1.8%. People per sq.km. 24.

Peoples: Over 27 peoples.
West Atlantic (15 groups) 59.5%. Balanta 230,000; Manjako 90,000; Papel 85,600; Mankanya 28,000; Beafada 27,000; Bijago 21,000; Jola 15,000.
Fula (5 groups) 23% 195,000.
Mande (5 groups) 14%. Mandingo 104,000; Nalu 6,900; Soninke 4,100; Soso 2,560.
Other 3.5%. Creole, Cape Verdians, Guineans.

Literacy 6%. **Official language:** Portuguese. **Trade language:** Creole, spoken by 44% of the population. **Bible translations** 1Bi 3NT 4por.

Capital: Bissau 130,000. Urbanization 28%.

Economy: Ruined by the long independence war, famine conditions and lack of capital and infrastructure for development. Basic commodities are unavailable. Income/person $209 (1% of USA).

Politics: Independent of Portugal in 1974. Socialist government, seeking development aid from East and West.

Religion: Christians are free to witness and preach, though no new mission groups are being allowed to enter.
Animist 51.1%. Predominantly the coastal Balanta and West Atlantic peoples.
Muslim 42.5%. Fula, Mandingo, Soninke, Beafada are all Muslim; and Nalu, Soso, largely Muslim.
Christian 6.4%.
Roman Catholic 5.7%. 48,000a; 29,000m.
Protestant 0.7%. 5,840a; 3,200m. Denominations 3. Largest (adult members):
Evangelical Church (**WEC**) 3,000
Evangelical 0.7% of population.
Missionaries to Guinea-Bissau 33 (1:25,700 people) in one agency.

Religious Changes

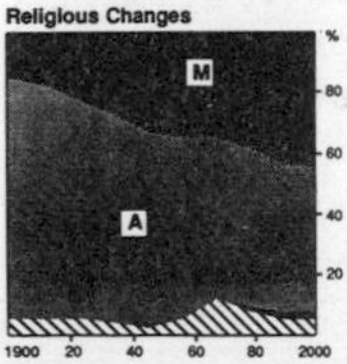

Evangelical Changes

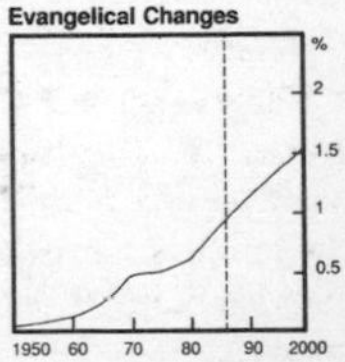

1. **There are unprecedented opportunities for evangelization and church planting**, for the majority of the people have never heard the Good News. Pray for continued open doors despite the teaching of Marxism in the schools and assiduous Muslim missionary work.

2. **The unreached are many.** Only four of the 27 peoples have a resident witness of local evangelical believers. The Muslim peoples are unoccupied, and Islam slowly extends among the animistic Jola, Manjako and Balanta. A specific recruitment and effort to evangelize the Muslim Mandingo, Fula, Beafada and Nalu is essential.

3. **There are growing churches among the Balanta, Papel and Bijago, and an emerging church among the Manjako.** Pray for a missionary vision among the Christians to reach out to unevangelized villages of their own peoples and on to the unreached coastal peoples such as the Jola, Mankanya and the many smaller tribes.

4. **The Church is strongest among the Balanta and Papel.** The Bijago churches need a move of the Holy Spirit to restore the believers to dedication and zeal. The "take off point" for the Church has yet to be realized. Many believers suffer persecution from heathen relatives, with loss of status, family rights, etc.

5. **The only Protestant mission is WEC** with workers based in eight centres. Living conditions are harsh, and health has been a major problem. The overworked little team needs reinforcing with evangelist/church planters, Bible teachers, translators and those with technical, medical and practical skills.

6. **Leadership training** through annual conferences, TEE, short-term Bible schools and a small residential Bible school is hampered by lack of teachers and the poverty of the churches to support students. Many churches are without adequate trained leadership.

7. **Literature is eagerly sought after,** but little is available in the one Christian bookstore. Russians, Cubans and other Eastern Bloc personnel often visit the store.

8. **Bible translation** is a pressing challenge. The Creole, Balanta and Bijago New Testaments are complete, but literacy programmes are inadequate. Work continues in Papel and Manjako. **SIL** workers are making a survey of translation needs.

9. **A Christian radio programme** aired once a week on the national radio has a wide audience. Pray both for quality, and lasting response. A cassette ministry for teaching and evangelism is lacking personnel. **GRI** has produced recordings in 31 languages.

GUYANA

(The Cooperative Republic of Guyana)

Caribbean

May 23

Area 215,000 sq.km. A narrow, developed coastal strip in northeast South America. The hinterland is forest-covered and underdeveloped. Much of the interior is claimed by Venezuela.

Population 979,000. Culturally part of the Caribbean. Annual growth 2.1%. People per sq.km. 5.

Peoples: Colonial importation of labour for the sugar industry has created the present racial diversity and political tensions.
East Indian 53%. Predominantly rural farmers.
African/Eurafrican 41%. Dominant in government, civil service and in urban areas.
Amerindian 4.7%. The majority in the sparsely inhabited interior. Carib (5 tribes) 20,500; Arawakan (4 tribes) 8,000.
European 0.8%. Mainly Portuguese.
Chinese 0.5%.

Literacy 91%. **Official language:** English. **All languages** 12. **Bible translations** 1Bi 1NT 6por.

Capital: Georgetown 223,000. Urbanization 30%.

Economy: In a state of collapse. The main exports are sugar and bauxite. State ownership, corruption and flight of skills have accentuated the pressures of world recession. Income/person $723 (5% of USA). Inflation 12%.

Politics: Independent from Britain in 1966. All four main political parties are varying shades of Marxist but polarized on racial lines. The Black minority government retains power by subtle discrimination, vote-rigging and state control of national life.

Religion: Atheism is officially propagated.
Hindu 35.6%. All East Indian.
Muslim 9%. Most East Indian, some Blacks.
Animist/Spiritist 3%. **Non-religious/Atheist** 2%.
Christian 50%. Nominal 10%. Affiliated 40%.

Roman Catholic 9.4% (officially 16%). Practising 25%. 92,000a; 49,000m.

Orthodox 0.9%. 9,000a.

Marginal groups 1.8%. 17,000a; 8,200m. Over 16 indigenous and foreign cults.

Protestant 28% (officially 33%). 274,000a; 105,056m. Denominations 51. Some of largest (adult members):

Anglicans	25,000
Seventh Day Adventist Church	17,000
Elim Pentecostal Church	8,500
Assemblies of God	5,600
Lutheran Church	5,600
Congregational Church	5,000
Methodist Church	4,900
Church of the Nazarene	4,000
N.T. Church of God	3,000
Brethren	2,600

Evangelical 8.7% of population.

Missionaries to Guyana 50 (1:19,600 people) in 16 agencies.

Missionaries from Guyana possibly 2.

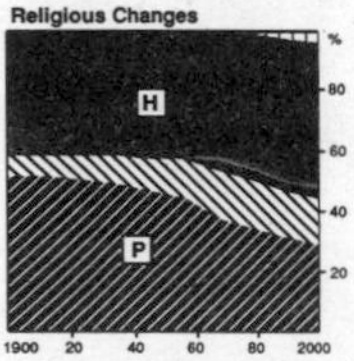

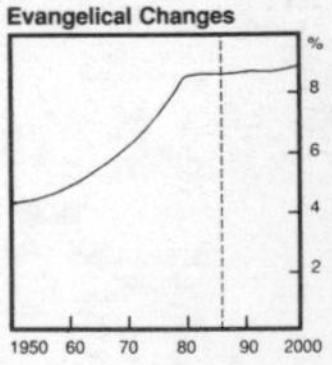

1. **Official atheism has led to pressures on Christian work** and confrontations between the authorities and Christian leaders. This hostility is beginning to backfire to the advantage of the gospel. Pray for all Christians in places of influence, for they need ethical rectitude and divine boldness to demonstrate the power of the gospel. Pray for God-fearing leaders for the country. The Marxist President Burnham died in 1985 and leadership succession is uncertain.

2. **Economic hardship and oppression** have caused many to emigrate and could cause a resurgence of racial rioting and even civil war. Pray that these times of stress may bring nominal Christians, as well as non-Christians, to faith in Christ.

3. **The Christian Church** is a mixture of dead nominalism and vital, vibrant evangelical fervour. The last 10 years has been a time of decline for the older churches, and rapid growth for Pentecostal churches and charismatic fellowships. Evangelical believers are found in all walks of life. Pray that present freedom to worship and witness may be used to the full. Sadly the racialism in politics affects the Christians too, so pray for unity that transcends culture.

4. **The tragic moral state of the Black population** calls for fervent prayer and witness to the delivering power of God. Almost all have been baptized as "Christians".

5. **The suffering East Indian majority** needs the gospel. 70% are Hindu and 18% Muslim, the majority of whom have not been effectively evangelized. Praise the Lord for the growing numbers of believers (almost entirely ex-Hindu). About 10% of the Indians are now Christian. The Pentecostal churches have had a significant impact (**AoG**, Elim, etc.). Little impression has been made on the Muslims.

6. **The Amerindians** have, to a great measure, been Christianized. Most are Catholic. Relatively few have a clear understanding of the gospel and are basically animists. Only a few isolated groups and villages are totally unreached. The **UFM** work in the south among the Waiwai and Wapishana has resulted in a growing, missionary-minded church despite many government restrictions. The Scriptures are being translated in the latter language.

7. **Christian education** at all levels is hampered by severe import restrictions on Christian literature and Bibles. Pray for the free flow of such. Pray for Bible schools, of which there are five, and for the training of leaders.

8. **Foreign missions** passed through some years of great curtailment in ministries and personnel. New visas have been granted more readily of late. Pray for all serving the Lord in economically discouraging circumstances. The Elim Pentecostal Church has the largest group of missionaries (14).

9. **Student work** of the ISCF(**IFES**) has borne fruit in 85 schools, but prayer is needed for a more stable and effective witness in the tertiary institutes and university.

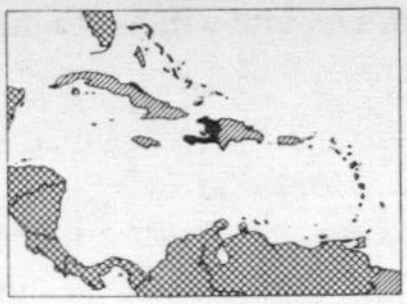

HAITI
(The Republic of Haiti)

Area 28,000 sq.km. Western third of the island of Hispaniola; shared with the Dominican Republic.

Population 5,800,000. Annual growth 2.3%. People per sq.km. 207. One of the most densely populated countries in the Americas. Many Haitiens have fled or emigrated to the USA.

Peoples: Black 94.5%, **Mulatto** 5%, **Other** 0.5%.

Literacy 25%. **Official language:** French (10% speak it). **Common language:** Creole.

Capital: Port-au-Prince 860,000. Urbanization 28%.

Economy: Largely agricultural, but overpopulation and soil erosion together with systematic large-scale commercial plunder by the corrupt elite made Haiti the poorest country in the Americas. Income/person $320 (2% of USA).

Politics: A slave revolt against the French in 1804 created the first black republic in the world. A troubled history of blood and dictatorships since then. The most recent dictators, the Duvaliers, had an unenviable record of severe repression. The harshness of the regime lessened in the 1980s. (Note: As we go to press in February 1986, news has come of the deposing of Duvalier. The military government promises to introduce democracy within three years.)

Religion: Catholicism is the state religion, but the real religion of the people is Voodooism: a mixture of African spiritism and witchcraft. There is freedom of religion.

Non-religious/Atheist 1.4%.

Spiritist approximately 75% but usually classified as "Christian".

Christian 98.4%. Affiliated 93%.

Roman Catholic 75%. Practising 20%. 4,960,000a; 2,880,000m.

Marginal groups 0.6%. 37,500a; 8,600m.

Protestant 17.2%. 1,130,000a; 410,000m. Denominations 30+ (many splinter groups). Largest (adult members):

Seventh Day Adventist Church	130,000
Baptist Conv. (**SBC**)	40,000
Church of God (Cleveland)	39,400
MEBSH (**WT**)	30,900
Episcopal Church	17,000
Church of God of Prophecy	14,000
Evang. Baptist Church (**UFM**)	14,000
Church of the Nazarene	11,700
Conservative Baptist (**CBHMS**)	11,000

Evangelical 12.3% of population.

Missionaries to Haiti 504 (1:13,000 people) in 60 agencies.

Missionaries from Haiti possibly 20.

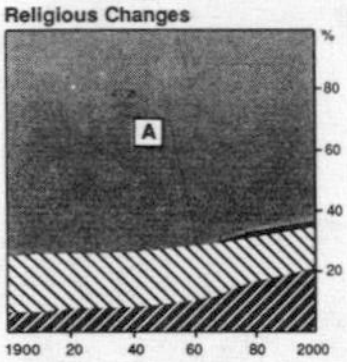

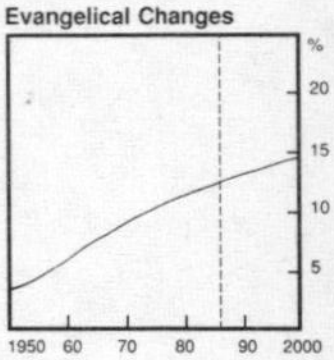

1. **Voodoo has a pervasive and powerful influence on all levels of society.** About 85-90% of all Haitiens, including nearly all Catholics and a minority of Protestants, are still in bondage to its practices. Satan's grip will only be loosened by warfare in the heavenlies.

2. **The continued, steady growth of the Protestants** is the result of widespread evangelism, Christian radio, community development and the evident power of Jesus to free people from the tyranny of Satan. Praise God for this.

3. **The manifest weaknesses of the Church need correcting for healthy growth.** The Protestants have had relatively greater impact on the more rural, poor and illiterate. Lack of commitment and understanding of the gospel, together with the poverty of congregations, limits the emergence of strong, well-taught, indigenous leadership to give adequate Bible teaching. Missionary vision is limited, but some Haitien missionaries are serving in surrounding lands.

4. **Poverty, disease and degradation** have stimulated a flow of financial aid and a wide range of community development projects. Over 40 Christian agencies are actively involved, including Salvation Army, **WV**, **TEAR Fund**, "Compassion" and Mennonites. Sensitivity and wisdom are needed to preserve the indigenity, morality and independence of the churches

and their leaders. Pray that every expression of Christian concern in these medical, agricultural, social and literacy programmes may draw folk to the Saviour. Pray also for the new government, that it may tackle the serious economic problems partially caused and certainly not solved by the Duvalier dictatorships.

5. **Leadership training** is hard to provide without foreign funds. Pray for the 12 Bible schools/seminaries and the many TEE programmes that seek to meet the need. Pray for Haitien leaders to be raised up who are men of faith and spiritual authority, and who are not diverted by material inducements.

6. **The Council of Evangelical Churches** is becoming a centre for fellowship, unity and research among believers; a vital need in the light of evident denominational rivalries.

7. **Missions continue to have a large input.** The largest are **WT** (79 missionaries), **UFM** (44), **OMS** (39), Wesleyans (18), Baptists (17), **WGM** (13). Pray for a humble sensitivity, avoidance of paternalism and a ministry of life through them to the churches.

H

8. **The less evangelized people groups:**
   a) **The Mulatto elite** — wealthy, French-orientated and isolated from the poor majority.
   b) **The refugees** — 50,000 in Florida; 10,000 in Bahamas, etc. There are churches among them, but their cultural and economic isolation makes this a hard ministry. **OMS**, Nazarene, Baptists, etc. have a ministry to them.

9. **Christian literature** is not widely available due to poverty, and its value is limited due to illiteracy. The long-awaited Creole Bible was published by the **Bible Society** in 1984. Pray that the Word may begin to transform and revive the flagging Church. Literacy programmes are a prerequisite.

10. **Christian broadcasting has made a deep impact.** Two key radio ministries, Radio Lumière (**WT** with five stations) and 4VEH (**OMS** in north) have a large following. Over 37% of the population listen regularly to Radio Lumière. Pray for social and spiritual impact in the lives of listeners.

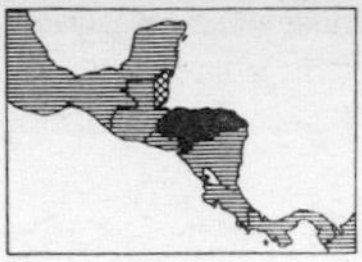

HONDURAS
(The Republic of Honduras)

Latin America

May 25

Area 112,000 sq.km. Guatemala to the west, Nicaragua to the southeast.

Population 4,372,000. Annual growth 3.4%. People per sq.km. 39.

Peoples
Mestizo (Ladino) and some **White** 84%.
Eurafrican 8%. Predominantly English-speaking Mulatto 240,000; Black Caribs speaking Garifuna 110,000.
Amerindian (5 groups) 7%. Only 1% using the original languages; Miskito 35,000; Jicaque 3,000; Sumo 2,000.
Other 1%. Palestinian and Arab 30,000; Chinese 2,000, etc.
Refugees — Salvadorian 40,000-70,000; Nicaraguan Miskito 25,000.

Literacy 60%. **Official language:** Spanish. **Other languages:** English on the north coast.

Capital: Tegucigalpa 550,000. Other city: San Pedro Sula 346,000. Urbanization 38%.

Economy: The broken terrain and unequal distribution of land and wealth have hindered development. Insensitive exploitation by multinationals and corruption of politicians have also helped to keep Honduras the poorest of the "banana" republics. Bananas and coffee are the main exports. Income/person $670 (5% of USA). Unemployment 40%.

Politics: Independent from Spain in 1821, but 134 revolutions by 1932. Military rule for much of this century. Democratic civilian government since 1984. The nation is deeply affected by the wars in bordering El Salvador and Nicaragua and the large US military commitment to the land.

Religion: The Roman Catholic Church is officially recognized, but there is separation of Church and State and religious freedom.

Non-Christian 1.8%. Muslim, Spiritist, Animist, etc.

Christian 98.2%. Affiliated 96.5%.

Roman Catholic 86% (officially 93%). Practising 18%. 3,750,000a; 1,948,000m.

Orthodox 0.14%. 6,500a. Mainly Lebanese.

Marginal groups 0.7%. 31,720a; 12,000m. Largest (adherents):

Jehovah's Witnesses	17,000
Mormons	13,600

Protestant 9.9%. 435,000a; 150,000m. Denominations approx. 50. Largest (adult members):

Assemblies of God	16,000
Church of God (Cleveland)	14,000
Brethren	13,800
Seventh Day Adventist Church	13,000
Prince of Peace	8,050
Free Pentecostal Church	8,000
Reformed Church	6,200
Central American Church (**CAMI**)	6,000

Evangelical 8.8% of the population.

Missionaries to Honduras 405 (1:10,800 people) in 50 agencies.

Missionaries from Honduras 0.

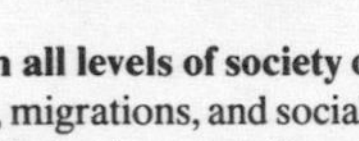

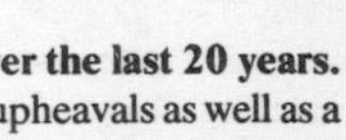

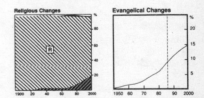

1. **Response to the gospel has been dramatic in all levels of society over the last 20 years.** This has been brought about by natural disasters, migrations, and social upheavals as well as a massive outreach by churches and missions through evangelism (Evangelism-in-Depth 1963/4, Luis Palau campaigns in '70s, etc.), distribution of Scriptures and literature and extensive use of radio. Pray that the fruit of this harvest will be conserved and mature in the growing churches.

2. **The Roman Catholic Church** has suffered from limited funds and personnel. Over 80% of the latter are foreign. Nominalism, pagan practices and immorality have been widespread, resulting in losses to Protestant churches. The whole structure of society must be permeated by the gospel.

3. **The Protestant churches** have grown steadily, but poverty and illiteracy have stunted maturity. The large missionary presence has not always led to happy fellowship between missionaries and churches. Pray for strong, stable, mature leadership. There are 16 Bible schools, one seminary and eight TEE programmes operating.

4. **There is an extensive variety of supportive ministries** — literature (13 bookstores), youth (CCC, IFES — 20 groups) the **Bible Society**, **MAF**, etc.

5. **The Amerindians** are gradually being assimilated into the Ladino culture. The few retaining their original cultures and languages are responding to the gospel.

6. **Missionaries are relatively numerous** — may their ministries result in a reversal of the flow, with Hondurans serving the Lord in other lands! The largest missions are **SBC** (37 missionaries), **WGM** (32), **CAMI** (31), **MAF** (13), and **AoG** (10).

7. **Needy peoples.** Only the Black Caribs and Jicaque (among whom **SIL** work) have proved unresponsive to the gospel until recently. The English-speaking Blacks are nominally Protestant, but with relatively few born-again believers. The small Arab and Chinese communities are unreached and unoccupied.

8. **The refugees** from El Salvador and Nicaragua have suffered and are dependent on Christian aid. Most of the Miskito are believers. **MAF**'s flying programme has been of great help.

Asia

May 26

HONG KONG
(The Crown Colony of Hong Kong)

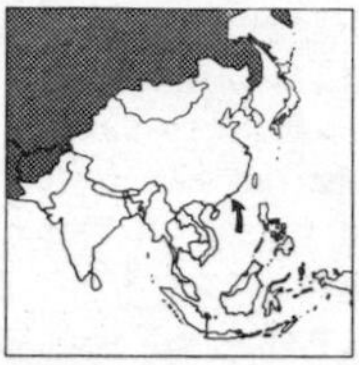

Area 1061 sq. km. A mountainous peninsula and 230 islands on the coast of Gwangdung Province of the People's Republic of China (PRC).

Population 5,400,000. It was 600,000 in 1945. Annual growth 1.9%. People per sq.km. 5,108. 40% of present population was born in the PRC. 500,000 refugees since 1975. One of the most densely populated areas of the world.

Peoples
Chinese 98.3%. Cantonese 81.5%, Hoklo 8.1%, Hakka 3.3%, Sze Yap 3%, Mandarin 2.8%.
Other 1.7%. British 28,000; Indians and Pakistanis 14,000.

Literacy 82%. **Official languages:** Chinese, English.

Capital: Victoria 990,000. Other city: Kowloon 2,800,000. Urbanization 92%.

Economy: Rapid growth to become one of the world's leading financial, industrial and trading centres. Hong Kong is the source of 40% of China's foreign exchange and the port for 30% of its exports. Uncertainty about the future has dampened the ardour of its ruthless capitalism. Income/person $6,000 (43% of USA).

Politics: British crown colony since 1846; reverting to China in 1997 as a Special Administrative Zone with guaranteed autonomy of government, legal system, finance and international trade.

Religion: A secular state with religious freedom, but PRC pressures and controls feared by many after 1997 despite official promises to the contrary.
Non-religious/Atheist 14.5%.
Chinese religions 62%. Still fairly popular. Over 900 Taoist and Buddhist temples in Hong Kong.
New religions 3.5%. Syncretic combinations of Chinese and world religions.
Muslim 1%. **Hindu** 0.2%. **Sikh** 1,000.
Christian 18.9%. Nominal 6.4%. Affiliated 12.5%.
Roman Catholic 4.9%. 270,000a; 116,000m.
Marginal groups (10) 0.6%. 29,700a; 14,200m.
Protestant 7%. 380,000a; 212,000m. Denominations 44 (also over 130 independent congregations). Some of the largest (adult members):

Baptist Conv. (**SBC**)	34,000
Church of Christ of China	22,700
Lutheran groups (7)	20,000
Anglican Church	15,870
Christian and Miss. Alliance	13,000
Methodist Church	8,600
Ling Liang Worldwide M.	7,500
Assembly Hall (Little Flock)	7,000
Assemblies of God	5,200

Evangelical 5.2% of population.
Missionaries to Hong Kong est. 540 (1:10,000 people) in over 50 agencies.
Cross-cultural missionaries from Hong Kong 46 (1:8,300 Protestants) in 17 agencies.

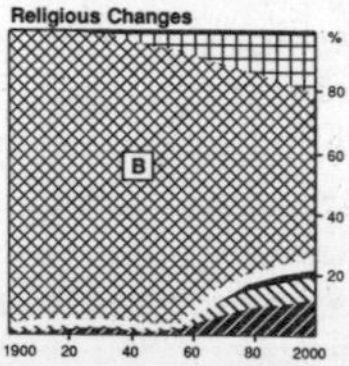

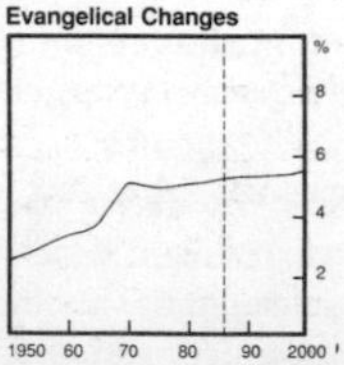

1. **The countdown to 1997 dominates the thinking of Hong Kong citizens.** Non-Christians are being forced to realize that money is not everything and that their idols will not help them. Christians see that time is precious, spiritual preparation vital, and present opportunities for evangelism strategic. Pray for right priorities for Christians and a doubling in church membership by 1997. Pray for close fellowship between denominations; a greater unity is essential in the light of impending changes.

2. **The Christian community** grew rapidly in the '60s, but growth has slowed. Church attendance is low, and there is a high rate of dropouts among young adults. Christians face many pressures in Hong Kong's crowded and intense atmosphere. Some churches are maintaining vigorous growth through evangelism - such as Ling Liang WWM, Assemblies of God, Baptists, and churches related to **CMA, OMS**, etc. Pray for both vitality and growth in the 660 churches.

3. **Christian leaders** have a key role to play in the next decade, but workers are too few. There are 500 students in 12 seminaries, over half being women. Pray for the present and future ministries of the Alliance Seminary (104 students), China Graduate School of Theology (45), Baptist Theological Seminary (35), etc. Pray also for the graduates as they move out to ministry in Hong Kong and overseas.

4. **Hong Kong's underworld of crime and secret societies** (37 Triad societies with 500,000 members) stimulates the drug-addiction, prostitution, theft, gambling and protection rackets that thrive in crowded living conditions in proximity to much material wealth. Few Christians have faced up to the appalling need of folk trapped in this evil way of life — and such need much prayer.

5. **There are many segments** of Hong Kong's society that are less well evangelized, such as:
   a) **The blue-collar industrial workers,** and the wealthy financiers and businessmen.
   b) **The Vietnamese refugees** — with some 40,000 remaining and with little hope of finding an alternative home to their crowded camps. **WV** and **YWAM** have a ministry to them.
   c) **The Chinese refugees** — most are housed in unhygienic squatter settlements, crowded little high-rise flats or boats in the harbours. Many are disillusioned and frustrated. A number of churches and missions have long sought to alleviate their needs physically and spiritually (**WV, OMF, ECF**, etc).
   d) **The village farmers and fisher folk**. There are few churches in the rural areas. Pray for the recently initiated programmes of evangelism.

6. **Many Chinese are seeking to emigrate all over the world before 1997.** This emigration could become a flood. Pray that many may find refuge in Jesus.

7. **Missionary agencies have multiplied** — partly through flight from China in the '50s, and partly to use Hong Kong as a base for ministry to other parts of Asia. Duplication of effort by "China Watchers" and supportive ministries is not unusual. Present ministries need to be vital and strategic. Continued missionary presence after 1997 may not be expedient. Major agencies being **SBC** (73), **SDA** (60), **CMA** (27), Lutheran Ch. — Missouri Syn. (27), **OMF** (22), **CCC** (18), **OMS** (12).

8. **The missionary vision of the Hong Kong Church is growing.** There is widespread interest in ministry to the believers in the PRC and in missionary work abroad. Pray that this burden may grow and not be hindered by fears for the future. The Hong Kong Association of Christian Missions is a focal point for 17 agencies. Pray for adequate sending structures and the sending of quality recruits overseas. The Chinese School of Missions is planned to open for intending missionaries in 1988.

9. **Ministry to the Chinese mainland** is fraught with problems yet vital for the believers in the unofficial groups in the PRC. Pray for sensitivity, wisdom and boldness for all committed to such outreaches. Pray that churches may be adequately prepared for future ministry in a changing situation.

10. **Student ministries** — dynamic growth through the HKFES(**IFES**) programmes in evangelism, Bible teaching and the widely read magazine *Breakthrough.* Over 5,000 students in secondary and tertiary institutions are involved. 12,000 Hong Kong students are studying

abroad, where the conversion rate is also high. May the impact of Christian graduates on Hong Kong society be decisive!

11. **Hong Kong is a vital nerve centre for media.** Groups such as Christian Communications Ltd., and **AO**, have made significant contributions. **Literature** is written, printed, published and distributed on a massive scale (**CLC, EHC, CMA**). Bibles are printed for the world, and the **Bible Society** has a key role. **Radio** studios prepare programmes for **FEBC, FEBA, TWR** and many other radio agencies. Pray that this role may continue beyond 1997.

Eastern Europe

May 27-28

HUNGARY
(The Hungarian People's Republic)

Area 93,000 sq.km. A landlocked, central European state on the River Danube.

Population 10,748,000. Growth rate -0.4%. People per sq.km. 115.

Peoples
Magyar (Hungarians) 91.1%. More than six million Hungarians live in surrounding lands or in the West.
Minorities 8.5%. Gypsy 600,000; Jews 95,000; Slovak 32,000; Croat 26,000; Serbian 20,000.
USSR Military, etc. 0.4%.

Literacy 98%. **Official language**: Hungarian.

Capital: Budapest 2,230,000. Urbanization 46%.

Economy: Less central control of the national economy gave considerable material progress until 1978. The effects of the recession since 1980 brought hardship to many, though Hungary's economy is one of the most free in E.Europe. Income/person $2,150 (15% of USA).

Politics: A Russian-engineered coup brought the Communists to power in 1947. The Hungarian uprising of 1956 brought terrible revenge from the Russians. 80,000 were killed, wounded or deported and 200,000 fled to the West. There has been a tactful liberalization of controls over the subsequent years.

Religion: Tight control of church leadership of the larger churches and harassment of those who protest was the pattern until recently. Restriction on church meetings, building programmes and literature production have been somewhat eased since 1981. Relationship between the authorities and Church has been steadily thawing.
Non-religious/Atheist 14%.
Jews 0.9%.
Christian 85.3%.
Roman Catholic 60.7%. Practising 14%. 6,520,000a.
Orthodox 0.6%. 60,000a. Denominations 6.
Protestant 24%. 2,580,000a; 738,000m. Denominations 17. Largest (adherents):

Reformed Church	2,075,000
Lutheran Church	430,000
Baptist Church	26,000
Ev. Christian Pentecostal	15,000
Seventh Day Adventist Church	9,600
Methodist Church	5,500

Evangelical 3.7% of population.

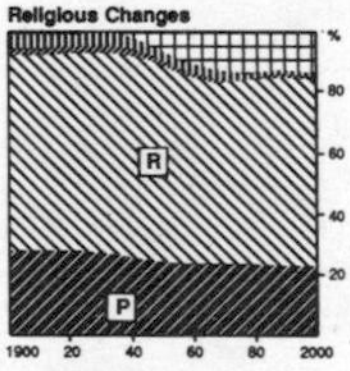

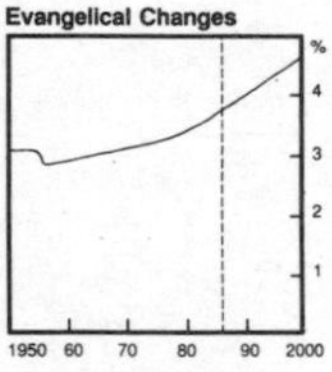

1. **Leadership of all denominations** is infiltrated by Communists, and most toe the Party line. These leaders seek to enforce government policies on pastors and churches that are often detrimental to the gospel. Most pastors have had to take an oath of loyalty to the state in order to preach. Pray that leaders may put loyalty to God and His Word first.

2. **Revivals in Hungary in 1939 and 1946** brought much life to sections of the mainline churches and some growth to smaller Free Churches; most of the latter are evangelical, but there is much nominalism in the larger denominations. Pray for pastors in the larger churches who are faithful witnesses in spite of the restrictions. Pray for a further move of God's Spirit in

these churches, of which there are encouraging signs. There is more freedom now than ever before for camps, conferences and evangelistic meetings.

3. **Illegal meetings** were forced on many groups of believers because of the tardiness of the government to recognize them or grant permission for more than a limited number of churches. Praise God for permission given for 12 new Baptist church buildings in 1984. Pray for a relaxation of restrictions. Pray also that Christians may make full use of present opportunities for witness.

4. **Open persecution is now a thing of the past**, replaced by a subtle propaganda that aims to enervate and emasculate the Church. Pressures, discrimination and dismissal of pastors who do not conform has occurred in the recent past. However, most Christians are content to live with the status quo, and too many have allowed compromise and lethargy to blunt their testimony. Pray that believers may be shaken from a dull conformity, live radiantly for the Lord, and make a decisive impact on their nation.

5. **Bible-trained leaders are few**. The larger denominations are free to run seminaries, though liberal theology is widely taught. The Baptist seminary is too small and will soon be enlarged, but, in other schools, far too few are coming forward for the ministry. The Free Churches have a united correspondence school.

6. **Young people** are turning to the Lord all over the country. For a long time youth meetings were not allowed and therefore went "underground", but now they are legally and socially acceptable. Disillusionment and restlessness is widespread among non-Christians. Drugs and alcohol have become so widely used that the authorities have asked Christians to help with the problem. Pray that they may, and be so in the power of the Spirit that the life-changing gospel may be seen by all.

7. **The scarcity of Bibles was long a problem.** Between 1949 and 1977 only 50,000 Bibles and Scripture portions were printed, and limited supplies imported legally and extra-legally. Praise God for the new edition of the Bible (1975) of which over 100,000 have been printed, and which is quite widely available. Praise God that the Bible has also been permitted as a "work of literature" in schools. Pray for the Bible's message to be read by the many who need it, and for the Holy Spirit to speak to them.

8. **Christian literature** is available in limited quantities in the two Christian bookstores for the whole country. The selection of titles is small, and there are too few good theological and Christian teaching books available. Pray for relaxations in publishing and distribution, evident in 1984, to continue. Pray for all who use various ways to make literature available.

9. **Christian radio** broadcasts from the **TWR** station in Monaco are valuable for evangelism and teaching. There is also a weekly half-hour service broadcast on Sunday on the national radio.

The West

May 29

ICELAND
(Republic of Iceland)

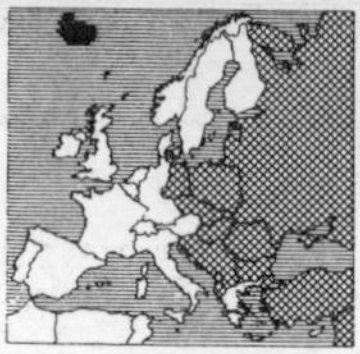

Area 103,000 sq.km. A large volcanic island in the North Atlantic; mountainous, largely barren with many large glaciers.

Population 237,000. Annual growth 1.2%. People per sq.km. 2.

Peoples
Icelander 98.5%. Original settlers came from Norway 1,000 years ago.
Foreign 1.5%. US military and Danish.

Literacy 100%. **Official language:** Icelandic.

Capital: Reykjavik 86,000. Urbanization 89%.

Economy: Prosperous, but very dependent on the fishing industry. Income/person $10,270 (73% of USA).

Politics: Parliamentary republic since independence from Denmark in 1944. A member of NATO.

Religion: The Lutheran Church is still recognized as the State Church, but there is religious freedom.

Non-religious/Atheist 2.1%.

Christian 97.7%. Affiliated 96.6%.

Roman Catholic 0.9%. Practising 40%. 2,200a; 1,560m.

Protestant 95.5%. Church attendance 10%. 226,000a; 162,000m. Denominations 11. Largest (adherents):

National Church (Lutheran)	214,000
Lutheran Free Church	7,300
Pentecostal Movement	2,100
Independent Lutheran	1,150
Seventh Day Adventist Church	1,100

Evangelical 3% of population.

Missionaries to Iceland 14 (1:17,000).

Missionaries from Iceland 6 (1:37,700 Protestants) in Africa.

1. **The Icelanders are nominally Christian,** but prosperity is causing a drift away from the churches and a growing interest in occultism and leftist ideology. The spiritist movement has a great influence in de-Christianizing Iceland, and more than 40% of the population has had involvement with the occult. Pray that these dark powers may be bound in the name of Jesus.

2. **There is much nominalism in both the Lutheran and the Free Church today**, and there are very few Bible-based churches where the new birth is preached. Pray for the Brethren and Pentecostal assemblies and also for the two groups of evangelical believers (Salvation Army and YMCA) indirectly linked to the State Church. Charismatic youth groups of UFMM within the State Church are bringing a more biblical perspective to some congregations. There may be no more than 2,000 truly born-again believers in the country. Pray for the growth of the evangelical witness.

3. **Evangelistic work** has been discouraging in the prevailing spiritual climate, but since 1980 more efforts are being made through evangelistic teams and extensive literature distribution (Pentecostal movement and **YWAM**). Pray for the ministry of these centres through evangelism and Bible teaching that they may be effective tools for the extension of God's Kingdom in Iceland and abroad.

4. **The KSF(IFES) work among the 3,000 university students** is encouraging, with around 200 members. Pray for those who love the Lord that they may maintain a glowing testimony where indifference is so widespread.

5. **The Bible Society published a new Bible version in 1981.** Pray for the ministry of God's Word through the 10,000 copies already in circulation.

6. **The missionary vision** is very small — with only three missionary couples of the national Church serving in Africa. Pray for an increase of this vision.

Asia

INDIA
(Republic of India)

May 30-June 5

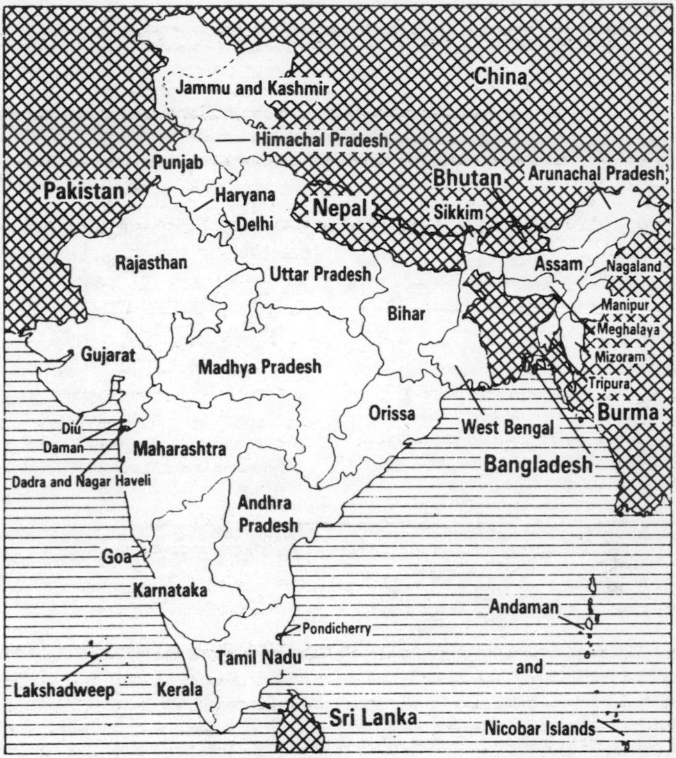

Area 3,204,000 sq.km. 22 union states and 9 union territories. Geographically India dominates South Asia and the Indian Ocean.

Population 748,000,000. Annual growth 2.2%; 17 million increase every year. People per sq.km. 233. Nearly 16% of the world's population is Indian, living on 2.4% of the world's land surface.

Peoples: The great racial, ethnic, religious and linguistic diversity makes a simple subdivision of the population difficult.

Ethno-Linguistic:

Indo-Aryan 72%. In N. and C. India.

Dravidian 25%. Majority in S. India.

Sino-Tibetan 3%. N. border and N.E. India.

Caste: A system that pervasively influences every religion in India, to a lesser or greater extent, but which is fundamental to Hinduism. Caste discrimination is forbidden by the constitution, but it is socially important for over 80% of the population.

Caste Hindus 64%. (Brahmin, Kshatriya, Vaisya, Sudra).

Harijan (Outcastes, Untouchables) 14%. Classified by the government as "Scheduled Castes".

Tribal peoples 7%, **Muslims** 12%, **Christians** 3%, etc., are considered outside the caste structure. The former are classified as "Scheduled Tribes".

Literacy 36%. **Official languages** 14: Hindi 31%, Telugu 8%, Tamil 7%, Urdu 5%, Gujarati 4.6%, Kannada 4%, Malayalam 4%, Oriya 4%, Punjabi 2.5%, Assamese 1.6%, Kashmiri 0.5%. **Nationally used languages:** Hindi and English; the latter being important in education. **All languages** 1,658 (1971 census), 329 listed by **SIL**. Those with over 5,000 speakers number 350. **Bible translations** 36Bi 25NT 54por. At least 13 NTs need a major revision.

Capital: Delhi 6,600,000. Other major cities: Calcutta 10,200,000, Bombay 10,000,000, Madras 6,900,000, Bangalore 4,000,000, Hyderabad 3,000,000, Ahmedabad 3,000,000, Pune 2,000,000, Kanpur 2,000,000. Urbanization 23%.

Economy: Agriculture and industry are both important. 74% of the labour force is agricultural, but rapid industrialization and urbanization is taking place. Remarkable economic growth has been offset by the high birth rate, illiteracy, prejudice, resistance to change, and bureaucratic inefficiency. Income/person $260 (2% of USA). Yet 300 mill. probably live below the breadline.

Politics: Independent from Britain in 1947. The world's largest functioning democracy. Troubled relations with surrounding nations; two wars with Pakistan and one with China. Internal tensions have arisen because of regional, caste, and religious loyalties that have sometimes broken out into violence and rioting.

Religion: India is a secular state that grants freedom to all religions to practise and propagate their faith. In practice there has been strong pressure from Hindu militants to prevent proselytization at a state and central level. Several states have discriminatory legislation against religious minorities, but the federal government has not followed this course.

Hindu 82%. Figure somewhat raised by the automatic inclusion of many of the tribal animists. Hinduism is a social system and philosophy and readily absorbs elements of any religion with which it comes into contact. Popular Hinduism is idolatrous. Intellectual Hinduism is philosophical and mystical and has a growing appeal to Western countries. India suffers under its fatalism, castism, 200 million holy cows, 33 million gods, etc., to its economic and spiritual detriment.

Muslim 11.8% (Muslims claim 13%). A widespread minority, but a majority in Kashmir and Lakshadweep, and growing among Harijans.

Sikhs 1.92%. Majority in Punjab. Many in armed forces.

Tribal religions approx. 1.5%. Among Scheduled Tribes.

Buddhist 0.7%. A small minority in the land of its origin. Majority among Tibetans, several N.E. tribes, and growing among Harijans in Maharashtra.

Jain 0.47%.

Other religions and persuasions 0.4%. **Baha'i, Zoroastrian** 75,000; **Jews** 6,000.

Christian 2.61% officially (churches claim 4%). A great variation in percentages in the different states.

Roman Catholic 1.55%. Strongest in the south and in Goa. Practising 70%. 11,700,000a.

Syrian Orthodox 0.24%. 1,840,000a. Predominantly in Kerala, southwest India; descended from churches planted by the Apostle Thomas in the first century.

Protestant 1.79%. More numerous in the south and northeast. 13,400,000a; 5,480,000m. Denominations 320+. Largest (adult members):

Church of South India (CSI)	600,000
United Lutheran Churches	464,000
Council of Baptist Churches in N.E.	400,444
Methodist Church of S.Asia	400,000
Salvation Army	400,000
Church of North India (CNI)	324,000
Mar Thoma Syrian Church	270,000
Presbyterian Church of N.E.	201,000
Telugu Baptist Churches	128,000
Seventh Day Adventist Church	124,000
Indian Pentecostal Ch.of God	105,000
Baptist Conv. of Northern Circars	84,500
Christian Assemblies/brethren	71,000
Church of God (Cleveland)	43,000
Assemblies (Bakht Singh)	approx. 42,000

Evangelical 1% of population.

Missionaries to India 900 (1:850,000 people), with a rapid reduction in numbers.

Missionaries from within India 4,200 in about 120 agencies. Not all are in cross-cultural ministries.

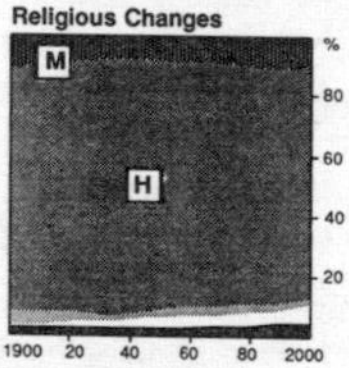

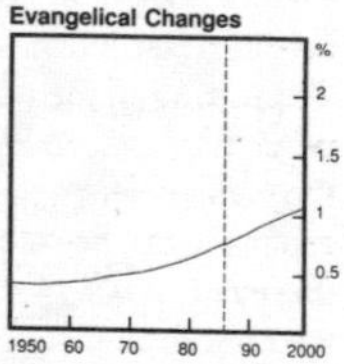

INDIA GENERAL

1. **Praise God for the past 250 years.** The Holy Spirit has used the labours of countless thousands of preachers, both Indian and expatriate, to change India and plant the Church. Although a minority, Christians are numerous and the Church is growing. Praise for:

a) **The great freedom to spread the gospel** despite efforts to limit this.

b) **Great people movements** among the Harijan "Untouchables" and tribal peoples which continue to this day.

c) **The spiritual awakening since independence**, manifest hunger for peace with God and response to literature and radio evangelism.

d) **Revivals** in South India and in 1976 in Nagaland.

e) **The new missionary burden** based on prayer that is stirring hundreds of churches.

2. **These advances are being contested by the enemy of souls.**

a) **Militancy among Hindus is on the increase.** Millions of despised Harijans have turned to Buddhism, Christianity and increasingly to Islam to escape the oppressive caste system. This has sparked violence against religious minorities, persecution of Christians, discriminatory legislation in some states and the forcible conversion of tribal people to Hinduism. Should such militants gain political control, communal strife would escalate. Pray that Christians may use present freedoms to the full and be prepared to stand firm for the Truth in love.

b) **Communism** has considerable influence in Tripura, West Bengal and Kerala. If economic disaster befell the land, that influence could spread. Pray that Christians may not be complacent in days of momentous change in India.

c) **Nominalism in the churches.** Mass movements to Christ were often inadequately discipled. The quality of life of many Christians deters non-Christians from putting their trust in Jesus. Christians have often become but another caste in a Hindu world. Revival is sorely needed to rid the churches of introspection, social climbing, petty squabbles and sin; to implant a love for the brethren irrespective of social origin; and to give a burden to evangelize.

d) **Severe restriction on the issuing of missionary visas in 1984.** The task of evangelizing India's millions is so great that the Church in India needs all the help it can get. Pray that this restriction may spur on a moving forward of India's 19 million Christians to evangelize. Pray also for ways in which foreigners may continue to cooperate.

3. **There is a rapid decline in the number of missionaries.** Most now serving have already given years of service to India. Pray for the wisest and most effective deployment of the missionaries remaining. Pray for eternal fruit through their ministry, both in the churches and among those outside of Christ, despite restrictions and discouragements. Some of the larger agencies are: **BMMF, CBFMS, CMA, ICF, OMS, WEC, IMI, CBOMB, TEAM,** and most are involved in church development ministries, some in institutions, but relatively few in pioneer work. Pray that visas may be issued, against all present trends, to those whom God is calling. They are needed!

4. **The growth of the churches has slowed since 1971.** In fact, between 1971 and 1981, the census recorded an increase of Christians in only Sikkim, Nagaland, Manipur, Meghalaya and Tripura; all in the northeast. In most states the Christians are stagnating or even declining in percentage. More growth is occurring in indigenous assemblies (i.e. such as those linked with the name of Bakht Singh) and Pentecostal groups, and also older denominations among tribal groups in the northeast. Few believers ever witness to non-Christians, and in some churches there may be no first generation converts out of Hinduism or Islam. The long-term impact on the churches of the aggressive evangelism and literature distribution teams of **OM** and **EHC** has been immense. Many believers have caught the vision as a result. Pray for more to become involved in evangelism, and pray for better coordinated, and more determined, evangelism of non-Christians by local churches — even if it does result in discomfort or persecution.

5. **Caste is one of the biggest issues facing the Church.** Most Christians are of Harijan or scheduled caste origin, and are not yet liberated from what is little more than a legitimized racism. The ambivalent attitude of Christians is a problem to higher caste Hindus who are attracted by the gospel but repelled by the low social origin of Christians, and a stumbling block to Harijans who are put off by castism among Christians. Pray that Christians may formulate and clearly preach biblical standards that liberate Christians to be a new people in Jesus and that do not prevent Hindus bound by caste from coming to Him.

6. **The evangelical witness is a growing force in the Church today.** Praise God for outstanding, mature leaders of international stature in both the older and newer denominations. Pray for:

a) **The Bible to be given its rightful place** in both the theologically liberal and more evangelical denominations. In the former, dialogue and universalism have replaced evangelism and conversion. In the latter there is little solid teaching, expository preaching or application of teachings to the real and pressing needs of India today.

b) **The Evangelical Fellowship of India** has more than 100 cooperating evangelical bodies. It is having a significant impact in maturing, stabilizing and mobilizing the believers through weeks of prayer and conventions; through pastors' retreats; and coordinating missionary outreach, literature production, Sunday School courses, TEE (under title TAFTEE), as well as backing the Union Biblical Seminary.

c) **The Federation of Evangelical Churches of India (FECI)** is the fruit of the work of over 15 smaller evangelical societies (both denominational and interdenominational). Pray that this body may overcome internal problems to become a mighty force for the evangelization of the land.

7. **The training of Christian leaders is of crucial importance.** The lack of dedicated Christian workers prepared to leave all for the sake of Christ is the biggest factor limiting the growth of the Church. There is an average of one pastor for eight churches and 400 villages across the country. Some pastors must care for 200 congregations. Pray for:

a) **Degree-level seminaries**, of which there are over 40. A minority are theologically evangelical. One such is **Union Biblical Seminary** in Pune, with 207 students and backed by 26 evangelical denominations and agencies. Pray for a stream of warm-hearted workers, anointed by the Spirit, to move out from these institutions to India and beyond.

b) **The multitude of Bible schools.** Evangelical institutions are full. Only 10% of all those trained for Christian work go out into evangelistic or pioneer church planting ministries. Pray that this percentage may increase.

c) **TEE** is widely used **for training church leaders.** The best known is "TAFTEE" with many thousands of students. The multiplication of leaders by all means possible is essential.

8. **The exciting growth of Indian missions deserves much prayer.** The rate of growth in numbers of Indian missionaries exceeds the decline in foreign missionaries. Many denominations have sent out cross-cultural missionaries (e.g. CSI, Methodists, Mar Thoma, Baptists of Nagaland, Presbyterians of Mizoram, etc.). In the '60s and '70s a multiplicity of Indian interdenominational missions sprang up, many, especially from the south, linked with the EFI-sponsored **India Missions Association**. Some of the more significant agencies are **IEM** (with 192 workers) and Friends Missionary Prayer Band (260). Pray for:

a) **Wise leaders** who have both vision and sensitivity to the problems of cross-cultural outreach.

b) **Effective sharing** of training, information and skills. The task is so enormous that co-operation is essential.

c) **Adequate cross-cultural preparation** for missionaries. The inter-mission **Indian Institute of Cross-cultural Studies** begun in 1980 is a blessing, but has been started by the Church Growth Research Centre.

d) **Efficient research of the needs.** No complete survey of India's unreached people groups or distribution and growth of the churches has ever been undertaken. Pray that the unfinished task may be carefully researched and the challenge put before believers all over India.

9. **Indians unreached.** No area of the world has such a diversity and concentration of unreached peoples. Some of the broader categories are mentioned here; others will be found under individual states below.

a) **The North India plains** with their teeming millions have very few churches and believers.

b) **The rural population.** 75% of Indians live in the 600,000 village communities. Very few of these have a Christian congregation. In North India there is an average of one church for every 2,000 villages. Few Indian missionaries have concentrated on this big majority.

c) **The great cities** with their exploding populations. Many areas are unreached, and few adequate strategies have been proposed to reach them. Many live in abject poverty and have no homes. One million live on Calcutta's streets alone.

d) **There are reckoned to be 3,000 major ethnic groups** (castes and tribes). In only 22 are Christians a significant minority. In a further 50, Christians are a small minority. Far more cross-cultural evangelism is needed to evangelize every people group.

e) **The higher castes** have shown little open response to the claims of Christ. Pray for the Brahmins (the priestly castes), Kshatriya (the warrior castes) and Vaisya (merchant castes) that pride of descent may be replaced by conviction of sin and faith in the Lord Jesus. Pray for the right approach to win and disciple each group.

f) **The Muslim minority** of 88 million is one of the most accessible for Christian witness in the world. Muslims ruled much of India for 600 years. There is a marginally greater responsiveness today, and about 1,000 Muslims are known to have come to Christ. There are about 100 Christian workers committed to this ministry. Pray specifically for Ishmaelites Salvation Society (ISS) and Intercessory Ministry among Muslims (IMAM), two of a number of Indian missions that are dedicated to this hard and costly ministry.

g) **Young people** are neglected in the churches through lack of manpower, training and interest. How much more needy are those who are unchurched! Youth For Christ, **SU**, **CCC** and others are seeking to reach out to some.

h) **Students** number five million in 120 universities and 4,500 colleges. Calcutta University has 120,000 students! The only effective evangelical witness on a national level is the **Union of Evangelical Students of India (UESI-IFES)** with groups in most campuses and 24 staff workers. Pray for a clear, vibrant witness to the thousands of non-Christian students. Pray for their growth and integration into local churches. There are no **UESI** groups in Kashmir, Punjab or Rajasthan.

i) **Tibetan refugees** (100,000) are scattered through India in special areas and camps. There are 12 churches and 17 pastors among them, but the majority remain bound in their superstitions and Lamaistic Buddhism. The **Tibetan Christian Fellowship** carries a special burden for their evangelization in India and elsewhere.

j) **Leprosy sufferers number 3.2 million**. Christian agencies, especially **The Leprosy Mission**, have a ministry of love to some.

10. **Help ministries.**

a) **Literature**. The prodigious growth of the writing, publishing and distributing of Christian literature has been a major factor in breaking down opposition to the gospel. EHC (**WLC**) teams have gone through India *three* times, leaving literature in the majority of homes. **OM** teams distribute 12-14 million pieces of literature annually. **SGM** dispatched four million Scripture portions in 1982. Christian publishers and bookstores contend with problems in lack of local writing talent and in high costs in a poor land. The Evangelical Literature Fellowship is a major coordinating body. Pray that millions may be reached and gathered into churches through these ministries.

b) **Bible Correspondence Courses** have proved most successful. 60-70 centres send out BCCs. The centre linked with **TEAM** has courses in 22 languages. Over two million have completed at least one course.

c) **The Bible Society** has long had a remarkable ministry, distributing 60-100 million portions of Scripture or Bibles annually. Other organizations are also supplying and distributing Scriptures — such as **World Home Bible League,** and **Bharatiya Bible League.** Pray for these agencies.

d) **Bible translation** is a major need. A new effort as great as that of William Carey and his team 180 years ago should be mounted. At least 13 NTs must be revised and maybe more than 200 need translation teams. There are 39 languages in which work is in progress. The Indian Bible Translators are training and preparing teams to tackle others. IEM workers are translating eight NTs. Pray for more Indian Bible translators to be raised up. A major new Hindi Bible translation is under way.

e) **The Gospel Recordings Assoc. (GRI)** has a unique ministry in India's complex linguistic diversity. There are now recordings on cassettes and records in 350 languages and dialects.

f) **Christian medical work** has had to be streamlined with the run-down of missionary staff. **The Christian Medical Assoc.** has the oversight of 430 institutions with both Indian and expatriate medical workers. **The Emmanuel Hospitals Assoc.** has responsibility for all the institutions that were run by evangelical missions. Pray for the witness that goes out from these hospitals to the many patients, that this may lead to many seeking the Saviour. Pray for the **Evangelical Nurses Fellowship** with groups in many hospitals.

g) **Christian radio** has won a huge audience among Christians and non-Christians. Although there is no Christian broadcasting in India, more than 20 studios turn out programmes for **FEBC** Manila, **FEBA** Seychelles and **TWR** Sri Lanka. "**Back to the Bible**" programmes from the latter have been singularly effective. 1,100 hours of broadcasting in 22 languages is beamed into the land from these stations alone. Pray for wise, long-term strategies that will lead to effective evangelism and church planting — perhaps by radio alone. Pray radio churches into existence, as has happened in the USSR and China.

11. **Indians overseas number 6.3 mill.** Many have migrated for work or to settle on all five continents. Indians form a significant part of the population in two countries in the Americas (Guyana and Trinidad), two in Africa (Mauritius and Natal, South Africa), and two in Asia-Pacific (Fiji and Malaysia). There are large minorities in the Middle East, East Africa, Europe and Canada. Some efforts are being made to evangelize them, but fruit has been limited in most areas.

INDIA – STATES

How can such a country be adequately covered here? The areas of need, the health of the Church and the challenge of unreached peoples are so varied; so *most* of the states and union territories are briefly covered below. Most of these states are far larger than the majority of nations dealt with in far more detail elsewhere in this book. A few smaller states and territories have been omitted for reasons of space.

ANDHRA PRADESH

Population 59,400,000. People per sq.km. 215.

Languages 150. Telugu 71%, Scheduled tribes (36) 4%.

Religion: Hindu 86%, Muslim 8%, Christian 4% (RC 30%, Protestant 68%).

1. **Andra Pradesh has the fourth largest Christian population of any Indian state**, yet there appears to be a serious decline in numbers since 1971. 90% of Christians have come from Scheduled Caste and a few lower caste Hindu groups in great people movements between 1866 and 1940. There are not many non-Christians being won to Christ today. Pray that Christians may make an impact on the 96% of the population outside the churches.

2. **The unreached:**

a) **Several middle caste groups** are receptive, but few have yet come to Christ. Pray for a breakthrough for Jesus in every caste group.

b) **All 36 tribal groups** are, at best, minimally reached. **IEM**, **EHC** and others have seen some fruit among the Koya, Yerukala, Lambad, and Gond, but this is still a hard pioneer field. Most languages have no Scriptures at all.

ARUNACHAL PRADESH

Population 722,000. People per sq.km. 8. Remote, and politically sensitive, mountainous region bordering on China.

Languages 24 tribal groups with many subdivisions.

Religion: Animist 50%, Hindu 30%, Buddhist 14%, Christian 6%.

1. **The Church is growing fast despite persecution**. There are groups of believers among the Adi, Nishi and Tangsa, but most of the churches have been destroyed, atrocities perpetrated against believers and the believers scattered. Pray that their faith and love may be strengthened. Few are literate, and little of the Scriptures is available in their languages.

2. **Anti-Christian legislation** has been passed due to certain elements opposed to the gospel. Hindu missions are free to operate, but no Christian activity is permitted. Pray for the restoration of constitutionally guaranteed religious freedom. The peoples of Arunachal are some of the most backward and illiterate in India, whereas Nagaland to the south is one of India's most educated and Christian.

3. **Most of the people are animists and sun worshippers**, some tribes in the west are Buddhist, but nearly all are unreached. Pray this territory open, and for Indian missionaries to be allowed to enter.

ASSAM

Population 22,300,000. People per sq.km. 284.

Languages 60. Assamese 60%, Bengali 20%, Nepali, etc. 8%, Scheduled Tribes (23) 12%.

Religion: Hindu 71%, Muslim 24%, Christian 4.6% (RC 18%, Protestant 81%).

1. **Christian growth has been fast among the receptive tribal peoples.** The largest churches are Baptist, Lutheran and Presbyterian. Naga and Mizo missionaries have taken on what Western missionaries started. Lack of evangelists, church planters, Bible teachers and translators limits faster growth.

2. **The unreached:**

   a) **The indigenous majority Assamese** are mostly Hindu. They are fast becoming a minority in their own state because of illegal Muslim Bengali immigration from Bangladesh. This resulted in bitter violence and killings, but an amicable settlement was achieved in 1985. Pray that the new climate of peace may be conducive to the spread of the gospel. Pray, too, that the few Christian Assamese and Bengali may exercise a loving ministry among the two estranged peoples.

   b) **Many tribal groups** are only partially evangelized such as the Boro 1,000,000; Miri 360,000; Kachari 300,000; Mikir 220,000; yet churches are being planted among them.

BIHAR

Population 76,200,000. People per sq.km. 450. Overpopulated, poor, and has India's lowest literacy rate.

Languages 77+. Hindi 44%, Bhojpuri, Maithili, Magahi 35%, Urdu 9%, Scheduled Tribes (30) 10%, largest: Santal 2,400.000; Oraon 1,200,000; Munda 976,000; Ho 750,000.

Religion: Hindu 82.7%, Muslim 14.4%, Animist 1.6%, Christian 1.1% (RC 50%, Protestant 50%).

1. **Bihar has been known as the graveyard of missions.** Missionary input has been relatively small, and most has been into the tribal areas. The need is great among the non-tribal majority. Pray that Satan's grip may be broken.

   a) **58 million Biharis** in the 24 central and northern districts are in one of the least evangelized parts of India. There are 40,000 "Christians", but only 50 known among the Aryan majority who make up 84% of the population.

   b) Among the 11 mill. **Muslims** there is not one single Christian worker.

   c) **Most of the tribes are animist in background.** Even the Munda are only 25% Christian. There is a lack of labourers to reap among these increasingly responsive peoples.

   d) **In the capital, Patna** (800,000), there are fewer than 100 evangelical believers.

   e) **The only known believers in three districts of North Bihar** (6 mill.) are Christian workers and their families.

2. **Christians are an insignificant, despised and discouraged minority.** 90% are tribal people, of whom few have a personal faith because of lack of workers, biblical teaching and literature in their languages. The largest denominations are the Lutherans and CNI. Yet people movements among the Santals, Oraon and Munda continue; and others such as the Ho, Sauria, Paharis (FMPB), and Tharus (**RBMU**, FMPB) are opening up to the gospel.

3. **The Ganges Outreach '83** coordinated by **OM** and involving 400 Christian workers was the largest evangelistic assault ever made on this needy state. Pray for fruit in changed lives, revived churches and vision for evangelism.

GUJARAT

Population 37,584,000. People per sq.km. 203.

Languages 64. **Gujarati**, the state language, is spoken by 80% of the population. Scheduled Tribes 14%, largest: Bhil two mill.

Religion: Hindu 89.5%, Muslim 8.6%, Jain 1.4%, Christian 0.39% (RC 64%, Protestant 30%).

1. **Gujarat**, Gandhi's birthplace, has been polarized by high caste Hindu violence against Harijan and Muslim communities. Pray that genuine peace may come to hearts through the gospel, and that communal tensions may open closed communities to the Lord Jesus.

2. **The Christian Church**. The largest church groups are CNI, Methodist, **CMA** and Pentecostal. These groups are growing and there are people movements in progress in at least eight tribal groups. The impact of **OM** team evangelism has been decisive in mobilizing many congregations of late. Pray for vital witnessing by local believers.

3. **The unreached**. All sections of the community are in this category. Pray out labourers to:
   a) **Saurashtra**, the S.W. peninsula, has 10 million people and seven Christian congregations. The Amreli district has one million people and no known believers.
   b) **North Gujarat** has more Muslims. There are very few Christians in the area.
   c) **Most of the tribal groups are unevangelized**. FMPB has an outreach to the Bhil and IEM to the Dangi tribes (140,000) and the Garasia (60,000), among whom a response has begun.
   d) **The Parsees** (11,000 of India's 75,000 in Gujarat), a well-educated, wealthy people of Persian origin who follow the Zoroastrian religion. Few have ever believed and little work has been attempted, yet they no longer strongly adhere to their religion.

4. **Large Gujarati communities** have grown up in E. and C. Africa and in Britain. Most have become wealthy traders but although surrounded by Christians, there has been little success in evangelism.

JAMMU and KASHMIR

This much disputed territory is divided between Pakistan and India. Part of the remote Ladakh region adjoining Tibet has been occupied by China. Two-thirds forms the Kashmir part of the state of Jammu and Kashmir. It is the only Muslim majority state in India.

Population 6,700,000. People per sq.km. 30.

Languages 74. Most speak Kashmiri.

Religion: Muslim 64%, Hindu 32%, Sikh 2.2%, Buddhist 1.2%, Christian 0.14%.

1. **Kashmir and neighbouring Himachal Pradesh and Haryana States have the lowest percentage of Christians for any state in India.** There are about 10,000 altogether. Most are immigrant groups or of low caste Hindu origin in the South. Evangelicals number a few hundred. Pray for workers, open hearts and the planting of new groups of believers.

2. **Several Western missions (CAM, WEC, etc.) and now a number of missions of South and NE Indian origin have sought to witness in the area.** Pray for the work of the Kashmir Evangelical Fellowship across the state, **IEM** among the Tibetan-related peoples and others.

3. **Unreached peoples** — all are in this category. Pray for:
   a) **Kashmiri Muslims** who are becoming more militant for their faith. There are a number of smaller Muslim peoples such as the Baltis, Gujars, etc., who are unreached. Only about 30 Christians have come from within the Muslim community.
   b) **Tibetan Buddhists** from a number of different people groups in the mountainous north and northeast have been only marginally evangelized.
   c) **The high caste Brahmin Pandits of Kashmir** are only 5% of the population but very influential. No known Christians.
   d) **The Dogras of Jammu** have some Christian outreach but few believers.

4. **In neighbouring Himachal Pradesh** (4,500,000) there are numerous local languages and only 4,000 Christians. Few are born-again. 96% of the population are Hindu. The only evangelical advances of note are the **OMS**-related Evangelical Church outreach in Simla and **IEM** church planting in the Kulu Valley. This is a very needy area.

KARNATAKA (formerly Mysore)

Population 40,827,000. People per sq.km. 212.

Languages over 19. Kannada, the state language, is spoken by 65% of the population. Scheduled tribes (53) 0.9%.

Religion: Hindu 85.7%, Muslim 11.3%, Jain 0.8%, Christian 2.1% (RC 66%, Protestant 33%).

1. **Karnataka is the least receptive of India's southern states.** Almost all the Hindu caste groups and the Scheduled tribes are unreached. The few Christians are culturally isolated from them, and few have a vision to evangelize outside their community. Almost all Christians are concentrated in Bangalore and the south of the state. The Baptists are the fastest growing denomination.

2. **Bangalore City** is the Indian headquarters for many Christian churches, and more than 90 Indian missions (The India Missions Association, **IEM**, Quiet Corner) and agencies (**The Bible Society**, **GRI**, **SGM**, **EHC**, International Correspondence School of **AoG**, India Bible League, **FEBA**, etc.). The Methodists and CSI are strong in the area. Pray that Karnataka's privileged Christian community may be revived.

KERALA

Population 28,400,000. People per sq.km. 732. India's most literate, prosperous and densely populated state.

Languages 63. The majority speak Malayalam. Scheduled tribes (68) 1.3%. Most have their own language.

Religion: Hindu 58.1%, Muslim 21.3%, Christian 20.5% (Syrian Orthodox 33%, Catholic 44.5%, Protestant and Mar Thoma Syrians 22%.)

1. **The Syrian Christians** are the direct descendants of those evangelized by the Apostle Thomas. They form the majority of Kerala's Christians and are members of Orthodox, Catholic and Protestant denominations. They have high social status but have become little more than a caste within Hindu society, and few have broken out to become vital witnesses to those of other cultures. There are, therefore, few converts out of non-Christian religions in the churches. Pray that Eph. 2:13-17 may be true for these Christians.

2. **Kerala has numerous Protestant denominations.** Movings of the Spirit over the last 100 years brought multitudes of both nominal Syrian Christians and low caste Hindus to faith in Christ. There are strong mainline, Brethren and Pentecostal congregations. There has been spiritual decline over the past 40 years — castism within the churches is an unmentioned reality, foreign funds and materialism have stimulated divisions. A revived Church in Kerala would have a deep impact on all of India.

3. **Unreached peoples.** Some Christians in Kerala are beginning to catch a missionary vision for the unreached religious, caste and tribal groups in their state and beyond. Yet social barriers are high, and believers need to be liberated from the spirit of caste to both evangelize other social groups and welcome converts as brethren in their fellowships.

   a) **Of the 68 small tribal groups only three or four have Christian groups**; most are Hindus, animists or demon worshippers. Only seven have over 10,000 people. Kerala Christians need to catch a vision to reach them — praise God a few have.

   b) **The Malabar Muslims or Mapilla** are very strong in some districts and number 5.5 mill. A few are becoming Christians through the ministry of IMAM, ISS, **OM** and others, but resistance to the gospel is high. Pray for them.

   c) **Of the higher and 68 Scheduled Castes of Hindus,** there have been people movements to Christianity from among only six or seven of the latter.

d) **The Union Territory of Lakshadweep** (Laccadive Islands). 45,000 Malayali-speaking people related to the Maldivians live on this archipelago of coral atolls. Almost all are strongly Muslim. No Christians or churches are known. The few efforts to bring the gospel to them have been bitterly resisted.

MADHYA PRADESH

Population 57,100,000. People per sq.km. 128. India's largest state.

Languages 223. Hindi 56%, Chatisgarhi 20%, Other 4%. Scheduled tribes (61) 20%, half of which are Gonds.

Religion: Hindu 93% (most of tribal people actually animistic), Muslim 4.8%, Jain 0.9%, Animist 0.3%, Christian 0.67%.

1. **This state was one of the last to open up for missions and is one of the most resistant to Christianity**. It is strongly Hindu with stern laws limiting conversions to Christianity. The small Christian community is growing, but slowly. The great majority are Catholic, and most are Harijan or tribal in origin. Pray for the overturning of opposition to the gospel in high places and in individual hearts. The whole state is a pioneer mission field.

2. **There are a large number of unreached tribal peoples**. The Bastar District, India's largest, is reputed to be the most primitive too. Nine or more tribal groups make up 80% of the population, and only now are the first missionaries beginning outreach to some of them (**IEM**). Many languages in M.P. have nothing of the Scriptures.

MAHARASHTRA

Population 68,544,000. People per sq.km. 222.

Languages and dialects 226. Marathi 90%, Other 4%. Scheduled tribes (approx. 162) 6%, largest: Bhil, Varli, Kokni, Kolam.

Religion: Hindu 81%, Muslim 9.6%, Buddhist 6.3%, Jain 1.5%, Sikh 0.2%, Christian 1.3% (RC 90%, Protestant 10%).

1. **The Christians are a small minority** concentrated in towns and cities, especially in Pune and Bombay. 40% never attend church; court cases, bitterness and quarrelling are common among them. The Protestant community is scattered and very small, and few of them have a personal experience of salvation. The **OM**-coordinated Love Maharashtra campaign of 1981 stimulated Christians to evangelize non-Christians. Pray that revival, growth and outreach may become part of the life of the churches.

2. **Unreached areas and peoples:**

a) **Bombay** (Mumbai) has a large minority of Catholics, but evangelical churches are few.

b) **Many Hindu caste groups, Muslims and Buddhists** are unreached, and little effective evangelism and church planting is being directed to them.

c) **Tribal groups** such as the Bhil, Konkani, Gond, Gowli, Korku and Kolam have not responded readily to the gospel. **IEM** has an outreach to the last three. Less than 1% of the four million tribal people are Christian.

d) **The Konkani people** of the neighbouring territory of Goa (formerly Portuguese) are predominantly nominal Catholic. Evangelical believers are few.

e) **The Jains**, 1 mill. of India's 3.5 mill., live in Maharashtra. This prosperous community with their own religion has scarcely been touched with the gospel in a culturally appropriate way.

MANIPUR

Population 1,600,000. People per sq.km. 71.

Peoples: Meitei (Manipuri) 64%. Scheduled tribes (28) 36%.

Religion: Hindu 60%, Muslim 7%, Animist 2%, Christian 31% (RC 8%, Protestant 92%).

1. **Nearly all the tribal people have become Protestant over the past 80 years.** Baptist and Presbyterian churches are numerous, but there have been many divisions. There are many vital Christians with a vision for outreach and missions. Pray for revival to sweep through these churches as in Nagaland to the north.

2. **Of the indigenous peoples, only the majority Meitei are unreached** but an upsurge of interest of late has resulted in 2,000 coming to Christ. A nationalistic spirit is causing a rejection of Indian Hinduism. Pray that many may come to Christ.

NAGALAND

Population 911,000. People per sq.km. 55.

Peoples: Naga tribes (26) 85% speaking 60 languages and dialects, Hindi, Bengali 15%, Assamese, Bihari.

Religion: Hindu 14%, Animist 4%, Muslim 1.7%, Christian 80%.

1. **Nagaland is unique!** It is the only predominantly Baptist ethnic state in the world. Revival dramatically changed the moral and spiritual climate in 1976-78. Almost all Nagas are now Christian. There are probably proportionately more born-again believers in this state than any other in the world. The revival is overflowing to other states. Materialism, internal divisions, Hindu pressures and Naga nationalism are all dangers that can quench the fires of revival.

2. **Missionary vision blossomed** as a result of revival. Christians made a solemn covenant in 1980 to live for, and further, world evangelization. They are trusting God that 10,000 missionaries will be sent out from Nagaland. Pray for the **Nagaland Missionary Movement,** and pray that this vision may be obeyed and fulfilled. There are many obstacles to missionaries leaving Nagaland.

3. **Mizoram** (500,000) to the south is a union territory. Nearly all Mizos have become Christian in great awakenings (Presbyterian, Baptist and numerous indigenous groups), and they have initiated a number of vigorous missionary outreaches to other parts of India. There are over 300 Baptist and Presbyterian Mizo missionaries. Pray that the new generation of Mizo may retain the spiritual vitality of their elders.

ORISSA

Population 28,400,000. People per sq.km. 182.

Languages 68. Oriya 76%. Scheduled tribes (62) 20.5%.

Religion: Hindu 95% (including many animist tribal people), Muslim 1.6%, Animist 1%, Christian 1.9% (RC 45%, Protestant 55%).

1. **Anti-conversion laws in Orissa** have not slowed the growth of the Church but created added interest in the gospel. Significant people movements among the six million tribal peoples are gathering many into the churches. Pray that this movement may be well discipled and thousands brought to a living personal faith in Christ. Pray that church leaders may be courageous in the face of opposition from the Hindus. Revival is sorely needed in the older churches.

2. **Unreached peoples abound.** Of the 62 tribes, only nine have a large Christian presence, and 25 are without any Christians; the rest are marginally reached. Fifteen languages used by over 10,000 speakers are without the Scriptures. In only one Hindu caste group has there been a significant turning to God. Most of the Oriya-speaking majority are unreached.

PUNJAB

Population 18,300,000. People per sq.km. 361. Punjab is India's "breadbasket", a fertile wheat-growing area.

Languages 40. Punjabi 70%, also Hindi, Urdu, Nepali, Sindhi, etc. There are over 30 small minority tribal groups.

Religion: Sikh 60.7%, Hindu 36.9%, Muslim 1%, Christian 1.1% (RC 30,000, Protestant 160,000).

1. **Punjab is the only state where Sikhs are in the majority**. As is well known, this state has seen much violence, killings, and Sikh extremist activities, including the assassination of Mrs Indira Gandhi, during 1984-85. In July 1985 an accord was signed between the central government and the leading religious/political party. Pray that these events may open the hearts of Sikhs and Hindus to the Lord Jesus. Response has hitherto been minimal among the upper class Sikh Jats.

2. **Most of the Christian community originated in the last century in mass movements** from the depressed Chamar and Chuhra castes of Hindus and Sikhs. The Christians are underprivileged, generally nominal and discouraged. May God revive them! Evangelism through Pentecostal churches and the Indian Evangelical Team is bearing fruit, halting the decline in numbers. IET has 320 workers in Punjab, Haryana, etc. and has already planted 352 churches. The Ludhiana Christian Medical School and Hospital has a worldwide reputation for Christian care and witness. Pray for a dynamic Punjabi Church to emerge.

3. **The unreached are many**. Forty-five caste groups are untouched, and there are churches in only two of the 30 tribal groups.

RAJASTHAN

Population 38,400,000. People per sq.km. 113.

Languages 39+. Rajasthani and Hindi in the majority. Scheduled tribes (13) 11%, largest: Mina 2 mill., Bhil 1.8 mill.

Religion: Hindu 89%, Muslim 7%, Jain 1.8%, Sikh 1.4%, Christian 0.12%.

1. **Christians are a tiny minority within minority castes and tribes**. There are about 45,000 Christians (60% Catholic) in the state. Pray for the little CNI, Pentecostal and Brethren congregations. Anti-conversion laws and Hindu pressures have not stopped the steady growth in number of believers. Most of the evangelism has been through **OM, EHC**, and Rajasthan Bible Institute teams. Only nine of the 25 districts have any established Christian work.

2. **Unreached peoples:**

a) **The Bhil** 1,500,000 and **Mina** 2,000,000 are Hindu/animist and only now beginning to respond to the gospel. Most of the Christians are of these groups.

b) **The Meo** 2,000,000 are Muslim; no Christians are known.

c) **The higher caste Hindus**, especially the warlike Rajputs, have shown no response to the gospel.

TAMIL NADU

Population 51,633,000. People per sq.km. 396.

Languages: Tamil 82%, Telugu 9%, Kannada 3%, Urdu 2%, Malayalam 1%. Scheduled tribes (33) 2%.

Religion: Hindu 89%, Muslim 5%, Christian 5.8% (RC 2.5 mill., Protestants 1.8 mill.).

1. **The Christian presence is strong and growing** in a receptive population. Madras has 695 churches — more than any other city in S. Asia; 8% of the population is Christian. Although caste distinctions are strong, a number of caste groups have large Christian minorities. There is a spirit of prayer and revival in both older mainline churches and evangelical and Pentecostal groups. This is generating an enthusiastic growth of missionary vision for tribals and N.India. There is a multiplicity of denominations and Christian organizations. Pray that these believers may make an impact on India.

2. **The unreached:**

a) **Over 16 large caste groups** have resisted the gospel.

b) **In all the 36 tribal groups** there are less than 1,000 Christians. Pray for the Badaga (400,000) and Kurumba (700,000) among whom there are a few believers. IBT and **IEM** have a ministry among them. Pray for other unreached such as the Irula (100,000), Tuda (800), etc.

c) **The Tamil-speaking Muslims**, the Labbai, are fairly strongly Islamic. ISS has an outreach to them.

SIKKIM

Population 353,000. People per sq.km. 48. Himalayan state surrounded by Nepal, China, Bhutan and India; annexed by India in 1975.

Languages: Nepali 75%, the political "underdogs"; Lepcha 14%, the original people; Tibetan (Bhot) 10%, the politically dominant group.

Religion: Hindu 67%, Buddhist 28.7%, Muslim 1%, Christian 2.2%.

1. **There are about 7,000 Christians**, mainly Lepcha and Nepali with a few Tibetans. Most are linked with the CNI. There is but one church building and a growing number of house churches. Christians have suffered persecution at times. Western missionaries may not enter, but a few Indian missionaries are seeking to evangelize these predominantly unreached peoples.

TRIPURA

Population 2,300,000. People per sq.km. 215.

Languages: Bengali 70%, Tripuri 16%. Scheduled tribes (30) 14%.

Religion: Hindu 90% officially, but including 20% animists as Hindu. Muslim 7%, Buddhist 2.7%, Christian 1.3% (mostly Baptist).

1. **Bengali immigrants have effectually taken over Tripura** from its indigenous inhabitants over the past 30 years. Oppression and social exclusion of the tribal peoples led to a violent backlash in 1980, and also to an unprecedented openness to the gospel. A dramatic people movement has been taking place since 1970. Six tribes are now Christian, and at least seven are rapidly becoming so.

2. **The Christians have suffered persecution** from animists among their own people, Communists in government circles, and extremist Hindu groups who alternately bribe and coerce Tripuris to become Hindu. Pray for the Church to thrive in the midst of persecution and communal violence.

3. **The unreached**. The **Bengali** majority is unresponsive. There are only 120 Christians known among them. Other **indigenous tribes** are ready to respond, but workers to reach them are lacking.

UTTAR PRADESH

Population 121,400,000. People per sq.km. 411. India's most populous state.

Languages 88. Hindi 85%, Urdu 10%, Kumaoni 1.5%, Garhwali 1.4%. There are six Scheduled tribes.

Religion: Hindu 83.3%, Muslim 16%, Sikh 0.4%, Jain 0.13%, Christian 0.15% (RC 50,000, Protestant 120,000).

1. **Uttar Pradesh is the home of Hinduism, Buddhism and Jainism**, but has given no home to the gospel. It is one of the darkest and most needy parts of the world. Millions of pilgrims visit Varanasi, the "holy" city of Hinduism on the Ganges River, but few find the Living Water that only Jesus can give.

2. **Christians are a tiny minority** of outcaste (Chamar) and tribal (Dom) origin. Most are nominal and rarely attend church. There is a stream of reversions to Hinduism. There are only about 150 little evangelical fellowships in the whole state, which is almost one per million people. Evangelists and church planters are desperately few. But pray for the missionaries of **AoG**, the All India Prayer Fellowship, **IEM**, and Friends Missionary Prayer Band who are planting churches in the state.

3. **The unreached are many:**
   a) **Bhojpuri Hindi** (25,000,000) are physically and spiritually poor. Very few believers.
   b) **The Kumaon** 1,700,000; **Jaunnaris** 70,000; **Tharus** 35,000; and **Buksa** 10,000 have little gospel witness.

c) **The Garhwalis** (1,500,000) are unresponsive, but a few have believed through the work of **IEM**.

d) **The Muslims** are a large but unreached minority of 19,000,000.

e) **Students** are a challenge! **UESI** has only four student groups for 21 universities and 407 colleges.

WEST BENGAL

Population 59,300,000. People per sq.km. 675.

Languages 85. Bengali 84%, Hindi 5%, Santali 3%, Urdu 2%, Nepali 1%. There are 36 Scheduled tribes.

Religion: Hindu 77%, Muslim 21.5%, Christian 0.6% (RC 240,000, Protestant 70,000).

1. **Christians are a tiny minority among Bengalis**. Nominalism is rife, and the life style of Christians has frequently been a hindrance to Hindus and Muslims receiving the gospel. The Assemblies of God and some Brethren and Baptist churches have a clear evangelical witness, but some reckon that there are only 5,000 born-again believers in the whole state. **TWR** broadcasts 31 hours per month in Bengali.

2. **Calcutta is a huge and tragic slum** with the lowest urban standard of living in the world. It is named after the Hindu deity Kali, the goddess of destruction. Pray for the destruction of Satan's kingdom there.

3. **The majority of Christians in the state are tribal**, mainly Santal, Munda and Oraon. Even these groups are only partially evangelized; others have scarcely been touched with the gospel. There are too few workers to reach them.

4. **The Muslims** are in the majority in central districts. They are unevangelized.

INDONESIA
(The Republic of Indonesia)

Asia

June 6-13

Area 1,920,000 sq.km. 13,500 islands of which 3,000 are inhabited and cover 9,500,000 sq.km. of the Indian/Pacific Oceans, 27 provinces.

Population 168,400,000. The world's fifth most populous nation. Annual growth 2.2%. People per sq.km. 88; varying from Java's 700 to Irian Jaya's two.

Peoples. Major races:

Malay 94%. Seventeen languages with more than one million speakers of which the largest are: Javanese 42%, Sundanese 13.6%, Madurese 7%, Minangkabau 3.3%, Batak 2.9%, Sumatran Malay 2.9%, Bugis 2.8%, Balinese 2.1%.

Chinese 4%. Many are becoming integrated into the Indonesian majority. Only 20% still use Chinese dialects. Scattered throughout the nation.

Irianese/Papuan peoples 1.2%. In Timor, Alor, Halmahera and Irian Jaya.

Other 0.8%. Arabs, Indians, Europeans, mixed race.

See more detail under separate islands.

Literacy 64%; rising rapidly. **Official language:** Indonesian. Its increasing use is both unifying the nation and lessening the importance of smaller languages to the younger generation. **All languages** 583; 17 spoken by more than one million speakers; 238 spoken in Irian Jaya. **Bible translations** 8Bi 21NT 39por.

Capital: Jakarta 9,086,000. Other cities: Surabaya 3,054,000; Bandung 1,878,000; Medan 1,600,000; Semarang 1,056,000. Urbanization 24%.

Economy: Based on agriculture and oil. Enormous potential with impressive growth over the last 20 years. A rise in living standards is being slowed by overpopulation in Java, difficult communications by land and sea and cumbersome bureaucracy. Inflation ('83) 15%. Income/person ('82) $516 (4% of USA), but higher in Menado (Minahassa), North Sumatra and Jakarta.

Politics: Independent from the Netherlands 1945-49 after 350 years of colonial rule. The abortive

Communist coup in 1965 radically moderated the political orientation of the country. A strong presidential military-civilian government. President Suharto seeks to balance tendencies to religious extremisms and local secessionist nationalisms in this culturally diverse nation.

Religion: Monotheism and communal peace are the bases of the government ideology of "Pancasila". All are free to choose to follow Islam, Hinduism, Buddhism, or Christianity; but the numerical and political strength of Islam is frequently exercised to give it preferential treatment and limit Christian expansion. There are, therefore, some restrictions on open proselytism.

Muslim 78-80%. This figure needs to be qualified. 29% of the electorate voted in 1982 for parties that seek to make Indonesia an Islamic state. 43% could be defined as Quranic Muslims, living by many of Islam's tenets. A further 35% are statistical Muslims, who, though enumerated as Muslims for the census, are actually followers of the Javanese mystical religion that predates Islam, or else animists who have (to a lesser or greater extent) accepted some of the outward aspects of Islam. Islam is strongest in Sumatra, Java and in many coastal areas in the east.

Animist 5.1%. Discouraged by the government but strong among some peoples in Irian Jaya, E. Timor, Sumba, and inland Sumatra, Kalimantan, Sulawesi, etc. Folk Islam followed by the majority is strongly influenced by animism.

Hindu 3.1%. Majority on Bali and among Tengger in E. Java.

Buddhist/Chinese religions 1.22%. Mainly Chinese.

Non-religious/Atheist 1.4%. Mainly Chinese and underground Communists.

Christian 11.2%. Church figures indicate 13.2%. A large number of known "sympathizers" would further increase this total — hence the graph.

Roman Catholic 3.5%. In the majority on Flores and East Timor. Practising 74%. 4,900,000a; 2,600,000m.

Foreign and indigenous marginal groups 0.1%.

Protestant 9.7%. 16,100,000a; 7,100,000m. Denominations 250+. Largest (adherents):

Regional Reformed Churches (32) (Dutch and Swiss missions)	5,600,000
Pentecostal Churches (72)	4,200,000
Lutheran Churches (13) (German and Scandinavian missions)	3,000,000
KINGMI (**CMA**)	325,000
Seventh Day Adventist Church	168,000
GIIJ (**UFM, APCM, RBMU**)	100,000
GMI (Methodist)	94,000
Churches related to **WEC-IMF**	30,000
Churches related to **TEAM**	20,000

Evangelical 4.3% of population.

Missionaries to Indonesia 1,400 (1:120,000 people) in 109 agencies.

Missionaries from within Indonesia approx. 420 (1:38,000 Protestants).

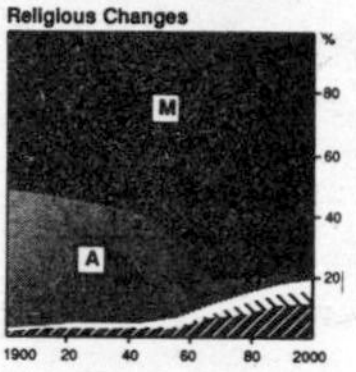

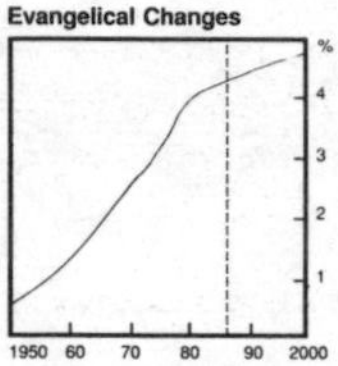

1. **Praise God for the thrilling growth of the Church!** One of the most significant movements to Christianity in history has been accelerating over the past 20 years in this land. God has used many means to bring this about:

a) **The Communist coup** of 1965 and its bloody aftermath in which maybe 500,000 sympathizers perished, and many became Christian.

b) **The fierce Muslim reprisals** on the Communists offended many — especially in Java. Many nominal Muslims turned to Christ.

c) **The government recognition** of four religions impelled many animists to consider the claims of the gospel.

d) **The rising extremism of certain Muslim groups** together with such legalisms as forbidding the eating of pork makes Christianity more attractive to some.

e) **The lives of Christians** and their vibrant, fearless witness in a society influenced by the power of the occult.

f) **The Spirit of God working in hearts** to give revivals in Timor, Java, Irian Jaya and E. Kalimantan, and great people movements in some areas.

2. **Could Indonesia be on the threshold of an even greater ingathering?** Look at the growth rates of Protestants: 6% per year in 1975 rising to 8% in 1980. So far the greatest gathering of souls into the churches has been confined to certain parts of the country. Pray the complete harvest in!

3. **The influence of Christians is greater than their numbers would indicate.** It must be used wisely. Their high urban population with many well-educated among them means that Christians have a significant impact on the nation's wealth, industry, civil service and military

forces. Many recent conversions have been from among the most influential in the country. Pray that the believers may live lives worthy of their Lord. Pray that they may not fear to testify in the face of opposition. The enemy of souls is not unaware of the situation.

4. **The rapid growth has its dangers** — cover these in prayer, that the enemy's counterattacks may be neutralized and turned to good.

a) **Too much publicity** which exalts man or the miraculous (as with Timor) or which provokes the attention of those who would oppose the ongoing work of the Spirit.

b) **Too few teachers and disciplers** for those seeking the Lord. Many traditional churches cannot cope with the influx, and the new seekers just increase the population of nominal Christians.

c) **The growth of error.** Inadequate teaching and nominalism has led to multiplicity of errors, growth of liberal theologies, and syncretic Christianity loaded with occultism and heathen thought patterns.

5. **The worldwide Islamic "revival"** has had its impact on Indonesia. Great efforts are expended, with some success, to Islamize animistic and nominal Muslims by liberal use of money and construction of mosques in every non-Muslim village and town. Pray for the 64 million uncommitted, nominal Muslims and animists that they might search for the truth and find the Saviour. Pray that the worldwide Islamic awakening may cause Muslims to re-examine their own religion in the light of the Scriptures — this *is* happening!

6. **The Muslim backlash** to the growth of the Church in predominantly Muslim areas of Sulawesi, Sumatra and especially Java has been marked by violence, looting, destruction of churches and, at times, persecution of Christians by some extremist elements. Christians need both tact and boldness. Pray that the pressures on them may bring a greater unity. Pray that Christians may use spiritual, and not carnal weapons, and thus win the fierce heavenly warfare.

7. **There is considerable scope for Christian work**; even mass evangelism. Christians need sensitivity to make use of present opportunities to the full. The government has the unenviable task of preserving communal peace in the face of vociferous and potentially explosive Islamic extremist groups. Muslim organizations constantly press for curbs on proselytization of Muslims and the activities of missionaries. Pray for the leaders of Indonesia, and for the maintenance and extension of present freedoms.

8. **Revival in Indonesia?** Praise the Lord for the work of the Spirit in the '60s and '70s in West Timor and C. and E. Java, and in the great cities in the '80s. Evangelistic prayer meetings have mushroomed, evangelical groups and churches multiplied and the Pentecostal movement spread dramatically across the country. Yet the need in most areas *is* revival. Nominalism, deadness in the churches, internal politics, divisions and carnality are still very evident. The majority of "Christians" still need a conversion experience. This is especially true in the traditionally Christian areas; some, such as Menado, Timor and Maluku, have been "Christian" for hundreds of years. Please look at the different areas on pp. 234-239 for more detail.

9. **The need for spiritual leaders of maturity for the churches has never been greater.** The pastor is of importance in Indonesian church life because the majority of Christians follow the Reformed and Lutheran tradition inherited from the Netherlands and Germany. The rapid growth of the Church has far outstripped the supply of full-time workers. Some reckon 20,000 new leaders will be required before 1993. So pray for:

a) **The rapid development of effective lay leadership**. There are only 10,200 trained pastors for 24,000 churches in the country, and most of the other 40,000 recognized leaders have had little training.

b) **The widespread use of TEE programmes** — now being refined by **SBC**, **CMA**, and many others. Many pastors have had inadequate training and need to be retrained and fired with new zeal. All too many need to be born of the Spirit.

c) The multitude of evangelical, **primary level, Bible schools** in rural areas of Kalimantan, Sulawesi, and Irian Jaya, many of whose students have had little schooling.

d) A wide range of **secondary level Bible schools** across the country run by many churches — often evangelical.

e) **The twenty degree-level seminaries.** Some of them are liberal in theology. Pray for foreign and national faculty members who are evangelical. Pray also for the vital project sponsored by **OMF** in printing the New Bible Commentary and Dictionary which is helping to counteract the influence of liberal books being published in Indonesian. Pray for an increase of evangelical pastors in the large and influential regional Reformed and Lutheran Churches.

f) **The nine evangelical seminaries** are bulging with both potential and students — Malang (**ECF**), KINGMI (**CMA**), Baptist (**SBC**), Bandung, Jogjakarta (**CNEC**) and Batu (**IMF-WEC**) with about 1,130 students all told and a further three Pentecostal seminaries. Pray for an outflow of life through graduates from these institutions to old and new churches and to the mission fields of Indonesia and beyond.

g) **The Fellowship of Evangelical Theological Schools** was founded in 1981. Pray for close fellowship and cooperation in training leadership, and for a flowering of biblical theology in the Church.

10. **The Chinese** are being absorbed into Indonesian society but are often unpopularly wealthy. A large part of the industrial, financial and trading world is controlled by them. The Chinese have been responsive to the gospel over the last 50 years, and now about 13% are Protestant (in Chinese and Indonesian-speaking congregations) and 6% are Catholic. There are fine leaders and strong mission-minded congregations in Java and elsewhere. Pray that Chinese Christians may contribute much to the vitality, growth and missionary outreach of the Church in Indonesia; they often live among totally unevangelized peoples.

11. **The development of a missionary vision.** The history and background of Indonesian Christianity is unique and can be significant for world evangelization. Pray for:

a) The churches to be gripped by the challenge of hundreds of unreached peoples in their own country and in other lands of Asia and Africa. The financial and manpower resources are there.

b) The sending out of Christians as individuals, teams and communities to migrate to unevangelized areas with a vision for church planting is not hard in an increasingly homogenous society. Christians will need to be set free from tribalism and local loyalties.

c) A growing number of indigenous missionary agencies are being formed for cross-cultural missionary work. There were 13 in 1980 — the largest being **IMF** (280 workers), GKIJ (180), KINGMI (67), GKMI (40). Most of the work is within Indonesia, but a growing number are going out to Europe, South America, Asia and Africa.

d) Indonesians who are working with international missions like **OMF, WEC, OM, YWAM, CCC**, etc.

12. **The Transmigration Scheme** is one of the world's largest peaceful resettlements of people ever organized. Vast areas of virgin territory in Sumatra, Kalimantan, Sulawesi and Irian Jaya have been opened up for migrants from overpopulated Java and Bali. 3,500,000 were relocated by 1984. These new settlements have been hard on the newcomers with harsh conditions, poor soils and communications. Yet among these migrants there is an openness to the gospel, and Christian groups have thrived. Pray that these Christians may be lights for the Lord in areas never before evangelized — especially in Sumatra and Sulawesi.

13. **Young people** are a vital mission field, but so little is specifically aimed at evangelizing and discipling them. There are 27,000,000 children in primary and 5,000,000 in secondary schools. Response rates at evangelistic outreaches are consistently high.

14. **Students in universities** number 400,000 in 43 government universities and 388 private colleges. PERKANTAS(**IFES**) has only six full-time staff but with exciting growth of groups on campuses in 19 cities and in high schools in 17. Over 20% of university students are Christian — they need to be mobilized for Jesus. There has been dramatic expansion since 1980, but many schools and campuses have no evangelical student body.

15. **The work of missions** has been blessed of God despite the obstacles of geography, bureaucracy and the spirit world. Praise God for fruitful ministry of Dutch and German missions before World War II and many other international missions since then. Stand with these brethren in the battle:

a) **For visas** which are hard to obtain. Pray for those who wait for years for missionary visas.

b) **For patience** in the face of endless bureaucracy and red tape.

c) **For government officials** to be sympathetic to the presence and work of missionaries.

d) **For effective evangelistic outreach** when everything seems contrived to hedge in foreigners with restrictions.

e) **For warm relationships with church leaders,** who may not have a close walk with the Lord. Humility and tact are needed to win the confidence of these key men who have the potential to influence so many Christians. **OMF**, **ICF**, etc. have a vital ministry within traditional churches — but openings for effective teaching and mobilizing ministries are not easy to obtain.

There are concentrations of missionaries in W.Kalimantan, Irian Jaya and Java, but a great lack in Sumatra, Nusatenggara, Sulawesi and E.Timor. Pray that this land may remain open for missionaries from abroad. The largest evangelical missions are **SIL** (151 missionaries), **CMA** (141), **CCC** (134), **NTM** (128), **MAF** (98), **OMF** (75), **WEC** (64), **TEAM** (61). The major openings for missionaries today are in Bible teaching, leadership training, church planting and supportive ministries. There is a strong emphasis on training Indonesians to take over missionary ministries.

16. **Supportive ministries:**

a) **Bible translation and distribution.** The **UBS** have 34 translation projects in Irian Jaya, and a programme to publish common language translations in 12 major languages. **SIL** has a growing team involved in 22 language projects, but there are over 300 languages requiring Scripture translation work. This is one of the major unmet Bible translation challenges in the world today. The need for local vernacular translations is still great despite the rapidly spreading use of Indonesian.

b) **Literature**. There is an insatiable appetite for good Christian literature, but too little is widely available at a price people can afford. Numerous indigenous and mission groups have an extensive printing and publishing ministry — notably the Christian Publishing Society (with which **OMF** is cooperating), S. Baptists, **AoG** and various Pentecostal groups, **CLC** (with nine bookstores), **AO** (concentrating on pastoral teaching and follow up literature), Emmaus (widespread BCC programme). Pray for literature to meet the need.

c) **Gospel recordings** are now available in 350 languages and dialects (**GRI**); 200 of these are in Irian Jaya. The potential for using this evangelistic and teaching tool has not been adequately exploited. It is too easy to lean heavily on the use of imperfectly communicated Indonesian.

d) **Missionary flying** is a blessed boon to Christian workers in this huge, rugged island world, but it is costly and dangerous. In some areas of Kalimantan, Sulawesi and Irian Jaya missionary work would be impossible without it. **NTM**, **RBMU**, SDAs, and **MAF** (with 98 workers) have flying programmes. Pray for the staff and for safety of the planes. Pray also for efforts made to fulfil government requirements to train Indonesian pilots.

e) **Practical ministries** — development programmes, preventative medical programmes, and literacy can all provide opportunities for sharing the gospel (**WV**).

f) **Christian radio. FEBC** broadcast 108 hours per month in Indonesian and 30 in Javanese. The whole radio ministry could be increased and diversified.

THE ISLANDS OF INDONESIA

Each major island or island archipelago is so unique and complex that some of the more significant are handled separately from west to east.

The map on page 229 will help locate them.

SUMATRA

The world's fifth largest island. A vast potential storehouse of minerals and agricultural produce, but much is untamed jungle, swamp and volcanic mountains, with very poor surface communications.

Population 30,000,000.

Religion: Muslim 79%, **Animist** 3%+, **Buddhist** 2.4%, **Hindu** 0.7%, **Christian** 14.6% (RC 2.6%, Protestant 12%).

1. The Christians are almost entirely confined to five major groups of peoples:

   a) **Bataks** who speak four major languages and number 3,100,000. The Toba are 80% Christian, the Lutheran Churches being the oldest and largest; the Simalungun 30% Christian; Karo 25%; Mandailing-Angkola 10%.

   b) **Nias Islanders** (325,000) are 62% Christian and are almost all Lutheran Christians.

   c) **Mentawei Islanders** (43,000) are 50% Christian.

   d) **Chinese**, a large minority are Christian.

   e) **Javanese transmigrants** maybe 5% Christian.

Pray that the gospel may break out of ethnic cocoons to the Muslim majority around them.

2. **Revival is the greatest need.** There is considerable growth now among the Karo Bataks, and much new life coming to Chinese, Javanese and Batak communities through the vigorous evangelism of Methodists, Baptists, Pentecostals and others. Yet the large traditional churches are steeped in pagan practices — especially among the Nias people and the majority of the Toba Bataks. They know little of the new birth. The Nias people have an archaic Bible which few understand. These large Christian communities amongst such dynamic people have the potential to affect all of Indonesia.

3. **Sumatra** is one of the most neglected and needy parts of the world (though parts of N. Sumatra are an exception). The Dutch colonial administration forbade the preaching of the gospel to Muslims, so mission work outside the above Christianized areas has begun only in the last 40 years. Pray in more workers. There may be no more than 30 foreign missionaries in the whole of the island. Much of this pioneering work has been done through **IMF**, **WEC**, and Methodist missionaries, with **OMF**, **ICF** and others loaning missionaries to existing denominations.

4. **The unreached:**

   a) **The strongly Muslim peoples need to be reached** — the **Aceh people** of the northern tip; 2.2 million sophisticated and ardent Muslims, but with only 40 known believers, all resident outside the area, and no church or New Testament. **The Minangkabau** of West Sumatra with many scattered throughout Indonesia. 6.3 million people with only about 1,000 Christians — almost all of these being on Java. **Sumatra Malay** — 12 million in Jambi, Riau, S. Sumatra, etc., speaking numerous dialects. **Lampung-Komering** — 2 million in the southern province of Lampung. There are hardly any Indonesian or foreign missionaries concentrating on these 22 million people.

   b) **The less strongly Muslim peoples** may present more opportunities for witness — the 800,000 Mandailing-Angkola Bataks, 170,000 Gayo of N. Sumatra, 100,000 Simeulue islanders also with no missionary outreach at present.

   c) **South and Central Sumatra has 38 unreached peoples.** Of the 160,000 Christians, only 2,000 are indigenous to the area — mainly the Serawai of Bengkulu. Six of these tribes are small animist groups — only two of which are now being reached, one being the Kubu (**WEC-IMF**). Others are virtually without a witness. Denominations in the area are developing cooperative strategies to reach out to the Rejang 1,000,000; Pasemah 200,000; Ogan 50,000; Semendo 40,000; Bengkulu; Lembak; Pekal; MukoMuko; Bathin and Abung peoples. Little has been done to evaluate the need. Gospel recordings, literature and the Scriptures will have to be made available. Pray for the right approaches and for churches to be planted within each group.

JAVA

Fertile; densely populated; culturally, economically and politically dominant in the nation.

Population 99 mill. (60% of Indonesia's population).

Religion: Quranic Muslim approx. 45%, **Statistical Muslim/Kebatinan/Animist** 49%, **Hindu** 1.3%, **Buddhist** 1%, **Christian** 3.6% (RC 1.5%, Protestant 2.1% — unofficially considerably higher).

1. **Praise God for the receptivity of the Javanese and Chinese peoples to the gospel.** Since 1965 many churches, Reformed, Pentecostal and other Evangelicals, have been growing in excess of 10% per year. Pray in the full harvest! Possibly 22% of the Chinese and 7% of the Javanese are now Christian.

2. **There have been touches of revival among Chinese and Javanese** in some areas in the past. That is the need today. Syncretism among the Javanese and materialism among the Chinese are snares. Trust God for the full mobilization of the resources of the Church for evangelizing Java and beyond. There are also many Minahassan, Ambonese and Batak Christians in the great cities.

3. **The large, receptive Javanese population** must be reached *now.* Pray for churches and missions seeking to reach out to less well evangelized areas — Banten in the northwest, Jogjakarta in the centre, and many rural villages without a witness. Major church planting missions: **SBC**, **CMA**, **OMS**, **WEC**, and now **TEAM**. Pray for wise strategies, close co-operation, and good Indonesian leadership for these advances.

4. **Jakarta**, the great mother city, is now 10% Christian. Over 2,000 evangelistic prayer meetings and Bible studies are known to exist in the city. Church planting proceeds apace. A spiritual awakening is going on in that city which could dynamically affect every people group in the country. Many non-Christian ethnic minorities have scarcely been touched with the gospel; millions live in slum conditions.

5. **Unreached peoples.** The other three major ethnic groups are tragically resistant and neglected:

a) **The Sundanese.** 30 million in W. Java — the largest unreached people group in the world. Staunchly Muslim but with underlying animism and the old Sundanese religion. Several areas still adhere to the latter, resisting Islam but showing response to the gospel since 1978. Christian Sundanese number about 10,000, but most are nominal and culturally isolated from the Muslim majority; the largest church, the Pasundan Church, believes more in coexistence than evangelism. Persecution is assured for those who become Christians. Born-again Christians number but a few hundred. There is no evangelical Sundanese church. Only about three full-time and 30-50 part-time workers are committed to their evangelization. There is a dearth of workers, suitable literature and adequate airing of radio programmes. The new version of the Bible was released in 1983. Pray that quickening interest evident among the Sundanese may become concern, conviction of sin and commitment to Christ. The Sundanese Missionary Fellowship coordinates new thrusts to evangelize them. **CMA, SBC** and others also seek to reach them.

b) **The Madurese.** 10 million in E.Java and Madura Island. There are no known Madurese churches, only a few hundred nominal Christians and a handful of born-again believers. This hot-headed, needy people has rejected all efforts hitherto to reach them (**WEC**, etc.). There are now no resident missionaries on Madura Island.

c) **Tenggerese.** 400,000 Hindus around Mt. Bromo in E. Java have refused Islam and have shown little response to the few attempts to reach them with the gospel. A few individual believers, no churches.

d) **The Banten Javanese** on the northwest tip of Java have not been evangelized.

BALI

Population 2,673,000.

Religion: Hindu 88.8%, **Muslim** 10%, **Buddhist** 0.6%, **Christian** 0.9% (RC 0.4%, Protestant 0.5%).

1. **Bali is an island of great spiritual darkness,** demonic oppression and the occult under a "beautiful" bondage of Hindu culture and intricate ceremonies. 1.5 million tourists are attracted to this island annually. Balinese need the liberating power of the gospel. The whole Bible in Balinese has just become available.

2. **Balinese Christians are few.** The cost of discipleship is high, and converts to Christ have to face much ostracism and persecution when they break off from their families' way of life. Pray for the witness of the Christians — mostly of KINGMI (CMA) and the Reformed Church.

3. **Balinese who have migrated** to Sumatra and elsewhere are far more open to the gospel. There have been people movements of Balinese to Christ on Sulawesi.

W. LESSER SUNDA ISLANDS (Lombok, Sumbawa)

Population 2,950,000.

Religion: Muslim 96%, **Hindu** 2.6%, **Christian** 0.5% (RC 0.3%, Protestant 0.2%).

1. **These staunchly Muslim islands are some of the least evangelized in Indonesia.** The 6,000 Protestants are mainly immigrant peoples in the towns (Javanese, Timorese, Chinese). There are no known Indonesian or foreign missionaries seeking to reach the Muslim majority.

2. **The unreached:**
   a) **The Muslim** Sasak (1,800,000) on Lombok, the Sumbawa (500,000) and the Bima (450,000) on Sumbawa Island. There are just a few Scripture portions in Bima and Sasak.
   b) **The Hindu Balinese** — 80,000 on Lombok.
   c) **The partly animistic Donggo** (15,000) on E. Sumbawa among whom there are a few hundred Christians (CMA).

E. LESSER SUNDA ISLANDS (Flores, Lomblin, Alor, Wetar, W.Timor)

Population 3,000,000.

Religion: Muslim 7%, **Animist** 16%, **Hindu** 0.4%, **Buddhist** 0.5%, **Christian** 76% (RC 48%, Protestant 28%).

1. **Flores** is 90% Catholic but steeped in pagan and idolatrous ritual involving snake worship. Born-again Christians are very few and largely Timorese. No language of Flores has any Scriptures. The Manggarai 400,000; Ende-Lio 300,000; Lamaholot-Solar 250,000; Sikka 180,000; Ngade 70,000 need to be evangelized in their own cultural setting and language. Muslim minorities among the Solorese (140,000 and Manggarai (25,000) are totally unreached.

2. **Sumba** is now one of the less evangelized animistic areas of Indonesia. There are only 22,000 traditional Protestants, and 90% of the population is basically animist. Only E.Sumban (125,000) has a New Testament. No Scripture is available for the other six languages. What a challenge for Indonesian missionaries!

3. **West Timor.**
   a) **Praise God for the outpouring of the Spirit** in 1965-8, and continued working since then. Unusual miracles, deep repentance and thousands of conversions from occultism, Islam and sin resulted. About 20% of the Timorese were converted. There has been an outflow of life to other parts of Indonesia. Timorese serve the Lord as missionaries on four continents.
   b) **The large Reformed Church was blessed by the revival,** and other groups also, such as Pentecostals and CMA, have grown as a result. Pray for the consolidation and maturing of the fruit of revival. The majority of the population is Protestant, but witchcraft is still a potent force.

c) **Unreached peoples:**
Sabunese (90,000) are 80% animist, 20% nominal Christian. Few are born-again. Black magic is widespread.
Ambenu Timorese live in Oikusi, the western enclave of former Portuguese Timor. Most are nominally Catholic.
Belu Tetun are 40% animist, 60% Catholic-animist. Few know the Lord.

EAST TIMOR

Population 587,000.

Religion: Animist 15-75%, **Muslim** 2%, **Christian** 34-84% (RC 30-80%, Protestant 3.4%). Majority of Catholics very nominal hence the second percentage may be more realistic.

1. **The sufferings of this former Portuguese colony have been terrible.** Five centuries of colonial neglect followed by the collapse of the administration in 1976 led to bitter civil war and Indonesian intervention. After 10 years, fighting continues. Famine and war have resulted in many casualties. Pray that these tragic events may give an opportunity for the gospel to spread.

2. **For years this land was one of the world's dark spots.** Only in the past 20 years have Christian groups emerged in Dili and on the small island of Atauro. Since the Indonesian take-over, about 20,000 Timorese have become Protestant but with a minimal knowledge of the gospel.

3. **Over 20 languages are spoken; few speak Portuguese or Indonesian.** What an urgent need for evangelism, church planting and Bible translation! For this, peace must be restored. The largest groups are Tetun 300,000; Kemak 50,000; Tukudede 50,000; Galoli 50,000; Fatakulu 25,000.

KALIMANTAN

The Indonesian three-quarters of the island of Borneo.

Population 7,227,000.

Religions: Muslim 64%, **Animist** approx. 15%, **Hindu** 2.7%, **Buddhist** 1.1%, **Christian** 17.4% (RC 9.4%, Protestant 8%).

A vast, underpopulated land of rivers and forests with few roads.

1. **The growth of the Church has been most significant among the two million Dyak peoples.** In E.Kalimantan **CMA** work has resulted in a large, revived and strong church among the Kenyah and Kayan peoples. In C.Kalimantan many of the 200,000 Ot Danum and 300,000 Kapuas peoples are nominally of the Reformed Church — but with little evangelical theology. In W.Kalimantan many Dyak tribes have been responding to the gospel in people movements — **CMA** and **WEC** among the Iban-related groups, **RBMU**, **CBFMS**, etc. among the Land Dyak peoples. About half the Dyak are still animists, and many of the Christians need a better understanding to be free from the power of the evil one.

2. **The churches are not mature enough** to cope with the inflow of transmigrants and the modern world. There are some Bible schools at both primary and secondary level and TEE programmes for leadership training, but more facilities to train leaders is an urgent need.

3. **The unreached:**
a) **The large Malay population** of four million along the coasts and up the rivers is strongly Muslim. Nothing is being done to evangelize them, and they have no known churches. They are concentrated in less-evangelized South Kalimantan.
b) **The immigrant Javanese** (nominally Muslim), Balinese (Hindu), Bugis (strongly Muslim) etc. number over one million. They live in transmigrant settlements and in the oil-boom towns of the east. The growing churches of the Javanese could minister to other ethnic groups around them, but they need the vision to do so.

c) **The animist peoples of the interior. NTM** has an expanding ministry to over 10 tribes in W. and now C.Kalimantan. The complexities of reaching isolated tribal groups are immense, survey work hard, and living conditions difficult. Pray for more pioneers willing to reach out to these hard-of-access but receptive peoples. The Ot Danum and Barito peoples are the least evangelized.

d) **The Chinese** are 25% of the population in W.Kalimantan but have proved less responsive to the gospel than elsewhere. Pray for the witness of Chinese Christians and churches on the coast, in Pontianak and up the Kapuas river.

MALUKU

Population 1,506,000.

Religion: Muslim 30%, **Animist** 10%, **Buddhist** 0.3%, **Hindu** 0.1%, **Christian** 59% (RC 5.5%, Protestant 53%).

A medley of 1,000 small islands and over 100 language groups.

a) **Ambonese, S.Halmaherans and many other groups** are Protestant; the large Moluccan Reformed Church has over 500,000 adherents. Revival is needed.

b) **Unreached peoples** — the Muslim Ambonese, Halmaherans, and the largely animist peoples of Ceram, Buru, Taliabu, Halmahera, etc. need to hear the gospel in their own heart languages. The **AoG** and **NTM** are seeking to meet some of that need on the latter islands. **SIL** has made a survey and is moving in translation teams. Pray for the evangelization of these long-neglected peoples, and labourers to achieve this goal.

SULAWESI

Population 10,900,000.

Religion: Muslim 65.7%, **Animist** 10%, **Hindu** 2.0%, **Buddhist** 0.7%, **Christian** 21.5% (RC 2.6%, Protestant 18.9%).

This large crab-like island is a complex medley of races and religions.

1. The Christians are concentrated among three major peoples.

a) **The Sanghir-Talaud** (278,000) and the five Minahassa peoples (420,000) of the northeast tip of Sulawesi have been Protestant for three centuries or more. They are among the wealthiest and best-educated peoples of Indonesia, but materialism, nominalism, poor church attendance and occultism are rife. There is little concern for the evangelization of the Muslim and animist majority of the island.

b) **The Toraja** (1,000,000 with eight languages and 30 dialects) are now 50% Christian, mostly adherents of the four Reformed Churches. Few have a personal experience of the Lord. Tradition — especially a morbid preoccupation with death — still grips many. **OMF** has a ministry of help within the Reformed Church; **CMA**, Salvation Army and several Pentecostal groups have a growing work among them.

2. **Unreached peoples — The Muslims** are very strong in some areas.

a) Among the **Bugis** (2,000,000) and **Macassarese** (1,600,000) of S.Sulawesi with colonies all around the coast. Trading is their major occupation. Islam is orthodox for Indonesia. There are about 800 Buginese Christians, and 3,000 Salyar Macassarese — the latter being one of the few significant Muslim groups responding in any numbers to the gospel in Indonesia.

b) Among the **Gorontalo** (400,000) of the north and the **Bungku-Mori Toraja** of the southeast where animistic practices are more prevalent. There are small churches indigenous to these peoples, but response is slow and many areas are untouched.

3. **The Animists.** There are numerous isolated tribes and offshoots of the major peoples scattered around Sulawesi's rugged coast and steep mountain valleys. Indonesian Christians need to catch a vision for their evangelization. **NTM** is working in three of these people groups.

4. **Bible translation** needs are only now being systematically evaluated. Pray for **SIL** teams tackling translation projects in Sulawesi, and for other teams to be called for this vital ministry.

IRIAN JAYA

The western half of New Guinea, the world's second largest island. See Papua New Guinea for the eastern half. Ruled by Netherlands until 1963. Some of the most wild and inhospitable terrain on the surface of the earth.

Population 1,292,000.

Religion: Muslim 4% rapidly increasing through immigration of Javanese, **Animist** 12%, **Christian** 84% (RC 23%, Protestant 61%).

1. **Praise God for the people movements that have brought stone age peoples to faith in Christ from most of the 250 tribes.** Those on the north coast in the last century (Reformed Church), in the more densely populated highlands (**APCM, CMA, RBMU, UFM**, etc.), the "Bird's Head" (**TEAM**) and southern swamps (**TEAM, RBMU**) have responded in this way. Over 80% of the indigenous population is Christian.

2. **Strong, Bible-centred, maturely led national churches are the great need** as modernization, education and a growing flood of transmigrants, often Muslim, enter the island. Christians must face up to the challenges of tribalism, syncretism and separatist politics, which are beginning to sap the spiritual energies of some churches.

3. **The missionary force has been depleted over recent years.** So much remains to be done — pioneer evangelism, church planting, Bible translation, leadership training, etc. Pray for new recruits. Praise God for the remarkable missionary army that has opened up this island. Pray for **MAF** with 10 planes and seven bases in their essential ministry in the roadless and dangerous interior. There have been a number of bad accidents in recent years.

4. **The unreached.** There are still tribes unpenetrated by missionary pioneers, others have shown but minimal response. Some of these are:

  a) **Twelve unreached peoples in the Bird's Head** area (**TEAM**).
  b) **Many isolated groups in the southern Lowlands** (**TEAM, RBMU**).
  c) **The Baliem Dani** (50,000) have not been so responsive as the Western Dani.
  Pray that Irianese believers may have a stronger missionary vision for these unreached peoples. Praise God for the Dani and other tribal churches that have already sent out over 280 missionaries to other Irianese groups.
  d) **The Muslim Javanese** who may number 1,000,000 in 1990 through transmigration.

5. **Communicating the gospel in the heart language** amongst such linguistic diversity is a great problem. Many languages are spoken by only a handful of people. Many missions, as well as **SIL**, are involved in Bible translation and in recording gospel messages on tape — of the 435 dialects known, **GRI** has recorded 263.

Middle East

June 14-16

IRAN

(Islamic Republic of Iran)

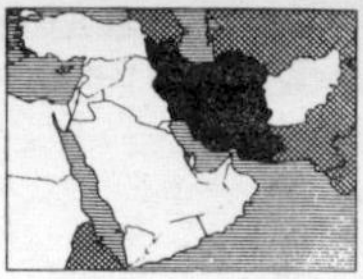

Area 1,648,000 sq.km. A central desert ringed by mountains.

Population 45,100,000. Annual growth 3%. People per sq.km. 27.

Peoples: Over 45 peoples/tribes speaking at least 23 distinct languages. Many are small nomadic groups.

Indo-Iranic (22) 76.8%. **Persian** (speaking Farsi) 22,300,000, the dominant people. **Kurds** 3,800,000; also the related **Luri-Bakhtiari** peoples 3,400,000.

Turkic (18) 21%. Azerbaijani 7,600,000; Turkoman 710,000; Afshar 370,000; Qashqa'i 230,000, etc.

Arab (2) 1.5%. **Other** (5) 0.7%. Armenian 150,000(est.); Assyrian 40,000(est.); Jews 50,000. Non-Muslim groups decreasing by emigration since the revolution.

Literacy 44%. **Official language:** Farsi. **All languages** 31. **Bible translations** 4Bi 4por.

Capital: Tehran 6,700,000. Other cities: Rai 1,100,000, Qazvin 1,000,000, Isfahan 1,000,000, Mashad 1,000,000. Urbanization 50%.

Economy: Material progress under the Shah was reversed by the religious bigotry, national paranoia, and violence that followed the 1979 revolution. The Gulf War has caused severe strains in the oil-based economy. Income/person $2,500 (1982, 18% of USA).

Politics: The progressive, West-leaning, but unpopular Shah was deposed in the Shi'ite Muslim Revolution, and a theocratic Islamic Republic formed in 1979. Regional loyalties and anarchy brought the country close to civil war and ruin. The invasion by Iraq in 1980 was the start of the bitter Gulf War. 200,000 Iranis have died in the conflict. Restive ethnic minorities and the repression of political and religious opposition may have violent consequences.

Religion: Shi'a Islam is the state religion. All deviations from Islam are liable to mean severe persecution. Other religious minorities tolerated.

Muslim 98%. Shi'a 91%, Sunni 7% (Kurds, Baluchis and Turkoman). Iran is the power house for exporting Shi'ite revolution to the Middle East and beyond.

Baha'i 0.8%. 340,000 followers of a Persian world religion founded in 1844. Severely persecuted as a heresy of Islam.

Parsi (Zoroastrian) 0.09%. 39,000 followers of Persia's ancient pre-Islamic religion.

Jews 0.09%. 40,000 (est.) Farsi-speaking Jews, many of whom are descendants of those exiled to Persia at the time of Daniel.

Christian 0.4%.

Orthodox Churches (4) 0.34%. 153,000a., 100,000m. Largest (adherents):

Armenian Apostolic Church	140,000
Nestorian Church (Assyrians)	12,000
Roman Catholic 0.03%.	17,000

(3 different rites — Chaldean, Latin and Armenian.)

Protestant 0.02%. 8,700a; 3,990m. Denominations 20. Largest (adult members):

Evangelical Church (Presbyterian)	2,730
Pentecostal Churches	1,800
Episcopal (Anglican)	1,200

Evangelical 0.02% of population.

Missionaries to Iran 0.

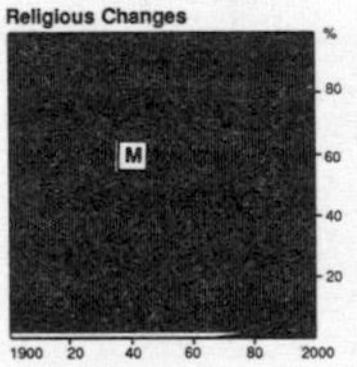

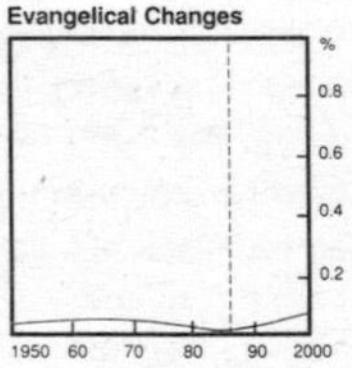

1. **The 1979 Revolution has been a blessing in disguise**. Islam has been shown to be a system worse than that which it replaced. Muslims are seeking answers. May the tragedy, hatred, cruelty, bloodshed and religious fanaticism open hearts to the Prince of Peace and doors for the gospel.

2. **Since 1979 Irani Muslims have shown a greater response to the gospel than ever before**. Disillusionment with Islam is muted, but widespread. In 1979 there were only several hundred believers from a Muslim background. The response has come both from Iranis within and outside the country. Pray that these might be the first-fruits of an abundant harvest.

3. **The minority ethnic Christian groups** have not been singled out for harassment. Churches have continued to function despite fear and uncertainty, though many Christians are emigrating.

Armenians and Assyrians are 95% of the Christian community, but most are nominal. Pray for a work of the Spirit in the Eastern, Catholic and small Protestant churches.

4. **The events of the last few years have dynamized many of the Protestant churches.** Low church attendances, personality clashes, lack of vision and witnessing characterized them in the past. Many Protestants have fled, but their numbers have been more than made up by conversions in churches that fearlessly preach the gospel. Christians have been challenged to stand for the Saviour and have had remarkable freedom to distribute literature and testify. Pray for the many hundreds of seekers from non-Christian religions.

5. **The Episcopal Church**, with many members of Muslim origin, has suffered particularly. Several leaders and believers have suffered martyrdom and imprisonment. All those converted out of Islam are under pressure, but some are fearless for the truth in spite of the danger. Pray for those who have had to flee to other lands; they need fellowship and help.

6. **About three million Iranis live outside Iran**, in lands where they can be evangelized. The major concentrations are in USA, W.Europe and in the Gulf States. Most are refugees, some are students. In many countries little Christian fellowships are springing up as disillusioned Iranis turn to the Lord — the majority from Islam. Pray for these Christians to be prepared for witness in Iran one day.

7. **Missions**. There are no longer any missions working in Iran. Pray for those labouring among the Irani diaspora, and for others to be called into this key ministry. Pray open the door to the many unreached peoples in Iran. How else can they hear?

8. **Unreached peoples**. There are only about 500 Protestants outside the tiny Armenian and Assyrian communities. Forty-five or more peoples have never heard the gospel, in seven there are a few individual believers, but no churches.

a) **There are 66,438 villages in Iran**. Only about half-a-dozen have a resident Christian witness.

b) **There are 178 towns and cities**, but only approx. 30 organized Protestant churches.

c) **Major segments of the population are hardly touched with the gospel** — the strongly Islamized universities, children, women, the densely populated Caspian coastal plain, the seven million semi-nomadic and nomadic tribes, etc.

d) **The Kurds, Luri, Bakhtiari** have no more than a few dozen known believers among 7.2 million people.

e) **The Turkic peoples** total 9.3 million with very few believers; many of the groups have never been evangelized.

f) **The Baha'i followers**. There are no known believers to have come from this religious group that has suffered so much. Little has been done to specifically evangelize the world's 4.5 million Baha'i. Pray that God may raise up such an outreach.

g) **The Refugees**. Over 500,000 Afghans in the east.

h) **The Baluch and Brahui** of the southeast.

9. **Christian literature is in surprisingly great demand**, but supplies and distributors are limited. Praise God for the courageous colportage work of Irani Christians, several Christian bookshops, and street bookstalls, as well as the work of the Bible Society. Pray for the unhindered dissemination of this literature. Pray also for cassettes, videos, BCCs, Bibles and literature distributed by **OM**, **IMI** and others before the revolution. Bibles are now being printed in Iran, but only four language groups have a Bible; many languages are without anything of God's Word.

10. **Christian radio** has even more importance since the departure of all missionaries. **ICF/FEBA** air a daily programme "Radio Voice of Christ" in Farsi. Broadcasting is directed to Iran by **FEBA** (16 hours per month from Seychelles) and **TWR** (9 hours per month from Monaco). Pray for those who prepare programmes, and for an increase in hours and languages.

Middle East
June 17

IRAQ
(Republic of Iraq)

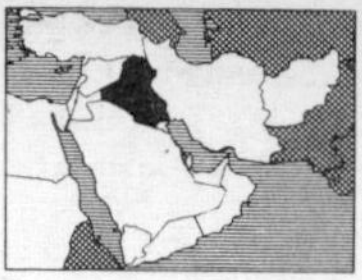

Area 435,000 sq.km. The site of the biblical Assyrian and Babylonian Empires.

Population 15,475,000. Annual growth 3.4%. People per sq.km. 36.

Peoples: Ethnic and religious diversity is responsible for much of Iraq's agonizing recent history.
Arabs 77%. Almost all Muslim; Shi'a 54%, Sunni 23%. Migrant Egyptians 300,000.
Kurds 18%. Mostly Sunni Muslim, but 135,000 are Yezidis, followers of a syncretic form of Islam. The Kurds have been fighting intermittently for autonomy or independence in their northern mountains since 1919.
Other minorities 5%. Turkoman 386,000; Luri 230,000; Farsi 120,000; Assyrian 60,000; Romany 50,000; Armenian 40,000; Chaldean 35,000; Circassian 9,000.

Literacy 41%. **Official languages:** Arabic, Kurdish in Kurdish districts. **All languages** 18. **Bible translations** 3Bi 1NT 1por.

Capital: Baghdad 6,492,000. Other city: Basra 1,000,000. Urbanization 76%.

Economy: Oil-based economy (since Genesis 11!); profits are used for industrialization. The war with Iran since 1980 has been a serious economic setback.

Politics: A violent revolution in 1958 overthrew the monarchy. Bloodshed and violence ever since with confrontations and wars against the Kurds and Iran. Military setbacks have altered the political stance of Iraq with uncertain future consequences.

Religion: Islam is the state religion. Christians are tolerated, but occasionally discriminated against.
Muslim 95.8%. Of which 62% are Shi'a, 38% Sunni and 0.9% Yezidis.
Non-religious/Atheist 0.5%.
Christian 3.4%
- **Roman Catholic** (4 different rites) 2.6%. 410,000a.
- **Orthodox** 0.7%. 110,000a. Denominations 6.
- **Protestant** 0.02%. 4,200a; 1,960m. Denominations 12. Largest (adult members):

Arab Evangelical Church	585
Episcopal Church	180

Evangelical 0.02% of population.
Missionaries to Iraq 0.

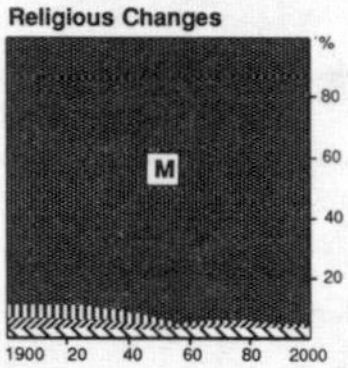

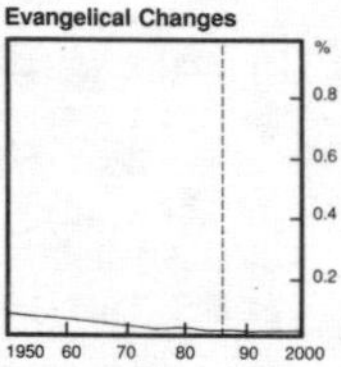

1. **The deep woes through which Iraqis have passed are decisively changing the nation.** Praise that it is God in control of this situation. Pray that there might be opportunity for the gospel to be freely preached. The land is completely closed for any form of open evangelism. The few foreign missionaries were expelled in 1969.

2. **Islam has almost complete ascendancy**, and it is virtually impossible for a Muslim to openly confess Christ and live. Pray that the centuries of prejudice and hatred may be broken down, and that Muslims may come to the Lord. Pray that the long agony of the Gulf War may help to bring a new day for the gospel in Iraq.

3. **The Christians are** confined to minority communities that never succumbed to Islam over the centuries. They are in a multiplicity of ancient Eastern churches and Catholic traditions divided on ethnicity, language, doctrines and personalities. They are a harassed, declining minority. Over 14,000 Christians fled to the West in 1972-77. Pray for real life in the Spirit among them.

4. **Evangelical believers.** Almost all are in the two major cities; years of discrimination and periods of more severe persecution have discouraged them. They are often more concerned with survival or emigration than in seeking creative ways to proclaim Christ to non-Christians. Pray for a joy and radiance to shine from them. Most of the few pastors serving the Lord are Egyptian.

5. **Unreached peoples**. Only the Armenian, Chaldean and Assyrian minorities are majority Christian. All the other peoples are almost completely unreached. Pray specifically for:

a) **The Arabs** 12 million. There is only a handful of Arab congregations in the country. The Shi'ite Arabs of the south, the 100,000 nomadic Bedouin, and the Marsh Arabs of the Tigris-Euphrates delta are particularly needy.

b) **The Kurds** 2.8 million. They are part of the tragic Kurdish nation divided up between the nations of Turkey, Iran, USSR and Syria, as well as Iraq. Among the 20 million Kurds there are only several congregations of believers, one or two of which are in Iraq. Bible translations and new initiatives to reach them with the gospel are planned.

c) **The minority groups**. No Christians or Christian outreach to the Turkoman, Luri, Farsi, or Romany are known.

6. **Pray for other means for preaching the gospel to Iraqis**.

a) **Christian literature** is almost unobtainable inside Iraq. The Bible Society was closed in 1979. Pray for the entry of suitable literature and Bibles from outside the country and for its wide distribution and impact.

b) **Christian radio broadcasts** are one of the few means available for evangelism. Pray for the Arabic broadcasts of **TWR** (Monaco and Cyprus) and **FEBA** (Seychelles).

c) **Christian cassettes and videos** could be very useful tools.

W. Europe
June 18-19

IRELAND
(Irish Republic)

Area 70,300 sq.km. 80% of the island of Ireland. Northern Ireland is a constituent part of the United Kingdom of Great Britain and Northern Ireland.

Population 3,600,000. Annual growth 1%. People per sq.km. 51. Millions of Irish have emigrated all over the English-speaking world — especially to the USA.

Peoples
Irish 96.3%. Predominantly of Celtic origin, but now using English as their first language.
UK citizens 3%. Gypsy 8,000.

Literacy 99%. **Official languages:** English, Gaelic. Latter spoken as first language by 3% of population.

Capital: Dublin 990,000. Urbanization 60%.

Economy: Industry, dairy farming and tourism are important. Member of EEC. Income/person $4,810 (24% of USA). Unemployment 16%.

Politics: Ireland was partitioned in 1920 between the 26 predominantly Catholic Celtic counties and the six predominantly Protestant Scots Anglo-Saxon counties of Ulster in the north. Independent from UK in 1922. Parliamentary republic since 1949. Politics heavily influenced by the division. Irish politics have been bloody, complex and emotive. Its roots are ethnic; its origin, England's attempts to subjugate and colonize Ireland; its reason, supposedly religious only because the Irish Celts clung to Catholicism when the English followed the Reformed teaching. Most Southern Irish want to see a reunited Ireland. Several Irish Republican Army factions, supported by an extremist minority, aim to achieve that dream through violence and are a threat to democratic government in both parts of Ireland.

Religion: The Catholic Church has no official link with the state, but its influence on all aspects of national life gives it a strong voice, which is generating considerable discussion and political polarization. There is freedom of religion.
Non-religious/Atheist 0.4%. **Jews** 0.1%.
Christian 99.4%. Affiliated 96.3%.
Roman Catholic 92.5%. Practising 90%. 3,330,000a; 2,230,000m.
Marginal groups (4) 0.2%.
Protestant 3.6%. 130,000a; 62,500m. Denominations 30. Largest (adherents):

Church of Ireland (Anglican)	90,000
Presbyterian Church in Ireland	19,000
Methodist Church	5,200
Indigenous churches/groups	2,000
Brethren	1,800
Baptist	700

Evangelical 0.6% of population.
Missionaries to Ireland approx. 140 (1:25,700 people) in 24 agencies.

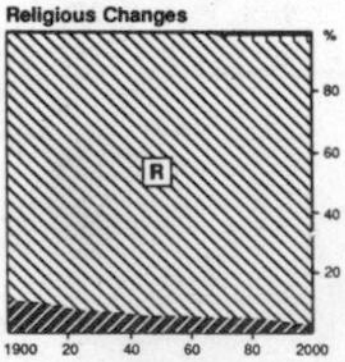

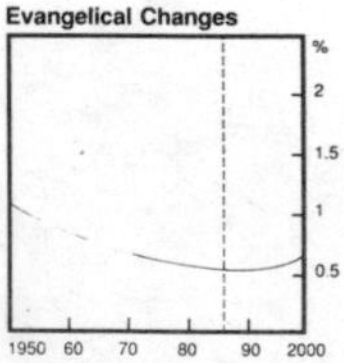

1. **The Catholic Church** has a remarkable position in the country. Practising Catholics are numerous though declining in percentage as young people question the traditional conservatism of the past. There are over 22,000 priests and members of monastic orders, and a further 5,900 Irish Catholic missionaries serving overseas. Widespread availability and use of the Bible is generating a spiritual hunger for reality.

2. **A spiritual awakening is taking place**. Its origins are in the dissemination of the Scriptures (**SGM, UBS**), widespread evangelistic activities (Irish Mission of Presbyterians, Ireland Outreach, Faith Mission, Irish Evangelistic Band, **OM** and many others), and the charismatic renewal within the Catholic Church. The latter is in decline, but from it have emerged hundreds of Christians in Bible study and prayer groups, the nucleus of an indigenous Irish church. Pray that this movement may grow in depth, knowledge of the Word, effective leadership and a viable identity untainted by the political overtones of Irish Catholicism and Protestantism. Pray for the Irish Bible school at Coalbrook which has the vision of training leadership for this move of the Spirit. The freshness, vitality and vision of these believers needs to be channelled into evangelism and missionary outreach.

3. **Protestants in Southern Ireland** have been in decline for 60 years through emigration and nominalism. They have become almost irrelevant to the evangelization of the Catholic majority. A few small evangelical groups — Baptists, Elim, and several N. American denominations are holding their own numerically. Pray for revival, ability to adapt culturally, a return to a high view of Scripture and a vision for outreach.

4. **Evangelicals are a very small community** and have made little impact on politics (only one Protestant in Parliament), education, the armed forces and public life because of their lack of influence in universities. **CCC** has 19 workers and **IFES** a further two committed to campus evangelism, but evangelical groups are few and small.

5. **Young people** have been responsive. **SU** has a growing and key ministry, 1,500 to 2,000 children attend evangelical camps every year run by United Beach Missions, **SU**, Bible Club, **CEF**, etc.

6. **Missionaries are now resident in every county.** Most are from N.Ireland or USA. There has been much evangelism, but more must be done to teach and encourage leadership in the emerging indigenous house fellowships. The present need is not a multiplicity of foreign denominations, because of the deep suspicion of anything foreign and Protestant. Agencies include Irish Mission (Presbyterian), Faith Mission, **EMF**, **GEM**, **UFM** and **CCC.**

7. **Less reached peoples:**
   a) **The central, southwestern and western counties** have few evangelicals.
   b) **The Gypsies** are an illiterate, neglected minority.
   c) **The Gaelic-speaking minority,** who live mainly in the rural west.

Middle East
June 20-21

ISRAEL
(State of Israel)

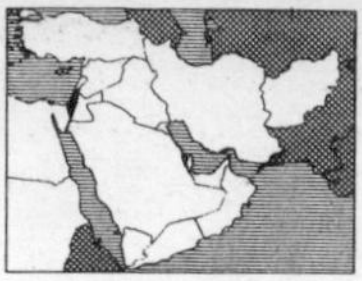

Area 20,700 sq.km. In 1967 Israel occupied the West Bank of Jordan (5,880 sq.km), Gaza Strip (378 sq.km) and Syrian Golan Heights. The Sinai Peninsula was occupied at the same time but was returned to Egypt by 1982.

Population 4,300,000. Annual growth 1.9%. People per sq.km. 207. A further 1,200,000 Arabs etc. live in occupied areas of Gaza, West Jordan and Syria.

Peoples (including Israel and occupied areas for conveniences of presentation).
Jews 66.5%. Immigrants from 102 nations; the most recent waves of immigration from USSR, Rumania and Ethiopia. A further 13,000,000 Jews worldwide.
Palestinian Arab 33%. Israel 653,000; Gaza 450,000; West Bank 725,000. A further 2,600,000 Palestinians scattered through Middle East and the world.
Other 0.5%. Armenian, Circassian, Western, etc.

Literacy 91%. **Official languages:** Hebrew, Arabic. Numerous immigrant languages from all over the world are spoken. **Indigenous languages** 9. **Bible translations** 3Bi 2NT.

Capital: Jerusalem 450,000, but not recognized as such internationally. Tel-Aviv 1,353,000. Urbanization 90%.

Economy: Modern, sophisticated industrial state. Military expenditure (30% of GNP), economic isolation in region and a mounting international debt is affecting living standards and bringing stresses to society. Inflation reached 1,000% per year at times in 1984. Income/person $5,360 (38% of USA).

Politics: The founding of Israel in 1948 ended 1,900 years of exile for the Jews. Five wars in 1948, 1956, 1967, 1973 and 1983-5 with surrounding states have exacted a heavy price on Israeli society. The conquest, occupation of South Lebanon in 1983 and withdrawal by 1985 has been a shock to the nation and has sharpened internal political divisions.

Religion: Freedom for all religious groups to work unhindered within their own communities, but proselytization is discouraged. Orthodox Judaism has much political leverage despite being a small minority. Statistics include Israel and all occupied areas in June 1985.
Jews 66.5%. 6% are Orthodox, also many other groupings. About 30% Jews are religious. Several divergent forms of Judaism: Karaites 12,000, Samaritans 300.
Muslim 30.6%. Almost entirely Sunni, but also the semi-Muslim Druze 55,000.
Christian 3.2%
Roman Catholic 1.7%. 74,000a; 43,700m. Three rites: Melkite, Latin and Maronite. Almost entirely Arab.
Orthodox 1.1%. Arab and other minorities. 48,500a; 29,000m. Denominations 8. Largest (adherents):

Greek Orthodox Church	43,000
Armenian Apostolic Church	2,500

Protestant 0.26%. 9,300a; 5,100m. Denominations 60+. Largest (adult members):

Messianic Assemblies approx.	1,400
Episcopal Church	1,320
Baptist Convention (SBC)	510
Lutheran Church	200

Evangelical 0.24% of population.
Missionaries to Israel 350 (1:12,300 people) in about 40 agencies.

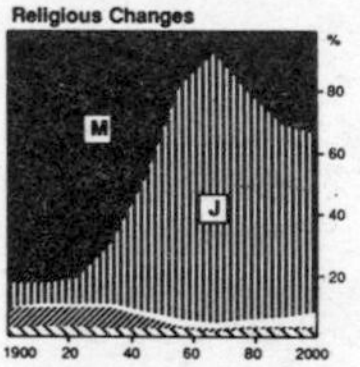

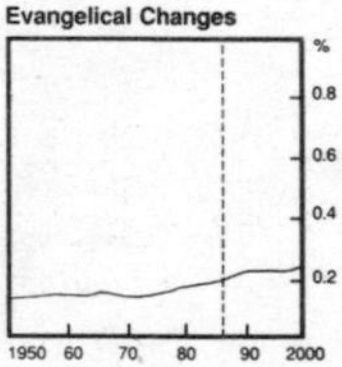

1. **Israeli Jews are sometimes harder to evangelize than those of the Dispersion.** Most have returned to their ancient land in unbelief. Pray for this hardness to be removed (Rom. 11:25), and for the promised harvest (Rom. 11:31).

2. **The idealistic dreams of Zionism have been shattered by the realities of life in modern Israel.** Social and economic stresses, religious and political divisions and the constant state of war-readiness have disturbed the nation. Pray for the peace of Jerusalem and Israel, and that Jews might find in their Messiah the peace that the world cannot take away.

3. **The social status of Messianic believers can be difficult**. Except for the Anglicans, Protestant churches do not have status as a recognized legal community. It is forbidden to influence a minor (under 18 years of age) without parental consent. There have been incidents of intimidation, violence and damage to churches at the hands of Jewish extremists during the early '80s. Pray for the government, and for a relaxation of attitudes that discriminate against Christians.

4. **The dislike of Christianity is a barrier to be overcome in Jewish minds**. "Christian" nations are seen to be destroyers of the Jewish nation whether by persecution (as in the Holocaust) or by proselytization. Pray that the gospel may be understood as a fulfilment of their Jewish heritage and that a widespread turning to Christ might come. Since 1960, it is estimated that worldwide about 50,000 Jews have found the Messiah.

5. **Praise God for a marked increase of evangelical believers among the Jews**. Numbers have quadrupled since 1975 to about 1,800 in 25 Messianic assemblies and also various denominational groups. Mature leadership is developing and a vigorous indigenous music and literature being produced. The emergence of a younger generation of leadership is a prayer target. Pray for unity among the few believers; this has been a serious problem in the past. There are numerous small denominational and interdenominational groups of foreign origin; few are viable congregations.

6. **Protestants are more numerous among the Palestinian Arabs.** The largest groups are Anglican, Baptist and Brethren, and most originate from the traditional Christian minority. Born-again Arab believers are a minority among the 6,000 Protestant Arabs. There is an unprecedented openness among Palestinian Muslims and freedom to share Christ with them, but there are, as yet, only three groups of believers of Muslim origin. Pray for the outreach of Arab believers to them. Pray also for close and warm fellowship between believers of both Jews and Arabs despite communal tensions; this is the objective of the United Christian Council of Israel.

7. **The missionary force** is variously estimated at between 350 and 1,500. Some of the larger agencies are CMJ (Anglican, 48 workers), Church of Scotland (47), **SBC** (46), **OM** (20), Norwegian Lutherans (12), **CWI** (9), and **MT** (5). Years of seed sowing and breaking down of long-held prejudices against Christianity are now bearing fruit, but missionary work can be frustrating and discouraging. Many come with unrealistic visions and find little fulfilment or identification with local believers. Pray that all called of God may find viable ministries, effective means of contact with non-Christians and sweet fellowship with local believers. Friendship evangelism, literature distribution, and encouragement of believers are the major means of service.

8. **The unreached:**

a) **Over 1.5 mill. Jews were born overseas**. Many still speak the languages of their lands of birth, and must be reached through that medium. Pray especially for the **Russian Jews,** many of whom are non-religious, and also for the 15,000 **Falasha** (Black Jews) who arrived from Ethiopia in 1985.

b) **Of the 100 towns and 800 villages in Israel** only a handful have Jewish or Arab congregations.

c) **Palestinian Arabs** are a people that most want to forget, or exploit for political ends. 1,800,000 are registered as refugees in 61 camps in surrounding lands. Pray for a fair settlement of the intractable Palestinian problem. Pray for the evangelization of the 95% of them who are Muslim. Only a few dozen believers from a Muslim background are known, yet Palestinian Arabs are more open to the gospel than ever before.

d) **The 55,000 Druzes** with their syncretic religion live in 17 villages of Israel. Only a handful have believed.

e) **The 45,000 Bedouin** in 22 tribes live in the Negev in the south.

9. **Supportive ministries.**

a) **Literature** is of unusual importance for the spread of the gospel due to the multiplicity of languages and paucity of Christians who witness. Pray for the Yanetz and Baptist publishing houses and the production of an increasing selection of Hebrew and Arabic

Christian literature, and the nine Christian bookshops. There are two Hebrew Messianic periodicals that have a readership beyond the Christian community. Too few believers are engaged in distribution. Pray that Jews may read the NT and find the Living Word. 12% of all homes have a NT. Pray for the project of annotating the Hebrew NT.

b) **Radio — TWR** broadcasts only 1.25 hours a month in Hebrew. Pray for an increase in hours and impact.

c) **Student work** is in its infancy. **IFES** has four groups with about 80 believers of Arab and Hebrew background. Leadership is the key prayer target.

10. **The Jews of the Dispersion** are declining in numbers through a lower birth rate, mixed marriages, secularism and conversions to other religions. There are now about 13,000,000 outside Israel. The largest concentrations are in North America 6,500,000; USSR 2,700,000; France 650,000; Britain 400,000; and Argentina 300,000. There are two million Jews in New York. In the USA there is much openness; elsewhere less so. Pray for the ministry of **Jews for Jesus, MT, CWI**, Churches Ministry to the Jews etc. Pray for a greater sensitivity on the part of Gentile churches towards the maintenance of a messianic testimony among Jews. Little is being done for Jews in the USSR, France and Argentina. The work involves long hours of loving, patient ministry to individuals and families.

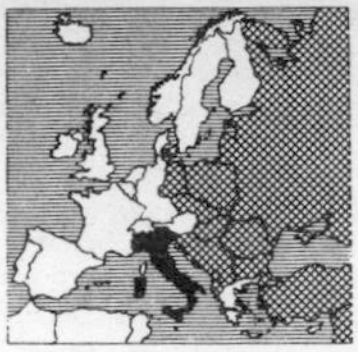

ITALY
(The Italian Republic)

The West

June 22-23

Area 301,000 sq.km. A long peninsula that dominates the central Mediterranean Sea.

Population 57,400,000. Annual growth 0.1%. People per sq.km. 192.

Peoples
Italian 95.2%. Deep cultural differences exist between the wealthier, and more radical northerners and the poorer, more conservative southerners.
Sardinian 2.2%. Speaking many Sard dialects.
Tyrolean 0.5%. In the northeast, speaking German.
Friulian/Ladin 0.8%. In the north.
Other European 0.5%. Albanian 260,000; French 70,000; British 25,000; Greek 15,000; Gypsy 12,000.
Middle Eastern 0.35%. Almost all Muslim.

Literacy 94%. **Official language:** Italian.

Capital: Rome 3,839,000. Other cities: Milan 6,940,000; Naples 4,116,000; Turin 2,171,000; Genoa 1,195,000; Florence 1,106,000. Urbanization 72%.

Economy: Highly centralized and inefficient government could have brought economic ruin had it not been for the drive of the private industrial sector and the initiative of the "black" (illegal) economy. The north is very industrialized. Income/person $6,830 (48% of USA). Inflation 14%.

Politics: United as a single state in 1870. Republican democracy since 1946. Weak and unstable succession of 45 governments since the war but with an underlying social stability. National frustration was expressed in the '70s by anarchy, terrorism and increasing support for the Communist party, one of the largest and most democratic outside the Eastern Bloc.

Religion: Roman Catholicism ceased to be the state religion in 1984. All religions have equal freedom before the law.

Non-religious/Atheist 18.3%. Almost all were baptized in the Catholic Church.
Muslim 0.35%. **Jews** 39,000.
Christian 81.1%. Affiliated 80%.
Roman Catholic 78.9%. Practising 15%. 45,300,000a.
Orthodox 0.07%. 38,000a.
Marginal groups 0.5%. 284,000a. Over 6 cults.
Largest (adherents):

Jehovah's Witnesses	251,000
New Apostolic Church	20,000
Mormons	12,000

Protestant 0.78%. 450,000a; 300,000m.
Denominations 22 larger and 125 small groups.
Largest (adult members):

Assemblies of God	190,000
Waldensian/Methodist Church	31,000
Brethren assemblies	15,000
Salvation Army	12,000
Lutheran Church	10,000
Seventh Day Adventist Church	5,300
Baptist Union	4,250

Evangelical 0.6% of population.
Missionaries to Italy 420 (1:137,000 people) in 57 agencies.
Missionaries from Italy approx. 20 (1:22,500 Protestants).

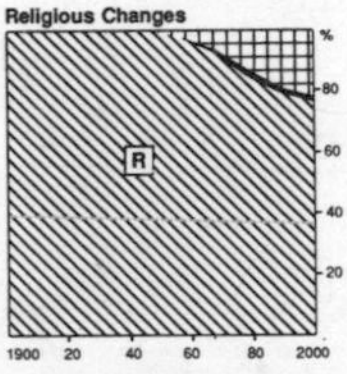

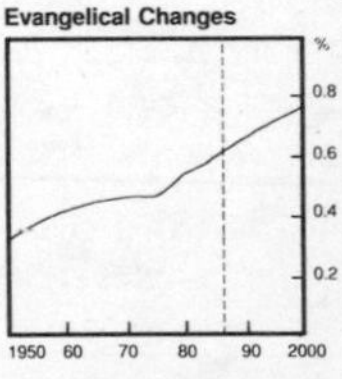

1. **Persecution of Protestants continued for nearly 800 years.** Today's freedom to preach the gospel is a new experience, but the response has been meagre, and indifference to spiritual truths widespread. Pray for decisive breakthroughs for the gospel.

2. **The long-powerful Roman Catholic Church** has lost over nine million members in this generation. The decline in the number of priests and of influence has been dramatic. Pope John Paul and his charisma has returned the Church to a far more traditional stance, which is slowing the decline. Although many Italians despise and ignore the Church, its traditions and mind-set still permeate every aspect of national life, and church attendance remains one of the highest in Europe. In their disillusionment many have sought ideological refuge in Marxism and cults, or reverted to witchcraft and spiritism. The bonds of Satan must be broken by prevailing prayer.

3. **Evangelism by Evangelicals has been sporadic.** The response of radical leftists and religious traditionalists has been indifferent or hostile. The task has been made no easier by the tireless efforts of the Jehovah's Witnesses and the 600 Mormon missionaries.

4. **The most unreached sectors of the population:**
   a) **About 1,500 of Italy's communities** have an established evangelical witness. The other 31,500 are unoccupied.
   b) **Three provinces**, Trento and Belluno in the northeast (where **ECM** ministers) and Macerata have no organized Protestant churches.
   c) **Sardinia,** a Mediterranean island nation with a limited autonomy, has 1,600,000 people with their own language and culture. There are only about six Protestant churches, a handful of Christian workers and a **CLC** bookstore. Suspicion of outsiders, fear, vendettas, the occult and the activities of JWs all make any evangelistic outreach very difficult.
   d) **The materialistic cities.** Milan has only 18 Protestant churches for 6,000,000 people. Many cities and towns have little or no established witness.
   e) **The 980,000 students in 44 universities.** There are only 60-80 active Christians in five cities linked with the GBU(**IFES**) and a few others with **CCC**. **OM** teams have occasional outreach to this community.
   f) **Sicily** is an island of 5,500,000 people. The baleful influence of the violent Mafia has helped to keep the island in poverty and underdevelopment. There are a number of churches and missions (including **WT**) on the island.

5. **The unreached minorities:**
   a) **Muslims** have rapidly grown in numbers to around 200,000 through an influx of refugees (Ethiopians, Africans, Iranis, Iraqis), migrant labour (North Africans), and immigrants (Arabs, Egyptians). Only a few workers (**SIM**, etc.) are committed to this minority.
   b) **Albanian** communities in Calabria in central and southern Italy number some 260,000 still speaking four archaic dialects of Albanian. No specific outreach to them has been undertaken.
   c) **The minorities in the northeast** — the **Friulians, Ladins, Slovenes** and **South Tyrolean Germans** all have their own distinctive cultures and languages, but little direct effort is being made to reach these staunchly traditional Catholics with the message of new life in Jesus.
   d) **The Greek and Croatian minorities** in the south.

6. **The Protestant church is weak** with little growth. The Brethren and Assemblies of God have made great gains in the past, but their growth has halted. Most denominations are small and often introspective. Protestantism is still seen as a foreign sect even though the world's oldest Protestant denomination, the Waldensians, is indigenous in origin. Sadly, Marxian influence has made deep inroads into the latter as in several other older denominations. What a need for revival and strong, clear biblical teaching!

7. **There is a dearth of Italian Christian leaders** both at a national and pastoral level in Protestant churches. There are less than 100 students at the five denominational and two interdenominational Bible schools and seminaries. The best known is the IBE (**GEM**) in Rome. Very few churches fully support their own pastors, and many leaders are dependent on foreign funds. The labourers are too few for the immense task. Internal conflicts and disunity among leaders within congregations, between denominations and between churches and missions are all too frequent and sap the spiritual vitality of the witness.

8. **Italy needs missionaries** — but of the right calibre. The casualty rate has been unacceptably high in the past. The pressures from spiritual forces and entrenched opposition to their message expose any personal inadequacies in a missionary. Pray out to the harvest field those with spiritual stamina, emotional maturity, and God-given faith. Some significant missionary groups in the country are **GEM** (21), **CBFMS** (19), **BCU** (19), **CCC** (18), **SBC** (15), **ECM** (11), **WT** (11), **WEC** (7), **AoG** (5), **EMF** (3). All mission groups, especially the interdenominational, have had traumatic histories. Ministries most needed are in discipleship and church planting.

9. **Literature and Bible distribution** have not had a wide impact due to the reluctance of Italians to read. There are about 14 Christian organizations with bookshops — including **CLC** with eight bookstores. The new common language Italian Bible was published in 1984. Pray for a hunger for God's Word and desire for wholesome Christian literature.

10. **Christian radio and TV** has become an extraordinary tool for evangelism since government control of broadcasting was relaxed. There are 600 private TV stations in Italy now! There are 80 evangelical local radio stations and many other commercial stations that broadcast evangelical programmes. Many churches and missions have developed ministries in radio (including **HCJB**/WRMF, **ECM**, **BCU**, **GMU**, **WT**, etc.). Pray that in all this multiplicity of effort there may be fruitful cooperation to produce relevant, dynamic programmes. Many recent conversions in Italy have been through this medium. Adequate follow up is a problem. Anarchy on the radio waves may force a change in the law; pray for balanced legislation and wise use of this medium.

11. **Vatican City** is an independent city state of 0.43 sq. km in the heart of the city of Rome. The total population is about 1,000. It is the administrative and spiritual capital for the worldwide Roman Catholic Church. Pray for:

a) **The Pope** who exercises such an influence within and beyond the Church he leads.

b) The Roman Catholic Church in this period of intense turmoil and change. Pray for a work of the Holy Spirit within this huge body. The increasing prominence of the Bible in Catholic circles is a positive development.

c) **A mighty moving of the Holy Spirit** in this Church would have worldwide significance.

Africa

June 24-25

IVORY COAST
(The Republic of Ivory Coast)

Area 322,000 sq.km. On the West African coast between Liberia and Ghana.

Population 10,100,000. Annual growth 2.8%. People per sq.km. 31. Massive immigration from surrounding lands, especially Burkina Faso and Mali.

Peoples: Over 70 languages spoken.

Africans indigenous to Ivory Coast 74%.

Kwa (17) 30%. Baoulé, 1,600,000, are the dominant people today. The 15 coastal Lagoon peoples 735,000; also Agni 441,000; Akan 90,000.

Krou (24) 14%. Bete 493,000; Gueré 260,000; Dida 204,000; Wobe 123,000; Kru (6) 85,000; Godie 36,000; Nyabwa 27,000.

Gur (37) 12.2%. Senoufo (30 dialects) 900,000; Koulango 183,000; Lobi 62,000, etc.

Mande (9) 10%. Malinké 554,000; Dyoula 162,000; Maou 95,000; Ligbi 70,000.

S. Mande (9) 8%. Yakouba 462,000; Gouro 150,000; Gagou 38,000; Toura 34,000; Yaoure 23,000; Wan 17,000.

Foreigners 26%.

Burkinabé (Upper Voltan) 1,200,000; Malian 530,000; Guinean 160,000; Lebanese 100,000; Ghanaian 75,000; Nigerian 65,000; French 45,000.

Literacy 32%. **Official language:** French. **All languages** 69. **Bible translations** 2Bi 7NT 16por.

Capital: Abidjan 2,800,000. Other city: Yamoussoukro 100,000 (has been proclaimed the new capital). Urbanization 38%.

Economy: Developed and diversified with French expertise since independence. Agriculture is the backbone of the economy, but rapid deforestation, growing unemployment and uncertain political future are braking growth rate. Income/person $720 (5% of USA).

Politics: Independent of France in 1960. One-party presidential government under Houphouet-Boigny. Two decades of stability threatened by the President's failure to resolve the succession problem. Tribal competition, the unfulfilled expectations of the educated youth and a high number of foreigners could spell trouble in the future.

Religion: Religious freedom. The government is very sympathetic to missions.

Animist 40%. Generally stronger in the centre and west, many tribes still predominantly animist.

Muslim 25%. Strong in the northwest and in Abidjan.

Christian 35%. Nominal 14.6%. Affiliated 20.4%.

Roman Catholic 10%. Practising 33%. 1,010,000a; 545,000m.

Marginal groups 5.6%. 566,000a. Large number of syncretic bodies of Ivorean and Ghanaian origin.

Protestant 4.8%. 485,000a; 171,000m. Denominations 25. Largest (adherents):

Eglise Prot. du Centre (**CMA**)	120,000
Eg. Prot. Methodists	120,000
Assemblies of God	75,000
Union des Eg. du G. (**MB-UFM**)	60,000
Conv. Baptiste (**SBC**)	8,000
Eg. Adventiste (SDA)	8,000
Alliance des Eg. Ev. (**WEC**)	6,500
Assoc. des Eg. du N. (**CBFMS**)	6,000

Evangelical 3.7% of population.

Missionaries to Ivory Coast 450 (1:22,400 people) in 28 agencies.

Missionaries from Ivory Coast 1.

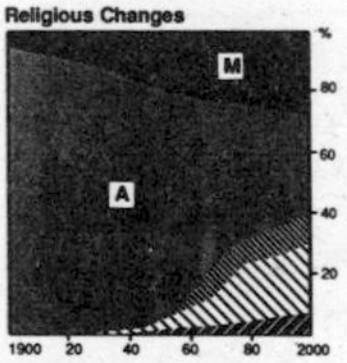

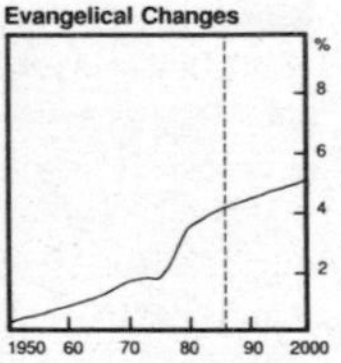

1. **Praise God for the last 25 years of relative tranquility, economic progress and stability of the country.** This could change. Pray for open doors and hearts in this day of abundant reaping.

2. **The preaching of Prophet Harris from Liberia in 1914-15 brought over 120,000 coastal people out of fetishism and darkness.** The initiative was lost as missionary help arrived "too little and too late". Many syncretic indigenous churches multiplied and grew out of that movement. The Methodists arrived in 1924 and were once the largest Protestant community, but liberal theology and nominalism are widespread among the diverse coastal peoples. Pray for a new wave of evangelism and church planting.

3. **The Catholic Church** has made a deep impact through an extensive educational system. Many Ivoreans are nominally Catholic as a result. Catholics are 50% of the population in Abidjan, a large minority in the south and among the upper and middle classes. The lack is a personal relationship with the Saviour.

4. **Evangelical groups** had a late and slow start; **CMA** entered the land in 1930. Since 1973 most churches have grown at between 10% and 30% per year. This is especially true of the Baoulé in the centre (**CMA**), Yakouba and Guere in the southwest (**MB-UFM**), and churches in Abidjan (**AoG**, Baptists and others). Pray for the spiritual health of believers. The major issues: materialism, growth of syncretistic ideas, breakdown in church-mission relationships and lack of concern for cross-cultural evangelism.

5. **Leadership for the churches** is the big bottleneck. Many denominations have one trained pastor for every 10-20 congregations. Congregational giving has been poor despite relative prosperity. Nearly every denomination lacks sufficient pastors, and lay leadership is often ill-trained for pastoral and teaching roles. Many of the larger denominations have French or vernacular Bible schools or TEE programmes. The inter-church secondary level Bible seminary at Yamoussoukro is vital for the future. Pray for the calling out and training of more leaders of high calibre.

6. **The Evangelical Federation founded in 1960** had become a uniting fellowship for promoting Bible training, nationwide evangelistic efforts and pastors' retreats as well as setting up the Evangelical Publishing Centre, but real fellowship between churches and agencies is deficient. Pray for spiritual unity and cooperation among national Christian workers and between nationals and expatriates.

7. **Missions have made a great effort over the past 15 years,** and God has blessed these endeavours. Yet much remains to be done, even in peoples among whom there are already churches. Only among the Baoulé, Wobe and Yakouba are Evangelicals over 5% of the population. Many villages and towns are unevangelized. Pray for decisive breakthroughs among the animistic Bete, Dida, Godie, Nyabwa, Guere, Kru in the southwest (**MB/UFM**-31 missionaries), Gouro, Gagou and Kouya (**WEC**-47), Baoulé and Agni (**CMA**-35) in the centre, Senoufo (**CBFMS**-66), Akan, Lobi and Kulango (Free Will Baptists-22) in the north. The greatest limitation is the lack of experienced workers for nearly all ministries in partially reached and unreached peoples, and in supportive ministries.

8. **Peoples that are both unreached and unoccupied by any mission/church group are not so many;** but pray for the evangelization of the following:

a) **The strongly Muslim peoples of the northwest:** Malinké, Dioula and Fulani (45,000) — among whom more work is being directed by **WEC**, **CBFMS**, **SIM**, **SBM**, but where response has been minimal — and the unoccupied Wassulunka (15,000) and Bambara (12,000).

b) **Marginally occupied peoples** in the Free Will Baptist area in the northeast: Birifor, Tegesie, Lorhon; **WEC** area in the centre: Mona, Nwan, Yaouré, Kouya, Maou, Toura; **MB-UFM** area in the southwest: Toura, Nyedebwa, Dida, Bete. The multiplicity of small tribes necessitates more cross-cultural workers. **NTM** is seeking to help in the northeast and later in southwest peoples.

c) The large **Lebanese** and **French** communities. There is little specific ministry among them and there are very few Evangelicals.

9. **Islam has grown rapidly** during this century — from 5% in 1900 to 25% today. Tribal groups in the north and pockets of people in tribes all over the country are becoming Muslim. Urban concentrations of Muslims are high and so are conversion rates among new immigrants to the cities. Nearly half of Abidjan's population is Muslim. Pray that Christians may be zealous to win non-Muslims while they can, and also show more concern for the Muslims themselves.

10. **Abidjan's exploding population, which doubles every four years, is the strategic key for evangelization of both Ivory Coast and Burkina Faso.** Every people of these two lands has a significant community in the city, but most are neglected. There are 16 church planting

missionaries in the city representing nine churches/missions, but this is not adequate. Over one million Muslims are scarcely touched with the gospel. There are only 75 churches in the city — the more significant being those of the **AoG**, **SBC**, **MB**, and now **CMA**.

11. **The large influx of foreigners** presents unusual opportunities for evangelizing those who are separated from the strong ties of their tribal cultures. Over a quarter of the population is foreign. So little has been done to evangelize the Burkinabé, Malians, Guineans, and colonies of Mauritanians in many towns. Pray that churches and missions may seize present opportunities before these people become Muslim. The most responsive have been the Mossis from Burkina Faso.

12. **Young people are responsive**, and wherever churches have been willing and able to minister specifically to them, there has been fruit. The liberty for teaching Scripture in public schools is exciting but underused through lack of qualified personnel. **SU** is making a vital contribution in school evangelism and discipleship. The **IFES** Francophone Africa HQ is in Abidjan, and there is a good GBU group (**IFES**) in the university. Both **CCC** and Navigators are commencing a student ministry.

13. **Literature**. Pray for the bookstores and depots of various missions — Bible Society, Maison de la Bible, **CLC** (Abidjan), **MB** (Man), **UFM** (Gagnoa), Cons. Bapt. (Korhogo), etc. Pray also for the inter-mission/church Evangelical Publication Centre in Abidjan which coordinates much of the production of evangelical literature for all Francophone Africa — publishing books, cassettes and an evangelistic magazine for children. Pray for this valuable ministry and for solutions to many problems: lack of qualified staff (especially French-speaking), financial pressures and lack of good distribution outlets.

14. **Bible translation** is one of the most pressing and demanding ministries for Christian workers. A considerable number of national and expatriate workers are involved in 27 translation and literacy programmes linked with **UBS** and various church/mission groups. **SIL**'s contribution in a number of projects is especially significant — many being among the superficially Christianized people of the south. Only two languages have the whole Bible, seven the New Testament and sixteen only portions. Possibly 24 other languages await translators. **GRI** has recorded 41 languages and dialects. Pray for newly translated Scriptures to take root in the hearts of the people.

15. **Radio work** — The ELWA (**SIM**) Francophone Africa programme and follow up work is now based in Abidjan. Pray for the provision of staff, cooperating churches willing to help with programmes and fruitfulness in these under-evangelized lands.

JAMAICA
(The Dominion of Jamaica)

Caribbean

June 26

Area 11,000 sq.km. Beautiful, fertile, mountainous island south of Cuba.

Population 2,358,000. Annual growth 2.2%. Emigration at the high rate of 1.5%. People, per sq.km. 214.

Peoples: African 76.3%, **Eurafrican** 15.1%, **Chinese** 1.2%, **Indian/Afro-Asian** 3.4%, **European** 3.2%, **Other** 0.9%.

Literacy 87%. **Official language:** English.

Capital: Kingston-St.Andrew 801,000. Urbanization 53%.

Economy: Ten years of recession and infatuation with Cuban-style socialism damaged bauxite, sugar and banana exports and drove away the tourists on which the country depended. Economic misery, 27% unemployment, poverty in the urban shanty towns and a high crime rate were the results. The government elected in 1980 has reversed the trend, but the economy remains precarious. Income/person $1,300 (9% of USA). Unemployment 20%.

Politics: Independent of Britain in 1962 as a parliamentary democracy. Reasonably stable politically despite the economic disarray.

Religion: Freedom of religion.
Non-religious/Atheist 2.3%.
Spiritist, Cultist 7.3%. Rastafarian, Pocomanian, etc.
Hindu 0.3%. **Muslim** 0.2%. **Baha'i** 0.2%.
Christian 89.5%. Nominal 37.3%. Affiliated 52.2%.

Roman Catholic 8.4%. Practising 20%. 198,000a; 115,000m.
Orthodox 0.1%. 3,000a.
Marginal groups 5%. 122,000a; 65,000m. Over 118 cults of Western and African derivation. Largest (adherents):

Revival Zion	35,000
Jehovah's Witnesses	23,684

Protestant 38.6%. 910,000a; 430,000a. Denominations 62. Largest (adult members):

Seventh Day Adventist Church	120,000
Anglican Church	51,000
Baptist Union	40,000
N.T. Church of God	33,000
African Meth. Episcopal Zion Ch.	30,000
Methodist Church	16,000
Church of God of Prophecy	15,100
United Church	14,500
Salvation Army	8,000

Evangelical 14% of population.

Missionaries to Jamaica 120 (1:19,700 people) in 33 agencies.

Missionaries from Jamaica 44 (1:20,700 Protestants) excluding those serving Jamaican communities abroad.

J

Note: Jamaica and the other English-speaking states and territories of the Caribbean are both diverse and jealous of their independence, yet they have a similar history and development politically, socially, culturally and spiritually. We have, therefore, grouped together prayer items for the 16 island states and territories that were recently or are currently ruled by Britain. These are:

A. **Independent States**
Antigua, Bahamas, Barbados, Dominica, Grenada, Jamaica, St. Christopher-Nevis, St. Lucia, St. Vincent, and Trinidad & Tobago. For statistics, see in alphabetic order of countries.

B. **British Colonies**
Anguilla, Bermuda, British Virgin Islands, Cayman Islands, Montserrat, and Turks & Caicos Islands. For statistics, see British Antilles (p. 115).

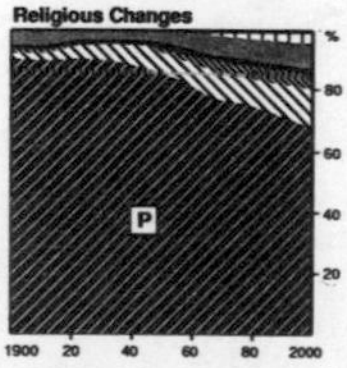

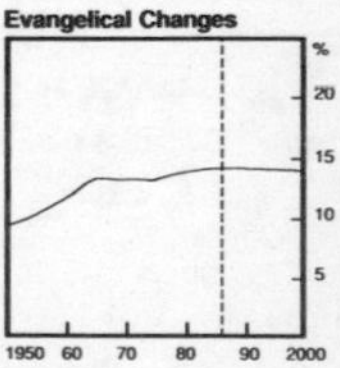

1. **The Caribbean is a paradise gone wrong, and now an ideological war zone.** The potent mix of poverty, overpopulation and limited hopes for future development makes it a breeding ground for revolution for many newly independent, scarcely viable Caribbean states.

2. **The economic and political traumas of the past 15 years have shaken the Caribbean.** The unconverted have become more receptive and Christians more aware of their responsibilities to both evangelize and influence the standards of society. Praise God for this. Violent changes cannot be ruled out. The widening gap between the rich and poor in the region could be disastrous.

3. **Political instability** and exotic extremism in Dominica, Grenada and Jamaica sent ripples of anxiety through the Caribbean. Pray that God may overrule in the affairs of men. With many new, inexperienced, little governments battling to solve the insoluble, Christians must be ready for the possibility of atheistic persecution and indoctrination of the youth. In Grenada in the early '80s, this had begun. Pray that committed Christians may be placed in leadership roles in their nations.

4. **Materialism and wealth** have sapped the spiritual vigour of Christians in the more prosperous Caymans, Bahamas, Bermuda and Virgin Islands.

5. **Christianity is a cultural veneer to most.** It is reckoned that 90% of Bahamians, 70% of Jamaicans and over 50% of most islanders rarely attend church. Confused family relationships, lax morality and increasing crime are rife. Pray for a surge of new life and revival through the churches. Pray for the young people and children — many are turning away to Marxism, spiritism, Rastafarianism and other off-beat life styles because of the inconsistent lives of their elders and the turmoil in their own hearts.

6. **The Protestant Church has had an exciting past** of revivals, ingatherings and missionary endeavours. Few areas in the world are better evangelized. Evangelicalism is strongest in the many Baptist and Pentecostal groups. Believers are often superficial, legalistic and moved by emotion rather than obedience to God's Word. Yet there are the stirrings of revival again in Jamaica and Antigua; may it come! Blessings in Jamaica will affect the Caribbean and beyond!

J

7. **The Evangelicals are numerically strong** and form a high proportion of the population on some islands. Baptist, Holiness and Pentecostal groups are generally growing. Pray for mature, dynamic churches with effective indigenous leadership to emerge in every denomination. The moral climate makes pastoral counselling and church discipline a touchy and difficult issue.

8. **The post-war missionary wave has vitalized the evangelical witness in these territories.** There are now about 604 missionaries serving in these 16 territories and states. Praise the Lord for the vital contribution of **SBC** (52 missionaries) in 13 territories, Church of the Nazarene (38) in 7, **WT** (26) in 5, Church of God of Prophecy in 16, Church of God (Cleveland) in 12, as well as a number of Jamaican missionaries in many islands. The high density of missionaries can create national-missionary tensions; love and sensitivity in avoiding paternal and economic dominance is needed for maximum fruitful ministry and growth of the Church.

9. **Christian leadership** is all too often lacking in depth, maturity and consistency of Christian standards. Many of the finest leaders have emigrated. Pray that an anointed, prophetic ministry may be provided by pastors and leaders in the churches throughout the islands. Praise God for those faithfully serving the Lord in the face of discouragements.

10. **Leadership training** is provided in four Protestant seminaries and 53 Bible schools (14 in Jamaica alone). Staff and students alike constantly need the fresh touch of the Lord on their lives. A stream of well-trained, Spirit-filled pastors and leaders must flow out to the many struggling churches in the islands. TEE programmes are run by **WT** for use all over the Caribbean from the Evangelical Institute of Christian Education.

11. **The missions outreach of the Caribbean churches.** In the last century Jamaican and other island missionaries made a decisive contribution to the evangelization of the Caribbean and West Africa, yet today this vision has dimmed. Poverty, lack of teaching and lack of vision are responsible. Pray for the Jamaican International Missionary Fellowship, its promotion of missions in churches and schools, its School of Missionary Training and its missionaries sent out into cross-cultural work. Pray for the Caribbean churches to catch again a vision for world evangelization.

12. **Several million English-speaking islanders have emigrated to Britain and now to North America.** The Caribbean emigrant communities face economic and social pressures. Young people are frustrated and often unemployed. They are rejecting the religion of their parents.

13. **The less reached islands and peoples:**

a) **Several major islands**, including Dominica and St. Lucia, are predominantly Catholic, and the Evangelicals are a small minority.

b) **Many of the smaller islands and cays** are poor and isolated, with little clear preaching of the gospel — e.g. the Grenadines, Barbuda, Anguilla, etc.

c) **The Rastafarians** are a growing force in Jamaica and 12 other Caribbean states. They reject the Western world view and champion Black consciousness, exotic life styles and drug use. They need the Saviour. They number 70,000 in Jamaica, and possibly 180,000 in the Caribbean, USA and UK.

d) **The East Indians** are a major segment of society in Trinidad. Muslim and Hindu communities have migrated to most of the larger islands where very little specific outreach to them has been attempted. There are 30,000 in Jamaica, 5,500 in Grenada, etc. A number have become Christians.

e) **The Chinese**: 38,000 in Trinidad, 26,000 in Jamaica and small colonies throughout the Caribbean. Most have become nominal Catholics. There is a lively Chinese Christian Fellowship in Jamaica. **TEAM** has a church planting ministry among Chinese in Trinidad.

f) **The Caribs**, the indigenous Amerindians, are reduced to 2,500 and only exist as a community on the east coast of Dominica. They have lost their language but not their identity. They attract tourists, but not yet evangelical witnesses. A sensitive approach to these nominally Catholic but practising animistic people will be necessary.

g) **Haitien refugees** in Bahamas number about 20,000. These destitute people need spiritual help. **WT** has a ministry among them, and there are three churches established.

14. **Christian literature.** High literacy levels and lack of reading materials at affordable prices is a challenge. The enormous problems for publishing and distributing literature are created by the difficulties of communication, inflation and lack of foreign exchange in the widely scattered islands. **CLC**'s ministry has been unique. Thirty-eight workers in eight nations run bookstores, bookmobiles, correspondence courses, and publish the successful *Caribbean Challenge*, an evangelistic/teaching magazine with a 30,000 circulation in 29 countries. The latter is based in Jamaica. Pray for an increase in sales, literature workers and fruit from this ministry.

15. **Student ministries.** The **IFES** ministry is the oldest and strongest movement in student work in the region. The combined ministry of **SU** and **UCCF** in the Student Christian Fellowship of Jamaica has resulted in 200 high school and 21 tertiary student groups and an expanding literature ministry. There are now 80 groups in Trinidad and 40 in Barbados, but smaller islands are less well covered. Pray for workers in student ministries, and for an expansion of the work. Pray that a strong, clear presentation of the Truth to students may vitally influence future leadership of churches and nations in the Caribbean.

Asia

June 27-30

JAPAN
(Nippon)

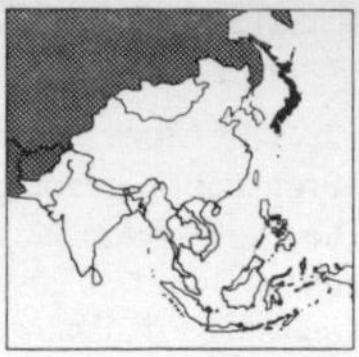

Area 372,300 sq.km. A 3,000 km. arc of four large islands (Honshu, Hokkaido, Shikoku, Kyushu) and 3,000 small islands in N.W. Pacific. Mountainous; only 13% can be cultivated.

Population 120,800,000. Annual growth 0.6%. People per sq.km. 324. Concentrated on the narrow coastal plains.

Peoples
Indigenous 99.3%. **Japanese**; **Ainu** 20,000 (19 dialects; dying language).
Foreign 0.7%. Korean 720,000; Chinese 55,000.

Literacy 100%. **Official language:** Japanese. **Bible translations** 3Bi 1por.

Capital: Tokyo. Major conurbations: Tokyo-Yokohama-Kawasaki 21,600,000, Osaka-Kobe 10,000,000, Fukuoko-Kita-Kyushu 3,100,000, Nagoya 2,200,000, Kyoto 1,500,000, Sapporo 1,500,000, Hiroshima 1,000,000. Urbanization 78%.

Economy: The world's most powerful export-oriented economy despite lack of oil and raw materials. Inflation 3%. Income/person $10,100 (72% of USA).

Politics: Stable democratic constitutional monarchy since 1947.

Religion: Freedom of religion is guaranteed to all by the constitution. In practice social and family pressures restrict that freedom.
Non-religious/Atheist 12.3%-60%. Many claim no personal religion, but follow the customs of Japan's traditional religions.
Shinto/Buddhist 20-60%. Polytheistic, ancestor-venerating Shintoism has been much modified by Confucianism and Buddhism. Many follow both Shinto and Buddhist teachings.
New religions (over 120) 23.5%. Most are Buddhist and some Shinto offshoots. Largest (adherents):

Sokka Gakkai	17,000,000
Risshokoseikai	5,500,000
Seichonoie	3,700,000

Christian 2%. Affiliated 1.3%. Many nominal and backsliding Christians.
Roman Catholic 0.34%. Practising 34%. 405,000a; 283,000m.
Orthodox (2) 0.02%. Greek Orthodox 24,700a.
Marginal groups (10+) 0.51%. 610,000a; 430,000m. Some claimed figures appear inflated! Largest (adherents):

Unification Church (Moonies)	270,000
Spirit of Jesus Church (Unitarian)	120,000
Jehovah's Witnesses	92,022
Mormons	71,000
Original Gospel Movement	47,000

Protestant 0.44%. 534,000a, 309,000m. Denominations 120+. Largest (adherents):

United Church	192,000
Baptist Convention (**SBC**)	26,500
Presbyterian Ch. of Christ	12,300
Seventh Day Adventist Ch.	11,500
Immanuel Ch. (Wesleyan Miss.)	10,500
NIKK (**JEB**)	10,200
Japan Holiness Ch. (**OMS**)	9,720
Assemblies of God	9,000
NDKK (**TEAM**)	7,100

Evangelical 0.23% of population.
Missionaries to Japan 2,570 (1:47,000 people) in 140 agencies.
Missionaries from Japan 160 (1:3,300 Protestants) in 48 agencies.

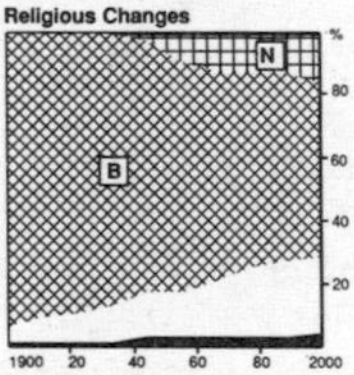

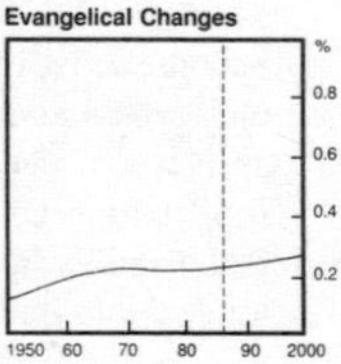

1. **Japan is a mixture of exciting openness and challenging unresponsiveness.** Warfare in the heavenlies is real. Areas of definite concern and contest:
   a) **The people** are polite, hardworking and sincere, yet are too absorbed in the things of this life to give heed to the gospel. Most see the value of a religion, 30% have a definite religion, but only 20% believe in the existence of God.
   b) **The period of post-war openness has passed**. Shintoism is once more a growing influence with a resurgence of Japanese nationalism. Pray for a new openness.
   c) **The growth of Sokka Gakkai** in the 1950s and '60s, and other new religions, as well as the success of aberrant versions of Christianity such as the Moonies, JWs, Mormons and Unitarian Pentecostals, is a challenge.

d) **A network of churches and Christians** through the land, but with minimal impact on their surroundings. Personal contacts are essential to get newcomers to a Christian gathering.

2. **The Church in Japan** grew steadily between 1945 and 1960, but both Catholic and Protestant percentages have hardly changed since. Conversions have only just exceeded the loss rate. Evangelicals are, on the whole, growing, but growth has been exaggerated by inclusion of fast-growing sects in those figures. Many Christians are praying that 10% of Japan may be Christian by AD 2000. The breakthrough has definitely not yet come. Pray for:

a) **The United Church:** a 45-year-old union of Presbyterian, Methodist and Congregational Churches. Liberalism and violent controversies in the late '60s, stirred up by leftist young pastors over social action, have blunted evangelistic outreach and speeded the decline in membership. Pray for a moving of the Spirit and a return to biblical theology in this and other denominations.

b) **The smaller and younger evangelical churches** of Arminian (Holiness), Calvinistic (Reformed) and Pentecostal persuasion are almost all growing in numbers, evangelistic zeal, effective organization and missionary vision. Some such are related to the work of **JEB, TEAM, AoG, Nazarene Church, IFCG, OMS**, etc. Most are linked together through membership in the Japan Evangelical Alliance. The latter sponsored two Congresses on Evangelism (1974, 1982). Widespread cooperative evangelism through Billy Graham Crusades, Evangelism-in-Depth, etc. have drawn together believers in outreach. Many denominations are active in evangelism and in the planting of new churches, though on a relatively small scale.

3. **Leadership training** is being ably done through at least 23 denominational and interdenominational Bible schools and seminaries. The great hope for the future of the Church is the high quality of many of Japan's pastors and church leaders. May their numbers be mightily increased! Pray for more men and couples to be called into pastoral and missionary work and come for training.

4. **Specific weaknesses in the churches:**

a) **Lack of biblical teaching**. Christians need complete renewal of their minds. The pervasive influence of the spirit world, philosophies and superstitions must be replaced by a vibrant theology, and a head and heart knowledge of the greatness and holiness of God.

b) **The minority complex**. Christians are a tiny minority in a society where consensus is important. Too few families have come to faith, and individuals feel exposed.

c) **Nonactive membership and backsliding are widespread**. Church attendance is low, with only 33% of Protestants regularly going to services; though in evangelical denominations the percentage is much higher.

d) **The lack of breadwinning men in the churches**. The drive for success and desire to satisfy the demands of employers make it hard for the men folk to openly identify with and become active in a church. Women are in the great majority in most congregations.

e) **Too few viable, active congregations**. Too much is left to the pastor. Pray for pastors and laymen in evangelical churches to work together more in persistent, innovative outreach to non-Christians.

f) **Formality in worship services**. May more life, more joy, and a Japanese hymnology be infused into them!

5. **The growing missionary vision**. The number of missionaries sent out from Japan is remarkable for the size of the Protestant Church. They now serve in 27 countries. Churches have generally little vision of the need for missions, or understanding of the problems of cross-cultural missions and missionaries. There is a small orientation course backed by a number of Japanese churches and missions. One significant indigenous agency is the Antioch Mission.

6. **Missions**.

a) **First-term missionaries**. Japan remains one of the easiest countries for missionaries to enter, but then the difficulties begin! The difficulty of the language and script, the complexities of the culture, the bewildering strands of a web society, the pervading influence of the unseen spirit world are all barriers to adaptation and communication for the missionary. Acculturation takes years, and many missionaries are still in that tearful stage. Pray for them.

b) **Missionary agencies** are usually small and cooperation inadequate. Most are involved in church planting and evangelism, but few have found *the* key to growth. Pray for leaders, for the right strategies, and above all for Spirit-anointed ministries. Major agencies in such ministries are: **SBC** (177 workers), **TEAM** (172), **OMF** (115), **SEND** (67), **NLM** (60), **CBFMS** (40), **AoG** (33), Liebenzeller Mission (36), **WEC** (32), **OMS** (22), **CMA** (16), **IMI** (13), **JEB** (10). There are a number of significant missions from Germany, Finland, Sweden, Norway, Switzerland, etc. 240 missionaries serve in the United Church.

c) **Opportunities for missionary service** are many. The most needful are evangelism, church planting and teaching. Many have used the teaching of English as a good opening for introducing the gospel.

7. **Needy peoples and areas.**

a) **Of Japan's eight regions** Kyushu, Chugoku, Chubu and Tohoku have proportionately the fewest churches and most counties with no evangelical congregations.

b) **The Burakumin** (3 mill.) are descendents of the former outcastes and still suffer a degree of social ostracism. Many have become followers of Sokka Gakkai. Most live in the central Kinki region.

c) **The Ainu**, a non-Mongolian race that first settled in north Japan. They have almost assimilated into Japanese culture, but a resurgence of Ainu culture may mean a specific Christian outreach is required.

d) **Koreans** are an unpopular and despised minority that is much discriminated against. Many live in urban slums. They are sharply divided in their allegiance to the two Koreas. About 60% align themselves with Communist N.Korea. There are 66 churches among Koreans; proportionately fewer Christians than in S.Korea, though more than in the Japanese population as a whole.

e) **Chinese in Japan** are predominantly in business in the larger cities. The great majority are still followers of the Chinese traditional religions. Only 1.5% are Protestant (800 adherents in 12 churches).

8. **Student witness is a strategic ministry**. There are some 950 colleges with two million students. The largest work is that of KGK(**IFES**) with groups in 219 colleges and 1,600 students linked to them. National, foreign and associated staff are hard pressed to take advantage of the tremendous opportunities. **Navigators** with 41 workers and **CCC** with 15 expatriate staff also have an impact. Apathy, atheism and Marxist philosophy are widespread, but many students are favourable to Christianity, though commitment to Christ is a step that few are prepared to take. There is need for a witness in secondary schools.

9. **Christian literature**. A deep impact is being made by an increasing number of indigenous publishers, who are producing a growing range of better quality materials. Christian literature is said to play a part in 70% of conversions. There are over 70 Christian bookstores, two large networks being Word of Life (**TEAM**) with 20 stores and **CLC**, with 11 stores and 45 workers. There are also 90 publishers and 25 Christian presses. The *Bible* is the best selling book in Japan.

10. **Christian radio and TV** is one of the most fruitful means of contact with non-Christians. Pray for:

a) **Three weekly Christian TV programmes** watched by audiences of 4-8 million (**Rex Humbard, PTL Club, Christian Broadcasting Network**).

b) **Many radio programmes aired in Japan**. (Pacific Broadcasting Assoc. — **TEAM**, etc.)

c) **Foreign Christian stations: FEBC** in Korea, Philippines and USA broadcast 70 hours per month, **TWR** in Guam 178 hours, **HCJB** in Ecuador 31 hours. The latter has a team of three Japanese handling letter response.

d) **Millions of Japanese young people belong to short wave listeners' clubs**. Many hear the gospel.

e) **Follow-up** and gathering of enquirers into churches.

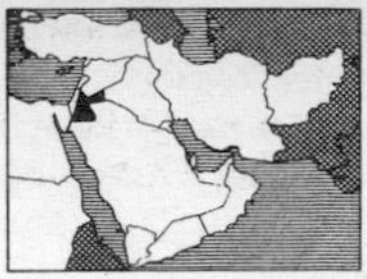

JORDAN
(The Hashemite Kingdom of Jordan)

Middle East

July 1

Area 98,000 sq.km. This includes West Jordan (5,880 sq.km. of Palestine) under Israeli military occupation since 1967.

Population 3,600,000. (incl. one mill. Palestinians still living in W. Jordan). Annual growth 3.8%. People per sq.km. 37.

Peoples
Arab 97%. Palestinian 2,300,000, East Bank Jordanian 1,500,000. Also many Lebanese refugees and Egyptian labourers.
Indigenous minorities 1.7%. Circassian (Cherkess) 47,000; Armenian 5,000; Kurd 5,000; Turkmen 4,000; Chechen 1,000.
Immigrant workers 1.3%. Pakistani 20,000, Indian, Filippino, Chinese, etc.

Literacy 80%. **Official language:** Arabic. **All languages** 8. **Bible translations** 2Bi 2NT 1por.

Capital: Amman 1,160,000. Urbanization 60%.

Economy: Remarkable recovery from three Palestinian wars, the loss of the more fertile West Bank of Jordan and massive influx of refugees. Economy helped by rich deposits of phosphates, the Lebanese civil war, Western aid and earnings from surrounding oil-rich states. Little unemployment. Income/person $2,000 (1981, 14% of USA).

Politics: Part of Turkish empire until 1918. Independent from Britain 1946. The first 25 traumatic years of war with Israel, influx of refugees and confrontations with neighbouring Arab states have been followed by 12 years of relative tranquillity and political stability. Constitutional monarchy with King Hussein having executive powers.

Religion: Islam is the state religion, but the constitution prohibits discrimination and promotes the free exercise of religious belief and worship.
Non-religious/Atheist 2.1%.
Muslim 93%. Almost entirely Sunni Islam; 3,000 Alawites, a few Druzes and Shi'ites.
Christian 5%. 184,000a; 102,000m. Almost all are descendants of the ancient eastern churches. Figures are approximate since some include Christians on the West Bank, others do not.
Orthodox (4 groups) 2.5%. 90,000a; 50,000m.
Roman Catholic 2.2%. 79,000a; 47,900m.
Protestant 0.48%. 17,300a; 9,000m. Denominations 20. Largest (members):

Episcopal Church	3,900
Lutheran Church	1,014
Church of the Nazarene	400
Baptist Convention (**SBC**)	350
Assemblies of God	250
Conservative Baptist Church	240
Alliance Church (**CMA**)	170

Evangelical 0.27% of population.
Missionaries to Jordan 160 (1:22,500 people) in 24 agencies.
Missionaries from Jordan 5 (?).

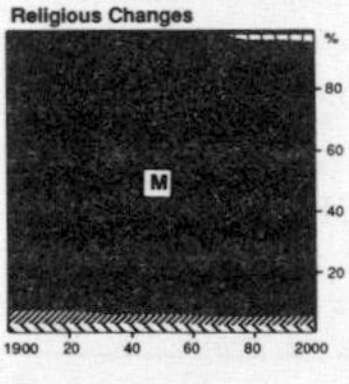

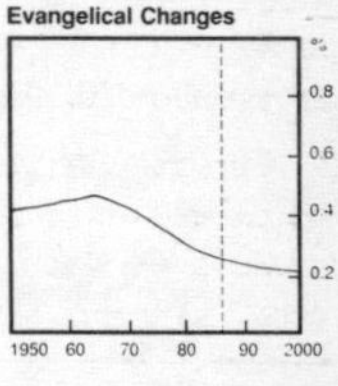

1. **Jordan is a haven of stability and comparative religious freedom.** Pray for the government and for the maintenance of that religious freedom in the face of rising extremism among some Muslims. Jordan is a key centre for many Christian activities — language learning, literature preparation and distribution, etc.

2. **The Christian community** has been in steady numerical decline for years due to lower birth rates, high rate of emigration, influx of Muslim refugees, etc. Yet Christians are found in all walks of life and often in positions of great influence. Most are Orthodox, Catholic, or traditional Protestant. Most need the touch of God on their lives that the Muslim majority may be blessed through them.

3. **Evangelical churches** are few, 9 in Amman and 16 in the whole country. The most influential are those of **CMA, Nazarenes, CBFMS**, Free Evangelical, and **AoG**. There are less than 7,000 Evangelicals, but there is some growth through effective witnessing. Most conversions are from the nominal Christian community. The constant loss of leadership potential through emigration is a drain on the tiny body of believers. Sadly, of the many who go to other

lands for Bible training, few return. Youth work has been fruitful in recent years. Pray for more Jordanian believers to be called to full-time work.

4. **The foreign missionaries'** supportive ministry of encouragement to national believers and their role in media and literature ministries is strategic. However, the sensitive political and religious situation does not make it easy. Pray that their lives may shine for Jesus, and that they may use all opportunities for witness. Asian missionaries could possibly be more acceptable and welcomed than Westerners. The largest agencies are **SBC** (39 workers) and **CBFMS** (8).

5. **The unreached** — the vast majority of the population. Pray especially for:

a) **The Muslim majority.** Very few have ever heard the gospel clearly presented. Pray for a sensitive witness to Muslims. The most successful methods have been through literature, films, cassettes, friendship evangelism and home meetings. Pray for the happy incorporation of converts from the majority community into fellowships of believers.

b) **The Palestinians** are now a majority in Jordan. Many have been integrated into Jordanian life, but others are still refugees housed in large UN-run camps. Disillusionment, bitterness and frustration have made deep wounds which only the Man of Calvary can heal. Pray for the few Christian Palestinians in the camps; witnessing and literature distribution is possible but risky.

c) **The 240,000 Bedouin** — many are still nomadic, and many others are in the army or reachable in cities and hospitals. Hardly any known believers.

d) **The people in the drier** east and south of the country.

e) **The minorities** — especially the proud and wealthy Cherkess, once Christian but now Muslim, and also the Kurdish and Chechen communities.

6. **The missionary vision of the believers is growing,** but more could be done. There are already Jordanian believers serving the Lord in secular work all over the Middle East — some in closed lands such as Saudi Arabia, Yemen, Libya, etc. Others have become well known all over the Arab World as evangelists and radio preachers.

7. **The ministry of media.** The paucity of Christians and the difficulties placed in the way of open witness to the majority community enhances the importance of radio, cassettes, video, films and literature. Pray for **FEBA**'s Arabic programmes beamed in from Seychelles, and for the wide and wise dissemination of gospel cassettes and video.

8. **Literature** in Arabic is becoming more widely available. Pray for effective distribution of books, magazines and tracts. Pray also for the work of the Bible Society in a ministry that is also strategic for the surrounding nations, where restrictions on Christian work are severe.

KAMPUCHEA (CAMBODIA)

(Democratic Kampuchea)

Asia

July 2

Area 181,000 sq.km. Southwest Indo-China.

Population 6,200,000. Annual growth 2.1%. People sq.km. 34. In 1975 the population was 7,735,000. Reduced by 3,000,000 in the 1975-79 holocaust, and accompanying wars, famines and flight of refugees.

Peoples: (Approx. percentages only, due to radical changes since 1975.)
Khmer 74.8%.
Major indigenous minorities 10.6%. Kui 400,000; Cham 220,000; Lao 100,000.
Immigrant peoples 13%. Vietnamese 680,000 settlers and military, Chinese 120,000.
Tribal peoples 1.6%. 12 peoples — Sheng 30,000; Mnong 20,000; Jarai 20,000; Rhade 12,000; Brao 10,000; also smaller groups of Somrai, Chong Pear, Laman, etc. totalling 11,000.

Literacy 30%. **Official language:** Khmer. **All languages** 18. **Bible translations** 1Bi 2NT 2por.

Capital: Pnomh Penh 500,000 (2,500,000 in 1975). Urbanization 16%.

Economy: Rich agricultural potential. Reduced to bare subsistence because of the devastation to land and people by war, massacres, political isolation and socialist bureaucracy.

Politics: Independent from France in 1953. The Marxist Khmer Rouge takeover in 1975 was followed by one of the most savage slaughters in this century. Almost all former military personnel, civil servants, educated or wealthy people and their families were killed, and the nation turned into a vast labour camp. The Vietnamese occupied the country in 1978. War between the Vietnamese and Khmer Rouge and non-Communist nationalists continues. The Pnomh Penh government is supported by Vietnam, but is not recognized internationally.

Religion: Strongly Buddhist until 1975. Christians were persecuted 1965-70. After 1975 the Khmer Rouge sought to eradicate all religion; 90% of Buddhist priests and most Christians perished. Since 1979 there has been less open persecution, but Christian gatherings were made illegal in 1983. Estimated percentages:
Buddhist 85%. They openly practise again, but under government control.
Non-religious/Atheist 9%. **Animist** 3%.
Muslim 3%. Almost entirely Cham.
Christian 0.07%.
Roman Catholic 0.02%. An estimated 2,000, mainly Vietnamese.
Protestant 0.05%. Probably around 2,000 believers.

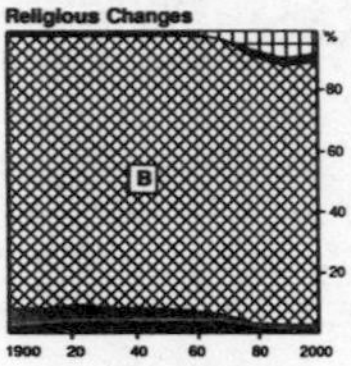

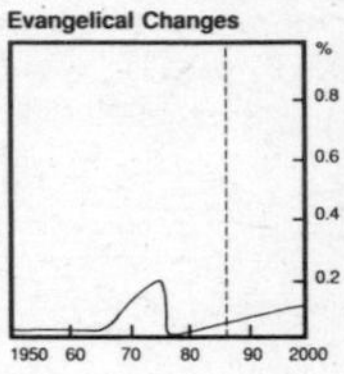

1. **The terrible genocide of 1975-79 haunts this tragic nation.** The survivors are depleted and demoralized; widows and orphans are numerous. The people fear the return of the Khmer Rouge and see the Vietnamese occupation as the lesser of two evils. Yet there is no freedom for the gospel, and the great majority have never heard of Jesus.

2. **For centuries Buddhist Cambodia fiercely resisted the light of the gospel**, yet since 1970 there has been an awakening. Between 1970 and 1975 the Church grew from 700 believers to 6,000. This church was the fruit of 42 years of faithful witness by **CMA** missionaries. Most believers died in 1975-79, but some escaped to the free world. In refugee camps in Thailand and in USA, France, UK, Canada etc., an ingathering of thrilling proportions has taken place. There are now over 200 Cambodian churches outside Kampuchea. Praise God that a Khmer Church is a growing reality, but pray for these believers in exile.

3. **The Church is again "underground".** In 1983 limited freedoms were withdrawn by the Communist authorities, and the last Khmer pastor had to flee. The Church is scattered, infiltrated and watched. Believers can only gather informally, yet they are free of direct government control. Pray for perseverance, boldness in witness, and confidence and security in the Rock of Ages. They lack teaching, literature and mature leadership.

4. **A flood of refugees fled the country after 1978.** About 400,000 fled to Thailand, many of whom were moved on to Western countries. There are still about 100,000 long-term refugees in Thailand and a further 250,000 straddling the fortified border territory between Thailand and Kampuchea. Pray for those seeking to minister to their physical and spiritual needs (**YWAM, WV, SAO, TEAR Fund, CMA**).

5. **The Khmer in exile are responsive to the gospel.** Labourers able to minister in Khmer are few. **CMA** and **SAO** in Europe, and **CMA** and other agencies in N. America are caring for them. There are possibly 160 Khmer churches in the West now, mostly in the USA. Pray that the Holy Spirit may build up a strong Khmer Church with vision for outreach and for the evangelization of their homeland.

6. **The unreached.** Most of the population is totally ignorant of the existence of the gospel. Specific groups for prayer:

   a) **The Cham Muslims.** Several individual believers but no churches known. Refugee communities live in Sumatra (Indonesia), Malaysia and 2,000 in USA.

   b) **The Chinese** have suffered especially severely, and relatively few remain in Kampuchea.

   c) **The Kui and Hmong** were beginning to respond to pioneer outreach before Communism came.

   d) **The smaller tribal groups** are all unreached. **SIL** continues research with a view to Bible translation in their languages. At least 10 may need translators.

   e) **The Vietnamese** are a growing minority. No known believers or groups in Kampuchea.

K

7. **Help ministries** from the Free World.

   a) **Christian radio** is the major means for encouragement of believers and evangelism. **FEBC** broadcasts 46 hours per month in Khmer, and for shorter periods in eight tribal languages, which are also spoken in Vietnam. Pray for the native speakers who prepare and broadcast the messages. It is illegal to listen to the **FEBA** programmes.

   b) **Literature** is going into Kampuchea, but only in small quantities. Pray for the spread of God's Word through the country.

   c) **Aid ministries. WV** and the Mennonites have medical teams in Kampuchea, the former in a paediatric hospital in the capital. Open witnessing is forbidden, and foreigners are under continual surveillance. Pray for spiritual fruit despite limitations.

KENYA
(Republic of Kenya)

Africa

July 3-4

Area 582,600 sq.km. Much of the north and east is desert. Most people live in the better watered plateaus of the south and west. Only 9.5% of the land is cultivated.

Population 20,200,000. Annual growth 4.1%. The highest natural increase in the world. People per sq.km. 35.

Peoples: About 65 ethnic groups.

Bantu peoples 67%. Over 30 peoples: Kikuyu 4,200,000; Luyia 2,200,000; Kamba 2,200,000; Gusii 1,200,000; Meru 1,100,000; Mijikenda (9 peoples) 969,000; Embu 250,000; Kuria 120,000; Mbere 100,000; Pokomo 60,000.

Nilotic peoples 29.5%. Over 16 peoples: Luo 2,900,000; Kalenjin (5 groups) 2,000,000; Maasai 280,000; Turkana 260,000; Samburu 100,000; Sabaot 95,000.

Cushitic peoples 2.6%. Two major groups: Somali (6) 430,000; Oromo-Boran (5) 130,000.

Other 0.9%. Asian 80,000; Arab 40,000; European 40,000.

Literacy 65%. **Official languages:** English, Swahili. **All languages** 55. **Bible translations** 14Bi 5NT 9por.

Capital: Nairobi 1,830,000. Other major city: Mombasa 520,000. Urbanization 16%.

Economy: Predominantly agricultural. Good growth following independence was not maintained after 1976 due to world recession, lack of oil, drought and a high population growth. Income/person $340 (2% of USA).

Politics: Independent from Britain in 1963. One party republic. Relatively stable despite complex tribal divisions that make all political decisions a delicate balancing act.

Religion: Freedom of religion. Government very sympathetic to Christianity. Many Christians in high leadership positions, including the President.

Africa traditional religions 12.8%.

Muslim 6%. Majority among coastal Swahili/Arab, Pokomo, Digo and N.E. desert Somali, Boran, etc.

Baha'i 1.1%. **Hindu/Sikh/Jain** 0.3%.

Christian 80%. Nominal 15%. Affiliated 65%.

Roman Catholic 20.5% (officially 29%). 4,143,000a; 2,200,000m.

Orthodox Church 2.2% (officially 2.7%). Indigenous groups linked with Greek Orthodox and Coptic Churches.

Marginal groups 13% (officially 23%). 2,600,000a; 1,200,000m. Over 152 groups, some close to mainstream Christian doctrine, others very syncretic.

Protestant 29.3%. 5,925,000a; 2,500,000m. Denominations 60+. Largest (adult members):

Africa Inland Church	540,000
Anglican Church (CMS)	520,000
Presbyterian Church (**C of S**)	380,000
Pentecostal Assemblies (**PAoC**)	192,000
Seventh Day Adventist Ch.	190,000
Pentecostal Ev. Fell. (Elim)	105,000
Full Gospel Churches (FFFM)	90,000
Methodist Church	80,000
Salvation Army	49,000
Baptist Convention (**SBC**)	27,000
Assemblies of God	25,000
African Gospel Church (**WGM**)	15,000

Evangelical 26.5% of population.

Missionaries to Kenya 1,850 (1:11,000 people) in about 100 agencies.

Missionaries from within Kenya est. 100 (1:59,000 Protestants).

Religious Changes

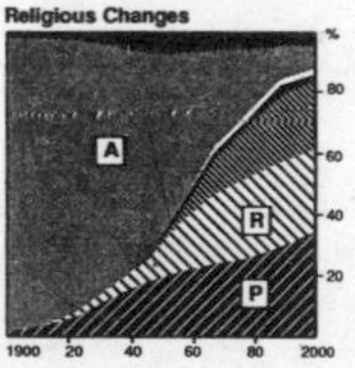

Evangelical Changes

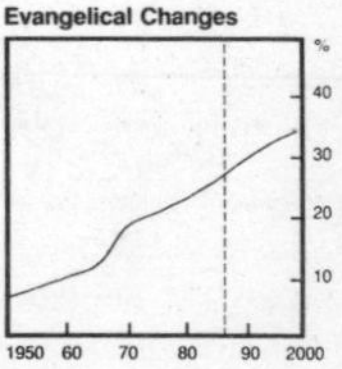

1. **Praise God for the great freedom to preach the gospel since independence**, for the receptiveness of the people and for the exciting growth of the Church. Three-quarters of the population claim to be Christian, and Christians are found in every stratum of society. Pray that present opportunities may be used to the full.

2. **The Protestant churches have grown fast**, and the proportion of Evangelicals is high. The East African Revival (1938-1960) made a deep and lasting impression on the Anglican, Presbyterian and Methodist Churches. A high proportion of church leaders have their spiritual roots in that movement of the Spirit. Legalism, divisions, materialism, and personality clashes have adversely affected this movement. Other evangelical and Pentecostal

groups have also grown. One of the largest denominations is the Africa Inland Church (planted by **AIM**), which has spread to nearly every part of the country.

3. **Rapid growth** has brought its problems:
 a) **Nominalism** is becoming a serious problem among second and third generation Christians. Revival is needed again.
 b) **Tribalism and tribal customs** have caused endless divisions and a multiplicity of independent churches, some theologically orthodox, others little removed from the old tribal religions. Pray for a unity that transcends culture and personalities.
 c) **Too few trained leaders**. There are over 33 seminaries/Bible colleges. The Scott Theological College (AIC-**AIM**) and St. Paul's United Theological College (Anglican, Presbyterian, Methodist) are significant institutions. The Nairobi Evangelical Graduate School of Theology serves all of Anglophone Africa and in 1985 had 22 students. There are also numerous TEE schools. Pray for these, and for lives to be set on fire for God through them. Pray for more graduates to be fully and adequately supported by their congregations — a need in all denominations. **Daystar** in Nairobi holds specialized courses for church workers enriching the ministry of those participating.

4. **Missionary vision among Kenyan Christians is growing**, though few congregations have grappled with its implications. There may be over 100 Kenyans serving the Lord cross-culturally as missionaries, though only a handful have moved to other lands. **AIC** has commenced a Missionary Training College in Eldoret. The African Gospel Church, Anglicans and others have also sent out cross-cultural missionaries. In 1986 there is to be an international missions conference for African students in Nairobi — pray for lasting vision to be implanted.

5. **Missions have served long and sacrificially in Kenya**. Much of the church work is entirely under Kenyan control, and missionaries generally serve under indigenous leadership, whether in pioneer outreach, Bible teaching or in service ministries. Some significant agencies: **AIM** (299 workers), **SBC** (124), **PAoC** (69), **WGM** (51), **AoG** (42), CMS (41), **IMI** (23), **CBOMB** (17).

6. **Over half the population is under 15**. Youth ministries are vital. **SU** has made a deep impact on secondary schools, and also **IFES** with lively groups in universities and colleges. Pray for the integration of Christian students into local churches; this is not easy, but their contribution is essential.

7. **Recent breakthroughs** among less responsive pastoral peoples are cause for much praise. The efforts of many Kenyan and expatriate workers in preaching and famine relief have begun to bear fruit. Famines, tribal warfare and radical social changes have been used by God to open hearts among the Maasai, Pokot, Turkana, Mukugodo, Njemps and Samburu. The pioneer work of AIC-**AIM** in most of these groups is noteworthy, though numerous agencies are involved too. Yet less than 10% of these peoples are committed Christians, and the work is still in its early stages.

8. **Unreached peoples**. Probably about 12% of the peoples of Kenya belong to peoples little affected by the gospel, though only a few are unoccupied by missions:
 a) **The Somali in the N.E. and cities**. The five clans of Somalis are all Muslim. About 20 Christian workers (AIC/**AIM, SIM, CBOMB** and Mennonites) are reaching these people. There are three small groups and 50 believers.
 b) **The pastoral tribes of N. Kenya** are predominantly animistic and nomadic. Anglicans, Lutherans, AIC and Pentecostals work among them but converts are few. Pray for the Boran 75,000; Samburu 73,600; Gabbra 32,000; Rendille 21,800, and for the emergence of truly indigenous churches.
 c) **The Muslim coastal strip.** The Digo 160,000; Bajun 40,000; Orma 35,000 and Upper Pokomo 23,000 are all Muslim. AIC, Methodists and Pentecostals work among these peoples. **CBFMS** are opening a new ministry among the Digo. The 220,000 Giriama are beginning to respond through the work of eight denominations, but the work is in its early stages.

d) **The Asian community** has become insecure since the disastrous expulsion of Asians in Uganda and destructive riots in Kenya in 1982. Over four languages are used. Hindus and even some Muslims have come to the Lord, and there are now five churches planted among them (**IMI, AIM**). **IMI** has the vision for a church planting work in every Asian community of East and Central Africa.

e) **The coastal Swahili/Arab** are strongly Muslim. Little has been done to reach them in Mombasa, Lamu, etc.

9. **Bibles** are available in many languages. The ongoing work of the Bible Society in publishing, distributing and translating is appreciated. **SIL** has seven teams in Kenya and they are already working on translations for four of the 16 languages that may need a NT. **GRI** has recordings available in 57 languages and dialects.

10. **Supportive ministries.**

a) **Aid programmes** through many of the above agencies, **TEAR Fund**, **WV**, etc. have played a significant part in opening the way for the gospel in the more arid and famine-stricken areas. Pray for those involved in a hard and difficult ministry.

b) **MAF** has a well-developed ministry, flying to many parts of E.Africa and N.E.Zaire from their base in Nairobi. Without this ministry much Christian work would come to a halt. **AIM-Air** also has an extensive flying programme in the region.

11. **Nairobi is one of the key communications centres in Africa**. Many international Christian organizations have their continental offices based there. One such is **AEAM** (Assoc. of Evangelicals of Africa and Madagascar). The latter has played a key role in promoting evangelical unity and ministries in theology, training, literature and fellowship. Pray for this work and its extension through Africa.

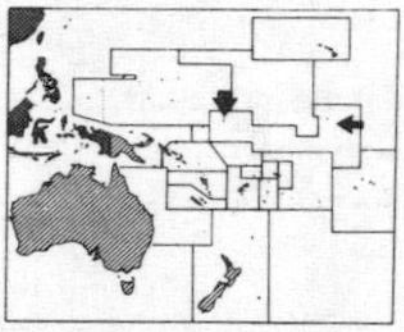

KIRIBATI
(The Republic of Kiribati)

Pacific

July 5

Area 728 sq.km. Three archipelagos — Gilbert Is., Phoenix Is., and 33 islands strung across 2,000,000 sq.km. of Central Pacific.

Population 62,000. Annual growth 1.6%. People per sq.km. 85.

Peoples: Micronesian 91%, **Polynesian** 4%, **Euronesian** 4%, **European, Chinese** 1%.

Literacy 95%. **Official languages:** Kiribati, English.

Capital: Baraiki 1,800.

Economy: Dependent on copra and fish; subsistence economy. Income/person $480 (3% of USA).

Politics: Independent from Britain in 1979.

Religion: Freedom of religion.

Baha'i 5.3%.

Christian 94.7%.

Roman Catholic 48.4%. Practising 49%. 30,000a.

Protestant 46.2%. 28,700a; 12,700m. Denominations 5. Largest (adult members):

Kiribati Protestant Ch. (**LMS**)	11,000
Church of God	1,030
Seventh Day Adventist Church	700

Evangelical 5.7% of population.

Missionaries to Kiribati 4 (1:15,500 people) in 2 agencies.

Missionaries from Kiribati 3 (among Kiribati in Nauru).

1. **The once strong Congregational Church** is losing members and pastors to other Protestant groups and also to RCs, Baha'i, Mormons, etc. The theological college in Tarawa is not evangelical. Pray for a return to biblical preaching and NT Christianity to counteract nominalism and underlying power of the occult.

2. **Evangelicals are in a small minority.** Only on some islands of Kiribati are there evangelical congregations. The Church of God is growing, and new workers are being trained for advance in their Bible school. Pray that every island may have a clear, resident gospel witness. Most needy are the migrant labourers on Nauru (see p. 310), outlying island groups and the little state of Tuvalu (see p. 417).

Asia
July 6

KOREA (North)

(Democratic People's Republic of Korea)

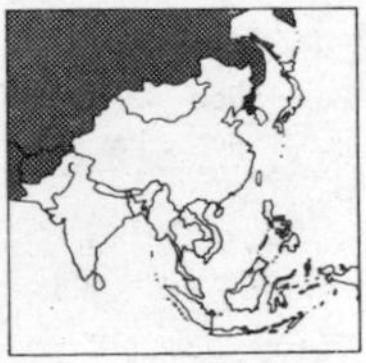

Area 121,000 sq.km. The larger part of the Korean peninsula, but climate more rigorous.

Population 20,082,000. Annual growth 2.3%. People per sq.km. 166. Two and a half million people died in the Korean War, two million more fled from the north to the south at that time.

Peoples
Korean 99.3%, **Chinese, Russian** 0.7%.

Literacy 91%. **Official language:** Korean.

Capital: Pyongyang 1,501,000. Urbanization 64%.

Economy: Heavily industrialized and very centralized socialist economy. Income/person $620 (5% of USA).

Politics: Occupied by Japan 1910-45. On Russian insistence, Korea was partitioned after World War II. A Communist regime was installed in 1948 in the North. North Korea invaded South Korea in 1949. The Korean War dragged on until 1953. The large North Korean armed forces continue to threaten a second invasion. One of the most oppressive Communist regimes in the world. There are occasional hints of a reunification of the Koreas, but the fortified border between them is one of the most impenetrable in the world.

Religion: All religions have been harshly repressed. Many thousands of Christians were murdered during and after the Korean War. Religious affiliations are unknown, so the figures given are estimates.
Non-religious/Atheist 60%.
Korean religions 39% (Buddhism, Animism, Confucianism, etc.)
Christian 1%.

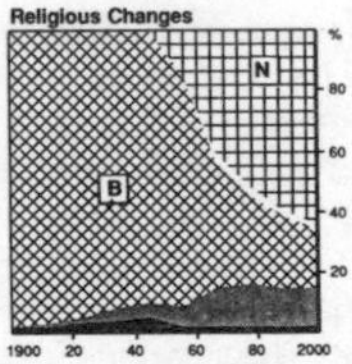

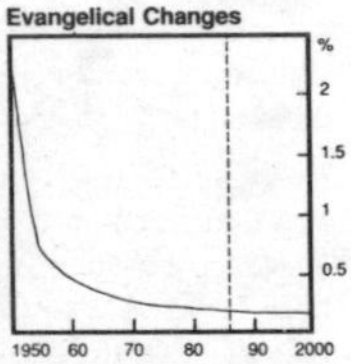

1. **The leader of North Korea and his son** have been almost deified by adulatory propaganda. Pray that the time may soon come when the Lord Jesus may be openly worshipped rather than a mere man.

2. **Organized Christianity was destroyed by the Communists.** Yet in 1945 there was a large and growing Church with about 400,000 Christians. Nearly all believers were killed or fled to the South. Pray that the land may open again for the gospel.

3. **The Church in North Korea** is one of the most persecuted on earth. There are no known churches or pastors left, though government spokesmen admit to 5,000 Christians in the country. Pray for the secret Church in its long years of suffering.

4. **The gospel can only enter by ingenious means** — floating literature ashore from the sea, balloon packages by air, etc. The most useful is **radio. FEBC** broadcast 428 hours per month from Manila. Other stations in South Korea also broadcast many hours of Christian programmes weekly.

KOREA (South)

Asia

July 7

Area 98,500 sq.km. Southern half of Korean peninsula. Mountainous; only 22% is arable.

Population 42,700,000. Annual growth 1.7%. People per sq.km. 434.

Peoples
Korean 99.8%. An ancient and cultured nation.
Other 0.2%. US military and Chinese (30,000).

Literacy 92%. **Official language:** Korean.

Capital: Seoul 10,028,000. Other major cities: Pusan 3,781,000; Taegu 1,848,000; Inchon 1,158,000. Urbanization 57%.

Economy: Rapid industrialization and growth since the Korean War. The economy has reached "take off" with high export earnings. The permanent state of confrontation and military preparedness before invasion threats from the North are a strain on the economy. Income/person $2,010 (15% of USA).

Politics: The Japanese occupation (1910-45), the Russian imposed division of Korea (1945-48) and the Korean War in which the Communist North invaded the South (1950-53) have moulded the attitudes and politics of South Korea. Strong military-civilian government slowly becoming more democratic. High degree of stability.

Religion: There is complete religious freedom unless that freedom is used by religious leaders to attack government policies. The government has been favourable to Christianity, seeing this as an ideological bulwark against the Communist threat.
No professed religion 14%. Including secularists, non-religious and many Shamanists (animist).
Buddhist 33%. Strong until 15th century, and with post-war resurgence.
Confucian 12%. Official religion until 1910. Both Buddhism and Confucianism have made a deep impact on Korean culture.
New religions 10.6%. Over 250 syncretic non-Christian religions, most of recent origin.

Muslim 0.1%. A growing movement among Koreans.
Christian 30%.
Roman Catholic 4.4%. Practising 66%. 1,900,000a; 1,060,000m.
Foreign and indigenous marginal (at least 13 groups) 1.6%. 660,000a; 220,000m. Largest (adherents):

Unification Church (Moonies)	500,000
Jehovah's Witnesses	77,428
Mormons	36,000

Protestant 24%. 10,200,000a; 4,370,000m.
Denominations 61. Largest (adherents):

Presby. Ch. in K. (Haptong)	1,389,200
Presby. Ch. of K. (Tonghap)	1,373,600
Methodist Church (4 groups)	1,007,600
Baptist Convention (**SBC**) (4 gps)	505,300
Full Gospel C. Church (Cho)	500,000
Korean Evang. Ch. (**OMS**) (3 gps)	461,000
Chr. Assemblies of God (6 gps)	293,200
Presby. Church in ROK	273,700
Koryo Presby. Church	250,800
Seventh Day Adventist Church	134,500
Other Presbyterian (28 gps)	3,231,200

Evangelical 18% of population.
Missionaries to Korea 610 (1:70,000 people) in 60 agencies.
Missionaries from Korea 360 (1:28,300 Protestants) in 17 sending agencies working in 37 countries. Just over half are cross-cultural missionaries.

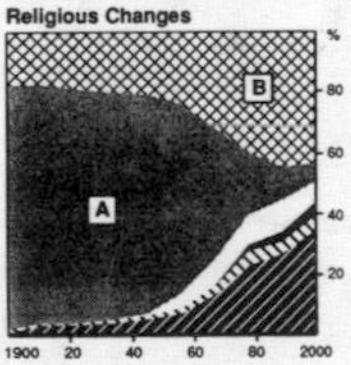

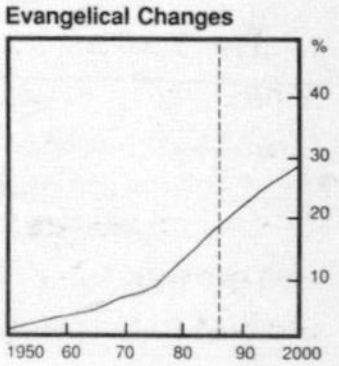

1. **Praise God for the spiritual awakening in Korea** and the evident work of the Holy Spirit. Here is a selection of the superlatives!

a) The first Protestant church was planted in 1884. By the centenary in 1984 there were nearly 30,000! About 4,900 of these are in the capital.

b) The largest congregation (Full Gospel Central Church), and the largest Presbyterian and Methodist congregations in the world.

c) The largest evangelistic campaign (Billy Graham 1973).

d) The largest Christian mobilization (CCC Explo '74, World Evangelization Crusade '80). 2,700,000 attended one meeting.

e) The largest baptismal service since Pentecost (in the Army, which is now 65% Christian).

2. **Praise God for a Church founded on sound indigenous principles**, blessed with many seasons of revival and refined by years of suffering. A strong, praying Church has emerged that is reaching out to every part of society. Seven churches a day are being planted. Pray that materialism and the cultural acceptability of Christianity may not blunt this growth. Korean Christians are praying that 50% of their nation may be Christian by the end of the century.

3. **There is another side – the Church in Korea needs prayer and revival.** The massive influx of people has been only partially discipled. The Church is often Christian in confession, Confucian in structure and Buddhist in thought. The deficiencies are many; pray for their rectification.

a) **Formality, legalism, authoritarian leadership** and lack of emphasis on a personal relationship to the Lord and his Word mean that many earnest Christians and pastors need genuine repentance and faith. Born-again Koreans are dynamic, courageous soulwinners, once the Holy Spirit is in full control. There must be a radical deliverance from old pre-Christian values that are contrary to the gospel.

b) **Divisions have afflicted every major denomination.** Nearly 60% of all Protestants are of one or another Presbyterian group, but there are over 30 such. The causes have been ecumenicism, doctrine, power struggles and personality clashes among church leaders. Emphasis has been on the right doctrine at the expense of fellowship with the Lord and the unity of the Body. Pray for a spirit of love and reconciliation among believers.

c) **Emphasis on the external** is often shown by pride in statistical church growth and desire to heap up theological qualifications by those in leadership. Pray for a Spirit-given humility, Christlikeness and faithfulness in discipling their flocks. The pastor has a high standing in Korean society.

4. **Leadership training is moving into mass production!** The largest theological seminaries in the world are in Korea. Several Presbyterian seminaries and KEC (**OMS**) have over 1,000 students. There are 283 theological institutions, 38 of which are seminaries turning out over 500 graduates a year. Yet there is a shortage of trained pastors for rural churches and for missionary outreach. Pray for a greater emphasis on expository preaching and a warm personal relationship with the Lord Jesus in these institutions.

5. **Young people** are a restive yet responsive section of the community. Non-denominational groups such as the University Bible Fellowship, IVCF(**IFES**), **CCC** and **Navigators** are all active and making an impact on the 124 colleges and university campuses. Denominational suspicion of para-church groups has led to a confusing profusion of church groups on many campuses. Pray that students may find the delight of personal Bible study. **SU** has a vital role to play in producing Bible study materials.

6. **Less reached peoples and sections of the population.** The widespread evangelism and church planting of the last 30 years have left few unexposed to the Truth. Rural areas are less well served than the cities. The **Chinese** are more needy; only 1.4% are Protestant and only 9 Chinese churches exist. **Islam** is growing and there are now 20,000 Korean Muslims – many as a result of Islamic missionary work among Koreans labouring in Saudi Arabia.

7. **The missionary vision of the Korean Church** is growing dramatically, but there is little understanding of channelling mechanisms and cross-cultural awareness or training in the churches. **The Asian Missions Association** is seeking to rectify this. Koreans moving overseas tend to go to expatriate Korean groups; pray for a greater input to unreached peoples. The enthusiasm, and rugged dynamism of Koreans can be a great asset in mission. Both denominational and interdenominational groups have bold plans to increase their number of Korean missionaries. Pray for Koreans already serving overseas; they face acute problems in cultural adaptation and the education of their children. Four significant missions are Korean International Mission, Mission to Muslim Lands, Korea Harbour Evangelism and World Concern Korea.

8. **Missions in Korea** have a valuable servant role in giving a fresh perspective to biblical teaching, personal holiness and, increasingly, training Korean missionaries for cross-cultural work. A number of mission agencies have made a major impact in church planting — several Presbyterian agencies, **SBC** (111 workers), **TEAM** (18), **AoG** (18), **OMS** (16). **OMF** loans workers to minister within established churches. **OMS** missionaries have planted the largest denomination in Asia originating from a faith mission.

9. **Christian literature**. The Bible in Korean has gone through many translations and has become part of the culture. The range of theological and devotional books is rapidly increasing, and there are many Christian bookstores (Word of Life Press, Voice [**CMA**], **CLC**, **TEAM**, etc.) and publishers (**IVCF**, **CLC** etc). Pray that this ministry may help to form a strong, Bible-literate church.

10. **Christian broadcasting** has a strong base with three large Christian radio networks. All broadcast to both Koreas (415 hours per month), and **FEBC**-Cheju and **TEAM**-Seoul broadcast to China, USSR, Mongolia, etc.

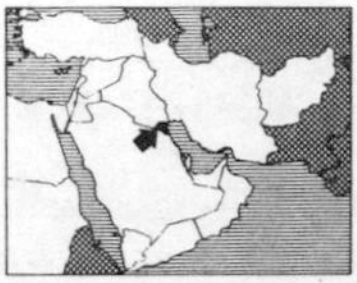

KUWAIT
(State of Kuwait)

Middle East

July 8

Area 17,000 sq.km. A wedge of desert at the north-east end of the Arabian Gulf.

Population 1,900,000. Annual growth 3.2%. People per sq.km. 111. High rate of entry of immigrant labour in '70s. Population in 1912: 35,000.

Peoples: Two-thirds of the population is foreign.
Arab 69%. Kuwaiti 33%, Jordanian/Palestinian 20%, Iraqi 5.3%, Egyptian 4%, Syrian 3.7%, Lebanese 2.8%.
Kurd 13%, **Irani** 6%, **Baluch** 0.4%.
Other foreigners 11%. Indian, Pakistani, Filippino, Westerners, etc.

Literacy 85%. **Official language:** Arabic.

Capital: Al Kuwayt 506,000. Urbanization 94%.

Economy: Exploitation of large oil fields is financing industrial and trading development. One of the world's richest states. Income/person $18,180 (129% of USA).

Politics: Parliamentary monarchy; fully independent from Britain in 1961. Extensive aid given to Iraq in the Gulf war.

Religion: Sunni Islam is the state religion. Immigrant religious minorities are permitted some worship facilities.
Muslim 90%. Sunni 70%, Shi'a 30%.
Hindu 2%. **Baha'i** 0.2%.
Christian 7-8%. Nominal 5%. Affiliated 2.8%.
Roman Catholic 1.5%. 27,500a.
Orthodox 1%. 18,400a. Denominations 5.
Protestant 0.35%. 6,600a; 3,400m. Denominations 7. Largest:

Mar Thoma Church	930
Pentecostal Churches	800
National Evangelical Church	570
Anglican Church	420

Evangelical 0.23% of population.
Missionaries to Kuwait 0.

1. **The shadow of the Gulf War and Shi'ite Muslim fundamentalism has disturbed Kuwaitis.** Pray that the wealthy Kuwaitis may become more receptive to the gospel. Possibly less than 2% have ever handled a Bible or heard the gospel. There may be only one family of Kuwaiti believers.

2. **Kuwaitis travel** as tourists, businessmen and students (2,500 in USA). Pray that they may meet Christians willing to share their faith.

3. **The majority of the Christian community** is concerned with amassing wealth, and few have any real commitment to church attendance, much less evangelism. Pray that the negative effects on the Muslims may be nullified by a work of the Holy Spirit.

4. **A number of expatriate ethnic minorities are unreached.** Pray for an effective witness to the Kurds, Iranis, Baluch, Bangladeshis, etc. Some of these groups could be responsive.

5. **Expatriate Christians** are forbidden to proselytize and suffer considerable difficulties in efforts to meet openly together. Pray for a greater freedom to worship and witness, and pray that they may win opportunities to speak of the Saviour. There are Protestant gatherings in 16 languages. The focal point is the Evangelical Church planted by the Reformed Church of America.

6. **Other means of proclaiming the gospel must be fully exploited.** Pray for:
   a) The wise use of **Christian video** and **cassette tapes.**
   b) **Radio broadcasts. FEBA** (Seychelles) is on the air 12 hours per week in Arabic. Pray for a response.

Asia

July 9

LAOS

(Lao People's Democratic Republic)

Area 237,000 sq.km. A landlocked, jungle-covered land in Indo-China.

Population 3,800,000. Annual growth 2.3%. People per sq.km. 16. The majority live in the lowlands along the Mekong River.

Peoples: Massive emigration 1975-79. Only estimates can be given.
Lao 61%. Related to Thai.
Tai 11%. Tribal Tai of centre and northeast.
Sino-Tibetan peoples 9%. Mainly in north; related to peoples in China. Hmong 120,000; Yao 65,000; Phunoi 32,000; Lũ 18,000; Akha 5,000; Lahu, etc.
Malayan peoples 16%. In north, Khmu 340,000; in mountains of the south over 40 smaller tribes: Brao, Alak, Kasseng, Ngeq, So, etc.
Other 3%. Vietnamese 60,000; Chinese 40,000; Russian and East European 2,000.

Literacy 31%. **Official language**: Lao. **All languages** 70. **Bible translations** 2Bi 7NT 9por.

Capital: Vientiane 308,000. Urbanization 16%.

Economy: Subsistence agricultural economy. Steady recovery and economic betterment from 30 years of warfare and devastation. Little trade with other countries. Income/person $80 (0.6% of USA).

Politics: Independent from France in 1949 as a constitutional monarchy. Lao and Vietnamese Communist forces finally conquered the land in 1975. Virtually a satellite of Vietnam, yet Marxism is not applied vigorously!

Religion: Fears of religious persecution faded as the government moderated its anti-religious stance. The practice of both Buddhism and spirit propitiation continues unhindered. Considerable freedom for Christians to worship and witness.
Non-religious/Atheist 6%.
Animist 33%. Majority of tribal people; also strongly embedded in Buddhist peoples too.
Buddhist 58%. Majority of lowland Lao.
Muslim 1%. Cham minority.
Christian 2%. Approximate figures:
  Roman Catholic 0.8%. 32,000a.
  Protestant 1.2%. 47,000a; 23,300m. Denominations 4. Largest (adult members):

Laos Evangelical Ch. (**CMA**)	17,000
Brethren (**CMML, OMF**)	5,000

  Evangelical 1.2% of population.

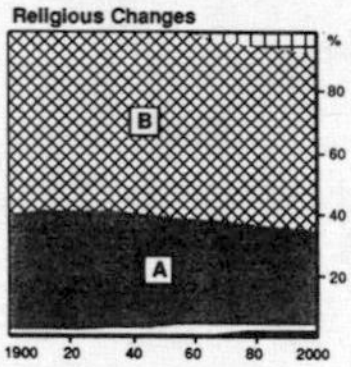

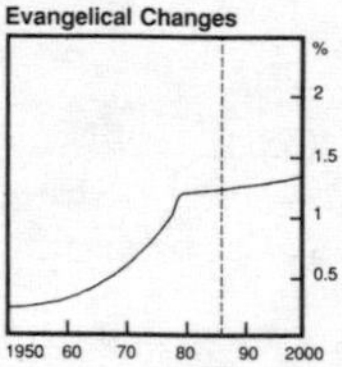

1. **Only a few areas and ethnic groups have ever been evangelized.** Laos needs to hear the gospel. **Brethren** and **CMA** missionaries laboured for years with little fruit. Now the land is closed to foreign missionary work. There are some foreign Christian relief workers serving in the country.

2. **Persecution refined the Church.** The early years under Communism were hard. Weak Christians fell away, those that remained had to learn to trust in God and not in Western help. Ideological confrontations and restrictions brought a deeper appreciation of the gospel. About two-thirds of the Christians fled to Thailand, yet after the decline the Church has grown and matured.

3. **The Christians doubled in number between 1976 and 1983.** Many young people are being converted in the relative freedom that now prevails, but initial commitment is rarely followed by maturity and consistent Christian living. Pray that all believers may use the open door for witness. There needs to be a missionary vision for unreached ethnic groups — most believers are Lao, Hmong, Khmu, and some Brao.

4. **There are only a few pastors and leaders**, most having left the country. Pray for informal training of developing leaders in several areas. Few are able to teach the Scriptures in depth. Pray for the development of closer fellowship links among the 130 or so congregations around the country.

5. **The Hmong** turned to the Lord in large numbers through the ministry of **CMA** missionaries in the '60s. 70% fled to Thailand and the West after resisting the Communist takeover for years. 35,000 still languish in Thai refugee camps. Possibly 10-20% of this people are now Christian. Pray for believers who remain in Laos.

6. **The Church in exile.** There may be 700,000 Laotians scattered around the world. **CMA**, **SAO** and others have a ministry among them. There are about 100 Hmong churches in USA, France and French Guiana, but the scattered little communities and diversity of languages complicate this ministry. There are few full-time workers fluent in these languages.

7. **Unreached peoples in which there are no known churches.**
   a) **The Tai tribes** speaking nine languages.
   b) **The northern tribes**, many of whom have responded to the gospel in neighbouring China and Thailand. Political conditions never allowed missionary penetration.
   c) **The small southern tribes** were being evangelized for the first time from 1957-63, but war prevented the planting of churches among most of these peoples. They are deeply enmeshed in the fear of spirits. In only four of the 40 tribes have small churches emerged. Small groups of refugees from these tribes are now in Europe, N. America and Thailand, where they could be reached.
   d) The **Vietnamese** and **Chinese** have been only marginally evangelized.

8. **Help ministries.**
   a) **Bible translation.** Over 50 languages may require Bible translations. Several projects are continuing in the free world. Pray for ways and means to put God's Word into the hands of minority groups in Laos. **Gospel Recordings** are available in 87 languages and dialects.
   b) **Christian radio** is a valuable means of teaching. **FEBC** broadcasts for 30 hours in Lao and 15 hours in Hmong each month. Pray for those who prepare the programmes.

L

LEBANON

(Republic of Lebanon)

Middle East

July 10-11

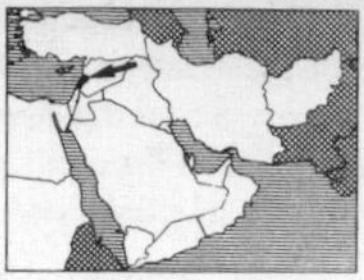

Area 10,400 sq.km. E.Mediterranean coastal state. An enclave between Israel and Syria. The site of ancient Phoenicia.

Population 2,600,000. Annual growth 2.1%. People per sq.km. 250. Since 1975 over 500,000 Lebanese have fled or emigrated, and a further estimated 200,000 have lost their lives in ten years of warfare.

Peoples
Arab 89% of which 44% are immigrant settlers, refugees and workers. Syrians 700,000; Palestinians 370,000; Egyptians 75,000.
Other minorities 11%. Armenians 177,000; Kurds 70,000; Samaritans 15,000 etc.

Literacy 87%. **Official language:** Arabic; French is widely used among Christians. **All languages** 5. **Bible translations** 2Bi 1NT 1por.

Capital: Beirut 1,200,000. Urbanization 76%.

Economy: Trading, banking and tourism were once profitable and made Lebanon the commercial centre of the Middle East. The ten-year agony of civil wars and foreign interventions have reduced the land to ruins and poverty. Recovery will take decades. Income/person $1,100 (8% of USA).

Politics: French mandated territory 1919-1941. Independent in 1941 as a republic, with a constitution based on a delicate balance related to the size of each of the 17 recognized religious communities. The influx of 400,000 Palestinian refugees between 1948 and 1976 upset the status quo. The Palestinians virtually took control of south Lebanon as a base of operations against Israel in the 1975-76 civil war. Foreign forces from Syria, other Arab countries, and Western nations intervened in costly but vain attempts to quell the communal fighting. Israel invaded in 1982 to destroy Palestinian power, but in doing so unleashed a further wave of violence as Druze and Shi'a militia sought to improve their political leverage at the expense of the Christians. Lebanon has been polarized into community "cantons" and all semblance of central government control has been lost. The Israeli withdrawal in 1985 is likely to lead to Syrian forces taking over much of the country.

Religion: Freedom of religion; the only Arab state that is not officially Muslim. The distribution of power according to the size of each community was frozen at 1932 levels. The rapid increase in size of the Muslim population, and especially the under-represented Shi'a, is one of the basic reasons underlying the present conflict. There are 17 recognized religious communities: five Muslim, one Jewish and 11 Christian.
All figures are estimates. The last religious census was in 1932 when Christians were 53.7% of the population.
Non-religious/Atheist 3%.
Muslim 67%.
Shi'a 32%. A majority in south and Bekaa Valley in east, and in Beirut. Numerically and militarily the dominant community since 1985.
Sunni 28%. Majority in Beirut, Tripoli and north-east, mainly Syrians and Palestinians.
Druze 7%. Majority in Chouf mountains east of Beirut. Their beliefs differ much from the teachings of Islam.
Christian 30%. Rapid decline through war and emigration. Majority in East Beirut, central and north Lebanon.
Roman Catholic 19%. 485,000a; 270,000m. Six different rites. Largest: Maronites, Melkites, also Armenian, Syrian, Chaldean and Latin. Maronites are politically dominant.
Orthodox 10%. 255,000a; 144,000m. Seven different eastern churches using the Arabic, Armenian and Assyrian languages.
Protestant 1%. 25,700a; 10,400m. Denominations 35. Largest (adult members):

Union of Evang. Armenian Churches	4,260
National Evangelical Church	1,760
National Evangelical Synod	1,700
Arab Episcopal Church (Anglican)	1,100
Seventh Day Adventist Church	700
Baptist Convention (**SBC**)	590
Church of God	300

Evangelical 0.56% of population.
Missionaries to Lebanon 262 in 1973, about 80 in 1985 (1:32,500 people).
Missionaries from within Lebanon 9 (1:2,900 Protestants) in 2 agencies.

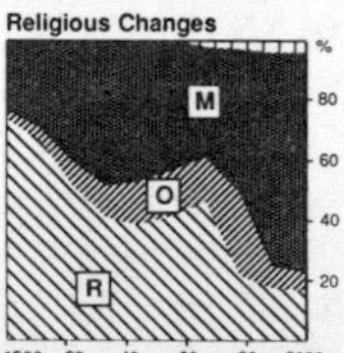

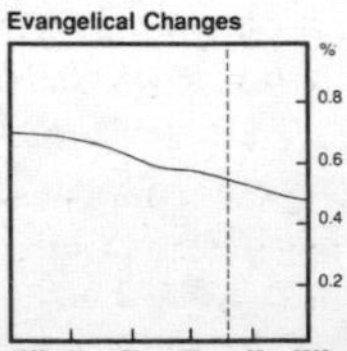

1. **Hatred and revenge have brought death and tragedy to all.** Deep repentance and a forgiving spirit must come before reconciliation is possible. Yet in the sorrow and tensions responsiveness to the gospel has increased. Both Muslims and nominal Christians are seeking the Saviour in different parts of the country. Pray that the centuries-old barriers to the understanding of the Truth may be swept away.

2. **The country has been ravaged for 10 years by foreign and community armies**, and is, in effect, ungovernable. Pray for community leaders of all religions, and pray that a national government may emerge that exalts righteousness and justice.

3. **The hatred and cruelty of Muslim militia on Christian communities has been returned in kind.** The retention of political power, and promotion of denominational interests, have had preeminence over pure Christian living and preaching the gospel. The bewildering variety of Catholic, Orthodox and Protestant bodies is hardly a witness to non-Christians. Pray that the pressures on all Christians may be redemptive and bring the Church to its **primary** commitment to the Kingdom of God and its extension. There is a healthy interest in Bible reading and renewal in sections of the influential Maronite Church and the Armenian Orthodox Church.

4. **Protestantism is seen as a threat to both traditional Christians and to Muslims**, and also appears foreign. Eighty per cent of all Protestants are from the Armenian community; only 20% from the Arab majority. Many of the cultural and doctrinal views of the missionary church planters have been absorbed by local believers, bringing further divisions to the Body. Pray for the believers, their unity, fortitude, protection and witness in this complex situation. Many pastors and members have emigrated recently, but conversions almost make up for this loss.

5. **Leadership in the Protestant churches** is at a premium. The evacuation of many missionaries, the collapse of the economy and the emigration of leaders has hampered outreach and growth. The **Lebanon Bible Institute** had to close, but was resurrected as the **Mediterranean Bible College** in 1984. The Baptists (**SBC**) and **AoG** have Bible schools too — the only residential theological institutes for Evangelicals in the Arab world. Pray for staffing, supply of needs, and for students in these difficult times.

6. **Lebanon has been one of the key centres for Christian ministries to the whole Middle East**. Much of this outreach has been limited or stopped altogether. Pray for the restoration of freedom and a resumption of this role for the blessing of the whole region. Pray especially for these ministries:

a) **The Bible Society** has been a major contributor to the spread of Christian literature and Bibles. Pray for staff, supplies, distribution of God's Word and openness to it.

b) **Christian literature** production has been severely disrupted; much has been transferred to Cyprus, Europe and elsewhere. Pray for the Evangelical Carmel Mission, **OM, MECO**, Arabic Literature Mission, Christian Arabic Literature League, Baptists, etc., who are all publishing and distributing literature for Lebanon and the Arab world.

c) **Radio.** Both **FEBA** and **TWR** maintain studios and produce programmes in Beirut despite the danger and destruction. The **FEBA** studio was destroyed in August 1985. The "Voice of Hope" Christian station in south Lebanon broadcasts the gospel 24 hours a day, locally and to all the Middle East, with some impact and response.

d) **Student work. IFES** has three staff workers based in Beirut who serve isolated Christian students throughout the region. The spiritual needs of students are great but almost entirely unmet at present.

e) **Missionaries** continue to minister where and when they can. Major missions are **SBC** (20 workers), **OM** (20), **MECO** (14). Many have had to leave because of the danger from war and kidnapping. Pray for their safety and effectiveness. Most are involved in literature, radio, relief work and teaching.

7. **The enormous task of reconstruction and rehabilitation is an opportunity to demonstrate Christian love and concern**, and open hearts for the Lord Jesus. **CMA, MECO, WV, YWAM** and others have committed personnel and resources to 130,000 who were blinded and maimed as a result of the hostilities, and for these victims much could be provided.

8. **The unreached.** The social consequences of personal conversions to Christ are immense, so those coming to Him have been few, but praise God for greater openness now. So pray for:

a) **The Druzes.** Well organized, but close-knit community with a secretive religion. Response to the gospel has been minimal.

b) **The Shi'ites** are newly powerful, militant, radical and hostile to any Western influences. Pray that they may discover the emptiness of a religion without Christ.

c) **The Kurds:** a despised and ignored but more responsive minority.

d) **The Palestinians:** a tragic, stateless people. There are Christians among them, some evangelical, but the majority are Muslim and unreached.

Africa
July 12

LESOTHO
(Kingdom of Lesotho)

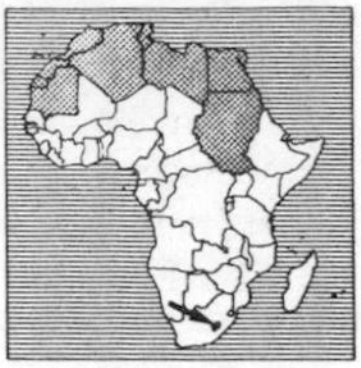

Area 30,300 sq.km. A mountainous, landlocked country completely surrounded by South Africa. Only 10% is arable.

Population 1,520,000. This includes 180,000 men working in S.African mines. Annual growth 2.6%. People per sq.km. 50.

Peoples. Five distinct peoples: Sotho 90%; Zulu and Xhosa 9%; Mixed race, European and Asian 1%.

Literacy 71%. **Official languages:** Sotho, English. **All languages** 4. **Bible translations** 3Bi.

Capital: Maseru 82,000. Urbanization 6%.

Economy: Serious overpopulation, unemployment, lack of resources and severe soil erosion keep the country poor. A large part of the labour force works in S.Africa, and their earnings are vital to the economy; but employment opportunities are decreasing, and the future is bleak. Income/person $470 (3% of USA).

Politics: Independent from Britain in 1966 as a parliamentary monarchy. The constitution was suspended in 1970 due to political unrest. Foreign policy is dominated by tension between the economic reality of dependence on S. Africa and dislike of its racial and political policies. There was a military coup in 1986.

Religion: Political tensions have limited some outreach activities. The Catholic Church is influential.

African traditional religions 6%. **Baha'i** 1%.

Christian 93%. Affiliated 91%. Many non-practising.

Roman Catholic 43%. 654,000a.

Marginal groups (over 210) 18%. 273,000a.

Protestant 30%. 450,000a; 174,000m. Denominations 50+. Many small groups of S.African origin. Largest (adherents):

Lesotho Ev. Ch. (PEMS-DEFAP)	300,000
Anglican Church	100,000
Church of God (Pentecostal)	16,000
Assemblies of God	2,000
Dutch Reformed Ch. in Africa	1,900

Evangelical 2.7% of population.

Missionaries to Lesotho approx. 90 (1:17,000 people) in 25 agencies.

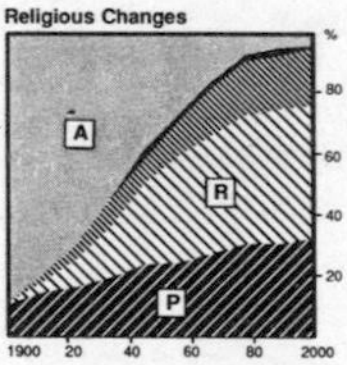

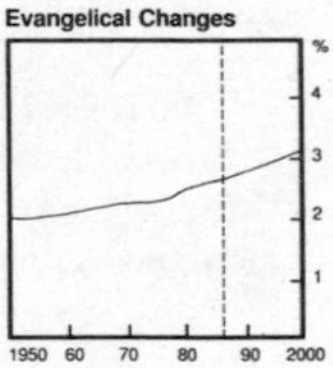

1. **Lesotho's tragic poverty is both physical and spiritual.** The great work of French missionaries of the Paris Evangelical Missionary Society is in decline. The daughter church has only 36 pastors and few candidates for the ministry in the theological school. Nearly all the older churches are very nominal. Since 1960, Protestants have declined from 33% to 22% of the population.

2. **The Roman Catholics have invested vast sums of money and manpower in the country.** The entire cabinet, the Prime Minister and also the King, are Catholic, and most of the schools and hospitals are run by the RCs. There is considerable intolerance of Protestant work by

some chiefs and officials, and Protestants sometimes suffer discrimination in schools and the health services. Pray for many to turn to a biblical faith.

3. **The evangelical witness has been weak for years.** However, over the 10 years since 1975 there has been improvement, with growth in small Pentecostal and Dutch Reformed Church congregations. Other evangelical missions are entering the land for aid programmes, church planting and Bible teaching (**AIM**).

4. **The churches are very weak.** Congregations are almost entirely made up of women, the few men present usually being illiterate. Many men spend most of the year in South Africa. Consequently, it is almost impossible to build up lay leadership, adequate family life and giving for the Lord's work. Pray for the conversion of more men and the planting of strong churches all over the land.

5. **Less evangelized areas.** Almost all claim to be Christian, but superstition and witchcraft are commonplace. Pray for:

a) The bewildering variety of brightly robed, **syncretic indigenous churches** among whom there is little knowledge of the Truth. A sensitive approach to them is needed.

b) **Isolated mountain communities**; many have never heard the gospel clearly. **MAF**'s flying programme, with three planes, is spearheading a new thrust of evangelism. It is an asset in medical and agricultural aid programmes by Mennonites (19 workers) and other missions in a land where roads are often non-existent or impassable.

c) **Migrant workers in South African mines** are being evangelized by **AEF**. Pray for this key ministry.

d) **Embittered refugees from South Africa**, many of whom live in the Maseru area.

e) **Young people**. Both **SU** and **IFES** have a young, small work.

LIBERIA
(Republic of Liberia)

Area 111,000 sq.km. Coastal state between Sierra Leone and Ivory Coast.

Population 2,200,000. Annual growth 3.1%. People per sq.km. 20.

Peoples: There are 16 major ethnic groups divided in three language families:
Mande 52%. Kpelle 435,000; Mandingo 300,000; Gio 171,000; Mano 148,000; Loma 111,000; Vai 60,000; Bandi 59,000; Mende 9,000.
Kru 35%. Bassa 341,000; Grebo (5) 202,000; Kru 166,000; Krahn 79,000; Belle 11,000; Dey 11,000.
West Atlantic 8%. Gola 97,000; Kissi 72,000.
Non-tribal Liberians 5%. Descendents of the original ex-slave settlers.

Literacy 30%. **Official language:** English. **All languages** 31. **Bible translations** 6NT 6por.

Capital: Monrovia 300,000. Urbanization 39%.

Economy: Mining of iron ore and diamonds, export of rubber, timber and coffee and a large "flag of convenience" fleet of ships could make this land prosper. Years of institutionalized corruption and failure to develop the economy have been followed by the inability of the new government to cope with the situation. The country was close to economic collapse by 1985. Income/person $470 (3% of USA).

Politics: In 1847 Liberia became Black Africa's first independent state. The dominance of the Liberians of American origin ended in the coup of 1980. The military government has become increasingly unstable.

Religion: Liberia was founded as a Christian state. There continues to be freedom of religion.
Traditional religions 41%. Strongly entrenched and institutionalized secret societies. Relatively few Liberians are uninvolved.
Muslim 21%. Majority among Mandingo and Vai, and increasing in Western peoples.
Christian 38%. Nominal 20%. Affiliated 18%. Only 25% of Christians attend church regularly.
Roman Catholic 1.8%. 39,000a.
Marginal groups (70+) 4%. 82,500a.
Protestant 13% (23% would claim to be Protestant). 282,000a; 127,000m. Denominations 40+. Largest (adherents):

Baptist Convention (**SBC**)	50,000
United Methodist Church	35,000
Lutheran Church	25,650
Episcopal Church	20,000
Assemblies of God (**PAoC**)	18,000
African Methodist Episc. Church	13,000
United Liberia Inland Ch. (**WEC**)	6,500

Evangelical 7.1% of population.
Missionaries to Liberia approx. 480, (1:4,600 people) in 45 agencies.
Missionaries from within Liberia 5.

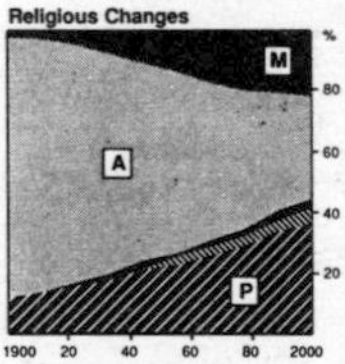

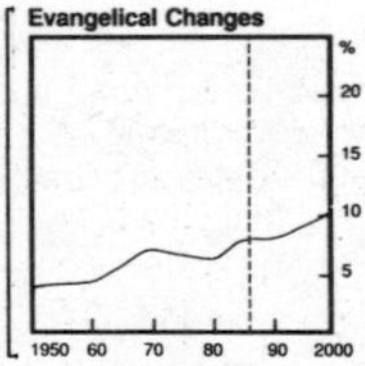

1. **The first Protestant churches served the needs of the freed slaves** who founded Liberia. They were culturally isolated from the inland peoples and had little vision to evangelize them. Nominalism, secularism, immorality and alcoholism have been serious problems in the churches. Pray for revival.

2. **Inland the progress of the gospel has been slow**. The unhealthy climate, diversity of languages, lack of Scriptures and a low literacy level hindered the earlier wave of missionaries. In the east and centre of the country there are churches in most communities, but far fewer among the peoples in the west. Generally, the churches are stagnating, lacking in trained leadership and vision for evangelism. Many vigorous indigenous churches have sprung up among the Bassa, but they often make up with enthusiasm what they lack in knowledge of the Word. Compromise with polygamy, secret societies, ancestor worship and witchcraft is widespread even among church leaders. Pray that Christians may fearlessly live and proclaim the liberating Truth, even if it results in ostracism.

3. **The effects of the social upheavals since the 1980 revolution have been far-reaching.** People are seeking a national identity and showing a renewed interest in both Islam and the gospel, and the power of the secret societies has begun to lessen. Pray for a decisive breakthrough of the Spirit.

4. **Trained, spiritual leaders are insufficient for the task**, especially with the steady reduction in missionary personnel. Many leaders have had no formal training. Pray for the raising up of fearless men and women of God who will bring back the churches to biblical standards. There are 10 Bible schools in the country. One of note is the **Africa Bible College** for more advanced students. ELWA (**SIM**) runs a radio Bible school.

5. **The missionary thrust of the Liberian Church has hardly started.** A few pastors have sought to evangelize other peoples for short periods within Liberia and over the border in Guinea. Pray for enthusiasm and long-term commitment by Christians to obedience to the Great Commission. Nearly all the nations round about have a large unevangelized population.

6. **Islam has grown more rapidly** in recent years. Islamization of the Bandi, Mende, Gola and Dey is rapid. Arab oil money has been liberally used to build mosques and train Muslim missionaries. Other peoples may turn to Islam. Pray that Christians in Liberia may seize present opportunities to evangelize both Muslims and pagans. Muslims see Liberia as the key country for winning all of West Africa to their faith.

7. **Less reached peoples.** About six peoples are without a viable Christian testimony, most being in the west where Islam is stronger. New thrusts are beginning to each of them:

a) **Vai** are nominally Muslim but becoming open to Christianity in some areas (**SIM**).

b) **Bandi** are rapidly turning to Islam and could be wholly so in 10-15 years. The small Christian community is shrinking (**SIM**).

c) **Loma** are strongly fetishist and less than 1% Christian (**CRWM**).

d) **Gola** are largely Muslim, but a few are turning to Christ (**SIM**).

e) **Krahn** in NE are only 4% Christian and bound by fetish worship. Christians are declining in numbers (**PAoC**).

f) **Mandingo** are the strongest Muslim people in the country and have gained almost a monopoly of trade. Only a handful have believed, and they suffer persecution. Pray for **SIM**'s outreach to them.

There are a further 12 peoples among whom the Church is hardly viable.

8. **Missionaries have had a long, hard uphill struggle** to see gospel breakthroughs. Some missions have laboured for years and packed in, leaving little permanent result. The work of **PAoC**, **WEC**, **AoG**, etc. has resulted in evangelical congregations, but much remains to be done. Bible teaching and discipling in the churches, pioneer evangelism in less reached peoples, and rural development programmes are key needs. A new wave of missions is moving out to less reached peoples: **SIM** (Mandingo, Bandi, Gola), **CRWM** (Loma), **NTM** (8 groups in SE) etc. Some larger agencies are: **SIM** (111 workers), **SBC** (59), Baptist Mid-Missions (30), **PAoC** (13), **CRWM** (11), **WEC** (10).

9. **Bible translation** has gained momentum through the work of Lutheran Bible Translators, **WEC** and several older missions. There are 11 languages in which NTs are being translated, and there are possibly 13 that may need a translation programme. Illiteracy is a serious problem. **GRI** has recordings in 39 languages and dialects.

10. **Liberian youth are frustrated and want answers to the meaning of life.** **LIFES** has a ministry to university students, and **CCC**, **Youth for Christ** and **SU** to high schools. Pray that many might become vital witnesses for the Lord.

11. **Radio ELWA (SIM)** is Africa's best known Christian broadcasting station. The impact of this station, with its radio, TV, school for missionaries' children, hospital, film library and TEE programme, in Liberia and beyond is incalculable. Previously resistant peoples in Guinea and Liberia have responded because of the radio ministry. Over 44 languages are aired in 1,148 hours of broadcasting every month. Pray that the large missionary and Liberian staff may work harmoniously together and have an eternally fruitful ministry. Pray for the extensive outreach to N.African and W.African Muslim peoples.

Middle East

July 14-15

LIBYA

(Socialist People's Libyan Jamahiriya)

Area 1,760,000 sq.km. Agriculture on Mediterranean coast; over 90% Sahara desert.

Population 4,000,000. Annual growth 3.5%. People per sq.km. 2.

Peoples
Libyan Arabs 68%.
Indigenous minorities 4%. Berber peoples (4): (Zenaga, Tuareg) 120,000; Saharan peoples (2): Teda 20,000; Zaghawa 5,000(?).
Foreign workers 28%. Egyptian 350,000(?); Pakistani 25,000; South Korean 10,000; North Korean 3,200; Westerners; Indian; Bangladeshi, etc.

Literacy 37%. **Official language:** Arabic. **All languages** 8. **Bible translations** 1NT 1por.

Capital: Tripoli 1,200,000. Urbanization 64%.

Economy: Almost entirely oil-based. Wealth gained in '70s used to export leftist and Islamic revolution all over the world. The rapid decline in oil revenues in the '80s has moderated these maverick interventions. Income/person $7,500 (53% of USA).

Politics: Former traditional monarchy overthrown in 1969 revolution. Ghadaffi's revolutionary republic has subverted governments in most of the surrounding lands and beyond in its attempts to promote Arab unity and Islamic solidarity.

Religion: Sunni Islam is the state religion, but secularizing influences are strong. No form of Christian witness to Libyans is tolerated.
Muslim 93%. All Libyans and most of the foreigners.
Buddhist 0.6%. Korean, Sri Lankan, Chinese.
Christian 6%. Nominal 3.6%. Affiliated 2.4%.
Orthodox (4 national denominations) 1.4%. 54,300a. Largest:
Coptic Church (Egyptian) 45,000a.
Roman Catholic 1%. 40,000a, Maltese, Egyptian, etc.
Protestant 0.14%. 5,600a; 3,400m. Denominations 6. Largest: Korean Presbyterian, Union Church, Anglican Church.

1. **No open evangelism is possible**. The last missionary outpost was closed in 1960. There is not one known group of Libyan Christians. No witness to the Berber or southern oasis peoples has ever been attempted. Pray Libya open for the King of Kings.

2. **The Christian community** is large, nominal and foreign. There are some lively groups of evangelical Christians among the Western oil experts (Union and Anglican Churches), Korean construction workers (Presbyterians) and Pakistani labourers; but few are able to communicate with the indigenous majority. The tense political and security situation also hinders any witness by believers. Pray that the Word of God may have free course among both the expatriate communities and the indigenous peoples.

3. **Alternative means for preaching the gospel:**
a) **Radio**. One of the only ways of directly reaching Libyans. **TWR** (Monaco) is the key station for the area. Radio School of the Bible (**NAM**) is one of the most profitable programmes. Follow-up is virtually impossible. Pray for eternal fruit.
b) **Literature and cassettes** may enter only by devious means. Pray for the conversion of censors! BCCs by mail very rarely get through.
c) **Libyans overseas**. Refugees from totalitarianism, diplomats, students and businessmen could be introduced to Christ by believers in other lands.

LIECHTENSTEIN

(Principality of Liechtenstein)

The West

July 16

Area 160 sq.km. Sandwiched between Switzerland and Austria.

Population 28,000. Annual growth 1.8%. People per sq.km. 173.

Peoples: All German-speaking, of which Liechtensteiners are 63%.

Capital: Vaduz 5,000. Urbanization 30%.

Economy: Manufacturing, banking and tourism. Wealthy. Income/person $16,000 (115% of USA).

Politics: Constitutional principality in customs and monetary union with Switzerland.

Religion: The Catholic Church is the State Church, but freedom of religion guaranteed to all.
Non-religious/Atheist 1.5%.
Christian 98.2%. Affiliated 96%.
Roman Catholic 90%.
Marginal groups 0.25%.
Protestant 5.8%. 1,610a; 992m. Reformed Church, Lutheran Church and Adventists each have one congregation.
Evangelical 0.15% of population.

1. **Liechtenstein is one of the last remaining vestiges of the Holy Roman Empire.** Few have ever heard of the necessity of a personal faith in Christ.

2. **There is not a single fully evangelical fellowship functioning in the country.** The three Protestant congregations are liberal or Adventist; there are several committed believers within these. In 1985, the first open evangelistic campaign ever held was organized by an international team of British, Norwegian and Swiss believers. It was an exciting beginning with some seeking the Lord. Pray that groups of committed believers may emerge as a result.

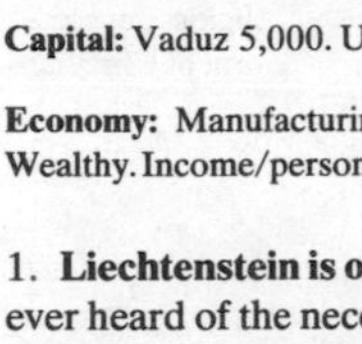

LUXEMBOURG

(The Grand Duchy of Luxembourg)

The West

July 17

Area 2,600 sq.km. The smallest of the Benelux, or Low Countries.

Population 366,000. Annual growth 0%. People per sq.km. 140.

Peoples
Luxembourgers 76%
Foreigners 26%. Portuguese 29,000; Italian 22,000; French 11,000; German 7,000.

Literacy 98%. **Official language:** French. **Spoken language:** Letzburgisch (Germanic language).

Capital: Luxembourg 80,000. Urbanization 78%.

Economy: Steel making and international finance and agencies are important. Income/person $12,190 (87% of USA).

Politics: Parliamentary monarchy in economic union with Belgium and Netherlands. A member of EEC, and Headquarters of many EEC institutions.

Religion: Freedom of religion. The Catholic Church is effectually the State Church.
Christian 94%. Affiliated 86.6%.
Roman Catholic 84.3%. Practising 50%. 308,000a; 244,000m.
Marginal groups 0.8%. 2,900a; 1,500m. Largest (adult members): Jehovah's Witnesses 1,129.
Protestant 1.5%. 5,200a; 3,000m. Denominations 15. Largest (adult members): Protestant Church of Luxembourg 1,800.
Evangelical 0.1% of population.
Missionaries to Luxembourg 12 (1:30,500 people).

1. **The land is Catholic by tradition and culture**; revolutionary changes in the Church elsewhere have passed it by, and few have clearly heard the gospel in their own language. Pray for the spiritual liberation of this land.

2. **Evangelical Christians are a very small minority** within the already small, but nominal, Luxembourg and foreign Protestant community. There are more Jehovah's Witnesses than born-again believers. Pray for the small fellowships of the Free Church, Mennonites, Assemblies of God and Baptists, and for the four Reformed Congregations. Pray that there may soon be a strong indigenous body of believers as most are scattered and lack real fellowship. There is a handful of expatriate Christian workers in the country and some who make visits from surrounding countries.

3. **A few isolated evangelistic efforts** through **OM**, Teen Challenge's coffee-bar and others who have sown the seed, but the visible breakthrough is yet to come.

4. **The Letzburgisch language** is spoken by the majority as their heart language. Most are fluent in French and German, but a Bible in their language could be a key opening for the light of the gospel.

Asia
July 18

MACAO
(The Province of Macao)

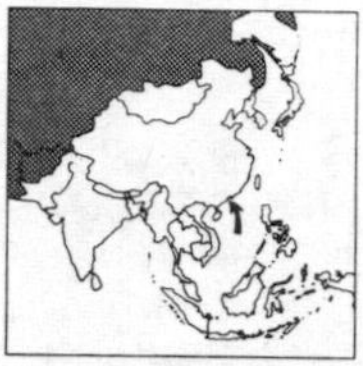

M

Area 16 sq. km. A tiny peninsula 64 km. west of Hong Kong on the coast of Gwangdung Province of China.

Population 415,000. Between 100,000 and 200,000 refugees entered illegally since 1979. Population may be 500,000.

Peoples
Chinese 92.5%. Mainly Cantonese speaking.
Burmese 4%. Many still speaking Burmese.
Macanese 2.7% (mixed race). **Portuguese** 0.3%.

Literacy 82%. **Official language:** Portuguese. **Trade language:** Cantonese

Capital: Macao 308,000. Urbanization 98%.

Economy: Flourishing on entertainment and gambling, some light industry and as a base for the international gold market. Income/person $2,300 (17% of USA).

Politics: Rented by the Portuguese in 1577. Became a Portuguese Colony in 1887, considered a Chinese Territory under Portuguese administration since 1974. Negotiations are under way for the full resumption of control by the Peking government.

Religion
Non-religious/Atheist 18%.
Chinese religions 66%.
Christians 16.4%. Affiliated 12.4%
Roman Catholics 11%. 45,500a; 26,800m.
Protestants 1.4%. 6,000a; 2,470m. Denominations 18. Largest (adult members):

Baptist Convention (**SBC**)	1,032
Chinese Evangelical Church	390
Seventh Day Adventist Church	370

Evangelical 1.6% of population.
Missionaries to Macao 20 (1:20,700 people) in 5 agencies.

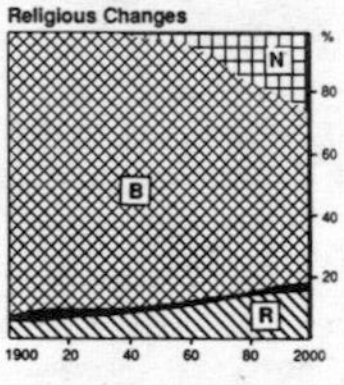

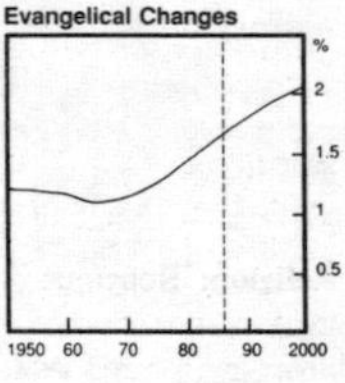

1. **Unreached peoples:**
   a) **The nearly 200,000 refugees from the PRC and Vietnam** have suffered much and are open to the gospel.
   b) **The 12,000 Burmese** refugees still use their home language. There is now one growing church among them.

c) **The Macanese** and **Portuguese** are staunchly Catholic, but have little personal experience of the gospel.

d) **Those in the entertainment industry** — so full of vice.

2. **The Protestant Church is small, introspective and weakened** by emigration and high turnover of leadership. There are now 25 churches and 18 pastors being assisted by 11 missionaries (**SBC, CCC, ECF, SwAM**); the latter are heavily committed to educational and social programmes. What a mission field for Hong Kong Christians! Macao's first Bible school was opened in 1982 and has 16 students.

3. **Macao was the first base for Protestant missions to China.** Today it is one of the most needy but open fields for missions in Asia. Witnessing in this idolatrous, sinful territory is not easy. Recent evangelistic outreach by **CCC** and others has sharply increased church attendances.

MADAGASCAR
(Democratic Republic of Madagascar)

Africa

July 19

Area 587,000 sq.km. A 1,600 km.-long island in the Indian Ocean 600 km. off the coast of Mozambique.

Population 10,037,000. Annual growth 2.8%. People per sq.km. 17.

Peoples

Malagasy 98%. 18 groups of mixed African, Arab and Indonesian origin speaking a single Indonesian related language. The Indonesian ethnic element is strongest in the highlands.

Other 2%. Indian 15,000; Arab 12,000; Chinese 10,000; French; Réunionese; Comorian.

Literacy 44%. **Official languages:** Malagasy, French.

Capital: Antananarivo 820,000. Urbanization 22%.

Economy: Mainly agricultural, with good potential; but worsening communications, hasty nationalizations, and central government control have prevented growth. Income/person $290 (2% of USA).

Politics: Independent from France in 1960. One party republic with a revolutionary socialist government since 1975. During the '80s the Marxist emphasis has been watered down.

Religion: Religious freedom for recognized religions and churches, despite the anti-Christian propaganda and Marxist instruction in schools since 1975. As revolutionary fervour wanes, the status of Christians improves.

Traditional religions 43.3%.

Non-religious/Atheist 2%.

Muslim 1.7%. One Malagasy ethnic group is Muslim, three partly so. Arabs, Comorians and some Indians also Muslim.

Christian 53%. Affiliated 45%.

Roman Catholic 21.3%. Practising 44%. 2,138,000a; 1,176,000m. Stronger among coastal lowland peoples.

Marginal groups (20) 1.3%. 120,000a. Mainly syncretic Christo-pagan groups.

Protestant 20.8%. 2,090,000a; 626,000m.

Denominations 11. Largest (adherents):

Ch. of Jesus Christ in M. (orig. LMS, PEMS, Friends)	1,300,000
Lutheran Church	600,000
Episcopal Church	78,000
Seventh Day Adventist Church	39,000

Evangelical 1.8% of population.

Missionaries to Madagascar approx. 110 (1:91,000 people) in 13 agencies.

Missionaries from Madagascar 3.

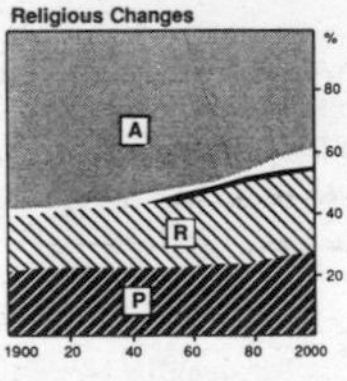

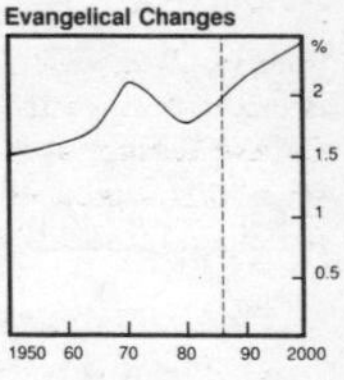

1. **Praise God for increased freedom for Christians** as the country moderates its Marxist rhetoric. Pray for this generation to be fully evangelized and for economic and political conditions that further this.

2. **The Lord worked in power in the last century**. Persecution from heathen rulers and then by Roman Catholics, after the French gained control of Madagascar, strengthened the Protestant Church which grew from 5,000 members in 1861 to one million in 1900. Pray that God may do it again! There have been touches of revival in the Lutheran churches of the south and northwest, but in the main, spiritual life has drained away; a shell of robes, liturgies and ceremonies remains. Most Christians have no knowledge of the basics of the gospel.

3. **A revival of paganism followed independence**. The power of Jesus to deliver from magic and demon possession must be demonstrated before people can fully trust in Him alone. There are few believers able and willing to confront the powers of darkness, yet since 1980 there has been an evident increase in spiritual concern. An indigenous lay movement of "shepherds" with an emphasis on healing and exorcism has, in fact, led to considerable growth in church membership of some Lutheran churches.

4. **Spiritual deadness and theological confusion are the dominant features of the Church**. Liberal theology that accommodates astrology, heathen customs and Marxism is held to by many pastors today. Pray for liberal theological schools to return to a biblical theology. Pray for the establishment of a good evangelical Bible school. TEE has been developed by **CBFMS** missionaries.

5. **Evangelical believers are few today** and confined to some Baptist and Pentecostal groups, and sections of the Lutheran Church. There is an indigenous Pentecostal fellowship based in the capital called "Jesus Saves" which is growing particularly rapidly. Pray for the work of GBUM(**IFES**) with two staff workers, 30 groups and 1,300 members in the university and high schools, as also for **SU**. The influence of these two fellowships on the country is out of all proportion to their numbers. Many young people are catching the vision to form evangelistic teams. Pray for a return to biblical Christianity and that a wave of evangelism will sweep through the land.

6. **The Malagasy Bible has been available for 150 years**. It has a treasured place in the culture. Pray that its message may enter hearts. The Bible Society has a vigorous distribution programme, but lack of foreign exchange limits the number available. All Christian literature is in short supply. There are few good, spiritual books in Malagasy. The Lutherans have a large printing press.

7. **Unreached areas and peoples:**
   a) **Many thousands of villages** have no gospel witness and are still openly pagan.
   b) **The Comorian minority** (only a few left since 1976) and the **Malagasy Tankarana** (40,000) are wholly or predominantly Muslim. No specific outreach has been made to them.
   c) The coastal **Sakalava** in the west, and **Antiamoro** in the southeast have very few committed believers. They are partly Muslim.
   d) The **Chinese** and **Indian** minorities have never been specifically evangelized.

The poor state of the road system makes itinerant evangelism very difficult to maintain.

8. **Missionaries are few in number**. The largest groups are those of the Norwegian Lutherans in the north, American Lutherans in the south, the newer **CBFMS** (6 missionaries) assisting an indigenous Baptist group, **AIM** (4) working with the Bible Society and **SU**, and several Pentecostal missionaries. Entry is not easy, but missionaries able to serve with Malagasy Christians in evangelism, literature, church planting and Bible teaching are needed. Pray the way open for others to enter.

9. **Christian radio programmes** are broadcast by **TWR**-Swaziland for 15 hours per month, and by **FEBA**-Seychelles for 28 hours per month. Pray for the content and impact of these programmes.

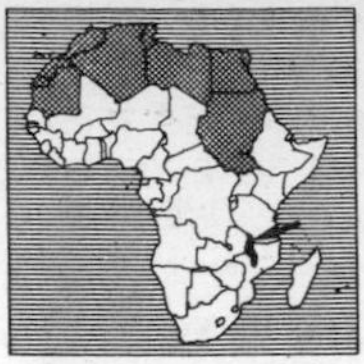

MALAWI
(Republic of Malawi)

Africa

July 20

Area 118,000 sq.km. Central African state extending along Lake Malawi and its outflow river, the Shire. Landlocked and virtually an enclave within Mozambique.

Population 7,100,000. Annual growth 3.2%. People per sq.km. 60.

Peoples. All ethnic groups over 20.
Nyanja group 59%. Chewa-Nyanja 2,800,000; Angoni (Zulu invaders being culturally absorbed) 639,000; Tumbuka (8 groups) 426,000; Sena 300,000.
Other **northern peoples** 7.3%. Ngonde 300,000; Tonga 213,000.
Other **southern peoples** 33%. Lomwe 1,300,000; Yao 994,000.
Others 0.8%. Mozambiquan, European, Asian 5,000.

Literacy 26%. **Official languages:** Chewa and English. **All languages** 12. **Bible translations** 7Bi 1NT 2por.

Capital: Lilongwe 120,000. Largest city: Blantyre-Limbe 525,000. Urbanization 12%.

Economy: Relatively poor; lacking in natural resources and sufficient agricultural land. Many Malawians work in Zimbabwe, South Africa, etc. Income/person $210 (1% of USA).

Politics: Independent from Britain in 1964. One party republic. Has been fairly stable and economically viable under existing leadership.

Religion: Freedom of religion, though the banning of Jehovah's Witnesses in 1969 led to persecution of that sect.
African tribal religions 15.7%.
Muslim 16.3%. Almost entirely Yao people, but also some Asians.
Christian 68%. Affiliated 61%.
Roman Catholic 23.4%. Practising 45%. 1,660,000a; 885,600m.
Indigenous marginal groups (120+) 2.5%. 175,000a.
Foreign marginal groups (3) 1%. 74,000a.
Protestant 34.3%. 2,440,000a; 734,000m.
Denominations 32. Largest (adult members):

CCAP (**DRC**, Ch. of Scot. FCS)	est.	472,500
Seventh Day Adventist Church		57,000
Anglican Church	est.	39,000
United Evang. Ch. (ZEM-NM)	est.	29,000
Baptist Convention (**SBC**)		22,000
Int. Ch. of Foursquare Gospel		21,000
African Baptist Assembly		18,000
Churches of Christ	est.	13,000
Seventh Day Baptist Church		7,100
African Evang. Church (**AEF**)		4,800

Evangelical 14.8% of population.
Missionaries to Malawi 220 (1:32,000 people) in about 30 agencies.
Missionaries from within Malawi 40(?) (1:61,000 Protestants).

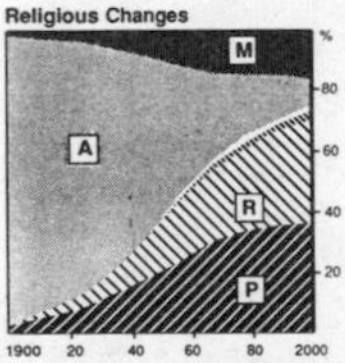

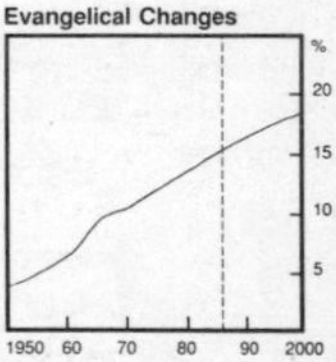

1. **Praise God for the relative peace, freedom for the gospel, and receptivity of the people.** Surrounding lands have suffered from wars, famines, and restrictions on the preaching of the gospel. Pray for future stability.

2. **Malawi is probably the most receptive country in central Africa.** Years of evangelical witness in many areas, the significant impact of **SU** in schools, SCOM(**IFES**) in the universities and colleges, **NLFA** in churches and a multiplicity of prayer groups and house meetings are part of the reason. The 1983 Blantyre inter-church crusade was a time of harvest **(AE)**. The gospel is reaching into every section of society, and in places there is a revival atmosphere.

3. **Church growth has been consistently large for the last 30 years.** The key denomination is the CCAP; formed by a union of the churches planted by the S.African Dutch Reformed Church, Free Church of Scotland and Church of Scotland missions. The former is evangelical; the latter two less so. Pray for revival in this large church. Other smaller churches listed above have experienced even greater growth in recent years. Pray that second and third generation Christians may come to personal faith and be enthused by the gospel.

4. **Full-time workers are too few to reap the harvest** and conserve it in the churches. The relative poverty of most rural congregations means that few can afford to support an adequately trained full-time pastor. Pray for many to be called, and pray for increased facilities to prepare them for the ministry. There are six Bible schools and seminaries. Pray for the CCAP theological school at Nkhoma, that it may maintain a clear evangelical stand.

5. **Islam** has been a veneer over the Yao people's culture, but a determined effort is being made to strengthen Islamic institutions, train Muslim Malawians for the spread of Islam, and build mosques all over the country. Pray for a greater concern for the Muslims in Malawian churches. Response from among Muslims in the last decade has increased, but few are concentrating on the seven Muslim areas.

6. **Missionary work** is more for supporting existing churches in training and outreach. A number of missionaries are still involved in institutional work. Pray for a deep heart identification with Malawian believers and fruitful ministries in this day of opportunity. Largest agencies are **SBC** (39 workers), Church of Scotland (24), **AEF** (24), USPG (Anglican) (22), **AoG** (16).

7. **Less reached peoples:**
   a) **The Muslim Yao**. About 5% have become Christian, but too few workers are committed to this specialized outreach.
   b) **The few northern Ngonde** are Christianized but not many have a vital personal faith.
   c) **The Sena and Lomwe in the south** are part of larger tribes that live in neighbouring Mozambique. The Sena especially are largely unevangelized in that land. Pray that Malawi Christians may make an impact for God on war-torn Marxist Mozambique.
   d) **The Asian Community** of Indians and Tamil Sri Lankans is unreached. Only sporadic attempts are made to evangelize these Hindu and Muslim peoples.

8. **Bible and Christian literature distribution**. The Bible Society has a full programme in revising existing versions of the Bible. Only in Yao and Lomwe is there a need for further translation (of the OT) and completion of the NT in Sena. Literature is avidly sought after, but the cost prevents wider distribution.

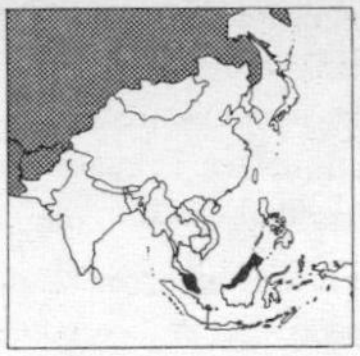

MALAYSIA
(The State of Malaysia)

Asia

July 21-22

Area 330,000 sq.km. Two distinct parts: Peninsular (West) Malaysia on the Kra peninsula of mainland Asia (**PM**), and East Malaysia (**EM**) consisting of the territories of Sarawak and Sabah on the northern third of the island of Borneo.

Population 15,700,000 (83% in **PM**). Annual growth 2.2%. People per sq.km. 48.

Peoples
Malay 48%. This figure includes some Muslim Orang Asli and all Indonesians (Javanese 136,000; Banjarese 45,000; Minangkabau 12,000, etc.). Predominantly rural, but influential in politics and civil service. A majority in **PM** only.
Chinese 36%. Speaking over 9 major dialects; majority Hokkien, Cantonese, Hakka and Teochew. Influential in commerce and business.
Indian 9%. Tamil 1,040,000; Punjabi 40,000; Malayali 36,000; Telugu 30,000, etc. Mainly poor estate workers or urban.
Orang Asli 7% ("Original People" tribal groups). In **PM** 75,000, **EM** 873,000 in about 80 tribes.

Literacy 59%. **Official language:** Malay. **All languages** 117. **Bible translations** 9Bi 9NT 12por.

Capital: Kuala Lumpur 1,397,000. Urbanization 35%. Chinese and Indian majority in urban areas.

Economy: Vigorous growth since independence through the development of oil, mining, agriculture and industry. Income/person $1,870 (13% of USA).

Politics: Independent from Britain in 1957 as the Federation of Malaya. Sabah and Sarawak joined to form the Federation of Malaysia in 1963. Recent years have been dominated by the efforts of the politically powerful Malays to extend their influence over the non-Malay half of the population in educational, economic and religious life. These have strained inter-ethnic relationships.

Religion: Sunni Islam is the official and favoured religion in **PM**, and there is continual pressure to apply the same in **EM** where Islam is a minority. It is illegal to proselytize Muslims, but considerable effort is expended to induce animistic tribal people and Chinese to become Muslim.
Muslim 53%. Malays, some Indians and a few ethnic minorities in **EM**.
Buddhist and Chinese religions 28%.
Hindu 7%. Almost entirely Indian.
Animist 3% (?). Many tribal animists are classified as "Muslim".
Non-religious/Atheist, **other** 3%.
Christian 7%. Affiliated 5%. The Church statistical situation is confusing and unclear for many denominations!

Roman Catholic 2.9%. Practising 60%. 460,000a; 244,000m. Mainly Chinese and Eurasian.
Marginal groups (6+) 0.1%. 14,500a.
Protestant 2%. 320,000a; 150,000m. Denominations 48. Largest (adult members):

S.I. Borneo (**OMF**)	50,000
Methodist Church	40,000
Anglican Church	20,000
Assemblies of God	7,500
Protestant Ch. of Sabah	7,200
Baptist Convention (**SBC**)	4,700
Christian Brethren	2,000

Evangelical 1.2% of population.

Missionaries to Malaysia est. 150, fairly rapid reduction in numbers.
Missionaries from within Malaysia est. 40 (1:8,000 Protestants) in 10 agencies.

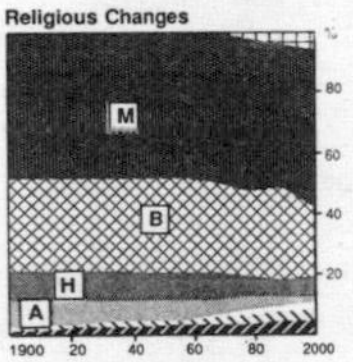

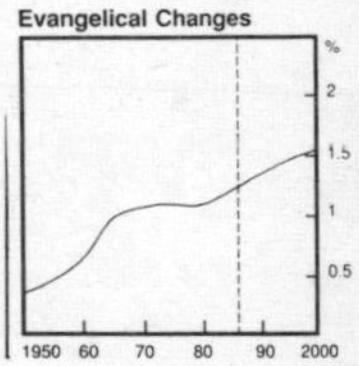

MALAYSIA – GENERAL

1. **The Muslim half of the population** has been politically and socially divided through an extremist minority pressing for radical Islamic reforms. This has brought stress to the whole country, an acceleration of Muslim missionary activities among non-Muslims and also discriminatory legislation and actions against non-Muslims. Pray for inter-racial harmony and true freedom of religion.

2. **A creeping erosion of freedom of religion by the Muslim authorities** has limited Christian activities and outreach. Many Chinese, Indian and tribal Christians have been over-intimidated by the turn of events. Pray that:

a) Believers may humbly, lovingly, but firmly stand for their heavenly right to proclaim the gospel.
b) Christians may obey God rather than man, even if this may mean discomfort or material loss.
c) There may be unity among churches in common matters affecting the practice and propagation of religion in the multiracial and multireligious Malaysian context. The Christian Federation of Malaysia formed in 1984 may help in this.

3. **Malay is now the only national language**, and all education is in this medium. This has forced non-Malay speaking congregations to adapt, Christian literature to be written in Malay, and the Bible to be translated and printed in modern Malay. Pray that this may help non-Malay Christians to make a greater impact on the unreached Malay people. The transition has been difficult for Christians, but presents great opportunity for the gospel.

4. **Leadership training** is of added importance as the missionary force declines. There are about 15 Bible schools or seminaries in the country (6 of these being of the **SIB** in **EM**). Too few are responding to the call to full-time work and many churches are without pastors.

5. **Christian literature** is widely available in English, and there are over 24 Christian bookshops, but there is very little available in the Malay language. Pray for writers, publishers and distributors of literature in this language, and for its effective dissemination to non-Christians. **The Bible Society** is legally recognized; pray for its ministry, and also for the wide acceptance and impact of the new Malay Bible.

6. **Young people** have been responsive in these years of flux and pressure. Agencies such as **YFC**, **CCC**, **Navigators**, **SU**, **IFES**, etc. have had a wide impact on school and university students. The rapid and painful change of education from English to Malay has brought stress to many. Pray that this may ultimately enhance the evangelization of all ethnic groups.

7. **Overseas students.** A large number of Malaysian Chinese and Indians are unable to obtain university places in the country, so they study overseas. Eighteen per cent of the Chinese become Christians during their period overseas, but relatively few become active for Jesus in their homeland after graduation.

8. **Missionaries are a dwindling force** because of decline in their numbers through the "10 year rule" and denial of visas for new workers. Pray for the most effective use of present missionaries and wise future strategies for tent-makers, short-termers, and visiting missionaries that will help the Church to greater maturity and outreach. Pray that these limitations may stimulate many believers in the country to volunteer for full-time service. The largest agencies are: **OMF** and **SBC**.

9. **Malaysian Christians are rising to the challenge of missions**. Some are serving as missionaries within Malaysia (Chinese in **PM** and tribal Christians of **EM**); others have moved overseas. Pray for the development of this vision in the churches and those preparing for, or who have gone into, missionary service. Their numbers must be multiplied to evangelize Malaysia's unreached peoples.

PENINSULAR MALAYSIA

Area 132,000 sq.km. or 40% of the nation.

Population 13,188,000.

Peoples
Malay 53%, **Chinese** 35.2%, **Indian** 10.5%, **Orang Asli** 0.65%. Senoi 40,000 and Proto-Malay (Jakun) 35,000; 14 tribes of Semang (Negrito) 2,200.

Religion: Muslim 56%, **Chinese/Buddhist** 31%, **Hindu** 8.4%, **Non-religious** 0.7%, **Christian** est. 3% (officially 2.1%).

1. **The Church is embattled** — externally with restrictive pressures on evangelism and construction of church buildings, and internally through materialism, inability to adapt to rapid Malayanization and industrialization. Pray for greater liberality by both federal and state

governments in granting sites for church buildings. Many young people backslide through non-Christian family pressures. Pray for revival and emphasis on biblical priorities. The majority of Christians are Chinese, though a higher proportion of Indians (8.4%) are Christian.

2. **Unreached peoples.** The task of reaching the many unreached must now be a Malaysian responsibility; the potential in human and financial resources are there! Pray for:

a) **Malays who cannot be evangelized by normal means.** The few hundred Malays who have believed have suffered social ostracism, loss of legal rights, privileges, jobs etc.; and some have had to leave the country. There is more openness among urban Malays and those living in S.Thailand and Singapore, but few Christians are actively reaching out to them. Pray for Christians to tactfully, but fearlessly, share the Good News with them. Malay Christians meet together in some house groups or in multi-ethnic churches, but there are no viable Malay churches. Pray for the right evangelistic and church planting strategy to be revealed and applied.

b) **The Chinese.** The **PM** Chinese have been far less responsive than those in **EM**; materialism and traditional religions are strong. Only 3.5% are Christian, the majority being RC. Presbyterian and Pentecostal denominations are growing, but mostly among the urban middle-class English-speaking Chinese. There are no churches using Hainanese (200,000 people), and the Hakka, Teochew and Kwongsai are little better served. Rural and small town Chinese are patchily evangelized. There is religious freedom, but few are using present opportunities for witness and church planting.

c) **Orang Asli** have, in the main, been untouched by the gospel because of Malay opposition and the lack of vision of Christians. Yet most of the Orang Asli tribes dislike Islam and its restrictions and remain bound by animism. Methodists and Lutherans have planted a number of churches among the Senoi, who are now about 20% Christian. Many peoples need translations of the Scripture.

d) **Indians.** There are many Tamil Christians, but few among the poor estate labourers. Other Indian ethnic minorities are unreached — Punjabis (mostly Sikh) with 62 known believers, Telugus etc. The Indian Muslims number some 50,000; there has been no specific outreach to them. The Tamil Bible Institute (**AsEF**) is training Christian workers to reach Indian communities with the gospel.

SABAH (formerly North Borneo)

Area 81,000. Wealthy and underpopulated.

Population 1,208,000. Annual increase (3.8%) high due to immigration of Muslim Moros from Philippines and Indonesians.

Peoples: Languages 53; **Kadazan** 28%, **Chinese** 21%. **Bajau** 11.4%, **other tribal peoples** 18.6%, **Immigrants** etc. 15% (mostly Muslim), **Malay** 6%.

Religion: Muslim 51%, **Christian** 27%, **Animist** 10%, **Non-religious** etc. 12%.

1. **The inter-ethnic and inter-religious tensions have been acute.** Crude and forceful Muslim proselytism among the indigenous peoples and favoured immigration to Muslims from surrounding lands did not help, though a non-Muslim coalition government was elected in 1984. Pray for the breaking down of satanic opposition to the gospel.

2. **Churches have grown rapidly** among the Chinese, Kadazan and other tribal peoples through the work of the Basel Mission, Anglicans and **BEM**. The **SIB** has over 210 congregations in Sabah. Nominalism, the drift to the cities of tribal peoples and serious lack of full-time workers, are unresolved problems for the churches.

3. **Unreached peoples:**

a) **The Muslims** are untouched — the coastal Bajau 137,000; Filipino Moros 120,000; Indonesians; Malays. Local Christians need much grace and courage to overcome the cultural, political and religious barriers to reach them.

b) **Some tribal groups**, such as the Kadazan and Dusun, arc only partially evangelized, though there have been large people movements among them. Few languages have a NT, but **SIL** has 14 teams of translators working in Sabah. Pray for them. There are virtually no other missionary personnel left.

SARAWAK

Area 121,000 sq.km.

Population 1,508,000.

Peoples: Indigenous peoples 50%, **Chinese** 30%, **Malay** 19%.

Religion: Christian 29%, **Muslim** 26%, **Animist** 33%, **Non-religious** etc. 12%.

1. **Sarawak has experienced a series of thrilling movements of the Spirit over the last 50 years.** Through the work of **BEM-OMF** and others, people movements and revivals have taken place in many tribes. The **SIB** daughter church has over 240 congregations, six Bible schools and a work in more than 10 peoples, with a vigorous outreach to towns and unreached peoples. Praise God for this and pray for a retention of the spirit of revival in the up-and-coming generation. The coastal churches among the Chinese are more nominal, though nearly half the Chinese now profess to be Christians.

2. **The Church is under pressure** through materialism in the towns and severe pressure from Muslims in some rural areas. Pray that believers may not only stand firm in their faith, but become more bold in their witness. Pray that many young people may be called and adequately supported in full-time service. Pray also that as missionary support is reduced, the leadership in the churches may be able to handle the complexities of national politics and the nurture of churches scattered over a land with many transport difficulties outside the towns.

3. **Unreached peoples:**

   a) **The Muslims in the coastal areas** are not open to the gospel, but many Chinese and indigenous Christians live around them.

   b) **The Sea Dayaks (Iban) and Melanau** have begun to respond to the gospel after years of indifference or nominal commitment to Christianity, but Christians and Christian workers are too few to make use of present opportunities.

   c) There are many smaller groups that are unevangelized.

Asia

July 23

MALDIVES

(Republic of Maldives)

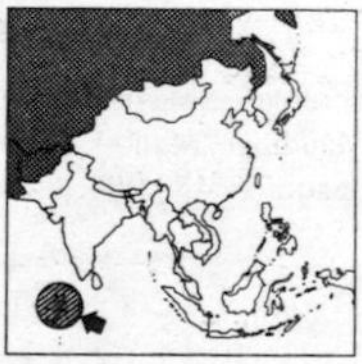

Area 298 sq.km. Twelve clusters of 1,200 coral atolls 600 km. southwest of Sri Lanka, 202 of which are inhabited.

Population 177,000. Annual growth 3%. People per sq.km. 594.

Peoples: Maldivian, a people of Sinhalese origin. Small minorities of Indian, Sri Lankan, etc.

Literacy 41%. **Official language:** Divehi, related to Sinhalese, but with its own script.

Capital: Malé 30,000. Urbanization 20%.

Economy: Fishing and tourism are important. Lack of fertile soil and fresh water, and the high population density keep the people at subsistence level. Income/person $180 (1% of USA).

Politics: Long tradition of isolated independence. The nominal British protectorate terminated in 1965. Republic since 1968. The government cultivates international links with Islamic and non-aligned nations.

Religion: Islam is the only recognized religion, and the government is committed to greater Islamization both as an end in itself and as a means of preserving national unity.

Muslim: Officially 100%.

Christian: A handful of Sri Lankan, Indian and other expatriates.

1. **Are the Maldivians the least evangelized people on earth**? There are no Scriptures available, no Christian radio programmes, there have never been any resident missionaries, and there are no known Maldivian Christians on the islands.

2. **There is a deep suspicion of Christianity** which has been enhanced by tactless actions of Christians in the past. Pray for the removal of prejudices, and for the true message of Christ to be heard and understood.

3. **There are a few expatriate Christians residing in the country** as professionals or supervising aid programmes. Some have a personal faith; pray that they may earn opportunities to tactfully share it.

4. **Maldivians travel to other lands** as sailors, students, etc. Communities of Maldivians live in several Indian and Sri Lankan coastal cities. Pray that ways and means may be found to bring some to Christ.

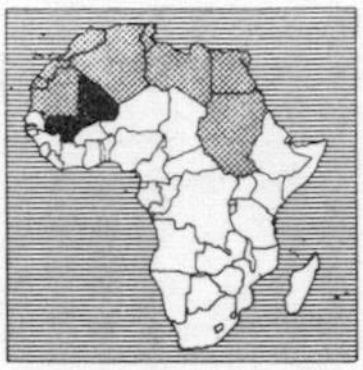

MALI
(Republic of Mali)

Africa

July 24-25

Area 1,240,000 sq.km. Landlocked state. Dry southern grasslands merge into the advancing Sahara Desert.

Population 7,700,000. Annual growth 2.8%. People per sq.km. 6.

Peoples: 35 ethnic groups.
West African peoples 93%. Bambara 2,500,000, the dominant people of Mali; Fulani 1,000,000; Soninké (Sarakulé) 593,000; Songhay 477,000; Mandingo/Maninka 470,000; Dogon 447,000; Senoufo 439,000; Minianka 308,000; Bobo 154,000; Kassonké 115,000; Bozo 77,000.
Other 7%. Tuareg 385,000; Maure (Hassaniya) 123,000.

Literacy 11%. **Official language:** French. **Trade languages:** Bambara, Fulani. **All languages** 21. **Bible translations** 2Bi 3NT 5por.

Capital: Bamako 750,000. Urbanization 18%.

Economy: At best a poor agricultural land, but prolonged droughts since 1970 have devastated the country and caused massive population movements and suffering. Famine aid has not produced long-term improvement. Income/person $150 (1% of USA).

Politics: The modern descendant of the great Malian empire. Independent from France in 1960. A one-party republic that has moved from a state controlled system to a more free market economy. The stresses caused by drought and famine could bring instability.

Religion: Freedom of religion is staunchly maintained by the government despite Muslim pressures to stop Christian missionary work.
Muslim 81%. Slowly increasing.
Traditional religions 17%. Strongest among the Dogon, Bobo, Minianka and Senoufo peoples in the southeast and east.
Christian 1.7%.
Roman Catholic 1.1%. 88,000a.
Protestant 0.58%. 45,000a; 17,000m. Denominations 9. Largest (adherents):

Alliance Church (**CMA**)	32,000
Evangelical Prot. Church (**GMU**)	11,000
Prot. Church of Kayes (**UWM**)	850
Evangelical Baptist Church	100

Evangelical 0.58% of population.
Missionaries to Mali 160 (1:48,000 people) in 14 agencies.

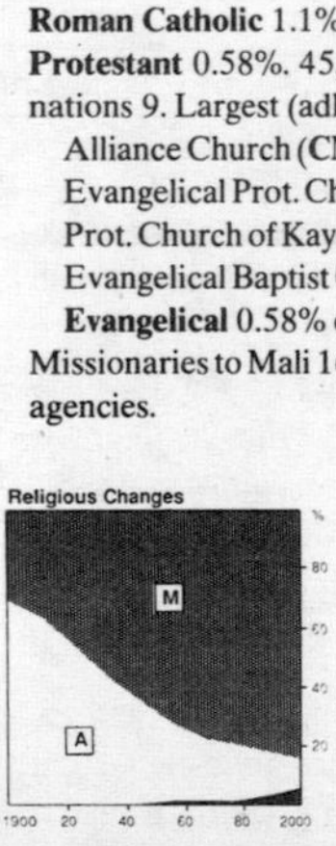

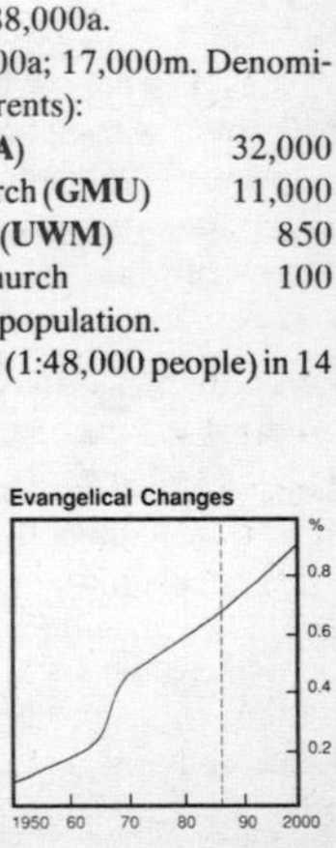

1. **This land is wide open for the gospel**; missionaries are welcome, but the labourers are so few. For years there were only four Protestant missions — **GMU** in the centre among the Bambara, **CMA** in the east among the Dogon, Bobo, Minianka and Senoufo, **UWM** in the west among the Maninka and Evangelical Baptists in the north among the Songhay. Only in the **GMU** and **CMA** areas have strong churches emerged. Other missions have entered since 1980, but this is still a needy pioneer field. Major mission agencies: **CMA** (35 workers), **GMU** (30), Ev. Baptist (20), **UWM** (13), **RSMT** (13), **CRWM** (8).

2. **The Sahel Famine has been a major disaster. Famine relief given by Christians has brought an openness to the gospel and an increasing response.** Yet political change or Muslim pressure could alter this. Pray that present opportunities may not be lost by default. Pray for agencies involved in famine relief (**WV, SBC**, as well as the church planting missions listed above) that they may contribute both to the long-term wellbeing of the people and to the planting of churches.

3. **Although Christians are concentrated in only five ethnic groups, there is vigour and growth.** The turning to God has been most dramatic among the Dogon and Bobo. Only 10% of believers are from the Muslim majority. Material poverty limits funds for training and supporting pastors. The Bible schools in the country are therefore struggling. Seventy per cent of believers are illiterate. Pray for the rapid growth of believers in maturity and numbers in this day of opportunity. Pray for a decisive breakthrough among the more Muslim peoples.

4. **The unreached peoples of Mali**. Only three peoples are more than 1% Christian — Bobo (8% Protestant), Dogon (3.5%) and Minianka (2.4%). These are the least Muslim of Mali's peoples.
Pray for:

a) **The Bambara** are key people for the evangelization of the country, yet they are only 0.3% Protestant. Pray for the work of **GMU**, and more recently, **CMA** and **AoG** among these people. Pray for the Bambara Church. There have been breakthroughs for the gospel since 1974, with 2,500 turning to the Lord in Nonkon, north of Bamako; but follow up is an urgent need in the light of the activity of syncretic indigenous cults in the area.

b) There have been the beginnings of a response with a few Christians among the **Maninka (UWM), Songhay** (EB) and **Senoufo (CMA).**

c) Pioneer work among the **Soninké** and **Maure (RSMT), Fulani** (Norwegian Lutherans, **CRWM, CMA**), and Senoufo (**CMA**) is being undertaken, often using rural clinics and development help at village level as a means of contact with the people.

d) **Peoples not yet occupied by Christian workers** number 12. Namely the Guinea Manenka 200,000; Diawara 120,000 (among the Soninke); Manenka-Kita 75,000; Kagoro 60,000; Fulanka 55,000, etc.

e) **The Niger inland delta fishermen**, the Bozo 80,000 and Somono 50,000 are Muslim, and there are no known Christians.

f) **The Tuaregs** have been made destitute by the famine and have lived on the political margin of society since independence. This proud Berber people have suffered much, but there is no Christian presence among them.

g) **Bamako** is a growing city, and more church planting should be initiated (**GMU, CMA** and others).

5. **Help ministries**.

a) **Bible translation**. At least seven languages may need translation teams, and work is in progress in six. **SIL** has three teams in the southeast of Mali.

b) **Cassette tapes** are a vital evangelistic and teaching tool, and greatly appreciated. **GRI** has recordings in 25 dialects and languages.

c) **Christian programmes on Radio Bamako** and through ELWA (**SIM**) have a wide audience, and have opened many unreached villages to the gospel. From 1985 onwards Television Mali has offered Christians regular free TV time.

d) **Literature**. **GMU** has a literature ministry in the capital and **CMA** in Kontiala. Pray for literacy programmes, and production of suitable reading materials in the various indigenous languages as well as for Bambara Christian literature.

MALTA
(Republic of Malta)

The West

July 26

Area 316 sq.km. Three small but strategic islands in the central Mediterranean.

Population 365,000. Annual growth 0.8%. People per sq.km. 1,157.

Peoples: Maltese 97%. **Other** 3%. Italian 5,000; British 1,000; Libyan 1,000.

Literacy 90%. **Official languages:** Maltese, English. Maltese is related to Arabic.

Capital: Valletta 16,000. Urbanization 85%.

Economy: Tourism and light industry are important. Unemployment 20%. Income/person $3,710 (26% of USA).

Politics: Independent from Britain in 1964. Parliamentary republic since 1974. The socialist government has emphasized nonalignment in international affairs.

Religion: The Catholic Church is the State Church, and very influential but in bitter confrontation with the socialist government. This conflict has resulted in greater freedom of religion than ever before.
Non-religious/Atheist 2%.
Muslim 0.2%. Libyans, etc.
Christian 97.5%. Affiliated 95%.
Roman Catholic 94%. Practising 80%. 337,000a.
Marginal groups (5) 0.14%. Jehovah's Witnesses 500a.
Protestant 0.42%. 1,500a. Denominations 5. Expatriates 1,460a. Maltese 40a.
Evangelical 0.05% of population.
Missionaries to Malta 3 (1:120,000 people).

1. **Malta is possibly free Europe's least evangelized land**, despite being probably the first nation to embrace the gospel — after Paul's shipwreck on the island. Few have ever heard a clear presentation of the gospel and come to a living faith, although a high degree of religious devotion is shown by so many.

2. **Protestant activity among Maltese was illegal before 1964**. There is still much opposition to the preaching of the gospel, and any activities of this kind are still undermined. There are those in authority who have shown friendship for the cause of the gospel. Pray that this, and the widespread disillusionment among the younger generation with the hypocrisy of traditional Christianity, may open the land and its people to the message of Life. Some are turning to the JWs.

3. **The few Maltese believers** are associated with a little Gospel Hall and an Assembly of God Church. Pray that these little groups and their leaders may grow and prosper. Catholic charismatic groups that studied the Scriptures have been pressurized by the hierarchy and have dwindled to become quite ineffective.

4. **The Malta Mission was founded in 1982**. This agency is committed to evangelizing the islands and helping the Maltese believers. A quickening pace of evangelistic crusades and literature evangelism (Christian literature has been placed in every home) have led to conversions. Pray for lasting fruit and continued government permission for these and the entry of missionaries. For the first time there are now several resident missionaries on the islands. Hitherto Christian workers have only been able to make occasional visits.

5. **New converts find it difficult** to integrate and identify with the despised little groups of believers. Pray for the combined outreach of believers as they witness by means of door-to-door evangelism and informal meetings in homes.

6. **The Maltese Bible was published in 1980.** There has been widespread interest, but pray that people may read it and be drawn to real faith in Christ. Newspaper advertisements for the Bible and the widespread distribution of NTs by the Gideons are bearing fruit.

7. **Christian literature** is very limited in quantity and variety. Pray for an effective Christian literature centre. A "Way of Salvation" Bible Correspondence Course is now legally advertised and circulated by the Malta Mission.

8. **Many Maltese have emigrated to other lands:** Australia 100,000; Britain 40,000; Canada 20,000, etc. Pray that they may be won to Christ, and that some of these may return to their homeland with the gospel.

Caribbean

July 27

MARTINIQUE

See Guadeloupe on p. 198.

Middle East

July 28

MAURITANIA
(Islamic Republic of Mauritania)

Area 1,031,000 sq.km. The land is entirely desert except for the north bank of the Senegal River on the southern border.

Population 1,890,000. Annual growth 2.9%. People per sq.km. 2. 75% nomadic in 1970, now 25% because of drought.

Peoples
Maures 75%. A mixed Arab/Berber people speaking Hassaniya Arabic. A predominantly pastoral or trading people. Black Maures or Haratine are slaves or descendants of slaves and form half of the Maure population.
Berber 1.5%. Zenaga and some Tuareg.
Black African 23%. Toukoulor 180,000; Fula 100,000; Soninké 50,000; Wolof 10,000; Masna (speaking Aouker) 7,000. Most are settled farmers in the south and despised by Maures.
Other 0.5%. French, Senegalese, Togolese, etc.

Literacy 17%. **National language:** Arabic. **Official language:** French. **All languages** 6. **Bible translations** 1Bi 1por.

Capital: Nouakchott 500,000. Urbanization 30%.

Economy: By 1985, 14 years of severe drought had devastated the economy. Earnings from abundant minerals and fishing limited by corruption. Income/person $440 (3% of USA).

Politics: Independent from France in 1960. Military government and a long series of military coups that are a continuation of Maure tribal warfare. The tensions between the growing Haratine and Black population and the dominant White Maures could portend more violence.

Religion: Islamic state; no proselytizing of Muslims permitted.
Muslim 99.6%. All Sunni.
Christian 0.2%. All expatriates, no Mauritanian Christians in the country.
Roman Catholic 0.2%. About 4,000 Black Africans and French.
Protestant. About 25 Black African and European believers.

1. **There is not one indigenous Mauritanian believer or church in the country.** Everything seems against a change: Islam entrenched for 1,000 years, low literacy level, no Scriptures, no radio broadcasts in Hassaniya Arabic, and laws that forbid any Mauritanian to renounce Islam. The "strong man" must be bound. There *will* be a redeemed people from this land!

2. **Expatriate Christians** have opportunities for technical and professional employment, but economic, climatic and spiritual conditions are harsh. Pray for all seeking to live for Christ. May they see the planting of a Mauritanian Church. Fellowship opportunities are limited.

3. **Mauritanians live in Senegal** (70,000), **Mali** (90,000), **Ivory Coast, etc.** Their numbers are swelling through the addition of drought refugees. Only in Senegal has the first definite ministry to them begun (**WEC**). Only two or three Mauritanian believers are known in all W. Africa.

4. **Unreached minorities:**
   a) The restive **Haratine**.
   b) The desert **Masna** people of central Mauritania.
   c) **The Senegal River Valley peoples:** Wolof, Toukoulor, Fula, Kasonke, Soninke. Christian work among them in Senegal and Mali is in its infancy, and there are no churches yet planted.

MAURITIUS
(The Dominion of Mauritius)

Africa

July 29-30

Area 2,045 sq.km. One larger and three smaller islands in the Western Indian Ocean 800 km. east of Madagascar. Rodriguez Island is 500 km. to the east.

Population 993,000. Annual growth 1.4%. People per sq.km. 486.

Peoples: No indigenous peoples; all immigrants.
Indians 66%. Over 20 original home languages, largest: Hindi 214,000; Bhojpuri 186,000; Tamil 70,000; Urdu 60,000; Telugu 27,000; Marathi 22,000. Politically dominant.
Creole 29%. Mixed African and European.
European 3.6%. French 33,000; British 2,000; Other 600. Controlling most of larger businesses and sugar estates.
Chinese 2.1%. Prominent in retail trade. Majority Hakka, minorities of Cantonese and Mandarin speakers.

Literacy 89%. **Official language:** English, yet the French culture and language is dominant. The most widely spoken language is French Creole. **All languages** 48.

Capital: Port Louis 169,000. Urbanization 44%.

Economy: Heavily dependent on tourism, production and export of sugar. Agricultural and industrial diversification is being encouraged. Over-population is a major problem. Income/person $1,150 (8% of USA).

Politics: Independent from Britain in 1968 as a parliamentary democracy within the Commonwealth. A French colony until 1810. The political power of the majority Indian community is resented by the Creoles, and inter-ethnic tensions are not far under the surface.

Religion: Freedom of religion tempered by strong tendency for Indianization, and, by implication, Hinduism. All religious and missionary activity directed to evangelizing Hindus is regarded with disfavour.
Hindu 49.6%. A large variety of sects.
Muslim 16.6%. Mostly Indian Sunnis, with some Shi'a and Ahmaddiya.
Buddhist/Chinese religions 0.5%, **Non-religious** etc. 2%.
Christian 31.3%.
Roman Catholic 26.7%. 265,000a; 143,000m. Creoles, French and most Chinese.
Protestant 4.6%. 45,200a; 22,100m. Denominations (11). Largest (adherents):

Assemblies of God	32,000
Anglican Church	5,500
Seventh Day Adventist Church	3,200
Presbyterian Church	610

Evangelical 3.5% of population.
Missionaries to Mauritius 15 (1:66,000 people) in 7 agencies.

1. **Mauritius has been a forgotten mission field**. The evangelization of the Indian majority has only just begun and is difficult to achieve with limitations on the entry of missionaries.

2. **Strong ethnic and religious loyalties hinder the progress of the gospel**. To the Indians conversion to Christianity is a step loaded with political and ethnic overtones — of "becoming a Creole". Pray for wise and effective strategies to reach out to the 490,000 Hindus and 160,000 Muslims in both Creole and the Indian languages used by the older people.

3. **Most older churches are in gradual decline**, and are traditional and nominal. The charismatic movement made a big impact for a while on the RC Church and the Anglicans, but most of those converted have now formed their own groups. Few really have a personal faith in Christ.

4. **Evangelical Christians** are predominantly Pentecostal. The Assemblies of God have grown rapidly and now have 70 congregations. However, numerous splits, doctrinal extremes and immature, untaught leadership have been problems. There are also a number of smaller evangelical congregations — notably three linked with **AEF**, two with the Southern Baptists and several Presbyterian congregations. There are few trained and effective Mauritian evangelical leaders.

5. **There is a great openness among young people**. They are less bound by ethnic loyalties, and there are exciting opportunities for witness among them in the multiracial schools. Many have been touched by the gospel but are held back from open commitment by family pressures and from liberal church leaders. **Youth For Christ** has a good outreach through youth centres, and **IFES** and **CCC** are linked with small evangelical groups in the university. There are too few labourers for the responsive age group.

6. **Missionary work is limited**. Numbers of workers should be increased, but visa restrictions need to be relaxed. The great need is for church planters, disciplers and Bible teachers to mobilize Mauritian believers in effective evangelism. **AEF** has five missionaries in the land.

7. **Specific unreached minorities:**
   a) **The Muslims**. There are only one or two known believers, and no specific outreach to them.
   b) **Rodriguez Island Creoles** are 98% Catholic. **AEF** and the Assemblies of God have recently commenced outreach to them.
   c) **The upper-class French community** of 33,000. Nominally Catholic; very few committed believers.
   d) **Major Indian languages** are Bhojpuri, Hindi and Urdu, all representing large unreached language groups in India. Little evangelism is done in these languages.
   e) **The Chinese community** has become largely Catholic. Evangelical believers number only around 200 in three to four congregations of the Sino-Mauritian Evangelical Church and Chinese Christian Fellowship.

8. **Help ministries:**
   a) **The Bible Society** has a vital role in distributing the Scriptures in all the island territories of the Indian Ocean — Seychelles, Reunion, Comores, etc.
   b) **There is only one Christian bookshop (AEF)**; a greater distribution of pre-evangelism and discipleship literature is a big need.
   c) **Christian radio broadcasts** from **FEBA** Seychelles are beamed to Mauritius; 21 hours per month in French and in Indian languages.

MAYOTTE

See Comores on p. 147.

MEXICO
(The United Mexican States)

Latin America

July 31-Aug 2

Area 1,973,000 sq.km. Latin America's fourth largest country. Much of the country is arid or semi-arid; only 11% of the land is arable.

Population 80,484,000. Annual growth 2.9%. People per sq.km. 41. Massive illegal emigration to USA hardly alleviates the explosive population growth. Five million Mexicans live in the USA, increasing by 800,000 illegals per year.

Peoples
Spanish/Amerindian (Mestizo) 55%.
Amerindian 29%. 21.3% speaking Spanish only. Six million Indians still speak 236 languages. Major groupings: Aztec 4,800,000; Maya 2,700,000; Otomi 2,100,000; Zapotec 1,800,000; Mixtec 1.600,000; Totonac 240,000; Mazahua 160,000; Mazatec 160,000, etc.
Spanish and other European 15.3%.
African origin 0.5%. **Other** 0.2%.
Central American refugees 150,000.

Literacy 80%. **Official language:** Spanish, the world's largest Spanish-speaking nation. **All languages** 237. **Bible translations** 2Bi 71NT 41por.

Capital: Mexico City 18,535,000. Other cities: Guadalajara 3,483,000; Monterrey 2,622,000; Puebla 1,022,000. Urbanization 72%.

Economy: Mixed but increasingly dependent on oil since 1975. Rapid population growth and overspending of new wealth led to massive international debts ($85 billion in 1985). The radical correctives imposed have increased unemployment to 40% and inflation to 80% with a rise in urban and rural poverty. The collapse of oil prices and the earthquake that damaged Mexico City in 1985 have postponed the likelihood of early economic recovery. Income/person $2,250 (16% of USA).

Politics: Independent from Spain in 1821. Republic with what is virtually a one-party democracy since 1910. Increasing social pressures for political change.

Religion: Secular state with freedom of conscience and practice of religion, but with careful legal controls on Catholics, Protestants and others.
Non-religious/Atheist 3.4%.
Jews 0.1%, 57,000; **Baha'i** 28,000; **Muslim** 25,000.
Christian 96.4%. Nominal 4%. Affiliated 92.4%. Doubly affiliated 2.4%.

Roman Catholic 88% (officially 90.5%, but with many defections to other beliefs). 70,800,000a; 37,500,000m.

Marginal groups (16) 1%. Largest (adherents):

Jehovah's Witnesses	388,000
Mormons	295,000

Protestant 4%. 3,200,000a; 1,300,000m. Denominations 250. Largest (adult members):

Union of Ind. Evangelicals (Pente.)	270,000
Seventh Day Adventist Church	210,000
Assemblies of God	120,000
Baptist (SBC)	65,000
Presbyterian Church	53,000
Church of God (Cleveland)	29,000
Church of the Nazarene	21,700

Evangelical 3.1% of population.

Missionaries to Mexico 1,700 (1:47,000 people) in 84 agencies.

Missionaries from Mexico approx. 98 (1:33,000 Protestants) in 3+ agencies.

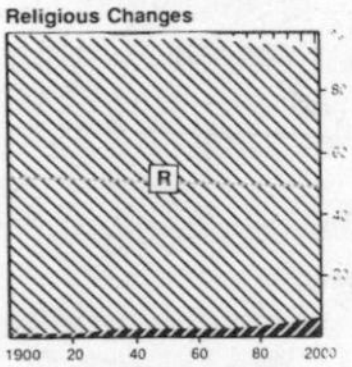

1. **This dynamic, growing nation is searching for an identity** in its Hispanic and Indian roots. This leads to a fierce nationalism and demonstrations of independence from its large northern neighbour, the USA. This is often expressed in anti-Protestant populist propaganda. Pray that Mexicans may find their true identity in a personal faith in Christ.

2. **The deep economic crisis together with the population explosion** could precipitate chaos. It is reckoned that nearly half of the 35 million children suffer from the devastating effects of malnutrition and promiscuity. Pray for the government as it seeks to grapple with endemic corruption, the debt crisis, unemployment and the unfulfilled expectations of the poor. Pray that these situations may break down prejudices to the message of the gospel.

3. **The Roman Catholic Church** lost its political and economic power in the 1910 revolution but retains a visible cultural dominance. Most Mexicans are culturally Catholic but still bound by sin, narrow traditionalism and syncretic religious practices. The power of the ancient gods and spirit world has yet to be broken in the Spanish-speaking majority and, more especially, in the Christo-pagan Indian minority groups.

4. **The growth of Evangelicals has been dramatic over the last two decades** — as the above graph shows. Much of this growth has been among the lower classes, urban migrants and some Indian tribes in the southeast. Along the northern border and Caribbean coastal states there is scarcely a town or village without an evangelical witness. Aggressive evangelism by local churches; crusades of Billy Graham, Luis Palau, and others; and people movements among Indian groups have multiplied congregations. Pray for:
   a) Bold new initiatives planned for the last years of the '80s.
   b) Retention and maturing of new converts to become committed disciples of Christ.
   c) A greater spiritual fellowship and unity in the complex and fragmented evangelical church.

5. **Persecution, war and economic depression** all hindered evangelism and church growth until the 1940s. There has been rapid growth of indigenous and mission-related churches since then, with the most marked growth among Pentecostals and SDAs. During the '80s the growth has attracted negative attacks in the press. Evangelicals are portrayed as anti-Mexican spies or destroyers of Mexican culture and unity. Pray that believers may demonstrate the meekness and love of their Saviour.

6. **Leadership training is the key to the future health of the Church.** There are over 100 Bible schools and seminaries training thousands of future leaders at all levels; from tribal languages to degree-awarding schools, as well as numerous TEE programmes. Pray that spiritual depth as well as sound teaching may be imparted to the students. Doctrinal shallowness, error and also moral and personal relationship breakdowns have impaired the growth of the Church.

7. **The missionary vision of the Mexican Church** has only begun to take off during the '80s. Pray for the growth and nurture of this burden. Most Mexican missionaries come from independent Pentecostal churches.

8. **Foreign missionaries'** legal position is both ambiguous and restrictive. Visas have been a battle to obtain. Almost all are US citizens, so they need great sensitivity and tact in their cultural adaptation to overcome the perceived disadvantages of their origin and wealth. Openings are many for missionaries in children's and youth work, evangelism and church planting, and especially in leadership training. The largest agencies in Spanish-speaking work are **CCC** (153 workers), **SB** (86), **CAMI** (63), Baptist Bible Fellowship (58), **GMU** (19), and in Indian work **SIL** (303) and **NTM** (68). Pray that their ministries may assist the Church to be what God desires. Mexico could be a fruitful field for Asian and Latin missionaries.

9. **Unreached peoples and areas:**
   a) There are few strong churches in the **central states** Sinaloa, Durango, Zakatekas, Nayarit, Jalisco, Michoacan; the **southern Pacific coast states** of Oaxaca and Guerrero; and the **Yucatan peninsula** in the east.
   b) **Many Indian peoples** are resistant or unresponsive with only a handful of believers. Vital church planting ministries must be expanded to build on the impressive Scripture translation programme of **SIL**. Pray for efficient research and analysis of the need for church planting by Mexican and foreign workers, especially in Oaxaca and Yucatan. Pray for the expanding work of **NTM** in four tribes as well as for the extensive work of the Presbyterians and others. There may be as many as 100 ethnically isolated Indian peoples without a viable indigenous church.
   c) **The many conservative Catholic towns and cities** where evangelical witness is limited and introverted.
   d) **The capital, Mexico City,** with its concentration of abysmally poor and little-evangelized slum dwellers. These six million people increase by the addition of 1,600 new immigrants daily.
   e) **The Guatemalan and Salvadorean refugees.**

10. **Outreach to students** has become exciting, but how small are present efforts in the face of the need! There are over one million tertiary-level students in the country — 150,000 in Mexico City alone. Pray for the wide-ranging ministries of **CCC** (on campuses and among churches), for **IFES**, and also for outreach to high school students.

11. **Christian broadcasting** has been forbidden to Evangelicals since 1980. Pray for expanded programming beamed into Mexico from stations in the USA and Central American border areas and from **TWR** in Bonaire, Netherlands Antilles (p. 315). Building up audiences and follow up ministries is not easy, so may God give the increase.

12. **Bible translation and distribution.** Pray for the praiseworthy printing and distribution work of the **Bible Society** in both Spanish and Indian languages. There remains much translation work to be completed. No Indian language has the whole Bible in print (several are in preparation). One hundred and twelve languages have at least one book of the Bible, 71 have New Testaments. Pray for the notable work of **SIL** since 1936, with 62 New Testaments completed, 86 in translation and with 51 languages yet to be tackled. Their work is under vitriolic attack by secular humanists, anthropologists and some Catholic leaders — pray that their objective of the New Testament in every language may be obtained, and visas provided for workers to achieve this.

13. **Supportive ministries** — to mention a few:

a) **Gospel Recordings** have messages available in 180 of the 236 languages, a vital tool in the complex linguistic situation. Pray for recordists, new recordings, wide distribution and eternal fruit.

b) **MAF** has a key role in the mountainous and inaccessible regions of the southern part of the country.

c) **Literature** has been hard hit by the serious state of the economy. Few can afford expensive literature. Less than 5% of all literature is written by Latin Americans.

14. **Migrant Mexican labour in California and other border states of the USA** has long been a feature of national life. Their numbers are unknown but may be as many as six to eight million (many illegals). There are many opportunities for them to hear the gospel. Pray for evangelistic and church planting work in Spanish by **CAMI**, **GMU** and many denominational workers in these areas.

Pacific

Aug 3

MICRONESIA

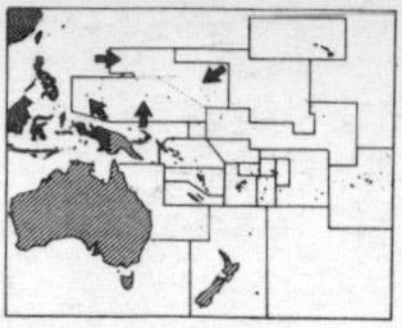

Area 1,950 sq.km. 2,000 islands of the Caroline, Marshall and Mariana archipelagos in 7 million sq.km. of the N. Pacific. 100 are inhabited.

Population 155,000. Annual growth 2.8%. People per sq.km. 80.

Peoples
Micronesian 87%. Speaking 14 languages.
Chamorro 11%. Mixed race Micronesians.
Polynesian 1%. Speaking two languages.
Other 1%. US Citizens, Chinese.

Literacy 90%. **Official language:** English. **All languages** 17. **Bible translations** 1Bi 5NT 2por.

Economy: Coconuts, agriculture and tourism. Very small scattered islands that have not been adequately developed since 1945. Much poverty and frustration on the part of local inhabitants at the neglect of the US administration. Income/person $1,000 (7% of USA).

Politics: US administration under UN Trusteeship (1947-78). Four self-governing states; one of which is a federation of a further four micro-states. Full independence from or free association with the USA is being discussed.

Name	Area (sq.km.)	Population	Capital
Belau	460	14,000	Koror
Fed. States of Micronesia (Yap, Truk, Ponape, Kosrae)	830	86,000	Kolonia
Marshall Islands	180	36,000	Majuro
N. Marianas	480	19,000	Saipan

Religion: Complete separation of church and state, and freedom of religion.
Other religions 2.6%.
Christian 97.5%. Nominal 7.7%. Affiliated 89.2%.
Roman Catholic 45.2%. 70,000a; 38,190m.
Indigenous and foreign marginal groups (4) 5.6%. 8,700a.
Protestant 38.4%. 59,500a; 30,900m. Denominations 12. Largest (adult members):

Prot. Church of E. Truk	10,850
Prot. Ch. in Caroline Is. (Liebenzell)	8,000
United Ch. of Christ in Ponape	7,100
Assemblies of God	5,842
United Church in Marshall Is.	1,350

Evangelical 19% of population.
Missionaries to Micronesia 48 (1:3,200 people) in 10 agencies. Some missionaries based in Guam serve Micronesia.

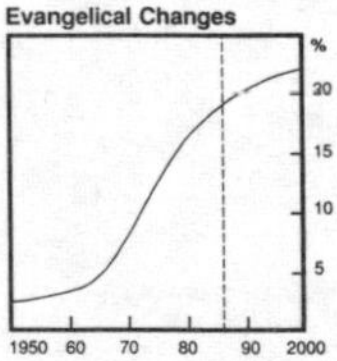

1. **Although Christianized for a century or more,** many small island communities need spiritual help. The great distances and poor communications hamper all evangelistic, pastoral and literature distribution work. Pray for Christians seeking to serve these isolated peoples.

2. **Evangelical missions.** Most noteworthy is the work of **Liebenzell Mission** with 18 missionaries working in Belau and the Fed. Rep. of Micronesia; also the more recent work of **AoG** in the Marianas and Marshalls. The people have often been unresponsive, but churches are growing through these ministries. The **AoG** has three Bible schools and **Liebenzell** one. Christian workers for many island communities are few.

3. **The Bible Society,** based in Guam, has performed a remarkable service in initiating new translation projects, revising archaic Scripture portions and providing new reader scriptures. Pray for translators, consultants and distributors of God's Word. At least six other language groups will need NT translations.

4. **Christian radio. FEBC** has built a powerful station on Saipan, with eight expatriate workers, for broadcasting to the USSR and E.Asia and to the local Chamorro people. Pray for this growing, but expensive, project — that there might be much fruit for eternity.

MONACO

(The Principality of Monaco)

The West

Aug 4

Area 1.5 sq.km. The second smallest state in the world. On France's south coast.

Population 27,000. Annual growth 0.8%. People per sq.km. 18,000. Annual influx of 600,000 tourists.

Peoples: Moneqasque 15%, **French** 58%, **Italian** 16.6%, **Other** 10.4%.

Literacy 99%. **Official language:** French.

Economy: One of the world's most luxurious holiday resorts. Income/person $11,000 (78% of USA).

Politics: Independent city-state with a traditional monarchy under French protection.

Religion: The Roman Catholic Church is the state religion.
Jews 1.7%.
Christian 98.2%. Affiliated 95.1%.
Roman Catholic 88.9%. **Orthodox** 0.4%.
Protestant 5.9%. 1,650a; 800m. French Reformed and Anglican.
Evangelical 0.3% of population.
Missionaries to Monaco 47. Mainly serving in the **TWR** work.

1. **No open evangelism is permitted,** and the evangelical presence is very small in the Protestant community. The local residents and wealthy tourists need to hear the gospel.

2. **Trans World Radio's base is here,** and from Monaco 800 programmes a week in 34 languages are broadcast on powerful medium and short wave transmitters. The broadcasts to "closed" Muslim and Communist lands are a unique and fruitful means of ministry in evangelism and church planting.

3. **A network of studios produce programmes** for transmission from Monaco to the Muslim world (e.g. **GMU** and **NAM** for North Africa) and Europe (German **TWR**, etc.). The staff needs prayer, as do the listeners. The difficult but key follow up ministries are often the only fellowship links that new believers can enjoy.

Asia
Aug 5-6

MONGOLIA
(The Mongolian People's Republic)

Area 1,565,000 sq.km. Grassland, forested in north, three major mountain ranges and the great Gobi Desert. Known as Outer Mongolia before 1911.

Population 1,800,000. Growth rate 2.7%. People per sq.km. 1.

Peoples: Four groups for which schooling is provided.
Halh Mongolian 71%. Language has developed over the last 60 years under different influences from Mongolian spoken in China or Inner Mongolia.
Other minorities (a further 10%) such as the Durbet, Buryat, Bayad, Dariganga, Urianhai, Zaxchin, Darhat, etc. now use Halh and are largely absorbed into the Halh majority.
Russian 13%. Both native to Mongolia, and also Soviet specialists and army personnel.
Kazakhs 4%. In the far west.
Chinese 1.6%.

Literacy 100%. **Official languages:** Halh Mongolian; Russian used as second language in schools, etc. **All languages** 11.

Capital: Ulaan Baatar 350,000. Urbanization 46%.

Economy: Pastoral agriculture (large herds of sheep, cattle, horses, camels and goats), mining and light industry. The latter is developing rapidly.

Politics: Centuries of Manchu rule and Chinese domination rule ended in the revolution of 1921 with Soviet help. A People's Republic declared in 1924, thus becoming the second state in the Socialist Bloc.

Religion: Promotion of scientific atheism.
Non-religious/Atheist 66%.
Lamaistic Buddhism 32% (?). Was once the national religion — an overlay of Buddhistic teaching on Shamanism which contained a high degree of demonology. Only one working monastery and also a monastery school remain, both supported by the government.
Muslim 2%. Among the Kazakhs.
Christian — no official figures given.

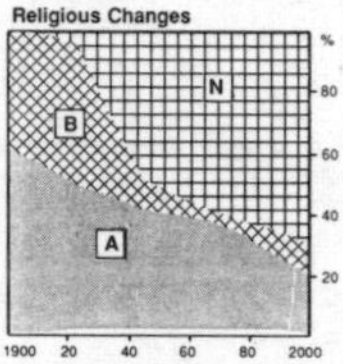

1. **After 60 years of atheistic teaching** little but superstitious remnants of the old religion remain. Pray that the spiritual void may be filled by the Lord Jesus Christ.

2. **One of the least evangelized countries in the world.** Pray it open for the gospel. In this century there has been long-term mission work only in Inner Mongolia, which is part of the People's Republic of China — see on p. 137.

3. **Pray for a current translation of the Mongolian New Testament** to be made available; some portions are already in print. The script of several older translations is no longer in use and those translations are little understood today.

4. **Pray for other unreached peoples:**
   a) **The Kazakhs** 72,000, were largely Muslim.
   b) **The Chinese** 6,000 or more.
   c) **The Russians** 200,000, generally live in special areas and camps and come from all over the USSR. Believers are not selected for such service.

5. **Christian radio broadcasts in Halh Mongolian** — there are none at present, pray that they may become a reality. Many Mongolians can speak Russian — pray for broadcasts in that language beamed to the region.

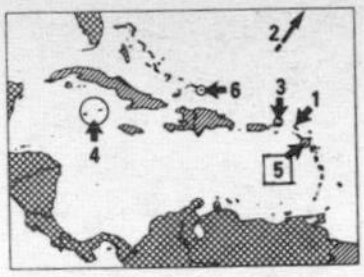

MONTSERRAT
(Colony of Montserrat)

Caribbean

See British Antilles on p. 115.

MOROCCO
(The Kingdom of Morocco)

Middle East

Aug 7-8

Area 447,000 sq.km. Northwest corner of Africa. A further 160,000 sq.km. of former Spanish Sahara claimed and occupied by Morocco in 1976. Fertile coastal areas, barren Atlas mountains inland and Sahara Desert to south and southeast.

Population 24,300,000. Annual growth 2.9%. People per sq.km. 54. Nearly one million Moroccans live and work in Europe.

Peoples
Arabic-speaking 65%. Culturally Arab, but predominantly Berber with Arab admixture.
Berber-speaking 34%. Three main languages: Shluh (speaking Shilha) 4,100,000 in south; Beraber (speaking Tamazight) 2,500,000 in centre; Riff 1,360,000 in north. There are numerous tribal dialects and sub-dialects. Also Black Berber Haratine and Tuareg of the Sahara.
Other 1%. French 100,000; Spanish 20,000; Jewish 20,000, etc.

Literacy 24%. **Official language:** Arabic. French and English are widely used. **All languages** 5. **Bible translations** 1Bi 3por.

Capital: Rabat 1,212,000. Other cities: Casablanca 3,000,000; Marrakech 1,700,000; Fez 1,200,000. Urbanization 49%.

Economy: Mainly agricultural, but phosphate deposits in Morocco and the Sahara are large and important with 70% of world's proven reserves. The cost of the Sahara war is straining the faltering economy. Income/person $750 (5% of USA).

Politics: Independent kingdom in 1956. Formerly French and Spanish protectorates. A limited democracy with an executive monarchy. The dominant political issue since 1974 has been the occupation of the Western Sahara and the subsequent warfare to retain it.

Religion: Islam is the state religion. The government is committed to the preservation of Islam as the religion of all Moroccans. Other religious groups are tolerated so long as they confine their ministry to expatriate communities.
Muslim 99.6%. Almost entirely Sunni.
Jews 0.1%. 20,000 Sephardic Jews, the remnant of a large community that has emigrated to Israel.
Christian 0.27%. Foreign 97%. Moroccan 3%.
Roman Catholic 0.25%. Practising 10%. 60,000a; 33,600m. French, Spanish, etc. Only 500 Moroccans.
Protestant 0.01%. 3,460a; 1,780m. About 60% Moroccan. Denominations 10. Largest (adherents):

Indigenous fellowships	1,250
French Reformed Church	1,000
Anglican Church	800

Christian expatriates in Moroccan ministries inside and outside country approx. 100.

1. **Islam has so completely replaced Christianity that little remains of a once large church**. Pride in Morocco's glorious past as a centre of civilization and Islamic learning, and prejudice against the truths of Scripture are barriers to the acceptance of the gospel. 80% of the population have had no contact at all with the gospel. Pray for individual hearts — and the entire nation — to be opened for messengers of the Cross

2. **Praise God for a new and unprecedented level of interest in the gospel**. Yet every advance is bitterly contested by the enemy, and every possible obstacle to the witness of national

and foreign believers is exploited. Over the land lies the blanket of a spirit of oppression that grips all but those with a strong faith in the Lord Jesus and His victory. Pray that interest may lead to concern, conviction, conversion and congregations.

3. **The government refuses to recognize the legality or even the existence of an indigenous Moroccan Church**. For individuals who become followers of Christ, this lays them open to charges of treachery, illegal contacts with foreign organizations, and to prison sentences for not adhering to Islamic practices such as the fast month of Ramadan. For church groups it is very difficult to find meeting places or arrange Christian marriages and burials. Pray for the king and those in authority, and for a radical change of policy that will give greater freedom to Christians.

4. **The Church in Morocco is becoming a reality**. Growth in the number of believers, Christian marriages and Christian fellowship groups, has been slow, but the momentum has picked up. There are possibly 1,000 believers and eight cities in which Christians gather in little groups. Yet few could be considered viable, organized churches. Pray for the planting of a church in every city and town. Pray that these believers may radiate the peace and joy of the indwelling Saviour. Pray for real and deep trust and fellowship to replace the all-too-common fear and mistrust even among believers, so that they may be willing to meet together despite the cost. Pray that a vital, vibrant Moroccan Church might come into the visible despite set-backs in 1984/85 due to government persecution.

5. **Intimidation of seekers and persecution of believers** has steadily increased since 1968 because of the advances. This has taken many forms: lengthy police interrogations, ostracism, expulsion from employment, family harassment and occasional imprisonment. In 1984 some informal groups had to cease gathering for a time. Believers need encouragement, a strengthened faith, deliverance from the fear of man and a heavenly boldness in the fiery trials they are undergoing.

6. **It is hard for leaders to be trained and openly recognized in the hostile environment**. There is a low-key TEE programme which is benefitting some mature believers. Pray that there may soon be a God-given, Spirit-gifted leadership for every group of believers.

7. **Christian radio and BCCs** have been so successful that every effort has been made to hinder or discredit the ministry. **GMU** was forced to move their radio and literature base to Malaga, Spain, and **NAM** to Marseille, France, from where the work continues. Pray for:

a) **GMU, NAM** and **Brethren** missionaries, as well as North Africans, working to write, print, distribute literature and prepare radio programmes for north Africa.

b) **Christian radio broadcasters: TWR, IBRA, ELWA** beaming programmes to the region; programme content and times to be appropriate, length and regularity of broadcasts to be improved.

c) **A suitable long-term strategy** for effective church planting through radio and literature.

d) **Postal services** to function without interference by the authorities. Many BCCs have been intercepted.

e) **BCC students** to persevere despite difficulties. Over 150,000 have signed on for courses prepared by **GMU, NAM**, etc.

f) **Adequate follow-up** that does not put seekers or new believers at risk. More national believers need to be involved.

g) **Conviction, conversion, cell groups and churches** to be the fruit.

8. **Missionary work**, as such, is no longer permitted, and all mission centres are closed. Christian workers remain on in various secular roles as nurses, teachers, etc., and contrive quietly to share their faith and encourage believers. Praise for others moving out to join them! May their lives radiate the life of Jesus. May they have a tactful boldness and faith for a harvest despite surveillance, pressure and discouragements. Pray the way open for other Christians to enter to replace the many who have had to leave. Major missions in the past have been **GMU, BCMS, NAM**, Immanuel Mission, and **Brethren**.

9. **The Berber peoples were nominally Christian until Islam came.** Arabization is being resisted, and there is a revival of Berber culture and script. Some are seeking an identity in their Christian past. Pray that many might follow in the faith of their illustrious Berber forebears of the early Church — Tertullian, Augustine, etc. Pray also for:

a) **Church planting.** There is not yet a single Riff, Shilha or Tamazight-speaking congregation. Pray for those who have a vision to see this happen. Pray for wise and creative strategies to achieve this.

b) **The individual believers**, many isolated and illiterate.

c) **The daily 15-minute Shilha or Tamazight broadcasts** prepared by **GMU**, and transmitted by **TWR**; also for an increase in programme time. Many listen in spite of the brevity. There are no broadcasts in Riff.

d) **Bible translation.** The Tifinagh Berber script is now legal in Morocco. Scriptures in Shilha and Tamazight are being translated. Pray for a wise choice of words in the confusion of dialects, and for the dissemination of God's Word among the people.

10. **Western Sahara** is a barren desert land. The total population was no more than 150,000 when Spain relinquished its control. Morocco controls the useful third with a large army, while Polisario Sahrawi forces control the rest. Forty thousand Sahrawi now live in the Moroccan area, and 110,000 in refugee and guerrilla camps in nearby Algeria. There has been no known effort to evangelize these nomadic Arab-Berber Sahrawi tribes.

11. **Moroccans have migrated** in large numbers in search of employment. There are 640,000 in France where **NAM** and others have a ministry among them; 105,000 in Belgium (**GMU**); 100,000 in Netherlands; 44,000 in Germany. Others may be reached when they visit Gibraltar and the towns of Ceuta and Melilla, Spanish enclaves on Morocco's Mediterranean coast.

Africa
Aug 9-10

MOZAMBIQUE
(People's Republic of Mozambique)

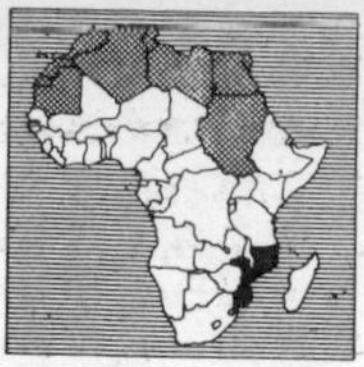

Area 802,000 sq.km. Southeast African state with 2,800 km. coastline on the strategic Mozambique Channel.

Population 13,900,000. Annual growth 2.8%. People per sq.km. 17.

Peoples

African peoples 99%.

Northern peoples 44%. Makua 4,300,000; Lomwe 1,200,000; Makonde 320,000; Yao 250,000.

Central peoples 22%. Sena-Nyungwe 1,600,000; Shona-Ndau 1,100,000; Nyanja 350,000.

Southern peoples 33%. Tsonga (Shangaan) 1,600,000; Ronga (Tswa) 600,000; Chopi 800,000; Tonga 10,000.

Other 1%. Portuguese 30,000, Mixed race 30,000, Russian, etc.

Literacy 24%. **Official language:** Portuguese. **All languages** 23. **Bible translations** 8Bi 2NT 6por.

Capital: Maputo 1,040,000. Urbanization 13%.

Economy: Subsistence economy despite fertile agricultural land and rich mineral deposits. Restrictive colonial exploitation, followed by overhasty application of Marxist economic theories, have limited the development of resources and infrastructure. Drought, floods and widespread guerrilla warfare have further paralysed and impoverished the country. Income/person $120 (1% of USA).

Politics: A Portuguese colony for 470 years. Independent in 1975 as a Marxist-Leninist state after a long and bitter war of independence. Widespread opposition to the central government's policies stimulated a dirty guerrilla war that has made chaos, a state of armed anarchy and starvation a way of life to most people.

Religion: Marxist-Leninist ideology is propagated and promoted. Until 1982 government policy was "all-out war on the churches" and "destruction of religious superstitions". A more conciliatory and flexible approach to religion since then, but present legislation and attitudes are ambiguous and varied.

Non-religious/Atheist est. 5%.

Muslim 13%. The majority among the Yao in northwest and coastal Makonde and Makua.

African traditional religions 59.5%.

Christian 21%.

Roman Catholic 13%. 1,562,000a. The Church suffered a serious decline after independence because of its links with the colonial regime.

Marginal groups (100+) 0.4%. 56,000a.

Protestant 6.4%. 890,000a, 379,000m. Denominations 30. Largest (adherents):

United Baptist (**AEF**, Scand. Bapt.)	160,000
Pentecostal Assemblies (**PAoG**)	75,000
Presbyterian Ch. (Swiss Miss.)	70,000
Anglican Church	65,000
United Methodist Church	60,000
Seventh Day Adventist Church	57,000
Assemblies of God	35,000
Church of the New Covenant	25,000
Church of the Nazarene	22,000
Free Methodist Church	15,000

Evangelical 4.5% of population.

Missionaries to Mozambique est. 20.

Religious Changes

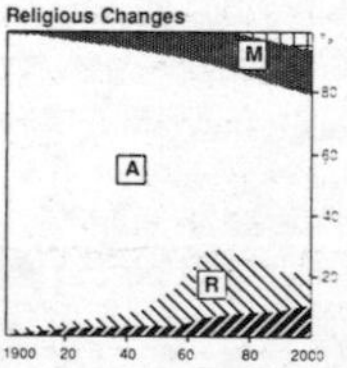

Evangelical Changes

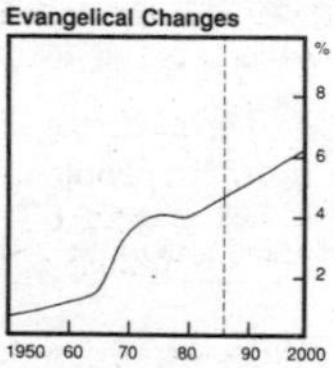

1. **Mozambique has never known religious freedom**. Protestants were severely limited in their outreach, and sometimes persecuted, in the time of Portuguese rule. Persecution of all Christians was particularly severe after independence and until 1982. Missionaries were expelled, Christian leaders intimidated and imprisoned, and many churches and institutions seized or destroyed. Discriminatory legislation was passed to limit Christian gatherings to recognized church buildings and prevent evangelism. Since 1982, the military and economic situation has brought an easing of the pressures and made Mozambique more open for the gospel than ever before. Praise God for this, but pray for complete religious freedom and peace for this tormented land.

2. **The long succession of political, military and natural calamities** has created a great hunger for reality and peace with God. Widespread responsiveness is evident, and churches

are growing — in some areas dramatically. Pray that the spiritual needs may be met, and that the whole land may open up for the preaching of the gospel. Mozambique has the largest unreached population in Africa south of the equator.

3. **The Church has emerged stronger from its years of suffering.** Before independence, most Protestant Christians were in the southern three provinces, where there was considerable nominalism. New life and renewed outreach has resulted in packed churches and church growth among the Assemblies of God, Baptists, Free Methodists and Anglicans. In the central provinces there were few churches, but there has been exciting growth in the Assemblies of God and Nazarene Church over the last few years. In the north the Baptist Union (ex-**AEF**) has grown dramatically from 1,500 baptized members in 1959 to over 80,000 in 1985, mostly among the Lomwe. A huge harvest is being gathered, but the churches do not have the resources to handle the influx.

4. **Christian leaders have been under great pressure to compromise their faith and their congregations** through intimidation and fear. The only recognized interdenominational body is the Christian Council of Mozambique, but not all members are evangelical. Pray for bold, clear, incisive leadership for each denomination.

5. **The training of leaders for the churches is woefully inadequate**. The few pastors often have responsibility for 10-20 churches, but not the income or means of travel to give sufficient time to pastoral care. Over 80% have had no formal training, and there are not the finances or facilities available to obtain it. The one seminary (the Union Theological Seminary) has a strong liberal-Marxist tendency. Pray for the establishment of local Bible schools, TEE schemes, etc. This is now permitted by the authorities. Pray for the provision of Mozambiquan and expatriate teaching staff. The Emmaus Bible Correspondence School is proving valuable to many, but limited postal services hinder its wider use.

6. **Almost all the few missionaries had to leave in 1975**, but since 1982 expatriate Christian workers have been permitted to make pastoral visits and engage in Bible ministry on the invitation of Mozambiquan churches. Some missions have been invited to resume ministries forcibly ended in the '70s. Pray for denominational and interdenominational agencies such as the Baptists, **AEF, AIM** and others who are preparing and sending in workers. There are about 20 Brazilian, N.American and European workers serving the Lord in Mozambique. Conditions are extremely difficult and even dangerous; they need prayer. Pray also for those to be called who will be able to strengthen and encourage the Church at this crucial time. Pray for wise strategies for their deployment, and sensitivity and humility in relationships between agencies and churches. Many Zimbabwean Christians are deeply involved in ministry over the border in the central provinces.

7. **Unreached peoples**. Despite church growth among some peoples, most of the central and northern peoples are unevangelized:

a) **The Makua** are the largest animistic unreached people in Africa, possibly the world. 20% are Muslim, 10% Catholic and only a few are born-again believers (mostly through Baptist Lomwe missionary work).

b) **The partly Muslim peoples** of the north: the Yao (among whom the Anglicans have a growing work), the Makonde (some Christians through Brethren work in Tanzania) and the coastal Swahili. There is only one known church in the northeast province of Cabo Delgado.

c) **The peoples of the Zambezi valley** — especially the Sena, Kunda, Podzo, Nyungwe, Mazaro. Only in the last few years have any Sena churches been planted.

8. **Bible translation and distribution**. The Mozambique Bible Society has a bookshop and great freedom to operate, but lack of Bibles, foreign currency, means of distribution, etc. limit this ministry. Many projects for new translations or revisions have also been hampered. Government efforts to minimize the use of local languages was reversed in 1982, and **SIL** is planning to send in workers for promoting the study of Mozambiquan languages and help in Bible translation. This is needed in at least five and possibly 10 languages — especially in Makua, Kimwani and Sena.

9. **Christian literature** is in very short supply, but it is legally imported. There are two bookstores that stock Christian literature. Several agencies in Zimbabwe (Lifeline) and S.Africa (Frontline Fellowship) have vigorous itinerant literature distribution ministries.

10. **Christian radio has an important teaching role. TWR** in Swaziland broadcasts in Tswa and Tsonga, and both **TWR** and **FEBA** (Seychelles) broadcast in Portuguese. Both stations are cooperating in publicity and programming. There is also need for programming in Sena and Lomwe-Makua. Shortage of radios and batteries limit the audience.

11. **Relief and development programmes** by Christian agencies are welcomed by the government because of widespread hunger and destitution. **WV** and others have been engaged in supplying basic needs to many. **MAF** has several planes involved in these programmes, but flying conditions are tricky. Pray that these efforts may strengthen believers and stimulate evangelism.

Africa
Aug 11

NAMIBIA
(Southwest Africa)

Area 823,000 sq.km. A predominantly desert land. Most people live on the central plateau and the better-watered northern border regions adjoining Angola.

Population 1,128,000. Annual growth 3%. People per sq.km. 1.4.

Peoples: Five races, 11 distinct groups speaking 23 languages.
Ovambo 49.5%. Six tribes along the border with Angola.
Kavango etc. 22.1%. Kavango 117,000; Herero 85,000; Caprivi peoples (4) 43,500; Tswana 7,500.
Hottentot 11.6%. Damara 77,000; Nama 54,700.
White 5.6%. Afrikaans 38,500; German 19,000; English 6,500.
Coloureds 4.2%.
Bushmen 2.8%.
Rehoboth Basters 2.5%.
Others 1.7%.

Literacy 57%. **Official languages:** English, Afrikaans, German. **All languages** 23. **Bible translations** 6Bi 3NT 5por.

Capital: Windhoek 178,000. Urbanization 45%.

Economy: Relatively prosperous with mining of diamonds, uranium and other minerals the mainstay of the economy. Livestock farming and fisheries are also important. Heavily dependent on South Africa for manufactured goods. Income/person $1,760 (13% of USA).

Politics: A former German colony; ruled by South Africa since 1915. The 20-year shuffle towards independence has been fraught with international controversy and diplomacy, bitter warfare between nationalist and South African forces in the country and in neighbouring Angola, and confusion among the various peoples within the country.

Religion
Traditional religions 11%. **Non-religious** 3%.
Christian 86%. Adherents 85%.
Roman Catholic 15%. Practising 39%. 175,000a; 105,000m.
Indigenous marginal groups (40) 5%. 42,000a.
Foreign marginal groups (5) 0.8%. 8,500a.
Protestant 64%. 727,000a; 313,000m. Denominations 30. Largest (adult members):

United Evang. Lutheran	207,000
Dutch Reformed (DRC-NGK)	42,100
Ch. of England in S.Africa	16,000
Full Gospel Church of God	9,000
African Methodist Episcopal	7,800

Evangelical 17% of population.
Missionaries to Namibia 239 (1:4,700 people) in 20 agencies.
Missionaries from Namibia est. 12 (1:60,600 Protestants).

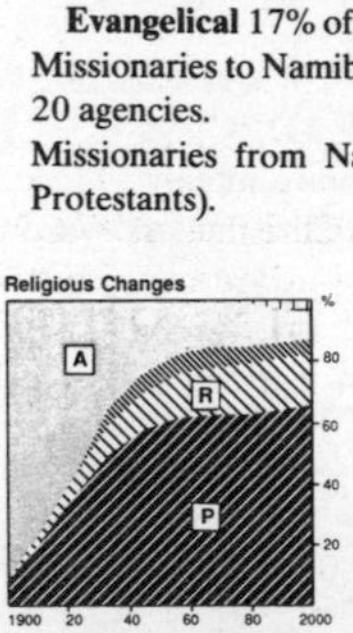

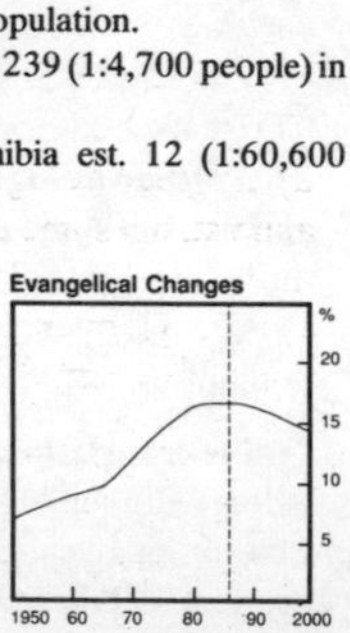

1. **The political future of Namibia** calls for believing prayer. Pray for a peaceful settlement fair to all Namibians, and for a government that will uphold Christian values.

2. **Namibia is one of Africa's most Christianized lands**, yet biblical truth and true spirituality are in short supply. Christian leaders need prayer that they stand for the gospel rather than ideologies or sectional interests. Only Christians can adequately bridge the tensions and hatreds that divide the diverse ethnic groups. Pray for a deep spiritual revival.

3. **The evangelical witness has been strengthened** in recent years through new missionary thrusts by the **DRC**, **AEF/AIM**, **YWAM**, Baptists and Church of England in South Africa. Evangelicals are relatively few in the German, Herero, Damara and Nama communities; but much stronger among the Ovambo and Afrikaans. Pray for a unity in the gospel that transcends race and denomination.

4. **Leadership training.** The major seminary in the country has been much influenced by Black and Liberation theology to the spiritual impoverishment of students passing out into the ministry. Several smaller Bible schools make a stronger evangelical stand. Pray for the raising up of many dedicated Christian leaders at such a critical time in the nation's history.

5. **The Ovambo and Kavango peoples** live along the northern border. They have suffered the most in the warfare. Christian work has been seriously hampered, and pressures on the Christians have been severe. These sensitive peoples have proved very responsive to the gospel — pray that their present sufferings may lead to a deeper commitment to Christ.

6. **The independent churches** among the Herero, Basters and Nama are an expression of protest at exploitation and discrimination in the past, and, in the case of the Hereros, virtual genocide in 1905 when 80% of the Herero were slaughtered after an uprising against German colonial rule. A large part of the Herero follow syncretic churches that mix pre-Christian and Christian teachings. Pray for the tactful and sensitive approaches of **DRC** and **AEF/AIM** missionaries seeking to reach the Herero, and trust the Lord for conversions and discipling work in three centres.

7. **Twenty-five percent of young people** are in schools. They face acute pressures from the more traditional old people and the radical young political movements. The evangelical SCM has 6,000 members in 20 of the 55 secondary schools and is making considerable impact. Pray for the full emergence of a vital interracial student movement.

N

8. **Missionaries in both the older and newer missions** need acute sensitivity and understanding as they minister in an emotionally charged political situation among a strongly traditional Christian population.

9. **The less reached peoples:**

a) **The Bushman tribes.** Most are animists, some have become Christians (**DRC**), but cultural adaptation for these simple, nomadic desert dwellers is hard. Dependence on alcohol has ruined the lives of many.

b) **The Caprivi peoples** — the Mbukushu (20,000), Mafue (16,000), Yeyi and Subiya peoples are 50% animist. Some have become Catholic and Adventist, but Evangelicals are very few.

c) **The Himba** or Kaokoveld Herero are 94% animist, and about 5% are at least nominally Christian (Lutheran and **DRC**).

d) **Angolan refugees** are mainly Ovambo, Kavango and Mbukushu. The majority are animist, but some are Christian. **AEF/AIM** have established 30 preaching posts. Pray that the believers may have an impact on both Namibia and Angola.

e) **The German and English-speaking** communities are much influenced by secular humanism, and vital, witnessing groups of believers among them are relatively few.

10. **Bible translation.** The **UBS** has seven new translation projects in smaller languages — including Mbukushu and four Bushman dialects. Full Bibles are being prepared or revised in four major languages. Pray for this work, and for the impact of God's Word on the hearts of the readers. **GRI** has produced recordings in 21 languages of Namibia.

Pacific
Aug 12

NAURU
(The Republic of Nauru)

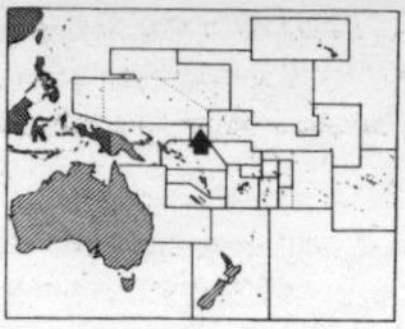

Area 21 sq.km. A single phosphate-covered coral island 300 km. west of Banaba, Kiribati.

Population 8,000. Annual growth 1.3%. People per sq.km. 381.

Peoples
Nauruan 58%.
Foreign 42%. Other Pacific Islanders (mainly Tuvalu and Kiribati) 3,200; Chinese 640; European 560.

Literacy 100%. **Official languages:** English, Nauruan.

Economy: Nauruans are among the richest peoples in the world. Phosphate mining is the source of this wealth, which is being used to finance shipping, air transport, insurance, offshore banking, etc. Income/person $11,000 ('82) (80% of USA).

Politics: Independent in 1968 as a republic.

Religion: Freedom of religion.
Non-religious/Atheist 8%.
Chinese religions 7.7%.
Baha'i 1.6%.
Christian 83%. Nominal 16%. Affiliated 67%.
Roman Catholic 27.5%. 2,200a.
Protestant 39%. Congregational Church 3,100a; a few unorganized groups of Christians.
Evangelical 2% of population.
Missionaries to Nauru 3 (1:2,700 people).

1. **The wealth of Nauruans** contrasts markedly with the relative poverty of surrounding island states. Materialism has sapped the people of spiritual concern. Church life is at a low ebb. There are few evangelical believers.

2. **The immigrant phosphate workers** — Chinese, Tuvalu and Kiribati islanders — need to hear the gospel, for few of them know the Lord.

Asia

Aug 13-14

NEPAL
(Kingdom of Nepal)

Area 141,000. A mountain-ringed Himalayan state between China (Tibet) and India.

Population 16,000,000. Annual growth 2.4%. People per sq.km. 113. Very unevenly distributed. Most live on the overpopulated hills and in the Kathmandu valley; many are migrating to the lowland Terai in the south.

Peoples: Over 30 major ethnic groups; numerous smaller groups. Two main ethnic components, with considerable intermingling:
Indo-Aryan (from south and west) 79%. Nepali 8,800,000; Maithili 1,830,000; Bhojpuri 1,120,000; Tharu 686,000; Awadhi 438,000; Rajbansi 77,000; Dhanwar 14,000; also eight other languages.
Tibeto-Burman (from north and east) 20%. Thamang 768,000; Newari 630,000; Magar 400,000; Rai (21 dialects) 321,000; Gurung 238,000; Limbu 236,000; Sherpa 110,000; Sunwar 29,000; also 34 other languages.
Other 1%. Santali 29,000; Munda; Indian; European.

Literacy 20%. **Official language:** Nepali, the first language of 55% of the population. **All languages** 76. **Bible translations** 6Bi 1NT 21por.

Capital: Kathmandu 430,000. Urbanization 6%.

Economy: An isolated subsistence economy. The terrain is difficult and in habitable regions there is a high population density. The development of roads, agriculture and social projects has been slow. Main foreign exchange earners are tourism, agriculture and Gurkha soldiers. Heavily dependent on foreign aid. Income/person $170, with 40% living below the poverty line (1% of USA).

Politics: Political isolation from the outside world ended in 1951. The king has executive powers in a partyless government system. A gradual process of democratization has been accelerated by mounting unrest.

Religion: The world's only Hindu kingdom. Hinduism is the state religion, and it is unlawful to convert anyone from the religion of their fathers. Open Christian evangelism is illegal.
Hindu 89%. Much intertwined in Buddhism and a strong, underlying animism. A complex caste system exists despite its illegality since 1963.
Buddhist 7%. Lamaistic Buddhism is dominant among the Tibeto-Burman peoples. The Buddha was born in Nepal.
Muslim 3.5%. Predominantly in the Terai.
Christian 0.3%. Almost entirely Protestant Evangelicals.
Roman Catholic about 250 adherents.
Protestant 0.3%. 47,000a; 26,000m.
Missionaries to Nepal approx. 600 (1:26,700 people) in two large inter-mission fellowships and several independent agencies.

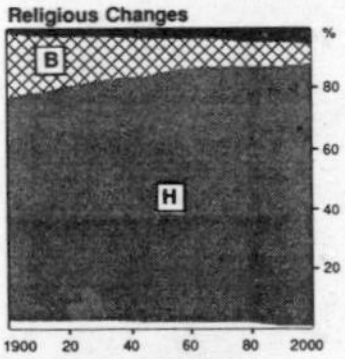

1. **Praise for the growth of the Church in Nepal.** For years witness among Nepalis was only possible in north India, but in 1951 the land opened a little for the gospel. In 1960 there were about 25 baptized believers; in 1985 this had grown to around 25,000. Most of the growth is in the last 10 years. In some places whole villages have come to Christ, in others whole families. There are nearly 400 larger or smaller worshipping groups scattered across the country and in all of the major ethnic groups. Most are linked to the **Nepal Christian Fellowship**, an umbrella fellowship for a wide variety of groups.

2. **The political situation is tense and potentially explosive.** Pray for peace and enough freedom for the gospel to allow the whole land to be evangelized as soon as possible.

3. **Persecution has been intense at times.** In 1985 there were 50 Christians awaiting trial, and some were in prison for infringing the anti-conversion laws. Those who profess Christ are liable to one year in prison, and those who baptize them six years. Some Christians have recanted under pressure; many others have become more fervent and bold. Pray for valiant believers who risk all for the sake of the gospel as itinerant preachers, teachers and literature evangelists. Pray also for those who are suffering for their faith.

4. **Leadership is the critical bottleneck.** No training institutions are allowed, and training courses have to be low-profile. It is not easy for Nepalis to obtain Bible training outside the country. There are only about 9 full-time Nepali pastors, and they must frequently itinerate to teach believers in isolated groups. Pray for adequate training methods and for committed believers to be called to this exacting ministry.

5. **Doctrinal extremes and error are easily followed, and divisions on racial and doctrinal grounds** have emerged of late. Pray for a deep commitment to biblical truth and also to the unity of the Body. Pray also that this vigorous young Church may become a means of blessing to the struggling and nominal Church in nearby north India.

6. **Unreached peoples.** All people groups are in this category; pray through the list above! The majority of believers are Nepali-speaking, and increasingly among the Newar, Tamang and Chepang (10,000); but other peoples have few believers.
   a) **The Awadhi and Maithili** of the Terai have been unresponsive.
   b) **The numerous Tibeto-Burman, and frequently Buddhist, peoples** are often isolated in mountain communities that have not been exposed to the gospel.
   c) **Tibetans**, both refugees (100,000) and those in the little "kingdom" of Mustang in the north.
   d) **The Muslims** are untouched.

7. **Missions have played a remarkable role** in improving health, agriculture and education in a land hampered by disease, low life expectancy and illiteracy. Relationships with the government can be delicate, and visa applications are carefully screened. Pray for wisdom and grace for leaders and missionaries, and for the entry of called workers. Pray for radiance of life and freedom of speech in all contacts with Nepalis as the medical workers minister in hospitals, dispensaries, leprosy and health programmes, and others in educational institutions. Many Nepali Christians owe their conversion to the loving practical ministries of expatriates and the fervent witness of local believers. Pray also that the missionaries may be a blessing to the Nepali believers. The **United Mission to Nepal** is the largest body with 381 missionaries representing 38 agencies from 22 countries. The **INF** has a further 100 workers in the west of Nepal. There are several other foreign and Indian agencies also working in the country.

8. **Nepalis outside the country:**
   a) There are about eight million living in India, Bhutan, etc. Over the years groups of Christians have come into being in these lands. There is a Nepali Bible school in Darjeeling, W.Bengal.
   b) **Gurkha soldiers** are world renowned for their bravery. Thousands serve in the Indian and British armies in Hong Kong, Britain, Brunei, etc. All are recruited in Nepal, many being Gurung and Rai. Pray for outreach to these soldiers — some have been converted in Hong Kong.

9. **Other help ministries**:
   a) **Bible translation** is in progress in 15 languages, but practical and spiritual obstacles to their completion are many. Pray for all committed to complete these projects. There are about 43 languages without any Scriptures at all.
   b) **The Bible Society** labours under great difficulties. Pray that all barriers to the importation, printing and distribution of God's Word may be broken down.
   c) **Christian literature** may not be printed in Nepal without permission and is almost impossible to import, yet it is widely acceptable to the people. There is one Bible Society bookshop and several other literature outlets; pray for these and itinerant colporteurs. Some have been arrested and imprisoned for such activities. **Christian Media Nepal** has an ambitious programme for promoting literacy among believers and producing locally printed literature, books, cassette tapes, filmstrips and films. Pray for this ministry.
   d) **Cassette tapes** are a useful evangelistic and teaching tool, but players are not widely available. **GRI** has recorded 62 languages and dialects.
   e) **Bible Correspondence Courses** have long been a key means of outreach, but the programme lacks funds and personnel to continue effectively.
   f) **Radio** is underused, and only six hours of broadcasting is available monthly — from **FEBA** Seychelles.

NETHERLANDS

(The kingdom of the Netherlands)

The West

Aug 15

Area 41,000 sq. km. Over 30% is below sea level.

Population 14,500,000. Annual growth +0.4%. People per sq.m. 354.

Peoples
Indigenous 91.2%. Dutch 12,800,000; Frisian 460,000; Gypsies 1,200.
Ex-colonial 4.1%. Dutch-Indonesian 320,000; Surinamese 260,000; South Molukkan 45,000; Antilles 33,000.
Immigrant communities 4.6%. Other EEC countries 160,000; Turkish 150,000; North African 105,000; Chinese 45,000; Yugoslav 14,000.

Literacy 100%. **Official language:** Dutch (Nederlands).

Capital: Amsterdam 1,000,000. Other cities: The Hague (seat of government) 700,000; Rotterdam (the world's busiest seaport) 1,100,000. Urbanization 88%.

Economy: A strong industrial and trading economy. A member of the EEC. Unemployment 18%. Income/person $9,910 (70% of USA).

Politics: Stable democratic constitutional monarchy.

Religion: Complete freedom of religion, but with a strong and steady secularization of society.
Non-religious 28%. Also includes nominal Christians who have no affiliation to a church.
Muslim 2.1%. North African, Turk, Indonesian and some Surinamese.
Hindu 0.7%. Surinamese Asian and Sri Lankan Tamil.
Jews 0.2%. Before World War II it was 1.4%.
Christian 69%. About half attend church.

Roman Catholic 39.2%. 5,650,000a; 3,955,000m. Predominantly in southern provinces.
Marginal groups 1%. 133,000a; 82,000m. Largest (adherents):

Jehovah's Witnesses	46,700
Protestant Union (Unitarian)	18,000
New Apostolic Church	12,500

Protestant 28.7%. 4,130,000a; 1,360,000m. Predominant in north and centre. Denominations approx. 150. Largest (adult members)

Reformed Church (NHK)	616,000
Reformed Churches (GK)	480,050
Reformed Ch's (Liberated) (VGK)	60,850
Fell. of Pente. Ch's & others	40,000
Christian Reformed Ch's (CRK)	38,500
Mennonite Church	26,300
Ev. Lutheran Church	21,070
Neth. Reformed Ch's (NRK)	17,600
Remonstrant Brotherhood	13,000
Baptist Union	12,000
Free Evangelical Churches	7,450

Evangelical 8% of population.
Missionaries from Netherlands 1,100 (1:3,800 Protestants) in over 75 agencies. Over 85% are evangelical.
Missionaries to Netherlands approx. 160.

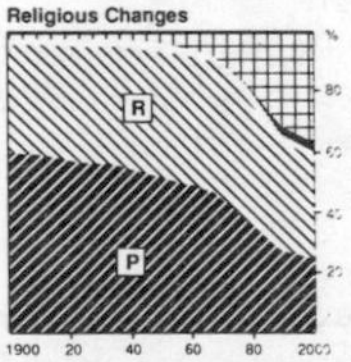

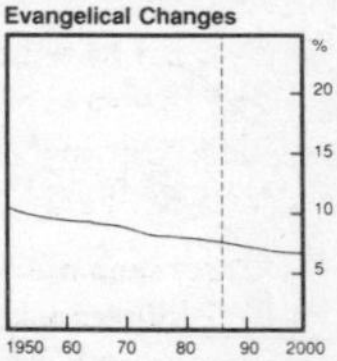

1. **Netherlands has a great history of struggle for religious liberty, and of revival, ministry to refugees and suffering for the Word of God**. The younger generation is generally free-thinking, churchless and more concerned with horizontal than vertical issues. The land has gained a reputation for drugs and loose living. Pray for revival. Praise God for a growing awareness for church renewal.

2. **The Catholic Church** has a strong liberal element that has had worldwide influence, and which has caused great strain on relationships with the Pope. Numerical decline has accelerated over the past 10 years. Pray that the independence and spirit of enquiry among the Dutch may be harnessed by the Holy Spirit in a return to vital biblical Christianity for the blessing of the world.

3. **The Protestant Church** has strong roots in Calvinism, but has suffered serious decline this century, with the percentage of Protestants falling from 61% in 1900 to under 30% in 1985. Formalism, numerous theological differences, liberal theology and secularization have all played their part in accelerating this. Nearly every denomination has liberal, neo-orthodox,

orthodox and evangelical factions. During 1986 the NHK and GK will unite — pray that its basis might be God's Word. Pray for a return to a warm personal faith, scriptural holiness of life and a burden to evangelize the many unchurched Dutch and immigrant communities. There is a pervasive universalism which has robbed many Evangelicals of their cutting edge in evangelism; pray for conviction of the biblical truth of the lostness of man outside of Christ.

4. **The evangelical upsurge** is an encouraging feature today, and nearly all evangelical groups and ministries are thriving in the midst of national decay. Pray for:

a) **The multiplication of evangelical groups — often meeting in homes**. These are denominational (Free Church, Pentecostal and mainline Evangelical) or Christian inter-denominational workers — Women Aglow Fellowship (Pentecostal) and De Christenvrow (Reformed). The latter have been instrumental in bringing spiritual life to many women. This development is beginning to break up the deadening traditionalism associated with church services. Effective church planting among those alienated from traditional denominations is still limited. Many in the country have grown up with no concept of the gospel.

b) **Evangelische Omroep:** an interdenominational evangelical broadcasting organization that functions as part of the national radio and TV system. It has become a strong unifying force for Reformed evangelical believers. Its message of life and hope on five hours of TV and 38 hours of radio programming per week is widely appreciated and effective.

c) **The Evangelical Missionary Alliance** (1973), and the **Evangelical Alliance** (1979) which have become rallying points for evangelism and missions.

d) **The multiplication of evangelistic, revival and youth agencies. Youth for Christ, YWAM**, and many other groups are making a vital impact on churches and on young people. Pray that these endeavours may turn the tide of evil which is sweeping through the nation.

e) **The continued growth in the number and quality of evangelical Bible schools.**

f) **Christian literature:** there are over 120 Christian bookshops, and a growing variety of good literature and good Bible versions. **CLC** has six shops and a bookmobile.

5. **Young people:** Unemployment and life without God in a permissive society have made young people more responsive than for generations. Pray for:

a) Street evangelism, coffee bars, camps, outreach to drug addicts through **Opwekking, Jong en Vrij, Teen Challenge, YWAM, CCC,** etc.

b) **University students** live in a high-pressure ideological battle zone where it is hard to stand for Jesus. Pray for **Navigator** and **IFES** groups on many campuses. About 1,000 students are affiliated to groups linked with the latter.

c) **A challenge to missions and outreach** that will give young people a cause for which to live and die.

6. **Interest in foreign missions has grown fast.** The EMA has a membership of 60 indigenous and international mission agencies with over 800 missionaries. Pray for church fellowships to get the vision and support this growth. Dutch missionaries are making a significant contribution in Eastern Europe (**OD**) and the Middle East, and in Bible translation and evangelical aid programmes.

7. **Praise God for the input of international missions in Netherlands**. There are approximately 70 expatriate workers assisting indigenous ministries such as **YFC, IFES, ECM, BCU, GEM**, etc., and over 90 long-term **YWAM**ers.

8. **The unreached:**

a) **The great, secular cities. Amsterdam is a trend-setting city for Europe** in finances, tourism and drug distribution. Over half the population claims no religious affiliation. The city has become well known for its large drop-out population. For over 10 years the city has been a special target for prayer. Twenty-five evangelical groups and churches have been cooperating since 1976 to reach out to this city. Seventy **YWAM**ers minister in the city in a strong urban missions programme which is becoming an example of creative evangelism in decaying world cities.

b) **The Muslim minority**. Moroccans and Turks are the largest communities. All are guest workers and have many problems with housing and unemployment. Only a handful have become believers. Pray for those seeking to reach them — SVEOM, Gospel for Guests, **YWAM** in Amsterdam, de Kandelaar in Rotterdam, etc.

c) **The many other language groups** among visitors, guest workers, refugees who pass through or reside in the country. Pray that they may hear the gospel rather than be swallowed up in materialism and sin. Specialized efforts for many of these groups are needed — especially the Chinese (12 known churches) and Southern Europeans.

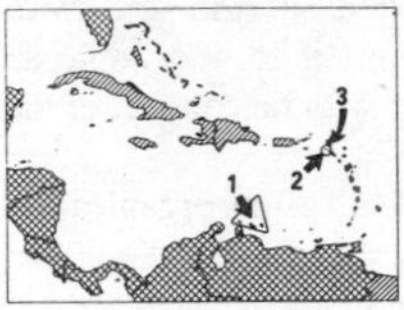

THE NETHERLANDS ANTILLES

The West

Aug 16

Area 961 sq.km. Three larger, barren islands, Curacao, Bonaire and Aruba off the coast of Venezuela, and two and a half smaller islands in the Leeward islands 800 km. to the northeast. St. Maartin is shared with France.

Population 270,000. Annual growth 1.3%. People per sq.km. 280.

Peoples
Creole 87%. Mixed race — African, Amerindian, Dutch, and 40 other nationalities.
European 6.1%. Mainly Dutch. **African** 4.9%. **Other** 2%, Chinese, Jewish, etc.

Literacy 95%. **Official language:** Dutch. **Common languages:** Papiamento (84% of the population) in southern three, English in the northern two and a half islands.

Economy: Heavily dependent on extensive oil refining industries, but made wealthy thereby. The closure of most of the refineries 1983-85 has created a major economic crisis for the country. Income/person $4,200 (30% of USA).

Politics: Integral part of Kingdom of Netherlands with domestic autonomy and parliamentary democratic government. Independence is expected in 1991.

Religion
Non-religious/Atheist 2%.
Jews, Muslim, Buddhist, etc. 1%.
Christian 96.8%. Nominal 6.3%. Affiliated 90.5%.
Roman Catholic 80%. Practising 57%. 216,000a; 127,000m.
Marginal groups 2.1%. Largest: Jehovah's Witnesses 2,100m.
Protestant 8.3%. 22,400a; 8,700m. Denominations 42. Largest (adult members):

Seventh Day Adventist Church	2,100
Methodist	1,330
Evangelical Church (**TEAM**)	880.

Evangelical 2.7% of population.
Missionaries to Netherlands Antilles 135 (1:2,000 people) in 10 agencies.

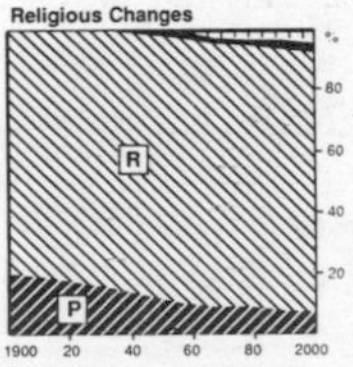

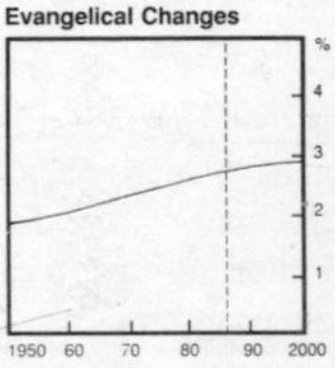

1. **Openness to the gospel has not resulted in a great harvest.** Moral laxity, superstition and the growing marginal sects show how few understand the message of salvation.

2. **Evangelical witness has progressed slowly.** A vital, growing church in every island is a target for prayer. **TEAM** has concentrated on evangelism and church planting among the Papiamento-speaking majority, and the 11 daughter churches are a large part of the evangelical witness. There are estimated to be 20 evangelical congregations on Aruba, but inter-denominational rivalry is a major blot on the testimony of the Church.

3. **The whole Bible in Papiamento** has been translated by **TEAM** and the **Bible Society.** Little Christian literature is available in this language.

4. **Christian radio** is a significant ministry which involves most of the Protestant missionary force. **TEAM** concentrates on local Papiamento broadcasts from Radio Victoria, and **TWR** on Latin America and the world from their powerful station on Bonaire.

Pacific
Aug 17

NEW CALEDONIA

(Territory of New Caledonia and Dependencies)

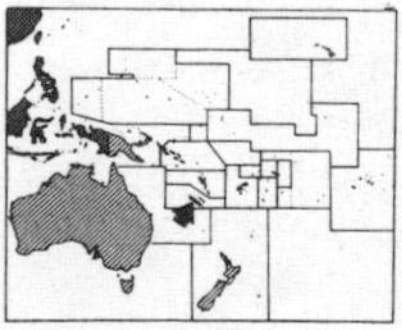

Area 19,000 sq.km. One large 400 km.-long island and many smaller ones 1,500 km. northeast of Queensland, Australia.

Population 157,000. Annual growth 1.4%. People per sq.km. 8.

Peoples
Indigenous (Kanak) 43%. Melanesian (31 groups) 65,300; Polynesian (1) 2,000.
Immigrant Pacific islanders 15.4%. Wallisian 13,000; Tahitian 7,000; Futunan 3,000; Vanuatan 1,300.
Other immigrant peoples 41.6%. French 55,000; Javanese 6,000; Vietnamese 2,600.

Literacy 91%. **Official language:** French. **All languages** 40. **Bible translations** 4Bi 1NT 1por.

Capital: Nouméa 90,000. Urbanization 72%.

Economy: Nickel mining, agriculture. French prosperous, but Kanaks relatively poor and deprived of most of the farmland. Income/person $7,790 (55% of USA).

Politics: Overseas territory of France since 1946. The indigenous Kanaks are frustrated in efforts to win independence in the face of the intransigent local French population. Tenseness and violence as polarization between Kanaks and French settlers increases — to the embarrassment of the metropolitan French government.

Religion: Freedom of religion in a secularized society.
Non-religious/Atheist 5%. Mainly French.
Muslim 4%. Mainly Javanese. **Baha'i** 0.4%.
Buddhist 0.3%. Mainly Chinese/Vietnamese.
Christian 90%. Nominal 7.5%. Affiliated 82.5%.
Roman Catholic 60.5%. Practising 42%. 95,000a; 53,300m.
Marginal groups (3) 1.7%. 2,700a.
Protestant 20.3%. 31,800a; 7,700m. Denominations 5. Largest (adult members):

Evangelical Church (PEMS)	3,680
Free Church	2,000
Assemblies of God	1,600.

Evangelical 8.3% of population.

Missionaries to New Caledonia 18 (1:8,700 people) in 4 agencies.

Missionaries from New Caledonia 3 (1:10,600 Protestants).

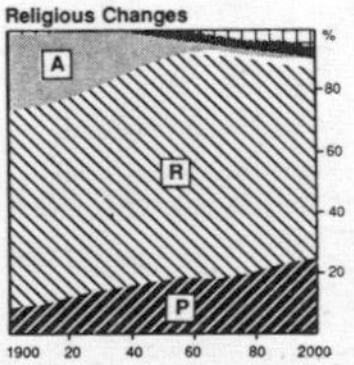

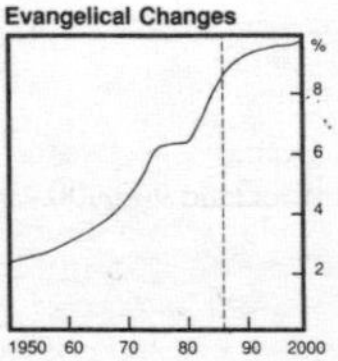

1. **The political tensions** inevitably affect spiritual life and church growth. Pray for a wise solution to the territory's political turmoil; one that will also further the evangelization of this land with relatively few evangelical believers. Drunkenness, immorality and materialism are especially common among young people.

2. **The Protestant churches,** though often liberal in theology, have a higher proportion of evangelicals and evangelical leaders than those in France. The Free Church and Assemblies of God have a vigorously growing work with a multitribal base. Pray for the witness of believers in difficult times — most villages and towns have no evangelical group. Most churches are in the interior; Nouméa and the Isle of Pines are almost entirely Catholic.

3. **Missions.** The first missionary was a Tongan. Later LMS work was taken over by the PEMS. This territory has been seriously neglected by evangelical missions. The entry of **AoG** in 1963 and later of **SIL** was providential. Pray for these missions and for the entry of new French-speaking, church planting missionaries.

4. **Unreached peoples:**

a) **The indigenous Melanesians** are superficially evangelized. Animist practices and cargo cults have been prevalent in the past. Little has been done in the many local languages to communicate the gospel to the heart.

b) **The immigrant Muslim Javanese, Buddhist/Catholic Vietnamese, Catholic Wallisian** and **French** have very few evangelical believers among them. Pray for specific evangelistic outreach to them.

5. **Bible translation.** At least five and possibly 32 languages require Bible translation programmes. Only one indigenous language has a NT. **SIL** now has one couple commencing translation. Other teams must be prayed out. What a challenge for Australian, French and New Guinean missionaries. **GRI** has recorded messages in only five of the languages.

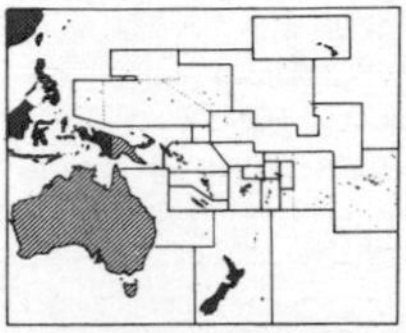

NEW ZEALAND
(The Dominion of New Zealand)

Pacific

Aug 18

Area 268,000 sq.km. Two main islands 1,800 km. southeast of Australia.

Population 3,210,000. Annual growth 0.3% People per sq.km. 12.

Peoples
European 85%. Predominantly of British origin.
Polynesian 14%. Indigenous Maori 300,000; immigrant Samoan 43,000; Cook Islanders 26,000, etc.
Other 1%. Chinese 20,000; Indian 12,000.

Literacy 98%. **Official language:** English. **All indigenous languages** 2.

Capital: Wellington 358,000. Largest city: Auckland 900,000. Urbanization 83%.

Economy: Highly efficient agricultural industry, and rich in natural resources but far from export markets. Income/person $7,410 (52% of USA).

Politics: Independent dominion in British Commonwealth since 1907. A stable parliamentary democracy.

Religion: Freedom of religion; no established church.
Non-religious/Atheist and other 26%.
Other religions 0.7%. Hindu 7,000; Buddhist 5,000; Jews 3,300; Muslim 2,600.
Christian 73%.
Roman Catholic 15.6%. 500,000a; 335,000m.
Marginal groups (17) 3.3%. Majority among Maori. 106,000a; 64,000m. Largest (adherents):

Mormons	39,590
Ratana Church	36,550
Jehovah's Witnesses	18,066
Ringatu	6,000

Protestant 51.4%. 1,714,000a; 457,000m. Denominations (62+). Largest (adherents):

Anglican Church	740,000
Presbyterian Church	510,000
Methodist Church	130,000
Baptist Union	55,000
Brethren	24,250
Salvation Army	20,000
Assemblies of God	20,000
Indig. Pentecostal	12,000

Evangelical 16.7% of population.
Missionaries to NZ approx. 150.
Missionaries from within NZ 1,560 (1:1,100 Protestants) in 50 agencies, of which 220 are based in NZ.

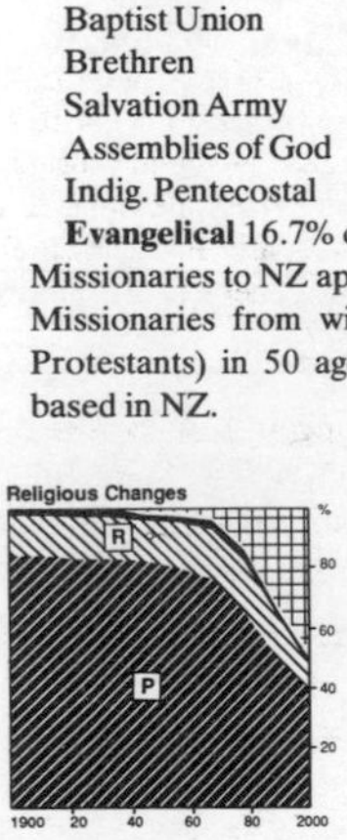

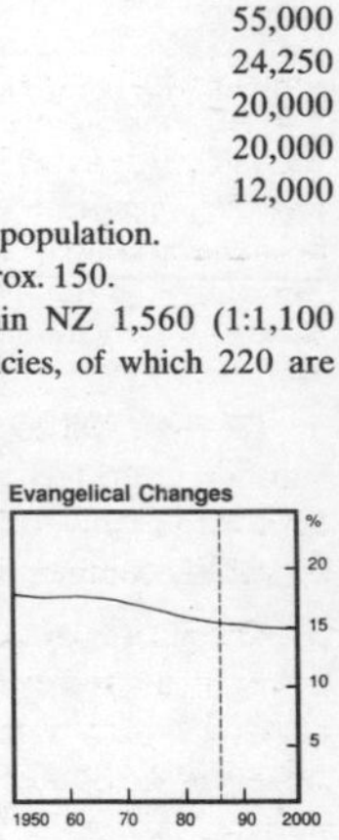

1. **In nearly every denomination there has been a breath of new life since 1960.** The Holy Spirit has brought a freshness of worship, freedom in fellowship, and emergence of new patterns and structures to many congregations. All the English-speaking world sings the Scripture choruses that came out of this move of the Spirit! Yet the longed-for revival has yet to come.

2. **The prevailing trend of New Zealand society is, as in many Western lands, secular materialism and a turning away from God.** Pray that the many believers may make a greater impact on society, its standards and its institutions.

3. **Charismatic renewal has brought about widespread changes**. Nearly every denomination has been affected. The impact has been greater than on any other English-speaking nation. Liberal denominations have declined in numbers, the evangelical minority in the Anglican and Presbyterian Churches has grown and Pentecostal and independent renewal fellowships have multiplied, as has the Baptist Union. Pray for a maturing of new life and vigour, an emergence of adequate leadership and structures to lead the Church, and a channelling of more effort into missionary outreach.

4. **New Zealanders have an exciting record for missionary endeavour**, with missionaries serving all over the world. Pray that this vision be nurtured by pastors and leaders, and that the Church may continue to be outward looking. There are 9 Bible schools and seminaries in NZ; pray that missions may be fundamental to the instruction given. About 30% of all Bible school students are at the Bible College of New Zealand in Auckland.

5. **The Maori people** have begun to reassert themselves after years of cultural decline. Most are Christian in name, but the gospel needs to become more fully Maori yet true to Scripture. Traditional Protestant churches have been too superficial and there is little missionary vision. Syncretic sects (Ratana and Ringatu, etc.), and the Mormons have gained a large following. Too much initiative and leadership is still in non-Maori hands, and there is still no Maori Bible school.

6. **Other ethnic minorities**.
   a) **Polynesians** have immigrated to NZ seeking employment. Large communities of Samoans, Tongans and islanders from the NZ-administered Cook, Tokelau and Niue Islands live in the cities. Auckland is, in fact, the city with the world's largest population of Polynesians. Most are Christian, many being Congregational. Church attendances are high, but church is more a social event. Pray that the Holy Spirit may break down the barriers of nominalism, tradition and status in these rather exclusive communities.
   b) **Indians**. A rapidly growing group. Most of NZ Muslims and Hindus are Indian. No specific outreach until recently, though a number have become Christians. **AsEF** is commencing a ministry among them.
   c) **Chinese**. Although 75% claim to be "Christian", only 12% of these attend church regularly. There are about 10 churches with a large Chinese membership. May they be challenged to daring discipleship and missions.

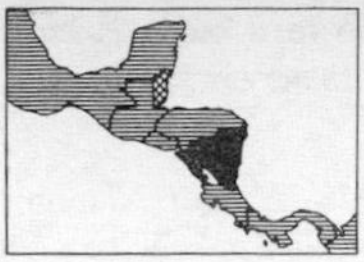

NICARAGUA
(Republic of Nicaragua)

Latin America

Aug 19

Area 130,000 sq.km. The largest of the Central American republics; poor communications with the Atlantic coast.

Population 3,218,000. Annual growth 3.3%. People per sq.km. 25. Most live in the Pacific lowlands and adjacent highlands.

Peoples
Spanish-speaking 83%. Ladino (Eurindian) 68%, European 14%, Amerindian 1%. Three Hispanicized peoples: Matagalpa 20,000; Monimbo 10,000; Subtiaba 5,000.
English/Creole-speaking 12%. African and Afro-Indian 390,000; Black Carib. 2,000; Rama (Amerindian) 1,000.
Amerindian dialects 4.7%. Miskito 160,000; Sumo 7,000.
Other 0.3%. Chinese 3,500, etc.

Literacy 61%. **Official language**: Spanish. **All languages** 6. **Bible translations** 1Bi 2NT.

Capital: Managua 858,000. Urbanization 80%.

Economy: Diversified agricultural economy. Destitution of the economy by the depredations of the former dictatorship and revolutionary wars. The Sandinista government instituted a vigorous programme of health, literacy, land redistribution and reconstruction, but the collapse of agricultural prices and confrontations with surrounding states and the USA have further impoverished the land. Income/person $900 (6% of USA).

Politics: Independent republic since 1838. The rather brutal and corrupt Somoza dictatorship ended in the 1979 revolution after a bitter civil war. The Sandinista government set up a junta of national reconstruction, an alliance of social democrats and Marxists. Since 1983 the radical left has become more influential, but the implementation of fully Marxist policies has been hampered and moderated by the bad military and economic situation. Several guerrilla movements are operating against the government.

Religion: Secular state. The new regime promised freedom of religion. Sporadic excesses and abuses of that freedom have occurred. Since 1983 government policy is moving to politicization, and control of churches and evangelism.
Non-religious/Atheist 3%.
Christian 96.6%. Affiliated 89.7%.
Roman Catholic 78.4%. 2,520,000a; 1,340,000m.
Marginal groups (4) 2.1%. 66,000a; 25,000m.
Protestant 9.3%. 298,000a; 119,000m. Denominations 55+. Largest (members):

Assemblies of God (Span.)	22,000
Moravian Church (Eng.)	18,200
Seventh Day Adventist Church	15,600
Apostolic Ch. of Faith in Jesus Christ	8,500
Church of God (Cleveland)	8,400
National Baptist Convention	7,680

Evangelical 6.3% of population.
Missionaries to Nicaragua 141 in 1973, possibly 60 in 1985.
Missionaries from Nicaragua 0(?)

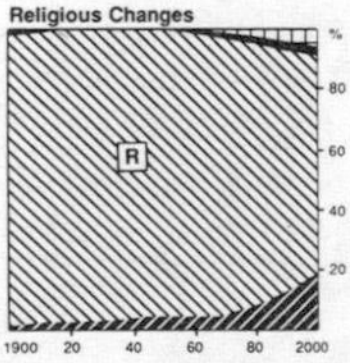

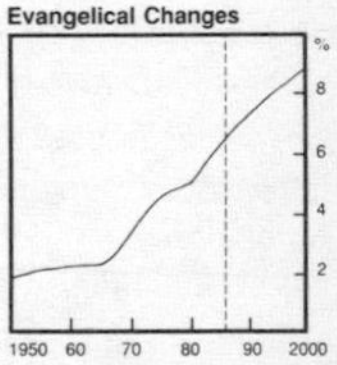

1. **Nicaragua is a land of agonizing contradictions**. The events surrounding and following the 1979 revolution are clouded by a miasma of propaganda. Christians inside and outside the country are divided and confused about their response. Pray for discernment.

2. **The turning to God since 1972 has been miraculous.** God used many means:

a) The devastating earthquakes that destroyed Managua brought evangelical churches and agencies together in a beautiful cooperation resulting in multiplied conversions.

b) Aggressive evangelism through Evangelism in Depth, mass crusades (notably of Luis Palau and others), also church outreaches.

c) The acute sufferings since 1977 due to war have made people seek after God.

Evangelicals have grown about 12% a year for the last 15 years, and are becoming a significant minority. In 1960 Evangelicals were only 2% of the population.

3. **CEPAD, The Evangelical Committee for Relief and Development**, emerged as one of the major cooperative bodies for evangelicals after the 1972 earthquake. CEPAD enjoys acceptance with the government and credibility with many Evangelicals. The National Council of Evangelical Pastors is an alternative body more fully representative of evangelicals in 65 denominations, and about 800 of the 1,500 evangelical pastors are members. Pray that evangelicals may continue that record without compromise to the Truth or to their primary responsibility to evangelize.

4. **The attitude of Christians to politics is a burning issue**. Many are supportive of much good that the Sandinista government has done, others are opposed to their Marxist policies. Pray for unity among true believers and wisdom as to how to respond to efforts by the new leaders to politicize and even limit the activities of churches. Few Christians have faced up to the challenge posed by liberation theology.

5. **There is a crisis in the Catholic Church**. The hierarchy is strongly anti-Marxist, but many parish priests are convinced by the arguments of liberation theology. Church attendances are dropping, and few Nicaraguans are becoming priests.

6. **Leadership training** is of enhanced importance in the light of pressures on the churches. There are eight evangelical theological institutions. Pray for national staff, maintenance of their loyalty to the Bible, and clarity of presentation to students.

7. **The English/Creole and Miskito-speaking Christians** on the Atlantic coast have suffered intensely through tactless handling by government forces in the early days after the revolution. Forcible removal and collectivization was resisted, and 25,000 Miskito people fled to Honduras. There are many believers among these peoples; pray that their sufferings may draw them closer to God. The Moravian Church is the largest Christian denomination among them.

8. **Young people** live under exceptional pressures. Heady revolutionary fervour and national pride hardens the hearts of unbelievers and dampens the desire of believers to share their faith. Pray that personal relationship to Christ may be seen as more important than the claims of the state.

9. **Less reached sections of the population:**
   a) **The militarized youth** that have known little but propaganda and war.
   b) **The hispanicized Indians** are nominally Catholic, and few active evangelical congregations exist among them.
   c) **The Black Caribs** are still largely animist, though there are churches among them.

10. **Missionaries** still in the country need tact and sensistivity to maintain fruitful links with national and spiritual leaders. Relationships between nationals and expatriates have been difficult in the past. The missionary numbers are dwindling because many are of US origin. The priority in ministry is in Bible teaching.

11. **The post-revolutionary literacy drive** was highly successful. The government asked for 800,000 NTs and Bible portions (**UBS**) for distribution to the newly literate. Pray that this may bear fruit, and that there may continue to be freedom for distribution of Christian literature and Bibles.

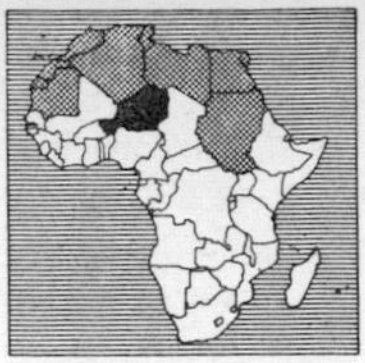

NIGER
(Republic of Niger)

Africa

Aug 20-21

Area 1,267,000. Sahara desert in centre and north. Only the southwest and a narrow strip along the Nigeria border in the south are savannah grasslands.

Population 6,500,000. Annual growth 2.8%. People per sq.km. 5.

Peoples: All peoples 25.
Black African peoples (22) 90.7%. Hausa 2,800,000; Djerma 942,000; Fulani 696,000; Songhai 357,000; Kanuri 356,000; Maouri 123,000; Manga 104,000; Zaghawa 78,000; Kurfey 65,000; Gurma 40,000, etc.
Tuareg 9%. Predominantly nomadic in the north.
Other 0.3%. French, etc.

Literacy 8%. **Official language:** French. **Trade language:** Hausa. **All languages** 14. **Bible translations** 2Bi 3NT 2por.

Capital: Niamey 298,000. Urbanization 16%.

Economy: Mining of uranium and other minerals was bringing some economic development to this impoverished land, but in the '80s the Sahel famine, collapse of the uranium market and Nigeria's closure of the common border devastated the economy. Ninety per cent of the population live at bare subsistence level at the best of times. Income/person $240 (2% of USA).

Politics: Independent from France in 1960. Republic with military government. Stability reduced because of economic stresses and Libyan interference.

Religion: A secular state with freedom of religion. There are pressures to make the country more Islamic.
Islam 86%. Sunni Muslims, many linked with Sufi brotherhoods. Islam is strongest among the settled Fulani, Kanuri, Hausa city dwellers and Tuareg.
African traditional religions 13%. Only two peoples have resisted Islam: the Kurfey and Maouri.
Christian 0.4%. Affiliated 0.28%. Almost all French Catholics — many nominal.
Roman Catholic 0.17%. 11,000a. Only a few Niger citizens.
Protestant 0.08%. 5,000a; 2,400m. Denominations 6. Largest (adherents):

Evangelical Church (**SIM**)	2,900
Evangelical Baptist Church	750

Evangelical 0.07% of population.
Missionaries to Niger 193 (1:33,700 people) in 12 agencies.

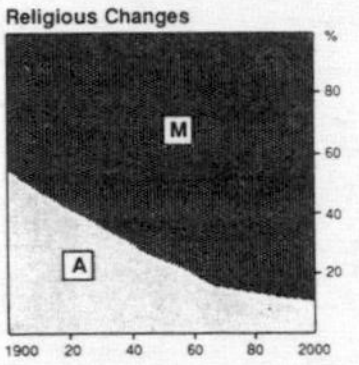

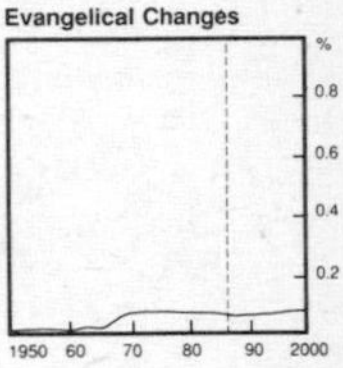

1. **This Muslim land is open for the gospel**, and Muslims are more receptive than ever before, yet response has been very small. Islam is strong and well organized. An Islamic university has opened near Niamey. Pray that the land may remain open, and that every social, religious and spiritual barrier to the knowledge of the Lord may be removed. In 1981 some restrictions were placed on missionaries preaching; new missions must limit their activities to social welfare.

2. **There are too few missionaries to cover all the opportunities.** Pray out labourers into this difficult and long-resistant land. The loving ministry of missionaries in about seven Christian aid agencies and missions, through health education, rural improvement and other aid programmes has won credibility for the gospel and created a new interest among Muslims and pagans. **SIM** has 113 missionaries and is by far the largest agency, with a wide range of ministries, including the only mission hospital in the land. Pray for sensitivity in helping the small, young churches and their leaders to maturity.

3. **The Church in Niger** is small and weak, yet believers have shown courage and initiative in evangelism. There has been an increase in church planting in several areas since 1980. Believers are often isolated and widely separated; few are literate or have had consistent Bible teaching, and in only two peoples have churches been planted. Pray that the little groups of believers may make a decisive impact on their needy land and its peoples.

4. **Leadership in the churches.** There have been problems due to lack of fellowship, co-ordination and maturity — pray! There are two Bible schools (one in Hausa and one in French), both initiated by **SIM**. The latter also serves Burkina Faso and Benin. Pray for the emergence of a mature, educated, articulate leadership. **SIM** runs small TEE programmes in nine centres.

5. **In only six peoples are there missionaries labouring.** Only among the Gurma (Baptists) and Hausa (**SIM**) have churches emerged. Pray for pioneering work among these and also:

a) **The Tuareg,** once rich, but impoverished by the Sahel famine and dependent on aid. The selfless ministry of missionaries from **SIM**, Baptist International Missions and Sahara Desert Mission opened the hearts of some, and there are two or three small groups of believers. **SIM** missionaries are translating the Scriptures.

b) **The Djerma** still 25% animist, with only 50 believers. Evangelical Baptist missionaries have laboured long, but no breakthrough has yet come among this resistant people.

c) **Manga** (Kanuri) in the east among whom **SIM** has a good entry and where there is the beginning of a response. **SIL** is translating the Scriptures for them. There are now about 10 believers.

6. **Unreached and unoccupied peoples are numerous.**

a) **The Songhay, Kurfey, Wogo** (30,000), **Kado**, who are Muslims living along the Niger River in the southwest.

b) **The Fulani** — both the settled Sokoto and nomadic Fulani of the west, and the less Islamized nomadic Fulani across the whole country. There are some believers in surrounding countries, but only about 10 known in Niger. Radio ELWA broadcasts in Fulani, and one **SIM** couple is committed to this people.

c) **Non-Muslim minorities:** Kurfey (50,000), Maouri (120,000) speak Hausa and are similar to the Maguzawa of Nigeria. **SIM** has some contact with them.

d) **The nomadic peoples of the Sahara** notably the Tubu in the northeast, and Zaghawa near Lake Chad and west of Agades.

7. **Young people** have been the most responsive, yet little has been done to minister to this key section of the community. There is a small GBU(**IFES**) group in the university, but most of the believers are from other African lands.

8. **Distribution of Christian literature** is limited due to illiteracy and poverty. There are only two Christian bookstores in the land. Much remains to be done in Bible translation. At least seven languages may need translation work.

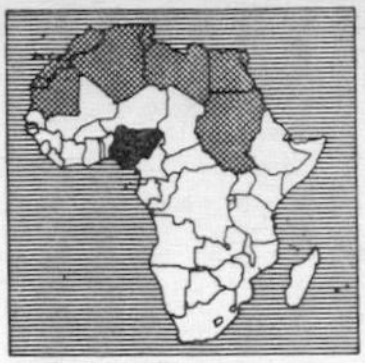

NIGERIA

(The Federal Republic of Nigeria)

Africa

Aug 22-25

Area 924,000. Tropical forest in south, merging into savannah in the north. Divided into 19 states to minimize the impact of ethnic loyalties on national politics.

Population est. 91,200,000. No reliable census since independence; the northern population is likely to be overestimated. Annual growth 3.1%. People per sq.km. 99. Africa's most populous state.

Peoples: Over 426 known. The major groups are: Yoruba 17.8%, Ibo 17.5%, Hausa 16.8%, Fulani 10.3%, Tiv 5.6%, Kanuri 4.7%. See more details under regions.

Literacy 30%. **Official language:** English. **Trade languages:** Hausa in north and centre, Yoruba in southwest, Ibo in southeast. **All languages** 408, though some say 510. **Bible translations** 15Bi 33NT 48por.

Capital: Lagos est. 4-5 mill., capital being transferred to Abuja in central Nigeria. Other major cities: Ibadan 4,000,000; Ado-Ekiti 1,400,000; Port Harcourt 500,000. Twenty-five cities of over 100,000 people. Urbanization 28%.

Economy: Rich in agricultural land and mineral resources. Vast oil wealth in the '70s raised educational and living standards, but also stimulated gross misuse of public funds. Grandiose prestige projects, spectacular corruption, incompetent management and neglect of agriculture were the result. The collapse of oil prices then quickened both the collapse of the economy and the fall of the corrupt civilian government in 1983. Solutions to Nigeria's economic woes are not yet in sight. Income/person $760 (5% of USA), but the cost of living is high.

Politics: Independent from Britain as a federal state in 1960. Colonial history further polarized the widely differing cultural, religious and educational systems between the Muslim feudal north and the traditional religion/Christian capitalist south. These differences underlie the tensions, coups and Biafra Civil War (1967-70), and attempts by the Muslim north to retain political control. The civilian government ousted in 1983 was predominantly Muslim, as was the military regime that followed. The latter found it difficult to cope with the economic crisis, and there was widespread disillusionment, which led to another coup in 1985. The new military government appears to be more vigorous in dealing with the inherent malaise in the structure and economy.

Religion: Freedom of religion, but most post-independence governments giving preferential treatment to Islam. Statistics for religions and churches given below are nearly all estimates.

Muslim 36%. Muslims claim up to 60%, non-Muslims as low as 30%. Dominant in federal and military leadership until 1985, and in northern states.

Traditional religions 15%. The majority in numerous peoples in the Middle Belt, but influential in both Muslim peoples of north and west, and Christian peoples of the south.

Christian 49%. Nominal 18%. Affiliated 31%. Large numbers claim to be Catholic, Protestant, etc. but are not affiliated to any church. *All* statistics are approximate but given to indicate the growth of the Church.

Roman Catholic 6.6%. (12% claim to be RC.) Practising 40%. 6,040,000a; 3,323,000m.

Indigenous marginal groups (800+) 5%. 4,560,000a. A profusion of syncretistic denominations.

Foreign marginal groups (20+) 0.4%. Over 20 cults. Largest (adult members):

Jehovah's Witnesses	113,360

Protestant 19%. (28% would claim to be Protestant). 17,584,000a; 5,800,000m. Denominations 140+. Largest (adult members):

Anglican Church		1,000,000
Evang. Chs. of W.Afr. (ECWA/**SIM**)		650,000
TEKAN (**SUM**)	est.	400,000
Nig. Baptist Conv. (**SBC**)		400,000
Christ Apostolic Church	est.	400,000
Nigerian Chr. Fellowship	est.	350,000
Apostolic Church		320,000
Assemblies of God		275,000
Church of God Mission	est.	250,000
Gospel Faith Mission	est.	200,000
Methodist Church		160,000
Qua Iboe Church		83,000

Evangelical 14% of population.

Missionaries to Nigeria est. 950 (1:96,000 people) in about 60 agencies.

Missionaries from within Nigeria est. 740 (1:23,500 Protestants) in about 10 agencies. About 60 of these are outside Nigeria.

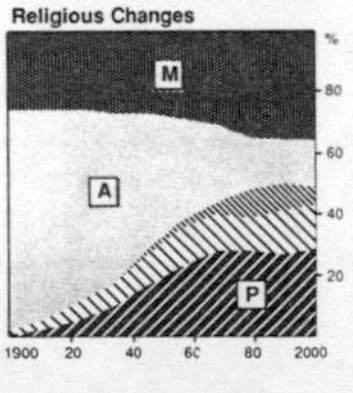

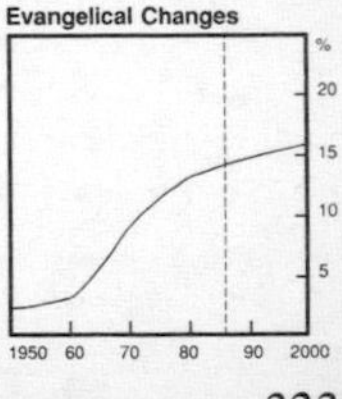

1. **Praise God for the growth and dynamism of the Church in Nigeria.** There have been three great waves of growth: first in the last century on the coast through denominational missions; the second through predominantly interdenominational agencies, such as **SIM** and **SUM**, in the Middle Belt; and since the '60s and '70s, among the more educated through a large number of indigenous denominations and independent fellowship groups. Much of the latter is Pentecostal/Charismatic in flavour, enthusiastically evangelistic and rejects deep-seated witchcraft practised by many who claim to be Christians.

2. **The political and economic crises of Nigeria** have brought frustration and despair to millions. Unless the hearts of men are changed, little improvement can be expected. Pray for a spiritual awakening in the country, and pray that Christians of exemplary life may become decisive in national life. Pray for a government that can unite the country, restore and maintain high ethical standards in all areas of administration, and deal impartially with both Muslims and Christians.

3. **Islam is seeking to gain full control of Nigeria.** The conversion of pagans by bribery or coercion and the limitation of Christian activities and outreach have increased in areas where there are Muslim rulers. In some areas of the north there has been intimidation of Christians, and destruction of churches. Christians are both unsure how to react and unprepared for active, loving witness to Muslims. There have been a number of extremist Muslim riots during the '80s with considerable loss of life. Pray that the forces of darkness may be bound and captives set free. There are congregations in some cities that are almost entirely of Muslim origin.

4. **The Nigerian church** has grown with an influx of millions of non-Christians over the past 30 years. Pray for the correction of inherent dangers:

a) **Massive evangelism without adequate discipling and biblical teaching.** Witchcraft, polygamy, tribalism and secret societies are serious problems which have not been adequately faced.

b) **Materialism, position and power seeking, and selfishness** have further harmed the spiritual impact of churches. Divisions, fragmentation and a profusion of indigenous denominations and sects are the results.

c) **Second generation nominalism** in both traditional and younger churches is becoming a problem of enormous proportions. Where the Holy Spirit has not broken through, immorality, corruption and sin can be just as prevalent among "Christians" as among the unsaved.

d) **The rapid growth of the Aladura Churches** and other syncretistic, indigenous churches is a challenge for Bible-believing Christians.

5. **Praise God for Nigerian leadership** that has emerged for churches and a multiplicity of agencies and ministries. Almost all foreign mission work is under the supervision of local leadership. Yet the rapid growth of the Church and the enormous social and economic changes over the past 20 years have placed great strains on the leadership.

a) **There are not enough mature, qualified leaders.** So pray for the 45+ seminaries and Bible schools and the expanding TEE programmes run by many churches. Pray also for the provision of suitable Nigerian and missionary staff.

b) **There is a serious generation gap.** Many older pastors are not able to meet the needs of better educated congregations, and few churches can adequately meet the needs of young people who are often more at ease in English.

c) **A strong individualism** in many leaders has led to divisions and the starting of many one-man ministries and agencies that are especially prevalent in the eastern states. Pray that Christian leaders may be Christlike in their relationships with one another, submitting to one another in love.

6. **Young people have responded to the gospel in huge numbers**, and it is among them that there is such a move of the Spirit today. It is especially in the secondary schools and universities that this is most evident.

a) **Scripture Union** in the south and **Fellowship of Christian Students** in the north have had a big impact on secondary schools through a network of groups in most schools. Pray for the overworked travelling secretaries, Christian teachers who act as advisers and for wise and effective student leadership. Enthusiasm has sometimes taken groups into doctrinal extremes.

b) **NIFES** is the world's second largest body affiliated to **IFES** with over 20,000 members in the 17 universities, etc. Pray for those in leadership nationally and on the campuses, and for a depth of teaching and experience that will enable them to become Christian leaders in society. Relatively few graduates become active in local churches.

c) **Christian Students Social Movement** (CSSM) has been doing much to mobilize prayer among students for the nation and the world.

7. **Missionary help is desired by the churches**, but visas are becoming difficult to obtain. Pray for the issue of visas and a more sympathetic attitude by immigration authorities. The rapid growth of the Church, and the number of unreached areas and peoples, mean that the churches need all the help and encouragement they can get. Pioneer evangelism and church planting, Bible teaching and leadership training, Bible knowledge, teaching in schools, a wide range of supportive and aid ministries and training Nigerian missionaries are key ministries needed today. Pray for harmonious, helpful relationships between Nigerian and expatriate workers, not easy to maintain in the stresses of modern Nigeria. Some of the larger agencies are **SUM** (260 missionaries), **SIM** (200), **SBC** (130), **QIM** (41).

8. **Literature is vital for the growth of the Church.** It is avidly sought but in short supply.

a) **Authors** — too few Nigerians are writing relevant Christian books and literature; too much is foreign and superficial.

b) **Printing** has become an acute problem through strict import controls for paper and printing equipment, etc. A number of Christian agencies are seeking ways of setting up more printing presses. Pray that ways and means may be found to print more Christian literature at a price which the people can afford.

c) **Publishing.** Christian publishers — such as ECWA Productions, TEKAN Publications, Baraka Publications in the north, Christian Media Fellowship and **SU** — publish books, magazines, Sunday School materials and Bible-reading notes; but all are frustratingly limited by the economic situation and need prayer.

d) **Distribution**. There are over 300 Christian bookstores in Nigeria, 36 of ECWA, 30 of TEKAN; but there is an alarming lack of books and Bibles to sell due to severe import restrictions. Pray for viable solutions.

9. **Electronic evangelism and teaching** has become important in modern Nigeria.

a) **Cassettes and records** are an essential component for evangelism and teaching. In numerous smaller languages this is the only convenient way of communicating the Good News. **GRI** has recordings in 430 languages and dialects. Pray for a wider use of this medium and for more Nigerians to be involved.

b) **Television** is widely used, and Christian programmes produced by churches and agencies in Nigeria are snapped up by many state TV stations. However, in some states restrictions and prohibitive prices have reduced access to such facilities. **NLFA** studios produce a variety of TV programmes, but more studios are needed. Pray for better production facilities and wise programme selection that will make a lasting impact on Christian and non-Christian viewers.

c) **Films and filmstrips** are effective evangelistic tools. ECWA Media is one agency which produces the latter and maintains a good library of the former. Hundreds every month make decisions for Christ through this medium.

d) **Radio.** ECWA (**SIM**) maintains two studios and produces 37 programmes weekly in six languages for transmission over ELWA (Liberia). Muryar Bishara studio (**SUM**, Lutheran) produce programmes in Hausa and Fulani and seek new outlets for their broadcasting.

10. **Bible translation is still a massive task.** Many missions and Nigerian churches are involved in over 39 translation projects. Of especial mention is the oversight of the Bible

Society and the translation work of Nigerian Bible Translation Trust, the indigenous continuation of the work of **SIL**. The latter has translation teams working in 10 languages. However, only 33 languages have a NT, and over 310 have nothing of the Scriptures. Pray especially for Nigerian Christians to catch a vision for this ministry.

11. **The Great Commission is becoming a concern of Nigerian Christians.** In spite of the serious social and economic obstacles, the number of missionaries sent out by churches and agencies is increasing. The stimulus of Lausanne 1974, the Nigeria Congress on Evangelism 1975, the founding of the **Nigeria Evangelical Missions Association** (**NEMA**) in 1982 have all helped to push this vision. The **Evangelical Missionary Society** of ECWA has by far the largest number of cross-cultural missionaries (622 in 1985), but TEKAN, Baptists, Anglicans and others have sent out a considerable number. Young evangelical, interdenominational agencies are multiplying and reaching out to the unreached in Nigeria and beyond. Some such are **Calvary Ministries** (41 workers), **Christian Missionary Foundation** (25), and **Nations for Christ** (9). Pray for them. The acute problem of sending financial support out of the country holds back many Nigerians from working in other countries of West Africa. Pray for these difficulties to be overcome, and for the Church in Nigeria to make an impact for God on the Muslim areas of Africa.

12. **The unreached**. No accurate survey of Nigeria's unreached peoples and areas, nor of Nigeria's churches, has ever been made, but **NEMA** is now undertaking it. Pray for this. Some estimate that there could be 37 people groups accounting for 30 million people yet to be reached.

NIGERIA REGIONS

Regional descriptions help in understanding the highly complex social and religious situation. Religious percentages are approximations.

THE SOUTHEAST

States: Anambra, Cross River, Imo, Rivers.

Population 21,600,000.

Major peoples: Ibo 16,000,000; Ibibio 4,300,000; Igala 100,000. About 110 other indigenous languages.

Religion: Christian 80%, Traditional religions 17%, Muslim 3%.

1. **The region was pioneered by Presbyterians, Catholics, QIM,** etc. The Christians are in a large majority. The civil war was a harrowing time, and through the suffering came spiritual deepening and revival to many congregations. During those five years the Qua Iboe Church greatly increased its membership; and the Apostolic Church, Baptist, **AoG**, ECWA, TEKAN, Church of God Mission and other Pentecostal groups also multiplied. Outreach has been vigorous.

2. **There is a lack of full-time workers because of the lack of means to support them**; pray for more to be called and equipped for evangelistic, pastoral and missionary service.

3. **Unreached peoples and areas.** The Igala to the north, and some peoples of the Niger River and Delta, and Cameroon border areas are less evangelized. The need must be better researched, and local believers mobilized for cross-cultural outreach, church planting and Bible translation to those groups who are more needy.

THE SOUTHWEST

States: Lagos, Bendel, Ondo, Ogun, Oyo.

Population 22,000,000.

Major peoples (figures for whole nation): Yoruba 16,000,000 Edo 3,00,000; Ijo 1,800,000. Thirty-eight other indigenous peoples.

Religion: Christian 60%, Traditional religions 15%, Muslim 15%.

1. **The Christian majority** is predominantly Anglican, Methodist and Baptist, the result of mission endeavour in the last century, and also major indigenous denominations such as Christ Apostolic Church, Gospel Faith Mission and Church of God Mission. It is respectable to be a Christian, but occultic influences, the Ogbuni cult, secret societies, as well as worldliness, stagnation and lack of outreach are common among Christians. There are many indigenous Pentecostal groups springing up in the region. Pray for revival, and a greater awareness and concern for Muslim Yoruba and other unreached peoples in the region and beyond.

2. **Unreached areas and peoples**:

a) **The growing cities** are insufficiently evangelized despite the profusion of denominations. Lagos has a bad reputation for spiritual deadness and sin. There are many young, enthusiastic evangelists, but there is little coordination or conservation of the fruits of their efforts.

b) **The Muslim Yoruba** are a large minority in the cities and northern part of the region. Few Christians have sought to evangelize them. Pray especially for the large Muslim population of the city of Ilorin.

c) **There are ethnic groups and areas** along the Benin border and in the east where Christian penetration has not been great.

d) **Areas along the lagoon** and riverine parts of Lagos, Ondu, Ogun and Bendel are unreached.

THE MIDDLE BELT,

the southern half of the old northern region.

States: Kwara, Niger, Plateau, Benue, Gongola. (Culturally, S. Kaduna and S. Bauchi belong to this region.)

Population 17,300,000.

Major peoples: No dominant group, but a medley of over 230 languages, most using Hausa as a trade language. Largest: Tiv 5,100,000, Nupe 1,800,000

Religion: Muslim 30%, Animist 25%, Christian 45%.

1. **The region was pioneered at great cost in the early years of this century by SIM in the west and centre, and SUM** (a family of eight denominational and interdenominational missions) in the centre and east. The ministries of these missions have been merged with, or absorbed into, their large daughter churches. (Evangelical Churches of West Africa or ECWA (**SIM**) and Fellowship of Churches of Christ in Nigeria or TEKAN (**SUM**).) Pray for the continuing work of **SIM** and **SUM** missionaries in their self-effacing ministry of support and help to these churches in their maturation and outreach.

2. **The churches have grown dramatically** over the last 30 years. Some denominations experienced 400% growth in the last 15 years. The churches are almost entirely evangelical with a vigorous evangelistic outreach. New Life For All proved most successful in this area and many believers were mobilized for profitable outreach. Pray for the continued (though in a lower key) **NLFA** outreach through witness teams in the centre and north of the country. Pray for the spiritual growth of believers and also for the conversion of the younger generation — nominalism is becoming a problem. The Anglicans and the Baptists are making a significant contribution to the evangelization of the area.

3. **Muslim missionary activity** has been most marked in this region. Considerable efforts are made to win over pagans and backsliding Christians. Pray that these attempts may be frustrated by conversions to Christ. Pray that Christians may overcome historic hatreds and personal fears for courageous witnessing to Muslims in love.

4. **Unreached peoples**. There are 60-70 people groups in the region which have shown minimal response to the gospel, but the overall situation is inadequately researched. There are four main areas where many unreached peoples live.

a) **The Gwoza Hills in the northeast** (North Gongola State and South Borno State). The area has become a spiritual battleground, with some peoples turning from paganism to

Islam and others to Christ. Over 23 peoples live in the area. Pray for the peoples in the heart of the battle — Guduf, Hidkata, Dghwede and Matakam.

b) **The Mountain regions in the east around Yola in Gongola State** are the home of numerous peoples, some scarcely touched by civilization. Over 50 peoples live in the area, many unreached. Pray especially for pioneer outreach to the Mumuye 600,000; Chamba 130,000; Bata 50,000, etc.

c) **Some resistant people in Plateau State** are still predominantly animist such as the Bassa 120,000; Afo 35,000, etc.

d) **Along the Niger River and Benin border** there are numerous unreached and partially reached peoples — pray for the Muslim Nupe, pagan Kambari 130,000; Gbari Yamma 100,000; Dukawa 73,000; Busa 60,000; Kamuku 25,000, etc. The Dukawa and sections of the Kambari are now turning to Islam in large numbers. Only a handful of Christian workers are attempting to reach them.

THE NORTH

States: Sokoto, Kaduna, Kano, Bauchi, Bornu.

Population 30,000,000.

Major peoples: Hausa 15,300,000; Fulani 9,300,000; Kanuri 4,500,000. About 40 other smaller groups north of the Middle Belt.

Religion: Muslim est. 77%, Animist 15%, Christian 8%. Latter mainly in South Kaduna.

1. **There have been great gospel advances into this Muslim area** over the last 20 years. There is a slow but steady trickle of Muslims being converted and churches planted in both the Muslim centres of Sokoto and Kano as well as in the rural areas. Pray for a greater harvest in coming days. Converts out of Islam face considerable opposition and hostility from relatives. Most of the Christians are from further south; pray for their witness to be effective among their Muslim neighbours.

2. **The need for missionaries. SIM** and **SUM** have sought to evangelize in this area for many years, but the work has been hard. Praise God for the increasing missionary concern of the Nigerian church for the evangelization of the north. Pray for the calling of ex-Muslims into full-time service, and also for their training as missionaries to Muslim peoples.

3. **Unreached peoples:**

a) **The Fulani** are a strategic people right across Africa. Their origin was in Senegal, but their greatest number is in Nigeria where nine million of the possibly 16 million Fulani live. They form both the strongly Muslim ruling class in Nigeria and also the nominally Muslim nomadic cattle grazers over much of Nigeria and the Sahel. About 93% of Nigerian Fulani are Muslim. There has been a growing response through ECWA-**SIM** and others, and there may now be 2,000 Christians. In 1983 the **Joint Christian Ministry in W.Africa** was formed to specifically coordinate evangelism, literature, radio, and training ministries. Pray for vital churches to be planted that will effectively meet the spiritual needs of the nomadic people. Pray that Christians in W.Africa might be enthused to reach them. If the gospel gripped the Fulani, all W.Africa would be affected! Many of the urban Fulani speak only Hausa and must be reached through this language.

b) **The Hausa** are known as Muslims; very few have ever believed on the Lord Jesus. Yet about 30% of the Hausa only claim to be Muslim to the casual enquirer and are actually pagan. The majority of these are known as **Maguzawa**, a people with their own distinctive culture, and among them an exciting turning to Christ is going on. Many new ECWA, Anglican, Baptist and other churches are being planted in rural areas. Another pagan group, the **Gwandarawa** (200,000), is also beginning to respond (ECWA). Pray for large numbers of Hausa to be won to Christ in this day of opportunity.

c) **The Kanuri of Borno State** are strongly Muslim, and have been so for 1,000 years. There are only 25 known believers among the 4,500,000 Kanuri after years of witness by COCIN-**SUM** missionaries. Bible translation is progressing, but the key to the hearts of the Kanuri has yet to be found. Pray that the breakthrough may soon come.

NIUE

See Cook Islands on p. 150.

NORWAY
(Kingdom of Norway)

The West

Aug 26

Area 324,000 sq.km. Also Arctic dependencies of Jan Mayen and Svalbard (Spitzbergen) Islands 62,000 sq.km. One of the four Scandinavian countries, a long, fjord-indented, mountainous land.

Population 4,200,000. Annual growth 0.2%. People per sq.km. 13.

Peoples
Norwegian 97.7%. Descendants of the Germanic Vikings.
Other minorities 2.3%. Sami (Lapp) 30,000; other Scandinavian 46,000.

Literacy 96%. **Official languages:** Norwegian (Bokmål and Nynorsk).

Capital: Oslo 726,000. Urbanization 71%

Economy: Strong and wealthy industrial state with high earnings from oil, mining, fishing and forest products. Income/person $13,820 (98% of USA).

Politics: Independent from Sweden in 1905 as a parliamentary monarchy.

Religion: The Lutheran Church is the official religion of the state, but there is complete freedom for other denominations and religions.
Non-religious/Atheist 3.4%.
Muslim 0.4%.
Christian 96.2%.
Roman Catholic 0.4%. 17,000a. Predominantly immigrant communities.
Marginal groups 0.5%. 19,000a. Mainly Jehovah's Witnesses.
Protestant 95.3%. 4,000,000a; 2,900,000m. Denominations 36. Largest (adherents):

Church of Norway (Lutheran)	3,850,000
Pentecostal Assemblies	44,000
Salvation Army	42,000
Ev. Lutheran Free Church	19,641
Methodist Church	17,500
Baptist Union	12,500
Mission Covenant Church	12,500

Evangelical 20% or more of population.
Missionaries from Norway 1,539 (1:2,600 Protestants) in 40 agencies and 44 lands.
Missionaries to Norway 75 in about 12 agencies.

1. **There is much spiritual life in Norway** through the influence of Pietism, prayer and revival movements within the State Church over the past 300 years, which have left a strong evangelical heritage. Yet today believers long for revival. Pray for a fresh outpouring of the Spirit that will thrust out more soul-winners and evangelists.

2. **The Lutheran Church** is unique in Europe, for although it is the State Church, most of the pastors are theologically evangelical. Most Norwegians, though, have little understanding of the new-birth. Many voluntary organizations have sprung up within the Church with a burden for home and overseas evangelism. Pray that this large Church may not be moved from its biblical basis, and may be continually freshened by the work of the Holy Spirit.

3. **The Free Churches** are a small but significant minority, yet only a few of the Pentecostal groups and Baptists are showing any growth at all. Pray that this stagnation may end, and that a new vision for evangelism may emerge.

4. **Theological training** in university theological faculties and Bible schools has generally been evangelical; pray that this may continue. Pray that many may be called into Christian service at home and abroad.

5. **More needy areas and peoples:**
   a) **Oslo and the surrounding area** has a low number of evangelical Christians.

b) **The Sami** are nominally Lutheran, but committed believers are relatively few. Their language and culture are very different to Norwegian. **EMF** has a work among them.

c) **Immigrant minorities** need to be reached. There are 15,000 Muslims, mainly from Pakistan and the Middle East. A number of Latin American refugees have settled in Norway.

6. **Norway has made a great contribution to world evangelization.** This little land has sent out proportionately more missionaries than almost any other nation in the world. There are about 14,000 mission support groups of believers in Norway. The land has the potential to send and support more — pray them out! There is a new concern for evangelizing unreached peoples.

Middle East

Aug 27

OMAN
(The Sultanate of Oman)

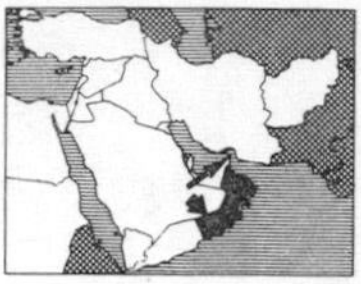

Area 212,000 sq.km. Southeast coast of Arabia and the strategic tip of the Musandam Peninsula that dominates the entrance to the Arabian/Persian Gulf.

Population 1,200,000. Annual growth 3.1%. People per sq.km. 6.

Peoples
Indigenous citizens 85%. Arabs 900,000; Mahri 80,000; Baluch 50,000; Persian 38,000; Indian 30,000; African/Zanzibari 22,000.
Foreign workers 15%. 70% of the workforce is foreign. Expatriate Arabs, Indians and Pakistanis 80,000; Iranis 60,000; British/US 5,500.

Literacy 21%. **Official language:** Arabic. **All languages** 5. **Bible translations** 2Bi 1por.

Capital: Muscat 85,000. Urbanization 8%.

Economy: A latecomer as a Middle Eastern oil producer. Oil revenues are financing agricultural and industrial diversification. Income/person $6,240 (44% of USA).

Politics: Feudal monarchy until 1970. Enlightened absolute monarchy since then. Guerrilla insurrection in Dhofar Province 1963-77 backed by Communist South Yemen.

Religion: Ibadi Islam is the state religion. Catholics and Protestants legally permitted to establish churches for the expatriate communities.
Muslim 97.4%. Ibadis in majority, minorities of 7% Shi'ites (many being Irani), 4% Sunni.
Hindu 1%, **Non-religious** 1%.
Christian 0.5%.
- **Roman Catholic** 0.4%. 4,200a.
- **Orthodox** 0.01%. 130a.
- **Protestant** 0.15%. 1,800a; 780m.
  - **Evangelical** 0.1% of population.

Missionaries in Oman 15 (1:80,000 people) in 2 agencies.

1. **Rapid social change** together with war and tensions in the Gulf have begun to break up the stability of the old traditional culture. May this make people receptive to the gospel.

2. **Indigenous Christians** may number 40 in two small Arabic-speaking groups. There are no known believers among any of the minority groups indigenous to Oman; the Mahri villages of Dhofar, Baluchi of the eastern coast or the Indian middle-class traders.

3. **Almost all Christians are among the expatriate work force** — Westerners, Pakistanis and Indians. Pray for a pure life style and glowing witness for believers to their own communities, as well as to indigenous groups. There are several Western and Indian pastors serving these fellowships.

4. **Cross-cultural outreach** must be through Christian "tentmakers" in the future. The Reformed Church of America has maintained a good medical work since 1890. Samuel Zwemer, the famous missionary to Muslims, began his mission work in Oman at that time. The hospital, clinics and missionary workers have been incorporated into the government health service. Pray that by some means the gospel may be proclaimed.

5. **Other means of witness.**

a) **Five family bookshops** (Danish Reformed Church) have a literature outreach in many languages.

b) **Christian radio broadcasts are clearly heard from** FEBA-Seychelles. There is a sizeable audience, and some have come to the Lord.

c) **Over 1,600 Omanis are studying in the West.**

O

Asia

Aug 28-31

PAKISTAN
(Islamic Republic of Pakistan)

Area 804,000 sq.km. Arid mountains in the north and west. Sind desert in southwest. Vast irrigation schemes in the fertile Indus valley.

Population 99,200,000. Annual growth 2.7%. People per sq.km. 123. Over half the population lives in the Punjab.

Peoples
Punjabi 60%. Speaking Punjabi and Urdu. Their dominance is resented by other minorities. They live in the northern plains.
Sindhi 12%. Speaking Sindhi. In the south.
Pushtu-Afghan 15%. Speaking Pushtu and Dari. Numerous tribes and clans, and augmented by Afghan refugees. Majority in Northwest Frontier Province and North Baluchistan.
Baluch 3.5%. Speaking Baluchi. In the west and also in East Iran and South Afghanistan. The 800,000 Dravidian Brahui live among them.
Indian refugees (of 1947) 8%. Speaking Urdu.
Other minorities 1.5%. Tribal groups in the far north (27) 700,000; Tribal Mawari Bhil and Kohli (16 tribes) 700,000.

Literacy 18%. **Official languages:** Urdu, English. Urdu is becoming widely used by all. **All languages** 50. **Bible translations** 6Bi 1NT 8por.

Capital: Islamabad 335,000. Other cities: Karachi est. 8,000,000; Lahore 3,600,000; Rawalpindi 2,000,000; Faisalabad 1,600,000; Peshawar 1,000,000. Urbanization 29%.

Economy: Predominantly agricultural. A large textile industry. Remittances from Pakistanis living and working in Europe, North America and Middle East are the largest source of foreign currency. The large army, and influx of millions of refugees from Afghanistan and Iran, have strained the country's resources. Income/person $390 (3% of USA).

Politics: Independent from Britain at the partition of India in 1947. Constant instability and three wars with India over Kashmir and East Pakistan. (The latter became independent as Bangladesh in 1971.) There was a military takeover in 1977. The regime has sought to further Islamize the nation's institutions and legal system. The Soviet occupation of Afghanistan, and subsequent resistance by Afghans to the invaders, has exposed Pakistan to increased secessionist pressures and the threat of political destabilization.

Religion: Islamic republic. The government is pursuing its policy of Islamization of the legal system, taxation and public life, despite widespread popular misgivings. Minority religions are safeguarded in the constitution, but the situation is both delicate and unclear for non-Muslims.
Muslim 96.6%. Sunni 70%, Shi'a 27% (including the unorthodox Ismaili), Ahmaddiya 3%. The latter are not considered Muslims by the government and are persecuted, and many driven underground.
Hindu 1.6%. Tribal peoples of Sind and some Sindhis and Punjabis.
Christian 1.6%. Affiliated 1.5%.
Roman Catholic 0.5%. Practising 37%. 471,000a; 254,000m. Punjabis and also Goanese in Karachi.
Protestant 1%. 974,000a; 445,000m. Denominations 44. Figures very approximate. Largest (adherents):

Church of Pakistan	400,000
United Presbyterian Church	250,000
National Virgin Church (ex-Presby)	52,000
Salvation Army	50,000
Un. Ch. in Pak. (Lahore Ch. Counc.)	42,000
National Methodist Church	32,000
Assoc. Reformed Presbyterian Ch	25,000
Full Gospel Assemblies (SFM)	12,000
Pakistan Christian Fell. (**ICF**)	2,600
Indus Christian Fell (**CBFMS**)	2,500
International Missions (**IMI**)	2,500
Evangelical Alliance Ch. (**TEAM**)	1,100

Evangelical 0.2% of population.
Missionaries to Pakistan 680 (1:146,000 people) in about 40 agencies.
Missionaries from within Pakistan est. 10.

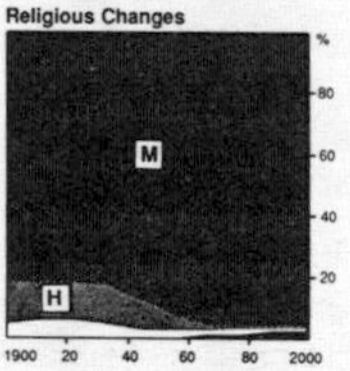

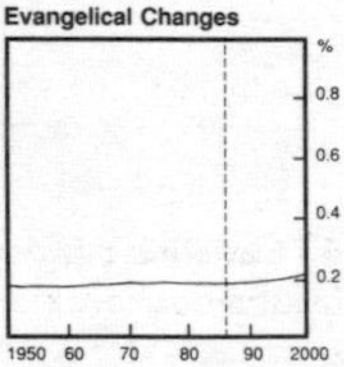

1. **Pakistan is one of the most open Muslim lands for the gospel.** Despite Islamization, Pakistanis are proud of their record of religious freedom and tolerance. Commonwealth citizens are free to live in Pakistan and serve the Lord, but few have taken up the opportunity. Many missions are asking for workers. Pray that the door may remain open; Islamic fundamentalism or Communist plottings from Afghanistan could limit the present freedom.

2. **Muslims have never been so open to the Good News as now**. Pakistan's turbulent recent history, military setbacks and secularism have made many receptive to new ideas. Islamization was instituted to unite the nation, but it has increased sectarian violence. Many are disquieted and disillusioned, and fear the full implementation of Islamic law and practices. Yet despite openness, social pressures limit conversions from among Muslims. Pray for more workers called and equipped to evangelize Muslims and love them into the Kingdom. Pray for the planting of live churches of converts out of Islam, and praise that this is beginning to happen in the cities.

3. **Unevangelized peoples and areas abound.** Pray for:

a) **Baluchi and Brahui**. 75% of the 4,500,000 Baluch live in Pakistan. There are only about 10 known Christian Baluch in the world. Seven hundred thousand live and work in Karachi; Baluchistan is largely desert and not open for expatriate workers. There are no known Christians among the Brahui, who live among them. Pray for the new thrust of **RSMT**, **WEC** and others to this strategic and restive people.

b) **The peoples of the N.W.Frontier** on the Afghan border are predominantly Pushtu, and famed for their warlikeness. There are only a few believers and no known churches of Pushtu speakers. (**ABC**, **TEAM**, **RSMT**, **OM** all have workers in the area.) Over one million Pushtu-speaking people live in Karachi.

c) **The mountain tribes of the northern mountains and Pakistani Kashmir**. Over 27 small peoples live in the districts of Kohistan, Swat, Dir, Chitral and Gilgit. For years no Christian witness was possible, but now pioneer thrusts are being made into the region through medical workers. The 3,000 Kalash are largely animist, but turning to Islam since 1975. All the other peoples are Muslim — Sunni, Shi'a, and Ismaili. Pray especially for the 60,000 Burushaski of the Hunza, the 60,000 Tibetan-related Balti, the 200,000 Khowaris of Chitral, the 100,000 Shina, as well as the numerous smaller groups. There is not one known church among any of these peoples.

d) **The Sindhi and Punjabi majority** on the Indus plain. Christians are almost exclusively from the Hindu minorities that were originally at the bottom of the social order. Few Muslims have been evangelized. There is no known ethnic Sindhi church.

e) **Karachi** is a city of many languages and peoples. Every community in Pakistan is represented, and this is one of the key areas for the evangelization of the non-Christian majority of Pakistan. Pray for workers to be set apart for each community in the city — pray especially for the many Urdu-speaking "mujahir", (those who fled from India in 1947), Baluchi, Pushtu, Ismaili Muslims (400,000), Afghan refugees (100,000) and Irani refugees (15,000). The few Protestant churches cater for the needs of the Punjabis and other minority groups; they are small and the Christians discouraged.

f) **Afghan refugees** have been pouring out of their land since 1978 and probably number four million. There are 330 government refugee camps in which most of the poorer refugees live. Forty-six per cent of the population are children, and the rest predominantly women as the majority of the men are looking for work or fighting the Russian occupation forces. They are mainly Dari speaking, but many Pushtu, Uzbeks and other ethnic groups are represented. Never have Afghans been so open for and to the gospel, but only a few Christian workers are permitted to give material and spiritual aid to them. Pray for **ABC** and **SERVE** workers who are committed to this ministry.

g) **The 3,500,000 Ahmaddiya Muslim sect** is militantly missionary minded. Few have ever come to Christ.

4. **Christian missions have been working in the land since 1833**. Christian standards and institutions have had a deep impact on the country. Presbyterians, Anglicans, Methodists and, later, Salvation Army missionaries pioneered the work. There was a great turning to the Lord from six of the 30 scheduled Hindu castes between 1890 and 1930. This was accompanied by revival in 1904. Other missions, predominantly evangelical, entered Pakistan at or after independence. Most of the latter work together in the Pakistan Evangelical Fellowship and in a number of inter-church/mission projects. Some larger missions are **OM** (78 — mostly short-term workers), **BMMF** (57 workers), **TEAM** (42), PCF(**ICF**) (30), CMS (29), **CBFMS** (15), **ABC** (11), **WEC** (11), **IMI** (10), **RSMT** (8). The great majority of missionaries are serving

within the existing church structures; only a minority in pioneer evangelism and church planting. There are many openings for service. Most missionaries are from the West, but an increasing number come from Asian lands.

5. **Church growth** is occurring only among some of the Mawari and Kohli tribes in the southwest (**BMMF**, **PCF**, **CBFMS**), and in several cities. Decline is more evident. Yet there are reachable and potentially responsive segments of society — refugees, Hindus of Karachi, and marginally reached tribes in the southwest. Pray for a prayer burden among Christians and the right strategies for today's Pakistan.

6. **The Christians are almost all Punjabi-speaking** of Hindu derivation. Many are still illiterate. Most are second, third and fourth generation Christians who lack spiritual life and teaching. Tragically, some churches in Pakistan are riven by squalid leadership struggles, court cases, factionalism and schism. As a result, the leaders have lost credibility, and the members have become demoralized. Some Christians are drifting away from the churches, adopting Muslim customs and marrying Muslim partners. Pray for:

a) **Spiritual unity and revival**.

b) **Pakistani church leaders and pastors**. Some are walking in the Spirit, but others are not born-again. Praise God for a new generation of young leaders emerging.

c) **A vision to reach out to Muslims**. Only a handful of Pakistani Christians are full-time in such an outreach. **OM** teams have challenged many believers to become involved in outreach — pray that this challenge may affect whole congregations too.

d) **A missionary vision**. Large numbers of Pakistanis work in the Middle East, Christians among them. Pray for the preparation and witness of 'tentmaking' missionaries in these closed lands — a vision of **BMMF**. The St. Andrews Sending Fellowship in Lahore supports four workers in cross-cultural outreach.

7. **Leadership training**. There are four small theological colleges and Bible schools, the best known being the inter-church/mission theological seminary and United Bible Training Centre at Gujranwala. Too few respond to the call of God, and lack of finance limits many. Pray that a higher proportion of Pakistani Christian leaders may be able to serve in national churches without the support of foreign agencies. The TEE (PACTEE) programme is useful, but there is a lack of personnel and teaching materials in local scripts. There are 200 students in 15 centres.

8. **Christian literature is much in demand** despite low literacy. Pray for:

a) **The MIK Christian Publishing House** pioneered by Brethren missionaries, where a wide range of Christian literature, including **SGM** publications, is translated, edited and published.

b) **The Bible Society** has a bold Bible printing, translating and distributing programme and aims to increase distribution outlets from 250 to 1,000 between 1984 and 1990.

c) The huge quantities of Christian literature distributed by **OM** teams every year.

d) **ELS** (**CLC**) book shop and literature outreach in Karachi.

9. **Bible translation** is an ongoing ministry. Most major languages have a Bible or NT, but considerable revision work, research, and pioneer translation is needed, especially in the northern languages. There are six languages now in translation — one key project is the Baluch NT. **SIL** has a number of projects "on the go". Pray for all involved.

10. **Bible Correspondence Courses** have proved a most useful means of evangelizing Muslims and teaching Christians. Pray for both the inter-mission Pakistan Bible Correspondence School and the courses run by the Swedish Pentecostals. Pray for the staff and students, and that there will be eternal fruit.

11. **Youth work** has not yet developed sufficiently, and is a major item for prayer. Good work is being done by **SU**, **CEF**, **CCC**, Church Foundation Seminars and **YFC**, but the labourers equipped for these specialized ministries are few. Pray for PFES(**IFES**) who have 9 staff workers and an expanding ministry in universities. Six of the 12 universities now have groups. Pray for the ministry of **SU** staff workers.

12. **Christian radio** is limited by the small number of programmes aired, and the lack of short-wave radios in Pakistan. Pray for the recording studios where programmes are prepared in three languages. **TWR** broadcasts for two and a half hours in Urdu; and **FEBA** 25 hours in Urdu, seven in Pushtu and only one in Punjabi. Pray for an increase in the latter and a wider linguistic range of broadcasts. There is nothing in Baluchi or Sindhi.

13. **Pakistanis have emigrated all over the world in recent years** — especially to the Middle East, North America, Britain and Australia. Very few Muslims of Pakistani origin have come to Christ in these lands, and Christians have done relatively little to rectify this situation.

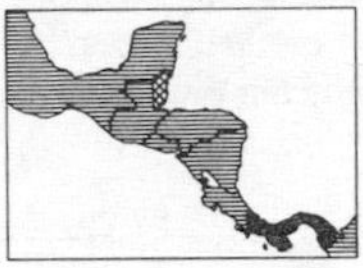

PANAMA
(Republic of Panama)

Latin America

Sept 1

Area 77,000 sq.km. The narrowest point of the Central American isthmus, and bisected by the Panama Canal. The former Canal Zone (ex-US) 1,432 sq.km.

Population 2,140,000. Annual growth 2.2%. People per sq.km. 28.

Peoples
Spanish-speaking 79%. Ladino (Eurindian) 1,400,000; European (Spanish descent) 190,000; African origin 85,000.
English/Creole-speaking 10%. West Indians, US civilians and military; both groups declining through assimilation and emigration.
Amerindians 5%. Speaking eight languages, Guaymi(2) 50,000; Kuna(2) 38,000; Choco(3) 12,000; Buglere 2,500.
Asians 6%. East Indians 90,000; Chinese 33,000; Lebanese, etc.

Literacy 80%. **Official language:** Spanish. **All languages** 12. **Bible translations** 3Bi 1NT 8por.

Capital: Panama City 851,000. Urbanization 60%.

Economy: Petroleum products, revenues from the canal and large "flag of convenience" fleet of ships, and agriculture are the main sources of income. Income/person $2,070 (15% of USA).

Politics: Republic which became independent in 1903. A succession of strong military and weak civilian governments. The USA returned the Canal Zone to Panama in 1979 whilst retaining some controls until 2000.

Religion: A secular state with religious freedom.
Muslim 4.5%. East Indians, Lebanese, etc.
Non-religious/Atheist 1.8%, **Baha'i** 1%, **Animist/Spiritist** 0.8%, **Hindu** 0.3%.
Christian 91%.
Roman Catholic 78%. 1,700,000a; 939,000m. A further 10% were baptized Catholic but now are associated with other groups.
Marginal groups (4) 1%. 21,300a; 8,000m. Rapid growth. Largest (adherents):

Jehovah's Witnesses	14,000
Mormons	7,270

Protestant 11.8%. 252,000a; 98,500m. Denominations 50+. Largest (members):

Int. Ch. of Foursquare Gospel	27,500
Assemblies of God	18,000
Seventh Day Adventists	12,000
Baptist Convention (**SBC**)	6,550
Episcopal Church	4,700
Church of Christ	4,600
Tribal churches (**NTM**)	3,800
Church of God (Cleveland)	2,700

Evangelical 9.8% of population.
Missionaries to Panama 210 (1:10,200 people) in 36 agencies.
Missionaries from Panama 4 (1:63,000 Protestants).

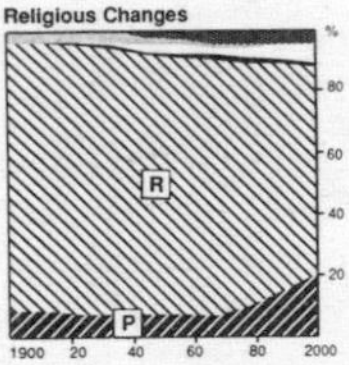

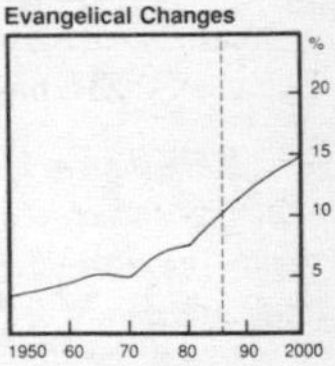

1. **The famous canal dominates the politics and economy of this "crossroads" nation.** Nominally Catholic, Catholicism is an irrelevant cultural heritage, and spiritual lethargy is widespread, secularism increasing and sectarian groups active. Pray for an outpouring of the Spirit on this strategic land.

2. **Growth among Spanish-speaking churches** was good between 1935 and 1960, but has slowed considerably since. Denominational rivalries, a paucity of mature national leadership in many churches, and a lack of solid Bible teaching and sustained evangelism in congregations are areas of weakness. However, the two major Pentecostal denominations are growing fast. In 1935 there were 38 organized Protestant churches; in 1985 there were over 1,200.

3. **The English-speaking churches** among the West Indians are static or in decline; several Pentecostal denominations are an exception to this.

4. **Amerindians** have been responding to the gospel. The extensive church planting ministries of numerous denominations and missions have been fruitful. All eight peoples now have viable churches. The Bible translation programme of **SIL**, with 14 workers in six languages, was seriously hampered by the government's request in 1981-83 for the termination of this ministry. Pray that the goal of NTs for each language may still be achieved by 1988, despite the upheavals. Pray for the full flowering of a vital and truly indigenous church in each people.

5. **Theological training** is provided by 11 schools and seminaries, as well as four TEE programmes. Pray for more Panamanians to be called into full-time service. Strong, mature leadership is needed to dynamize the church and combat widespread activities of cultic groups.

6. **The less reached sections of the population:**
   a) **The upper-middle classes** had remained aloof from the gospel until the mid '70s. A number of lively charismatic fellowships have been started since then.
   b) **The Chinese** are rapidly being assimilated, but many still speak Cantonese and Hakka, and few have been evangelized. Most are nominal Catholics or follow the traditional Chinese religions. There are four Chinese missionaries now ministering to them, and there are two small congregations.
   c) **The East Indians** are mostly Muslim, though some are Hindu. There is no specific outreach to them.
   d) The 3,000 **Jews** are unreached.

7. **The missionary presence** is large for such a small population. The majority are committed to pioneer situations among the 128,000 Amerindians. Pray for wise deployment and sensitive avoidance of a paternalistic attitude. The largest agencies are **NTM** (70 workers), **SBC** (25), **AoG** (14), **CAMI** (13). **GMU** (12).

8. **Christian literature** is distributed by the Bible Society and a dozen bookstores (one of **CLC**); almost all in the Canal Zone. Poverty, illiteracy and low interest in reading limit the impact. Pray for the dissemination of literature nationally and internationally from these centres.

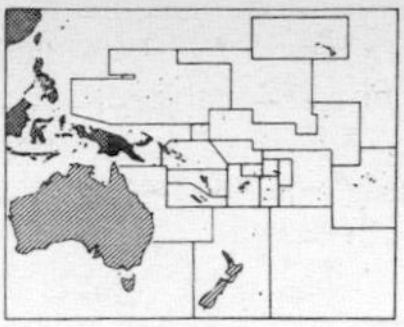

PAPUA NEW GUINEA

Pacific

Sept 2-3

Area 462,000 sq.km. The eastern half of New Guinea and numerous smaller islands to the north and east. New Guinea, the world's second largest island, is shared with Indonesia where West New Guinea is called Irian Jaya, see p. 229. A land of earthquakes, high mountains, torrential rainfall and thick jungle.

Population 3,300,000. Annual growth 2.7%. People per sq.km. 7; 72% live in New Guinea Territory to the north, 28% in Papua to the south.

Peoples: 1,000 small tribes speaking 700 languages. Ethnically and linguistically the world's most complex nation, whose cultures have been moulded by successive immigrations, geography, sorcery, fear and warfare.

Melanesian 99%. A term to express a common predicament rather than a common culture! Components of Papuan, Negrito, Austronesian, Melanesian and Polynesian origin. A large number of isolated languages spoken by several hundred to several thousand people. The 140,000 Enga are the only people with numbers over 100,000.

Other 1%. Other Pacific Islanders, Chinese, Australian, etc.

Literacy 42%. **Official language**: English. **Trade languages**: Tok Pisin in centre and north, and gradually replacing Hiri Motu in Papua. **All languages** 696. **Bible translations** 5Bi 67NT 103por.

Capital: Port Moresby 341,000. Urbanization 13%.

Economy: Largely a subsistence agricultural economy, but with a developing mining industry and considerable economic growth. The very difficult terrain, climate and frequent earthquakes make the development of adequate communications difficult and expensive. Income/person $790 (6% of USA).

Politics: New Guinea was a German colony until World War I. Independent from Australia in 1975 as a stable parliamentary democracy. The government has wisely handled tribal and regional loyalties by a policy of decentralization.

Religion: Freedom of religion. Many Christians are in government and the whole country is permeated with Christian values. Local nationalists and humanist anthropologists are exerting pressures to limit the activities of churches and missions.

Animist 3%. Many nominal and superficial Christians are still practising animists.

Cargo cultist 2%. Over 40 syncretic movements combining heathen and Christian elements with material gain.

Baha'i 0.7%.

Christian 94%. Affiliated 83%.

Roman Catholic 27.4%. 904,000a; 536,000m.

Marginal groups 1.9%. 62,000a.

Protestant 54.1%. 1,790,000a; 810,000m.

Denominations 44. Largest (adherents):

Evang. Lutheran Church	480,000
United Church	394,000
Evangelical Alliance (incl. all faith mission and other evangelical groups)	310,000
Anglican Church	156,000
Seventh Day Adventist Church	119,000
Bethel Pentecostal Tabernacle	62,000
Wabag Lutheran Church	60,000
Baptist Union	32,700
Assemblies of God	31,000
Brethren assemblies	29,000

Evangelical 21% of population — but many of these are without a personal knowledge of salvation.

Missionaries to Papua New Guinea approx. 2,300 (1:1,430 people) in about 40 agencies.

Missionaries from within PNG est. 100 (1:18,000 Protestants).

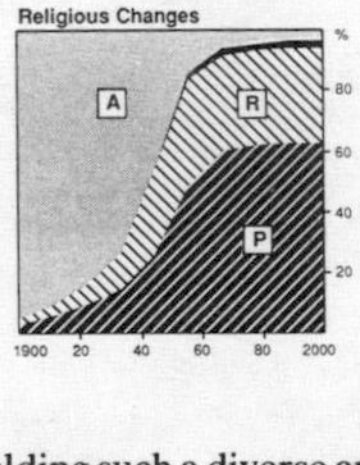

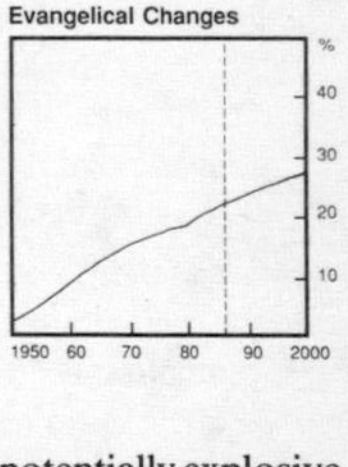

1. **The government faces a daunting task** in welding such a diverse and potentially explosive variety of tribes into a single nation. Tribal fighting and revenge killings are still fairly frequent occurrences, and the social dislocation caused by half-educated young people flocking to the cities has bred serious urban violence. Pray for the leaders of this land, and pray that they may seek the guidance of God in the affairs of their nation.

2. **Ever since 1904 mass movements have been occurring in many tribes.** Now 96% of the people would *claim* to be associated with a church or mission. Western technology and the gospel have revolutionized the stone age tribal societies — in earlier years along the coast, and in the last 30 years inland and in the highlands. Praise God for the miracles already seen in the lives of many individuals and some peoples.

3. **Early missionaries suffered disease and martyrdom to plant the Church.** A number of Western and South Seas missionaries were actually eaten by the tribes they sought to evangelize. The large investment of missionary personnel in health, education, technology and evangelism has significantly changed the land and its people. Pray for:

a) **Good relationships between expatriate and national workers.** The large number of missionaries can hinder fellowship and encourage paternalistic attitudes.

b) **A greater emphasis on relating the gospel to local cultures.** The widespread use of trade languages by missionaries and failure to major on Bible translation (until recently) has hampered the indigenization of the gospel message and often encouraged a superficial acceptance of Christianity.

c) **Those involved in translation and literacy** programmes. Few have the vision and burden, and local people often fail to see the need. The indigenous Bible Translators Association is a developing ministry of **SIL**.

d) **Those involved in health, education and rural development programmes**, which are fundamental to the emergence of strong indigenous churches that can relate to modern life in the rapidly developing nation.

e) **Those committed to pioneer work, church planting and discipling church leaders.** Workers are needed for all these and other ministries. The larger mission agencies are **SIL** (735 workers), **NTM** (246), Lutheran agencies (160), **APCM-UFM** (100), Baptist groups (100), Liebenzell Mission (48), **SSEM** (15).

4. **The initial penetration of most tribes is complete.** Massive people movements have resulted in a nominal and superficial Christianization of the majority, without achieving their deliverance from witchcraft, spirit and ancestor worship. Fears and superstitions have dominated them for millennia. In the areas earlier evangelized by Lutheran, LMS, Methodist and Anglican missionaries, widespread disillusionment and falling away has occurred, with drunkenness, cargo cults, and heathen customs openly pursued. Pray for revival, deep repentance, and cultures revolutionized and beautified by the gospel. Such has occurred in the East Sepik Province in **SSEM**, Brethren and Baptist areas, and also in North New Britain Island. There is also healthy growth in Pentecostal and charismatic fellowships in the urban areas.

5. **The young Church faces acute problems.**

a) **Diversity of languages** makes it hard for the emergence of trans-cultural fellowships of churches, and hinders the flow of blessing from one area to another.

b) **Illiteracy and lack of the Scriptures** results in spiritual apathy, slow growth and exposure to error. Pray for the increased provision of Christian literature for the newly literate and the better educated.

c) **Poorly trained leaders.** There are about 14,000 pastors and church workers, but over 85% have had little or no formal schooling. Many do it as a job with little burden for their flocks. There is a large generation gap between them and the better educated youth.

d) **Ecumenism is polarizing the churches.** There is a growing emphasis on the PNG equivalent of African theology (looking for revelations of God in pre-Christian religions).

e) **Denominational rivalry** confuses the people and impairs spiritual unity.

6. **Leadership training is a priority.** Many small Bible schools are run by churches and missions. There are also about 13 denominational theological colleges as well as the fine inter-denominational **Christian Leaders' Training College** with 200 students where leaders for evangelical churches all over PNG and the Pacific are trained (**APCM**, **IEM**, **SSEM**, etc.). Pray for:

a) **Men and women called of God** to full-time service as pastors, missionaries, etc. The lure of highly paid secular jobs is strong for those with a good education.

b) **Bible teachers** who can impart a love for God's Word to students and a desire to apply its truths to their own cultures.

c) **The provision of spiritual, articulate Christian leaders** who will decisively influence the spiritual life of the nation and establish the Church on biblical foundations.

d) The two urban centres of CLTC being set up in Port Moresby and Lae.

7. **The PNG church has, generally speaking, not understood the missionary challenge.** Some have become cross-cultural missionaries in church planting and Bible translation in PNG, but far more should catch the vision. Only about 10 Protestant missionaries have left PNG for other lands. **The Missions Prayer Group** is being used of God to stimulate concern, and some of its members are preparing for overseas service.

8. **The aeroplanes of missionary organizations are essential for the work of missions.** Many areas are only accessible by air, but flying conditions are some of the worst in the world with thick jungles, high mountains, much cloud and treacherous weather conditions. Pray for the flying staff of **MAF** (with 54 workers, 20 planes and a helicopter), of **SIL** (with four planes and two helicopters), of **NTM** (with three planes and one helicopter), and all who service these planes and travel in them. Within the space of one week in 1979 **MAF** lost two planes and pilots in the island of New Guinea.

9. **Unreached peoples and areas.** Only a minority of PNG peoples are unevangelized and unoccupied by missions.

a) **Possibly 20 different unreached peoples** live in the Star Mountains on the Irian Jaya border or in the Fly and Sepik River valleys and swamps.

b) **Small island peoples** — the Mortlock and Tasman Island **Polynesians**, the **Gumasi** of the d'Entrecasteaux Islands, and the Sud-Est of Tagula Island are unreached.

c) **Cargo cult peoples.** Wholesale conversions from Christianity to cargo cults have deeply affected 13 peoples on Manus Island.

d) **Hundreds of nominally Christian peoples**, where born-again believers who live all-out for Jesus may be only a handful. A new wave of pioneer evangelism is necessary.

10. **Bible translation** is the major incomplete missionary task. The profusion of small languages and extreme difficulty of travel make this a difficult and demanding task. The widespread use of trade languages in churches hinders the realization of the need and blunts the urgency. Translation teams are definitely needed for 160 languages and possibly for a further 280. **SIL** members have already completed 34 and are working on a further 160! Many translators work among peoples where there is no viable evangelical witness. The Bible Society is deeply committed to translation and distribution programmes. The most urgent task is the completion of the long-delayed Bibles for the two major trade languages.

11. **Key media** for prayer:

a) **Local radio** is a vital link used by churches and Christian workers for information and the spreading of the gospel, and Kristen Radio has a good studio for national and regional broadcasting on the national radio network.

b) **Christian cassettes** are essential for evangelism and teaching where equipment is readily available but speakers in the many languages are not. **GRI** has recorded 616 languages and dialects.

c) **Christian literature.** There are four main publishing groups: Christian Books Melanesia (Brethren), Evangelical Brotherhood Church, Kristen Press (Lutheran) and the Bible Society. Much excellent material is being produced, and there are Christian bookstores in most towns.

Latin America
Sept 4

PARAGUAY
(Republic of Paraguay)

Area 407,000 sq.km. Landlocked nation. The Paraguay River divides the more developed east from the forests, marshes and ranches of the Gran Chaco.

Population 3,600,000. The majority live within 100 km. of the capital. Annual growth 2.8%. People per sq.km. 9.

Peoples
Spanish/Guaraní-speaking 85%. Almost entirely Mestizo of Guaraní Indian and Spanish descent.
Portuguese-speaking 10%. Brazilians in northeast corner of the country.
Indian tribes 1.7%. Fifteen small groups totalling 50,000, the majority in the Chaco.
Other immigrant minorities 3.3%. German 60,000; Russian 28,000; Japanese 8,000; Korean 4,000.

Literacy 85%. **Official languages:** Spanish, Guaraní 90% of population speak the latter. **All languages** 21. **Bible translations** 1Bi 6NT 4por.

Capital: Asunción. 950,000 (including satellite towns). Urbanization 39%.

Economy: Mainly agricultural. Development hindered by distance from the sea and lack of mineral resources. The completion of the world's largest hydro-electric project in 1988 on the Paraná will give a boost to the economy. Income/person $1,400 (10% of USA).

Politics: Independent from Spain in 1811. Devastating wars with surrounding nations in 1864-70 and 1932-35. Military regime since 1954 with a highly centralized presidential government. Only a token opposition is permitted.

Religion: The constitution guarantees religious liberty, but Catholicism is the official religion of the country.
Non-religious/Atheist 0.6%. **Animist** 0.7%.
Christian 98.3%. Affiliated 96%.
Roman Catholic 91.5%. Practising 40%. 3,300,000a; 1,790,000m.
Marginal groups (2) 0.3%. 11,270a.
Protestant 4%. 136,000a; 52,100m. Denominations 51. Largest (adult members):

All Mennonite groups (7)	13,000
Lutheran Churches (2)	7,827
Baptist Convention (**SBC**)	3,800
Seventh Day Adventist Church	3,800
Anglican Church (**SAMS**)	2,800
Assemblies of God	2,000
Church of God (Cleveland)	1,206
Brethren	1,200

Evangelical 2.5% of population.
Missionaries to Paraguay 235 (1:15,300 people) in 28 agencies.

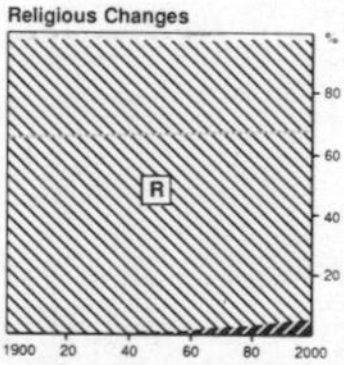

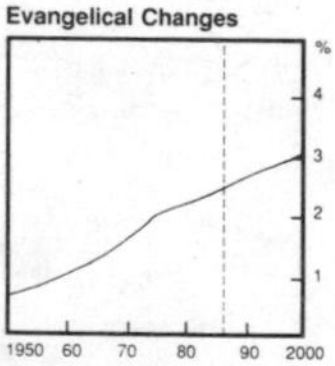

1. **Praise God for a rising expectancy of a great harvest.** The impact of Luis Palau's evangelistic crusades in 1976 and 1982 was nationwide. In the latter over 10,000 decisions were recorded. In the 1983 Rex Humbard crusade many more sought the Lord. Pray that the thirst after God manifested then may continue and be satisfied, and result in church growth.

2. **A traditional, syncretic Catholicism,** with much emphasis on Mary and the saints, has a strong hold on the people. Pray that the spirit of idolatry and fear of man may be broken; the breakthrough will not come without this. Only a minority of believers are of the Spanish-Guaraní Mestizo majority.

3. **Indigenous Protestant church growth was slow and discouraging until the late '70s.** The greatest response was from isolated Indian or poor Mestizo sections of society. Many adherents were illiterate and dependent on missionary initiative and programmes. Dynamic indigenous leadership has been slow to emerge. Pray for a greater impact on all levels of Paraguayan society and the development of strong congregations with vigorous outreach. Growth has been more marked in Assemblies of God, Baptist and Brethren congregations.

4. **Nearly half of all Protestants are members of immigrant communities** isolated from the mainstream of national life, such as the Lutherans and Mennonites. Many of these churches

still use German. There are also six Korean denominations. Pray that these communities may integrate into Paraguayan society and contribute towards its evangelization.

5. **Christian leaders** need prayer. Pray that the unity created by the recent crusades might continue and grow. There has been discord and mistrust between denominations in the past.

6. **Work among the Indian tribes** has been fruitful, and a majority have become Christians through the work of **SAMS** among the Lengua Guaraní and Sanapana, **NTM** in seven tribes and **Mennonites** among the Lengua and Chulupe. Missionary aid projects are helping many communities to become self sufficient and viable in providing education and the Scriptures, and in initiating agricultural programmes. Pray for the young churches as they adapt to the national culture.

7. **Missionary help is needed**, and there is an open door for those who can humbly work alongside Paraguayan brethren and strengthen national leadership. The main ministries needing personnel are church planting, leadership training and Bible translation; at least 9 languages still lack a NT. The largest agencies are **NTM** (72 workers), **SBC** (40), **SAMS** (36).

8. **The Bible has received wide and positive publicity**. The Bible Society has supported mass distributions of Scriptures in schools, and in 1982-84 a Gospel of John was distributed in every home in the land. Pray that the Word may change many lives.

Latin America

Sept 5-6

PERU
(Republic of Peru)

Area 1,285,000 sq.km. Andean State. Three zones — dry coastal plain in the west where most of the cities and industry are located, high plateau which is agricultural, and upper Amazon jungles in the east.

Population 19,500,000. Annual growth 2.5%. People per sq.km. 15.

Peoples

Spanish-speaking 45% (majority Mestizo, minority white and black).

Amerindian 54%. **Highland peoples**. Quechua 9,200,000; Aymara 1,000,000; **Lowland peoples** 330,000 speaking 41 languages.

Other minorities 1%. Japanese 65,000; Chinese 60,000; other European, etc.

Literacy 88%. **Official languages:** Spanish, Quechua. **All languages** 86. **Bible translations** 1Bi 19 NT 24por.

Capital: Lima 5,627,000 including the port city of Callao. Other city: Arequipa 700,000. Urbanization 67%.

Economy: The combined effects of sudden climatic changes, world recession and destructive terrorism have brought the country to its knees and hindered necessary social and land reforms. Major social stresses are shaking society. Income/person $1,040 (8% of USA).

Politics: Fully independent from Spain in 1824. Return to Democratic government since 1980, but a Maoist guerrilla movement has brought increasing instability and an atmosphere of fear through spectacular acts of terrorism. The socialist government elected in 1985 has demonstrated commendable courage in tackling economic and social problems.

Religion: Religious freedom guaranteed in 1978 constitution, but in practice the Catholic Church still tends to be favoured and exercises a decisive influence.

Non-religious/Atheist 1%.

Animist 1%. Though at least 30% of nominal Catholics are in reality Christo-pagan.

Christian 98%. Affiliated 94%.

Roman Catholic 89.1%. Practising 20%. 17,400,000a.

Marginal groups (10) 0.86%. 167,000a. Largest (adherents):

Jehovah's Witnesses	75,080
Mormons	60,000

Protestant 3.6%. 692,000a; 285,000m. Denominations 85. Largest (adult members):

Assemblies of God	97,000
Seventh Day Adventist Church	60,000
I.E.P. **(EUSA, SIM)**	40,000
Christian & Missionary Alliance	15,000
Church of the Nazarene	12,400
Baptist Convention (**SBC**)	8,500
Church of God (Cleveland)	7,330
Evangelical Ch's of NE (**RBMU**)	4,000
Brethren	3,500

Evangelical 3% of population.

Missionaries to Peru 890 (1:21,900 people) in 60 agencies.

Missionaries from within Peru est. 110 (1:6,300 Protestants).

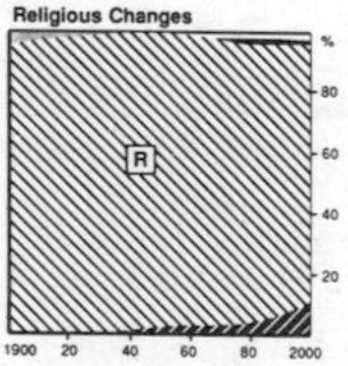

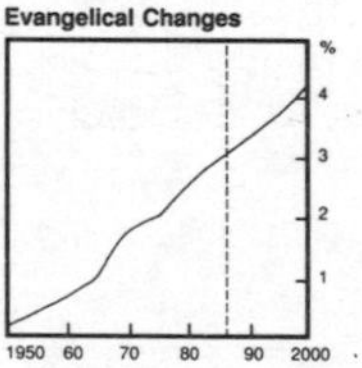

1. **A series of natural and social disasters have shaken the nation.** Severe droughts, floods and earthquakes, together with economic collapse and escalating violence have created uncertainty and fear. Many are seeking eternal solutions, and evangelical churches are growing. Pray for peace, for the government and for believers. Pray that Christians will see they have a strategic role to play in the nation at this time.

2. **The Catholic Church** is beset with problems; 80% of the clergy are foreign, and there is a growing polarization between the traditionalists and those who espouse liberation theology. Many are leaving the Church and turning to ideologies propagated by Mormons, Jehovah's Witnesses and Marxists. Pray that churches may more faithfully proclaim the attractiveness of Christ and the fulness of the gospel.

3. **Spanish-speaking evangelical churches** are growing apace, with many new congregations being planted every year. Growth has accelerated since 1980 in nearly all denominations — especially of **AoG**, IEP (**EUSA-SIM-RBMU**), **CMA** and Baptist groups. About 40% of evangelicals are Pentecostal. Pray that this growth may be maintained despite:

a) **Strong denominationalism** and lack of real fellowship between believers of different evangelical groups.

b) **More transfer growth than conversion growth.**

c) **A high rate of backsliding** and congregations hampered by resentments, moral failures, sin and divisions.

d) **Too little earnest prayer** for growth of believers and salvation of sinners.

e) **Too few leaders of maturity and spiritual depth.**

Pray for a unity among God's people that will glorify the Lord Jesus.

4. **The National Evangelical Council of Peru** has coordinated disaster relief programmes; it is becoming a focal point for communication between evangelicals and the authorities, and for research into the spiritual needs of the land. The **Peace and Hope Commission** is making a significant contribution to the whole concept of mission in Peru through its prophetic and relief and development work.

5. **The Quechua and Aymara peoples**, the descendants of the Incas, have begun to emerge from centuries of oppression, cultural deprivation, grinding poverty and isolation. Quechua was recognized as an official language in 1975. There is new growth, optimism and blossoming of Christianity in Quechua culture, with revival in some areas. Pray for:

a) **The millions of mountain Quechua and Aymara** still bound by superstitions of pagan and "Christian" origin. There are one million landless Quechua.

b) **The completion of Bible translation** in two major Quechua dialects (**EUSA, UBS**), and the undertaking of NT translation by **SIL** in 19 others.

c) **Acceptance of believers by Spanish-speaking churches.**

d) **The development of an indigenous**, biblical expression of the Body of Christ in hymnology, worship, literature and outreach.

e) **The training and support of pastors** for poor, isolated, largely illiterate congregations.

6. **Persecution of evangelical believers** at the hands of Catholics was severe at times in the past, but more recently there have been localized outbursts again despite the religious freedom. Since 1980, the savage guerrilla war has resulted in the murder of individuals, and several massacres of groups of believers. In the area of Ayacucho whole congregations have been scattered, and pastors have fled. Pray for protection, provision for the bereaved, and purity of testimony in these trials.

7. **Christian leaders are in short supply**. Doctrinal confusion, deficient theology and the multiplication of sects must be answered by clear biblical teaching, but few pastors have the gifts and training. Pray for:

a) **Leadership training**. The interdenominational Lima Seminary is strategic for Spanish-speaking countries (**EUSA, SIM, RBMU**, etc.). At least 20 other Bible schools are preparing workers for the ministry. TEE programmes are so necessary, but they are hampered by a lack of missionary and Peruvian personnel and adequate teaching materials. There is a lack of enthusiasm among those who would most benefit from them. Pray for the provision of more missionary Bible teachers at every level.

b) **Balance in preaching the gospel and addressing social concerns**. Some evangelical leaders isolate themselves from the burning issues of the day; others are infatuated by the challenges of liberation theology.

c) **Christian workers who serve in dangerous areas**. A number of pastors and leaders have been murdered in the guerrilla war.

8. **The cities** have a lower percentage of Evangelicals than the national average. Lima is the home of 30% of the population, many of whom live in abject poverty. Praise God for remarkable church growth in Lima through the ministry of **CMA, AoG**, Baptists, **SAMS, TEAM/RBMU**, etc. over the last 10 years. There were fruitful evangelistic crusades of the Luis Palau Team in 1984. Yet few have found the key to the evangelization of the sprawling slums of

Lima and the nurture of churches in that difficult environment, though **AoG** and **SAMS** have made a good beginning. There are only two Quechua-speaking congregations in the city. Pray for more fellowship and cooperation among churches for the evangelization of the cities.

9. **The Amerindians of the jungles** have increasingly responded to the preaching of missionaries of South American Mission, Swiss Indian Mission, **RBMU** and others. Much work must be done to prepare and equip believers to face with confidence the pressures of the outside world. Whilst there are churches or believers in many of the tribes, in most of them the majority are still bound by the powers of darkness. **SIL** has made a remarkable contribution through the ministry of 200 missionaries in providing Scriptures for many languages. Just a few tribes are still uncontacted or without groups of believers.

10. **Missions** have passed through difficult times, especially those from North America (75% of missionary force); anti-American press reports, spy scares, and the widespread activities of Mormons and Jehovah's Witnesses have not helped. The spreading scourge of terrorism adds new perils for the life and ministry of missionaries. The majority of the missionary effort is directed to pioneer work in the eastern jungle, Bible translation and leadership training. Reinforcements are needed, but visas are not easy to obtain; pray for a relaxation of restrictions. Praise God for the countermanding of the expulsion order of 1977 for **SIL**, and for renewed opportunities for Bible translation. Some larger agencies are **SIL** (287 workers), **RBMU** (60 in two branches), **SBC** (38), **CMA** (31), **EUSA** (29), **CoN** (14), **TEAM** (12), **SIM** (11).

11. **Unreached peoples.** Despite church growth and encouragement, Peru is still a pioneer mission field with needy areas and peoples.

a) **Needy areas** — many towns and villages in the high plateau (mainly Quechua, but also Mestizo), pioneer regions in the northeastern forests (both new settlers and some tribal groups).

b) **Ethnic minorities** — **Gypsies**, many still speaking Romany; **Chinese** (60,000) with only one church and one missionary couple (**CMA**).

c) **Social segments of society** — **upper class**, often wealthy, strongly Catholic and unreached by present evangelism; **slum dwellers** around the major cities.

12. **The witness among university students** is vital for the future of the Church in Peru. For years political agitation and leftist politics have involved many, but there is widespread disillusionment among them today. Pray for many to turn to Christ. ABU(**IFES**) has small groups in half the 35 universities, and two staff workers.

13. **Peruvian missionary interest** is awakening, but churches are often too introspective. **CMA** and the Baptists have commenced missionary programmes. AMEN (Association Misionera Evangelica a las Naciónes) is a young, interdenominational mission with great vision; some of their workers have gone to serve the Lord in Europe and other parts of Latin America.

14. **Christian radio** has a wide audience, both the local **Radio del Pacifico (TEAM)** in Lima, and the large international stations of **HCJB** Ecuador (Spanish and Quechua) and **TWR** Bonaire (Spanish), with many thousands of hours of broadcasting per month in Spanish, and 900 in Quechua dialects!

PHILIPPINES
(Republic of the Philippines)

Asia

Sept 7-8

Area 300,000 sq.km. 73 provinces; 7,250 islands, of which over 700 are inhabited, the largest being Luzon (116,000 sq.km) in the north and Mindanao (95,000 sq.km) in the south.

Population 56,800,000. Annual growth 2.5%. People per sq.km 189. Over 400,000 Filipinos working in 103 nations and on ships. About one million have emigrated to the USA.

Peoples
Malayo-Indonesian Filipinos 95%. Major languages: Cebuano 24.4%, Tagalog 23.8%, Ilocano 11.1%, Hiligaynon 10%, Bicol (many dialects) 7%, Waray 4.6%, Kapampangan 3.4%, Maranao 2.8%, Pangasinan 2.3%, Magindanao 2.2%, Tausug 1.5%, Samal 1%.
Tribal peoples 2.8%. In the more inaccessible mountainous areas of Luzon (46 tribes) 930,000; Mindanao (22 tribes) 490,000; Mindoro (6 tribes) 50,000; Palawan (6 tribes) 30,000.
Chinese 1%. Important in the commercial world.
Other 1%. US citizens, Vietnamese, etc.

Literacy 88%. **Official languages:** Filipino (based on Tagalog), English. **All languages** 151. **Bible translations** 9Bi 26NT 55por.

Capital: Metro-Manila 10,000,000. Urbanization 37%.

Economy: A mixed agricultural and industrial economy. Serious economic difficulties have worsened under the combined impact of the oil crisis, decline of export income, widespread corruption, social and political unrest and a series of natural disasters. Loss of international confidence in the country's future since 1983 has caused hardship, with rising unemployment, 50% inflation rate and widespread poverty. Income/person $760 (6% of USA).

Politics: A Spanish colony from 1565 to 1898; hence the Catholic majority and many Spanish customs. Ruled by the USA until independence in 1946. Martial law imposed in 1971 to combat Communist subversion, and the country became virtually a one-party republic. Political manipulation, mismanagement and abuse of civil liberties stimulated antipathy to the government and led to its downfall in 1986. The resulting frustration because of this increased support for the activities of Maoist guerrillas in rural areas. There is also a secessionist war being waged by the Muslims of Mindanao and Sulu. The new government in March 1986 is inexperienced, and its ability to handle the problems is not certain. The Republic is a member of ASEAN and an important ally of the USA.

Religion: Freedom of religion. Asia's only country with a Catholic majority. There was a state of cautious confrontation between the former government and Catholic leaders over the political situation.

Non-religious/Atheist 1.5%.

Animist 1%. Many nominal Catholics are still animist at heart. Majority among many of the tribal peoples.

Muslim 8.4%. Sunni Islam. Almost all in S.W. Mindanao, Sulu Is. and Palawan. Strong among the Magindanao, Maranao, Ilanon, Samal and Tausug; less strong, but in the majority, among eight other peoples.

Christian 89.2%. Many Christo-pagan.

Roman Catholic 63.6%, though a further 12% were baptized Catholic, but have left the Church. 36,150,000a; 19,240,000m.

Indigenous Catholic groups 8%. 4,500,000a; 2,600,000m. Over 120 groups have broken away from Rome. Largest (adherents):

Philippine Independent Church	4,200,000

Indigenous marginal groups 6.1%. Over 280 groups. 3,433,000a; 1,850,000m. Largest (adherents):

Iglesia ni Cristo	1,400,000

Foreign marginal groups 0.7%. 388,000a; 185,000m. Most rapidly growing and largest (adherents):

Jehovah's Witnesses	237,000
Mormons	76,000

Protestant 10.7%. 6,010,000a; 2,600,000m. Denominations 140. Largest (adult members):

Seventh Day Adventist Church	290,000
United Church	260,000
Christian & Miss. Alliance	185,000
United Methodist Church	166,000
Baptist Convention (**SBC**)	89,000
Assemblies of God	60,000
March of Faith	55,000
Conv. of Phil. Baptist Ch's	54,000
Int. Ch. of Foursquare Gospel	48,000
Evangelical Methodist Church	40,000
Episcopal Church	33,000
ABCOP (**OMF, SEND Int**)	16,000
Conservative Baptist Assoc.	15,000

Evangelical 6.4% of population.

Missionaries to Philippines approx. 2,300 (1:24,700 people) in about 120 agencies.

Missionaries from within the Philippines approx. 670 (1:9,000 Protestants) of which over 180 are serving in other lands.

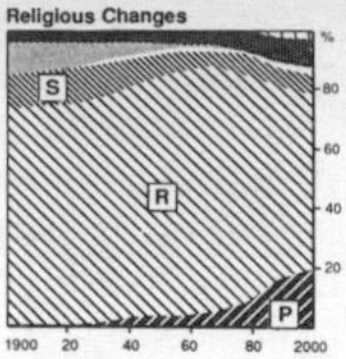

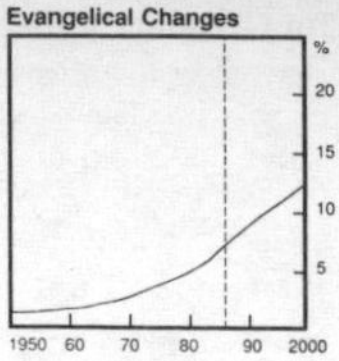

1. **Praise the Lord for dramatic growth in Protestant Churches since 1974**. There is an exciting harvest being won in this nation and the Protestant Church is becoming a major force in the life of the country. Rapid changes, uncertainty for the future, religious freedom, aggressive evangelism by growing churches and good Filipino leadership, are all factors promoting this expansion. Above all, prayer has been answered!

2. **The Roman Catholic Church is at a crossroads**. The political polarization of the nation is dividing the Church; many priests openly support leftist revolution. The study of the Scriptures has opened the hearts and minds of millions of Catholics to the need for a personal experience of the grace of God — some remaining in charismatic groups within the Church, many others joining Protestant Churches. Pray that this time of crisis may bring many to Christ. A large proportion of all Catholics are practising animists and spiritists.

3. **The sorry state of lethargy and stagnation in Protestant churches** after World War II was challenged by:

   a) **The impact of Pentecostalism**. Pentecostal denominations and charismatic fellowships have multiplied across the country. Many are indigenous in origin.

   b) **The Church Growth movement**. Studies, books and seminars on church growth revolutionized the thinking of Filipino Christian leaders (Fuller School of World Mission was instrumental in this).

   c) **International, regional and national congresses** on evangelization between 1966 and 1980 produced a ground swell of expectancy for growth.

   d) **The mobilization of many denominations in evangelism by means of home Bible studies through the Christ Only Way movement of 1970. OC Ministries** was used of God in this challenge, and the setting of church planting goals by many denominations during the '70s led to dramatic growth.

   e) **The Discipling of a Nation concept** taken up by many church leaders in 1979-80, with the goal of multiplying churches from 10,000 in 1978 to 50,000 by AD 2000, so that each community in the country would have a church. Pray that these goals may be achieved; the latest news is that growth goals are on target!

4. **The growing churches need prayer**.

   a) **Rapid growth** can lead to inadequate discipling and "poorly born" Christians. Pray for spiritual depth.

   b) **Funding** is difficult due to the poverty of churches and, all too often, there is a dependence on US funds.

   c) **Leadership** is inadequate. Praise God for many fine leaders, but they are too few. Pray for the 100+ seminaries and Bible Schools from postgraduate to primary level. Some key seminaries for prayer: The Alliance Biblical Seminary (**CMA**), ATS, FEBIAS (**SEND Int**) and FEAST (**AoG**). TEE programmes are many and vital if run well. Many of the better qualified Christian workers emigrate to the USA.

   d) **Fellowship across high denominational barriers**. The existence of many churches experiencing growth leads to competition. Pray for the work of Philippines Council of Evangelical Churches in its ministry of promoting unity, cooperation, confirmation and proclamation of the gospel.

5. **Ideological conflict increases in the midst of this growth**. Escalating violence between government and Communist guerrilla forces is involving civilians and churches. Pastors have been killed, and rural churches closed. Pray that Christian leaders may both prepare believers for suffering for the gospel, and speak out to address the ills of society that provide the soil

for Communist ideology to take root. Compromise of the truth in acquiescing with the status quo, or going along with violence, is easy. Pray for revival in the Church; such could save the Philippines from disaster.

6. **Praise the Lord for the missionary burden of Filipino Christians**! Cultural flexibility, use of English and simple life style have helped Filipinos to adapt well overseas as missionaries. Poor support and inadequate pastoral backing hinder the development of this movement. Some notable agencies are: **Philippines Missionary Fellowship** (140 missionaries), **New Tribes Mission** (60), **OMF Philippine Council** (106), **National Bible Translators** (40), **Asian Christian Outreach** (25). **PMF's** Missionary Training Institute and the Asian Center for Missionary Education specifically provide cross-cultural preparation for would-be missionaries.

7. **In recent years many new missions and missionaries have entered the land** but there are far more opportunities than there are workers to use them — in pioneer evangelism, church planting, Bible teaching, student work and in technical ministries. Pray for a humble sensitivity on the part of missionaries in a time when Filipino Christians are seeking an identity of their own rather than adopting N. American culture. Some larger agencies (all with a wide range of ministries) are: **SIL** (327 workers), **NTM** (160), **SBC** (160) **OMF** (144), **SEND** (94), **IMI** (83), **CMA** (71), **CBFMS** (78).

8. **Unreached peoples**. Praise the Lord for advances over the '70s and '80s to nearly every ethnic group in the country. A number of smaller peoples are unoccupied by expatriate or national missionaries. In many areas and peoples the work is still in its pioneer stages. **SIL** has achieved the commendable record of completing eight NTs, (by 1990 NTs in 52 languages should have been printed), and placing translation teams in 62 other language groups. There are only 19 definite translation projects left to tackle. Pray for the completion of this task, and that the Bible might enter into the culture and hearts of every people.

9. **The Muslim unreached.** By far the largest group of unreached in the country are the 14 Muslim peoples. In only *three* of these have churches been planted. Pray for the nearly five million Muslims who have been antagonized by the incursions of Spanish and Filipino "Christian" colonizers in the past.

a) **The Maranao** 1,500,000, **Magindanao** 1,200,000, and **Ilanon** 15,000 live in central S.W.Mindanao. There is a handful of Magindanao believers, but no known churches. **OMF**, **ICF**, **RBMU** and **SEND** are working together on a new outreach to them. **IMI** has 16 workers committed to these peoples in the north of the area.

b) The **Tausug** 780,000; **Samal** 560,000; and **Badjao** 6,000 of the Sulu Islands and Zamboanga have long been the burden of Alliance missionaries and pastors (**CMA**). There are 300 Christians and four churches among the Samal believers. There are only three or four Tausug and two or three Yakan believers. There are also some believers among the 300,000 partly Muslim Subanon, north of Zamboanga. **CMA** commenced a new work among the Tausug in 1985.

c) **The Muslim peoples of Palawan Island** are unreached. Pray for the Palawani (40,000), and Molbog (6,000) and also for the Jama Mapun (7,000) of nearby Cagayan Is. **SIL** has translation teams at work in these languages, but there are no known churches.

10. **The tribal unreached:**

a) The **Ifugao** 227,000; Bontoc 160,000; Kankanai 140,000; Kalinga 134,000; Tinggian 50,000, of the central mountains of N.Luzon, have begun to respond to the gospel and turn from animism. Many pockets of animism are unchallenged, but in most peoples, churches have come into being. Pray for the continuing translation and literacy work of **SIL** and other missions such as **NTM** and **RBMU** who are working to establish or strengthen the young churches.

b) Many small semi-nomadic **Dumagat Negrito** peoples live in N.E.Luzon. Few have become Christian and the task of church planting is complex. **NTM** has made a large investment of personnel to these peoples.

c) **The Mangyan tribes of Mindoro** are no longer unreached, though pockets of animism and opposition to the gospel remain. **OMF**'s work has resulted in a network of tribal churches, that have begun sending missionaries to tribal peoples, on Luzon. Second generation Christianity is now the problem. NTs in three languages will soon be printed.

d) **The tribes of Palawan. NTM** has missionaries in all six peoples, but work is in the pioneer stages.

e) **The 18 Manobo tribes of Mindanao.** Among the 490,000 people there may be but 1,500 believers in five of these tribes. Pioneer work by **CMA**, Baptists, and **OMF** continues.

Pray for churches to be planted that will be spiritually strong, and maturely led to cope with the influx of colonists, guerrillas and materialism that encroach on their old way of life and lands. Lowland Filipinos have often exploited the mountain peoples.

11. **The Chinese** number 500,000 but only 3% are Protestant. Many are Catholic. There are only about 70 predominantly Chinese congregations; most are wealthy, but few Chinese are prepared to volunteer for full-time service.

12. **Manila** is swamped by migrants. Eighty per cent live in shanty town slums. In the whole city of 10 million there are only 150,000 evangelical church members. Most of these are in the more affluent 20%, with few in the poorer areas. Pray for lasting results from the massive outreach "**Manila '85**" in which 50 church organizations cooperated. **Christ for Greater Manila** with 52 staff had a large part in the programme. The goal was for one million evangelical believers by the year-end! Pray also for effective, viable church planting in the slums.

13. **Student ministry** among the 1,500,000 students in the many universities has developed well despite the strong leftist element. Many groups are involved — **CMA, CCC, Navigators, AoG** and also the **IVCF** (**OMF** assisted) with 30 keen young staff workers. Pray for the development of strong witnessing groups in the universities.

14. **Literature** is extensively used by Christians. There are over 44 denominational and non-denominational literature agencies for printing, publishing and distributing reading materials. Pray for the work started by **OMF** (publishing house and network of bookstores), **CMA, CLC** and others.

15. **Christian radio.** Extensive use of radio and TV is made by Christians. Few countries are better served. **FEBC Philippines** has 20 stations from which 2,200 hours of programmes per week are broadcast in 61 languages and dialects to the Philippines and other parts of Asia. Pray for:

a) The 200 (mainly Filipino) staff that they may know the blessing of the Lord in their lives in ministries that are often behind the scenes.

b) The programming studios and programme producers, smooth running of broadcasting equipment, printing press and follow up ministries.

c) The spiritual impact on Filipino audiences. Many local stations are used for smaller language groups.

d) The fruitfulness of international ministries to closed Asian countries — especially China, Siberia, Indo-China, Burma.

POLAND
(The Polish People's Republic)

The West

Sept 9

Area 313,000 sq.km. Poland has the misfortune of being sandwiched between Germany and Russia.

Population 37,300,000. Annual growth 1%. People per sq.km. 119.

Peoples
Poles 96.6%. Over 10 million emigrants (65% in USA).
Minorities 3%. Ukrainian 256,000; Pomeranian 220,000; Byelorussian 220,000; German 73,000; Gypsy 70,000.
USSR Military, etc. 0.4%.

Literacy 98%. **Official language:** Polish. **All languages** 7. **Bible translations** 4Bi 1por.

Capital: Warsaw 1,770,000. Other major cities: Lodz 945,000, Cracow 800,000. Urbanization 58%.

Politics: A well remembered tragic history of wars and partition among powerful neighbours over the last 200 years. One quarter of the population died in World War II. The Soviet army imposed a communist regime in 1945. Popular discontent caused gradual liberalizations during 1980-81, but all this was revoked after the military takeover in December 1981 and imposition of martial law.

Religion: The Roman Catholic Church is too strong for the Communists to dominate or destroy, so there is more religious freedom than in any other Communist state. The Protestants have more freedom than for centuries because they are considered a counterbalance to the Roman Catholics.
Non-religious/Atheist 10%.
Jews 12,000 (3,500,000 in 1939).
Christian 89.8%.
Roman Catholic 87.3%. Practising 65%. 32,800,000a; 21,600,000m.
Orthodox 1.6%. 606,000a; 375,000m. Denominations 3.
Protestant 0.45%. 171,000a; 110,000m. Denominations 24. Largest (adult members):

Lutheran Church (German)	60,000
United Evangelical Church	20,000
Assemblies of God	8,500
Baptist Union	4,200

Evangelical 0.2% of population (0.5% including the members of Oasis).

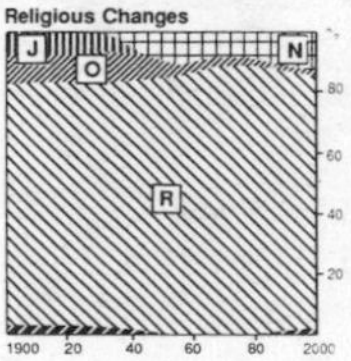

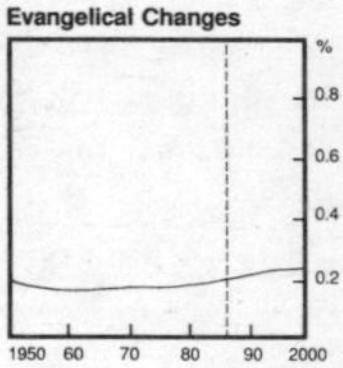

1. **This land is very open for Christian work**, but few pastors have a vision for evangelism. Many areas of the country are without an evangelical witness. Pray that the tragic events since 1981 may open many hearts for the message of the gospel.

2. **The Roman Catholic Church is very powerful,** and has successfully blocked all attempts by the atheist government to deprive it of its independence and freedom to work through its churches and institutions. The election of a Polish Pope has further strengthened the power of the Church. Many Communist Party members remain RC. The Church is really the centre of Polish nationalism and culture in the face of Russian imperialism. The Church is very conservative, and the effects of liberal theology and the charismatic movement are still small, but both Vatican II and the caution of the hierarchy in recent troubles are provoking greater freedom of thought and action among young Catholics.

3. **The many freedoms of both Roman Catholics and Protestants** could be taken away. Stepped-up government efforts to weaken the influence of religion are evident. There is little persecution of believers, but restrictions and difficulties are often placed in the way of their witness. Pray that there may be continued freedom for the propagation of the gospel, and enthusiasm by the few committed believers to evangelize their countrymen.

4. **Many thousands of young people** have turned from a nominal Catholicism to new life in Christ through the **OASIS** movement with Bible study groups and camps. Pray for this evangelical movement within the Catholic Church. There were 150,000 members in 1983.

5. **There is a great hunger among university students for spiritual reality.** Pray for conversions and for all who witness on the campuses.

6. **The evangelical churches** are a tiny, misunderstood minority. Pray for greater unity, evangelistic fervour and spiritual power among the believers. Pray for government building permits to be issued more readily to churches seeking to put up new meeting places. Praise God for growth in many congregations over the last three years. In some areas there was a touch of revival reported in 1985.

7. **The United Evangelical Church sponsors a Bible Institute** started in 1980, and now has 20 students. Pray for this unusual institution — one of the few in the Communist Bloc!

8. **Radio programmes** are prepared with the cooperation of several churches in Warsaw for broadcast from **TWR** Monte-Carlo. The government has given permission for this, but the privilege could easily be withdrawn. There is such a good response to these broadcasts that the evangelical churches have difficulty finding enough mature Christians to follow up the contacts. One Bible school in Poland has a special course to train radio follow up workers. Please pray too for the Polish staff of **TWR** in Monaco.

9. **Bibles in both the Protestant and Catholic versions are in very great demand.** Pray for the well used Warsaw depot of the Bible Society, from which Bibles (235,000 were printed in 1982) and Christian literature are freely sold and even distributed beyond Poland's borders. Pray for the spiritual impact of the new Polish Bible published in 1976.

10. **Literature** — a limited selection of Christian book titles are printed and distributed in the country. Pray for the provision of funds, supplies and permission to print adequate numbers — difficult in the present economic crisis. **WLC** has an office in Poland from which literature is being legally distributed to thousands of homes.

PORTUGAL
(Portuguese Republic)

The West

Sept 10

Area 92,000 sq.km. Europe's most southwesterly state. Part of the Iberian Peninsula which is shared with Spain.

Population 10,300,000. Annual growth 0.5% People per sq.km. 112.

Peoples
Portuguese 99%. Nearly 900,000 refugees from African colonies were added to the population at their independence in 1975. 1,200,000 are guest-workers in other European countries.
Other 1%. Mozambiquans, Angolans, Cape Verdians, British, etc.

Literacy 80%. West Europe's lowest level. **Official language:** Portuguese. **All languages** 3.

Capital: Lisbon 1,257,000. Urbanization 30%.

Economy: The 1974 revolution disrupted an already poor economy. Productive agricultural land and industrial development are limited. By 1985 the country was on the brink of bankruptcy, and only large international loans shore up the fragile economy. Membership of the EEC since 1986 may help to raise low living standards and employment. Income/person $2,190 (15% of USA).

Politics: 50 years of right wing dictatorship ended in 1974. Now a relatively stable parliamentary democracy despite a succession of short-lived coalition governments. The post-revolution leftist government granted independence to Portugal's colonies of Mozambique, Angola, Guinea-Bissau, São Tomé and Cape Verde Islands, which all have socialist or Marxist governments today. East Timor was annexed by Indonesia, and Macao will shortly be returned to China.

Religion: Freedom of religion since the revolution, but traditional Catholicism remains influential.
Non-religious/Atheist 8.3%, though many professed Communists claim to believe in God!
Muslim and **Hindu** 0.15%. Mainly Indian refugees from Goa and Mozambique.
Christian 91.6%.
Roman Catholic 90%. Regular practising 29%; high in north, low in south.
Marginal groups 0.75%. 77,000a; 30,000m. Very rapid growth. Largest (adherents):

Jehovah's Witnesses	72,000
Mormons	5,100

Protestant 0.78%. 80,000a; 53,700m. Denominations 29. Largest (adult members):

Assemblies of God	21,240
Brethren assemblies	7,000
Seventh Day Adventist Church	7,000
Baptist Convention (**SBC**)	3,500
Presbyterian	2,000

Evangelical 0.6% of population.
Missionaries to Portugal 240 (1:42,900 people) in about 30 agencies.
Missionaries from Portugal est. 8.

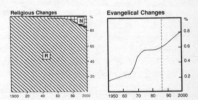

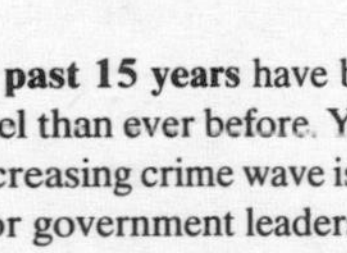

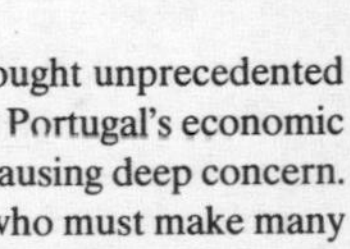

1. **Political and economic upheavals over the past 15 years** have brought unprecedented changes, including greater freedom for the gospel than ever before. Yet Portugal's economic plight has caused difficulty for many, and the increasing crime wave is causing deep concern. Pray for peace and stability for the land. Pray for government leaders who must make many uncomfortable decisions to safeguard the future; they need wisdom and determination.

2. **The religious freedom since 1974 has given many new opportunities for evangelism** through open-air evangelism, house visitation, literature, etc. Evangelicals have grown numerically, but the effort could have been greater. The growth of cults such as Jehovah's Witnesses and Mormons has been dramatic. Pray for a great mobilization of believers for outreach in this day of opportunity.

3. **Evangelical churches** have, generally, not grown fast, with the exception of the Assemblies of God and a few smaller groups. Praise the Lord for the steady increase in the number of evangelical churches (815 in 1980 to 930 in 1983). Pray for more pastors and full-

time workers to be raised up, and for more effective discipling and outreach. Lack of co-operation, quarrels and divisions have hindered more rapid growth.

4. **Bible training for new leaders is important.** Many leaders are ageing and there are few younger men to replace them. There are relatively few live spiritual leaders — and this is reflected in the spiritual condition of most evangelical churches. Pray for the five Bible schools/seminaries; **AoG** (51 students), **GEM** Bible Institute (24), Baptist (11), Presbyterian and the Antioch Bible School (ex-Brazil). There are about 80 doing the **GEM** TEE programme. Young people need to get a vision and burden for their own people and discipline themselves to prepare adequately to reach the lost.

5. **Unreached peoples in Portugal.** It is estimated that there are about 80 counties with over two million people who have never been confronted with the claims of Christ on their lives.

a) **The seven northern and northeastern provinces** are strongly traditional Catholic, and few evangelical churches exist. Brethren, Baptists, **AoG**, Missão Antioquia, **GEM** and **WEC** are initiating church planting programmes.

b) **The four provinces of the south** are poor and few people ever go to church. Many are Communist in their sympathies. Attendance at mass by people in Beja province is less than 3% of the population. Evangelical churches are few.

c) **New middle-class housing areas of Lisbon** are neglected.

d) **Madeira Island** (260,000) has only seven small evangelical churches, and the **Azores** (250,000) a further 18; most being Assemblies of God and Baptist. Four of the seven islands have no churches.

e) The **Muslim** and **Hindu Indians** are unresponsive; **AME** has a witness among them.

Pray that a church may be planted in each town of Portugal by 2000. There are over 80 without one.

6. **Portuguese migrant workers** in other countries of Europe need the gospel. Many live in barracks and hostels with little thought for anything but making money. It is difficult to reach them with the gospel and to plant churches among them. Pray for workers to evangelize the 900,000 in France, 110,000 in Germany and 30,000 in Britain.

7. **Missionary numbers have increased** since 1974. Relatively few really integrate into the culture or learn the language well. Pray for these barriers to be broken down. Unfortunately the importation of foreign ideas and teachings by some has further confused and divided the few believers, so pray for a humble sensitivity among all missionaries. Workers of quality are needed in the many unreached areas for ministry in evangelism, church planting and also for Bible training, music, etc. Short-term team evangelism by young people could also be productive. Some missions: **TEAM** (10 workers), **AoG** (18), **SBC** (20), **Brethren** (12+), **GEM** (11) **WEC** (7), etc. A growing number of Brazilian missionaries are entering the land, and finding acceptance once they realize that Portugal is different from Brazil.

8. **Literature has been much used in the conversion of the Portuguese.** Pray for:

a) The growing ministry of Bible production and distribution by the **Bible Society**.

b) **NUCLEO** has a vital coordinating ministry for the Body of Christ in research, publishing, printing tracts and distributing cassettes and films.

c) **CEDO** the quarterly gospel broadsheet ministry of **WEC** with 40,000 going out each edition all over Portugal and the world.

9. **Student work is still in its infancy.** The GBU(**IFES**) has groups in three of the universities. Marxism and antireligious feeling on the campuses is strong. **SU** and **CEF** have small, but useful ministries among school children.

10. **Christian radio and TV.** Pray for greater access for Evangelicals to radio and for openings in TV on Portuguese stations.

PUERTO RICO

Latin America

Sept 11

Area 9,100 sq.km. Greater Antilles; between Dominican Republic and the Virgin Islands.

Population 3,350,000. Annual growth 1.3%. People per sq.km. 368.

Peoples: European 74.8%, **African** 15%, **Eurafrican** 10%.

Literacy 90%. **Official Languages:** Spanish, English.

Capital: San Juan 1,360,000. **Urbanizaton** 67%.

Economy: Densely populated with few natural resources but much aid from USA. Industry and tourism are the main sources of income. Income/person $2,890 (21% of USA). Unemployment 22%.

Politics: Self-governing Commonwealth associated with the USA since 1898. The alternatives of independence and becoming a state of the USA are hotly debated.

Religion

Non-religious/Atheist, etc. 2%.

Christian 98%. Affiliated 95.7%.

Roman Catholic 65.8%. 2,200,000a; 1,260,000m. A further 14% of baptized Catholics have become Protestants, etc.

Marginal Groups 2.7%. 89,000a; 35,000m. All groups 17. Largest (adult members);

Jehovah's Witnesses	19,371
Mormons	5,000

Protestant 27.2%. 911,000a; 363,000m. Denominations 85. Largest (adult members):

Assemblies of God	80,000
Seventh Day Adventist Church	47,000
Pentecostal Church of God	35,500
Baptist Conv. (**ABFMS**)	20,000
Church of God (Cleveland)	17,000

Evangelical 20.8% of population.

Missionaries to Puerto Rico 180 (1:18,600 people) in 28 agencies.

Missionaries from Puerto Rico 25 (1:36,440 Protestants).

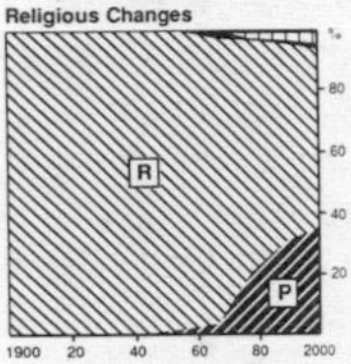

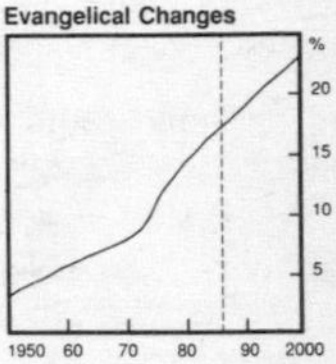

1. **A great harvest has been gathered into Protestant churches this century.** Widespread evangelism, a large missionary investment and many institutions have resulted in a large proportion of the population deserting the once dominant Catholic Church. The fastest growth has been among Pentecostal groups, SDAs and Baptists.

2. **The impact of Anglophone North American culture on the Hispanic Puerto Ricans has been far reaching.** This has created fertile soil for change, but also an identity crisis that affects politics, the Catholic Church and mission-church relationships among Protestants. Pray for the maturing churches and their leadership. A missionary vision is lacking.

3. **Less reached groups:**
   a) **Chinese** (2,000). A small Christian fellowship meets, but the majority are unevangelized.
   b) **Slum dwellers in the cities** live in a hopeless poverty trap.

4. **Overpopulation and unemployment have forced over 1.5 million Puerto Ricans to emigrate to the USA.** Sixty per cent live in New York where they form the lowest income groups. Many live in Hispanic ghettos where frustration has driven many to violence, drugs and immorality. Pray for all specifically ministering to this community.

Middle East

Sept 12

QATAR

(The State of Qatar)

Area 11,000 sq.km. Arabian Gulf peninsula that is almost entirely desert.

Population 285,000. Annual growth 3.7%. People per sq.km. 26.

Peoples
Indigenous Arabs 19%.
Foreign 81%. Arabs from surrounding lands, especially Palestine and Egypt 100,000; Pakistanis 77,000; Indians 36,000; Iranis 40,000; Western 3,000.

Literacy 70%. **Official language:** Arabic.

Capital: Doha 200,000. Urbanization 86%.

Economy: An oil economy with progress towards economic diversification. Income/person $21,170 (150% of USA).

Politics: Under UK protection until independence in 1971. Absolute monarchy.

Religion: The strict Wahhabi form of Sunni Islam is the state religion. Proselytism of Muslims is forbidden, but expatriate Christians are allowed to meet informally.
Muslim 92%. Sunni 88%, Shi'a 12%.
Hindu 1%.
Christian 6% (1980). Many are not actively linked with Christian groups. 10,000a; 1,450m.
- **Roman Catholic** 1.9%. Arab, Indian, Western.
- **Orthodox** 0.5%. Arab, Indian.
- **Protestant** 3.5%. Western, Arab, Asian. About 5 denominational groups.
  - **Evangelical** 1.4% of population.

1. **There are no known Qatari believers.** Pray for the expatriate Christians who have contact with Qataris that they may have opportunity to share their faith.

2. **The expatriate communities** have been drawn to the country for material gain. Pray that the witness of the small groups of believers among Indians, Pakistanis, Egyptians and Westerners to their own communities may be fruitful. Little has been done to reach out to other unevangelized minorities such as the Iranis, etc.

REUNION

(French Department of Réunion)

Africa

Sept 13

Area 2,510 sq.km. West Indian Ocean island 900 km. east of Madagascar. The largest of the Mascarene Islands which includes Mauritius.

Population 535,000. Annual growth 1.7%. People per sq.km. 213.

Peoples
Creole 91%. Very mixed; of European, African and Asian origin.
Other minorities 9%. French 18,000; Chinese 16,000; Comorian 14,000; Indian 7,500; Malagasy 4,000.

Literacy 98%. **Official language:** French. Common language: French Creole.

Capital: St. Denis 120,000. Urbanization 41%.

Economy: Unhealthy dependence on sugar cultivation and French aid. Income/person $3,710 (26% of USA). Much unemployment and emigration to France.

Politics: Overseas Department of France.

Religion: As France which is a secular state with freedom of religion.
Non-religious/Atheist 0.4%.
Muslim 2.2%. Mainly Gujarati Indians.
Baha'i 0.4%.
Hindu 0.2%. Tamil Indians. Many Tamil Catholics are practising Hindus.
Christian 96.3%. Affiliated 93.6%
Roman Catholic 92.4%. 494,000a; 277,000m.
Marginal groups 0.4%. Chiefly Jehovah's Witnesses 849m.
Protestant 0.8%. 4,300a; 1,770m. Denominations 4. Largest (adult members):

Assemblies of God	750
Evangelical Ch.(**AEF, AIM, SEM**)	250

Evangelical 0.56% of population.
Missionaries to Réunion 10 (1:53,500 people) in 5 agencies.

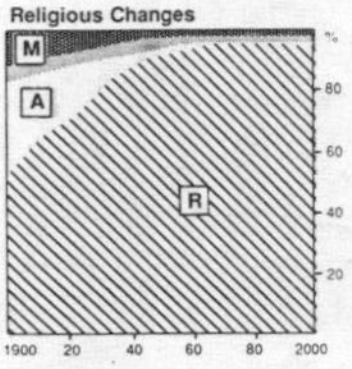

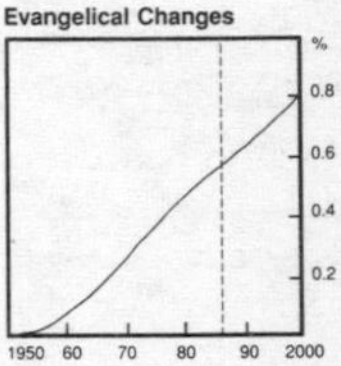

1. **The great spiritual need** is underlined by widespread alcoholism (much rum is made), loose morals and witchcraft. There is also much poverty — especially in the highlands. Catholicism is the stated religion of most people. This is still a pioneer field for missions.

2. **Réunion was, until recently, largely unevangelized.** Exciting church growth in both the Assemblies of God and the Evangelical Church has taken place since 1970. There are still areas without an evangelical witness.

3. **Missions.** For years French Assemblies of God missionaries pioneered alone. After 1970 **AEF, AIM** and Swiss Evangelical Mission workers pioneered a successful church planting programme; the resulting Evangelical Church now directs the work and invites missionaries for outreach and Bible teaching ministries.

R

4. **Mature leadership** for the young and rapidly growing churches is a priority. The Evangelical Church commenced a Bible school in 1984. Pray that this school may make an impact on all the five French-speaking island territories of the Indian Ocean, (Reunion, Mauritius, Comores, Seychelles, Madagascar).

5. **Young people** are a neglected group. Economic prospects are bleak. Little has been done to meet their spiritual needs through special literature, camps or youth programmes. **CEF** has started a ministry among children.

6. **Unreached peoples:**
   a) **The Chinese.** Many are nominally Catholic; only one known born-again believer.
   b) There are no churches functioning among the **Comorian** or **Malagasy**, or among the Hindu **Tamil** and Muslim **Gujarati Indians**.

7. **Christian literature and Bibles** have been widely distributed in the past 10 years through the Bible Society, SU and Evangelical Church. There is one small Christian bookstore.

8. **The French broadcasts from FEBA** Seychelles are well received. Pray for fruit from the 22 hours of broadcasting monthly.

Eastern Europe

Sept 14-15

ROMANIA

(The Socialist Republic of Romania)

Area 237,000 sq.km. Area is much reduced by Russian seizure of Bessarabia in 1940 (now the Moldavian Soviet Socialist Republic).

Population 22,800,000. Annual growth 0.9%. People per sq.km. 96.

Peoples
Romanian 84%. A Latin people descended from Romans settled in Dacia.
Hungarian 8.5%. In Transylvania.
Minorities 7.5%. Gypsy 700,000; German 300,000; Jew 106,000; Turk 100,000; Ukrainian 67,000; Serbian 65,000; etc.

Literacy 98%. **Official languages:** Romanian, Hungarian.

Capital: Bucharest 2,200,000. Urbanization 49%.

Economy: Rigid centralized control has nullified benefit of economic links with the West, and Romania is now Europe's poorest nation with a steady deterioration in 1981-83. Income/person $1,988 (14% of USA). Inflation 2.2%.

Politics: Communist coup in 1947 with Russian support. The very harsh and repressive Communist regime has followed a nationalistic, independent line since 1963.

Religion: The registered churches are very strictly controlled. Many evangelical believers are forced to worship in illegal groups because the government rarely allows the registration of new churches. Persecution of churches is the most severe of any of the Eastern European states.

Non-religious/Atheist 14%.
Muslim 1.2%. Predominantly Turks, some Bulgars and Gypsies.
Jews 0.5%. Steadily declining through emigration to Israel.
Christian 84.2%.

Orthodox 67.4%; 15,400,000a 10,700,000m. Denominations 6. Largest (adherents):

Romanian Orthodox Church	12,200,000

Roman Catholic 5.5%. 1,244,000a 900,000m.
Marginal groups 0.3%. 66,000a 48,000m.
Protestant 11%. 2,500,000a; 1,500,000m. Denominations 14 legally acknowledged. Largest (adult members):

Reformed Church		520,000
Baptist Union	(?)	340,000
Church of God		230,000
Assemblies of God		170,000
Lutheran Church		94,500
Brethren	(?)	63,000
Seventh Day Adventist Church		57,000

Evangelical 7.8% of population (11% if the Lord's Army Christians are included).

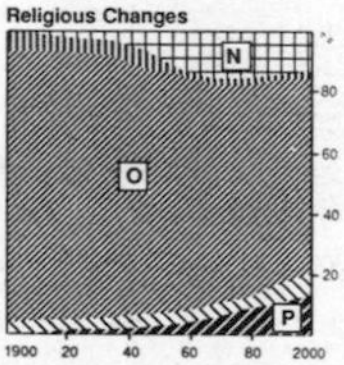

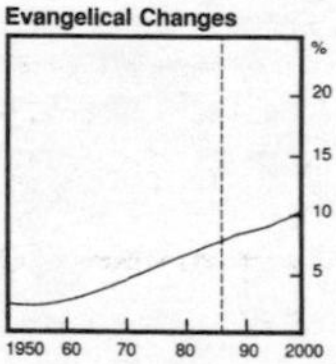

1. **Romania is experiencing the most widespread moving of God's Spirit of any Eastern European country.** Intense propaganda and persecution has stimulated this interest and also refined the Church. There are many thousands of baptisms in evangelical churches every year. Revival is most marked in the north, Transylvania and among the Gypsy minority. The rate of conversions has noticeably increased since the severe earthquake in 1977.

2. **The authorities have used every possible means to control the churches** — infiltration of informers, falsely accusing pastors and church leaders, and blackmailing them to conform to government demands in exchange for reduced persecution. Many leaders in the larger churches are therefore servile to the state. Pray for all Christian leaders in their unenviable situation.

3. **Persecution of all groups who refuse to conform has been particularly severe** — and the level of pressure has gradually increased between 1974 and 1986. Especially persecuted are the evangelical Orthodox "Lord's Army", Baptists, Brethren and Pentecostals, because of their vigorous evangelism and refusal to compromise the Truth. Pray that Western leaders may make the right representations to the government to adhere to international agreements on religious freedom. The ethnic minority churches are also under great pressure — Lutherans (German) and Reformed (Hungarian and German) in Transylvania.

4. **The forms of persecution are many** — blackmail, limitations on church buildings, baptisms, and youth work, violent disruption of meetings, destruction of "illegal" church buildings, heavy fines, imprisonments, enforced exile, dismissal from work and frequent house searches. Pray for our suffering brethren, that they may stand firm in the Lord and continue their courageous witness.

5. **The Lord's Army** is a remarkable, unofficial organization within the Orthodox Church with about 300,000 converted members and possibly another 200,000 sympathizers. Pray for this very significant movement, and its leaders, which was banned in 1949 and has also been severely persecuted.

6. **Trained leadership is in critically short supply.** The government restricts numbers and scrutinizes applicants to the Baptist Theological College and Pentecostal Bible School. In 1981 there were only 15 students in the former. Only three of the 160 Baptist pastors have had formal training, yet there are over 1,300 churches. Outstanding pastors have recently been forced into exile, further complicating the situation. Pray for adequate theological literature to be available (there is virtually none extant in the Romanian language) — all having to come from outside the country. Pray for alternative leadership training schemes.

7. **Bible distribution** is severely limited by government restrictions on importation of Christian literature from the West. Some shipments of legally imported Bibles were even recycled to make toilet paper and re-exported to the West. Locally published Bibles are occasionally issued, but are inadequate in numbers and rarely made available to nonconforming groups which most need them. Pray for all who risk their livelihood and even their lives and the economic wellbeing of their families for this vital ministry. Pray for the increased availability of God's Word and preservation of those Scriptures already in the land. The police continue to arrest believers with Bibles and destroy any stocks they find. A number of believers have received heavy prison sentences in recent times.

8. **Christian radio broadcasts** from Monaco (**TWR**) are a source of immense comfort and blessing to the believers, and a means of evangelizing the lost.

9. **Missionary vision.** Pray that Romanian believers may effectively use their strategic position to evangelize people of surrounding countries. There are many unreached minorities within Romania from these lands:

a) **Muslim:** Turk (100,000), Tatar (24,000), Bulgar, Gagauzi, etc.
b) **Jews**, many of whom have emigrated to Israel and the West.
c) **Greek** (12,000), among whom there are few born-again believers.

Africa
Sept 16

RWANDA

Area 26,000 sq.km. A mountainous country similar to its southern neighbour, Burundi.

Population 6,300,000. Growth rate 3.6%. People per sq.km. 242. Africa's most densely populated country.

Peoples
Hutu 85%. The dominant people since 1959.
Tutsi 9.7%. The former feudal ruling people.
Other 5.3%. Rundi 315,000; Twa Pygmy 25,000.

Literacy 25%. **Official languages:** French, Kinyarwanda.

Capital: Kigali 240,000. Urbanization 5%.

Economy: Very poor and overpopulated agricultural land with few natural resources. Income/person $250 (2% of USA).

Politics: Belgian mandated territory until independence in 1962. The Hutu revolted against Tutsi over lordship in 1959 and slaughtered many. Since 1973 the military government emphasizes national unity after years of intertribal mistrust and warfare.

Religion: There is freedom of religion.
Traditional religions 13.8%.
Muslim 8.6%. Rapid growth.

Christian 75.6%. Nominal 14.6%. Affiliated 61%.
Roman Catholic 39.7%. Practising 70%. 2,500,000a 1,375,000m.
Protestant 21.2%. practising 90%. 1,333,000a; 476,400m. Denominations 11. Largest (adult members):

Anglican (Ruanda Miss. CMS)	180,000
Seventh Day Adventist Church	130,000
Pentecostal Ch. (Swed. Pente.) (?)	100,000
Baptist Union	25,000
Presbyterian Church	18,000
Assoc of Baptist Ch's (**CBFMS**)	12,300
Free Methodist Church	10,300

Evangelical 16% of population.
Missionaries to Rwanda 134 (1:47,000 people) in 13 agencies.
Missionaries from Rwanda 0.

Religious Changes

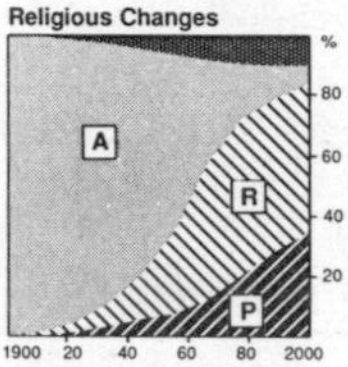

Evangelical Changes

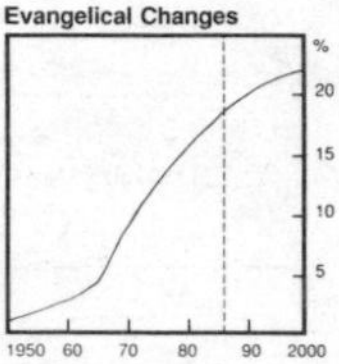

1. **Praise God for the open door for the gospel** and also for the noteworthy "Rwanda Revival" of the '30s in the Anglican Church, which spread to many denominations and lands in East Africa and beyond. Spiritual life is still evident, but much of the love and fire of that generation has gone. Pray that Christians may be an example to the nation that has been torn by the intertribal warfare and massacres of the '60s.

2. **There has been a fresh move of the Spirit** over the last 10 years among young people in all churches. Pray that this may result in a breakdown of the "generation gap" between them and the older Christians and a new vitality in all expressions of church life.

3. **There has also been a spontaneous movement of the Spirit in the Roman Catholic Church.** A very extensive network of prayer and Bible study groups sprang up all over the country. The emphasis on the Scriptures has gradually been replaced by increasing structure and control, and a reversion to a more conservative RC theological stance. Pray for the born-again believers within this church.

4. **Christian leaders of vision and spiritual calibre are needed.** Pray for those in training at the inter-church seminary in Butare and elsewhere in Africa and the West. All too often those who are highly trained find it hard to be satisfied with the ministry and support in a land of poor rural churches. Pray for the training of local leaders in the churches.

5. **Scripture Union** has a blessed ministry among young people of all churches, thus helping to lessen denominational rivalry. Pray for blessing on the daily Bible-reading notes and extension of this ministry to the churches, for this is often the only systematic Bible training most people get. Pray also for the **SU** programme to develop follow-up materials for new converts — few churches have a vision for this.

6. **The eviction of 70,000 Rwandans and their cattle from Uganda** in 1982 threatens the precarious stability of this overpopulated land. The 45,000 accepted into Rwanda have no hope of resettlement and face starvation. A considerable number of these are committed Christians. Pray for these people in their plight.

7. **The missionary force numbers about 134** in 13 different societies. Most are evangelical, some of the larger being: **Ruanda Mission**/CMS (40), Swedish **AoG** (30), **CBFMS** (9), Free Methodists (21). Pray that their life and witness may be a blessing and example to all.

8. **Unreached peoples:**
   a) The Muslims are a growing community. Much money has been poured into the country by Libya. Few Christians have either the burden or the knowledge to approach them with the gospel.
   b) The 25,000 Twa remain unreached, and few Christians are concerned for them.

SAHARA or WESTERN SAHARA

See under Morocco p. 303.

Caribbean

Sept 17

ST. CHRISTOPHER AND NEVIS

(The State of St. Christopher and Nevis)

Area 269 sq.km. in the Leeward Islands.

Population 45,000. Annual growth 1.8%. People per sq.km. 167.

Peoples: African 90%, **Eurafrican** 5%, **East Indian** 3%, **White** 1.5%.

Literacy 88%. **Language:** English.

Capital: Basseterre 18,000. Urbanization 45%.

Economy: Dependent on sugar and fishing. Income/person $829 (6% of USA).

Politics: Associated state of UK in 1967. Anguilla protested and reverted to British colonial status in 1980. Independence in 1983.

Religion: Statistics of Anguilla to the northeast included.

Christian 99.2%. Nominal 15.3%. Affiliated 83.9%.

Roman Catholic 7%. 5,740a; 4,000m.

Marginal groups 2.7%. 2,200a; 1,000m.

Protestant 74.2%. 60,800a; 28,000m. Denominations 26. Largest (adult members):

Methodist Church	8,100
Seventh Day Adventist Church	1,350
Baptist (2 groups)	1,050
Moravian	1,000
Church of God Cleveland	900
Church of God Prophecy	600

Evangelical 21.6% of population.

Missionaries to St. Christopher and Nevis 18 (1:4,500 people) in 7 agencies.

Missionaries from St. Christopher and Nevis 2 (1:30,000 Protestants).

Points for Prayer: See Jamaica on p. 255.

Caribbean

Sept 17

ST. LUCIA
(The State of St. Lucia)

Area 619 sq.km. Windward Islands; between Martinique and St. Vincent.

Population 127,000. Annual growth 2.2%. People per sq.km. 205.

Peoples: African 50.3%, **Eurafrican** 45.4%, **East Indian** 3.2%, **European** 1%.

Literacy 78%. **Official language:** English.

Capital: Castries 51,000. Urbanization 43%.

Economy: Manufacturing and tourist industries rapidly growing but with decline in agricultural exports. Income/person $1,060 (7.5% of USA).

Politics: Independent from Britain in 1979 as a relatively stable parliamentary democracy.

Religion: Freedom of religion.
Spiritist 2.3%.
Christian 97.4%.
Roman Catholic 83%. Practising 45%. 106,000a; 56,000m.
Marginal groups 1.4%. 1,800a; 620m.
Protestant 13%. 16,500a; 8,700m. Denominations 11. Largest (adult members):

Seventh Day Adventist Church	4,000
Anglican Church	1,850
Evang. Ch. of W.I. (**WT**)	700

Evangelical 4.8% of population.
Missionaries to St. Lucia 38 (1:3,300 people) in 5 agencies.
Missionaries from St. Lucia 1 (to French Guyana).

Points for Prayer: See Jamaica on p. 255.

The West

Sept 17

ST. PIERRE & MIQUELON
(Department of St. Pierre and Miquelon)

Area 242 sq.km. Eight rocky islands at the mouth of the Canadian St. Lawrence River, and south of Newfoundland.

Population 6,000 French. People per sq.km. 25.

Politics: Department of France; the last vestige of France's once vast North American possessions.

Religion: Freedom of religion.
Non-Christian 2% including Baha'i.
Christian 98%. All Roman Catholic but for a small group of Jehovah's Witnesses.

S

1. **This is the only territory in the Americas without a known Protestant Church**. Pray for the evangelization of these French fisher communities. **EHC** literature has been distributed. This is a possible field for French Canadian believers.

ST. VINCENT
(St. Vincent and the Grenadines)

Caribbean

Sept 17

Area 389 sq.km. Windward Islands; located between St. Lucia and Grenada. One larger island and the majority of the Grenadine islets to the south.

Population 118,000. Annual growth 2%. People per sq.km. 304.

Peoples: African 66%, **Eurafrican** 20%, **East Indian** 6%, **European** 4%, **Amerindian (Carib)** 2%, **Other** 2%.

Literacy 82%. **Official language:** English.

Capital: Kingstown 40,000. Urbanization 45%.

Economy: Agriculture and tourism are the mainstays of the economy. Underemployment and over-population becoming acute. Income/person $860 (6% of USA).

Politics: Independent from Britain as a parliamentary democracy in 1979.

Religion

Spiritist 2%. **Baha'i** 0.8%. **Other** 1.4%.

Christian 96%. Nominal 28%. Affiliated 68%.

Roman Catholic 16.8%. 17,300a; 9,000m.

Marginal groups 1%. 1,000a.

Protestant 50.3%. 59,300a; 19,000m. Denominations 18. Largest (adult members):

Anglican Church	5,700
Methodist Church	3,750
Seventh Day Adventist Church	2,120
Church of God (Cleveland)	1,670
Brethren	800
Evang. Ch. of W.I. **(WT)**	620

Evangelical 12.8% of the population.

Missionaries to St. Vincent 29 (1:4,000 people) in 8 agencies.

Missionaries from St. Vincent 0.

Points for Prayer: See Jamaica on p. 255.

SAMOA (WESTERN)

(The Independent State of Western Somoa)

Pacific

Sept 18

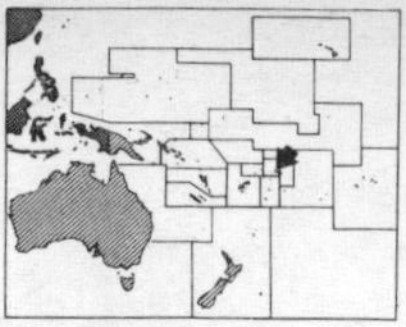

Area 3,000 sq.km. Three volcanic islands in the South Central Pacific. Six small islands to the east ruled by USA.

Population 164,000. Annual growth 0.9%. People per sq.km. 55. Over 30,000 Samoans live in New Zealand.

Peoples: Samoan 89%, **Euronesian** 10%, **European** 1%.

Literacy 90%. **Official languages:** Samoan, English.

Capital: Apia 35,000. Urbanization 22%.

Economy: Agriculture, tourism and remittances from overseas Samoans are the main sources of revenue. Income/person $500 (3.5% of USA).

Politics: Independent of New Zealand in 1962. Constitutional monarchy.

Religion: Freedom of religion.
Baha'i 2%.
Christian 98%. Nominal 5%. Affiliated 93%.
Roman Catholic 20.4%. Practising 78%. 33,500a; 16,750m.

Marginal groups 17.4%. 28,500a; 19,500m. Groups 5. Largest (adherents):

Mormons	25,860

Protestant 55%. 90,200a; 40,300m. Denominations 11. Largest (adult members):

Congreg. Chr. Church (LMS)	24,300
Methodist Church	10,700
Assemblies of God	3,200
Seventh Day Adventist Church	3,080

Evangelical 9.1% of population.

Missionaries to W. Samoa 30 (1:5,470 people) in 7 agencies.

Missionaries from W. Samoa approx. 50 (1:1,800 Protestants).

Religious Changes

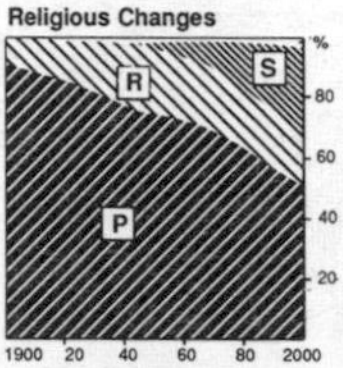

Evangelical Changes

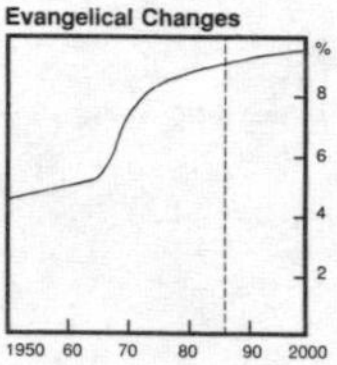

1. **The entire population was Christian by 1900,** and every village has a church. The basic structure of society remained intact with the coming of the gospel, and much pride, formalism and compromise is evident. The Mormons have made big inroads into the nominal Protestant community.

2. **There are no unreached peoples, but thousands have never been challenged to a personal commitment to Christ.** Evangelicals are growing in numbers through the Assemblies of God and several smaller denominations.

3. **For years many ardent Samoan missionaries traversed the Pacific,** but now that number is greatly reduced. Pray for renewed vision and zeal for the kingdom of God.

4. **Pacific Students for Christ** serves 11 countries, including Samoa, with student groups in 40 institutions. Pray for the evangelization of Pacific campuses.

SAN MARINO

(Most Serene Republic of San Marino)

The West

Sept 19

Area: 62 sq.km. An enclave in North Central Italy.

Population: 23,000 Sammarinese speaking Italian. A further 20,000 living abroad.

Politico-economic: Independent republic since AD 301. Income/person $8,000 (57% of USA).

Religion: Freedom of Religion.
Non-religious/Atheist 5%. **Baha'i** 0.5%.
Christian 94.5%.
Roman Catholic 92.3%. 20,000a.
Jehovah's Witnesses 0.7%. 160a.

There are no known groups of Protestant believers in the republic. Sadly, only Jehovah's Witnesses have succeeded in starting a group.

SAO TOMÉ & PRINCIPE

(Democratic Republic of São Tomé & Principe)

Africa

Sept 20

Area 964 sq.km. Two larger and several smaller islands in the Gulf of Guinea 200 km. west of Gabon.

Population 120,000. Annual growth 2.9%.

Peoples
African origin 90% from Angola, West Africa.
Creole/Portuguese 10%, many from Cape Verde Islands.

Literacy 42%. **Official language:** Portuguese.

Capital: São Tomé. Urbanization 32%.

Economy: Subsistence agriculture; cocoa the major export. Income/person $310 (2% of USA).

Politics: Independent from Portugal in 1975 as a one-party republic.

Religion: Secular state with freedom of religion.

Non-religious, traditional religions, etc. 3%.

Christian 97%. Affiliated 87.8%.
Roman Catholic 83%. 100,000a.
Protestant 3.2%. 3,800a; 1,600m. Denominations 4. Largest (adult members):

Assemblies of God	1,000
Evangelical Church	300

Evangelical 2.5% of population.

1. **The major Protestant witness** is that of the Assemblies of God with 12 congregations in the islands. There are several smaller groups, but the majority of the population is nominally Catholic. There are no missionaries.

Middle East

Sept 21-22

SAUDI ARABIA
(Kingdom of Saudi Arabia)

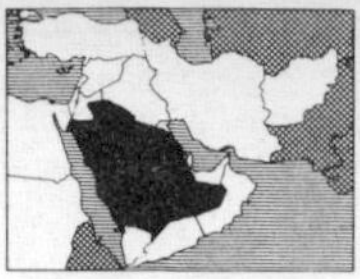

Area 2,150,000 sq.km. The main centre of the Arabian Peninsula, much of it desert and thinly populated.

Population 11,200,000. Annual growth 3%. People per sq.km. 5. In 1974, 27% of population was nomadic; this percentage is dropping rapidly through settlement schemes and industrialization.

Peoples (figures approximate)
Indigenous citizens 70%. Arab and small minorities of African Blacks, etc.
Foreign workers 30%. Yemenis 2,000,000; Other Arabs (Egyptians, Sudanese, Palestinian, etc.) 400,000; Koreans 300,000; Pakistanis 700,000; Filipinos 200,000; Indians 100,000; Iranis 78,000; US citizens 65,000, Bangladeshis 35,000, etc. However, numbers fell during 1984-86.

Literacy 13%. **Official language:** Arabic.

Capitals: Riyadh 1,650,000 (royal), Jiddah 1,360,000 (administrative), Mecca 658,000 (religious). Urbanization 70%.

Economy: An oil economy, possessing 25% of the world's known oil reserves. Oil revenues are used to improve services and communications, to develop industries and to finance Islamic advances around the world. Income/person $12,180 (86% of USA).

Politics: Absolute monarchy and a semi-feudal state with strict adherence to Islamic principles.

Religion: An Islamic state committed to the preservation of traditional Islam. All other religions are prohibited. Expatriate Christian gatherings are not allowed.
Muslim 94%. Sunni 90%, mainly of strict Wahhabi sect, Shi'a 9%, Ismaili 1%.
Other religions 3%. Unofficially followed by non-Christian migrant workers.
Christian 3%. Only a small minority are able to gather informally with other Christians — chiefly Koreans, Westerners, Filipinos, Indians, Pakistanis, etc.

1. **Saudi Arabia is one of the least evangelized nations on earth.** What a challenge to faith: no known believers, no indigenous churches, no Christian workers permitted to enter the country, and no Christian even allowed to set foot in Islam's holiest city of Mecca. Pray that this land, the heart of Islam, may see a demonstration of the power of the blood of the Lamb.

2. **Great efforts are made to shield the population from foreign influences** that could "corrupt" society. Pray that even this may stimulate a desire for the Truth and an openness to the gospel. Very few Saudis have heard the Good News, seen a Bible or met a true believer.

3. **Eight hundred million Muslims worldwide** bow daily in prayer towards Mecca, and 2.5 mill. pilgrims annually make the "Hajj" to visit the birthplace of Islam. Pray that many may have their eyes opened to see the emptiness and bondage under which they live, and embrace the freedom that there is in Christ.

4. **The Islamic missionary impetus** is coordinated by the Muslim World League in Mecca. Vast sums of money are used to propagate their faith around the world — aid to countries considered sympathetic, building mosques, sending missionaries, literature, radio, etc. The Saudi government denies to Christians the liberty to share their faith, yet they expect it for Muslims elsewhere. Pray for the King and leaders of Saudi Arabia.

5. **Saudi believers**, if there are any, have to hide their faith or risk death. Pray for such. Pray that living fellowships of believers may be planted despite the apparent impossibility.

6. **Expatriates** are often hard, materialistic, isolated and frustrated. Pray for an adequate witness to each in spite of the seemingly insuperable obstacles. The communities devoid of a witness are the Yemenis, many of the Pakistanis and the Iranis. Some Koreans have been converted to Islam. There are believers among the Korean construction workers, Filipino workers and nurses, Pakistani labourers and Western professionals. Pray for their witness to their own communities and beyond.

7. **Expatriate Christians** live under strict surveillance. Controls on any form of Christian gathering are tightened year by year. Any identified as leaders of house fellowships are expelled. Survival, let alone friendship evangelism, under these conditions is not easy. Few expatriates have extensive meaningful friendships with local people. The strain on expatriate wives is unusually intense. Pray for believers who maintain a tactful witness under arduous conditions.

8. **Other means of witness worthy of prayer**.

a) Loving witness by believers to **Saudi students, tourists and businessmen** visiting the West.

b) **Christian radio programmes** are proving effective, and many Arabs listen secretly. **FEBA** broadcasts 80 hours per month, **TWR** 39. **FEBA** also broadcasts in Korean to Saudi Arabia.

c) **The tactful circulation of Christian literature and video cassettes**. Christian literature and Bibles are banned.

Africa

Sept 23-24

SENEGAL

(Republic of Senegal)

Area 196,000 sq.km. Much of the land is arid with few natural resources.

Population 6,700,000. Annual growth +3.1%. People per sq.km 34. The majority live on the coast and in the area around the capital.

Peoples: All totals for peoples include those living in the Gambia.
Wolof groups 35%. Wolof 2,500,000; Lebou 100,000. Politically dominant. Strongly Muslim.
Fula groups 26%. Fula (Peul) 1,300,000; Tukulor 681,000.
Mande groups 12%. Mandingo-Maninka 672,000 (mostly in the Gambia); Soninke 152,000; Bambara 54,000; Jakanka 20,000; Jalonke 14,000. All Muslim.
Serer-Jola groups 21%. Serer 1,000,000; Jola 561,000. The largest pagan minorities are within these peoples.
Other minorities 4%. Maures 84,000; Balanta 68,000; Mankanya 61,000, and over seven other smaller groups.
Foreign minorities 2%. Lebanese, French, Cape Verdian.

Literacy 10%. **Official language:** French. **Trade language:** Wolof. **All languages** 33. **Bible translations** 2Bi, 7por.

Capital: Dakar 1,400,000. Urbanization 42%.

Economy: Agricultural base, heavily dependent on unreliable rains and groundnut cultivation. Income/person $440 (3% of USA).

Politics: Independent from France in 1960. Senegal has been one of Africa's most politically stable states. Senegalese forces quelled an attempted coup in the Gambia in 1981. In 1982 a Confederation was formed between the two countries. A gradual integration of armed forces, economics, and political life of the two countries is planned.

Religion: A secular state with freedom of religion. The three Muslim Sufi brotherhoods, the Muridiya, Tijaniya and Qadiriya are influential in political and economic life.
Muslim 92%. Sunni Islam, but over 85% of Muslims are members of the three Sufi brotherhoods. Strongest among the Fula, Tukulor and Wolof.
Traditional religions 4.6%. Predominantly Serer (30%), Jola (30%), and smaller peoples of the Casamance in S.W.
Christian 3.5%.
Roman Catholic 3.4%. Practising 70%. 230,000a; 133,000m.
Protestant 0.1%. 6,600a; 2,800m. Denominations 12. Largest (adult members):

Lutheran Church	1,200
Assemblies of God	600
Baptist Convention	175
Evang. Church of W.Africa (**WEC**)	100

Evangelical 0.09% of the population.
Missionaries to Senegal 290 (1:23,100 people) in 20 agencies.

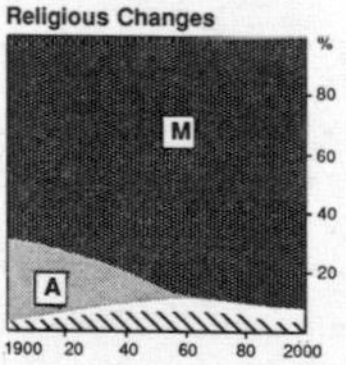

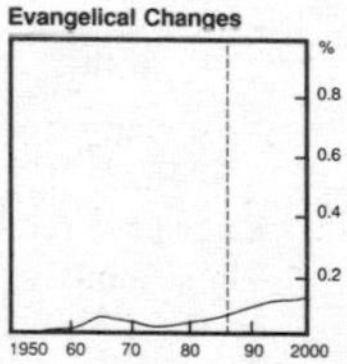

1. **Islam has grown rapidly over the last 50 years** from possibly 50% to 92% of the population, yet the land is wide open for the gospel! The highly organized and politically powerful Sufi brotherhoods claim 85% of all Muslims as members. Hitherto tolerance for other religions has been a point of pride. Pray for its continuance; extremists could insist on setting up a narrow, bigoted Islamic state. Pray for a breakthrough for the gospel among Muslims, and for an impact to be made on the Muslim brotherhoods.

2. **Christians are few,** though their influence is disproportionately great through their input into education. Most of these Christians are nominal and their life style gives little credit to the cause of Christ. Almost all are originally from a non-Muslim background and from the Cape Verdians, Serer and Jola peoples. Even among the non-Muslim groups the powers of darkness have yet to be routed.

3. **Evangelical believers are a rarity**. There may be no more than around 1,000 in all of Senegal. Only through the work of the **AoG** and Finnish Lutherans have groups of churches been planted, and these are only among the Serer and Bassari. Believers are scattered, often

poorly taught and under constant pressures from Muslim or heathen relatives to conform. The lack of believing girls tempts many young men to marry unbelievers or to immorality. Pray for a strong church to be planted in each ethnic group. Sadly, liberal teaching is affecting the young Lutheran Church, with increasing nominalism among members.

4. **There are very few Christian leaders**. There are probably no more than 48 full-time national Christian workers. The **AoG** runs a Bible school, and **CBFMS** a TEE programme. Pray that men of God may be raised up who can pastor believers and lead them out in effective evangelism.

5. **Missions in Senegal have struggled for years without much fruit**. **WEC** entered the Casamance in the south in 1936 among the Jola, Balanta and Fula, and later the Senegal River Valley in the north. Other pioneer missions have followed and there are now 14 church planting missions serving in the country. The largest are **NTM** (78 workers), **WEC** (44), Finnish Lutherans (30), **UWM** (22), **AoG** (14). Pray for more called of God to serve in this needy but open land. Pray also for encouragement among the missionary teams; most are young, inexperienced and short on leadership in a difficult, unresponsive field.

6. **Major areas of the country are virtually untouched with the gospel**.
   a) **Dakar**, the burgeoning capital, is a medley of peoples. Little is done to evangelize the ethnic communities. Most Christian work is administrative (serving missionaries elsewhere), or in French and to expatriate Westerners and Cape Verdians. Many areas need church planters. **SBC, UWM** and **AoG** have planted churches in the city.
   b) **The Senegal River Valley** in the north and northeast is a major development zone, with many changes coming. Only a few missionaries are working on this strategic frontier with closed Mauritania, among the Tukulor, Maure, Wolof, Fula, and Soninké (**WEC**, Lutherans, etc.). There is no church in the entire area.
   c) **The upper regions of the Casamance** in the east are more sparsely populated, and unevangelized. There is an **AoG** church in Tambacounda but the members are mostly Bassaris who have migrated there from another area seeking employment.

7. **Unreached peoples**. All but possibly the Serer are unreached. Pray for the:
   a) **Wolof**. The largest and most dominant people. They are strongly Muslim, and there are only about 30 known believers. **Brethren, CBFMS, WEC** and **ICF** missionaries are pioneering among this proud but resistant people. The **Lebou** around Dakar have no known believers.
   b) **Serer**, speaking two separate languages. Until recently they were strongly fetishist. Now many are becoming Muslim and Catholic. Only among some of the Serer has there been Protestant church planting (Finnish Lutherans and **AoG**). A considerable number of Serer have recently turned to Christ as a result of hearing Serer Scriptures on cassettes. The related Canguin are unevangelized.
   c) **Fula**. A pastoral people, some nomadic. Nearly all are Muslim. There are only a few scattered believers and two tiny groups meeting together. Lutherans work among the Fula in the north, and **WEC** have five workers committed to those speaking the Fulacounda dialect in the south.
   d) **Tukulor**. Muslim for 900 years, and only two known believers. Four **WEC** and **SIL** missionaries are working among them.
   e) **Jola**, speaking 13 major dialects. In the north of the Casamance they are nominally Muslim, and in the south strongly fetish worshippers. There are only about 50 committed believers (**WEC**, **SBC** and **SIL**). The breakthrough has yet to come to this, the last large pagan people of the country.
   f) **Maures**. All are Muslim. No known believers. The majority live in inaccessible Mauritania, though many are reachable in the Senegal River Valley (**WEC**).
   g) **The smaller peoples on the southern border** are pagan or nominally Muslims. **NTM** has a major thrust to evangelize the Balanta-Gonja, Manjak, Budik, Bainouk, Malinké, Jalonké, with plans also to reach the Badjaranké, Mankanya and Serer. Some work has been done among the Bassari and Konyagi (**AoG**), resulting in 200 Bassaris professing faith in Christ.

8. **Young people**. Many have flocked to the cities in search of employment. Their commitment to conservative Islam is not so great, but relatively little is being done to reach them. **SBC**, **UWM** and others have a youth work in Dakar. The **IFES** group in Dakar University is small but keen; however, all the members are non-Senegalese. Pray for an impact for God to be made on children and young people.

9. **Bible translation is one of the greatest needs**. There is still not a single NT in an indigenous language, though the Wolof NT is almost complete (**Brethren**, etc.), and progress is being made in Tukulor and Mandingo in the Gambia (**WEC**). Up to 20 languages may require translation teams; **SIL** is surveying the need. Work is in progress in Serer (Finnish Lutherans and **CBFMS**) and Budik (**NTM**). Many people read and write Arabic. There is great potential in publishing Scriptures in the local languages in a modified Arabic script. Pray for both translators and literacy workers to be called.

Africa
Sept 25

SEYCHELLES
(Republic of Seychelles)

Area 444 sq.km. 92 islands spread across 400,000 sq.km. of the Indian Ocean.

Population 72,000. Annual growth 1.9%. People per sq.km. 162.

Peoples
Creole 96%. Of African and French origin.
Minorities 4%. French, British, Indian, Chinese.

Literacy 62%. **Official languages:** French, English. Seychelles Creole is widely spoken.

Capital: Victoria 30,000.

Economy: Tourism, agriculture and fishing are the mainstays of the economy. Income/person $2,400 (17% of USA).

Politics: Independent from Britain in 1976. The coup of 1977 resulted in a one-party socialist government. The president has strong executive powers and relies on North Korean and Soviet military help to retain power.

Religion: Freedom for long-established denominations, but newer groups are not permitted to plant churches.
Non-religious/Atheist 1%.
Hindu 0.6%, **Muslim** 0.3%, **Baha'i** 0.3%.
Christian 97.6%. Affiliated 95%.
Roman Catholic 87%. Practising 35%. 62,600a; 37,000m.
Protestant 7.8%. 5,600a; 2,170m. Denominations 2. Adult members:

Anglican Church	2,000
Seventh Day Adventist Church	120

Evangelical 0.45% of population.
Missionaries to Seychelles 31 (1:2,300 people).

1. **Nearly all Seychellois claim to be Christian**, but are steeped in superstition and depend on the outward rites of baptism and confirmation. Immorality is a serious problem, and very few have a saving knowledge of Christ. Pray that full freedom for the preaching of the gospel may be granted, and pray that many within the recognized churches may be converted.

2. **Since 1970 over 15 informal Bible study groups** have sprung up on the largest island Mahé, with a number of Seychellois coming to the Lord. An indigenous Pentecostal group, which began in 1982, has rapidly grown to over 500 believers. Pray for lively, locally led fellowships to be planted all over the islands.

3. **Evangelical missionary work** has been confined to the large radio ministry of **FEBA** and a low profile ceramics vocational training project of **AIM** (with six workers). There is a growing variety of help ministries open for **AIM** missionaries in teaching, agriculture and medicine. Pray for continued acceptance for missionaries and an increase in personnel and opportunities for witness.

4. **The Seychelles Creole NT** is now being translated through the Bible Society of Mauritius. Pray for the rapid completion of this project and for the Word to make an impact on Seychellois society.

5. **FEBA has a radio ministry on Mahé.** The strategically placed islands enable 400 hours of broadcasting per month in 14 languages of S. Asia, 300 hours in eight languages of E.Africa, 100 hours in two languages of the Middle East to be aired. Many of these lands are closed to normal missionary work. Pray for:

a) **The preparation of programmes** in receiving areas in India, Middle East and Africa.

b) **Continued permission to broadcast** and for good reception in the target areas.

c) **Financial provision and efficient performance.** Equipment and running costs are expensive.

d) **The expatriate and national staff** to run the station and for their physical and spiritual health in a hot, humid climate.

e) **The growing response** from Muslims and Hindus in India and Pakistan and for adequate follow up among these enquirers.

f) **The Arabic broadcasts to the Middle East** and also for a settled studio in the area. (The Lebanese Civil war frequently disrupts the work of the Beirut studio.)

g) **For expansion of the African outreach** and news service in English which draws many listeners.

Africa

Sept 26

SIERRA LEONE
(Republic of Sierra Leone)

Area 72,000 sq.km. Small coastal state between Guinea and Liberia.

Population 3,600,000. Annual growth 1.7%. People per sq.km. 50.

Peoples: All ethnic groups approx. 74.
West Atlantic peoples (8) 47%. **Temne** 990,000; Limba 275,000; Sherbro 180,000; Fula 140,000; Kissi 78,000.
Mande peoples (7) 45%. **Mende** 1,050,000; Kuranko 155,000; Kono 128,000; Mandingo 76,000; Loko 76,000.
Kru peoples (2) 6%. Bassa 220,000.
Other 2%. Krio (Creole) 55,000; Lebanese 8,000; Asian 5,000; European 3,000.

Literacy 11%. **Official language:** English. **Trade language:** Krio (Creole) spoken by 20% of the population. **All languages** 20. **Bible translations** 1Bi 5NT 7por.

Capital: Freetown 516,000. Urbanization 28%.

Economy: Mining, especially iron ore and diamonds, is important. There has been a steady deterioration in the economy over the past 15 years due to mismanagement, smuggling and the world recession. Income/person $380 (3% of USA).

Politics: Independent from Britain in 1961. A one-party republic. Political and economic instability has increased since 1971, and several times the land has been on the brink of revolution.

Religion: Freedom of religion, but Islam has been growing in influence.
Traditional religions 50%, although over 90% would still be animistic in their world view. Strongest among the Kono, Kissi, Koranko, Limba and Loko.
Muslim 40%. Growing among most tribes, especially the Temne and Mende, the two largest peoples.
Christian 10%. Affiliated 8%.
Roman Catholic 1.6%. Practising 43%. 58,000a.
Foreign marginal groups 0.1%. 3,200a.
Indigenous marginal groups (10) 0.2%. 6,000a.
Protestant 6.1%. 210,000a; 105,000m. Denominations 27. Largest (adult members).

United Methodist Church	40,000
Methodist Church	28,000
Anglican Church	12,800
West African Methodist Church	12,000
Assemblies of God	2,000

Evangelical 1.5% of the population.
Missionaries to Sierra Leone est. 185 (1:19,500 people) in 18 agencies.

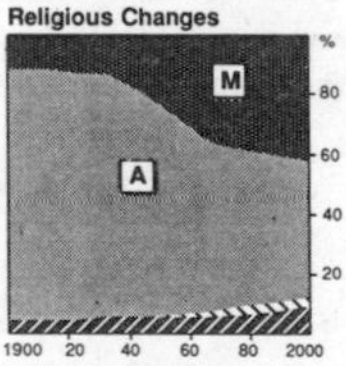

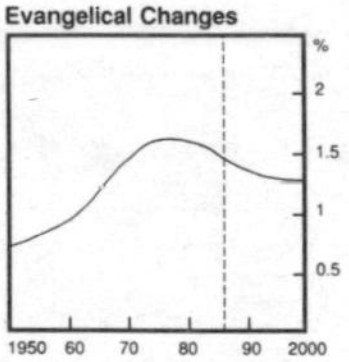

1. **Sierra Leone was the first West African country to be evangelized**, but after nearly 200 years of effort, only 10% of the nation even claims to be Christian. There is no significant church growth, nor is there a single denomination, Pentecostal or mainline Protestant, that has ever made a lasting spiritual impact on the country. Pray that the Christians may be electrified by the ministry of the Holy Spirit!

2. **The decay of public and private morality** has been so severe that the land faces a grim future despite its economic potential. Pray for wise and godly political leaders with foresight to be raised up, and for freedom to preach the pure gospel and make amends for past failures.

3. **Witchcraft and the all-pervading secret societies** have hardly ever been challenged and defeated by the power of the Cross. Both Islam and churches in general have avoided the confrontation that must come before breakthroughs can be seen.

4. **There are over 100 churches in Freetown**, but there is much nominalism, worldliness and sin among professing Christians. Almost the entire Krio population professes to be Christian, but their pride and lack of consistent Christian living is one of the major factors hindering the spread of the gospel to the tribal peoples whom they despised in the past.

5. **Churches in the hinterland** are a small minority surrounded by a sea of Muslim and pagan peoples. Illiteracy, feelings of inferiority, denominational rivalry, and lack of vibrant, growing churches have all combined to depress Christians. Pray for revival, and pray for the emergence of vital local leadership.

6. **The serious lack of trained and spiritual leadership** must be speedily rectified. There is little encouragement or incentive for young people to go into full-time service. The Sierra Leone Bible College is one of the few evangelical training institutes in the country; pray for this and the few rural primary level schools where leaders are trained.

7. **The first Protestant churches began in 1785**, yet after 200 years the land is still very much a pioneer mission field. A new beginning is required in many areas. The hardness of the field, the cultural inflexibility of earlier presentations of the gospel, and an overemphasis on institutions and schools have combined to limit the impact of earlier missionary efforts; many missionaries have been discouraged. Pray for those serving the Lord at this time, and pray for the calling of others. Some major agencies are: the Missionary Church (30 workers), Wesleyan Church (30), Lutheran Bible Translators (23), United Brethren Church (22), **AoG** (11), United Pentecostal Mission (6).

8. **Unreached peoples**. All but the Krio people around Freetown are still in this category. Pray for:

a) **Those peoples who are turning to Islam:** Yalunka (80% Muslim), Temne (70%), Mende (50%), Koranko (40%), Loko (40%). Few have the vision for their evangelization.

b) **Those peoples who are Muslim:** Fula, Vai, Susu and Bullom. Very few believers.

c) **Animistic peoples**. See list above. Only in a few localized areas among the Mende (United Methodist), Kissi (Assemblies of God), Limba (Wesleyan), Temne (Un. Pentecostal Mission, Wesleyan, Methodist) have there been a number of churches planted.

9. **Young people's work** has been fruitful, but not enough of that fruit has been conserved and matured in existing churches. **SU** and **YFC** have had a decisive impact on the more educated. **IFES** groups function on 9 university and college campuses.

10. **Christian radio**. Radio ELWA (**SIM**, Liberia) has had a considerable impact with many conversions and even churches planted in both remote and Muslim areas. Pray for this ministry, and also for those who prepare programmes.

11. **Literature. CLC** has a strategic and well-used bookstore in Freetown. Pray for the ministry of the written page. Pray also for the granting of permits for the importation of literature — these are often hard to obtain, and there are severe shortages of stock.

12. **Bible translation** is still a major need. At least six languages need to be translated. Translation teams are active in five languages; notably the Lutheran Bible Translators.

Asia

Sept 27

SINGAPORE
(Republic of Singapore)

Area 620 sq.km. One larger and 40 smaller islands of the southern tip off Peninsular Malaysia, and strategically located for communications and trade.

Population 2,600,000. Annual growth 1.1%. People per sq.km. 4,207.

Peoples
Chinese 76.5% speaking 12 dialects.
Malay 14.8%. Both of Malay and Indonesian origin.
Indian 6.4%. Predominantly Tamil.
Other 2.3%. European (25,600), Japanese (8,300), Arab (2,740), etc.
Literacy 86%. **Official languages**: English, Mandarin Chinese, Malay, Tamil. English to be taught as the first language from 1987.

Capital: Singapore is a city state. Urbanization 100%. Reputedly Asia's greenest and cleanest city.

Economy: Dramatic growth since independence to become one of the world's most efficient trading and financial centres. The world's second busiest port, with a growing 'high-tech' industrial base. The economic boom faltered in 1985.Income/person $6,620 (47% of USA).

Politics: Independent in 1965, on the partial break-up of the Malaysian Federation. The efficiency and foresight of the government has provided the basis and direction for the city-state's stability and economic growth.

Religion: Complete freedom of religion. Religion seen as a buttress for maintenance of moral standards.

Chinese religions 54%. Buddhism, Taoism, Confucianism.
Non-religious/atheist 13.2%. Mainly Chinese.
Muslim 17%. 99.5% of Malays, 21% of Indians.
Hindu 3.3%. 56% of Indians.
Other 1%. Sikh etc.
Christian 11.4%. Affiliated 8.7%.
Roman Catholic 3.9%. 98,000a; 68,000m.
Marginal groups 0.15%. 3,900a.
Protestant 4.7%. 122,000a; 80,000m. Denominations 20, also many independent congregations. Largest (adult members):

Methodist Church	approx. 10,500
Anglican	approx. 9,500
Assemblies of God	8,300
Presbyterian Church	7,500
Bible Presbyterian Church	5,000
Brethren	4,800
Baptist Conv. (**SBC**)	4,300

Evangelical 3.6% of population
Missionaries to Singapore approx. 255 (1:10,200 people).
Missionaries from Singapore approx. 90 (1:1,350 Protestants).

Religious Changes

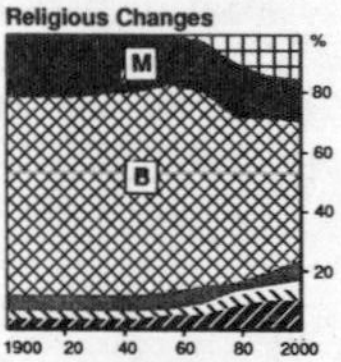

Evangelical Changes

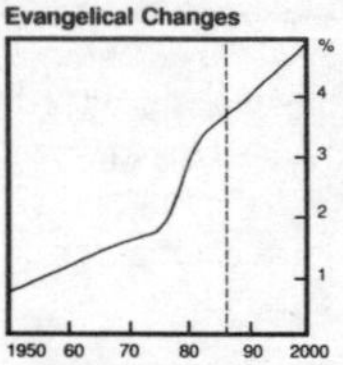

1. **The dynamism and growth of the Church in Singapore** over the past 15 years is cause for much praise to God. The rapid social change, economic development and increasing use of English are human factors in this growth. The receptivity of the Chinese and Indian Singaporeans, active evangelism of church and para-church organizations, and the concentration of committed, giving Christians in the little state are spiritual factors.

a) **The better educated** have been the most responsive. 12% of the population is Christian, but 28% of professionals, 35% of teachers, 36% of university students, 40% of doctors and 73% of present medical students are Christian.

b) **Vigorous church growth** with over 350 congregations in 1982; the fastest growing being the Assemblies of God, charismatic churches and Bible Presbyterians.

c) Most congregations are filled with **young people** who are predominantly first generation Christians.

d) There has been a rapid increase in the influence of **evangelical theology** in all denominations. What an impact the Church in Singapore could have on the world!

2. **The challenges facing the Church in Singapore**:

a) **How to maintain a spiritual cutting edge** in a time of increasing affluence.

b) **How to lessen the dropout rate** — maybe over 30% of those converted do not maintain their faith.

c) **Limited and expensive church building sites** — innovative methods to cope with further church growth are needed.

d) **Maintenance of adequate family life and witness** in high-rise flats and with high employment.

e) **The spirit of denominationalism** cripples the spiritual growth of a number of congregations.

3. **The unreached, and less reached of Singapore.**

a) **The Malay population** is staunchly Muslim, and for years their community has been fairly isolated economically. Christians of other ethnic groups have been hesitant to evangelize them because of the possibility of upsetting intercommunal relationships. However the rapid homogenization and relocation of the population could make the Malays more receptive. About 200 Malays have become Christians, but only 30-40 meet regularly together.

b) **Sections of the Indian community** — especially the Muslims, and Sikhs. There are many Indian believers, mostly from the Hindu majority community.

c) **The older, non-English-speaking population** is isolated by language from the many younger English-speaking Christians. The generation gap needs to be overcome.

d) How to evangelize the majority of **blue collar workers** among whom only 3.6% are Christian.

e) **International visitors** — tourists, seamen, students, etc., flock to the city, and provide unique evangelistic opportunities.

4. **Singapore has become one of the most strategic centres for world evangelization in Asia.** It is becoming a major missions training and sending base for **OMF, SIL, SIM, WEC, AsEF** etc. It is also the Asian headquarters for numerous Christian agencies, such as **SU**, Coordinating Office for Asian Evangelism (**COFAE**), Bible Society, etc. Pray that this little nation might become an ever greater blessing to the world.

5. **Bible training** in the 9 seminaries and Bible schools is becoming a key ministry for Christians all over Asia. Worthy of particular mention are the **Singapore Bible College** and **Far East Bible College** from where many young people have gone out to serve the Lord at home and overseas. The Discipleship Training Centre (**OMF**) is strategic for giving postgraduates a highly concentrated course in preparation for local and cross-cultural service. The latter has 285 graduates serving in 22 countries. **The Haggai Institute** has provided stimulating short-term courses for pastors and Christian workers from all over the world, especially Asia and Africa.

6. **Missionary vision** has rapidly developed. A major contribution has been through **OM** and its ship ministry which has both stimulated vision and given short-term cross-cultural experience to many. There are 42 Singaporeans with **OM**, eight with **OMF** and a number of others serving with international missions (**SIM, Navigators, WEC, AsEF, BMMF, SIL, YWAM** etc.) and local agencies.

a) Pray that local churches may both understand the vision for world evangelization, and its implications for them in support of those who are being called.

b) Pray also for the **OMF** Asia Missionary Training Institute which commenced in 1985.

c) Pray for more Singaporeans to commit themselves to long-term missionary work.

7. **Young people** are open to the gospel, and are the dynamic future for the country. The impact of youth ministries has been decisive — **SU**/ISCF has groups in 80% of all secondary schools. The VCF(**IFES**) has a strategic input among tertiary students — 1,500 of the 9,000 students are linked with VCF groups! **Teen Challenge** and others have made a major impact on drug addicts. **Eagles Evangelism** has used effective and innovative evangelistic outreaches. The **Navigators** have had a unique contribution with thousands discipled in educational institutions and in the armed forces. **Youth For Christ** has had an extensive ministry also. Pray for the effective integration of young people into local churches and mobilization for world evangelization.

8. **Foreign missions** have played a vital role in the evangelization and development of Singapore. Visas are no longer easy to obtain, nor is the need for foreign input so great. The major emphasis is on international ministries based in Singapore, and on Bible and missionary training. The largest missions are **OMF** (39, of which 12 are involved in local ministries) and **SBC** (26).

9. **Christian supportive agencies**

a) **Literature** is widely available. There are more than 37 Christian bookstores and over eight other publishers of books, magazines and tracts. Much literature is printed in Singapore and distributed in lands around the world.

b) There are over 176 para-church agencies involved in a large variety of spiritual and technical ministries.

Pacific
Sept 28

SOLOMON ISLANDS

(The Solomon Islands)

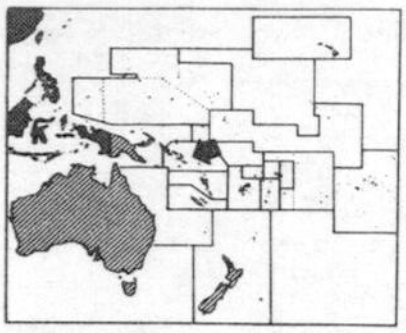

Area 28,800. Six major and many smaller islands southeast of New Guinea.

Population 273,000. Annual growth 3.5%. People per sq.km. 10.

Peoples: 62 languages spoken; numerous dialects. Only five spoken by over 10,000 people and a further 31 over 1,000.

Indigenous islanders 97.1%. **Melanesian** (50 groups) 218,000; **Papuan** (7) 28,000; **Polynesian** (7) 19,000.

Immigrant islanders 1.7%. From Kiribati, Fiji.

Other 1.2%. European 1,800, Chinese 500.

Literacy 72%. **Official language:** English. Trade language: Solomon Pijin, spoken by half the population. All languages 62. **Bible translations** 1Bi 13por.

Capital: Honiara 26,000. Urbanization 9%.

Economy: Agriculture and fishing are the mainstays of the economy. Income/person $640 (5% of USA).

Politics: Independent from Britain in 1978 as a parliamentary monarchy. Stable since independence.

Religion: Freedom of religion.

Animist 4%. **Cargo cult groups** (12) 2.8%.

Christian 93%. Affiliated 87.3%.

Roman Catholic 17.2%. 47,000a; 27,000m.

Indigenous Marginal groups (3) 2.9%. 7,800a.

Foreign Marginal groups (2) 1.2%. 3,200a.

Protestant 66.1%. 180,400a. 90,000m. Denominations 6. Largest (adult members):

Ch. of Melanesia (Anglican)	42,600
South Seas Ev. Ch. (SSEC-SSEM)	23,600
Seventh Day Adventist Church	14,000
United Ch. (Methodist — LMS)	8,160
Assemblies of God	1,050

Evangelical 32.3% of population.

Missionaries to Solomon Islands 132 (1:2,100 people) in 10 agencies.

Missionaries from Solomon Islands 130 (1:1,400 Protestants).

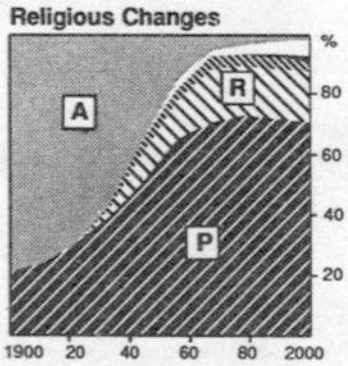

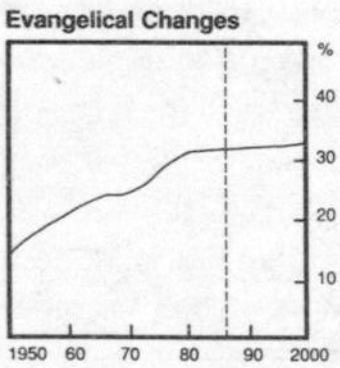

1. **Praise the Lord for the work of the Spirit in reviving power** in the SSE Churches in 1935, 1970, and in nearly all Protestant denominations in the '80s. People in all walks of life are coming to the Lord in churches, house groups and prayer meetings. There are strong, growing churches; dynamic leaders; and a remarkable missionary outreach, especially to Papua New Guinea.

2. **Island and tribal loyalties could create difficulties for the government.** Pray for wise leadership and continued freedom for the gospel. Its impact on the land has been great. The Prime Minister elected in 1985 is a born-again believer.

3. **The poor training of pastors** is the biggest bottleneck for growth in maturity and expansion of the Church. Pray for the six SSEC Bible Schools and the Anglican Theological College.

4. **Missions have made a major investment** in evangelism and in a wide range of institutional work. Largest missions are the **SSEM** (40 workers), Anglican Melanesian Mission (30), and **SIL** (25). In the future, major contributions of skills and gifts will be in teaching, youth work, training of cross-cultural missionaries and Bible translation.

5. **Unreached peoples.** The land has been so exposed to the gospel that only pockets of resistant pagans on Guadalcanal and Malaita hold out against the gospel. Yet the continued influence of syncretic or almost pagan "cargo cults", with massive exoduses from churches in the past, shows the need for a personal appropriation of the gospel by each generation.

6. **Youth ministries** are very important with the rapid population growth and numbers of third and fourth generation Christians. **SU** has vital groups in many of the high schools.

7. **Bible translation.** National believers are taking the initiative, and this long-underestimated ministry is now receiving the attention it deserves. Pray for the 17 translation projects in hand — **UBS, SIL** (with six teams); 26 projects remain to be tackled. The major need is for the completion of the Pijin Bible (the trade language). Only three languages of the 62 have an extant NT.

SOMALIA
(Somalia Democratic Republic)

Africa
Sept 29

Area 638,000 sq.km. The dry and barren Horn of Africa east of Ethiopia and Kenya.

Population 6,500,000. Annual growth 2.6%. People per sq.km. 10. 1,000,000 Ogaden Somali refugees now live in Somalia.

Peoples
Somali 95%. Five related ethnic groups speaking the same language. A further 1,700,000 Somalis live in East Ethiopia, Northeast Kenya and Djibouti.
Other African peoples 4%. Four small minority peoples along the Juba River and along the south coast.
Other 1%. Arab 40,000, Italian 2,000, Indian 1,000.

Literacy 6%. **Official languages:** Somali, Arabic, Italian, English. **All languages** 5. **Bible translations** 3Bi 1por.

Capital: Mogadishu 507,000. Urbanization 34%.

Economy: Subsistence pastoral economy. Sixty per cent of the population was nomadic in 1970, with heavy dependence on camel herding. Drought and irrigation schemes are reducing the nomadic population. The influx of refugees and continuing confrontation with Ethiopia is impoverishing the country. Income/person $250 (2% of USA).

Politics: British and Italian Somalilands united soon after independence in 1960. A revolutionary socialist government supported by the USSR followed the military coup of 1969. Somalia's defeat by Russian arms and Cuban forces in 1978 destabilized the government. There is considerable inter-clan rivalry and hostility.

Religion: All religions were opposed after the revolution, but attitudes to Islam have warmed and it is considered the official religion. The few Christian churches are tolerated but not free to evangelize.
Muslim 99.8%. Somalis have been devout Muslims for centuries. All are Sunni but for the few Shi'a Asians.
Christian 0.1%.
Roman Catholic 2,100a. Almost entirely Italian and other expatriates.
Protestant maybe 800 believers.
Christian aid workers in Somalia est. 38.

1. **This closed land** needs to be prayed open for the gospel. Only a few areas were ever exposed to the gospel, and this was just for a limited period of 20 years.

2. **The work of missions** ended in 1973-74 after some very difficult years of seeking to win Somalis under almost impossible restrictions. Yet the courageous witness of **SIM** and the Mennonites led to the conversion of a number of Somalis and also the translation of the Somali Bible.

3. **National believers** continue to live for the Lord under very difficult conditions. Many are isolated and it is hard to meet for fellowship. They face much opposition from both the authorities and their own families. Some believers took refuge in Kenya. Pray that God may preserve his own and bless their witness.

4. **Unreached peoples and areas:**

a) **N.Somalia** (formerly British ruled) has never had a resident missionary witness.

b) **The one million refugees from Ethiopia** live in 33 camps and in urban areas. They have little chance for future betterment. Most are dependent on aid programmes administered by 28 organizations; some, such as **TEAR Fund** and **WV**, are Christian. Opportunities for witness by Christian aid workers are difficult to obtain.

c) **The minority peoples** are unreached.

5. **About two million Somalis live in surrounding lands**; Ethiopia approx. 1,500,000; Kenya 430,000; Djibouti 153,000. **SIM-AIM**, **CBOMB** have a ministry to Somalis in Kenya, and **RSMT** in Djibouti. Pray for Christian aid workers and their tactful witness in refugee camps and among the destitute in Somalia. Pray that all these ministries may have an impact on closed Somalia, and that viable Somali churches may be planted.

6. **The Somali Bible** was published in 1977. Many NTs were handed out just before the expulsion of missionaries in 1974. Pray for Bible distribution through the post in Somalia and to Somalis in surrounding lands. The government-sponsored crash literacy programme should raise the literacy level and help others to read the Word.

7. **Radio broadcasts** are prepared by **SIM** in Kenya and transmitted daily by **FEBA** Seychelles. Response to the 33 hours of programming per month is good. This is the only direct way of reaching into the country.

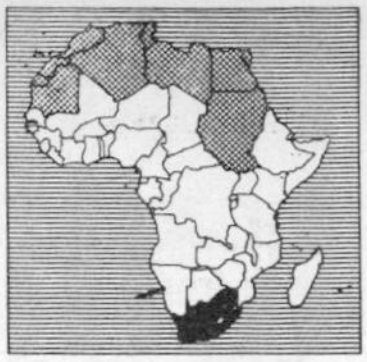

SOUTH AFRICA
(Republic of South Africa)

Africa

Sept 30-Oct 3

Area 1,222,000 sq.km. This includes:

1. Walvis Bay (an enclave on Namibian coast 1,124 sq.km.).

2. Four independent states: Transkei 45,000 sq.km., Bophuthatswana 40,000 sq.km., Ciskei 9,000 sq.km., and Venda 6,500 sq.km. These 'TBVC' states are not internationally recognized so are included here as part of South Africa.

Population 32,100,000. Annual growth 2.4% (White 1.2%, Black 2.8%). People per sq.km. 27. TBVC states 5,100,000, National states ("Homelands") 7,100,000. 52% of the Black population lives in the ten enclave states created by the government.

Peoples
Black 73%.
Nguni (5) Zulu 6,600,000; Xhosa 5,900,000; Swazi 1,000,000; S. Ndebele 477,000.
Sotho (3) North Sotho/Pedi 2,800,000; East Sotho/Tswana 2,400,000; South Sotho 2,200,000; North Ndebele 340,000.
Other (2) Tsonga/Shangaan 1,200,000, Venda 594,000.
White 15%. Afrikaners 2,700,000, English speaking 1,800,000. Portuguese 650,000; German 45,000; Greek 40,000.
Coloured (Mixed race) 9%. Predominantly descendants of slaves with Black, Khoi-Khoi (Hottentot), European and Asian blood. Ninety per cent live in the Western Cape Province. The Cape Malays are considered part of this community.
Asian 3%. Indians 77% in Durban area of Natal, Chinese 11,000.

Literacy 89%. **National languages**: Afrikaans, English. The 10 national independent states also use their majority language as the official language. **All languages** 28. **Bible translations** 17 Bi 1NT 1por.

Capitals: Pretoria (administrative) 865,000; Cape Town (legislative) 1,740,000; Bloemfontein (judicial) 220,000. **Other major cities**: Johannesburg/Soweto 3,500,000 (6,600,000 live in the Witwatersrand and South Transvaal industrial complex); Durban 1,100,000; Port Elizabeth 680,000. Urbanization 56% (Asians 91%, Whites 89%, Coloureds 77%, Blacks 31%).

Economy: The richest and most industrialized country in Africa (25% of GNP, 40% of industrial output). The world's biggest exporter of non-petroleum minerals — especially gold, platinum, chrome, diamonds and coal. Lack of water and erratic rainfall could limit growth. World recession, drought and worldwide opposition to the racial policies have further stimulated government overspending on the cumbersome administration of separate development (apartheid) and defence. Inflation and a severe decline in the economy since 1982 have been the result. Inflation 25% ('85). Income/person $2,450 (18% of USA). Whites, on average, earn three times that of Blacks.

Politics: The Union of South Africa was formed in 1910. A white minority parliamentary republic created in 1961. The new constitution of 1984 instituted a strong presidency and a limited sharing of power with the Coloured and Asian minorities, but created serious rifts in both the Afrikaner and other communities. The exclusion of Blacks (especially the urban population) from national politics and the compartmentalization of the races are the major unresolved issues which dominate every aspect of national life. Government policy continues to be:

1. To work towards independent Black states for each of the 10 ethnic groups.

2. To gradually dismantle the structures of discriminatory apartheid.

3. To form a constellation of ethnic states economically linked together.

Changes are coming, but too fast for the fearful Whites and far too slow for the frustrated Blacks. The deteriorating security situation, adverse world publicity and the economic crisis make more rapid changes essential. The economic and strategic importance of South Africa ensure that internal stresses have serious international consequences, both for surrounding Black states and the superpowers.

The 10 national states are enclaves within South Africa. All are overpopulated and very dependent economically on South Africa. They are the theoretical home for the 11 mill. Blacks in the White areas of South Africa (87% of the territory). Four have opted for political independence: Transkei 1976, Bophuthatswana 1977, Venda 1979, Ciskei 1981. All but Bophuthatswana are one-party states.

Religion: Freedom of religion. The racial issue has led to a rising level of church-state confrontations and divisions within denominations. Official statistics omit the four independent states, which are here included:
African traditional religions approx. 20%. The

more strongly so being Shangaan 49%, Venda 46%, Xhosa 25%, Zulu 25%.

Non-religious/atheist, etc. 5%.

Hindu 1.8%. Indians, mainly in Natal.

Muslim 1.1%. Cape Malays and Indians.

Jews 0.42%. Over 130,000 mainly in Rand area of S. Transvaal.

Christian 71.6%. Affiliated approx. 61%. (including TBVC states). Church statistics below are based on 1980 government census which excludes TBVC states and are thus not affiliated figures as elsewhere. Numbers of Christians will also now be lower than indicated in 1980 for older, mainline denominations and higher for rapidly growing younger churches.

Roman Catholic 10.1%. 3,200,000a. Growing among Blacks.

Orthodox 0.13%. Mostly Greeks.

African Independent Churches 22%. Over 3,700 groups. Largest (adherents):

Zion Christian Church	1,250,000
Nazarite Baptist Church approx.	500,000
St. John's Apostolic Faith Miss.	400,000

Foreign marginal groups 0.5%. Largest (adherents):

Jehovah's Witnesses	103,750
Mormons	9,000

Protestant 40% approx. 12,800,000a. Denominations probably 160. Largest (adherents of all races):

Nederduitse Geref. Kerk (DRC)	3,478,000
Methodist Church	2,113,000
Ch. of the Prov. of S.A. (Anglican)	1,517,000
Lutheran Churches	835,000
Presbyterian Church	499,000
Congregational Church (UCCSA)	407,000
Apostolic Faith Mission	303,000
Baptist Church	255,000
Full Gospel Church of God	169,000
Assemblies of God (various)	133,000
Church of England in S.A.	96,000
Other Pentecostal Churches	764,000

Evangelical 15% of population.

Missionaries to South Africa approx. 1,310 in over 80 agencies.

Missionaries from within S. Africa approx. 1,020 of which 240 serve outside S. Africa (1:12,500 Protestants).

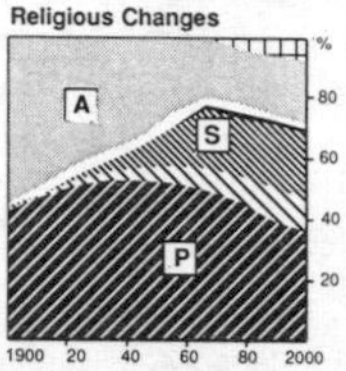

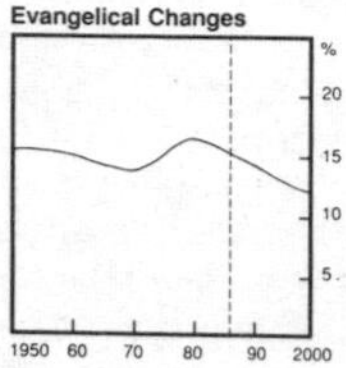

1. **The racial issue overshadows all others.** Pray for:

a) **The tensions and hatreds in society** to drive Christians into earnest prayer for the spiritual health of their nation.

b) **Courage for those in authority** to rectify injustices and implement policies that will bring about meaningful and nonviolent political changes.

c) **Christian leaders** to be uncompromising for both biblical truth and social justice. Few have the balance. Liberation theology has become a major emphasis in a climate where all legitimate means for change have been thwarted.

d) **The Church to be a true agent for reconciliation.** Christians need to put loyalty to their Lord before the security or advancement of their own ethnic group. There are Christians on both sides of the racial divide who advocate violence in either repression or in protest. Evangelical Christians have often been the least ready to speak out against the moral wrong of racial discrimination and sometimes violent measures used to enforce government policy, whilst being vocal against the equally moral wrong of violent protest for change. Pray for repentance from wrong attitudes and that credibility for a biblically prophetic role may be regained.

e) **True fellowship links** irrespective of language and race. Pray for those working to this end. Courageous attempts at bringing Christian leaders together for fellowship in conferences (such as the SACLA Assembly in 1979 and SACEL 1985 organized by **AE**). **Africa Enterprise** is playing a unique role in this ministry of reconciliation.

f) **The primary task of the Church for evangelism and missions** not to be lost, but re-emphasized.

2. **Praise for the positives:**

a) **The strength of Protestant Christianity** despite the widely publicized negatives. The Spirit of God is moving in all the major racial groups, and with touches of revival in some areas. There are large numbers of evangelical believers in the country.

b) **The increasing prayer concern** among Christians, and growth of interracial and interdenominational prayer movements.

c) **The growth through dynamic outreach of some Pentecostal churches** (Apostolic Faith Mission, Assemblies of God, etc.) **and the dynamic newer charismatic churches** (many within a loose association called the International Fellowship of Christian Churches). There are reportedly 100,000 believers associated with the charismatic churches.

d) **The impact of Christ For All Nations** evangelistic and healing campaigns, especially in Black urban areas and national states. CFAN has constructed the largest tent ever made!

3. **The missionary commitment of South African Christians** suffered severely because of the country's increasing political isolation since 1961. South African missionary outreach has been large, and some world renowned missionary thrusts have been of S. African origin — **NGK**(DRC) with a major outreach for many years to a number of African nations, South Africa General Mission (now **AEF**), **IHCF** (now with a worldwide ministry to and through medical workers), Africa Evangelistic Band, **Dorothea Mission**, and more recently **Africa Enterprise**, Christ For All Nations, etc. The **NGK** Mission is still the largest with 294 missionaries. Pray for:

a) **Renewed active involvement of churches in world evangelization.** The **NGK**, evangelical Anglicans, Baptists and Pentecostals are actively seeking creative new channels for ministry in other lands. Praise the Lord for enthusiasm for outreach to Muslims and to neighbouring Mozambique.

b) **South African Action for World Evangelization** which has a key ministry in publicizing, recruiting and channelling funds and missionaries to needy areas of the world through a variety of missions. **AE**'s Unreached Peoples Project. An African Society for Frontier Missions was formed recently.

c) **The effective development of Coloured and Indian missionary vision.** A number of Christians from these communities have moved overseas as missionaries — notably with **OMF, WEC,** etc. to Asia, Pacific, Europe and Latin America. The **South African Indian Missionary Outreach** was formed in 1983.

d) **The emergence of missionary outreach from the Black churches.** There is great potential, but obstacles for its realization are enormous.

e) **Africa Enterprise** which has an energetic outreach and teaching ministry to other parts of the world — but especially Africa.

4. **The White community.** Population 4,800,000.

Religion

Christian 91.8% (Protestant 83%, Roman Catholic 8.7%).

Non-religious, etc. 5.4%. **Jews** 2.6%.

The community has been shaken by the events of the past two decades. Yet much of the initiative for change and spiritual renewal must come from this section of the population. Pray for:

a) **Deliverance from materialism and fear** that inhibits objectivity and spiritual growth among Christians.

b) **The Afrikaners.** Most are members of the three major Reformed Churches. By far the largest of these is the theologically conservative **NGK.** There are many outstanding ministers and theologians as well as people of prayer in this church, and also much orthodox nominalism. Pray for the three theological seminaries (Stellenbosch, Bloemfontein and Pretoria). Pray that this church, with a large membership in all four major population groups, may become a catalyst for peaceful change and racial harmony.

c) **The English-speaking people** tend to be less religious than the Afrikaners. There is more liberal theology in the major denominations, yet remarkable changes are occurring in the Anglican Church through the charismatic movement, with a significant return to a more biblical theology and personal faith. The evangelical denominations such as the Baptists, Church of England in SA, Assemblies of God, etc., are growing steadily. However, many English-speaking people are alienated from the churches and need to be confronted with the gospel.

d) **The less reached: The Jews**, among whom there is a small, but growing number of Hebrew Christians. **The Portuguese** are predominantly Catholic and very conservative, but response through Pentecostal and **NGK** missions is increasing. **The Greeks** are neglected.

e) **Young people.** There are many denominational and interdenominational groups seeking to witness among them: Youth For Christ, **SU**, Student Christian Assoc., **YWAM, CCC** among young professionals, etc. Pray for young people to be won for Christ and to hear God's call into Christian service.

5. **The Coloured community.** Population 2,880,000 (mainly West Cape Province).
Religion: **Christian** 86% (72% Protestant, 10% Roman Catholic), **Muslim** 6.2%. **Non-religious/atheist**, etc. 7.8%.
Coloured leaders are pressing hard for real change in their political status as second-class citizens and are not satisfied with cosmetic adjustments.

a) **Their unfortunate past has left a legacy of social instability** which can only effectively be changed by the power of the gospel. Unstable family life, immorality and alcoholism are real problems.

b) **The churches** need revival. To most, religion and daily life are not closely related. Churches are often weak in leadership, nominal and introspective and there has been a large defection to sectarian groups. However the development of vital evangelical congregations with evangelistic and missionary outreach is moderately encouraging — especially among Pentecostal, **NGK** (NG Mission Church) and **TEAM** churches.

c) **Outreach.** Bethel evangelists of the **AEB** have seen much fruit from evangelistic outreach. Some churches have a fruitful ministry among sailors in Cape Town. Pray for many dedicated young people to be called into full-time Christian work. There are a number of good Bible schools for training leaders.

d) **The Cape Malays** (190,000, almost all in Cape Town) are considered part of the Coloured community, but are predominantly Malay and Muslim. They cling tenaciously to their customs and religion. Teams of Coloured Christians linked with **Life Challenge** are saturating Muslim areas with the gospel, and some are coming to Christ, but no real Malay church has yet emerged.

6. **The Asian community**
Population 920,000 (81% Natal, 14% Transvaal, 3.9% Cape Province). Predominantly Indian; some Chinese.
Religion: Hindu 62%, Muslim 19%, Christian 12.5% (Protestant 9.9%, Roman Catholic 2.6%), other 6.5%.
The Indian community has gone through traumatic social and economic changes since their arrival in Natal a century ago. Many are very Westernized.

a) **The bondage of Hinduism** is still very real despite a significant response to the gospel. A number of denominational and interdenominational agencies seek to reach them — such as the Pentecostals, **AEF, NGK, TEAM**, Church of England in SA, etc.

b) **The growth of the Church** — rapid during the '70s, but has slowed more recently. The major impact has been through the Bethesda Temple Full Gospel Churches (46,000 adherents), Apostolic Faith Mission (11,000), **AEF**-related churches (3,000), Baptist (3,500), Reformed Church in Africa (**NGK**) (2,000). The weaknesses evident are Hindu thought patterns and practices, and often a weak and divided leadership. There are at least three good Bible schools — pray for the calling and equipping of Indian pastors and missionaries.

c) **The Indian Muslims** (180,000) are a generally wealthy, tightly-knit community that has been fairly successful in resisting Christian evangelism, yet about 40% no longer believe Islam to be unique. Over the last 10 years Full Gospel Churches, Baptists, **AEF**, and **SIM** have developed specific ministries to them. "Jesus to the Muslims" is an agency committed to enable Christians to reach Muslims through literature, seminars, etc. There are only about seven full-time workers committed to Muslim outreach. About 200 have come to Christ from out of the Muslim community — they need prayer.

d) **The Chinese** (12,000) live mainly in Transvaal; many are still non-Christian; only about 600 are Protestant Christians, and a further 1,400 are Catholics. There are five denominations with Chinese membership.

7. **Black African communities**

Population 23,360,000.

Religion: Christian 76% (Protestant 35%, African Independent Churches 29%+).

African Traditional/no religion 24%.

a) **Black nationalism** has become a potent force. Politically this has led to violent protest in some areas and widespread rejection of the ideals of the dominant white community. This could lead to a rejection of biblical Christianity and persecution of true Christians. True believers need much prayer in this time of turmoil that they might keep their eyes on the Lord and not on circumstances. Pray that a purified, vigorous Church may emerge from these trials.

b) **Missionary work** began among the Blacks in 1799. Nearly every major denomination in Europe and North America has played a part in their evangelization. Heroic effort and tragic mistakes have marked its progress, leaving a legacy of fragmentation and serious deficiencies in the churches. The missionary force is greatly reduced, and most of the present thrust is for church development, leadership training, youth, literature and radio ministries. All cross-cultural workers need extraordinary wisdom in the tense and polarized situation, and special grace to bridge the barriers of race and culture. Pray for fruitful ministries for them in times of great difficulty and discouragement.

c) **The Church** is an extraordinary mixture. The rapid growth of the African Independent Churches is a challenge to more orthodox churches that have often suffered considerable decline and loss of spiritual vitality. Among more evangelical groups, growth has been more marked among the various Assemblies of God groups, Pentecostals, Nazarenes, **NGK**, etc. Major prayer points:

i) **Renewal** for the mainline churches, where nominalism, sin and pagan practices are common among professing Christians.

ii) **Development of many more deeply spiritual and well-taught church leaders.** Sadly some of the most prominent today are better known for their political activism than their spiritual authority.

iii) **The African Independent Churches** (AICs) have grown to include almost one-third of the Black population. Some are highly syncretic, others are more biblical in orientation, but need teaching. Efforts to provide theological training for AIC leaders have occasionally been successful.

iv) **Effective and close fellowship links** to be strengthened between Black and other racial Christian groups, and between orthodox and AICs.

d) **The urban areas**. Eight million Blacks live in satellite townships that ring S. African cities. Some, such as Soweto (Johannesburg), Kwa Mashu (Durban), Gugulethu (Cape Town), Sharpeville, etc., have become household names because of the violent events of the past two decades. Pray for:

i) **The churches, believers and their witness** in a society full of social stress, where tribal and family authority have broken down, and violence and fear are commonplace. Pray that, despite intimidation and pressures, believers may stand firm for Jesus, and be a powerful means of reconciliation.

ii) **Young people and children** who are particularly susceptible to the revolutionary fervour. Pray for all efforts to meet their spiritual needs — through the evangelical SCM, **Youth Alive**, etc.

iii) **Evangelical outreach** through churches and through mass evangelism (**Assemblies of God, Africa Enterprise, Dorothea Mission, Christ For All Nations**, etc.). The latter has had some notable crusades since 1975.

iv) **Islam** and other "-isms" which are making inroads into the city areas. Several mosques have been built of late.

e) **Migrant labourers** are a major feature of South African life because of restrictions on population movement. Over 1,500,000 people are in this category. Many men live separated from their families for long periods. Effective evangelism and church planting is hard, because of their social disruption and transient society. About 280,000 come from other lands such as Lesotho 150,000, Mozambique 60,000, Malawi 30,000, Botswana

29,000, and many more from the 10 national states. The mines draw many workers from all over S. Africa and beyond for longer or shorter periods. At any one time 400,000 are living in the large mine compounds of the Transvaal and Orange Free State. Pray for the outreach of the Mission to Miners (**AEF**), and **NGK** to these migrant workers. Pray that those won to Christ may be so effectively discipled that churches may be planted and strengthened in their homelands when their contract period ends.

f) **The 10 National States/Independent States** are a patchwork of larger and smaller ethnic enclaves within the area of S. African provinces indicated below according to the majority ethnic group, namely:

1. **Bophuthatswana:** population 1,490,000; 40% of Tswana. West Transvaal and North Cape Province. Fairly viable economy. **Christian** 90.4%, of which AICs form 24%. **Non-Christian** 9.6%.
2. **Ciskei**: population 738,000; 12% of Xhosa. East Cape Province. Independent 1981; government has a poor record on human rights. **Christian** 75%, **non-Christian** 25%.
3. **Gazankulu**: population 618,000; 40% of Shangaan/Tsonga. Northeast Transvaal. Economically backward. **Christian** 51%, **non-Christian** 49%. Only AICs and RCs growing significantly; mainline churches generally in decline.
4. **Kangwane**: population 185,000; 16% of Swazi. Northeast Transvaal. **Christian** 68%, **non-Christian** 32%. Massive growth of AICs from 28.6% in 1970 to 48% in 1980.
5. **KwaNdebele**: population 173,000; 35% of S. Ndebele. North Transvaal. **Christian** 85%, much nominalism; **non-Christian** 15%. AICs 50% of population.
6. **KwaZulu**: population 3,940,000; 60% of Zulu. Natal. Has refused independence. Very fragmented geographically. **Christian** 75%, **non-Christian** 25%.
7. **Lebowa**: population 2,020,000; 60% of Pedi. North Transvaal. Poor and economically unviable. **Christian** 57%, **non-Christian** 42%. Rapid growth of AICs and RCs. The Zion Christian Church, the largest AIC, is predominantly Pedi.
8. **Qua-Qua**: population 185,000; 9% of South Sotho. East Orange Free State. Very poor and overpopulated. **Christian** 88%, **non-Christian** 12%.
9. **Transkei**: population 2,562,000; 43% of Xhosa. Between Natal and East Cape Province. Independent 1976, one-party state. Good potential for economic viability. **Christian** 67%; **non-Christian** 33%.
10. **Venda**: population 349,000; 68% of all Venda. Independent 1979, now a one-party state. **Christian** 55%, **non-Christian** 45%.

Pray for:

i) **The complete evangelization of the pockets of non-Christians** — especially among the Venda, Shangaan, Pedi, and parts of Zulu and Xhosa.

ii) **The enlivening of Protestant churches**. The RCs and especially AICs are growing. The discouraging economic and political situation, and the absence of a considerable part of the active male population as migrant labour make effective church development very difficult. Lack of finance, dynamic leadership and spiritual vitality are prayer challenges.

8. **Christian literature**. Much is done in producing evangelistic and Christian discipleship literature in all languages by such as **All Nations Gospel Publishers** (with a worldwide distribution of tracts and booklets), **Roodepoort Mission Press** (Baptist Union), Africa Christian Literature Advance (**AEF**), and **NGK Press. The Bible Society** has a well developed programme for improved translations of the Scriptures — the last major languages to receive the Bible being the South Ndebele and Swazi. **SU**'s ministry through literature and to young people has been noteworthy. Few countries are better served with Christian literature, but pray that that which is distributed may be eternally fruitful.

9. **Christian radio and TV**. Many Christian radio programmes are broadcast daily by the S.A. Broadcasting Corporation and also by **TWR** from Swaziland and Bophuthatswana. These have a wide and appreciative audience in the major languages. Christian programmes on the four SABC TV channels are popular.

SPAIN
(Kingdom of Spain)

Europe

Oct 4-5

Area 505,000 sq.km. The major part of the Iberian peninsula, and including the Canary Islands off Northwest Africa, and the enclaves of Ceuta and Melilla on the North African coast.

Population 38,700,000. Annual growth 0.8%. People per sq.km. 77.

Peoples
Spanish 96%. Castilian 27,000,000; Catalan 6,900,000, Galician 3,200,000.
Basque 2.3%. Most in the four Atlantic provinces adjoining France. Many more Basques are being culturally absorbed into the Castilian majority. There is a strong separatist movement.
Gypsy 0.2%. Some claim that there may be 200,000.
Foreign 1%. German, French, Portuguese, British, Latin American, etc.

Literacy 93%. **Official language**: Castilian Spanish. Regionally official: Basque, Catalan, Galician. Spanish is now the third most widely spoken language in the world. **All languages** 5. **Bible translations** 3Bi 2por.

Capital: Madrid 4,000,000. Other major cities: Barcelona approx. 3,000,000; Valencia 1,000,000; Bilbao 1,000,000; Seville 1,000,000. Urbanization 77%.

Economy: The devastation caused by instability and the 1936-39 civil war impoverished the country. Steady growth through tourism and industry since 1968. Further radical changes are following Spain's entry into the EEC in 1986. Income/person $4,800 (34% of USA). Unemployment 22%.

Politics: Spain's tumultuous past moulds the present. The Muslim Moorish occupation lasted 700 years, ending in 1492. The worldwide Spanish Empire lasted for three centuries. The last two centuries have been ones of instability, civil wars and dictatorships; the latter under General Franco lasted from 1939 to 1975. Constitutional monarchy since 1975, and a gradual democratization and liberalization since then. Parliamentary democracy with more autonomy being granted to regions — especially for the Catalans and Basques. The left-wing ETA Basque terrorist campaign for full independence has plagued Spain since 1961.

Religion: Severe discrimination against, and even open persecution of, non-Catholics followed Franco's victory in the civil war. Traditional Catholicism became dominant. Gradual easing of discriminatory laws culminated in religious freedom being guaranteed in the 1978 constitution.
Non-religious/atheist 4%. Rapid secularization with many baptized Catholics no longer linked to the church.
Christian 96%. Affiliated 94%.
Roman Catholic 93.6%. Practising 25%.
Marginal groups 0.35% 135,000a; 57,000m. Rapid growth. Largest (adult members):

Jehovah's Witnesses	56,700
Mormons	7,200

Protestant 0.5% 193,000a; 63,700m. Denominations 20. Largest (adult members):

Filadelfia Ch. (gypsies)	13,500
Brethren	12,000
Evang. Baptist Union (**SBC**)	7,500
Seventh Day Adventist Church	5,000
Fed. of Indep. Churches (**TEAM**)	3,800
Assemblies of God	1,850

Evangelical 0.34% of population.
Missionaries to Spain 610 (1:63,400 people) in 88 agencies.
Missionaries from Spain: approx. 10 (1:19,300 Protestants).

Religious Changes

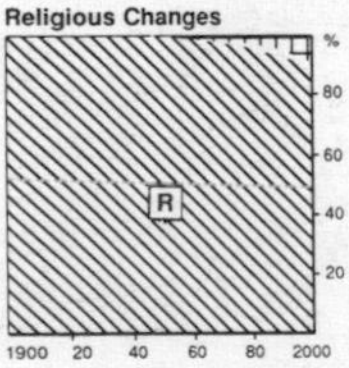

Evangelical Changes

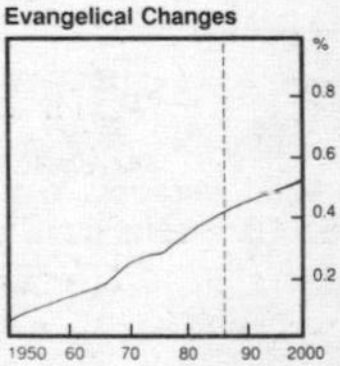

1. **The new era of liberty** gives a thrilling opportunity for the gospel. The stirrings of the Holy Spirit in Spain at the time of the Reformation were crushed by the Inquisition. For five centuries Spain had no liberty, and a repressive superstitious Catholicism dominated the life of the country. Pray that religious liberty may lead to spiritual liberty for many.

2. **The changes in Spain have not resulted in an openness to the gospel**. Satan's means of blinding people must be torn away:
   a) The rapid secularization of Spain has led to indifference to Christianity, a rejection of absolutes, a big drug problem and an alarming rise in crime.

b) Deeply ingrained superstitious Catholic practices and teachings have given a suspicion of any other view — especially foreign ones.

c) Evangelicals are often mistaken for Jehovah's Witnesses, whose activities are widespread and growing.

3. **The growth of the Protestant Church has been steady but disappointing.** The 6,000 Protestants in 1932 had increased to 20,000 in 1963 and 50,000 in 1986, but they are very unevenly distributed. Most churches are concentrated in Catalonia (esp. Barcelona), Andalucia and, to a lesser extent, around Madrid. Active Evangelicals are still only one in 1,000 in the whole country. The only major advance has been the exciting outpouring of the Spirit among the gypsies among whom there are many thousands of radiant, witnessing believers; their numbers may now be as high as 20,000.

4. **The challenges facing the Protestant Church**

a) **Liberation from the minority ghetto complex** after years of being a despised and officially rejected minority.

b) A determination to tackle the very real spiritual and social problems.

c) Willingness to witness and boldness to do so.

d) A vital indigenous expression of the gospel.

e) Greater cooperation in evangelism between the differing denominations.

5. **Leadership training.** The small size of the evangelical community, and the high level of unemployment make it difficult for the small congregations to support full-time workers, or for Christians to commit themselves to the work of the Lord. There are only about 400 full-time Spanish workers. The ministry of **OM, YWAM** and others has done much to enthuse young people — may this yield a copious supply of dynamic leaders for the future. Pray for the Evangelical Seminary and a Bible Institute initiated by **GEM**, as well as the several small Bible schools, and for the expansion of this ministry. **TEAM, OMS** and others have initiated TEE programmes.

6. **Little vision has yet been generated for world evangelization.** The need of unevangelized areas of Spain, and the nearby Muslim lands of North Africa are obvious targets for Spanish Christians. **OM** has done much to instil such a burden in the churches; there are eight Spanish **OMers.**

7. **There has been a considerable increase in missionaries and agencies since 1975**, yet the unoccupied areas are numerous. Two-thirds of the missionary force is concentrated in Madrid or around Barcelona. Pray for:

a) Others to be called to less evangelized areas.

b) Good and helpful relationships between expatriate and national workers.

c) Missionaries to effectively adapt to and serve the Church, and not stifle or divide it.

d) The high proportion of new missionaries who have particular need for pastoral care and effective integration into Spanish culture.

Some larger missions are: **SBC** (51 missionaries), **OMS** (41), **WEC** (41), **TEAM** (34), **AoG** (32), **GEM** (21), **CAMI** (15), **GMU** (13), **ECM** (7). Most are engaged in evangelism, church planting and Bible teaching. An increasing number of missionaries are coming from Latin America (approx. 30).

8. **The need of Spain is enormous.**

a) **Over** 15,000,000 live in towns, villages and districts where there is no evangelical church.

b) **Of the 15 regions** three have less than 10 Protestant churches — Cantabria (5), La Rioja (6) and Navarra (5). In these regions live 2,500,000 people.

c) **Of the 50 Provinces**, the 16 most needy for church planting are: Coruña, Valencia, Pontevedra, Seville, Barcelona, Oviedo, Alicante, Murcia, Orense, Badajoz and the sparsely populated provinces of Avila, Cuenca, Guadalajara, Soria, Teruel, Toledo which are almost without believers.

d) **Of the cities with over 40,000 inhabitants**, Mieres, Avila and Siero are without an evangelical church.

e) **Of the 8,022 cities**, towns and villages, only 419 have an evangelical witness.

f) The large number of drug addicts among young people —a specialized ministry is needed which **YWAM** and others are seeking to meet. This is a hard and frequently discouraging ministry, but very necessary.

9. **Unreached peoples**

a) **The Basques** are an ancient and proud people, but there is not a single Protestant church among them. The few churches in the four provinces (Guipúcoa, Vizcaya, Alava and Navarra) where Basques live, are Spanish speaking. There is only a handful of known believers among possibly 750,000 Basques in Spain. Only the beginnings of evangelistic and literature ministries have been made (**CAMI**, Baptists). The widely differing dialects in an already difficult language complicates the task. Pray for the indifference of this people to the gospel to be broken down.

b) **The 43 million tourists** each year from all over Europe.

c) **The Muslims** have a considerable influence in the cities of Granada, Cordoba and on the Costa del Sol where there are also communities of Spanish converts to Islam. **YWAM** and other groups are beginning to work among them.

10. **Students** are largely unevangelized. In 1967 there were 12 known evangelical students in universities. There are now about 500 — mostly among the 150,000 students on the three Madrid campuses. Pray for the consolidation of existing groups and the launching of new ones. Pray also for a viable secondary school witness to be started nationally.

11. **Ceuta and Melilla** (130,000) are small Spanish enclave towns on the north coast of Morocco. Thirty-five per cent of the population is Muslim. There are six small evangelical churches, three of which have some former Muslims in their membership. This is a strategic bridgehead for the gospel in North Africa. Pray for those seeking to use it for such.

12. **The Canary Islands**: an archipelago of seven larger islands off Africa's N.W. coast. Among the 1,440,000 inhabitants are but 1,800 believers in 43 small churches and fellowships — most being on the two larger islands. There is need for more evangelism on the smaller islands of Lanzarote, Fuerteventura, Gomera, La Palma and Hierro, and teaching for the scattered groups of believers.

13. **Christian literature** has been a major factor in church growth, yet the Spanish are poor readers, making literature work expensive and bookstores hardly viable. Pray for the 18 bookstores; **CLC** has three centres. Christian books are both imported and published in Spain, but too few are written by and for Spaniards. ***Ven*** is a gospel broadsheet with an increasing impact (**WEC**).

14. **Christian radio and TV.** Local radio stations carry evangelical programmes, and **HCJB** (62 hours per month) and **TWR** (one hour) broadcast into Spain. The national TV network broadcasts a 15-minute evangelical programme on TV once a month. There are also numerous opportunities for evangelical broadcasts on local radio. Pray that these means of proclaiming Christ may be effectively used.

Asia

Oct 6-7

SRI LANKA

(Democratic Socialist Republic of Sri Lanka)

Area 65,600 sq.km. Large island 80 km. southeast of the southern tip of India.

Population 16,400,000. Annual growth 2.1%. People per sq.km. 250.

Peoples

Sinhalese 72%. An Aryan people; largely Buddhist. Many castes — unusual for Buddhist societies.

Tamil 20%. (Lanka Tamils residents for over 1,000 years, mainly in north and east) 1,770,000; Indian Tamils (imported labourers in 19th and 20th centuries; mainly in highland tea plantations). The majority are Hindu.

Moor 6%. Arab-Tamil descent 950,000, Tamil descent 28,000.

Burgher 0.3%. European-Asian descent. Once privileged; many emigrating to Australia. Nearly all live in Colombo.

Veddah: Only 140 left of the aboriginal people.

Literacy 90%. **Official language**: Sinhala. Tamil and English are recognized as national languages. **All languages** 5. **Bible translations** 3Bi.

Capital: Colombo 991,000. Urbanization 24%.

Economy: Agricultural with tea and rubber the most important export commodities. Increasing industrialization since 1977. Subsequent rapid progress has been marred by the impact of the communal violence. Inflation, the cost of living and foreign debt are soaring. Tourism and trade are adversely affected. Income/person $320 (2% of USA).

Politics: Independence gained in 1948, as a parliamentary democracy, after 450 years of successive colonial administrations by the Portuguese, Dutch and British. Attempts to Sinhalize national life in 1956 and the attendant discrimination against ethnic and religious minorities provoked increasing communal violence and efforts by extremists to fight for an independent Tamil state in the north and east. The increasing scale of violence led to massacres, 150,000 Tamil refugees, and a state of virtual civil war by 1983. Polarization of the country is so deep that solutions are difficult to find.

Religion: Buddhism is the state religion and, as such, is protected and promoted. Although freedom for other religions is assured, there has been some discrimination against minority religions in taxation, employment and education.

Buddhist 69.3%. Almost entirely of the Sinhala community. Resurgence since 1956, and actively seeking the conversion of Christians, and stimulating Buddhist missionary activity round the world.

Hindu 15.4%. Almost entirely Tamil.

Muslim 7.6% Moors and Malays.

Christian 7.4%. Affiliated 7%.

Roman Catholic 6.3% 1,030,000a; 577,000m. Influential through a variety of social programmes.

Protestant 0.75% 124,000a; 59,600m. Denominations 30. Largest (adult adherents):

Church of Ceylon	48,800
Methodist Church	26,200
Salvation Army	5,500
Church of South India (Tamil)	5,300
Indep. Indigenous Churches	5,000
Ceylon Pentecostal Mission	5,000
Assemblies of God	3,500
Baptist Union	3,200
Apostolic Church	3,100
Fell. of Free Ch's (Pentecostal)	2,500
Foursquare Gospel Church	1,750
Apostolic Church	1,250
Seventh Day Adventist Church	1,000

Evangelical 0.2% of population.

Missionaries to Sri Lanka est. 90 (10:182,000 people) in 20 agencies.

Missionaries from within Sri Lanka: est. 12 (CPM which began in 1923 in Ceylon has established churches in India, Malaysia, UK, France, Canada, USA, Mexico).

Religious Changes

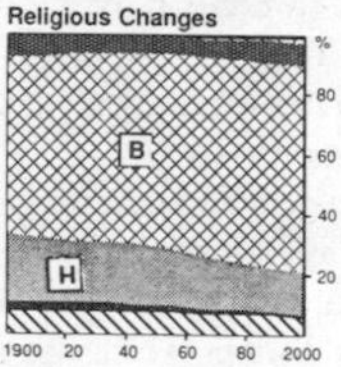

Evangelical Changes

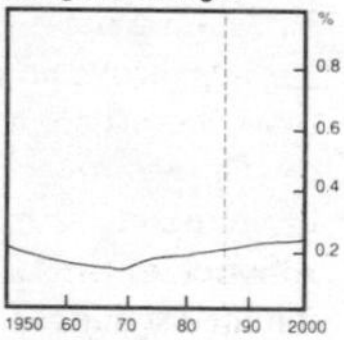

1. **Claimed by some to be the site of the Garden of Eden, but now an island of tears.** The ugly conflict between the Buddhist Sinhala and Hindu Tamil has brought disaster and death to many. The security situation in the north and east is limiting outreach and causing the closure of some churches. Many villages in the north have been turned into terrorist camps. Pray that the strife might humble the pride of the Buddhist in his religion of non-violence, and convince the Hindu of the futility of life without Christ. Praise God for the evidence of this already occurring.

2. **Sri Lanka is the only non-Muslim Asian country where the Christian Church has steadily declined in numbers and influence this century.** The causes:

a) Colonial suppression of national culture, language and imposition of Western national forms of Christianity.

b) The renaissance of national culture after independence and revival of traditional religion. Some nominal Christians have become Buddhists. Pray for a decisive reversal of these trends.

c) Hardly any evangelization by the mainline churches. Biological increase among Christians less than that among non-Christians.

3. **The Church** is one of the most nominal in Asia. Pray for a demonstration of the love and power of God in the lives of those who bear the name of Christ, and for a convincing unity among all true believers. Specific areas of weakness:

a) **Cultural isolation**, with Western worship forms, widespread use of English, and with obvious links to the colonial past. Most traditional churches are middle class and unable to relate to the poor.

b) **Liberal theology** has had a deadening effect. Dialogue rather than evangelism, church union rather than union with the Lord, and social concern rather than meeting heart needs have been the norm. Pray for the many congregations which are in decline that they may experience a renewing work of the Spirit.

c) **Limited outreach to non-Christian religions.** This has been hampered by an introspective attitude, a theology which suggests that the church's mandate is not to gain converts from other religions, and inconsistency in the lives of many Christians. Pray that believers may have the vision and faith for conversions from outside the Christian community and willingness for a simpler life style where there is such physical need.

d) **Lack of commitment to outreach** in unevangelized areas coupled with lack of faith for the finance needed to send church planters into villages.

4. **Theological education** has been a fundamental weakness and the need for full-time evangelists and pastors is acute. However, there are a number of evangelical training institutions including the **AoG** Bible School, Lanka Bible College, the Dutch Reformed Church Seminary, the officers' training school of the Salvation Army, and the Association for Theological Education by Extension. A number of independent churches have a clear evangelical stance.

5. **There are encouragements of better things to come:**

a) **The rapid growth of Pentecostal and charismatic groups**, with some very lively, evangelistic and caring fellowships and house churches with an uncompromising stand on the Scriptures. Several such: the Assemblies of God and the Fellowship of Free Churches.

b) **Other expanding evangelical groups** are the Kandy Bible Fellowship (**TEAM**), and Christian Fellowship Centre. There are a number of freelance evangelists working in many provincial and urban areas.

c) **Signs of hope in the older denominations.** Some Anglican congregations and the Salvation Army are seeing a new growth and evangelistic outreach. The Methodist Church has a vigorous lay-led revival movement. There is an increasing evangelical presence in most liberal denominations.

d) The growth of Evangelicals and evangelical agencies such as **CCC**, **YFC**, etc., in a time of increasing receptivity among Buddhists and Hindus. Pray for the young **Evangelical Alliance of Sri Lanka** which has a growing membership and influence. The latter has initiated significant publishing, TEE, and development projects.

6. **Missionary work** has been restricted by the authorities. New visas have been extremely hard to obtain. Pray for a change — the needs are so numerous that the resources of the Sri Lankan Church are inadequate for evangelism, church planting etc. Pray in a new generation of missionaries who are willing to learn the local languages and work in the vernacular. The largest agencies are: Salvation Army (10), **CCC** (9), **SBC** (6), Methodists (6), **OC Ministries** (6). Virtually none of the present missionary force is engaged in pioneer outreach.

7. **The Buddhist majority** continues to grow, but is in an ideological crisis, with many longing for national and inner peace, and freedom from fear. In recent years there has been mounting concern in the churches to express the gospel in a more relevant way. Pray that believers may actively reach out to Buddhists at this time.

8. **The tense Tamil community is angry and fearful**. Many have become refugees in the Jaffna area in the Tamil-majority north, in India, West Germany, Britain and elsewhere. Pray that Christian Tamils and others may have a fruitful and helpful spiritual ministry among them. Pray for church multiplication in this time of stress. The impartial, loving concern shown by believers of all ethnic groups to those suffering has been commendable.

9. **The unreached**

a) **The villages**: Throughout the land are rural communities that have never heard the gospel. Twelve million live in the 25,483 villages of Sri Lanka, but there are only 480 with Protestant Christian groups. Many areas are devoid of any witness at all. Pray for the indigenous **Margaya Mission** and **Lanka Village Ministries**, as well as other churches and agencies (**AsEF**, etc) seeking to meet that need. **EHC** has many field evangelists working in villages.

b) **The urban slums** are little evangelized. Most Christians are among the more prosperous. A few churches and groups are taking up this challenge — pray for the expanding work of **Jesus Lives Ministry**.

c) **Youth programmes are limited**; few agencies are making more than a localized impact. FOCUS (**IFES**) now has five groups functioning in eight universities, but the work has been severely affected by the national unrest. A number of urban evangelical churches have large youth fellowships; **YFC** and **CCC** have had considerable influence in the main cities. The vast majority of children and young people in the rural areas are out of reach of the gospel.

d) **The Indian Tamils** on the tea estates are a deprived and despised community. Little interest has been shown in their evangelization until recently. There is a mass awakening among them at the present time, and there are now over 2,500 believers among the estate labourers.

e) **The Moors** are generally traders, bureaucrats and farmers. Until recently there were few converts out of Islam, but through **Jesus Lives Ministry** over 100 Muslims have believed in Christ. The **AoG** has a good ministry among depressed Muslims in Colombo.

f) **The Malays** are syncretic Muslims, and potentially more open. Pray for a specific ministry to them.

g) **Other unreached social groups**: the educated Buddhists, coastal belt fishing communities, the Tamil and Sinhala refugees, and now villages being set up under the Village Re-awakening programme.

h) Tribal groups such as the Rodhiyas and Gypsies. **YFC** has some work among the former.

10. **Literature** is in great demand. Literacy is high, but good, cheap and culturally relevant literature is not being printed and distributed in sufficient quantities to make use of the opportunity. **SGM** have published much, but too few committed colporteurs are available. **EHC** has been successful in door-to-door distribution. There is a dearth of good pre-evangelism literature for Buddhists and Muslims.

11. **Christian radio** has not had much impact in Sri Lanka. **Back to the Bible** broadcasts through **FEBC/FEBA** have been most successful in other Southern Asian lands; a team of 22 work full-time in this ministry. **TWR** has been broadcasting since 1977 on medium wave to India and Bangladesh with remarkable effects. They have a large audience in 11 languages and 186 hours per month of programming.

SUDAN

(Democratic Republic of the Sudan)

Middle East

Oct 8-10

Area 2,506,000 sq.km. Africa's largest country. Desert in north, merging into tropical bush in south.

Population 21,800,000. Annual growth 2.9%. People per sq.km. 8. About 40% of the population is nomadic or semi-nomadic.

Peoples: Over 56 distinct ethnic groups, 597 subgroups. Many language families — Semitic, Cushitic, Nilotic, Nilo-Saharan, etc., too complex and unclear for breakdown here.

Sudanese Arab 51%. Predominant in centre and north.

Other African peoples 49%.

- **Southern provinces** 25%. Dinka 1,466,000; Nuer 800,000; Azande 360,000; Bari 300,000, Lotuko 200,000; Shilluk 190,000; Thuri 170,000; Toposa 160,000; Murle 70,000, etc.
- **North/northeastern peoples** 8%. Beja 1,100,000; Nubians 450,000; Tigre 190,000.
- **Darfur** 5%. Fur 400,000; Masalit 125,000; Zaghawa 120,000; Daju 80,000, Tama 60,000, etc.
- **West Africans** 6%. Fulani 100,000, etc.
- **Kordofan peoples** 5%. Nuba tribes (100 tribes speaking 37 languages) 900,000.

Refugees number 1-1.5 million. The majority from Ethiopia, many from Chad, some from Uganda. Just over half use Arabic as trade language.

Literacy 20%. **Official language**: Arabic, understood by 80% of the population. **All languages** 137. **Bible translations** 4Bi 14NT 10por.

Capital: Khartoum. Khartoum-Omdurman conurbation 2,258,000. Urbanization 21%.

Economy: Agricultural; cotton and peanuts being the major export commodities. The vast distances and inadequate transportation hinder development. The renewed civil war and the virtual collapse of the economy since 1983 have stopped big irrigation schemes and exploitation of southern oil deposits. Economic conditions in the south are tragic. Income/person $400 (3% of USA).

Politics: Independent from Britain and Egypt in 1956. Bitter fighting between Arab northerners and southern secessionists 1955-1972. After 12 years of uneasy peace, and a degree of autonomy for the south, fighting has broken out again. The erratic, and increasingly unstable, West-leaning government of President Nimeiry collapsed in 1985. The weak transitional government has been unable to stabilize the economy or end the debilitating war.

Religion: The strenuous efforts by Muslim northerners to impose Islam and Arab culture on the southerners has been one of the root causes for the present conflict. An Islamic republic — declared in 1983, with the imposition of Islamic sharia law on all citizens, — provoked anger among non-Muslims and vociferous anti-Christian propaganda and actions by Muslim fundamentalists. Muslim efforts to Islamize the southerners have been both crude and forceful.

Muslim 74%. Sunni Islam, with several powerful Sufi religious orders, the largest being Ansar, the followers of the famous Mahdi. Almost the entire northern population is Muslim.

Traditional religions 15%. Predominantly among southern tribes, Nuba Mountain peoples and some Darfur peoples.

Non-religious/atheist 1.2%. Mainly urban intellectuals.

Christian 9.8%. Affiliated 9.1%. Most statistics are approximate.

- **Roman Catholic** 5.2% 1,100,000a; 640,000m.
- **Orthodox** 0.8% 170,000a. Mainly Coptic in Nile Valley, and among Ethiopian refugees.
- **Protestant** 3.1% 650,000a; 190,000m. Denominations 11, largest (adherents):

Episcopal Church (Anglican)	(?)	520,000
Presbyterian Church	(?)	55,000
Sudanese Church of Christ (**SUM**)		40,000
Sudan Interior Church (**SIM**)		9,000
Africa Inland Church (**AIM**)	(?)	4,000

- **Evangelical** 1.6% of population.

Foreign Christian workers approx. 200 (1:110,000 people).

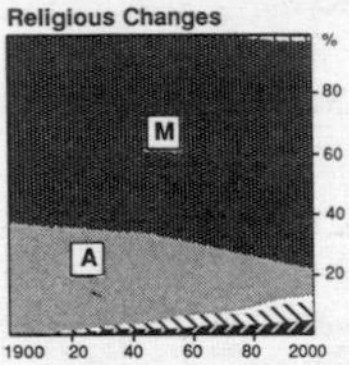

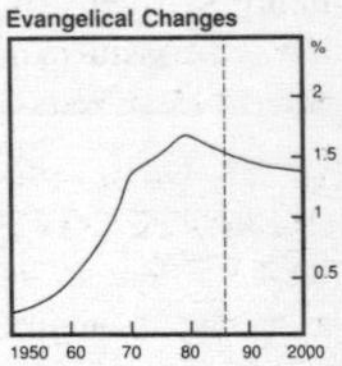

1. **The devastation due to war and famine appears unending.** Political and religious extremism, mistrust between Muslims and non-Muslims, as well as between the southern peoples themselves, are bringing despair. Pray that in all these disasters the Holy Spirit may soften hard hearts and give new openings for the gospel message of reconciliation.

2. **The Church has gone through 30 years of suffering, and periods of persecution.** Persecution has increased in intensity since the implementing of Islamic law. During the '60s many churches were destroyed, congregations scattered and pastors killed. Since 1983 some churches in the Nuba Mountains have been burnt down and great pressures applied to Christian leaders. Pray that Christians may grow in grace and boldness, and also demonstrate forgiveness and a concern for the evangelization of those who hate them.

3. **The growth of the Church since independence has been significant** in some areas. For many, Christianity has become a means of demonstrating opposition to the Muslims, but for others there has been a genuine work of the Spirit. Parts of the Anglican and Presbyterian Churches have experienced revival, and there have been significant people movements among the Nuer (Presbyterian), Mabaan, Uduk (**SIM**), parts of the Dinka (CMS), Toposa, Acholi (**AIM**), and some of the Nuba tribes (**SUM**). Yet in many Christianized areas there is a considerable degree of nominalism (both Catholic and Evangelical). Revival is needed.

4. **The needs of the believers in the south**:

a) **Physically they have virtually nothing.** Any development or health aid is but a drop in the bucket. Many diseases are endemic and spreading out of control.

b) **Tribalism** has become a divisive factor for churches.

c) **Young people** of the second generation are not being effectively reached; nominalism is increasing.

d) **Shortage of leadership** that can give congregations any effective Christian teaching.

e) **Little vision** or burden for evangelizing other ethnic groups, less for the Muslims.

f) **Christians are caught between the warring factions** and are confused and distressed.

5. **The Church in the Arab-speaking north is minute.** There are a number of Coptic Orthodox churches in the towns, but probably no more than 200 ethnic Arab evangelical believers. There is a large and growing body of Nuba Mountain Christians of the SCOC in the capital totalling several thousands, as well as smaller congregations of the Episcopal Church and the SIC. They all use the Arabic language. Pray that believers may effectively use the unusual openness of Sudanese to listen to the gospel.

6. **Leadership training** has been limited, and recently seriously disrupted again by the war. Pray for the AIC Bible School at Imatong, the SIC/**SIM** and SCOC/**SUM** joint Seminary at Melut meeting temporarily in Omdurman, and the Anglican Seminary at Mundri. Pray for the provision of adequate facilities, staff and Sudanese leaders for the churches.

7. **Christian work was severely limited in 1964** with the expulsion of expatriates working in the southern provinces. **SIM**, CMS and several other groups maintained a witness in the Khartoum area where many southern and Nuba Christians live. The return of a measure of peace in 1972 allowed a limited return of personnel for rehabilitation and development programmes in the south. ACROSS is a combining of evangelical agencies to serve Sudan in relief, rehabilitation and then development. The founder members were **SIM**, **SUM**, CMS, **MAF.** There are now 12 member bodies (including **AIM**, **TEAR Fund**) and a number of contributing agencies. Renewed fighting caused the withdrawal in 1983-85 of most personnel in the south, but in 1985 famine and refugee crises opened up aid and development programmes in the north (Darfur, Kordofan, Khartoum and among Eritrean refugees). Pray for:

a) **The 200 Christian workers** serving in the country in a time of great pressures, considerable danger and frustrating limitations. The emotional strains are acute.

b) **The opening up of this vast land for the preaching of the gospel.** Many areas in the north and south have never been evangelized.

c) **Favour in the eyes of the authorities** for Christian agencies, and the issue of visas for new workers.

d) **The redeployment of SIM and AIM workers** who have had to leave vital areas of ministry in the south.

e) **There are numerous opportunities for secondary school teachers** to work in government schools all over the country. Pray for the recruitment of the right ones.

8. **Bible translation** is still a major unmet need. At least 16 and possibly 97 languages will need to be tackled. Various translators are working in 18 languages, but some work has had to be continued elsewhere due to the chaos in the south. **SIL** entered in 1976 and has many openings for developing literacy and translation programmes; 27 projects are contemplated, 11 initiated. Pray for the **SIL** staff of 50 involved. Pray also for the newly formed indigenous Sudan Bible Translation and Literacy Association.

9. **Service agencies**
   a) **Special service planes** are a vital means for facilitating many ministries in the interior, but **MAF**'s programme has been curtailed. Pray for the granting of permission for flying. **AIM**, ACROSS, and **SIL** have permission for one plane each.
   b) **Literature. OM** has conducted some remarkable literature campaigns, with considerable interest generated. Pray for fruit.
   c) **The Bible Society** has faced hard times because of the national situation. Pray for the expansion of their translation, printing and distribution ministry. Scriptures on cassettes have proved valuable.

10. **The unreached**
   a) **Over 10 million Sudanese Arabs** in the northern five provinces have never heard the gospel, and only in four to five centres are there any seeking to reach them.
   b) **Darfur province** in the west never had a Christian presence until 1984 when Chadian famine refugees poured into the area. For a limited time ACROSS had workers in some of the camps where over 28 ethnic groups are represented. There is not a single known indigenous Christian among the Fur, Massalit, Zaghawa, Daju, Tama, Tunjur, Bideyat, Meidob, Fulani, etc., who make up 50% of the province.
   c) **The Red Sea coastal area** has never been evangelized, but now **RSMT** is seeking to win an entrance for the gospel among the hard and suspicious Beja.
   d) **Eritrean refugees** number 900,000. **MECO** and aid organizations are seeking to meet their temporal and spiritual needs. The Christian minority among them is severely pressurized by the Muslim authorities.
   e) **The Nuba Mountain peoples** are an island of non-Muslims in a sea of Islam. Whole tribes have turned to Christ (**SUM**, CMS); a few others have become Muslim. There are many unreached groups. The area is still closed to foreign missionary work.
   f) **The southern three provinces** are where the majority of the Christians live, yet there are many resistant peoples such as the Dinka, Shilluk, Nuer, etc., among whom there has been a limited response. Over 30 smaller and larger peoples in Equatoria province are mostly unreached, although among just one or two who have heard the gospel a response is beginning — Lotuka, Toposa, etc.
   g) **Student work** is in its infancy. There are small **IFES** groups in Juba and Khartoum; but the lack of effective leadership, Muslim obstructionism and unrest hinders the development of outreach.

Pray for these, and many other areas and peoples yet without a viable evangelical church.

SURINAME
(Republic of Suriname)

Caribbean

Oct 11

Area 163,000 sq.km. Northeast coast of South America between Guyana and French Guiana.

Population 393,000. Annual growth 2.5%. People per sq.km. 2.4. Almost all living on coastal strip. There are over 200,000 Surinamers in the Netherlands who emigrated in the mid-70s.

Peoples: Few nations could rival Suriname's ethnic diversity.
Asians 53%. Indians 155,000; Indonesians (nearly all Javanese) 67,000; Chinese 13,000.
African/Creole 42%. Creole (mixed race) 142,000; Black and Bush Negro 44,500.
Amerindian 3%. Six peoples 13,000.
Other 2%. Dutch, Portuguese, etc.

Literacy 80%. **Official language:** Dutch. Trade language: Sranen. **All languages** 16. **Bible translations** 3Bi 3NT 5por.

Capital: Paramaribo 70,000. Urbanization 66%.

Economy: Bauxite, rice and forest products are the mainstays of the economy. Income/person $3,520 (25% of USA).

Politics: Independent from Netherlands in 1975. A series of coups and attempted coups since 1980. Revolutionary military government since 1981. Communal tensions between Asian and Creole communities and the overthrowing of democracy are the underlying causes.

Religion: Freedom of religion continues despite the political upheavals.

Hindu 27.4%. East Indians.
Muslim 19.6%. Javanese and Indians. Sunni Islam and much folk Islam among Javanese.
Spiritist 5.5%. Largely among Bush Negroes.
Non-religious/Atheist 4%. **Baha'i** 1%.
Christian 42.5%.
Roman Catholic 21.6%. 85,000a; 44,000m.
Marginal groups 1%. 4,000a; 1,250m.
Protestant 19.9%. 78,000a; 19,660m. Denominations 22. Largest (adherents):

Moravian Church		56,000
Dutch Reformed Church		6,200
Lutheran Church		4,000
Evangelical Church (WT)		3,100
Seventh Day Adventist Church	est.	1,900
Pentecostal Churches (4)		1,205
Baptist Churches (2)		1,200

Evangelical 3% of population.
Missionaries to Suriname 140 (1:2,800 people) in 21 agencies.

Religious Changes

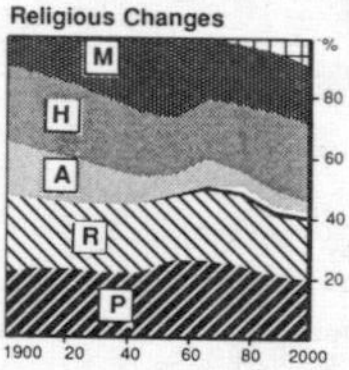

Evangelical Changes

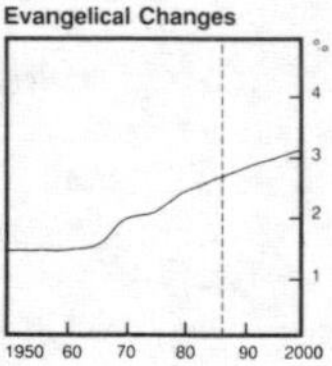

1. **The period 1975-1985 has been traumatic.** Religious freedom has been maintained, but the land needs a stable government that will ensure economic and communal wellbeing. Pray for the nation's leaders. There has been a growing spiritual hunger over this period.

2. **Christian leaders need to speak out for the truth and mobilize believers for outreach.** Materialism, sectarian growth, spiritism and Marxism have made great advances. There are four Bible schools (two Pentecostal, one Baptist and one **WT** Bible School for Amerindian interior churches).

3. **Both the Moravian and the Catholic Churches have a large following** in many ethnic groups. Few from these denominations know of the new birth and Christian belief is often mixed with spiritism. However, there are several key evangelical leaders in the Moravian Church, revival prayer groups and a spiritual awakening among the youth. Pray for them and for revival to sweep through the traditionalism of the majority of Christians. There are a number of small but growing evangelical and Pentecostal groups, but the number of born-again people is relatively low.

4. **Most of the six Amerindian peoples are now Christian. WT** has seen people movements among the Wayana, Akurio and Trio. The coastal Carib and Arawak are more needy. Pray for stability, maturity and indigenity to be maintained in the tribal churches; the pressures of the

missionary and the coastal cultures are overwhelming. There have been some who have reverted to old customs. Pray for the service of two **MAF** planes that make the ministry of **WT** practicable.

5. **Missions have had considerable freedom** despite a lack of full recognition by the government. There is a diversity of openings for missionaries in pioneer work, church planting, Bible teaching. Pray for the right recruits and a continued open door. Some major agencies are **SIL** (29 workers), **WT** (12), **IMI** (13).

6. **Less reached peoples.**

a) **Javanese** are Muslim, though often nominally so. The work of **IMF** and **IMI** has resulted in two congregations of believers, but most Javanese are unreached.

b) **Asian Indians** are predominantly Hindu and fairly entrenched in their religion. Only a small minority have become Christian, and there is not yet a single viable, evangelical church. Pray for the ministry of **IMI** and **WT** to these people. The Muslim community is unreached. One Indian missionary also labours among them.

c) **Chinese** are responding to the ministry of two Chinese **CMA** missionary couples, and there is now a single thriving congregation.

d) **The Bush Negroes** are descendents of escaped slaves who formed their own distinctive communities. Six district groups and languages have developed. Witchcraft and fear of spirits is widespread, but there are strong Christians among them (**WT** and **Baptists**). Many communities are only superficially evangelized.

e) **Guyanese refugees** number 20,000. There are several small churches among them (one being related to **WT**).

7. **Bible distribution** has increased greatly since independence. The **Bible Society** has a unique ministry in both disseminating the Scriptures and putting on a popular daily 20-minute TV programme. Pray that the people may be blessed and enriched through the entrance of God's Word.

8. **Bible translation** continues through the ministry of the Bible Society and **SIL**. Seven translation projects are being tackled. The Sranen Creole language is spoken by 80% and Sarnomi Hindi by 38%; NTs are being prepared in both these languages.

Africa
Oct 12

SWAZILAND
(Kingdom of Swaziland)

Area 17,400 sq.km. Small landlocked enclave between Mozambique and South Africa.

Population 647,000. Annual growth 3.1%. People per sq.km. 37.

Peoples

African 98%. Swazi 589,000; Zulu 15,000; Tsonga 15,000, etc.

Other 7%. British, South African Coloured, Portuguese, etc.

Literacy 39%. **Official languages:** Swati, English. **All languages** 6. **Bible translations** 4Bi 1NT.

Capital: Mbabane 25,000. Urbanization 26%.

Economy: Mostly pastoral and agricultural, but also some mineral production. Main exports: sugar, citrus, timber, paper pulp. Some manufacturing. Favoured with abundant water and irrigation. Not highly populated in some areas. Part of Southern African Customs Union and Rand Monetary Area. Income/person $890 (6% of USA).

Politics: Former Protectorate. Independence from Britain in 1968. A monarchy with King and Queen Mother having almost equal powers. Non-racial, non-party parliamentary democracy, though the king has considerable power and authority. Government conservative and traditional, with gradual changes towards modern political structures. Racial tensions of the Republic of South Africa and leftist ideology, and the civil warfare in Mozambique are having, inevitably, an impact on national affairs, particularly as refugees are fleeing from both sides.

Religion: Freedom of religion, with Christianity officially accepted. Most figures are approximate.

African traditional religions 30%.

Christian 70%. Affiliated 65%.

Roman Catholic 5.7%. 37,000a; 20,000m.

Indigenous churches in three main groupings 41%. 264,000a; 106,000m. Over 50 groups.

Foreign marginal 0.4%. 2,600a.

Protestant 18%. 116,000a; 50,000m. Denominations 33. Largest (adult members).

Evangelical Church (**TEAM**)	11,700
Church of the Nazarene	6,000
Assemblies of God	4,000
Anglican Church	3,700
Methodist Church	3,000
Free Evang. Assemblies	2,600
Africa Evangelical Church (**AEF**)	2,000

Evangelical 19% of population.

Missionaries to Swaziland est. 175 (1:3,700 people).

Missionaries from Swaziland est. 18 (1:6,450 Protestants).

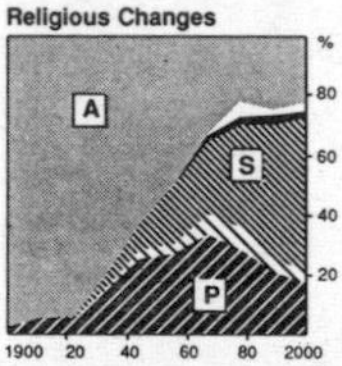

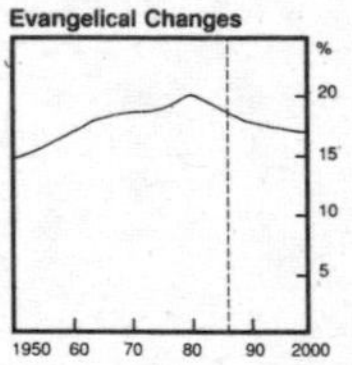

1. **Pray for a prepared united, revived Church**. Christianity is challenged by Communist ideology filtering over the border from Mozambique and entrenched traditionalism within the leadership of the country. Pray also for outreach teams and tent campaigns in towns and rural areas.

2. **The national believers** face many pressures if they want to live close to the Lord, for compromise is easy and materialism in the developing economy has a great attraction. As a result there are few believers who are willing to pay the price of going into full-time service for the Lord. There are five Bible colleges in the country. There are not many mature spiritual leaders in the ministry, though there are fine Christians witnessing in all walks of life.

3. **Nearly all mainline churches have stagnated for years.** There have been large defections from mission-planted churches since 1906 because of the failure to effectively express the gospel in a culturally relevant manner. The Zionist movement (indigenous churches that combine Pentecostal and traditional practices) has grown enormously in the rural areas. Some of these groups are open to the gospel; one group has invited a missionary to Swaziland to teach the Scriptures to their leaders and members. Over half all professing Christians belong to

independent indigenous groups such as these. Pray for good Bible teaching, real evangelistic concern, spiritual unity and a missionary vision among Protestant Christians.

4. **Most Protestant missions and missionaries are evangelical**, the largest agencies being **TWR** (50 workers), **CoN** (45), **CCC** (12), **AEF** (4), **TEAM** (4). The majority are heavily committed to institutional programmes and to radio ministry, and only a minority are in direct church development. Pray for a happy and close relationship between expatriates and national believers.

5. **Pray for the growth of the Christian Union** in the University College and other tertiary institutions, also for the work of **SU** in secondary schools. Pray that many young people may be converted and contribute much for the gospel in the land.

6. **Trans World Radio** has a powerful radio station in Swaziland, with an outreach to all of central, east and southern Africa, as well as to India and China; 280 hours of broadcasting a month goes out in 20 languages. Pray for the cooperation of churches and pastors in the countries to which **TWR** broadcasts both in the preparation of programmes and in the follow up of listeners who respond. Pray for broadcasts to the needy lands of Angola and Mozambique, and for the raising up of believers able to prepare programmes in the languages of tribes that have scarcely been touched with the gospel.

The West
Oct 13-14

SWEDEN
(Kingdom of Sweden)

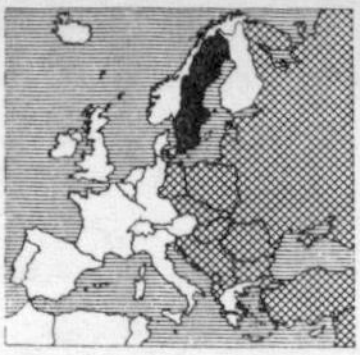

Area 450,000 sq.km. The largest of the Scandinavian countries.

Population 8,300,000. Annual growth 0%. People per sq.km. 18.

Peoples
Indigenous 88%. Swedish 7,300,000; Lapp 17,000 in the far north.
Other Scandinavian 5.5%. Finnish 335,000; Norwegian 60,000; Danish 60,000.
Other Foreign 6.5%. Mainly migrant workers and refugees: Yugoslav 55,000; Latin American 30,000; Greek 20,000; Assyrians from Iraq and Turkey 15,000; Turks (many Kurds) 20,000.

Literacy 99%. **Official language:** Swedish. **All indigenous languagues** 9. **Bible translations** 4Bi 1por.

Capital: Stockholm 1,600,000. Urbanization 83%.

Economy: Highly developed industrial state with an advanced social welfare system. Income/person $12,400 (88% of USA). Sweden has also one of the most taxed populations in the world!

Politics: Parliamentary monarchy. Strict neutrality has kept the nation out of all wars for 175 years. Fifty years of social democracy has moulded Sweden's way of life today.

Religion: The Lutheran Church is the State Church. All Swedish citizens are automatically members by birth unless they or their parents request otherwise. There is freedom of religion for other denominations and religions.
Non-religious/Atheist 30%.
Other 0.5%. **Muslim** 35,000; **Jews** 15,000.

Christian 69.5%, (though 96% of the population was, by default, born Christian).
Roman Catholic 1.9%. 123,000a. Predominantly immigrant minorities from South Europe and Latin America.
Orthodox 0.7%. 55,000a. Greek, Finnish, Russian, Ukrainian, Yugoslav minorities.
Marginal groups 0.6%. 45,700a; 27,100m. Majority Jehovah's Witnesses.
Protestant 66.3%. Predominantly Lutheran. Many members of other denominations retain links with the State Church.
Free Churches 3.6% of population. Largest (adult members):

Pentecostal Movement	100,000
Swedish Covenant Church	79,900
Swedish Evangelical Mission	24,200
Örebro Miss. (Baptist)	22,100
Salvation Army	21,700
Baptist Union	20,900
Swedish Alliance Mission	13,300
Holiness Union	6,100
Methodist Church	5,300

Conservative Evangelical 5.6% of population
Missionaries from Sweden 1,901 (1:2,900 Protestants) in 60 countries.

Religious Changes

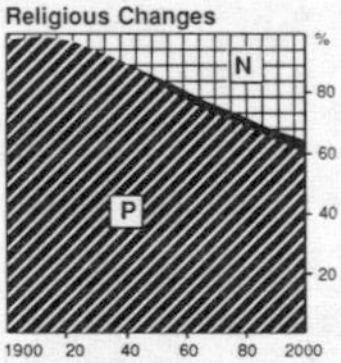

Evangelical Changes

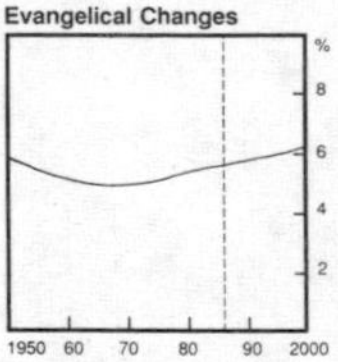

1. **In the last century Sweden was noted for its revivals**, but in this century for its permissive society and materialism. Pray for the government and leaders of the nation, as years of permissive legislation and erosion of respect for the things of God needs to be reversed. Pray for revival that will sweep through the nation.

2. **The spiritual need of the country** is shown by the decline of professing Christians from 99% of the population to 69% today. Only 3-4% of the population regularly goes to church. Over half the population have no real knowledge of the Christian faith, which has become a pleasantly impersonal cultural heritage with little practical relevance. Pray especially for the institutions and leaders of the State Church, and for a fresh moving of the Spirit within it. There is a growing evangelical minority among the pastors of the State Church.

3. **Membership in Free Churches** is higher than in any other Scandinavian country. Many are the fruit of earlier revivals, but only in three has there been no decline in numbers. The Covenant Church is theologically mixed, but most of the nation's finest evangelical leaders are to be found in it.

4. **All is not dark!** Praise the Lord for evidences of spiritual renewal in some areas. The Pentecostal and charismatic churches and fellowships are growing. Real life in the more informal home gatherings is encouraging. Many churches are majoring on evangelism. Cooperation between churches in fellowship and outreach has increased. The population, as a whole, has become more receptive; post-war idealisms have been cruelly disappointed. Pray for a mighty ingathering.

5. **Theological training** is a key prayer target. There are two main theological faculties at the universities, where many pastors are trained. This education is affected by the humanistic influence of the universities in general; pray for more lecturers who are truly evangelical. The free churches run eight theological schools with one to four-year courses including Örebro (170 students), SMF-Lidingö (100), SBF-Bromma (100), SAM-Kortebo (50). There are also many short-term Bible courses being held by most denominations, including the Pentecostals. Besides these there are a few independent Bible schools that run one to four-year courses such as NBI-**GEM** (60), Betel Institute (35), Torchbearers (70). Over 150 young people are trained annually in short-term courses held by **YWAM. OM** also has done much to motivate young people for evangelism and missionary service.

6. **Missionary outreach from Sweden** has been outstanding. The contribution of the Lutheran Church and all the free churches in more than 60 countries has been used of God. Pentecostal missionaries compose more than half of all present missionaries from Sweden. Pray for a quickening of this vision among young people for short-term and, even more, for long-term work. Sweden's unusual stand in world politics opens up many areas of the world for missionaries which are closed to other nations. Pray for the notable work of the **Institute of Bible Translation** in Stockholm with the vision to provide a translation of the NT in every language of the USSR.

7. **More needy areas and peoples.**

a) There are **rural and urban areas** with few evangelical churches; the latter being unevenly distributed due to localized revivals in the past.

b) **Political and religious refugees** from the Middle East, Latin America and Communist Bloc have been given a home in Sweden. They are frequently the most open section of the community to the gospel. Many of these minorities are unevangelized. There are a few workers among them. Pray especially for the 35,000 Muslims.

c) **The 5,000 Chinese**; three small groups of believers exist.

The West

Oct 15

SWITZERLAND

(Swiss Confederation)

Area 41,300 sq.km. Mountainous land; 26% unproductive, yet the Swiss Alps are one of the greatest tourist attractions in the world.

Population 6,500,000. Annual growth 0.2%. People per sq.km. 157.

Peoples
Indigenous 85.6%; of which German-speaking 74.4%; French-speaking 20.8%; Italian-speaking 3.9%; Romansch-speaking 0.9%.
Foreign 14.4%. (Only long-term residents). Italian 420,000; Spanish 110,000; German/Austrian 116,000; Yugoslavs 50,000; French 47,000; Turks 45,000; Portuguese 16,000; Czechs 11,500; Greeks 10,000; Tibetans 1,500, etc.

Literacy 99%. **Official languages**: German, French, Italian, Romansch. **Bible translations** 4Bi 2por.

Capital: Bern 287,000. Other major cities: Zürich 706,000; Geneva 335,000; Basel 365,000. Urbanization 58%.

Economy: A strong, stable industrial economy in spite of world recession. Unemployment only 1-2%. Both tourism and banking are important foreign exchange earners. Income/person $16,390 (116% of USA).

Politics: Federal democratic republic that has been at peace with its neighbours since 1815. The 26 cantons and half cantons have a high degree of autonomy.

Religion: The federal constitution guarantees religious freedom, but relationships between cantonal governments and the churches are decided locally. The post-Reformation confrontations between Catholics and Protestants helped determine the majority religion of each canton.

Non-religious/Atheist 4.1%. **Other** 0.2%.
Muslim 0.9%. Predominantly Turks, also Arabs and Yugoslavs.
Jews 0.3%.
Christian 94.5%. Much nominalism.
Roman Catholic 47%. 3,060,000a. Majority in 15 cantons; also many guest workers.
Other Catholic 0.2%. 15,500a. Over 32 groups.
Foreign marginal 1.4%. 88,000a; 40,000m.
Orthodox 0.6%. 37,000a. Greeks, East Europeans.
Protestant 45.3%. Majority in 10 cantons (one canton is shared with Catholics). 96% of all Protestants are linked with the 13 cantonal Reformed Churches, as also are many members of Free Churches. 2,940,000a. Denominations, largest (adherents):

Cantonal Reformed Churches		2,800,000
Pilgermission St. Chrischona		17,000
Pentecostal Free Ch. Assoc.	(?)	16,000
Methodist Church		10,000
Free Evang. Congregations	(?)	8,000
Baptist Union		3,200

Conservative Evangelical approx. 4% of the population.
Missionaries from Switzerland 1,232 (1:2,400 Protestants) in over 40 agencies.
Missionaries to Switzerland approx. 100.

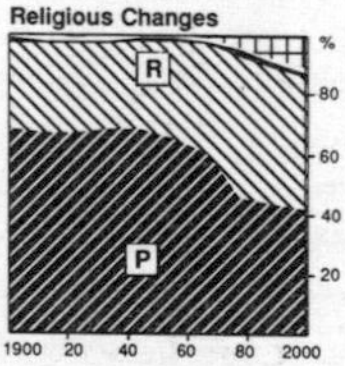

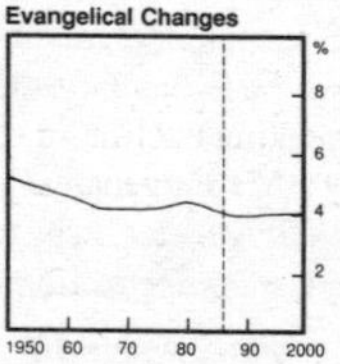

1. **Few today know of their national heritage through the great reformers Calvin and Zwingli**, or much of what real Christianity is. Materialism and a comfortable satisfied indifference prevails. However, there is a new spirit of inquiry among young people who seek a living faith. Pray that they may find the true way in Jesus Christ, and that the nation might be stirred again by the Holy Spirit.

2. **In the Catholic cantons**, predominantly in the south and centre of the country, the small evangelical witness is growing, and the centuries-old prejudices and religious polarization are breaking down. More Bibles are being purchased by Catholics than Protestants. Among both priests and laity there is a search after biblical truth. Pray that many may find it in a personal relationship with Jesus and come to assurance of salvation, and that a living fellowship of believers may come into being in every community.

3. **The manifest falling away in the Protestant churches** is cause for concern. Liberal and neo-orthodox theologies have sapped spiritual life, and replaced biblical preaching, evangelism and pastoral care with social and political activism. Pray for:

a) **The raising up of prayerful men and women of God** in both the leadership and the congregations, that through them, revival may sweep through the whole Swiss nation.

b) **That Spirit-filled pastors** within the Cantonal churches may be used to bring spiritual renewal to the many formal and shrinking congregations.

c) **That theological students** may become enthused by the Word of God, aim for a spiritual ministry, and not be ensnared by the dead theologies and human psychologies so often taught.

4. **Praise God for increased evangelical activity**, especially from within fellowship groups and in Free Churches. Many thousands are being reached through united evangelistic efforts under the umbrella of the Evangelical Alliance, but this has not really penetrated the mass of people outside the churches who never hear the gospel. The "Christ Day" celebrations of 1980 and 1984 in Bern were a testimony to unity in Christ among believers. Many service agencies are coming into being to encourage and build up local congregations. Pray for:

a) **A clear, consistent, united witness** by true believers in both Cantonal and Free churches.

b) **Effective evangelization** of the great majority who are only Christian in name.

c) **Ministry** among young people, students (with small **IFES** groups in French and German-speaking universities), drug addicts and alcoholics, etc.

d) **Outreach agencies** such as "**Action: New Life**", "**Christ For All**"(**WLC**), "**Pray for Switzerland**", etc.

5. **Bible training** is provided by a number of good institutions, and from them graduates have gone out into Christian service all over Europe and the world. Remember the:

a) **German-speaking seminaries**: FETA (Freie Evangelische Akademie, Basel) and St. Chrischona, and Bible Schools in Aarau, Beatenberg, Walzenhausen; and shorter-term Bible schools in Bienenberg and Gunten/Emmetten.

b) **French-speaking Bible schools**: Emmaus, Le Roc, Centre Biblique International and **YWAM.**

Pray that these may retain their spiritual cutting edge, and become a means of blessing and revival in Switzerland. Pray also for the calling of many into full-time work.

6. **The "Arbeitsgemeinschaft Evangelikaler Missionen" (AEM)** was formed in 1972 to strengthen and coordinate missionary vision and outreach — especially in the Free Churches; 33 agencies are members and from these 737 missionaries have been sent out. The "**Fédération des Missions Evangéliques Francophones**" (**FMEF**) has the same vision for the French-speaking Protestant churches in Switzerland and France; 200 missionaries have been sent out by **FMEF** agencies. There are a further 295 missionaries linked with denominational and other agencies. Pray for a greater awareness and sense of responsibility in Swiss churches for world evangelization, and support of the commendably large missionary force.

7. **The immigrant "guest workers"** are predominantly Catholic (Italian, Spanish, Portuguese, Yugoslav), Orthodox (Greek, Yugoslav) and Muslim (Turks, Arabs). Pray for each of the 19 ethnic minorities represented to be evangelized. There are a number of agencies and churches committed to this ministry such as MEOS, Tent Mission, etc.; most are linked together in the "Arbeitskreis fü Ausländermission".

8. **Local radio and TV stations** are well used by several Swiss Christian agencies, and have great potential for reaching the population.

Middle East
Oct 16-17

SYRIA
(Syrian Arab Republic)

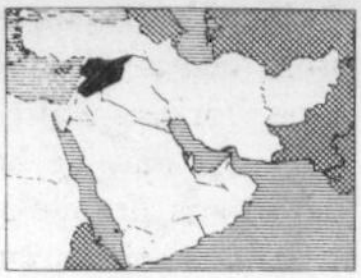

Area 185,000 sq.km. The site of some of the world's oldest civilizations; Damascus and Aleppo are reputedly the oldest continually inhabited cities in the world.

Population 10,600,000. Annual growth 3.9%. People per sq.km. 57. About 80% live on or near the Mediterranean coast.

Peoples
Arab 88%, of which Bedouin 800,000, and Palestinian refugees 240,000, are minorities.
Other minorities 12%. Kurds 670,000; Armenians 300,000; Turk/Turkoman 64,000; Assyrian 48,000; Circassian 30,000; Gypsy 20,000; Russians and East Europeans 7,000.

Literacy 44%. **Official language:** Arabic. **All languages** 8. **Bible translations** 3Bi 2NT 1por.

Capital: Damascus 1,741,000. **Other major city:** Aleppo 1,146,000. Urbanization 49%.

Economy: Development slowed by expense of maintaining a large, well-equipped army for internal security, defence against Israel and involvement in Lebanon. Income/person $1,680 (12% of USA).

Politics: Independent from France in 1946. Continuous internal upheavals until the coup in 1970. Relative internal stability under an Alawite minority, military-civilian socialist government. Fundamentalist Islam has fermented several revolts that were suppressed with much bloodshed. Efforts to bring communal peace and Syrian control in Lebanon have continued since 1973. The southwest Golan heights have been occupied by Israel since 1967.

Religion: Prior to 1973 Islam was the religion of the state. Since then it has been a secular state with Islam recognized as the religion of the majority, and all other minorities accorded definite rights and privileges.
Muslim 90%. Sunni 83%, Alawite 13%, Druze 3%, Ismaili 1%, Yezidi 0.2%.
Non-religious/Atheist 1.4%.
Jews 4,000.
Christian 8.6%. Affiliated 6.8%.
Roman Catholic 2.3%. 249,000a.
Orthodox 4.3%. 465,000a. Denominations 6. Largest (adherents):

Greek Orthodox (Arabic)	210,000
Armenian Orthodox	135,000
Syrian Orthodox (Jacobite)	82,000
Assyrian (Nestorian)	33,000

Protestant 0.23%. 25,300a; 13,000m. Denominations 17. Largest (adult adherents):

Union of Ev. Armenian Churches	10,000
National Ev. Synod (Reformed)	7,200
National Ev. Alliance (**CMA**)	3,400

Evangelical 0.1% of population
Missionaries to Syria 2.

Religious Changes

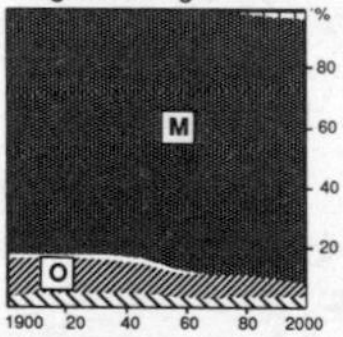

Evangelical Changes

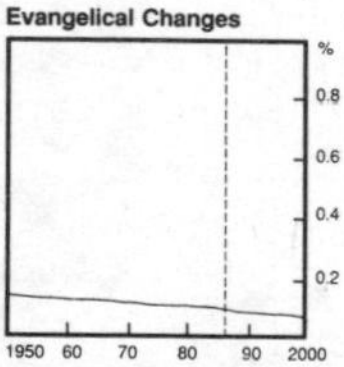

1. **Syria is a land of religious coexistence**. Tolerance for minority religions is tempered with surveillance of any activity that could provoke communal tensions. Christians find it hard to witness freely in these conditions, even when given the opportunity. Syria is one of the less evangelized nations on earth despite the large minority of traditional Christians.

2. **The Muslim majority has a false conception of what a true Christian is.** Pray that they may be enlightened by contacts with believers who have a holy life style and radiant witness. Muslims are in daily contact with traditional Christians, as are Syrian soldiers based in Lebanon.

3. **The Christians have stood up to Islam for centuries and survived**. Most Christians are Arab and 25% are Armenian; descendants of a multiplicity of Orthodox and Catholic traditions. Christians are an influential minority in the cities, professions, politics and the armed forces, but are a shrinking percentage due to a high rate of emigration to the Americas and Africa. Syria was once one of the great centres for the spread of the gospel. Pray that believers may recapture the zeal of the church of Antioch, and reach out to their compatriots with the gospel.

4. **The Protestant witness is small**, but churches are slowly growing. Almost all converts are from the traditional Christian minority. There are churches in most cities, but the lack of full-time workers and availability of training for leadership are serious limitations. Pray that believers may be both ambitious and original in seeking out opportunities to win non-Christians, despite official pressures. The major Protestant groups are those of the Alliance, Nazarene and Assemblies of God, as well as a number of thriving Armenian evangelical congregations.

5. **Conversions out of Islam are few and far between.** Spiritual bondages, social barriers and religious prejudices must be broken down before some can take the decisive step. For such individuals pray for perseverance in persecution, acceptance into fellowship by other believers and growth to maturity.

6. **Unreached peoples:**

a) **The Sunni Arab majority**. Very few have heard the gospel.

b) **The Alawites** are a poor rural community, but influential in the army and government. Their beliefs differ much from orthodox Islam, but little specific effort has been directed to them.

c) **The Druzes** are another heretical branch of Islam, but they have been unresponsive.

d) **The Kurds** of the north and northwest could be more receptive. Some are Orthodox Christian, others are Yezidis and Shi'a, but most are Sunni Muslim.

e) **The Bedouin, Circassian and Turkoman** minorities are solidly Muslim with no known Christians.

7. **Missionaries** are not allowed to reside in the country. Pray for those who pay occasional pastoral visits, and for a more open door to this needy land.

8. **The entry of Christian literature** was restricted for years, but since 1981 there has been much more freedom to import and distribute Bibles etc. Pray for the entry and dissemination of Arabic literature, and blessing to come to Christian and non-Christian readers. There are two Bible Society shops in the country.

Africa

Oct 18-19

TANZANIA

(United Republic of Tanzania)

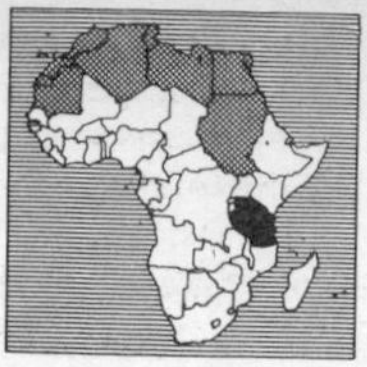

Area 946,000 sq.km. Mainland Tanganyika and Zanzibar (two offshore islands) 2,650 sq.km.

Population 21,700,000. Zanzibar 610,000. Annual growth 3.5%. People per sq.km. 23.

Peoples: Over 126 distinct ethnic groups.

African peoples 99%. Tribalism has not been as divisive a force as in many lands. Major groups: Sukuma 2,820,000; Rufiji (4 groups) 1,950,000; Rukwa (3) 1,090,000; Makonde 890,000; Chagga 800,000.

Other 1%. Hutu refugees from Burundi, 100,000 (?); Indian 70,000 and decreasing, Westerners, etc.

Literacy 85%. **Official languages**: Swahili, English. The use of Swahili is so widespread, it is even replacing local languages in some areas. **All languages** 115. **Bible translations** 11Bi 18NT 15por.

Capital: Dar es Salaam 1,500,000. Urbanization 14%.

Economy: Agricultural subsistence economy. Inefficient, centralized bureaucracy and an over-zealous nationalization of businesses and collectivization of rural communities into "ujamaa" villages have been detrimental. Lowered production, and a run-down of industry and services, together with severe drought in the '80s have seriously reduced living standards. Income/person $240 (2% of USA).

Politics: Tanganyika gained independence from Britain in 1961, Zanzibar in 1963. The two countries united as a one-party federal socialist republic in 1964, though Zanzibar has retained a considerable degree of autonomy. The retirement of the respected President Nyerere may eventually lead to a shift away from his socialist dream. There is considerable pressure for change and liberalization in Zanzibar.

Religion: Religious freedom; the government encourages religious education in schools.

Muslim 32.5%. The majority in Zanzibar (98%), along the coastal belt, and some peoples on the Mozambique border.

Traditional religions 19%.

Christian 47.7%. Nominal 12%. Affiliated 34%.

Roman Catholic 18.5%. 4,000,000a; 2,200,000m. Practising 44%.

Orthodox 0.1%. 15,000a.

Marginal groups 0.6%. 130,000a. Predominantly African indigenous churches.

Protestant 14.8%. 3,200,000a; 1,271,000m. Denominations 30. Largest (adult members):

Evangelical Lutheran Church	436,000
Anglican Church	306,000
Africa Inland Church (**AIM**)	200,000
Moravian Church	79,500
Seventh Day Adventist Church	53,000
Pentecostal Ch's in T. (ex-Swed)	42,000
T. Assemblies of God (**AoG**)	18,000
Pentec. Assemblies of T. (**PAoC**)	15,000
Brethren assemblies	12,000

Evangelical 9% of population.

Missionaries to Tanzania approx. 660 (1:33,000 people) in about 60 agencies.

Missionaries from within Tanzania approx. 10.

Religious Changes

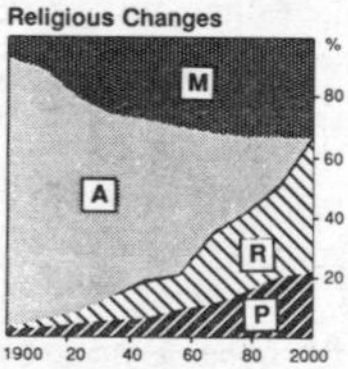

Evangelical Changes

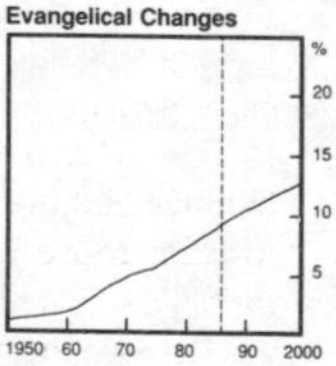

1. **Praise God for the growth of the Church!**
   a) **Revival** has renewed many churches over the past 30 years, and this continues today.
   b) There has been **vigorous outreach** to a receptive population.
   c) **Economic crises** and social disruption have made people more accessible and receptive than ever before. The collectivization of rural communities, though unpopular and an economic failure, has broken down traditional structures and opposition to the gospel. There has been rapid church growth in those areas where churches were prepared to make the effort to reach out.
   d) **Churches** all over the country, and especially in the cities, are full to overflowing.

T

2. **The growth of the Church** has been good, but patchy. Evangelical churches have been more successful. Pentecostal, Evangelical Anglican and AIC churches have grown fast; the large Lutheran Church more slowly. Yet there are problems:

a) There are extensive areas where the churches have stagnated; and many potentially open villages unreached.
b) Western cultural forms and formalism is common where revival has not touched the lives of churchgoers.
c) The lack of Christian workers and lay leaders.

3. **Leadership training** needs to be given top priority in the churches. Training facilities and funding are limited. Pray for the 15 or so Bible schools and seminaries in the country. Many need upgrading to higher levels to prepare leaders for an increasingly literate population. Extensive use is made of **TEE** and also **cassette Bible schools** for training local leaders.

4. **Response among young people** has been particularly encouraging. There has never been such responsiveness before. Workers for this ripe harvest are needed.
a) **Religious education** is taught in schools, and Christian teachers have had a big impact — more national and expatriate teachers are needed.
b) **SU groups** in schools are thriving and multiplying. Only the lack of staff workers prevents greater expansion.
c) **FOCUS groups (IFES)** in universities and colleges are large and evangelistic. Many students are being converted, including Muslims. Lack of staff workers is a hindrance to better national coverage and coordination of outreach and discipling.
d) **It is difficult to integrate young Christians** into the churches.

5. **Missionaries have a key supportive role**. The main thrust of the missionary force is in Bible and government teaching, technical ministries and outreach to Muslim areas. New workers are required. The largest groups of missionaries are Lutherans (from many lands), Anglicans (especially CMS from UK, Australia and New Zealand), **Brethren** (English and German-speaking), also **SBC** (78 workers), **AIM** (26).

6. **The Muslim challenge**. Between 1880 and 1960 Islam grew rapidly. That growth has slowed, and a small, but increasing number of Muslims are coming to Christ. Pray for decisive breakthroughs in every Muslim community. Pray also for the calling of those from a Muslim background into the work of evangelizing them.

7. **The unreached** — despite growth, great areas of need remain:
a) **The peoples of Zanzibar**. There are three distinct people groups on the two islands of Zanzibar and Pemba. The few Christians are largely mainlanders, and not indigenous. There are a few Quaker believers on Pemba; Anglicans and a few Pentecostals in Zanzibar. Pray for these, and the calling out of Tanzanians who will evangelize these island peoples. **SU** has initiated a work in Zanzibar. Pray that a new era of freedom for the gospel may come with the increasing liberalization now taking place.
b) **The Muslim coastal peoples**: Zaramo 450,000, Rangi 280,000, Luguru 480,000, Sambaa 500,000, Zigula 320,000, and the many urban coastal Swahili are almost entirely Muslim. More Tanzanian Christians need a vision to reach them. **AIM** is planning a new thrust in this area.
c) **The peoples on the Mozambique border.** The Brethren from Germany have worked and prayed for a breakthrough among the Islamized Makonde 890,000, Yao 390,000 and have only now begun to see the beginnings of a harvest. This is a key area for evangelizing unreached northern Mozambique.
d) **People are still following traditional religions**. Majorities in a number of peoples are still unresponsive to the gospel, some such being the Sukuma 2,820,000 and Zinza 100,000 in the AIC area in the northwest, the Arusha/Maasai 320,000, Barabaig 85,000, Iraqw 360,000, and Turu 450,000 in the Lutheran area in the north, the Nyamwezi 750,000 in the Anglican area in the centre, and the Safwa 80,000 and Nyakusa 400,000 in the southwest. However, in almost all there is a Christian presence.

8. **Bible translation** is a partially met challenge. The increasing use of Swahili lessens the need for translation into some languages. However there are 18 languages that definitely require a NT translation and possibly a total of 82. Pray for Tanzanian translators to be raised up and trained to meet the need. Bible and teaching cassettes have been widely used. **GRI** has recordings available in 70 languages.

9. **Christian literature** is vital for an increasingly literate nation, yet the poverty and difficulty of obtaining supplies hampers printing and distribution on a larger scale. Pray for more Tanzanians with the gifts and calling to write appropriate Christian articles and books. Pray also for the **Central Tanganyika Press** (Anglican) and **Africa Inland Press**, and for effective distribution of their products.

10. **Missionary flying** has become an essential service ministry in evangelism, and in leadership training programmes. **MAF** has aircraft based on six strategic locations. Pray for the 9 **MAF** families serving in this ministry.

11. **Christian radio** has more potential in Tanzania than in many African countries. The Lutherans and **IBRA** have recording studios. **FEBA** (Seychelles) broadcasts 115 hours per month in Swahili and 16 hours per month in English, and is clearly received.

THAILAND
(Kingdom of Thailand)

Asia

Oct 20-21

Area 514,000 sq.km. A fertile and well-watered land.

Population 52,700,000. Annual growth 1.9%. People per sq.km. 103.

Peoples: Four major peoples and numerous smaller groups.
Thai 80%. Four main groups. Central 19,000,000; Northern 6,000,000; Southern 4,000,000; Lao 12,500,000. The latter live in the northeast.
Chinese 12% or more. Thai-speaking 80%. A minority still use over six Chinese languages, mostly Chaochow.
Malay 3.2%. In the extreme south adjoining Malaysia.
Khmer 2.8%. Two main languages.
Tribal peoples 2%. Over 48 indigenous groups, most in the mountainous border regions. Six main groups: Mon-Khmer peoples (15 groups) 340,000; Karen (6) 280,000; Tai (9) 210,000; Miao-Yao (3) 156,000; Tibeto-Burman (10) 73,000; Austronesian (4) 8,000.
Refugees 1%. Kampucheans around 300,000; Laotians and Vietnamese 250,000; Burmese 15,000.

Literacy 84%. **Official language**: Thai. **All languages** 61. **Bible translations** 6Bi 7NT 10por.

Capital: Krung Thep (Bangkok) 6,043,000. Urbanization 17%.

Economy: Productive agricultural economy. Main exports are rice, pineapples, tapioca and rubber. The depletion of forest cover is worsening the cycle of droughts and floods. Rapid industrialization and development of mineral resources. The government is making a determined effort to eradicate the drug trafficking from the "Golden Triangle" in the far northwest of the country. Income/person $810 (6% of USA).

Politics: Never ruled by any Western power. Constitutional monarchy, with the popular king having a strong unifying and stabilizing role. The Vietnam War, increased Communist insurgency, and the huge influx of war refugees from Indochina created fears for the nation's future. There has been a succession of democratic and military governments.

Religion: Buddhism is the state religion, but there is freedom and all religions are seen as a bulwark against Communist ideology.
Buddhist 92%. Thai, Lao, Shan, some Chinese, etc. Much syncretism with spirit worship.
Muslim 4%. Malays and some Thai in the far south.
Chinese religions 1.6%. Many Chinese are included with the Buddhist figure.
Animist 1.4%. Among tribal peoples.
Christian 1%. Affiliated 0.72%.
Roman Catholic 0.4%. 212,000a; 114,000m. Stronger among Chinese and in Bangkok.
Protestant 0.31%. 167,000a; 81,000m. Denominations 33. Largest (adult members):

Ch. of Christ in T. (Presby, Bapt. etc)	35,000
Karen Baptist Convention	8,500
Seventh Day Adventist Church	6,800
Lahu Church	4,000
Ch. Fellowships relating to **OMF**	3,200
Ch. Fellowships relating to **WEC**	2,200
Gospel Church of Thailand (**CMA**)	2,110
T. Baptist Churches Assoc. (**SBC**)	2,100

Evangelical 0.2% of population.
Missionaries to Thailand approx. 1,030 (1:51,000 people) in 70 agencies.
Missionaries from within Thailand approx. 14.

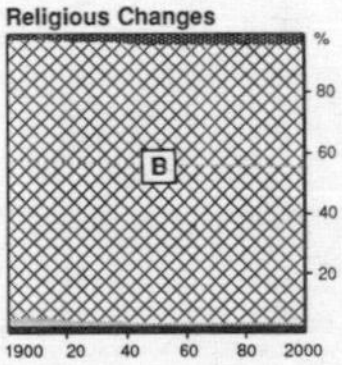

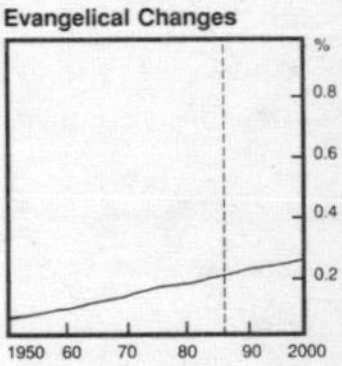

1. There is much for which to praise God — even in this land where the response has been so slow:

a) **Thailand means "Land of the Free"**. Praise God that it has remained so despite fears to the contrary.

b) **The marked increase in interest in the gospel since 1975** (the time of the fall of Vietnam). The emptiness of Buddhism has brought disillusionment to many.

c) **The increased emphasis on evangelism and church growth** by a new generation of Thai leaders, and widespread and effective use of media: radio, drama, cassettes, films and audio-visuals.

2. **The long-awaited spiritual breakthrough has yet to come** despite 160 years of intensive missionary effort. Prayer must break down:

a) **The fear that keeps people from Christ.** The social cohesiveness of Buddhism is strong, and Christianity appears foreign.

b) **The bondage of demonic powers is real.** Behind Buddhism is a complex world of venerated and feared spirits. Nearly every building has a spirit shelf and most Thai wear charms to ward off evil.

c) **The power of sin.** The social erosion caused by corruption, drugs and violence comes from the heart of man, but few have a concept of the need to repent.

3. **The slow growth of the Church is cause for concern.** The potential is great, but has yet to be realized. Pray for a much greater prayer burden and zeal to grip believers. Most of the congregations are poor, rural, and the believers are only partially literate. About half the believers are ethnic Thai, the other half are among the Chinese and tribal minorities. Pray for a life-changing move of the Spirit through the older and larger **Church of Christ in Thailand** (with which many denominational missions serve) and the younger more evangelical churches founded since World War II. In the **Evangelical Fellowship of Thailand** there are churches which are full members and others which are affiliated member churches; these together number 500 with a total of 50,000 adherents, 47 evangelical missionary and 30 Thai agencies. Nominalism, syncretism, a high rate of backsliding, lack of real spiritual concern among believers, lax church discipline and misuse of church funds have all been factors that have crippled the churches.

4. **A mobilization of believers is essential.** Pray for:

a) **Greater cooperation and less competition** among churches in aiming to plant a church in every community. There are 24,000 Buddhist temples, but only about 2,000, often small, Protestant congregations in the land.

b) **More training of believers** in evangelism; too few are both spiritually mature and willing to be active witnesses. There are over seven TEE programmes in operation.

c) **Preparation of leaders and church planters.** There were 16 Bible schools with 330 students in 1979, but many graduates do not go into full-time church planting or pastoral work. Pray for the **Bangkok Bible College** (initiated by **CMA** and **OMF**) and **Phayao Bible Training Centre** (**OMF**) and many denominational Bible colleges. Praise God, though, for some fine younger leaders who are coming to the fore in Christian work, but the great respect given to older people can be frustrating to the younger ones in the development of their ministry.

d) **Missionary vision** is slow in developing, but praise God for several Thai agencies and churches that have sent out missionary teams to other minorities. Pray also for those producing ***Doo Tert** (LOOK)*, a missionary broadsheet in Thai, through which the need for world evangelization is portrayed.

5. **Missionary work continues despite increasing government quota limitations.** The major involvement in the past was institutional; medical work and schools playing an important role in winning the first converts and planting the first churches in many parts of the land. The major emphasis is now on urban and rural evangelism, church planting and Bible teaching. Pray for:

a) **The calling, entry and preparation of new workers** to this exacting field. For many, two difficult languages must be mastered for effective communication.

b) **Safety.** Disease, road accidents and insurgency have led to the loss of a number of missionaries.

c) **Effective partnership** with Thai believers in strategic outreach.

d) **The major agencies. OMF** has 283 missionaries in five fields (among tribal peoples in the north, Thai in the centre, south and Bangkok, and Malay in the south). Other major agencies: **YWAM** (84 in refugee work and evangelism), **SBC** (79 missionaries), **NTM** (72 in tribal work), **CMA** (54 in the east) and **WEC** (46 in the northwest). There are 775 missionaries linked with the Evangelical Fellowship of Thailand.

6. **The unfinished task.** There are many and varied challenges:

a) **In many of the 72 provinces** there is scarcely a viable evangelical witness. Churches are more numerous in the north, in Bangkok and among tribal minorities.

b) **Bangkok** is sometimes called "sin city". Vice and violence are commonplace. A considerable migration of poor rural people to this seething metropolis is under way. Effective strategies must be developed to reach them. Pray for the church planting work of **AoG, SBC, CMA, OMF** and others there.

c) **The elite and middle classes** are well-educated, but little evangelized.

d) **There are about 12 unreached and unoccupied** tribal groups around the country. Many others still lack viable indigenous churches.

7. **Student witness** is small but growing. Twelve Christian hostels for students run by six agencies have proved valuable for discipling students and initiating Christian campus groups. **YFC**, TCS(**IFES**), **CCC** and an indigenous movement called Yuwakrit have begun to see conversions and growth of groups on campuses. The vast majority of this key group of people remains unevangelized.

8. **The Chinese** are an influential minority. They comprise nearly half the population of Bangkok, and control about 85% of the economy. Only 2% of the Chinese are Christian — mostly Catholic. There are about 70 Chinese Protestant congregations and 6,000 members. Pray that this key community may be well evangelized and become effective in witnessing to others. There is a lack of full-time workers from among them.

9. **The Muslim Malays** number 1,600,000 and nearly all live in the five southernmost provinces. There is political tension, and guerrilla activity in the area from Communists and Muslim fundamentalists. This is the only major Malay community in Asia open for evangelism, but after years of hard work **OMF** missionaries have seen only about 100 turn to Christ. Many others are held back by fear. Pray for the local believers and missionary team, and for their outreach. Pray also for the effective distribution of literature and the newly printed Jawi Malay NT.

10. **The tribal peoples** are beginning to respond in large numbers. This follows years of hard work by Baptists among the Karen, and **OMF** among eight tribes in the north with little fruit. The younger work of **NTM** in 11 tribes around the country is still in the pioneer stages. Many workers are needed to win and disciple tribal peoples. Pray for:

a) **The multiplying, but scattered congregations** among the northern Hmong (100,000), Lahu (37,000), Lisu (13,000), Akha (10,000) and Karen peoples. Lack of leaders, and second generation nominalism are problems. The Buddhist Shan (30,000) and animist Yao (30,000) have been less responsive.

b) **The pioneering work of NTM** among the Phu Thai (50,000), So (20,000), Thin (20,000) and Chaobon (1,000). The breakthrough has yet to come.

c) **The Kui, Khmu and Khmer peoples in the east who are unreached. CMA** works in the area, but there are insufficient workers to concentrate on them, especially the newly responsive Northern Khmer.

d) **Opium poppies** are the only lucrative cash crop for most of the northern tribes. The temptation for Christians to get involved, and the barrier to repentance of non-believers is acute. The narcotics trade breeds insecurity and violence. Pray for believers and missionaries in sensitive areas.

11. **Refugees** from war-torn Cambodia, Laos and Vietnam still flee to Thailand despite the danger of fighting on land and piracy at sea. The lot of the Cambodian refugees is particularly tragic. Pray for the 40 or so Christian agencies (such as **WV, CMA, OMF, SAO, YWAM**, etc.) with a service and spiritual ministry in the camps where up to 500,000 may be in residence at any one time. Some have been given homes in other lands, but for many this is a distant hope. Lively churches have sprung up in these camps.

12. **Bible translation** is still a major target for prayer. Many tribal language translations had to be converted from Roman to Thai script, which slowed translation work and delayed literacy. Work is in progress by a number of agencies in 16 languages. Between 18 and 30 languages may need translators. There are four different versions of the Thai Bible in circulation.

13. **Media evangelism and discipleship** have been well developed in Thailand. Pray that the following may prepare millions for the gospel and edify the Church:

a) **Traditional drama** with Christian themes is most effective.

b) **Radio** has had a wide impact. Forty-nine Thai stations air many hours of Christian programmes every day. **FEBC**, **IBRA**, Full Gospel Mass Communications, and Voice of Peace Studio all prepare a wide range of programmes.

c) **Cassette ministries** were first widely used in Thailand. The **Voice of Peace Studio** pioneered the use of evangelistic and teaching cassettes which are most effective in rural areas.

d) **Christian literature**. Over 1,000 Thai book titles published. There is increasing cooperation between publishers (such as **CLC**, **OMF** [Kanok], **CMA**, etc.). There are more than 10 Christian bookstores in the land. A number of massive literature campaigns are either under way or being planned. **EHC** has placed a piece of Christian literature in every home in Thailand, and is engaged in doing the same for a second time.

TOGO
(Togolese Republic)

Africa

Oct 22

Area 57,000 sq.km. The Atlantic coastline is only 56 km. long, but the little land stretches 540 km. northwards to the Sahel. Wedged between Ghana and Benin.

Population 3,000,000. Annual growth 2.8%. People per sq.km. 52.

Peoples: 21 major and many minor ethnic groups.
Ewe group 44%. Ewe 630,000; Watchi 290,000; Mina 180,000; Fon 55,000; Adja 30,000.
Kabiye group 22%. Kabiye 420,000; Kotokoli (Tem) 150,000; Tshamba 32,000.
Gur peoples 21%. Moba 150,000; Gurma 130,000; Nawdem 120,000; Lamba (Losso) 97,000; Konkomba 60,000; Bassari 40,000; Nateni 40,000; Ngangam 31,000; Mossi 10,000;
C. Togolese peoples 5%. Ife 75,600; Akposo 75,600; Akebu 35,000.
Other 8%. Yoruba 90,000; Fulani 50,000; Chokossi 46,000; Akan 30,000.

Literacy 18%. **Official language**: French. **All languages** 42. Only two indigenous languages used in education system: Ewe and Kabré. **Bible translations** 4Bi 4NT 3por.

Capital: Lomé 366,000. Urbanization 21%.

Politics: Independence from France in 1960. Numerous attempted, and several successful, coups. One-party military-civilian regime in power since 1967.

Economy: Mining phosphates and agriculture are important foreign currency earners, and economic growth has been moderate. The south is more prosperous than the drier north. Income/person $280 (2% of USA).

Religion: A limited degree of religious freedom to recognized religious groups. A period of intense anti-Christian rhetoric in the '70s has cooled to an official indifference. In 1978 twenty religious groups were banned; only the Muslims, Catholics and five Protestant churches are legally permitted to function.
Traditional religions 40.6%. Still very strong in most peoples.
Muslim 19%. Continued growth throughout this century. Muslims were only 4% in 1900.
Christian 40.4%. Nominal 16%. Affiliated 24.3%.
Roman Catholic 18.8%. 575,000a; 316,000m.
Foreign and indigenous marginal groups 1%. The 27 African indigenous churches are officially banned.
Protestant 4.6%. 138,500a; 41,000m. Denominations 8. Largest (adherents):

Eglise Evangélique	100,000
Assemblies of God (**AoG**)	15,000
Church of Pentecost	9,212
Baptist Assoc. (**SBC**)	6,000
Methodist Church	6,000
Evang. Baptist Church (ABWE)	1,000
Seventh Day Adventist Church	1,000

Evangelical 1.2% of population.
Missionaries to Togo 110 (1:27,300 people).

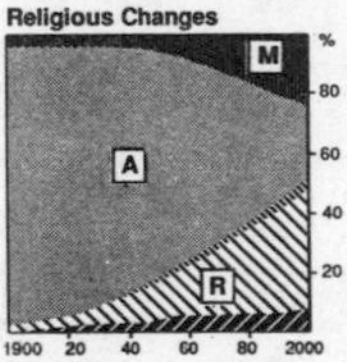

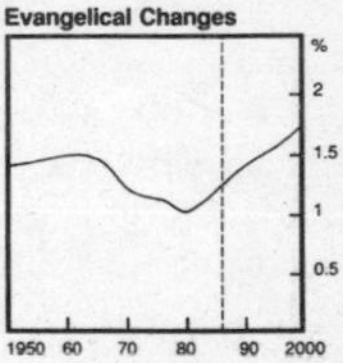

1. **Togo is the least evangelized non-Muslim country in Africa.** For years the door for Protestant missionaries was open, but the opportunity was lost. Entry for new missionaries is only practicable at present for service with existing missions. Pray for the entry of missionaries adequate to evangelize every people. There are at present only six missionaries serving in the northern 70% of the country, where 65% of the population and most of the ethnic groups live. The major evangelical missions are **AoG** (once mainly in the north, and now predominantly in the south) with 18 missionaries, **SBC** (21 missionaries), and **SIL** (33). The Assoc. of Baptists for World Evangelization has 35 workers in the south — mainly associated with a hospital in Kpalime in the southwest. The Missouri Synod Lutherans have recently begun a work among the Moba in the north.

2. **The long-established Eglise Evangélique and Methodist Church** have become very nominal and have very little evangelistic outreach. Their activities are almost entirely localized to the southern Ewe (Eg. Ev.) and Mina (Meth.), and there is little cross-cultural outreach. Pray for the ending of this tragic stagnation through an infusion of spiritual life into

these bodies. **Among the Ewe and Fon** an entrenched idolatry with strong secret societies has not been visibly challenged by the power of the gospel. Committed believers are few and the rate of backsliding is high. The percentage of active Protestant Christians in the population has not increased for 25 years.

3. **Evangelical churches have only recently begun to multiply.** The **AoG** have reached out to 12 peoples in the far north, and are seeing rapid growth in the south. The **SBC** have a growing work in the southern towns and capital. The Apostolic Church has a smaller work among the southern Ewe. Yet the gospel witness is still small, congregations scattered and labourers few.

4. **Leaders for the young churches are few**, and training facilities in Togo limited. The Baptist School of Theology and Assemblies of God Seminary in Lomé serve Francophone countries all over West Africa. Pray for Spirit-filled Togolese leaders to be raised up.

5. **Young people are largely unreached**. A godless and anti-Christian atmosphere prevails in most schools. Christians are few, and often pressurized. The work of **SU** in schools and GBU(**IFES**) in the university has grown slowly and is still in its infancy. There is a pressing need for a vital, nationwide outreach to high schools. Pray for a radical change in the situation. The **SBC** has a youth programme in Lomé.

6. **The growth of Islam during this century** has been marked and, as yet, unchallenged. There has never been any real attempt to evangelize Muslims or win those peoples being attracted to Islam. **SIL** has translation work among the Kotokoli and Chokossi, but where are the church planters to exploit the approaching availability of the Scriptures?

7. **Unreached peoples** — many in Togo:
   a) **The northern traditionalist peoples** among whom there is very little witness: Gurma, Konkomba, Ngangam, Lamba and Nawdem. There is a sprinkling of Christians and **AoG** churches in the area; but the majority are unreached. Accessibility is also a problem.
   b) **The 420,000 traditionalist Kabiye** are a strategic people in the centre/north. There are only five small **AoG** churches.
   c) **Many smaller traditionalist peoples in the south** — Fon, Mahi, Anago, Adele, etc. — are unevangelized.
   d) **The predominantly Muslim** Kotokoli and Tshamba in the centre, and Tamberma, Chokossi and Fulani in the north are totally unreached and unoccupied by missions.
   e) **Most of the towns and the capital have a high percentage of Muslims.** About 50% of Lomé's population is Muslim, but no specific outreach has been made to them.

8. **Bible translation** is a major need. Pray especially for the completion of the Kabiyé Bible now that it is one of the two indigenous languages used in education. There are at least four and possibly 15 languages into which the NT should be translated. Work is in progress in 14 languages — 9 of which are in the hands of **SIL** workers. Pray that there might be adequate teaming up of translators with evangelical church planters.

TOKELAU

See Cook Islands on p. 150.

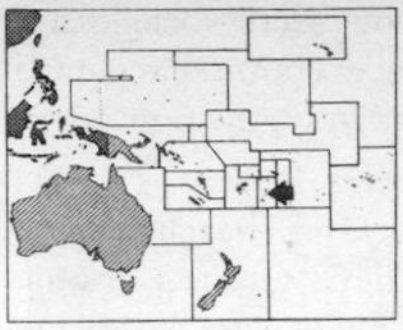

TONGA
(Kingdom of Tonga)

Pacific

Oct 23

Area 748 sq.km. Archipelago of 171 coral and volcanic islands 600 km. east of Fiji.

Population 108,000. Annual growth 2%. People per sq.km. 144.

Peoples
Polynesian 98.7%. Tongans (three related languages), a few other Pacific Islanders.
Other 1.3%. Euronesian, European, etc.

Literacy 100%. **Official language:** Tongan. **All languages** 3. **Bible translations** 1Bi.

Capital: Nuku'alofa 19,000.

Economy: Agricultural, with some tourism. Income/person $572 (1982. 4% of USA).

Politics: Constitutional Monarchy. Independent from Britain in 1970.

Religion: The Free Wesleyan Church enjoys a privileged position with the king as titular head. Freedom of religion.

Baha'i 3%.

Christian 97%. Affiliated 91%.

Roman Catholic 14%. Practising 65%. 15,000a; 8,700m.

Foreign marginal groups (2) 22%. 23,600a; 14,100m. Largest (adherents):

Mormons	23,490

Protestant 55.1%. 59,500a; 23,000m. Denominations 10. Largest (adherents):

Free Wesleyan Church	40,700
Church of Tonga	8,000
Free Church of Tonga	5,000
Seventh Day Adventist Church	4,200
Assemblies of God	1,375

Evangelical 7% of population.

Missionaries to Tonga 24 (1:4,500 people) in 6 agencies.

Missionaries from Tonga 12 (1:5,000 Protestants).

1. **The Tongan church** has had a glorious history of missionary outreach. Pray that the vision may be restored.

2. **The last century has been one of spiritual decline,** bitter schisms within the Methodist groups, and the rapid growth of Mormons to almost a quarter of the population. Oh, for revival!

3. **Leaders anointed of God** to proclaim the truth in love must be raised up. Unity among the evangelical groups is hampered by doctrinal extremes.

4. **Scripture Union** has had considerable impact on nominal Christians, with many coming to the Lord and with branches in nearly every village of Tonga.

Caribbean
Oct 24

TRINIDAD and TOBAGO
(The Republic of Trinidad and Tobago)

Area 5,128 sq.km. Two islands just off the coast of Venezuela.

Population 1,252,000. Annual growth 1.9%. People per sq.km. 240.

Peoples
African origin 42% and **Eurafrican** 14%. Predominant in civil service and cities; the majority on Tobago.
East Indian 42%. Predominant in agriculture, professions and trading. The bulk of the population is rural.
Chinese 3.1%. **European** 1.9%.

Literacy 92%. **Official language:** English.

Capital: Port-of-Spain 256,000. Urbanization 49%.

Economy: Predominantly agricultural, but oil revenues sparking off rapid industrialization. The sixth most wealthy country in Central and South America in income/person — $6,900 (49% of USA).

Politics: Independent from Britain in 1962 as a parliamentary democracy. The 30 years premiership of Dr E. Williams has been a time of stability except for a troubled period in 1970. Racial harmony and economic progress has been maintained.

Religion: Religious freedom is guaranteed.
Hindu 25% and **Muslim** 7.0% are almost entirely East Indians.
Baha'i 0.8%. **Spiritist** 0.4%. **Chinese religions** 0.5%.
Christian 66%.
Roman Catholic 29.4%. 368,000a; 210,000m.
Orthodox 0.5%. Two denominations.
Marginal groups (4) 2%. 25,000a 12,500m.
Protestant 33.7%. 422,000a; 135,000m. Denominations 55. Largest (adult members):

Anglican Church	29,000
Methodist Church	14,700
Pentecostal Assemblies	14,000
Seventh Day Adventist Church	13,500
Presbyterian	11,400
Open Bible Standard Church	9,000
Baptist Union	8,200

Evangelical 11% of population.
Missionaries to Trinidad 95 (1:13,200 people) in 20 agencies.
Missionaries from Trinidad 6 (1:70,300 Protestants).

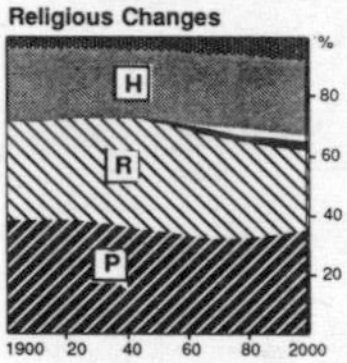

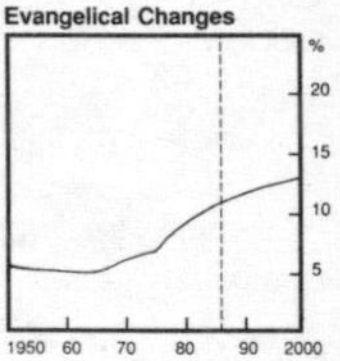

Many items for prayer are covered on p. 255, where Trinidad is included with other English-speaking Caribbean states.

1. **The East Indians are the largest non-Christian community in the Caribbean,** and present the greatest challenge. Traditional standards and strong East Indian links are loosening. Pray for a turning to the Lord Jesus. About 14% of all East Indians are now, at least nominally, Christian. **WT** has four churches among East Indian villages in central Trinidad amongst the Hindu and Muslim peoples.

2. **The 88,000 Muslim East Indians** have proved less responsive, but very little effort has ever been made to evangelize them.

3. **The Hindus have been more open.** The Presbyterians and now **TEAM**, **WT**, and several Pentecostal Churches are seeing a pleasing growth. Pray for the breakthrough!

4. **Religious instruction in public schools** presents an exciting opportunity for the gospel. In 1981 there were 118 Trinidad Christians engaged in this ministry. Pray for the young people of all races. **YFC**, **CEF** and **IFES** have work among students.

TUNISIA
(Republic of Tunisia)

Middle East

Oct 25

Area 164,000 sq.km. The site of notable civilizations: Carthaginian, Berber Christian and Arab Islamic. The smallest of the Maghreb nations of North Africa.

Population 7,156,000. Annual growth 2.3%. People per sq.km. 44.

Peoples
Arabic-speaking 97.5%. Mixed Berber and Arab descent.
Berber-speaking 1.5%. Six dialects/languages.
Other 1%. French 15,000; Jewish 10,000; Italian 5,000; Maltese 4,000, etc.

Literacy 42%. **Official language:** Arabic; French is widely used. **All languages** 8. **Bible translations** 1Bi 1NT.

Capital: Tunis 1,244,000. Urbanization 52%.

Economy: Rapid development after independence. Oil, tourism, agriculture and industry are all important foreign currency earners. Economic stagnation in the '80s and high unemployment are destabilizing the land. Income/person $1,290 (9% of USA).

Politics: Independent as a republic in 1956. President Bourguiba has ruled for 30 years, giving stability, continuity, and strong links with Western nations. Uncertainty about succession in leadership has provoked internal unrest and raised the likelihood of interference by neighbouring Libya or Islamic fundamentalists.

Religion: Islam is the state religion. The trend is to secularization rather than fundamental Islam. Not favourable to any form of Christian proselytism, but tolerance shown to foreign religious minorities.
Muslim 99.5%. Sunni, with minority of Ibadi Kharija on Djerba Island.
Christian 0.26%. Almost entirely foreigners.
Roman Catholic 0.25%. 18,000a. French, Italian, Maltese.
Protestant 0.01%. 450a, 240m. Denominations 7. Largest: Reformed, Brethren, Pentecostal.

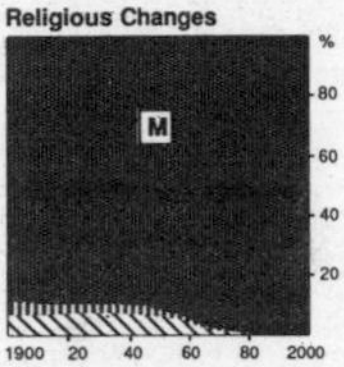

1. **In early centuries the Christian Church was strong.** Schism, heresy, foreign invasions and finally Islam brought about its demise. There are only about 50 indigenous evangelical believers today. Pray that a living, growing Church might become a reality again in this land.

2. **Indigenous believers** are often isolated, fearful, weak in their faith and prone to backslide or to marry a Muslim. To some, emigration is an easy option. Only a few have dared openly to share their faith. May they become "a threshing instrument having teeth" in the hands of the Lord!

3. **There is a leadership crisis**, with no mature leaders for the three small groups of believers. Pray that some may be raised up for the upbuilding of the Church. TEE courses are available and are a useful training tool.

4. **Almost all Christians are foreign** and predominantly Catholic. No missionaries are permitted; pray the land open. About a dozen evangelical Christians who are studying, teaching etc., are seeking to share their faith with non-Christians, also to encourage and help seekers and young believers. They need sensitivity and a persevering, servant spirit in a humanly discouraging situation. Pray in others called of God and with suitable professional skills. Pray for the English and French Reformed Churches' witness.

5. Specific unreached peoples:
   a) **300,000 Tunisians now live and work in France.** Present efforts to reach them are limited, but are being made (NAM, etc.).
   b) **Youth in Tunisia** are dissatisfied with the status quo and are looking for answers.
   c) **The Berber peoples.** Small communities of these indigenous peoples live in the rural areas and also the 65,000 Djerba islanders are unreached. There are no Scriptures in their languages.

6. **Christian literature** is not openly sold or distributed. Pray that a Christian bookstore may be permitted, and also the dissemination of Christian literature throughout the land. Pray for the development of a good Christian cassette and video programme.

7. **Bible correspondence schools and radio evangelism** have been the most potent combination for winning a hearing for the gospel. Pray for the thousands of Tunisian listeners and students. Pray for postal services to function smoothly and for conversions. Radio programmes in Arabic are beamed into Tunisia by **TWR** for 22 hours a month, and ELWA (**SIM**) for 69 hours. BCCs are prepared and sent out from both Spain (**GMU**) and France (**NAM**).

Middle East

Oct 26-28

TURKEY
(Republic of Turkey)

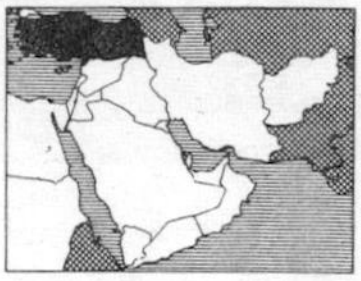

Area 781,000 sq.km. The country straddles two continents; 3% in Europe (Thrace), 97% in Asia (Anatolia), and controls the Bosphorus and the Dardanelles, the vital sea link between the Black Sea and Mediterranean. Its strategic position has made the area of prime importance through history.

Population 51,420,000. Annual growth 2.5%. People per sq.km. 67.

Peoples: There has been continued pressure on the ethnic minorities to conform to Turkish culture. Ethnic populations are therefore hard to assess.
Turks 80.2%. A Central Asian people that conquered and largely absorbed the indigenous peoples of the land from the eleventh century onward. The Turks are ethnically diverse, but culturally fairly homogenous. Distinctive sub-groups: Azeri 530,000 in the east, Yoruk 320,000 on the west coast.
Kurds 16%. An Indo-Iranian people in southeast Anatolia, probably related to the ancient Medes. Their ethnic identity is denied by the Turks.
Arabs 1.4% in South Anatolia adjoining Syria.
Muslim minorities 1.1%. Adygey 130,000; Laz 92,000; Georgian 90,000; Serbo-Croat 61,000; Albanian 61,000; Bulgarian 27,000; Gypsy 20,000, all of whom are being rapidly absorbed into the Turkish majority.
Non-Muslim minorities 0.3%. Armenian 60,000; Assyrian 25,000; Greek 8,000. Rapid decline through emigration. Note religious graph. There were 1,750,000 Armenians and 1,500,000 Greeks in Turkey in 1900.
Refugees 1%. Iranis 600,000; Central Asians poss. 50,000 from USSR and Afghanistan.

Literacy 62%. **Official language**: Turkish. **All languages** 29. **Bible translations** 7Bi 2NT 11por.

Capital: Ankara 2,300,000. Other major cities: Istanbul (Constantinople) 5,500,000; Izmir (Smyrna) 1,500,000; Adana 780,000; Bursa 620,000. Urbanization 45%. Rapid growth of cities with huge slum areas in which 65% of Ankara's population and 45% of Istanbul's live.

Economy: Political instability and social unrest together with world recession led to economic crises between 1973 and 1983. Steady recovery since then, but the land is only partially industrialized. Remittances from Turks in Europe are an important source of foreign exchange. Income/person $1,230 (9% of USA). Inflation (50% in 1984) and unemployment are high.

Politics: The Turkish Ottoman Empire once stretched across North Africa, Arabia, Western Asia and Southeast Europe. Its demise and final fragmentation in World War I led to revolution and the formation of a republic in 1923. Periods of social disorder and military rule gave way to a democratic government in 1983, but with the military still retaining considerable power. Turkey is a member of NATO, but is in dispute with fellow-NATO member Greece for long-standing historic reasons and over territorial rights in the Aegean Sea and the division of Cyprus.

Religion: Turkey's Ottoman Empire was for centuries the guardian of all the holy places of Islam and its chief protaganist. Since the sweeping reforms of the 1920s Turkey has officially been a secular state. In recent years Islam has become a more important political factor, making the lot of non-Muslim minorities more difficult despite the constitutional guarantee of religious freedom.
Muslim 99.5%. Sunni Muslims 85%. Alevi Shi'a 14% predominantly among Kurds. There are also Yezidis (a divergent syncretic sect) among the Kurds.
Christian 0.3%. Rapid decline. Almost entirely confined to national and foreign minorities.

Orthodox 0.23%. 120,000a. Denominations 10. Largest (adherents):

Armenian Orthodox Church		60,000
Greek Orthodox Church	(?)	23,000
Assyrian Orthodox Church		5,000

Roman Catholic 0.02%. 15,000a. Predominantly foreign residents and Assyrians.

Protestant 0.02%. 13,100a; 4,500m. Predominantly foreign residents and Armenians.

Evangelical — only about 750 indigenous believers, mostly Armenian, Assyrian and Greek. Maybe 250 believers from a Muslim background.

Foreign Christians serving in Turkey approx. 100 (1:500,000 people).

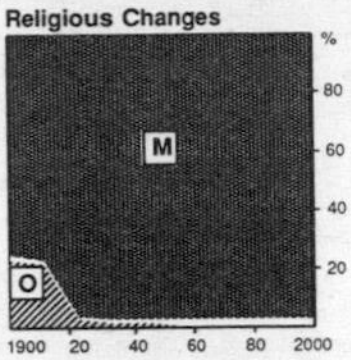

1. **Turkey is the largest unreached nation in the world.** Ironically Paul, the first great missionary to the Gentile world, came from Tarsus, and much of his early ministry was in what is now Turkey. Fifty million completely unevangelized people need to hear the gospel somehow and soon.

2. **Islamic fundamentalists** are applying strong pressure on the authorities to take a harder, and unconstitutional line against believers to hinder witnessing and Christian outreach. Pray that both the courts and state may uphold the laws protecting religious freedom.

3. **The barriers to the gospel appear insurmountable**:
   a) **History**. Turkey's long association with Islam and bitter wars with "Christian" European nations make conversion appear almost an act of treachery.
   b) **Culture**. To be a Turk is to be a Muslim, even if nominally so. Family pressure is usually acute on any who want to follow Christ. Every conversion to Christ is a miracle of grace.
   c) **Attitude**. A deep-seated resistance in the general public to anything Christian makes any form of witnessing difficult. A radical change in public attitudes must be prayed for.
   d) **Wrong understandings**. Evangelical Christians are lumped together with Armenian terrorists and Jehovah's Witnesses. Muslim misconceptions about Christian doctrine are also a major barrier.
   e) **The god of this world** has blinded them. In the name of Jesus we can pray for supernatural illumination!

4. **The Christian Church** as a whole is in decline, largely because of heavy emigration, but the number converted out of Islam is rising. Most Christians are nominal, introspective and are not evangelizing. The majority live in Istanbul. There are only about 700 known evangelical believers in the country, most of these being non-Turkish. Pray for a renewing work of the Spirit in Orthodox Catholic and the small Protestant groups. Some outstanding Christian leaders have come from these groups.

5. **The infant Turkish Church** needs much undergirding in prayer.
   a) Praise the Lord that there are eight or so small groups of believers in five areas. In 1960 there were less than 10 known believers from a Muslim background; now there may be 250.
   b) **There is only one functioning Turkish-led church.** There are five Turkish full-time workers, but most are ministering in other lands. Pray for mature indigenous leadership.
   c) **The rate of backsliding** is disconcertingly high. Family and social pressures on a new convert are intense. Most new believers go through a severe identity crisis on coming to Christ. Pray for perseverance, growth and development of warm, protective fellowships where there is also a greater reality and joy in worship!
   d) **Immaturity** is shown in personality clashes, doctrinal disputes and strong ethnic loyalties which have brought divisions and failure. Pray for a greater unity and trust among the brethren and for a greater liberty in worship and witness. Fear of man holds many back.
   e) **Emigration** is often a way out: to escape persecution, or to find a marriage partner; or else to find an adequate opportunity for public ministry. A strong, growing Church must become a reality in Turkey.

6. **Missionary work** began in 1821, but was soon directed to the more receptive non-Muslim minorities. Since 1960 renewed prayer and effort is slowly yielding fruit among the Muslims. Diverse means are employed. Pray for:

a) **Those called**, equipped and gifted for tentmaking ministries in this land where vital opportunities to share one's faith are hard to find.

b) **The right tentmaking opportunities** and strategy that will enable the whole country to be exposed to the gospel. Most are engaged in teaching, study or business.

c) **The right relationship** with indigenous believers — too many foreigners in an area can stifle the development of mature leadership.

d) **Acceptance, protection and fruitfulness** in a ministry where tensions, insecurity and discouragement abound.

e) **Short-term teams** of young people distributing literature — a major feature of present work. Great tact and courage are needed; "Christian propaganda" is an odious term.

f) **The 20 or so agencies** with a specific burden and calling to minister to Turks, and for the continuance of fruitful cooperation among them.

7. **Other means of witness** are profitably employed, and need prayerful support:

a) **Literature**. 3,500,000 pieces of literature have been distributed over the past few years in door-to-door work, postal evangelism, advertisements in the press, etc. Pray for fruit, and the development of effective ways of follow-up.

b) **Postal evangelism** through pen-pals, direct mail and correspondence courses has yielded a response. **Friends of Turkey** and other agencies are further developing this means of outreach. Pray that the postal system may function well and without interference.

c) **Radio outreach** in combination with literature distribution is generating a good response. **TWR** has 14 weekly programmes and **IBRA** two. Pray for favourable listening conditions and wide outreach. Pray, too, for the effectiveness of **TWR**'s Kurdish programmes.

d) **Ministry to the two million Turks** in Western Europe. Migrant labourers in Germany (1,550,000), France (160,000), Netherlands (150,000), Belgium (65,000), Switzerland (45,000) and Sweden (20,000) are far more accessible to Christian workers. A number of local churches and international agencies are seeking to evangelize them. Among such are **OM**, **WEC**, and **Orientdienst**. There are possibly 80 converted Turks as a result of this ministry. There is also a work among the 30,000 Turks in Australia. Pray for the multiplication of Turkish and Kurdish Christian groups in these areas and for these to make an impact on their homelands.

e) **Ministry among students** in Germany, USA and Britain.

f) **Use of audio-visual media**. Cassette and video tapes are valuable tools, but more good relevant materials must be produced and distributed. The film "Jesus" has been turned down by the censors; pray that this ruling may be changed and the Turkish version of the film widely seen.

8. **Unreached peoples**: The few Christian groups are almost all confined to the Istanbul and Syrian border areas. The rest of the country and its many cities and provinces are virtually without any witness. The capital has only 30 known believers; pray for 1,000 believers by 1990 — the goal for which many are trusting. Specific minorities for prayer:

a) **The Kurds**: there may be only two to three believers in Turkey, and no outreach in their own languages. Pray both for the penetration of their mountain homeland and expatriate Kurdish communities in Europe and North America with the gospel. Many follow the Alevi teachings, which give high regard to the Lord Jesus Christ, and are only nominal Muslims.

b) **The ethnic Muslim minorities** listed above. None have been evangelized in their own tongue; many are living in communities separated from the mainstream of national life.

c) **The Iranis** have been streaming over the border to flee the war and radical Islam in their homeland. Most are too poor and ignorant of other languages to emigrate elsewhere. No one is reaching them.

d) **The Central Asian refugees** from Communism; many from the unevangelized areas of the USSR and Afghanistan. There are Uzbeks, Kazakhs, Kirghiz, Tatars, Turkmen, etc.

9. **Bible translation**: Two versions of the Turkish NT are nearing completion — each for a different readership. Work on a new OT translation has yet to begin. Pray for all involved in translating, checking, printing and distributing the Word of God, and for these translations to have a deep and abiding impact on the people. There is work in progress in 11 minority dialects too.

10. **Christian literature** may be legally written, printed and distributed, but negative publicity, official intimidation, obstructionism and restrictions make life difficult for all involved. There is only one Christian bookstore in the country. The small number of Turkish Christian book titles is steadily being augmented. Pray for greater freedom to distribute literature; restrictions make life difficult for all.

TURKS AND CAICOS ISLANDS

(Colony of Turks and Caicos Islands)

Caribbean

See British Antilles on p. 115.

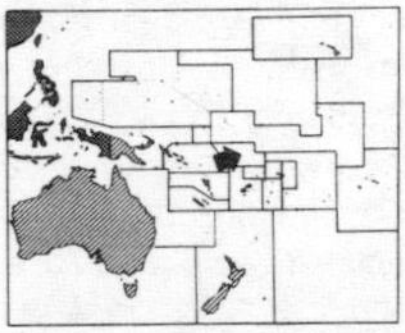

TUVALU

(The State of Tuvalu)

Pacific

Oct 29

Area 26 sq.km. Nine main islands south of Kiribati in the Central Pacific.

Population 8,000. Annual growth 1.3%. People per sq.km. 308.

Peoples: Polynesian 96%, **Micronesian** 2%, **Other** 2%.

Literacy 95%. **Official language:** English.

Capital: Fongatela 900.

Economy: Main export is postage stamps!

Politics: Formerly Ellice Islands. Independent from Britain in 1978 as a parliamentary monarchy.

Religion: Strongly Protestant; other religions not granted freedom until 1964.

Baha'i 5.3%.

Christian 94.7%.

Roman Catholic 1%. 80a.

Marginal groups (1) 2.3%. 180a.

Protestant 91.5%. 7,320a. All of the Tuvalu Church (LMS), but for a small group of Seventh Day Adventists.

Evangelical 4% of population.

Missionaries to Tuvalu 0.

Points for prayer: See Kiribati on p. 267.

UGANDA
(Republic of Uganda)

Africa

Oct 30-31

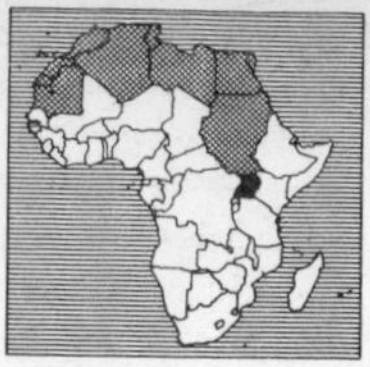

Area 236,000 sq.km. Much of the land is fertile and well watered. The climate is temperate in the highlands. Long known as the "Pearl of Africa".

NOTE. All following statistics are reasonable estimates; the anarchy and devastation since 1967 having been so great that accurate statistics are not available.

Population 14,700,000. Annual growth 3.5%. People per sq.km. 62. No one can estimate with accuracy the numbers who perished during Amin's dictatorship, and the subsequent civil wars, famines and tribal killings. Estimates vary from 800,000 to 2,000,000; 300,000 of these have been since 1981. Many more have fled into Kenya, Sudan and Zaire.

Peoples. Over 40 ethnic groups; three major divisions:
Bantu 65% (over 16 groups, mainly in west, southwest and south): Ganda 2,350,000; Ankole 1,200,000; Soga 1,175,000; Chiga 1,040,000; Toro-Nyoro 910,000; Nyaruanda 860,000; Luhya 400,000; Rundi 300,000; Konjo 250,000; Gwere 240,000, etc.
Nilotic 27% (12, mainly in the north and centre): Teso 1,220,000; Lango 800,000; Acholi 630,000; Karamajong 300,000; Alur 280,000; Padhola 230,000; Kakwa 90,000, etc.
Sudanic 6.4% (over 10): Lugbara 544,000; Madi 176,000, etc.
Other 1.6%. Kenyans, etc.

Literacy 40%. **Official language**: English, spoken by about 10% of the population. **All languages** 43. **Bible translations** 16Bi 3NT 10por.

Capital: Kampala 500,000. Urbanization 14%.

Economy: The fertility of the soil could have provided a healthy economic future. The expulsion in 1972 of the Asian community, who had played such a vital role in the economy, and the chaos in the years following, have reduced the land to poverty. Many areas have been laid waste by marauding soldiers — especially in the West Nile District and Luwero Triangle northwest of Kampala. Income/person $560 (4% of USA).

Politics: Independence from Britain in 1962. An attempt at delicately balancing the political powers of the southern Bantu kingdoms and northern Nilotic peoples ended in 1967, when the Northerner Milton Obote took complete control, favouring his own tribe, the Lango. Anarchy increased until Idi Amin seized power in 1971. The crazed dictatorship of Amin brutalized the country as the army pillaged and murdered with impunity. Amin's invasion of northwest Tanzania in 1978 provoked a vigorous response, and in 1979 Tanzanian and Ugandan exile troops deposed the military regime. Sadly, bitter tribal and political rivalries have continued with much bloodshed. The once prosperous southern peoples have suffered particularly through political isolation and military repression since 1979.

Religion: Under Amin there were restrictions and intense persecution of Christians (often for reasons of tribalism). For a time the Muslim minority was favoured. There is now freedom of religion. Most figures below are rough estimates:
Traditional religions 12%. Throughout the country, but only in a majority in four or five northeastern peoples, the Karamajong, Pokot, etc.
Muslim 5%. Most live in the northwest, but there are some sprinkled all over the country. No group has a Muslim majority, but there are large minorities among the Kakwa, Madi and Soga. Somewhat discredited since the fall of Amin.
Baha'i 2.8%.
Christian 80%. Nominal 9%, affiliated 71%.
- **Roman Catholic** 42.3%. 6,211,000a; 3,540,000m.
- **Orthodox** 0.14%. 20,000a.
- **African Indigenous Churches** 0.9%. 130,000a; 71,000m.
- **Protestant** 27.6%. 4,068,000a; 1,010,000m. Largest (adherents):

Anglican Ch. (CMS, **BCMS, AIM**)	3,700,000
Pentecostal Assemblies of God	(?) 80,000
Elim Pentecostal Fellowship	(?) 60,000
Church of the Redeemed	(?) 50,000
Baptist Union (**SBC, CBFMS**)	30,000

- **Evangelicals** 24.9% of population.

Missionaries to Uganda 190 (1:77,000 people) in 28 agencies.
Missionaries from within Uganda (?) 100. Many are exiles serving the Lord in other lands.

Religious Changes

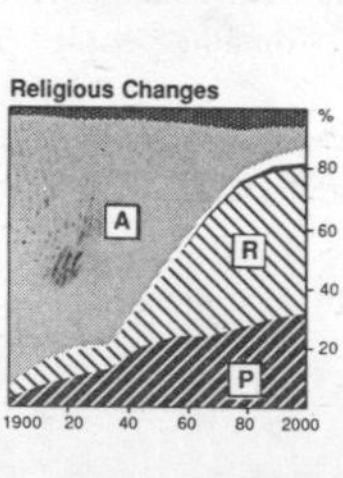

Evangelical Changes

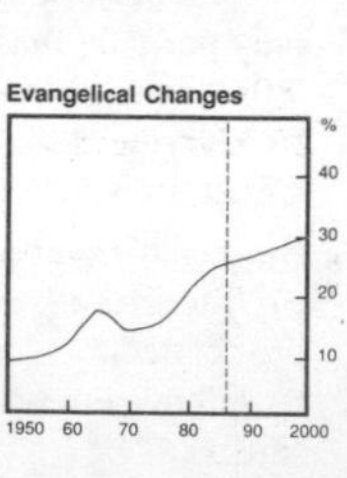

1. **Pray for the government.** The economic and moral devastation caused by 20 years of unrestrained murder, tribal hatreds, and corruption have left a legacy of deep bitterness. Only deep spiritual transformation can bring about an effective, lasting reconciliation and reconstruction.

2. **The persecution of Christians** during Amin's reign of terror was a dark time. Nominalism, formalism and failure to check tribalism in the churches prevented the Church from unitedly standing up for the right. The result was the destruction of many churches and institutions, the loss through death and exile of some of Uganda's finest Christian leaders, and heavy loss of life among Christians. Pray that:

   a) **There may be true reconciliation among Christians.** The sharp divisions between Protestant and Catholic, revived and non-revived, charismatic and non-charismatic have not been a credit to the gospel.

   b) **Christians** may be used to bring healing to the nation and salvation to men. Pray that evangelism and discipleship might be the priority.

   c) **Reconstruction** of fellowships, institutions, and church buildings may take place. Nearly all interdenominational and denominational groups were banned during the period 1973-77.

   d) **Ministry to the suffering may not be neglected.** Most congregations have a heavy burden to bear. There are reported to be 800,000 orphans and many widows.

3. **Praise God for revival and growth.** The East African Revival is now 50 years old, but still very much alive. The recent sufferings have led to deeper commitment, earnest prayer and renewed outbursts of revival. Charismatic, Pentecostal and Baptist groups have experienced good growth during the '80s.

4. **Ugandan missionary vision** has been expanded through exiled leaders and movements of refugees. Pray that the Ugandan believers may continue to develop missionary concern and send out workers to serve in other lands. Especially needy is nearby southern Sudan.

5. **The Refugees.** The ebb and flow of refugees within Uganda and to and from neighbouring lands has been enormous. There were estimated to be 800,000 Ugandan refugees in 1983. Pray for:

   a) **Stable political conditions** to help resettlement.

   b) **Aid** to enable the destitute to re-establish family life and a reasonable living standard. Many Christian aid programmes are involved; **TEAR Fund, WVI, AE,** Mennonites, etc.

   c) **Banyarwanda refugees** on the Rwanda-Uganda border. About 80,000 live in squalid camps and are rejected by both governments. Their economic status and long-term future is bleak.

6. **Christian leadership** for the growing Church is a pressing need. Many pastors bear responsibility for numerous congregations. Bible schools and seminaries will have to be re-equipped and staffed. Pray for the return and reintegration of former exiled leaders into the life of the churches.

7. **The return of missionaries has been welcomed.** Uganda needs everything! The dominance of Western agencies belongs to the past, so pray for a close fellowship between expatriates and Ugandan believers and the calling of those eager to serve the Church in reconstruction, development, Bible training and other ministries.

8. **Unreached peoples** are not many in this well-evangelized, but suffering land. Pray for:

   a) **The N.E. peoples** — Karamajong (300,000), Pokot (40,000), Jie (45,000) who are only partially reached nomadic peoples. They suffered particularly severely in the early '80s through famine.

   b) **Communities of Muslims** scattered across the country. Quite a number are coming to Christ. Pray for Ugandan believers to have an effective outreach to them.

9. **Supportive agencies**

   a) **Literature** is greatly lacking; adequate printing, publishing and distribution networks are needed.

   b) **Bible translation** is still needed in up to 10 languages, and progress is being made in 7 (**UBS**).

c) **Gospel recordings** have messages available in 32 languages and dialects.

d) **Students. FOCUS (IFES)** is very much alive and growing, but there is only one staff worker. Makerere University has a large FOCUS group. The vision is for a FOCUS group on every one of the 80 college campuses by 1990. **SU** has had a vital input to secondary school students.

e) **Christian radio programmes** on Uganda radio are being expanded, and are much appreciated. Pray for an effective ministry.

Nov 1-6

USSR
(Union of Soviet Socialist Republics)

Eastern Europe

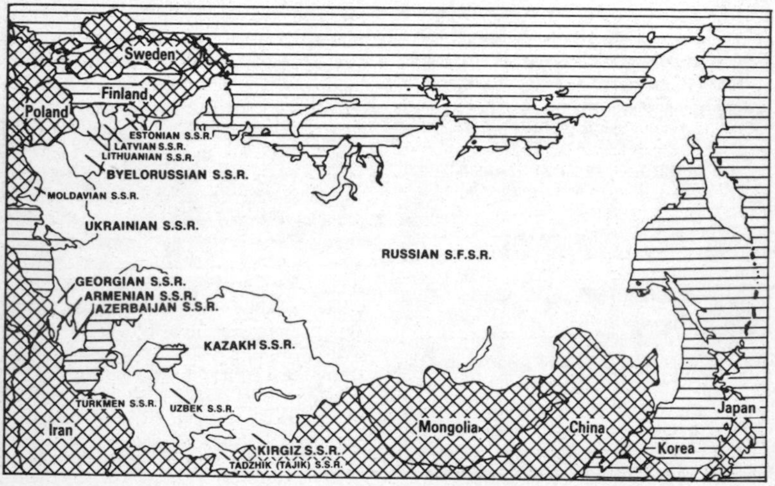

Area 22,402,000 sq.km. The world's largest country; nearly 11,000 km. from east to west and 4,000 km. from north to south. The USSR straddles 11 time zones. 24% of the USSR lies in Europe and 76% in Asia (Siberia).

Population 278,000,000. Annual growth 1%. People per sq.km. 12.5. The Slavic population is almost static, but some groups, particularly the Turkic peoples of Central Asia, are growing at over 3%. Large areas are uninhabited. 25% of the population lives in Siberia.

Peoples: An extraordinary mosaic of peoples came under Russian domination over the past several centuries. There are approximately 154 ethnic groups.

Indo-European 78.2%.

Slavic 72.8% (8 peoples). Russian 138,000,000; Ukrainian 43,000,000; Byelorussian 10,000,000; Polish 1,150,000.

Baltic 1.6%. Lithuanian 3,020,000; Latvian 1,518,000.

Iranian 1.3% (12 peoples). Tajik 3,400,000; Talysh 150,000; Kurdish 140,000.

Other 2.8%. Armenian 4,500,000; Romanian (Moldavian) 3,260,000; German 2,040,000; Ossetian 590,000; Greek 360,000; Gypsy (Jati, Romany) 337,000.

Altaic 16.5%.

Turkic 16% (24 peoples). Uzbek 15,000,000; Kazakh 7,800,000; Tatar 7,400,000; Azeri 6,500,000; Turkmen 2,430,000; Kirghiz 2,290,000; Chuvash 1,900,000; Bashkir

1,500,000; Karakalpak 350,000; Yakut 350,000; Crimean Turks 330,000; Uighur 250,000; Kumyk 226,000; Karachay 225,000; Tuvin 200,000; Gagauz 200,000.

Caucasian 2.5% (33 peoples). Georgian 3,900,000; Chechen 800,000; Avar 528,000; Kabardian 420,000; Lezgin 415,000; Dargin 310,000; Ingush 200,000; Adygey (Circassian) 120,000; Lak 110,000.

Finno-Ugric 1.7% (17 peoples). Mordvin 1,300,000; Estonian 1,100,000; Udmurt 770,000; Mari 670,000; Komi 500,000; Hungarian 180,000; Karelian 145,000.

Mongolian etc. 0.28% (12 peoples). Buryat 390,000; Kalmyk 160,000.

Jews 0.7%. About 1,900,000, but some estimate the number at double this due to strong pressures by the authorities to Russify them.

Other 0.16%. Over 10 other Siberian peoples totalling 31,000; Chinese 55,000; Korean 400,000.

Literacy 99%. It was 25% before the revolution. **Official language**: Russian spoken as first language by 56% of the population. Local languages are officially recognized in the various constituent SSRs and Autonomous Regions. Sixty-five languages are recognized as literary languages for use in the media. **All languages** 138. **Bible translations** 25Bi 5NT 34por.

Capital: Moscow 8,600,000. Other major cities: Leningrad 5,000,000; Kiev 2,500,000; Tashkent 2,100,000; Baku 1,700,000; Kharkov 1,600,000. There are 26 cities with populations over one million. Urbanization 64%.

Economy: Highly centralized socialist economy, with very little private ownership. The 'command' economy is both cumbersome and inefficient. Vast mineral wealth as well as an extensive agricultural output make the USSR the world's leading producer of wheat, butter, iron ore etc. The extremes of climate and collectivized agriculture make for low and erratic production figures. Over 15% of the nation's resources are spent on the armed forces. Income/person $6,350 (45% of USA).

Politics: The USSR came into being following the Bolshevik revolution in 1917. A federative socialist state consisting of 15 republics. The degree of autonomy of the constituent states is more nominal than actual. The government is led and dominated by the Soviet Union's Communist Party with its Marxist-Leninist ideology. The USSR sees itself as part of a world system that is in competition with the capitalist system and will sooner or later prevail over it. The former is probably the strongest military power on earth, but the criticism of the intellectuals, and restiveness of the numerous national minorities and the peoples of the East European satellite states is perceived as a continual threat to the stability of the country.

Religion: Marxism-Leninism is the official state ideology, of which atheism is an inseparable part. The strong opposition of the Communist Party to any religion makes mockery of the constitutional right of a citizen to profess a faith. There have been periods of severe persecution, with the closure of most churches, and imprisonment and murder of church leaders and believers. Persecution continues today, and is particularly severe against all who do not comply with the demands of the authorities. The state uses every means at its disposal to prevent evangelism and destroy the Church by rigid controls, discriminatory legislation, infiltration of agents, and also by intimidation and manipulation of church leadership even in the churches that have official recognition.

All statistics are estimates (possibly conservative). Even if the figures were accurately known it would be unwise to publicize them.

Non-religious/Atheist 52% and possibly up to 75%. For many, especially young people, it is inexpedient to profess any religion.

Muslim 18% ethnically; by profession around 12%; a large minority would claim to be atheist. Muslims are in the majority in six republics (Azerbaijan, Kazakhstan, Kirgizia, Tajikistan, Turkmenisten and Uzbekistan), nine autonomous republics and four autonomous regions. 75% of Muslims live in Soviet Central Asia adjoining Iran, Afghanistan and China. The majority are Sunni Muslim. The Azeri, Kurds and Talysh are Shi'a. Official Islam is government controlled by spiritual directorates in four different regions. There is a strong fundamentalist underground Islamic movement.

Jews 1.2%. Possibly over half are atheists. Two major groups: Western, and Eastern (Crimea, Georgia and Central Asia). They have suffered much persecution over the past 15 years, especially the many who have applied for emigration to Israel.

Shamanist 0.1%. Many of the smaller tribal peoples of N.Russia and Siberia are still animist — especially the Yakut, Chukchi, and also the Tungus and Samoyed peoples.

Buddhist 0.1%. The majority would not be practising Buddhists. Mahayana Buddhism among the Buryats, Kalmyks and Tuvinians. Some Koreans are also Buddhist. Officially recognized, but with a long history of repression by the Soviet authorities. Between 1933 and 1938 all 120 Buddhist monasteries were destroyed.

Christian 33%. Active adherents possibly 22%. Many are still baptized as children. Actual figures are only general estimates.

Orthodox 16.4%. 45,600,000a (?). Over 43 national or breakaway denominations. Largest (adherents):

Russian Orthodox	(?) 37,000,000
Armenian Orthodox	3,000,000
Georgian Orthodox	2,500,000
Other Orthodox groups	(?) 2,700,000

Roman Catholic 3.2%. 9,000,000a (?). Many Uniate Catholics have been compelled to be classified as Russian Orthodox.

Protestant 2.6%. 7,300,000a; 2,800,000m. Some officially sanctioned denominations, many unregistered groups, all totalling possibly 100. Largest (adherents):

AUCECB (registered)		3,000,000
Ev. Lutheran Ch. of Latvia		350,000
Ev. Lutheran Ch. of Estonia		250,000
Reformed Ch. of Transcarpathia		70,000
Other unregistered groups	(?)	1,500,000

Evangelical 2.5% of population. Higher if evangelical Orthodox and Catholic included.

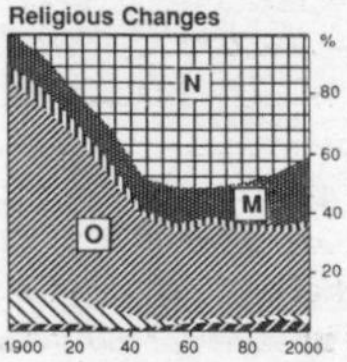

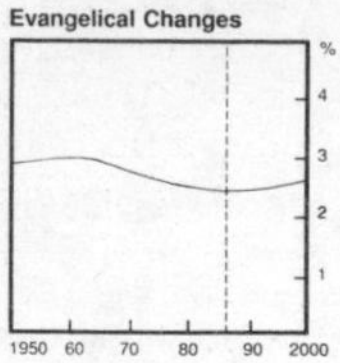

1. **The Church in USSR has suffered more severe and sustained persecution** than that of any nation in recent history. Yet there is much cause for praise:

a) **The survival and spiritual growth of the Church.** The steady drop in total numbers has been compensated by a corresponding increase in spirituality and commitment. There has been steady growth among Evangelicals; 100 years ago there were hardly any in Russia itself. There are a large number of deeply committed Orthodox and Catholic believers too.

b) **The bankruptcy of atheistic propaganda.** Enormous effort has been expended by the state to propagate atheism and discredit religion. The Marxist claim that the Church would wither away with the advent of Communism has not been fulfilled even with active efforts to destroy it. The proportion of believers steadily increases for many are converted as they grow older and become more disillusioned with atheism.

c) **The impact of radio** gospel programmes.

d) **The effectiveness of prison evangelism.** Christians imprisoned for their faith have been used in spreading the gospel to every corner of the land.

e) **The increasing worldwide concern** for the suffering Church and the needs of the many unreached peoples in the USSR.

f) **The evidence of spiritual awakenings** in some areas with many young people seeking the Lord. The Baltic States, Armenia and Central Asia are areas where revivals are reported.

2. **Specific churches** need prayer:

a) **The Orthodox Churches** survive under severe pressures such as the closure of 88% of all Russian Orthodox Churches, and infiltration of the leadership by agents of, or those prepared to compromise with, the atheist authorities. All spiritual leadership is severely repressed. Renewal has affected sections of the Orthodox Churches, but a moving of the Spirit is a great need. May the spiritual life existing be fanned to a flame and a biblical faith develop that will affect the whole land! The Georgian Orthodox Church has been reduced to 40 parishes, but the Armenian Orthodox Church has shown remarkable resilience, and over half the Armenians go to church regularly.

b) **The Roman Catholics** have suffered probably more than any other major ecclesiastical tradition. Most Catholics are now concentrated in Lithuania, Eastern Byelorussia and Western Ukraine. The Ukrainian Uniate Catholics have been savagely repressed.

c) **The Lutheran Churches** are predominantly national churches in the two Baltic States. The Russian occupation of these independent states in 1940 brought great suffering and years of persecution. There is an acute shortage of pastors. Many German-speaking people in the Volga region and Central Asia are also Lutheran.

d) **The Registered AUCECB** is a government-engineered union of Baptist, Brethren, Pentecostal and Mennonite churches that submitted to government restrictions, which, if rigidly enforced, make evangelical Christianity and effective outreach extremely difficult. In some areas the restrictions are not so rigidly enforced and congregations are packed. There are over 5,000 registered churches with 300 full-time and 30,000 part-time preachers. Official membership is 500,000, but is considerably higher in reality. Pray for the easing of restrictions, encouragement of believers, growth in grace of leaders and effectiveness in witnessing despite the limitations.

e) **The Unregistered Baptists and Pentecostals** have grown prolifically and have suffered intensely because of their refusal to compromise. In some areas the persecution has been particularly severe and the KGB (secret police) is very much in control of the situation. The majority of the present leadership is in prison or exile. Pray for:

i) **A new generation of younger leaders** to emerge.

ii) **Those in prison, also their families and children who suffer so much.** Maybe 400 leaders of the unregistered Baptists are behind bars in the infamous Gulags. Many Christian organizations in the West have details of such martyrs and their families for prayer and communication of letters of encouragement.

iii) **The "council of prisoners' relatives"**, which is a group of Christian women and relatives, formed in 1964 to inform the world of those who suffer for their faith. They are subject to much harassment and intimidation by the authorities, and need prayer.

iv) **The continued growth and multiplication of the churches**, and the conversion of persecutors and informers.

3. **Persecution is a very real factor for believers.** It takes many forms:

a) **Constant propaganda** and crude attempts at conversion to Communism at school, work and at home. Pray for believers to stand firm.

b) **Discrimination** in education, job opportunities and housing condemn many believers to a life of privation and poverty.

c) **Ambiguous legislation** which enables heavy fines and sentences to be handed down by courts for "criminal" activities.

d) **Psychiatric treatment.** To many atheists, those with a religious belief suffer from mental illness. Pray for believers suffering in such "hospitals" — some estimate that around 1,000 prisoners of conscience are being maltreated in this way.

e) **Imprisonment.** About 10,000 Christians are believed to have been sent to Siberian "gulags" or exiled for their faith. During the terrible purges in Stalin's rule during the '30s it is believed millions perished. Pray for those suffering because of their Christian testimony. Pray also for:

i) **Information** which is constantly needed in the West if help is to be given. Pray for the successful flow of reliable facts, dates and figures about imprisoned Christians and other acts of persecution.

ii) **Action by foreign governments** to protest more vigorously about the abuse of human rights by the violation of Christians' constitutional rights. The level of pressure on Christians has been steadily increasing during the '80s. The new Soviet leader Gorbachev promised to achieve that which his predecessors had failed to accomplish — to do away with the church and religion.

iii) Action by humanitarian and Christian organizations to press for changes for individuals and to the system. **Amnesty International** and **Keston College** in the UK have a good record in this.

iv) Alleviation of the persecution, and thwarting of the far-reaching plans of the authorities to extinguish the light of the gospel. The gates of Hell will not prevail . . .!

4. **The training of leaders is extremely difficult**, and almost impossible by normal means. Pray for:

a) **The Orthodox seminaries.** There are three Russian Orthodox seminaries and two academies with 2,500 students. There is also one Georgian and one Armenian seminary. Government control of the curriculum and student selection is tight. Pray that students may meet with God in their studies.

b) **Protestant institutions**: the Lutheran seminary in Tallinn, Estonia, is the only functioning one.

c) **The effective use of unorthodox means** of training by unregistered groups, in spite of the lack of Bible teachers, teaching materials, good Christian books, etc., which is a serious problem. Pray for the provision of both the means and teaching programmes being attempted through radio, TEE, etc.

5. **Young people and children** are singled out for abuse, mockery and harassment if they follow their parents in believing and refuse to join the Communist youth groups. It is illegal for parents to teach their own children about the Lord, or for churches to allow those under 18 to attend services. Pray for:

a) **The unity and preservation of Christian families.**

b) **Children placed in orphanages** after being removed from believing families. There are numerous cases of mothers and fathers being deprived of their parental rights.

c) **The courageous believers who do teach young people about the Lord.**

d) **Literature and radio programmes** specifically prepared to meet the spiritual needs of young people and children.

e) **Christian young men** who have to do their military service on leaving school. Some are subjected to severe persecution, many are sent to dangerous or inhospitable areas; many being put in the front line in Afghanistan, where the death toll has been high.

6. **Christian printing presses** have multiplied in the USSR despite the energetic efforts of the KGB. The work is dangerous; supplies are difficult to obtain and home-made presses hard to construct. Pray for those involved, and for their protection. There are reckoned to be only three million Bibles in the USSR.

7. **Missionary work in the USSR** is a vital necessity with so many unreached areas and peoples. Pray for:

a) **The Church in the USSR** to gain a vision and understanding of the need and opportunities among the peoples of Muslim, Buddhist and animist background. Survival has often taken precedence over cross-cultural evangelism.

b) **Christian students from other lands**. Many students have been sent by more socialist governments from Africa, Asia and the Americas to study in the USSR. Those known to be Christians can be isolated and subjected to a barrage of propaganda; yet in the midst of it all, they can be effective witnesses. Pray for many committed believers from all over the world to use the increasing variety of study programmes as a means of sharing their faith.

c) **Tourist missionaries**. Many possibilities for ministry in personal evangelism, encouragement of believers and conducting seminars on cross-cultural evangelism exist. However this will demand a high level of commitment and hard work in preparation among those called to such an exacting ministry.

d) **Agencies committed to evangelism** through literature, radio, cassettes, etc., and to encouraging the Church and those who suffer for their faith. Great wisdom, sensitivity and ingenuity are needed to be both effective and protective of the existing believers. Pray for the right balance among the agencies between cooperative fellowship and isolationist confidentiality. There have been conflicts and competition in the areas of finance, strategy and security.

8. **Islam's political power** was broken in the clash with Communism. There is a spiritual vacuum created by atheistic education, and an openness to the gospel never hitherto seen. Pray for breakthroughs in this bloc of people, probably the least accessible and least reached on earth. Pray also for the right ways of bringing the gospel to them:

a) **Through local believers**; mostly Russian and German. Helpful literature on how to reach Muslims is being translated and prepared, and evangelistic literature written.

b) **Through radio and literature**, but there are so few believers, and even fewer who are accessible enough to help in preparing programmes or literature.

c) **Through prayer mobilization** around the world.

9. **Numerous unreached Muslim peoples exist** despite the presence of a vibrant, growing Church among them. No real missionary work by Protestants has ever been permitted, and only among some peoples have Protestant churches become significantly numerous — especially in the Baltic States, and among the Germans, Karelians and Hungarians. Many other minorities remain virtually untouched — even when there are churches of other ethnic groups among them. Pray for the 33 Muslim peoples numbering nearly 50 million.

a) **Uzbeks,** most of whom live in Uzbekistan where they constitute almost 70% of the population. They are the USSR's largest Muslim group; only 30 or so believers are known among the 15 million Uzbeks.

b) **Kazakhs** (Sunni Muslims), many still semi-nomadic. There may be but 10 or so believers among the 7,800,000 Kazakhs.

c) **Kirghiz.** All are Muslim, three to five known believers among the 2,290,000 Kirghiz.

d) **Turkmen.** All but a handful are Muslim among 2,430,000 Turkmen.

e) **Tajiks** are related to the Persians, but are Sunni Muslims. Only a handful of believers are known.

f) **Azeri** in Azerbaijan are Shi'a Muslims. There are four known believers in the USSR; there are a few more in neighbouring Iran.

g) **Caucasus peoples** who are Muslim: Avars, Kabardians, Ingush, Adygey, Cherken, Abazar and Ossetians. No known churches among any but the Ossetians.

h) **Tatars and Bashkir** are the most northerly Muslim peoples in the world. Some are Orthodox Christians, but few are evangelical believers.

Non-Muslim unreached peoples:

a) **The Jews** are rediscovering their ethnic roots, but have been steeped in atheism. Pray that they may find their Messiah. 260,000 have emigrated to Israel and USA since 1968 where they can more easily be reached.

b) **The Siberian peoples** — numerous small Turkic, Samoyed and Tungku peoples have only had a superficial exposure to Christianity.

c) **The diverse peoples of the Caucasus** — a medley of languages and religions, many of whom have never been evangelized in their own tongue.

d) **The Buryat, Kumyk and Tuvinian** peoples have a Buddhist heritage, and are scarcely touched by the gospel. The Kumyks are the only indigenous Buddhist people in Europe.

10. **Assistance from the Free World.** Praise God that there are over 100 agencies outside the USSR seeking to bring relief to the Russian, German and other churches of the Soviet Union. Pray for:

a) **The provision and distribution of Bibles**; in many areas the shortages are extreme. On average it is reckoned that there is only one Bible for every 25 believers. Some come from the West, others are printed secretly in the USSR.

b) **The production and dissemination of good Christian literature** — hymn books, devotional and pastoral material, and literature for children are the great needs.

c) **Couriers** who require both wisdom and ingenuity as they travel and seek to supply some of the need. Many miracles are called for daily. Some travellers have been imprisoned for spreading "seditious" literature. This is in contravention of the USSR's signature to the UN Charter and Helsinki agreement concerning religious freedom.

11. **Bible translation** is an urgent necessity. Nearly half the population speaks Russian as a second language and 47 million cannot speak it at all. Only 64 of the 138 languages have even a portion of God's Word, and some of these are archaic, out of print, or in a script no longer used. This is a major challenge! Pray that the Bible might be made available in every language in the USSR. Plans are under way to have the NT ready in 1990 for all but two of the languages with more than one million speakers; the strategic NTs being those in Uzbek, Kazakh, Tatar, Turkmen, Kirghiz, Mari and Ossetian. Various agencies in the West are involved. Pray especially for the Institute for Bible Translation in Sweden with a remarkable ministry as co-ordinators in reprinting old, and translating new, portions and NTs in over 40 Soviet languages. The greatest bottleneck is finding believing translators and helpers among the non-Christian minorities.

12. **Christian radio** has been an exciting success story. Pray for:

a) **The 10 or more Christian stations** that ring the USSR; important ones being **FEBC** Manila, **HCJB** Ecuador, **TWR** Monaco. There is one short-wave radio for every two people in the USSR, and millions listen! Yet the ministry is expensive, and spiralling costs must be met to continue the ministry. Some reckon that over one million people have come to faith in Christ through this means.

b) **Those preparing radio programmes** need a deep understanding of the different cultures and intimate knowledge of the languages. Such are hard to find! This is especially true for the Central Asian Muslim peoples. Pray for the raising up of such individuals.

Pray also for **IBRA** Radio and other programming agencies, the former having a major input into the USSR by means of transmitting stations of **TWR**, Radio Trans-Europe in Portugal and Radio Mediterran in Malta. Programmes prepared by Earl Poysti are reputed to have an average audience of three to four million! Pray for conversions, planting of churches and edification of believers.

c) **Soviet jamming** can be disruptive, but is only partially effective. Pray against this!

d) **Follow-up** is complicated and demanding. Pray for adequate personnel and mechanisms for meeting the spiritual needs of enquirers. Letters come through despite censorship.

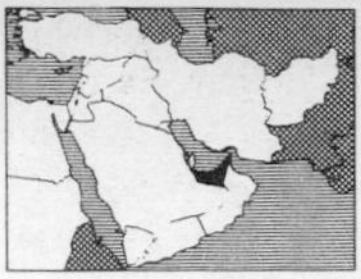

UNITED ARAB EMIRATES

(The United Arab Emirates)

Middle East

Nov 7

Area 84,000 sq.km. of desert and mountains on the Gulf coast of the Arabian Peninsula. Seven emirates: Abu Dhabi, Dubai, Sharjah (with large oil reserves) and Ras al Khaima, Ajmah, Umm al Qiwain and Fujaira (with no oil).

Population 1,300,000. Annual growth 2.3%. People per sq.km. 15. Massive legal and illegal immigration of expatriate workers until mid-'80s. Possibly only 12% of the population is native born.

Peoples
Arab 37%. Indigenous 12%(?), large numbers of Palestinians, Egyptians, Sudanese, Lebanese, Jordanians, etc.
Other migrant minorities 63%. Estimates: Iranis 325,000; Pakistanis 290,000; Indians 80,000; other Asians 55,000; all Westerners 50,000; Somalis 25,000, etc.

Literacy 26% among nationals, higher among expatriates. **Official language:** Arabic, but first language of only about 40% of population.

Capital: Abu Dhabi 150,000. Urbanization 81%.

Economy: Breathtaking advance from poverty to fabulous wealth in 20 years. Massive development schemes funded by oil wealth. Rate of growth has slowed since 1978. Income/person $21,340 (151% of USA).

Politics: The British protected Trucial States became a confederation of monarchies in 1971.

Religion: Islam is the official religion. Expatriate communities are free to worship and build churches, but non-Muslims are not allowed to proselytize. Statistics below are approximations.
Muslim 85%. Sunni 80%. Shi'a 20%.
Hindu/Buddhist etc. 6%. Indians, Sri Lankans, Thai.
Non-religious 2%. Mainly Westerners.
Christian 7%. Many nominal Christians.
- **Roman Catholic** 3.3%. 43,000a. Western, Arab, Filipino, Indian etc.
- **Orthodox** 1.4%. 18,000a. Arab, Indian.
- **Protestant** 2.3%. 29,900a. Numerous small groups and several church buildings of Anglicans, and independent Evangelical and Pentecostal expatriate groups.
- Expatriate Christian workers 45 (1:29,000 people).

1. **The radical changes of the last two decades** have made UAE citizens more cosmopolitan and open to new ideas. Many are in daily contact with foreigners and with all forms of media. Yet the effects of Islamic fundamentalism have increased restrictions on communicating the gospel. Pray for open doors and open hearts.

2. **Several Christian medical agencies** were invited in to serve the people; notably the **TEAM** hospital and clinic at El Ain, Worldwide Services and **MECO** maternity clinics in Fujaira and Sharjah. The continuance of these ministries is dependent on good relationships with the authorities. Christians serve in difficult conditions with little visible fruit. Pray that their faith for a harvest may be abundantly rewarded.

3. **Expatriate Christians** have considerable freedom for witness and worship. Pray for the various English, Arabic, Urdu and Indian language worship groups and congregations that meet. They need grace to evangelize their own ethnic groups in a materialistic society. They need even more grace to evangelize across cultural barriers to other unreached peoples.

4. **The unreached:**
   a) **The indigenous Arab population** — both urban educated and rural illiterate have had little exposure to the gospel. There is only a handful of believers among them.
   b) **The migrant Iranis,** Pakistanis and Iran Baluchi (60,000). Pathans, Somalis, Sudanese, Thai etc. have no known groups of believers among them.

5. **Media available for outreach** — several bookshops stock Christian literature. Video tapes can be widely used. The broadcasts from FEBA Seychelles reach the UAE. Pray for the effective use of all means to evangelize the wide variety of peoples and languages.

UNITED KINGDOM

(United Kingdom of Great Britain and Northern Ireland)

Area 244,000 sq.km. Two main islands: Britain and the northeast of Ireland. A union of four kingdoms: England 53%, Scotland 32.4%, Wales 8.5%, and Northern Ireland 5.8%. Also three small autonomous states which are dependencies of the British Crown: Isle of Man 588 sq.km. (island in the Irish Sea); Guernsey 78 sq.km. (five Channel Islands); Jersey 116 sq.km. (one Channel Island).

Population 56,600,000 of which England has 83.1%, Scotland 9.2%, Wales 5% and Northern Ireland 2.7%. Annual growth +0.1%. People per sq.km. 231.

Peoples

Indigenous Majorities 93%.

English 76%.	Predominantly Anglo-Saxon.
Scots 8%.	Anglo-Saxon and Gaelic.
Irish 5%.	Gaelic and Scots (including immigrants into Britain from the Irish Republic).
Welsh 4%	Predominantly Celtic.

Indigenous minorities 0.9%. Jews 410,000; Gypsies 85,000.

Immigrant minorities 6%.

South Asians 2.5%. Indian origin 700,000; Pakistani 250,000; Bangladeshi 200,000. Also refugees from East Africa 200,000.

West Indians 1.9%. From many Caribbean countries; almost all are Blacks.

Other 1.3%. Greeks 200,000; Italians 200,000; Arabs 150,000; Chinese 125,000; Africans 90,000; Turks 55,000; Vietnamese 20,000.

Literacy 95%. **Official language**: English; in Wales both English and Welsh. English has become the primary language of 700 million in the world, and become the major language of international communication. **All languages** 7 indigenous, many more immigrant languages (at least 128 in London alone). **Bible translations** in indigenous languages 4Bi 2por. There have been more translations of the Scriptures into English than in any other language.

Capital: London 10,100,000. Other major cities: Birmingham 2,800,000; Manchester 2,600,000; Bradford-Leeds 2,100,000; Glasgow 1,850,000; Liverpool 1,520,000; Newcastle-upon-Tyne 1,150,000. Urbanization 76%.

Economy: An industrialized economy — the world's first. Renewed economic growth in the '80s after years of decline through poor management, labour unrest, and the extent of public ownership in industry. The government has vigorously sought to rectify these with some success. Exploitation of North Sea oil has helped to stimulate recovery. High unemployment (13%) and continued industrial decline are causes for concern. Income/person $9,050 (64% of USA).

Politics: Parliamentary, constitutional monarchy. The UK was formed in 1801 as a Union of Great Britain and Ireland. Southern Ireland formally seceded from the Union in 1921. The British Empire which once covered one quarter of the world has become 60 independent states, most being members of the British Commonwealth. Since 1945 the transition from a world power to a European state linked to its own continent has not been easy. The UK is a member of NATO and of the EEC.

Religion: Complete religious freedom. The Church of England (Anglican) is recognized as the Established Church in England, and the Church of Scotland (Presbyterian) in Scotland. The Sovereign is recognized as the titular head of the Church of England.

Non-religious/Atheist: 26%. Many nominal "Christians" are actually secularists.

Muslim 2.7%. The actual number of Muslims is disputed, but is between 1 and 1.5 million, predominantly South Asians, but also Arabs, Turks, etc.

Jews 0.7%. Gradually declining.

Hindu 0.5%. **Sikh** 0.5%. Predominantly Indian.

Buddhist 0.2%. Chinese, etc.

Christian 69.4%. Nominal 20%. Affiliated 49.9%. Regular adult church attendance 11%; but with wide regional differences. See below:

Roman Catholic 9%. 5,100,000a; 2,315,000m. Predominantly lower class and many of Irish extraction. Highest percentage in northwest and London area.

Orthodox Churches 0.7%. 372,000a; 125,000m. Denominations 12. Predominantly Greek Cypriot, also many Eastern European refugee minorities.

Marginal 2.6%. 1,400,000a; 348,000m. Groups 14+. Largest (adult members):

Jehovah's Witnesses	97,945
Mormons	67,000
Spiritualist	53,000
Scientology	45,000

Protestant 48% including nominals. 31,200,000a; 4,900,000m. Many baptized Anglicans no longer attend church, hence the large adherent figure. Denominations 250+. Largest (adult members):

All Anglican/Episcopal (8)	2,058,000
All Presby./United Ref. (14)	1,483,000

All Methodists (6)		484,700
All Baptists (10+)		226,000
All "house" churches		120,000
All other Pentecostal Chs (15+)		95,000
Other independent Churches	(?)	85,000
All West Indian Ch's (numerous)		80,000
Brethren assemblies	(?)	65,000

Evangelical 7% of population.

Missionaries from within UK 5,800 (1:5,300 Protestants) in 102 agencies.

Missionaries to UK est. 580, increasingly so from the Third World and USA.

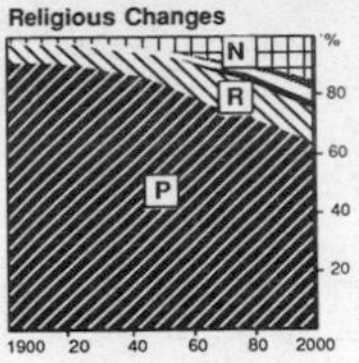

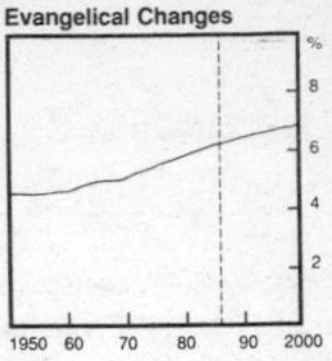

UK GENERAL

1. There is much for which to praise God:
   a) **The century-long** decline in church membership and attendances is slowing: many congregations are starting to grow, and there is an air of faith and expectancy that the long-awaited revival is round the corner. May it come; and may Britain become a spiritual blessing to the world!
   b) **Traumatic social change**, increasing violence and the breakdown of moral standards before the tide of secular humanism has shocked many to realize that something has gone seriously wrong. There is a willingness among young and old to consider the claims of Christ. Pray that millions may yield to Him! The campaigns of Billy Graham and Luis Palau during Mission England and Mission to London (1982-85) were respectfully received and fruitful. Effective church-based evangelism must become more important.
   c) **The renewal movement of the 1960s** brought radical changes to the ecclesiastical scene. Charismatic renewal has brought many hundreds of pastors and congregations from dead liberalism and traditionalism to lively worship and a love for the Bible. Many mainline churches have been affected, and a whole new family of fast-growing churches has come into being — often rather inappropriately named "house churches".
   d) **There is a new confidence among evangelical believers**. Decline is predominantly in non-evangelical congregations. Liberal theological institutions are nearly empty, and evangelical ones full to overflowing. An increasing minority of ministers in the Anglican Church and Church of Scotland are committed Evangelicals (approx. one-third of the total in each).

2. There is also much to stimulate earnest prayer:
   a) **Social breakdown** and increasing violence in the cities, divorce, drug abuse, immorality, and a helpless despair could take the country further down the road to disaster. Pray for a national repentance, and return to God that will once more restore this nation to the spiritual greatness that made it one of the greatest moral and spiritual forces in modern history. The government needs prayer that legislation may be both just and morally uplifting, and not passed for expediency.
   b) **The lack of concern of many evangelical believers for the spiritual and moral collapse around them.** Many believers are smugly ignorant of the stagnation and lack of outreach to the many without Christ and without hope. Revival is the need once more. There has been a national awakening every century for the last 800 years; the last was in 1859-60. Pray for a greater prayer burden to unite Christians to seek that blessing.
   c) **The influx of non-Christian religions**. Many of the spokesmen of Islam, Buddhism, etc. vociferously push for legislation that will favour their religions, and demand freedoms they would never grant Christians in their lands of origin. The mission field has come to Britain, but few stir themselves to win these people to Christ.

3. **Evangelical Christians** are growing in numbers. A much higher proportion of those going to church today are committed believers. The possibilities for faster growth through vigorous outreach are great, but too few believers have actively sought to befriend and witness to non-believers around them. Many of the fast-growing congregations are charismatic or Pentecostal in persuasion. Pray for:

a) **Unity in the Body**. There are many secondary issues that divide believers and denominations. The **Evangelical Alliance** has done much to encourage cooperative programmes, outreach and fellowship. **Mission England** (1982-85) was a time of drawing many believers together. Pray for effective cooperation in the future that will enable Evangelicals to reverse the moral slide of society, and win many to Christ.

b) **Increasing fervour and enthusiasm in worship has not been matched by a knowledge and understanding of the Scriptures**. Emotion rather than faith in the Scriptures can easily become a measure of spirituality. Pray for effective, balanced and yet faith-inspiring Bible teaching in the many growing congregations.

c) **A right balance between biblical separation and social involvement.** Too many Evangelicals turn a blind eye to the very real and serious social problems of the day. In the past Evangelicals have been the moving force for moral uplift and social change.

4. **The "house church" movement** or the **new churches** have rapidly grown to become a significant spiritual force in the nation. There are several different 'streams' within the movement. The worship style and teachings of these new churches are beginning to affect many older churches. Pray for:

a) A generosity of spirit for both the older and newer churches to listen to one another and learn for the upbuilding of the whole Body.

b) Further moderation of the over-authoritarianism that has been evident in some streams of the new churches.

c) Greater growth of the missionary vision for a lost world among all the groups in the movement, so that each one understands the need to break new ground, cross-cultural and racial barriers and take the gospel to the neglected peoples of this world.

5. **Theological training.** There is a shortage of trained pastors and Christian workers, but the great majority of those entering the ministry are evangelical believers. There are 108 denominational and interdenominational training institutions. Pray for many university theological departments and denominational theological colleges where liberal theology is often still taught — frequently to evangelical students. Pray also for the Bible schools such as: London Bible College, All Nations Christian College, Lebanon Missionary Bible College, Moorlands Bible College, Bible Training Institute in Glasgow, Birmingham Bible Institute, etc., where many are prepared for both home and overseas service.

6. **Young people** have been turning to the Lord in increasing numbers. Some churches and fellowships are predominantly made up of young people but, conversely, many of the more traditional churches have few. Young people flock in thousands to celebrations and conferences such as Greenbelt, Spring Harvest, the Dales Bible Week, etc. Pray for:

a) **Integration of young people into church life** and mobilization for service.

b) **Youth For Christ (YFC)** which has had a widespread impact across the country.

c) **Greater missionary vision**; few young people go to traditional missionary meetings, or have exposure to the challenge of an unreached world.

d) Those who go out on short-term missionary service with **OM, YWAM, Horizons**, etc., and pray that many may be called into full-time work as a result, as some have been already.

7. **Students** are exposed to great pressures in the secular education system. Many state schools have little religious activity, and much that there is, is formal and humanistic. A largely godless, materialistic, younger generation is being formed by it. Relatively few secondary schools have a live, outgoing witness from staff or from student groups. Pray for:

a) **The SU and Christian Union groups** in schools — for their growth and multiplication; and for Christian teachers to be used of God to help launch such groups.

b) **The campus Christian groups** among the 700,000 full-time students in colleges and universities. Their growth and diversity is encouraging, the main ones being: **CCC**, **Navigators**, and UCCF(**IFES**). The oldest and most widespread is the work of **UCCF** with **CUs** in nearly 600 colleges and universities, but a further 300 have no permanent group. Pray for mature, stable leadership, effective support and advice from the 35 travelling secretaries, and establishment of a viable witness in every college. The student population is one of the more receptive segments of society. The most difficult areas of ministry are the Polytechnics and the 190 scattered colleges in London.

8. **Missionary interest** has waned, and many congregations have never sent out their own missionary. There is a widespread conviction that either the job has been done, or that efforts should be concentrated on Britain's need. Pray for:

a) **A renewed commitment** by local congregations to world evangelization, to pray out their members to the areas of greatest need, and to adequately care for those who go.

b) **The 5,800 British Protestant missionaries** around the world, and that their numbers may be increased by dedicated long-term missionaries. About 26% of all UK missionaries are short-term workers.

9. **Unreached immigrant minorities**. Post-war immigration from the New Commonwealth (Third World states formerly ruled by Britain) on a large scale, brought in many ethnic minorities from lands that have had minimal exposure to the gospel, and where entry for missionaries is restricted or forbidden. Most have found homes in the larger inner cities; in Bradford 20% of the city is Asian. Pray for specific outreach efforts by:

a) **Local churches** — especially those in inner city areas surrounded by non-Christian minorities, but who have little vision and less preparation to make the effort to reach them. Many feel a sense of rejection by the indigenous majority, and have an unfavourably distorted view of Christianity. A number of agencies provide training for local churches for such outreach. Pray for those churches and City Missions who already have an active programme for evangelizing them.

b) **Teams of young people (OM, YWAM,** In Contact, etc.).

c) UCCF(**IFES**), **ISI** and others who arrange special training and outreach to the 71,000 **foreign university students**, and to many other foreign language students who come to Britain. About 20,000 of these are from Muslim lands, 15,000 are Chinese.

d) **Cross-cultural agencies** have committed workers to church planting and evangelism: **ECM** (33), **MECO** (25), **WEC** (12), **BMMF** (10), **IMI** (6), **RSMT** (5) and, increasingly, missions from non-Western countries. Pray for a better and more effective coordination and strategy to cover all the non-Christian minorities. Many towns and cities have totally unreached minorities.

e) **Literature**. Several Christian bookstores specifically stock materials for Asians (**CLC**, etc). ***SOON* gospel broadsheets** are produced in large numbers in English, French, Hindi, Urdu, Punjabi and Arabic (**WEC**).

Specific groups for prayer:

i) **The Muslim minority** has grown fast through a high immigration and birthrate. The majority are South Asians, and also many Arabs, Turks, etc. Also about 5,000 British have been converted to Islam. Muslim communities have become highly organized, and press constantly for legislation that will favour Islam. There are 1,200 mosques and 3,000 Koranic schools in Britain today. Yet Christians have been apathetic or fearful to witness to Muslims, and conversions have been few.

ii) **The Chinese**, many from Hong Kong and some from Vietnam. Only about 2% are Christian, but there is a growing number of Chinese churches and fellowships springing up. **Chinese Overseas Christian Mission** has an expanding ministry to them.

iii) **The Sikh community** (300,000) is highly visible, but little evangelized.

iv) **The Hindu community** has been slightly more responsive, and there are a number of Indian majority churches and fellowships in the Birmingham and London areas. However the outreach is only in some cities.

v) **The Arab community** and a large number of visiting tourists and business people who come from many "closed" Middle Eastern lands. Work among them is hard, but some come to the Lord through summer outreaches, and patient person-to-person evangelism.

vi) **The Southern Europeans** are nominally Christian; there are very few evangelical believers among the Orthodox Greeks (mainly from Cyprus) and Catholic Italians.

vii) **The Jews.** There has been a steady trickle of conversions to Christ, but the great majority remain unmoved by the gospel. Pray for the work of **MT** (26 workers), **CWI** (26) and the Anglican CMJ (12). Thousands of Jews who have come to Christ have been integrated into Gentile churches.

ENGLAND

Area 130,400 sq.km.

Population 47,000,000. People per sq.km. 360.

Capital: London.

Adult church members 13% of population. Adult church attendance 9% of population. Membership of major churches: Anglicans 39%; Roman Catholics 34%; Methodists 9.9%; Other churches 17.1%.

1. **The areas of need in England.** A few facts are given to stimulate prayer:
a) **Over 60% of the English** people have no real knowledge of the contents of the Bible, hence what the gospel really is. England is the most secular of the four kingdoms.
b) **Regular church attendance averages 9%.** About 46% of the population claims to be affiliated to the Church of England, but only 7% of them go to church regularly.
c) **The urban inner cities** of the industrial north, Birmingham and London are spiritual wastelands, with many dying congregations and closed churches, yet these are areas crowded with indigenous and immigrant communities that never enter a church.
d) **The rural areas** where 24% of the population live. Many villages have had no real resident gospel witness for a century or more. The **Datchet Evangelical Fellowship** and others are seeking to revive discouraged congregations and open closed chapels.

2. **England, and especially London, is the key to Islam's missionary strategy.** The Islamic Council of Europe is based in London. A big effort through exhibitions, public debates and sophisticated literature is being made to propagate Islam. The growing Muslim community give considerable energy in endeavouring to see the legal system changed to be more favourable to Islam. Pray for a greater concern about the growth of Islam and the need to witness to Muslims among British Christians.

3. **The West Indian Churches** have grown rapidly, but are isolated from the main stream of evangelical Christianity. There are about 150 church groupings and 1,500 congregations linked with the West Indian Evangelical Alliance. There is much spiritual life and vigour in these churches, but little real outreach from them. Pray that this concentration of evangelical believers may become motivated for evangelism of other ethnic groups and for foreign missions, and enjoy closer fellowship with other Evangelicals. Pray also for young people of West Indian origin — there is very high unemployment among them, and this leads to frustration and bitterness.

NORTHERN IRELAND

Area 14,100 sq.km.

Population 1,512,000. People per sq.km. 107.

Capital: Belfast 320,000.

Politics: The problems of Northern Ireland are but a continuation of the centuries-old tension between the Celtic Irish and Anglo-Saxon Scots-English. It happens that the former are Catholic and the latter largely Protestant. The partition of Ireland between the 26 counties of the South and six counties of Ulster did not solve the problem, for an indigenous and dissatisfied minority of Catholics who remained in Ulster under the British Crown still aspired to an all Ireland Republic while the majority of the people adhered strongly to the British link. The civil rights campaign of this minority in the late '60s degenerated into civil violence by extremist factions. The violence peaked in 1972, but has gradually declined to less than an eighth part of that peak. The Province is, at present, ruled directly from London.

1. **In the midst of the heartbreak and tensions of the past two** decades the Lord has been working. Many have come to the Lord — even from among those responsible for the bloodshed. Praise God for the reduction of the level of violence, and pray for a complete

restoration and preservation of peace. There has been much seed-sowing of the Word of God by local believers and by agencies such as the Faith Mission, **OM**, and many others. Fruit is beginning to appear in unexpected places!

2. **Within a 50 km radius of Belfast** is a higher concentration of evangelical churches than possibly anywhere in the world. These churches are full, and there are many committed, praying believers in all denominations. All Protestant denominations are generally far more evangelical than their counterparts in Britain. Pray that:

a) **Christians may be a means of reconciliation** and reconstruction in a province seriously harmed socially and economically by the events of the past decade.

b) **There may be a greater Bible-based spiritual unity and depth among believers**. A united witness to the life-changing power of the gospel is so necessary, because the communal violence was perceived by those outside to be caused by "religion".

c) **Christian leaders** may set an example in Christlikeness and not play on sectarian fears for political reasons.

3. **The missionary burden of Northern Ireland churches** is higher than elsewhere in the UK. Pray that this generosity in giving of money and personnel for world evangelization may continue!

SCOTLAND

Area 78,800 sq.km.

Population 5,207,000. People per sq.km. 66.

Capital: Edinburgh 622,000.

Adult church members 37%. Adult church attendance 17%. Adult membership of major churches: Church of Scotland (Presbyterian) 59.2%; Roman Catholic 37.7%; other churches 9.1%.

1. **Revivals** in past centuries and the localized revivals of the northeast coast in 1925 and Lewis in the Hebrides since the 1950s need to be repeated on a national scale.

2. **Scotland has sent out great men and women to bless the world** — such as: David Livingstone, Robert Moffatt, Mary Slessor, Eric Liddell, etc. May this good tradition continue!

3. **The stirrings of new life in the Church of Scotland is encouraging.** The rapid increase in numbers of evangelical theological students and ministers is changing the Church. Yet the general decline in membership and church attendance has not yet been halted. Pray that the renewed call for the re-evangelization of Scotland may be heeded.

4. **Of all the main denominations, only the Baptists have shown an increase in membership.** Pray for church growth all over Scotland, especially the areas where Protestant numbers are low. Strathclyde (includes Glasgow), Scotland's most densely populated area, has the lowest percentage of Protestants, and the Aberdeen area the highest percentage of non-church goers.

WALES

Area 20,800 sq.km.

Population 2,830,000. People per sq.km. 136.

Capital: Cardiff 630,000.

Adult church members 23%. Adult church attendance 13%.
Membership of major churches: Presbyterian 32%; Anglicans 28.5%; Roman Catholics 18.4%; other churches 21%.

1. **The Welsh revival of 1905-6** had an extraordinary impact on Wales, and also other parts of the world. Sadly the once full chapels in the coal mining and industrial valleys of South Wales are all-too-often empty and even falling derelict. Revival blessing was not retained in the churches. Pray that revival may come again.

2. **Wales is a land of many nonconformist and independent churches.** All are in decline. Only the Catholics and some smaller evangelical groups are growing in membership. The spiritual deterioration is perhaps more marked than in any other part of the United Kingdom.

The West

Nov 11-15

USA
(United States of America)

Area 9,373,000 sq.km. The world's fourth largest nation in both area and population.

Population 238,900,000. Annual growth 0.7% (0.3-0.5% due to immigration). People per sq.km. 25.

Peoples: A nation of immigrants with a greater diversity of ethnic origins than any other on earth. There are approx. 600,000 legal immigrants annually, and over 600,000 illegal immigrants.
Native Americans 0.7%. The 1,550,000 original inhabitants are broadly of three major groups:
- **Amerindians** 98% in 266 recognized ethnic groups in mainland USA.
- **Eskimo** (35,000) speaking five languages, and **Aleut** (4,000) together with Amerindians (16,000) speaking eight or more languages live in Alaska.

European origin 75.2%. The ethnic mix is so great, the relative contributions of different peoples is hard to determine. Probably German 28%, Irish 24%, English 22%, Scots 10%, etc.
African origin 11.3%. Most of their forebears came to America as slaves. Increasing immigration from Caribbean and Africa.
Hispanic 7.3% officially, but with illegal immigration from Mexico and Central America it may be 10%. Over 25 ethnic groups identifiable, who all speak Spanish. Mexican 60%, Puerto Rican 14%, Cuban 5.5%.
Asian and Pacific 2.1%. Rapid increase of **immigrants**: Filipino 1,200,000; Chinese 1,100,000; Japanese 800,000; South Asians 500,000, etc., and **refugees**, including 700,000 from Indochina (Vietnamese, Chinese, Cambodians, Hmong, etc.).
Other 4.1%. Jews 6,100,000, Armenians 1,000,000; Arabs 300,000; Haitians 300,000, etc.

Literacy 98%. **Official language**: English. There is continuing debate concerning the possible use of languages of ethnic minorities in the education system — especially Spanish. **All indigenous languages** 158, 49 of which are close to extinction. Numerous languages and dialects still used by immigrants from all continents. About 11% of the population use a language other than English in the home. **Bible translations into indigenous languages** 3Bi 6NT 46por.

Capital: Washington DC 4,000,000. There are 43 world-class cities of over one million inhabitants. Largest conurbations: New York 21,000,000; Los Angeles 12,400,000; Chicago 8,500,000; Detroit and Philadelphia 5,000,000; San Francisco 4,200,000; Boston 3,300,000; Houston 2,900,000. Urbanization 74%.

Economy: The most powerful economy in the world with an immense agricultural and industrial production. The state of health of the US economy has worldwide repercussions. The massive government deficit and adverse trade balance could precipitate future crises for the world economy, as well as for the nation itself. Income/person $14,090.

Politics: Independent from Britain in 1776 as a federal republic. The number of states has increased from the original 13 to 50 as the nation expanded westwards across the continent and Pacific. The strong democratic tradition, emphasis on private initiative and civil liberties have helped to make the nation great. The USA emerged from World War II as the leading industrial and military power in the world. Military involvement in the Vietnam conflict was a costly setback which temporarily weakened US resolve to promote democracy and resist aggression and oppression by Communist and other dictatorial powers. Since President Reagan's election in 1980 there has been a return of confidence to the nation.

Religion: Freedom of religion is written into the constitution. No state in the world has been so strongly influenced by biblical Christianity. The separation of State and Church enshrined in the constitution has been misused by liberal and anti-Christian minorities to limit the public exercise of religion and promote permissive legislation.
Non-religious/Atheist 9.7%.
Muslim 1%. Steady increase through immigration and conversion of Blacks to Islam.
Jews 3.2%. About one-third of all Jews in the world.
Christian 87%. Nominal 19.3%. Affiliated 67.7%. Overall regular church attendance est. 41% of population.
- **Roman Catholic** 23% (including nominals 31.6%). Practising 40%. 54,000,000a; 37,300,000m. About 30% of Roman Catholics are Hispanic.
- **Marginal groups** 3.6%. 8,400,000a; 5,075,000m. Number of groups exceeds 350. Largest (adult members):

Mormons	2,135,000
Jehovah's Witnesses	696,300

- **Orthodox** 2.2%. 5,000,000a; 3,400,000m. Denominations 55+. Most being of East European, Greek and Middle Eastern ethnic minorities.

Protestant 37.5% (including nominals est. 51%). 87,900,000a; 54,900,000m. Denominations est. 700+. The profusion and variety of national local and ethnic groups is too great to portray here!. Largest (adult members):

Southern Baptist Convention	14,200,000
United Methodist Church	5,700,000
Churches of Christ	2,460,000
Lutheran Church in America	2,200,000
Presbyterian Church (USA)	2,200,000
Lutheran Ch. Missouri Synod	2,000,000
Episcopal Church	1,900,000
American Lutheran Church	1,756,500
American Baptist Churches in USA	1,660,000

Largest groupings (with some overlap!) adherents:

All Evangelicals	53,800,000
All Baptists	27,000,000
All Methodists	14,000,000
All Pentecostals (denominational)	11,500,000
All Fundamental groups (?)	10,000,000
All Lutherans	8,700,000
All Presbyterian/Reformed	6,000,000

Conservative Evangelical 23% of population. Various Gallup polls estimate the number of adults over 18 who claim a "born-again" experience at around 34%; but this includes many who would not be theologically evangelical as defined in Appendix 5.

Missionaries from within the USA approx. 45,000, of which about 40,700 are serving in other lands (1:1,950 Protestants). Number of missionary sending agencies: over 370.

Missionaries to the USA approx. 6,200, many serving among their own immigrant ethnic groups.

Religious Changes

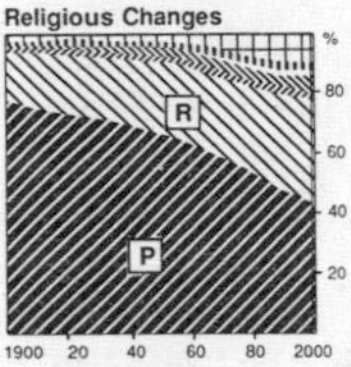

Evangelical Changes

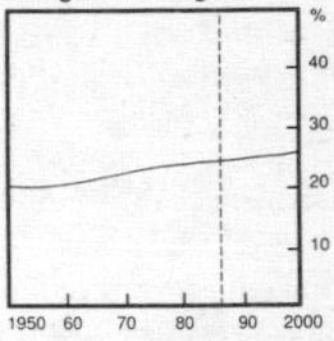

1. **The vitality, diversity and size of Christian organizations and activities** defy a detailed description. Many generalizations have to be made! How much we need to pray for this nation and its leaders. The spiritual and material resources of the USA are of such vital significance for the world and, more, for its evangelization. Here are a few facts:
   a) The USA has the largest number of professing Christians of any nation.
   b) Evangelicals in the USA are 22% of the world's total.
   c) There are 338,000 Protestant churches and 317,000 ordained full-time pastors/workers.
   d) The Protestant missionary force of 45,000 is about 55% of the world's total.
   e) The USA produces 25% of the world's wealth, but 76% of evangelical giving.
2. **There is much for which to praise God** in this great country.
   a) **A religious awakening** has been gaining momentum since the mid-1970's. The spiritual roots of the first settlers and founding fathers are being rediscovered. Young people are in the forefront of this interest in the things of God.
   b) **The USA is probably the most evangelized society on earth.** Major evangelistic campaigns of Billy Graham and many others have won a respect and credibility for the gospel. A multitude of effective outreach methods, tools, and programmes at individual, local congregational, state and national levels have won millions to a personal faith in Christ in the past decades.
   c) **A strong reaction** is developing against drug abuse, pornography, permissive legislation, abortion and crime. These evils have been encouraged by a vocal anti-religious minority, and promoted by unwise use of the media. The latter is the distorted image by which the USA is commonly perceived by foreigners.
   d) **Evangelical Christianity** has reappeared on the centre-stage of the national scene, and was a contributing factor in recent elections. Movements such as Moral Majority have become a major political lobbying force. Yet all this is not revival, and for that we must pray!
3. The potential perils of the resurgence of evangelicalism are matters to turn into prayer.
   a) **Popularity** can lower spiritual standards, bring in worldly attitudes, and lessen commitment to the Lord Jesus by those who bear His name. Divorce, among other wrongs, has become a major factor in Christian homes.
   b) **Political power** should be exercised with sensitivity. The Christian Right is likely to become a major influence on into the 1990s. It would be tragic to taint the purity of the gospel with political scandal. The promotion of regional or national interests could be at the expense of the credibility of the message the world needs.

c) **Christian leaders** with high moral principles are needed. However, in an increasingly mixed society, prejudice and intolerance could easily be manifested. Pray for the many Christians in key leadership positions of the federal and state administrations.

4. **The diversity and size in the Protestant churches** is extraordinary. Pray for:

a) **Spiritual unity**. A oneness in the Lord among those who are committed to Him is so needed. The luxury of perpetuating strong divisions over secondary issues such as church government, gifts of the Spirit, eschatology, definitions of biblical inerrancy, methods of evangelism and social issues is hampering the energetic furtherance of world evangelization.

b) **Church leaders** who need sensitivity and a servant spirit in a time when widespread use of the media can make some into nationally known figures.

c) **Effective in-depth Bible teaching**. This is not as common as it should be: spiritual entertainment can often be a substitute. Some have commented that many of the Lord's people are over-evangelized and underfed!

d) **Many of the mainline denominations** have been in decline for years, yet there is a healthy growth of the Bible-believing minority within them that is leading to renewed interest in evangelism and missions.

e) **The most significant growth** has been in evangelical Pentecostal and charismatic churches. May there be a corresponding growth in spiritual and Christian family life!

5. **Leadership training**. There are estimated to be over 200,000 preparing for full-time service in theological institutions. In the 194 major US theological seminaries, there was a 20% increase in student numbers between 1977 and 1982, a large majority being Evangelicals, though growth has levelled off since then. Pray for staff, students and a deep level of commitment to the cause of Christ worldwide.

6. **Young people** are one of the major areas of spiritual battle today. The bitter fruits of humanistic philosophies are now being harvested in the disorientation, rootlessness and rejection of authority by many. Yet in the midst of all this the Spirit of God has worked — in the Jesus Revolution of the '60s and the many movements that arose around that time. There is a wealth of effort, expertise and spiritual dynamism in the many youth-oriented ministries that are bringing many to Christ and involving them in Christian activities; to mention a few with worldwide impact: **OM, YWAM, CCC**.

7. **Student ministries** have flourished in recent years. The notable impact of the complementary ministries of IVCF(**IFES**), **Navigators**, **CCC** and others has led to effective discipleship and outreach on campuses. The large Urbana conferences of IVCF, and **CCC** efforts such as **Explo-86** have challenged many students with the needs of a lost world. The ministries of the **Navigators** and **CCC** have diversified into a wide range of activities in the USA and around the world.

8. **The Black community** numbers 27,263,000. Many live in the centres of the great cities. Unemployment, poverty, frustration, broken homes and one-parent families are tragically common and, in many ways, a legacy of their tragic origins and subsequent discrimination. The civil rights movement achieved much in changing attitudes to the Black community, but there remains a lot to be done to heal the wounds of the past. Pray for:

a) **The evangelization of the young people**.

b) **The conversion of Blacks who have become Muslims**, partly as a reaction against White Christianity. There may now be around 600,000 or more Black Muslims.

c) **The Black churches**. Many of the largest and most vigorous evangelical churches are Black, but they are isolated from the main stream of evangelical Christianity. Pray for a unity that transcends race among believers, and pray for a moving of the Spirit of God in the many churches with little spiritual life.

d) **Missionary vision**; this has been small. Black Christians could make a far bigger contribution.

9. **Ethnic minority churches** have sprung up all over the country. The most numerous and vigorous are the Korean churches. A growing concern for, and emphasis on, planting churches among less reached ethnic minorities is encouraging. Pray for:

a) **Effective cooperation and planning** to cover every ethnic minority community without a church. The efforts of such churches as **SBC, Nazarenes, CMA** etc., in this ministry are deserving of prayer.

b) **Effective evangelization of even smaller groups which must not be neglected**; these may provide vital means to reach their lands of origin by radio, literature and personal evangelism. Many new immigrants come from lands closed to mission work and from peoples without a viable indigenous church.
c) **The integration of ethnic minority churches into the main stream of American Christianity.** This becomes a major issue for the second and third generations who are less fluent in the languages of their parents.

10. **The native Americans** have suffered intensely in their encounter with European immigrants. They lost almost all their lands, their self-respect and much of their culture. Prejudice and insensitivity have been their lot to this day. Poverty, disease and unemployment are common among those on Indian reservations, and the 50% or so who have migrated to the cities. There has been a strong move among the younger generation to reassert their political and cultural rights. Pray for:
a) **Effective and vital churches.** There is a profusion of missionary and indigenous churches. Yet real in-depth impact has been meagre. There are about 2,500 congregations and 320,000 Christians of all kinds, but much nominalism is evident, even among the 16% that are affiliated to churches. The largest group, the Navajo (200,000), has, however, begun to respond in fairly large numbers.
b) **Bible translation** which has regained importance as local languages are revived. Over 50 languages are in common use, and **SIL** has teams working in 28.
c) **The evangelization of every reservation.** Of the 300 Indian reservations, 54 were surveyed recently and only 20% had a church led by a native American.
d) **The indigenous peoples of Alaska** who have retained their identity far more than in the mainland USA. Over 16 missions and churches have an input into these peoples, two such being Arctic Missions and **GMU**. The harshness of the climate, geographical isolation and economic stresses complicate the work of bringing churches to maturity. Many of the Aleut and Eskimo are traditionally Orthodox Church Christians, a legacy of the time when Russia ruled Alaska. Over 71% of the 65,000 indigenous people profess to be Christian.

11. **The less reached.** The variety and effort expended to evangelize the majority of US residents who do not regularly go to church means that few are unreached, but there are some groups who have not yet been effectively reached with the gospel.
a) **The Hispanics.** About 4% of the possibly 20,000,000 Spanish-speaking population are now evangelical believers. Over 1,200 Hispanic students in Bible schools are a promising indication of a greater harvest, but the proportion of believers in some Latin American countries is higher.
b) **The 6,100,000 Jews** are an influential minority. Over one-third of the Jews of the world live in the USA, and many especially in New York. The greater spiritual receptivity, especially among the middle-aged, has led to many conversions through literature, patient personal work and innovative outreach. Most notable is that of **Jews for Jesus** with 104 workers. There are about 300 full-time workers in over eight agencies committed to Jewish evangelism. About 80 Messianic assemblies have come into being as a result, but to what degree they should conform to Jewish culture is a matter of intense debate. A growing and more solidified opposition is arising against such missionary efforts.
c) **The sects.** Most of the more aggressively missionary sects such as Christian Science, Mormonism, Jehovah's Witnesses, Scientology, etc., have originated in the USA. There are reckoned to be 2,500 such sects and exotic cults. Specific efforts to reach such people must be made. Some successes have been seen among both Mormons and Jehovah's Witnesses.
d) **Foreign students** number around 300,000 or about 10% of the university student population. They come from 181 countries, 60% Asian, 15% Latin America, 13% African. About 120,000 are estimated to be Muslim, the largest single group being Iranian. The challenge of winning such to Christ is great, for many come from Communist

and Middle Eastern lands closed to the gospel. There are over 37 agencies specifically engaged in such ministries – some being **ISI**, IVCF(**IFES**) and **Navigators**.

12. **Christian radio and TV** have developed dramatically since 1961. The National Religious Broadcasters convention is now a major event. The impact of nationwide coverage by the **Trinity Broadcasting Network**, **PTL Network**, **Moody Broadcasting**, etc., is significant with possibly 61 million US citizens being regularly exposed to Christian radio and TV. There are now 200 Christian TV stations and 1,134 Christian radio stations; the latter being 12% of the national total of radio stations. Pray that the overall impact may be beneficial to individuals and to churches, and that the large sums of money involved may be wisely used and helpful for world evangelization.

US VIRGIN ISLANDS
(The Territory of the Virgin Islands of the USA)

Caribbean

Nov 16

Area 344 sq.km. In the Leeward Islands lying between Puerto Rico and British Virgin Islands. Three larger and 50 smaller islands.

Population 123,000. Annual growth 2.1%. People per sq.km. 358. Very rapid growth in '60s and '70s through immigration from other Caribbean islands.

Peoples: African 62.3%, **European/US** 16.4%, **Puerto Rican** 12%, **Eurafrican** 9%.

Literacy 95%. **Official language:** English.

Capital: Charlotte Amalie 17,000. Urbanization 14%.

Economy: Tourism is the mainstay of the economy, with over one million visitors a year. About half the working population is foreign, creating tensions in society. Income/person $6,500 (46% of USA).

Politics: Danish colony until 1917, when purchased by the USA. A self-governing unincorporated US territory.

Religion

Non-religious 1.5%. **Baha'i** 0.5%.

Christian 97.5%. Nominal 31.2%. Affiliated 66.7%.

Roman Catholic 23.2%. 28,500a; 16,200m.

Marginal groups (6) 2.8%. 3,400a.

Orthodox 0.5%.

Protestant (29) 40.2%. 49,500a; 22,800m. Largest (adult members):

Episcopal Church	6,875
Methodist	2,250
Moravian	2,200
Lutheran	1,540
Seventh Day Adventist Church	1,200

Evangelical 13.5% of population.

Missionaries to US Virgin Islands 70 (1:1,760 people).

1. **Tourism and the inflow of wealth have played havoc with the moral and social fabric of society.** Crime is widespread. Pray for the evangelization of tourists, those involved in the crime "industry", the many aliens and the local islanders themselves.

2. **The Christian Church has become very nominal and lacking in vitality.** The Evangelicals also suffer from this malaise. The two Church of God groups and the Nazarenes are growing through conversions, but the majority of the inhabitants, who live in an earthly paradise, are not heading in the direction of the heavenly one.

Latin America

Nov 17

URUGUAY
(Oriental Republic of Uruguay)

Area 176,000 sq.km. Located between Brazil and Argentina on the River Plate estuary.

Population 3,036,000. Annual growth 0.9%. People per sq.km. 17.

Peoples

Spanish-speaking 95.6%. Majority of Spanish origin, Italian 25%, Mixed race 5%.

Other ethnic minorities 4.4%. Jews 55,000; Germans 27,000; Brazilians 25,000; Russian 12,000 and many others.

Literacy 94%. **Official language:** Spanish.

Capital: Montevideo 1,505,000; about half the country's population live in the area. Urbanization 84%.

Economy: Once prosperous through agriculture. Loss of markets, economic stagnation and expense of maintaining welfare state have helped to lower living standards and destabilize political life. Inflation 45%. Income/person $2,490 (18% of USA).

Politics: Independent in 1828. A long tradition of democracy and civil liberties was ended by a brutal Communist terror campaign which began in 1968. The violence provoked a military takeover in 1973 which suppressed the terrorism with equal brutality. A civilian government was elected in 1985.

Religion: A complete separation of church and state, with no preference given for any religion.

Non-religious/Atheist 36%. **Jews** 1.7%.

Christian 62.1%. Affiliated 61.3%.

Roman Catholic 56%. Practising 18%. 1,702,000a; 1,226,000m. A further 19% of the population was baptized as Catholics but have left the church or become followers of another faith.

Marginal groups (6) 2.2%. 66,500a; 43,000m. Largest (adult members):

Mormons	19,300
New Apostolic Church	17,000
Jehovah's Witnesses	5,150

Protestant 3.1%. 94,000a; 38,000m. Denominations 50+. Largest (adult members):

Assemblies of God (2 groups)	9,200
Seventh Day Adventist Church	6,100
Waldensian Church	4,000
Methodist Church	3,600
Baptist Convention (**SBC**)	2,500

Evangelical 1.9% of population

Missionaries to Uruguay 115 (1:26,400 people).

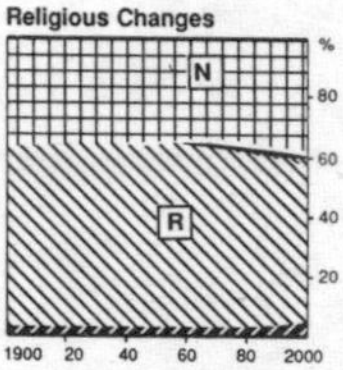

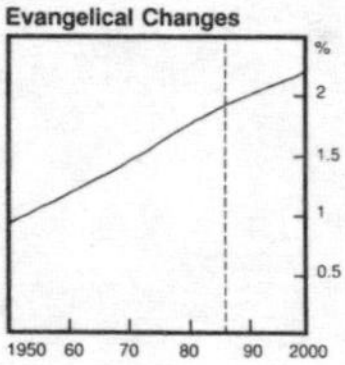

1. **The secular spirit** has made Uruguay Latin America's least Catholic country. Over one third of the people claim to be non-religious or atheist. Apathy to the gospel message has been widespread and the response slow. Pray for a change that will bring true liberty.

2. **The hurt and frustrations in society since 1968 hang like a shadow over steps towards full democratic rule**. Pray for the nation's rulers. Pray that these tensions may create a longing for spiritual reality.

3. **Protestant churches have grown, but only slowly.** The rate has increased since the successful 1978 Luis Palau national crusade in which many were confronted with the claims of Christ. Pray for a united effort from the local churches themselves to reach out to the whole population. The greatest growth has been among sectarian groups; the largest non-Catholic body is the Mormons. Several Pentecostal denominations, **CMA**, and **CoN**, have been growing.

4. **Leadership training** has improved with the increase in Bible schools and seminaries, of which there are at least seven, notably of Baptists, **AoG** and Mennonites. Liberal theology has limited the effectiveness of some denominations.

5. **Missions**. Uruguay has been an often discouraging field of service. Missionary pioneers laboured long for a relatively limited harvest. The pioneer stage is past and there are few unreached areas. Those called to minister in a loving servant role to the Church have much to

offer. Larger missions are **SBC** (30 workers), Gospel Mission of S. America (10), WEF Ministries (8).

6. **Less evangelized peoples:**

   a) The one large university is secular, and it is hard to establish an on-going and effective student witness. **CCC** has some workers committed to campus work. **IFES** has no group functioning.

   b) The **Jewish** and **Chinese** communities. There is no known specific ministry to them.

7. **Literature** is a vital Christian ministry in this highly literate land. **CLC** has a ministry through its bookstore and book mobile right through the country. **SBC** and the Bible Society have an extensive literature and Bible distribution ministry. Pray that the written Word may make a lasting impact. The recession has hindered sales.

Pacific

Nov 18

VANUATU
(The Republic of Vanuatu)

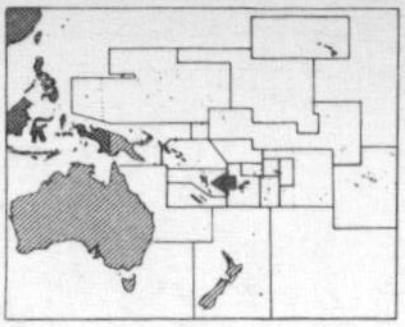

Area 15,000 sq.km. Twelve larger and 70 smaller islands southeast of Solomon Is. in S.W. Pacific. Formerly New Hebrides.

Population 138,000. Annual growth 3.2%. People per sq.km. 9.

Peoples: Over 106 indigenous languages and numerous dialects. Only 20 languages have over 1,000 speakers, none over 4,000.
Indigenous 95.4%. **Melanesian** (102) 131,600; **Polynesian** (3) 2,600.
Other Pacific Islanders 3.2%. From Wallis, Kiribati, Fiji, Tonga, etc.
Other 1.4%. French 700, English-speaking 700, Vietnamese 400, Chinese 150.

Literacy 61%. **Official languages:** Bislama, English, French. **All languages:** 107. **Bible translations** 4Bi 7NT 25por.

Capital: Vila 18,000. Urbanization 23%.

Economy: Agricultural subsistence economy. Income/person $510 (1982. 4% of USA).

Politics: Independent of Anglo-French Condominium in 1980 as a parliamentary republic in the Commonwealth. Independence marred by exotic secessionist movement on Santo Is.

Religion: Religious freedom.
Animist 4.5%.
Cargo Cultic groups (8) 11%.
Christian 84.5%. Affiliated 74.6%.
Roman Catholic 14.5%. Practising 79%. 20,000a.
Foreign marginal (2 groups) 0.2%.
Indigenous marginal (6 groups) 2.5%.
Protestant (9 groups) 57.4%. 79,200a; 33,600m. Largest (adherents):

Presbyterian Church	44,600
Anglican	17,000
Seventh Day Adventist Church	8,300
Assemblies of God	2,000

Evangelical 20.6% of population.
Missionaries to Vanuatu 96 (1:1,400 people) in 11 agencies.
Missionaries from Vanuatu 2 (1:40,000 Protestants).

Religious Changes

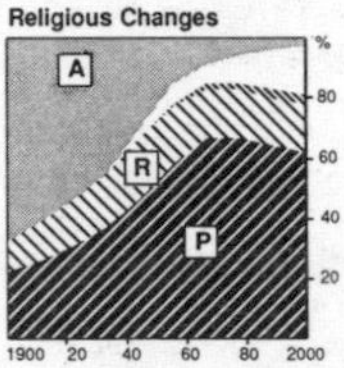

Evangelical Changes

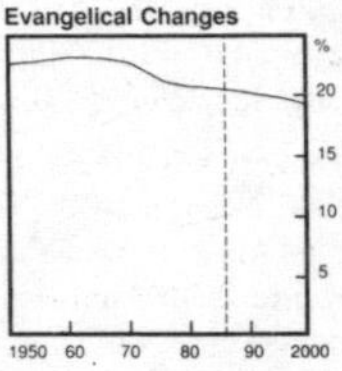

1. **Vanuatu's motto is "In God we stand".** Pray that the leaders of this complex little nation may be an example in doing so. There are Christians in the government.

2. **The Protestant church is numerically strong.** Mainly Anglicans in the north, Presbyterians in the centre and south. Some islands have been touched by revival, and there is much encouragement; however, in other islands and areas, spiritual life is at a low ebb. Pray for the training of leaders in the two Presbyterian and one **AoG** Bible colleges. Pray for Spirit-filled leaders who know how to apply Scripture to real life.

3. **Missionary martyrs in evangelizing these islands have been many.** On Erromanga six died for the evangelization of the, now, 400 people on the island. The church welcomes missionaries in a supportive role for teaching the Word. Pioneer work is also still needed for a number of smaller, superficially evangelized peoples, especially in Bible translation.

4. **Cargo cults and reversion to paganism** have been major problems over the past 40 years. There are also many nominal Christians who follow "Custom". Pray for decisive demonstrations of God's power in largely pagan Tanna, Aniwa, Santo and Vao.

5. **Bible translation** is the major unfinished task. Only two indigenous languages have the Bible (one is Bislama Pidgin — the trade language) and seven the NT. At least seven, and possibly 75, languages may require New Testament translations. **UBS** and **SIL** are involved in 9 projects. Pray for wisdom as to which of the small language groups warrant the effort, and for translation teams of expatriates and nationals. **SIL** is now working in three languages.

VENEZUELA
(Republic of Venezuela)

Latin America

Nov 19-20

Area 912,000 sq.km., with a long Caribbean coastline. A further 230,000 sq.km. of Guyana to the east is claimed by Venezuela.

Population 17,300,000. Annual growth 2.7%. People per sq.km. 19.

Peoples
Spanish-speaking 96%. Approx. composition: Mestizo 64%, European 22%, African 10%. The large Italian community has been almost entirely absorbed into the majority.
Amerindian 2.8%. Over 30 tribes. Largest: Guajiro 50,000; Warao 15,000; Piaroa 12,000; Yanomano 10,000; Carib 10,000.
Other 1.2%. Arabs 100,000; Chinese 25,000; Jews 20,000, etc.

Literacy 86%. **Official language**: Spanish. **All languages** 37. **Bible translations** 1Bi 6NT 11por.

Capital: Caracas 4,500,000. Other major cities: Maracaibo 1,050,000; Valencia 840,000; Barquísimeto 600,000. Urbanization 76%.

Economy: Oil is the major foreign exchange earner making Venezuela the most prosperous nation in Latin America. Diversification of the economy is being further encouraged by the decline in crude oil prices. There is an unhealthy gap between the very rich and the very poor. There is also an unhealthy foreign debt of $34 billion. Income/person $4,100 (29% of USA).

Politics: Independent from Spain in 1821. A succession of revolutions and harsh dictatorships ended in 1958. Since then there has been a stable democratic government. It is the first Latin American country to have a political party recognized as one founded by Evangelicals on reformation principles.

Religion: Religious freedom is guaranteed in the constitution. The Catholic Church regained official recognition in 1964 after years of strained Church-State relations, and has a pervasively influential position.
Non-religious/Atheist 1.5%.
Muslim 0.4%. Predominantly Arab, but also an inflow of Iranis.
Animist and Spiritist 2.2%. Among tribal Amerindians and also the Spanish-speaking majority.
Christian 95.8%. Affiliated 93.5%.
Roman Catholic 90%. Practising approx. 10%. 15,587,000a.
Orthodox 0.09%. 16,000a. Romanians, Greeks, Russians, Ukrainians etc., in 6 Denominations.
Marginal groups 0.7%. 113,000a; 35,400m. Largest (adult members):

Jehovah's Witnesses	25,300
Mormons	8,300

Protestant 2.6%. 450,000a; 187,000m. Denominations 74 with many independent churches. Largest (adult members):

Seventh Day Adventist Church		32,000
Assemblies of God		14,500
OVICE/AIEO (**TEAM**/ORM)	(?)	13,100
Brethren	(?)	10,000
Baptist Conv. (**SBC**)		8,300
The Native Church		7,500
Int. Ch. of Foursquare Gospel		4,000
Tribal Churches (**NTM**)	(?)	3,800

Evangelicals 2.1% of population.
Missionaries to Venezuela 510 (1:34,000 people) in about 36 agencies.
Missionaries from within Venezuela 12(?).

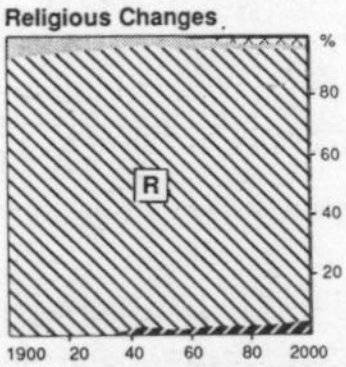

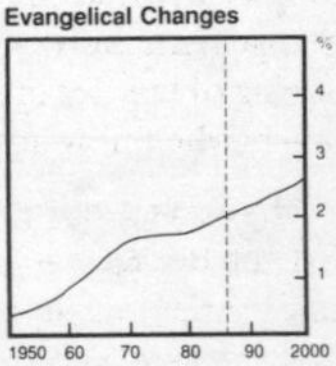

1. **Praise God for the open door for the gospel**, 30 years of stable government and the steady growth of evangelical witness. The country is ready for a spiritual harvest.
2. **The political stability** of the nation is threatened by the combined effects of the decline in the value of oil exports, inflation, the Central American confrontations and the narcotics traffic that has so affected neighbouring Colombia. Pray for all in authority, and for wise handling of the growing economic crisis.
3. **The Evangelicals** are growing steadily, though progress has not been spectacular. The encouragements:
   a) The good growth record of the Baptists and indigenous Pentecostal denominations. **Evangelism Explosion** has proved effective in a number of congregations.

V

b) **The increased fellowship** between some Venezuelan leaders of different denominations, and their desire to cooperate in evangelizing the many unchurched areas.

c) **The first missions congress** ever was held in 1985, giving a new sense of thrust and vision to the churches. Pray for this vision to result in recruits for cross-cultural missions at home and abroad.

4. **The areas of concern in the churches**

a) **Materialism** is a snare in this relatively wealthy land. It is hard for young people to commit themselves to full-time service, so labourers are few. Many pastors leave the ministry for secular employment when discouraged. Few are adequately supported, especially in rural areas.

b) **Petty legalism** in some Pentecostal churches has brought many into bondage rather than the true liberty there is in Christ.

c) **Divisions** within and between denominations have held back growth.

d) **The growth of the Mormons and Jehovah's Witnesses** has far exceeded that of Evangelicals — a ripened harvest is being reaped by those who proclaim error.

5. **Leadership training** is fundamental if present growth rates are to be maintained and urban areas evangelized. There are three seminaries. The **Seminario Evangélico Asociado**, started by **TEAM** and the Evangelical Free Church, has grown rapidly and serves many denominations. The **Evangelical Seminary of Caracas** serves both mainline and Pentecostal churches. The Baptists also have a Seminary.

6. **Opposition to the evangelization of the Amerindian tribes has been intense.** Some areas assigned to Catholic missions are closed to Evangelicals. In recent years there has been a vicious campaign launched by anthropologists, leftist politicians and some Catholic priests against evangelical missionaries, especially **NTM**. Unfounded accusations obviously made with ulterior motives have hindered the work of **NTM** (in six tribes) and **TEAM**/Orinoco River Mission (in a further six). Pray for:

a) **The defeat of slanderous attacks** on missions for harming the cultures of the indigenous people. Only a few thousand Indians still live in the old traditional ways.

b) **The opening up of the few remaining unevangelized tribes** for evangelical missionaries — possibly Venezuelan missionaries would be preferable.

c) **The continued ingathering** of Amerindians among the Guajiro, Maquiritare, Yanomano, Panare, Motilone, etc. Most of the larger tribes have now significant and growing churches.

d) **Bible translation work** which continues in 20 languages. Translation work may only be needed in a few languages. Pray for the impact of God's Word to be such that these peoples may be spiritually mature enough to cope with the inevitable encroachment of Spanish culture and all the trappings of civilization.

e) **MAF** which has two planes serving missionaries living in isolated jungle areas.

7. **The work of Protestant missions** has not been easy. To obtain visas is often a battle in faith. Comity agreements between the early missions hindered advance. Vigorous opposition by the Catholic Church earlier in the century, as well as the strong anti-foreign feeling, created barriers to harmonious relationships among missionaries and nationals. Only now are these obstacles disappearing. Pray for more missionaries for urban church planting and Bible teaching ministries, and for close and harmonious working together between expatriates and national workers. The largest missions: **TEAM** (109 workers), **NTM** (86), **SBC** (67), Evangelical Free Church (58).

8. **The less reached sections of society**:

a) **The upper and middle classes** have been less well evangelized. They constitute about 45% of the population. A number of missions and churches are beginning to concentrate efforts to reach these important groups.

b) **Caracas**, the capital, is less evangelized than the Amerindian tribes. There are only about 25,000 Evangelicals in 165 churches for a city of 4,500,000. In 1939 there were only two churches! Pray for a concerted effort to plant churches in every part of the growing city. There are about one million living in the *ranchos* (slums).

c) **Students**. Christian groups on campuses are generally small. More needs to be done to evangelize and disciple students.

9. **The unreached minorities**:

a) **Italian and Portuguese** immigrants are hardly touched by the gospel.

b) **The Arab** community has become prominent in commerce. Some are Orthodox and Maronite Catholics, but many are Shi'a and Sunni Muslims. No direct effort to evangelize them has been made. There is also a growing community of Iranis.

c) **The Jews** number 20,000. There is no permanent ministry directed towards them.

d) **The Chinese** are scattered through the country, predominantly in restaurant work. There are no known churches among them.

10. **Christian literature is in demand.** Economic conditions are adversely affecting costs and distribution. Both **TEAM**/Evangelical Free Church and the Baptists have publishing houses. **CLC** has a growing wholesale and retail distribution network. More literature workers are needed.

11. **Christian radio**. **TWR** Bonaire has a wide audience and many have been won to Christ and edified. Venezuelan Christians plan to start Christian FM and AM commercial stations for radio and, later, TV. Pray that needed permits may be granted.

Asia

Nov 21-22

VIETNAM
(Socialist Republic of Vietnam)

Area 330,000 sq.km. Occupying the entire 2,000 km. eastern and southern coastline of Indochina.

Population 60,500,000. Annual growth 2.2%. People per sq.km. 182. Possibly 1,500,000 have fled Vietnam since 1975.

Peoples
Vietnamese 86%. Predominantly coastal people; large cultural differences between northern and southern Vietnamese.
Northern ethnic minorities 7.2%. Predominantly Sino-Tibetan; Thai-Tai (19 groups) 2,500,000; Muong 800,000; Hmong (Meo) 350,000; Yao 150,000; Nung 100,000.
Southern ethnic minorities 5.6%. About 40 different groups. Predominantly Austro-Asiatic and Austronesian (Malay) in S. Highlands. Khmer 500,000; Cham 233,000; Jarai 200,000; Mnong 186,000; Koho 100,000; Hrey 100,000; Bru 70,000, etc.
Chinese 1%. About two-thirds fled to China and the West since 1975.

Literacy 55%. **Official language:** Vietnamese. **All languages** 62. **Bible translations** 2Bi 11NT 19por.

Capital: Hanoi 1,299,000. Other cities: Ho Chi Minh City (Saigon) 2,703,000, Danang 2,513,000. Urbanization 19%.

Economy: The destructive Vietnam wars have played havoc with the economy. High military expenditure, rigid socialist policies and world isolation prevent much progress. Widespread hunger and poverty. Income/person $600 (4% of USA).

Politics: Communist republic declared in North Vietnam in 1945. There has been continuous warfare since 1941, under the Japanese, against the French, South Vietnam, USA and all surrounding lands. N. Vietnam finally conquered the South in 1975, and Kampuchea in 1978-85. All of Indochina is controlled by Vietnam and is one cause of its isolation from non-Communist lands.

Religion: Government policy is the steady erosion of the influence of all religions in national affairs, and control of all organized religious movements. Pressures on Christians continue to be severe. Statistics below are approximations.
Non-religious/Atheist 22.5%.
Buddhist 54%. Numerous sects, and strongly permeated with Confucianism, animism and magic.
New religions 11%. Hoa Hao 1,800,000 (Buddhist offshoot), Cao Dai (Buddhist-Catholic syncretism) 3,600,000, etc.
Animist 4%. Minority ethnic groups.
Muslim 1%. Mainly Cham.
Christian 7.5%.
Roman Catholic 7%. 4,200,000a.
Protestant 0.5%. 316,000a; 106,000m. Main groups (est. members):

Evangelical Church (S)	80,000
Evangelical Church (N)	10,000
Other mountain churches	5,000
Seventh Day Adventist Church	3,600
Baptist Churches	1,900

Evangelical 0.5% of population.

Religious Changes

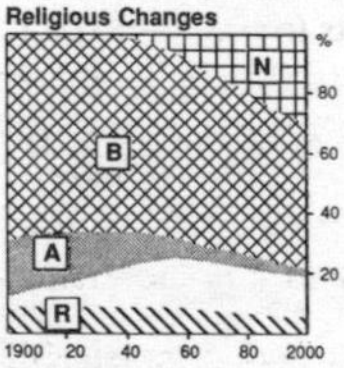

Evangelical Changes

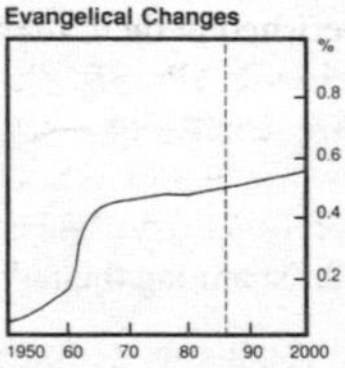

1. **The Communist occupation of South Vietnam** ended the war, but brought great hardship to the population. About one million were "resettled" in "New Economic Zones" (virgin jungle), many to die of starvation. Many who had links with the former government were sent to re-education camps, and about 1.5 million fled to other lands. Pray that the suffering Vietnamese may find solace in trusting in the Saviour.

2. **All open missionary work ceased in 1975. CMA** laboured for 64 years in Vietnam (for 50 years as the only Protestant mission). Other agencies arrived in the late '50s, notably **WEC, UWM** and **SIL** among the tribes, and Southern Baptists in the cities. In 1974 there were 280 missionaries in the land. Pray that the years of sowing the Word may now bring forth abundant fruit — among Hrey, Jeh and others.

3. **The Catholic Church has long had a big influence**. Restrictions and persecution have reduced the number of congregations and priests, but not the number of Catholics.

4. **The Protestant Church grew steadily** in the midst of war, despite massive movements of population, intimidation, terror and the murder of pastors. Almost half the Christians were in minority tribal groups among whom people movements to Christ have occurred. Praise God that this growth has continued despite Communist attempts to prevent it, and despite the flight of many believers from the country. There is a widespread hunger for God with many young people crowding into any church services that are permitted.

5. **The suffering Church today** has been largely forgotten in the West. News is sparse, mail censorship strict, and memories sad. May Christians in the rest of the world not forget their brothers and sisters, but pray for them.

a) **The Protestant Church in the North** is government controlled, but 77 congregations exist. Pray for these believers, isolated from any wider fellowship.

b) **The government is making strenuous efforts to gain control of the churches in the South**, but with limited success. Pray that Christians and leaders may stand firm for the truth. Compromise is easy. Pray also for unity amidst government-instigated efforts to divide them.

c) **Many congregations have been forcibly disbanded**, and buildings destroyed. This was especially true of rural tribal churches, and increasingly so for successful urban churches too. Pray for the small home groups meeting all over the country — may these become, as in China, the source of new life to millions.

d) **Pastors suffer much**. About 40 are still known to be in re-education centres, some being there for over 10 years. Ministry must be confined to their own congregation, and fellowship with other Christian workers is restricted. Economic hardships are severe.

e) **Believers suffer from the general economic crisis**, and also with relocation, job discrimination and exclusion from higher education. Pray for lives to be spared, their faith to be maintained and love multiplied towards their persecutors.

f) **Training of new leadership** is impossible except by informal methods. Pray for a new generation of leaders to be raised up for Vietnamese and ethnic minority churches.

6. **The mountain tribes have long been hated and despised.** For years their fields have been confiscated, their harvests stolen, and their numbers decreasing because of starvation and disease. The Hrey and Jeh became Christian in large numbers before Communism came. These Christians have suffered particularly severely.

7. **Vietnam's flood of refugees** has become a trickle, but hundreds of thousands have fled amidst terrible suffering. Who will easily forget the tragic **boat people**, many of whom perished in their attempts to reach freedom? (A high proportion were of the ethnic Chinese minority.) Pray for those still in camps in Indonesia, Malaysia, Thailand, Hong Kong, etc., with little chance of resettlement. Pray for those settled in: the USA 700,000, China 250,000, France 90,000, Canada 70,000, Australia 25,000, etc. Pray for Christian workers seeking to meet their spiritual and material needs. Praise God for the steady stream of conversions to Christ among them. Pray also for the Vietnamese churches in North America and Europe.

8. **Bible translation** is far from complete. **SIL** members were working in 24 languages before 1975, and work continues in three. Maybe 45 other languages still warrant NT translation; pray that this may be achieved. Pray for the distribution and preservation of minority language NTs and Scripture portions already translated.

9. **Bible and Christian literature** is in short supply. No open means of distribution remain. Many believers no longer have Bibles — especially the tribal peoples. Only 20,000 Bibles in Vietnamese have been imported since 1975.

10. **Christian radio programmes** of **FEBA** from Manila and Saipan have been remarkable in their scope and impact. They are a source of strength to tribal and Vietnamese believers, and widely heard despite shortage of batteries and radios, and the persecution of those discovered listening in. **FEBA** broadcasts 105 hours in Vietnamese each month and one to four hours in 22 other minority languages. Pray for first language speakers — for their provision and preservation to keep up the flow of programmes.

11. **Vietnam's unreached peoples**. Many minority groups could never be reached due to war or restrictions, others have only been minimally evangelized:

a) **The Muslim-Hindu Cham** of the Mekong Delta. A handful of believers only.

b) **The northern ethnic minorities**. Pray through the list above. A few refugees who fled to the South have heard the gospel. Eight hundred Nung believed as a result of radio broadcasts from Manila.

c) **A few southern ethnic minorities** have been less well evangelized. Pray for Christians in neighbouring tribes to reach out to them. There are many tribes with a high proportion of believers.

d) **Khmer**, some indigenous, and many refugees from Kampuchea live in the South. Few have been evangelized.

Pacific

Nov 23

WALLIS AND FUTUNA ISLANDS

(French Territory of Wallis and Futuna)

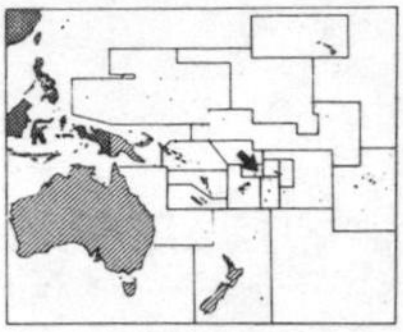

Area 274 sq.km. Three groups of coral islands 300 km. west of Samoa.

Population 13,000. A further 14,000 work in New Caledonia. Annual growth 2.7%. People per sq.km. 48.

Peoples: Polynesian 98.3%; **Uvean** 9,300; **Futunan** 4,500; **French** 1%.

Literacy 95%. **Official language:** French.

Economy: Based on export of labour and coconuts.

Politics: Overseas Territory of France.

Religion: Roman Catholicism is the only religion. Virtually a Catholic theocracy.

Roman Catholic 99%. Practising 99%.

1. **There are no known evangelical believers** on these isolated islands. No definite effort has been made by Protestants to establish a presence there.

2. **Over half the population works abroad** in New Caledonia or in Vanuatu. Pray that some may hear the gospel, believe and return with the message to their homeland.

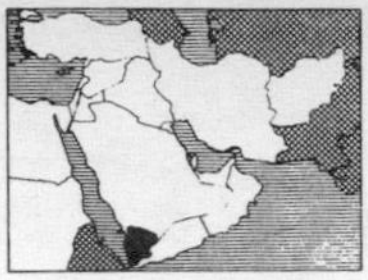

YEMEN, NORTH
(Yemen Arab Republic)

Middle East

Nov 24-25

Area 195,000 sq.km. In the mountainous south-west of the Arabian Peninsula.

Population 6,100,000. Annual growth 2.7%. People per sq.km. 31. The most densely populated and fertile land in the Arabian Peninsula.

Peoples
Arabs 98.4%. Admixture of Black Africans on coast.
Other 1.6%. Somalis 100,000, Indians and Pakistanis 12,000.

Literacy 20%. **Official language:** Arabic. **All languages** 3. **Bible translations** 2Bi.

Capital: Sana'a 274,000. Urbanization 12%.

Economy: Agricultural and pastoral economy, but heavily dependent on Saudi and Western aid, and also remittances from one and a half million Yemeni workers in Arabian oil states. Oil was recently discovered. Rapid development from a subsistence economy to a modern society. Income/person $510 (4% of USA).

Politics: Isolated feudal theocracy until 1962. Autocratic but moderate military-civilian rule is holding a delicate balance between the more traditional Shi'ite tribes of the north and east, and the Sunni of south and west. There have been coups, an 18-year civil war, and two wars with Marxist South Yemen since 1961. There continues to be talk of unification between the two Yemens.

Religion: Islam is the state religion and the stated religion of all Yemeni nationals.
Muslim 100%. Sunni 54%, Shi'a Zaidi in 400 tribes 45%, Ismaili 1%.
Christian: A few Yemeni believers and several hundred expatriates from the West and India.

1. **The nation's stability and social structure are threatened** by external attack, internal feuding, and the widespread use of the narcotic qat. The latter debilitating habit has diverted much valuable agricultural land into the cultivation of its leaves. Pray for spiritual liberation; as yet very few Yemenis have ever heard the gospel. May they, like their illustrious ancestor, the Queen of Sheba, seek for wisdom — from the One greater than Solomon!

2. **For 1,300 years the land was tightly closed to the gospel**. The government invited Christian agencies to initiate health and educational projects in 1964. At one time a number of agencies were involved, but conditions have become more restrictive and only a few remain. Pray that, despite all present trends, this land may be opened wide for the gospel, and also for the calling and entry of intrepid pioneer workers with the right professional skills.

3. **Several dozen Christian workers** in aid agencies live under discouraging restrictions. Earlier permission for them to share their faith and hand out literature to individuals has been withdrawn. Pray for the maintenance of their spiritual glow in the face of many attacks from the enemy of souls through discouragement, sickness, isolation from the wider Christian family and constant threats to their presence in the land.

4. **Yemeni believers** may number no more than a few dozen. The only little fellowship of believers was stopped by the authorities in 1974. Since then believers have been lonely and isolated, and some have suffered much. Pray that they may maintain their spiritual life and grow in grace and boldness. Pray that they might find adequate fellowship, and opportunities to share their faith.

5. **Christian radio programmes** from **FEBA**-Seychelles are clearly received. Many listen. Pray for lasting fruit and fellowships of believers to result.

Middle East

Nov 26

YEMEN, SOUTH

(People's Democratic Republic of Yemen)

Area 333,000 sq.km. At the strategic southwest tip of the Arabian Peninsula, and controlling the entrance to the Red Sea. Also the island of Socotra.

Population 2,116,000. Annual growth 2.9%. People per sq.km. 6.

Peoples
Arabs 91%. Over 1,300 clans or tribes.
Non-Semitic peoples (2) 1.5%. Mahri and Socotri.
Other minorities 7.5%. Indians/Pakistanis 50,000; Somalis 46,000; Black African 25,000; Communist Bloc military forces and advisers 10,000.

Literacy 21%. **Official language:** Arabic. **All languages** 4. **Bible translations** 1Bi.

Capital: Aden 450,000. Urbanization 38%.

Economy: Subsistence agriculture, fishing, oil refining and servicing USSR forces are the mainstays of the economy. Income/person $510 (4% of USA).

Politics: Independent from Britain in 1967. Soon afterwards a Marxist coup ousted the traditional rulers. For years the Soviet Union has subsidized and controlled the country which has become a major USSR military base. There have been two wars between the two Yemens interspersed with talk of unification.

Religion: Marxist-Leninist secular state which recognizes the Islamic cultural heritage, but steadily erodes the influence of all religion on national life.

Non-religious/Atheist 8%.

Muslim 92%. Sunni 95%, Shi'a 4.5%, Ismaili 0.5%.

Christian 0.01%. Several small groups of indigenous believers and a few expatriates.
Missionaries to Yemen 0.

1. **All mission work in the country was terminated in 1972** with the nationalization of all mission and church property. For years a few missionaries suffered and witnessed in this land but with very little fruit. Pray that the land may again be opened for the gospel.

2. **Communism is breaking down many traditional and Islamic barriers to the gospel**. Pray that Yemenis may seek the Prince of Peace in their ideological confusion.

3. **The literature distributed and witness** given before 1972 and present radio broadcasts by **FEBA**-Seychelles *will* bear fruit as prayer is made. There is a small, but steady response by letter to the broadcasts. Pray for secret listeners.

4. **The few national believers** still meet where and when they can, though lack of a legal place in which to gather makes it hard to maintain fellowship. They are under considerable pressure from both atheists and Muslims. Pray that they may not give way and compromise their faith or testimony. Pray that they may be used to win others to the Lord.

5. **Unreached peoples:** The whole population is in this category. Almost all previous evangelism that has been done was in the city of Aden. Many groups are totally unreached:
   a) **Tribes people of the Hadhramaut** in the centre and east.
   b) **Bedouin nomads** — 200,000 who are being forcibly settled by the government.
   c) **The urban minorities** of Pakistanis/Indians and Somalis.
   d) The non-Semitic **Mahri** of Hadhramaut and related **indigenous Socotrans** 7,000 on Socotra Island. The latter were Christian until the 16th century, but all are Muslim today.
   e) **The Russians, East Germans**, etc.

YUGOSLAVIA
(Social Federal Republic of Yugoslavia)

Eastern Europe

Nov 27-28

Area 256,000 sq.km. A Balkan state bordering on the Adriatic Sea.

Population 23,100,000. Annual growth +0.7%. People per sq.km. 90.

Peoples
Serbo-Croatian-speaking 70%. Four distinct Slavic peoples:

Serbian 39.4%. Predominant in centre and east, and mainly Orthodox.

Croatian 21%. Mainly in northwest and along Dalmatian coast. Predominantly Catholic.

Bosnian 6%. Serbian Muslims, but officially considered an ethnic entity in the central republic of Bosnia.

Montenegrin 2.6%. Mainly in the south coastal republic of Montenegro.

Slovene 8%. A Slavic people in the northwestern republic of Slovenia.

Albanian 7.8%. Majority in the Kosovo region adjoining Albania and many in Montenegro and Macedonia. Mainly Muslim; descendants of the ancient Illyrians.

Macedonian 6%. A Slavic people related to the Bulgarians in the far southern republic of Macedonia. Predominantly Orthodox.

Hungarian 2%. A large minority in Vojvodina region. Many are Catholic or Reformed Protestant.

Other minorities 7.2%. Romany Gypsies, maybe 300,000; Rumelian Turks 125,000; Bulgarians 36,000; Ukranians 30,000, etc.

Literacy 90%. **Official languages**: Serbo-Croatian, Slovene and Macedonian and, locally, six other languages. **All languages** 20. **Bible translations** 8Bi 3NT 3por.

Capital: Belgrade 1,600,000. Other major city: Zagreb 1,200,000. Urbanization 37%.

Economy: The world recession in 1979 exposed the inbuilt weaknesses of a bloated bureaucracy and excessive regionalization. There is a massive international debt, much unemployment and high inflation. The wide disparity in living standards between the wealthier north and poor south has further strained the fragile unity of the state. Average income/person $2,620 (19% of USA).

Politics: Modern Yugoslavia developed from fragments of the Austro-Hungarian and Turkish Ottoman Empire between 1878 and 1918. Communist republic formed in 1945, but non-aligned in world politics since President Tito's break with the USSR in 1948. Communism has not been so authoritarian as in other East European states. Yugoslavia is a federal socialist state consisting of six republics, two autonomous regions, three religions, eight major national groups and two alphabets! The fragmented and fierce nationalism of the various ethnic groups helped trigger off World War I, provoked intense civil war in World War II, and poses a flash-point for possible future conflict. Since Tito's death a complex collective leadership and devolution of power to the constituent republics has barely managed to keep the country together, and has hampered development and economic reform. Croatian and Albanian nationalisms are the two most sensitive issues today.

Religion: Atheism is actively promoted by the state in the education system. There is considerable religious freedom, though active proselytization is discouraged. There are restrictions on churches' social and cultural ministries, and some discrimination against Christians in job opportunities.

Non-religious/Atheist 18%. The Communist party has 2,200,000 members.

Muslim 11%. Bosnians, 80% of Albanians, Gypsies, Turks. Most are Sunni Muslims, a few are Shi'a. There are 2,250 functioning mosques.

Christian 71%. Affiliated 67%. Many are baptized, but do not attend church.

Orthodox 36.7%. 8,480,000a. Denominations 7. Mainly Serbians and Macedonians, a few Albanians.

Roman Catholic 29.7%. 6,860,000a. Mainly Slovenes, Croats and Hungarians and some Albanians.

Protestant 0.7%. 162,000a; 96,000m. Denominations approx. 40. Largest (adult members):

Lutheran Churches (3)	42,000
Reformed Church (Hungarian)	20,000
Pentecostal Churches (4)	(?) 11,300
Seventh Day Adventist Church	10,600
Baptist Church	3,650
Methodist Ch. (Macedonian & Hung)	1,850

Evangelicals 0.16% of population.

Foreign Christians serving Yugoslavians est. 25.
Missionaries from within Yugoslavia est. 10.

Religious Changes

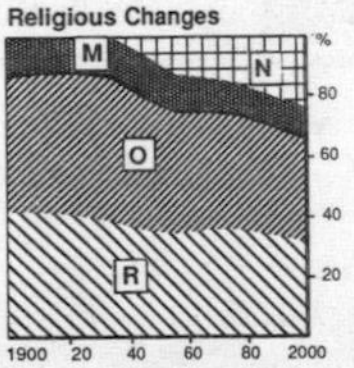

Evangelical Changes

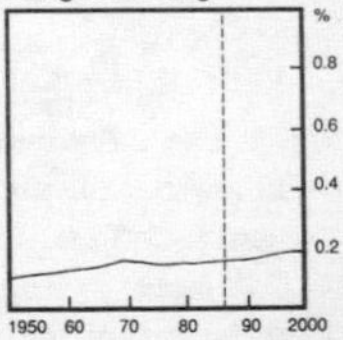

1. **The country is passing through a period of great stress.** The economy is in a bad state, and the complex one-party federal leadership is finding it hard to solve the regional inequalities, severe inflation and high unemployment. Pray for the present situation to heighten the spiritual awareness of the people.

2. **There has been considerable liberty for Christians since the '60s.** Pray for continued and greater freedom for the gospel. Yugoslavia is one of Europe's most spiritually needy lands, and few Yugoslavs have ever heard a clear presentation of the good news in Jesus. It would be tragic if Christians do not use to the full present liberty to reach out to the unconverted; there is a definite increase in hunger after God.

3. **The Church is one of the most formal in Europe** – this includes Orthodox, Catholic and most Protestant denominations, though renewal movements among Romanian Orthodox and Catholics are significant. A recent increase in religious fervour is little more than a reinforcement of ethnic prejudices. Most denominations are restricted to one or two peoples. The renewal movement in the older churches is very small. Evangelical believers are variously estimated at between 10,000 and 20,000. Pray for an outpouring of the Spirit that will halt the decline, enliven formal congregations, replace liberal theology with fervent biblical preaching and bring unity to the body of Christ.

4. **Evangelical believers** are in a tiny minority, and concentrated more among the Hungarian and Slovak minorities in Vojvodina. Congregations elsewhere are few and many areas are without an evangelical witness. Pray specifically for:

   a) **Unity**. Serious divisions exist because of strong personalities, ethnic and denominational exclusivism and doctrinal differences.

   b) **Growth**. Stagnation and decline is too evident. Several Pentecostal groups are growing. The Baptists are beginning to move out more in evangelism. Pray for a sense of expectation and faith, and growth of vision equal to the need.

   c) **Labourers**. Migration has removed many promising leaders who often never return. Pray for the calling of many with deep commitment to the evangelization of the land, and for the active backing of congregations.

   d) **Leadership training**. The *Biblijisko Teološki Institut* has a residential programme with students drawn from five denominations and nine nationalities, as well as a TEE programme in seven centres. This school is beginning to make a mark for God. Pray for the staff and students and their growth in the Lord, that they may have a vision for the lost and an understanding of the Word.

5. **Help from other lands**. It is not practicable for missionaries to enter as such. A number of Christians assist the Yugoslav Church in itinerant ministry, Bible teaching, etc. Pray for more assistance to be given. The Christians are so few and of limited means that any help is appreciated.

6. **Christian literature** is relatively freely available, especially in Croatian, Serbian and Slovenian, less so in other languages; There are Christian bookstores and presses in Zagreb and several other cities, with plans for bookstores in other centres too. There is a Bible Scoiety depot in Belgrade. Censorship exists, but is not a major problem; but the availability of printing supplies and distribution are. Much remains to be done to provide an adequate range and quantity of tracts, books, Bibles, etc., in all languages. The greatest need is for Macedonian and Albanian literature. Both these have only a NT; the OT is in preparation. Between 1975 and 1980 about 150,000 Scripture portions in 9 languages were printed in the country.

7. **Unreached peoples**: There are so few evangelical believers, almost every area, city, social and ethnic group could be called unreached. Pray particularly for:

   a) **The 2,300,000 Muslims**. Very little has ever been done to bring the gospel to any of the Muslim ethnic groups, nor has adequate relevant literature been provided for them. The Baptist Church has a vision to evangelize the Turkish minority.

   b) **The Albanians** (1,700,000) are 80% Muslim, and only sporadic efforts have been made to evangelize them. Praise God for the building of the first Albanian-speaking evangelical church in the world in 1985. Pray for the 100 or so Christians and their witness to Albanians in Yugoslavia, and possibly one day in sealed-off Albania. The NT was recently published by the Catholics.

c) **The Macedonians** (1,500,000) have recently received their first Bible. There are a few Methodist churches, and the number of committed believers is increasing.

d) **The Gypsies**. Scopia in Macedonia is the largest Gypsy city in the world, but is unreached. In 1984 an outpouring of the Spirit in south Serbia brought 100 Gypsies to the Lord. Pray that this movement may spread to related Gypsy communities all over the south Balkans.

8. **Yugoslavs working in Western Europe number almost 1,000,000**. Pray for their evangelization in Germany (613,000), Austria (160,000), France (70,000), Switzerland (50,000), Sweden (40,000). Among them are communities representing all of the diverse peoples of the country, especially from the poorer, less evangelized south. Some have come to Christ and returned home with a testimony. The work has been especially fruitful in Sweden.

9. **Christian radio programmes** are broadcast daily by **TWR** and **IBRA** in Croatian, seven times a week in Albanian, and weekly in Macedonian, Slovenian and Serbian. Pray for additional staff and air time.

ZAIRE
(Republic of Zaire)

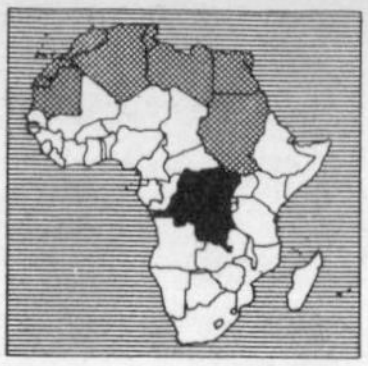

Area 2,345,000 sq.km. Covering much of Central Africa's rain forest. The heavy rainfall and extensive river systems complicate communications.

Population 33,100,000. Annual growth 2.9%. People per sq.km. 14. Large areas are sparsely populated.

Peoples: An estimated 200 ethnic groups, and many more sub-groups.
Bantu peoples 80%. Centre and south. Over 32 peoples with more than 100,000. Largest: Luba group 6,173,000; Mongo group 5,600,000; Kongo 4,000,000; Bemba 1,700,000; Songe 800,000; Tetela 650,000; Chokwe 550,000; Bbadha 500,000.
Adamawa Eastern 10%. Northern borderlands. Three peoples with over 100,000 each are: Zande 1,500,000; Ngbaka 800,000; Ngbandi 250,000.
Sudanic 6.7%. Northeast corner. Two peoples with 100,000 and over. Mangbetu 500,000; Lugbara 100,000.
Nilotic 2%. One major people on Uganda border: Alur 700,000.
Pygmy 0.4%. Many small groups in the northern forests.
Other 0.7%. Foreigners, Westerners, other Africans, etc.

Literacy 45%. **Official language**: French. **Trade languages**: Lingala-Bangala in north and northwest, Swahili in east and south, Luba in centre and Kongo-Tuba in west. **All languages** 192. **Bible translations** 20Bi 12NT 33por.

Capital: Kinshasa 4,200,000. Other major cities: Kananga 1,500,000; Lubumbashi 700,000; Kisangani 500,000. Urbanization 34%.

Economy: Vast mineral resources and agricultural potential. Post-independence chaos, widespread maladministration and corruption have enriched the powerful elite, but impoverished the nation. The road system hardly functions, trade is reduced to a trickle and profitable agricultural estates have reverted to forest. Africa's potentially most wealthy nation can no longer feed its own people, and is dependent on foreign aid. Some economies introduced since 1983 have brought slight improvements. Income/person $160 (1% of USA).

Politics: In 1960 Belgium hastily granted independence to an ill-prepared people, which led to eight years of violence, anarchy and secessionist wars. A military coup in 1965 brought General Mobutu to national leadership as an autocratic President of a one-party state. A measure of peace and stability has been restored. The sheer size, ethnic complexity and lack of communications in the country could imperil its future unity.

Religion: In 1972 the President decreed that only six organized religions were permitted to operate and own property: Catholic, one Protestant Church (ECZ), Kimbanguist Church, Orthodox, Muslims and Jews. The authenticity programme of the government between 1971 and 1978 placed increasing controls and limitations on Christian institutions and activities. Economic and social disasters forced a dramatic reversal, so that by 1980 there was considerable religious freedom once more, though with a continued subtle pressure that equates Christian commitment with a denial of national heritage. Zaire's size and lack of statistics and communications prevent accuracy in many of the following figures — especially for the African Independent Churches.

Traditional religions 8-12%. Pockets of peoples and areas where the response to the gospel has been less.

Muslim 1.4%. Sunni Muslims predominantly in eastern towns.

Christian 88-92%. Practising 62%.

Roman Catholic 42%. 14,000,000a; 8,100,000m.

African Indigenous Churches (?) 15-19%. approx. 6,000,000a.

Kimbanguist Church	(?)	4,800,000

Protestant 28%. 9,270,000a; 3,100,000m. Almost all of the 83 Protestant Churches are member communities of the Eglise du Christ au Zaire (ECZ). Most are evangelical, some more liberal, and others marginal in their theology. Some of the larger communities (adult members):

ECZ — Disciples of Christ	(?)	330,000
ECZ — Presbyterian		320,000
ECZ — CECA (**AIM**)		310,000
ECZ — Pentecostal (ZEM, UK)		151,000
ECZ — Baptist (**CBOMB**)		135,000
ECZ — Baptist (**BMS**, UK)		120,000
ECZ — Methodist (UMC)		115,000
ECZ — CEAZ (**CMA**)		98,374
ECZ — CECCA (**WEC**)		78,000
ECZ — CADELU (**RBMU**)		50,000
ECZ — CEHZ (**UFM**)	(?)	49,000
ECZ — Assemblies of God (USA)		38,000
Anglican Church		72,000

Evangelical 17.6% of population.

Missionaries to Zaire 1,300 (1:25,500 people) in 85 agencies.
Missionaries from within Zaire, very approx. 300.

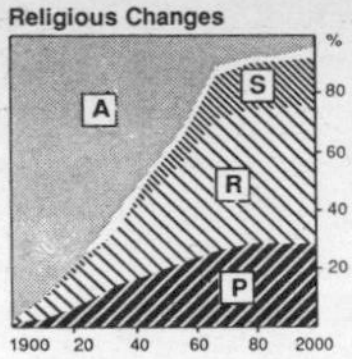

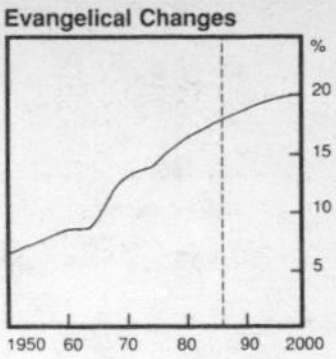

1. Praise items for:
   a) **The massive turning to Christ** (see graph!). The number of Christians has grown from 1.4% of the population in 1900 to 91% today. There have been powerful revivals in some areas before and after independence.
   b) **The costly service of missionaries**. Many lives have been laid down for Christ through sickness in the earlier years, and martyrdoms in the bloody aftermath of independence. In 1964 many thousands of Zairois and 34 Protestant missionaries were killed in the Simba Rebellion. The suffering was not in vain.
   c) **The impact of persecution** in the '60s, and then the government pressures in the authenticity campaign in the '70s led to a significant deepening of the spiritual life of many congregations, and increased outreach.

2. **The Church of Christ in Zaire (ECZ)** came into being through both government edict and pressure from some unscrupulous church leaders, though many evangelical leaders are now in favour of their membership in the ECZ. There have been positive benefits; the divisiveness of tribalism has been diminished, unnecessary competition reduced, administration rationalized and cooperation in training schemes and media increased. However, the negatives must be prayerfully counteracted.
   a) **The centralization of leadership** has harmed the development of effective lay leadership and congregational initiative. Hierarchical leadership structures have been encouraged — even to the extent of each community being encouraged to set up life-bishops. Christian leaders need wisdom and discernment in knowing where to draw the line on those who want authoritarian measures on doctrine, finance, and leadership structures. The structural rigidity is causing tensions between the older, less educated, and younger, more sophisticated pastors.
   b) **Worldly standards** among some leaders — power politics, pride of position, misuse of funds have frequently compromised the prophetic role of the Church. The Church has no clear, united message to a corrupt society. It is hard for men of God to maintain spiritual standards. The low level of support of pastors by churches discourages many who are not willing to use other less spiritual means of adding to their income.
   c) **Exposure to possible manipulation and interference by the state**. This has happened in the past and could be a major problem in the future.
   d) **Theological weakness**. Evangelical, liberal and even syncretic indigenous churches were brought under the same umbrella. The evangelical majority has been pushed aside, and more outspoken and less Bible-committed leaders have taken the limelight, helped by many smaller non-evangelical groups who have been invited as participating communities. Pray for a deep commitment to the authority of Scripture.
   e) **The effectual geographic compartmentalization** of the country by the ECZ has often blunted evangelistic zeal, left many areas devoid of any evangelical witness, and hindered cross-cultural outreach.

3. **Leadership training** at every level must be emphasized.
   a) **Lay leadership training** has not been given enough priority. It is hard to implement due to expense and the lack of both transport and personnel. Many congregations subsist on a poor spiritual diet. TEE is effectively used in only a few of the communities.
   b) **Bible Schools.** There are large numbers of primary local-language and trade-language Bible Schools, and a smaller number of French ones. They often function with slender resources and inadequate staff. Pray that spiritual and material standards may be constantly improved.

c) **The higher-level institutions** need prayer support. Some important ones are: **Institut Supérieur de Théology** in Kinshasa, the Bunia Seminary (**AIM, UFM, Brethren, WEC, CBFMS**), as well as several denominational schools. These are strategic for the provision of a new generation of well-educated pastors and leaders. Pray that spirituality among students and graduates may be more marked than intellectual pride or a nationalistic spirit that rejects anything foreign.

4. **The problem of nominalism has become acute**. The Church could experience decline, division and heresies unless the following problems are squarely faced:

a) **Cultures must be transformed by the power of the gospel**. Many areas are Christianized, but most are little more than baptized heathen. A stronger emphasis on personal conversion, committed discipleship and vigorous evangelism is needed.

b) **The young people** have high expectations of material improvement, yet most are educated in an ill-funded, largely church-run educational system. Low Christian standards among staff, and lifeless religious teaching, encourages indifference and rejection. Pray for a mighty move of the Spirit in the school system and the conversion of millions of young people.

c) **Materialism** is a snare. Wealth is usually found in the cities, and frequently obtained by underhand means. Widespread condoning of financial dishonesty by Christians devastates spiritual effectiveness.

d) **The growing cities** are a major need, and there has been insufficient vision or finance in most communities to plant churches in these key urban areas.

e) **The superficiality of Christian teaching and minimal understanding of the gospel**. Over 30% of "Christians" no longer attend church. Large numbers have become Christian with no clear grasp of repentance and faith in Christ. Animistic thought patterns, fear of witchcraft and syncretism are major problems. Pray that believers may recognize their inheritance in Christ and confront the forces of darkness in the power of the Spirit.

f) **The need for a vision for the lost**. Without this vision the churches will perish. Local and cross-cultural evangelism and missionary vision must be stimulated. Praise God for small beginnings by some Protestant communities in this respect (**CMA**, CECCA/**WEC**, Baptists, etc.).

g) **Leadership training** at all levels must be both increased and spiritually deepened if tomorrow's preachers are to have an anointed ministry which will edify the Church.

5. **Missionary involvement** is most needed in Bible teaching and discipling ministries, but is most demanded in development programmes, health and education. Pray for:

a) **A wise deployment of expatriate workers** and for the most effective use of their gifts.

b) **Harmonious relationships** between national and expatriate workers. There were many strains during the anti-foreign emphasis of the authenticity campaign. Missions are now, to a great degree, integrated into their daughter churches.

c) **Supply of needs**, and sensitive use of them.

Some major missionary agencies are: various Mennonite groups (130 workers), **Brethren** missionaries (80?), **BMS** (80), Presbyterians (65), **AIM** (51), **CBFMS** (48), **WEC** (39), **RBMU** (17); and **UFM** (10).

6. **The unreached** are few, but superficially Christianized peoples are more numerous. Special targets for prayer are:

a) **The intellectuals and the elite** — many in the cities are scarcely touched by a living witness to biblical Christianity.

b) **The vast swamplands northeast of Kinshasa** which are sparsely populated and under-evangelized. The 100,000 Mbole live in the area. Many other similar pockets of neglect exist. Pray for a more concerted research into where these areas and peoples are, and for church planting to be initiated.

c) **The peoples who have been less responsive**, and have a high proportion of non-Christians: the Azande (1,500,000), Hunde (300,000), Bira (40,000) and the many Pygmy groups in the north and northeast, and also the Kela (150,000), and Songomeno (60,000) in the southeast.

d) **The Swahili-speaking Muslim communities** (400,000) in eastern towns, Kinshasa and along the eastern border. There is no known outreach to them. There is a considerable missionary effort being launched by Muslims to spread Islam.

7. **Help ministries** have once more become a major responsibility of the churches. The government takeover of hospitals and schools in the 1970s was a disaster from which the health and education system is only slowly recovering. The administration and financing of these institutions is a constant drain on the time and energies of key personnel, yet the pressing needs cannot be ignored. Pray for right priorities, and effective use of:

a) **Health services**. There are a number of major and smaller hospitals run by different communities/missions such as BMS, ABFMS, **CMA** etc. One such is the inter-community/mission hospital at Nyankunde in the northeast (**AIM**, **Brethren**, Mennonites, **UFM**, **WEC**, etc.). Expatriate personnel are in constant demand.

b) **Education**. Many of the better schools are church run. The Catholics have made an enormous effort in this field; Protestants are under much pressure to do the same; but resources are limited, and committed Christian staff hard to find and retain. Pray that the educational system may also produce fine Christian leaders for the future.

c) **Transportation**. The breakdown in surface transportation has enhanced the importance of **MAF** and seven other flying agencies. Without the 38 aircraft and 34 flying personnel, missionary involvement, health programmes, and lay-training schemes would be seriously limited. Pray for safety in flying — much is over trackless forest — and for the provision of fuel, finance and personnel.

8. **Bible translation** is a major unfinished task. The profusion of languages led to an emphasis on trade-language evangelism which limited gospel penetration and stunted the development of indigenous Christian life styles, music and worship.

a) **At least 26 and possibly 144 languages** are in need of translation programmes by Zairois or expatriate believers.

b) **The Bible Society** is supervising 22 Bible translation programmes, and has the vision of making common language versions in all seven major languages by 1990.

c) **Research into translation is still needed**. **SIL** has done much towards this, and has involvement in five translation projects, and a consultancy ministry in a number of others.

d) **GRI** has messages available in 246 languages and dialects; a valuable resource in this land of many languages.

Africa

Dec 1

ZAMBIA
(Republic of Zambia)

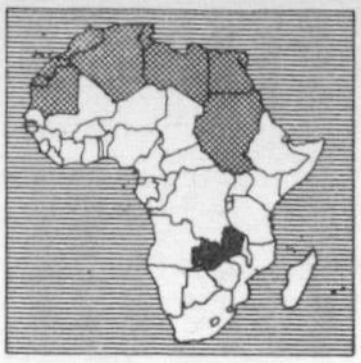

Area 753,000 sq.km. Landlocked country; still heavily forested.

Population 6,800,000. Annual growth 3.3%. People per sq.km. 9.

Peoples. There are 83 ethnic groups in five major groupings of Bantu peoples.
Indigenous 97%.
- **Bemba peoples** 37% (16 groups). Bemba 1,000,000; Lunda 180,000, etc.
- **Tonga peoples** 19% (over 6 groups). Tonga 820,000; Lenje 272,000, etc.
- **Nyanja-speaking peoples** 15% (over 5 groups). Chewa 800,000; Nsenga 360,000, etc.
- **Mambwe peoples** 8% (over 3 groups). Mambwe 200,000; Mwanga 150,000, etc.
- **Lozi peoples** 7%. Lozi 380,000, etc.
- **Other** 11%. Numerous smaller groups.

Foreign 3%. Angolan refugees 100,000(?); Europeans 30,000; Indo-Pakistanis 12,000.

Literacy 50%. **Official language:** English. **Trade language**: Bemba is spoken by 40% of the population. **All languages** 31. **Bible translations** 15Bi 7NT 3por.

Capital: Lusaka 1,100,000. Urbanization 43%.

Economy: Over-dependence on mining and refining of copper in the '60s and '70s distorted the economy. Agricultural development was neglected but is being re-emphasized. Wars and unrest in nearly all surrounding countries (Zimbabwe, Angola, Zaire and Mozambique) disrupted vital land links to the sea. This, together with the drastic fall in world demand for copper, and internal mal-administration, has brought great strains to the economy and a heavy foreign debt. Income/person $580 (4% of USA).

Politics: Independent from Britain in 1964. One-party participatory democracy with a strong, but respected leadership exercised by President Kaunda. Zambia has been severely affected by the revolutions and wars of surrounding countries.

Religion: Kaunda's Christian oriented, socialist humanism has been government philosophy. Complete freedom of religion exists with considerable privileges accorded to churches in religious education in schools and free radio/TV time for Christian programmes.

Note: Nearly all religious statistics are estimates; neither the government nor the majority of the churches have kept statistics.

Traditional religions 21%. Widespread, but in majority in some western and southwestern peoples.

Muslim 0.3%. Asians and some African immigrants.

Non-religious/atheist, etc. 1.7%.

Christian 77%. Nominal 19%. Affiliated 56.5%.

Roman Catholic 30.8%. 2,100,000a; 1,200,000m.

Foreign marginal 8.6%. 586,000a; 137,000m.
Groups 8. Largest (adherents):

Jehovah's Witnesses	393,400
New Apostolic Church	(?) 190,000

Indigenous marginal 5.4%. 370,000a. Over 70 groups.

Protestant 11.6%. 792,000a; 426,000m.
Denominations 43. Largest (adherents):

United Church	110,000
Seventh Day Adventist Church	90,000
Full Gospel Church (Cleveland)	(?) 76,000
Churches of Christ	(?) 70,000
Reformed Church (**NGK**)	50,000
Christian Brethren	50,000
Evangelical Church (**AEF**)	41,000
Baptist Convention (**SBC**)	(?) 30,000
Anglican Church	20,000
Brethren in Christ	12,800
Baptist Union of C.A.	10,000

Evangelical 7.3% of the population.

Missionaries to Zambia approx. 500 (1:13,600 people) in about 30 agencies.

Missionaries from within Zambia approx. 85 (1:9,300 Protestants); almost all within Zambia.

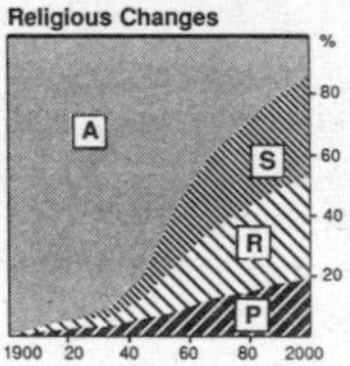

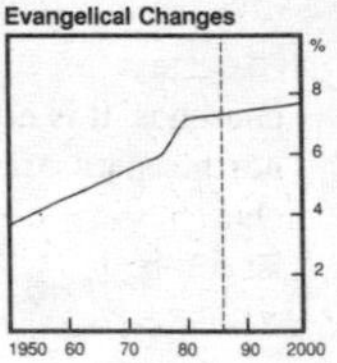

1. **Praise God for the impact of the gospel in Zambia in recent years.**
   a) There has been a widespread moving of the Spirit with many coming to personal faith in Christ from a nominal or sectarian Christianity.

b) Increased evangelization in urban areas of the copperbelt towns and Lusaka by Pentecostal, Baptist and Brethren believers. The growth of Pentecostal churches has been especially significant since 1979.

c) Outreach to rural areas that were once devoid of a clear gospel testimony.

d) The responsiveness of the youth with many making a greater level of commitment than previously known.

e) The increasingly strong evangelical witness in the United Church (the fruit of the work of LMS, Paris Evangelical Missionary Society, Church of Scotland and Methodist Missionary Society) is bringing new life and outreach in once dead and formal congregations.

f) The multiplication of groups of believers among the Angolan refugees. They have fled their war-torn, desolated land to the west.

2. **The negatives to be borne before the Lord in prayer**:

a) **The astonishing impact of foreign sectarian groups** such as the New Apostolic Church (many churches among the Lozi and in the southwest), and the Jehovah's Witnesses. It is reckoned that over 25% of the population has had involvement at some time with this latter sect. The past emphasis on institutions, made by mainline denominations, limited aggressive evangelism.

b) **The insidious danger of "scientific socialism".** Some government leaders are pressing for Marxist ideology to be taught in place of religious knowledge in schools.

c) **Widespread nominal Christianity**. Too many consider themselves Christian because of links with Christian institutions in their home areas. Many congregations have little biblical teaching and there are few who have a personal experience of salvation. This leaves them wide open to syncretic or foreign heresies. The rate of backsliding has been unacceptably high.

d) **Immorality** is a major problem among young people, and drunkenness among people of all ages.

3. **The maturing of the Church in urban areas is encouraging**. Strong, well-led English-speaking Baptist and Pentecostal Churches have developed over the last 10 years; although few older people are responding, many educated young people and professionals are coming to Christ. Pray that some of these may also be called into full-time work. There are insufficient Zambian church leaders from among the well-educated.

4. **Rural churches vary widely in spiritual quality and vigour**. Pray for:

a) **The many thriving evangelical congregations in the northwest** among the Luvale, Chokwe, Lunda, etc. (**Brethren**), Kaonde, Mbwela and Nkoya (**AEF**), Lamba, etc. (Baptist). The area has a high concentration of evangelical believers, but they need a greater vision for cross-cultural outreach to other areas of the land.

b) **The work of the Brethren in Christ and Churches of Christ among the Tonga peoples** in the south which has been fruitful; but some areas are only partially evangelized.

c) **The Reformed Church among the Nyanja peoples in the west** which is theologically evangelical, but formal and not growing.

d) **The Lozi and southwestern peoples and Bemba and northeastern peoples** who have very few evangelical congregations. Many have become nominally Christian, but because of unclear teaching, vast numbers have been swept into sectarian or syncretic indigenous churches. It is noteworthy that the Lumpa Church of the '60s had its greatest impact in northeastern areas where there was little evangelical witness. Pray for the planting of churches in these spiritually needy areas. The **AoG**, Pentecostal Holiness Church, **AEF**, **Brethren** and Churches of Christ have initiated new work in the northeast.

5. **The training of Christian leaders** is a priority, for many Christians are tossed about by every wind of doctrine.

a) **The Evangelical Fellowship of Zambia's** Theological College of Central Africa in Ndola is the first evangelical degree-awarding theological institution in Central Africa. Both the TCCA and the Pentecostal Bible School are full to capacity. There are also a number of lower level, local Bible Schools. Pray for spiritually and educationally qualified mature leaders to be prepared through these institutions.

b) **TEE** is widely used, but has only been partially effective. Lay training is a must.

6. **Young people.** **SU** has had a very significant impact in the secondary schools, with lively groups in most of them. ZAFES(**IFES**) has four staff workers and groups in almost every post-secondary institution. In some, over 10% of the student body come to Christian Union meetings. Many are being converted. Pray for adequate discipling and integration into church life when they finish their education. Many missionaries and Zambian believers have an extensive ministry in teaching the Scriptures in government schools.

7. **Missions have an open door**, but the emphasis is on working within the structure of the national churches, or in preparing Zambians for leadership. The largest are: **Brethren** (approx. 120 workers), **AEF** (75), Brethren in Christ (54) and **SBC** (48). Pray for wisdom, tact and humility for these brethren as they seek to help the Zambian Church. There are many opportunities for service: Bible teaching in schools, leadership training and the use of technical skills in radio, literature, etc.

8. **Less reached areas and peoples:**

a) **Many smaller peoples**, especially in the southwest, are minimally reached.

b) **The urban satellite towns** of Lusaka, the Copperbelt and Kabwe are spiritually needy. Many are squalid shanty settlements. Pray for the work of **DM** and others in evangelizing these areas where sin is rife.

c) **The European community is drawn from various nations.** Many have come on short-term government contracts or to work in the mines and are there just for the riches they can gain. Pray for the evangelization of this transient community. Pray also for the evangelization of such groups as the Communist Yugoslavs and Chinese, who are engaged in various development projects. There are some Zambian believers deeply concerned to witness to those from Communist lands — in fact, some Christians are witnessing in universities behind the Iron Curtain!

d) **The Indians are largely Gujarati-speaking.** The **IEM** from India has been invited to commence the first permanent work in this tightly-knit Muslim and Hindu community.

9. **Christian literature** is widely used, and there are a number of Christian bookstores (including four run by the Evangelical Church). The **Christian Literature Press** in Chingola has a significant role in publishing much evangelistic and teaching material for different groups.

10. **Bible translation** is possibly only needed in two to seven languages. The **Bible Society** has a continuing programme for upgrading existing versions and working on OT translations.

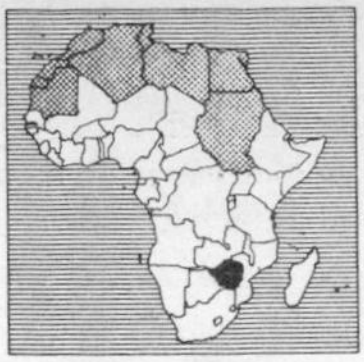

ZIMBABWE
(Republic of Zimbabwe)

Africa

Dec 2

Area 391,000 sq.km. Landlocked and dependent on surface routes through war-torn Mozambique and troubled South Africa for imports and exports.

Population 8,600,000. Annual growth 3.5%. People per sq.km. 22.

Peoples: About 30 ethnic groups.
Shona peoples 66%. Karanga 2,000,000; Zezuru 1,600,000; Manyika 1,000,000; Rozvi 680,000; Korekore 300,000; Ndau 300,000.
Ndebele peoples 18%. Ndebele 1,360,000; Kalanga 150,000 (Shona group being absorbed by Ndebele).
Other indigenous peoples 9%. Tsonga-Shangaan 260,000; Tonga 180,000; Venda 170,000; Tswana-Sotho 86,000; Kunda 50,000.
Other minorities 6%. Malawian 430,000; European 120,000; Coloured 25,000; Asian 18,000; Mozambiquan refugees.

Literacy 49%. **Official language**: English. **Trade languages**: Shona is widely spoken, Ndebele in the west. **All languages** 21. **Bible translations** 13Bi 3NT 2por.

Capital: Harare 900,000. Other major city: Bulawayo 500,000. Urbanization 24%.

Economy: Diversified economy, agriculture and mining of a wide variety of minerals providing export earnings. Considerable industrial development. The post-independence economic boom was slowed by serious drought, continued warfare in Mozambique and loss of skilled labour. Income/person $740 (5% of USA).

Politics: The Rhodesian declaration of independence from Britain by the white minority in 1965 led to prolonged and increasingly intense guerrilla warfare waged by two African nationalist groups. A British-mediated peace in 1979 led to a recognized independence in 1980. The government is ideologically committed to a one-party socialist state, but pragmatically permits a vigorous free market economy for the present. There is continuing guerrilla activity in the west, the homeland of the Ndebele.

Religion: The government favours Marxist-Leninism, but has promised religious freedom, and invited the churches to assist in national reconstruction. The government also made religious knowledge a compulsory subject in state schools.
Note: nearly all statistics are estimates. There never has been a census or much research concerning religious persuasion, and church life has been seriously disrupted by years of warfare.
Traditional religions 46.5%. Widespread in all areas, but in majority among the Tonga, Kunda, Ndau and Ndebele.
Non-religious/Atheist 1%.
Muslim 0.9%. Malawian Yao, Indians and some Shona-speaking Remba.
Christian 51.5%. Nominal 15.5%. Affiliated 36%.
Roman Catholic 9% (12.5% if nominals included). 760,000a; 413,000m.
African Indigenous Churches 10.9% (16% if nominals included). 937,000a; 416,000m. Over 130 groups. Largest (adherents):
African Apostolic Ch. of J. Marange 450,000
Foreign marginal 0.9%. Over 10 groups.
Protestant 15.3% (23.5% if nominals included). 1,310,000a; 537,000m. Denominations 61. Largest (adult members):

Anglican Church	(?) 92,000
Salvation Army	(?) 55,000
Seventh Day Adventist Ch.	55,000
United Methodist Church	(?) 48,000
Methodist Church	(?) 43,000
Reformed Churches (**NGK**)	(?) 35,000
Assemblies of God African	(?) 30,000
Apostolic Faith Mission	(?) 28,000
Evangelical Lutheran Ch.	17,100
Baptist Conv. (**SBC**)	(?) 15,000

Evangelical 7% of population.
Missionaries to Zimbabwe est. 600. (1:14,000 people) in about 50 agencies.
Missionaries from within Zimbabwe est. 80 of which about 30 serve abroad (both black and white Zimbabweans).

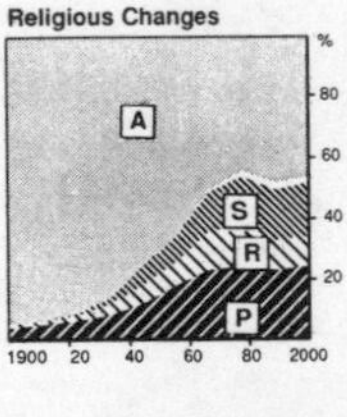

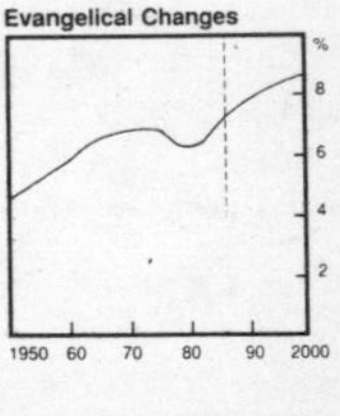

1. **The spiritual transformation** that has occurred in Zimbabwe is miraculous. The Holy Spirit is at work!

a) Despite the devastation and hurt of the war of independence, there has been an unprecedented openness to the Word of God. Many involved in the fighting have come to Christ.

b) Much evangelistic outreach in rural areas (Operation Fox-fire **AE**, etc.) and replanting of churches. The film **Jesus** has been widely and effectively used.

c) Evangelistic campaigns in the cities by **AE, DM**, Christ For All Nations, etc., have drawn many thousands to Christ. The CFAN campaigns in Harare and Bulawayo have been noteworthy.

d) Vigorous growth of some churches that have emphasized outreach — mainly smaller evangelical churches and indigenous and international Pentecostal groups.

e) Massive distribution of literature and Bibles to an eager readership.

2. **The brutality and horror of modern guerrilla warfare** brought death to 45,000, widespread destruction and moral collapse in many areas. There is continued warfare in Matabeleland, and life there has not returned to normal. Pray for peace, and for the balm of the gospel to heal ethnic and tribal hatreds. Pray for Christians involved in rehabilitation and aid programmes in the aftermath of both war and drought.

3. **Religious freedom is precious** and was hardly expected. Pray that the government may continue to maintain it and avoid ideological extremes. Persecution could come if Communist dogma is fully applied. Pray that believers may be adequately taught and spiritually prepared to use present opportunities, and to survive and grow even if persecution comes. There have been isolated incidents of pressure and intimidation of believers.

4. **For years the majority of churches stagnated**. The emphasis on institutional work; the lack of clear biblical teaching, and failure to ensure that pastors and church leaders had a vital living faith in Christ resulted in a large number of nominal, compromised Christians. The war changed that. In the sifting process many fell away and reverted to ancestor worship and witchcraft, but a stronger Church has emerged. Pray for:

a) **A spiritual unity that transcends race, tribe and denomination.** This is increasingly a reality in city churches of many denominations with strong multiracial congregations developing. The Pentecostal movement has suffered numerous divisions.

b) **A rebuilding of fellowships and meeting places** on stronger spiritual foundations than before, and conservation of the fruit of evangelism in the churches. Some Pentecostal and evangelical churches are growing fast.

c) **A clear stand** against the insidious pressures to compromise on ancestor worship and liberation theology which some church leaders advocate.

d) **A continued growth of vision for outreach** to needy areas and peoples in Zimbabwe and to other lands. Missionary concern for nearby Mozambique is growing; that land is wide open to Zimbabweans, but little evangelized. There are about 20 white and 10 black Zimbabweans serving abroad as missionaries in international agencies.

5. **Spiritual leaders of stature, courage and wisdom** are needed. Too few have had sufficient education to cope with increasingly sophisticated congregations. There is a serious generation gap between the more cautious, less well-trained, older pastors and the dynamism and relative immaturity of the younger in many churches. An evangelical theology relevant to Africa and clearly able to answer the strong voice of liberation theology among the younger Christian leaders is a need today. Pray for all 35 or so Bible schools and seminaries. Some for specific mention: the more ecumenical **Epworth College** where many of the mainline denominational pastors are trained and the evangelical **Baptist Seminary** in Gweru, **Reformed Church Seminary** in Mazvingo, and the **Theological College of Zimbabwe** in Bulawayo (EFZ-**AEF**). There are many secondary-level Bible schools: **TEAM, DM, AEF, AoG**, etc.

6. **Young people** have been deeply affected by the tumultuous events surrounding the time of independence. Political change did not give the expected benefits, and this is now the most open section of the population. Pray for outreach through the staff workers of:

a) **Scripture Union** which has had a decisive impact on the educated by their work in the secondary schools. The number of these schools increased from 250 in 1980 to 750 in 1983, and there are large active outgoing Christian groups in most of them. The camp ministry has been signally blessed. A smaller work in the primary schools is getting under way — pray that it may grow through an extensive programme of weekend camps.

b) **FOCUS(IFES)** which is responsible for Christian Unions among the 8,000 students in universities and colleges with 11 lively, growing groups. Pray that Christian graduates may become key leaders in the nation.

7. **The missionary force** was 996 in 1975, but was reduced during the war to less than 250. About 40 Catholic and Protestant missionaries and their children were killed in the crossfire of the fighting or were martyred. The most widely remembered was the Elim massacre when 13 missionaries and their families were slain; but praise God this was followed by the conversion of some of those responsible. The missionary numbers have risen again to around 600. Many are involved in serving the churches and in technical and reconstruction/aid ministries. Some of the larger mission agencies are **SBC** (71 workers), **TEAM** (33) and **AEF** (26).

8. **The less reached.** Zimbabwe has been extensively evangelized, but areas of need remain:

a) **The rural areas**, many of which suffered much in the war; in some areas there is relatively little spiritual life.

b) **The burgeoning cities**; much more and effective church planting is needed in new satellite townships springing up around the cities, where crime and frustration are common.

c) **Peoples**: The Tonga (180,000), Kunda (50,000), Nambya (30,000) and Dombe (15,000) of the Zambezi valley in the north are the least evangelized; evangelical believers are few, and little work has been done in their own languages. The Ndau in the southeast (**AEF**, etc.) and Ndebele and Kalanga in the west still have a high proportion of non-Christians and have proved less responsive than the Shona and Nyanja.

d) **The farming areas.** About 1,000,000 labourers and their dependents live on the large commercial farms, many owned by whites. About half are from Malawi and Mozambique. The CCAP(**NGK**), Salvation Army and others maintain an extensive ministry to these communities — especially to the Malawian Chewa-Nyanja speakers.

e) **Muslims** are few in number, but the least reached of all Zimbabwe's peoples. Most are Yao from Malawi (40,000), many are Indians in the main towns, and some are of the indigenous Shona-speaking Remba. They have their own secondary teaching to captivate the black youth.

f) **Mozambiquan refugees** fleeing the ongoing civil war in central Mozambique live in camps on the eastern border. Many are destitute and without Christ. Pray that many may be saved and return with the good news to their sparsely evangelized home areas.

g) **The Asians** are largely Gujarati-speaking and a closely-knit community which is not very open to the gospel. **AEF**, **TEAM** and local churches have an outreach to them, but there are no organized churches of Indian believers. They are 60% Hindu, 40% Muslim.

9. **Christian literature** has become a major ministry in Zimbabwe and beyond (especially Mozambique). Pray for:

a) **The Bible Society** with a huge Scripture printing and distribution programme. The government ruling for compulsory religious education has led to a massive distribution of Bibles, NTs and Scripture portions. In June 1985 a new start was made to revise the Shona Bible. A reliable revision is long overdue.

b) **Gospel Literature Lifeline** which has developed an astonishingly successful tract and follow up literature ministry. Two and a half million tracts were distributed in 1981; five million in 1984.

c) **Brethren in Christ** and **TEAM** bookstores which are a key part of the distribution of Christian literature. Pray for eternal fruit!

d) **CAVA** (Christian Audio Visual Action) which is, at present, the only major publisher of literature in Shona to counteract the renewed challenge offered by traditional animistic religion. About 20 books have been written and 42,000 printed in 1985 and distributed widely. Audio-visual materials are also produced.

10. **Christian radio** programmes are aired on the state radio and TV network. Many of these programmes are produced by churches and also by **TWR** Swaziland, in English, Shona (46 hours per month), Shangaan (15 hours), and Ndebele (14 hours). Many listen.

Dec 3

AUDIO-VISUAL EVANGELISM

Special Ministries

The extraordinary advances in technology are being harnessed for the gospel. Christian film making and TV programming have expanded enormously, and have had a significant impact worldwide. Several notable ministries are mentioned for prayer:

1. **The Moody 'Fact and Faith' film series** has long had a ministry among those influenced by a presentation of science moulded by a godless evolutionary materialism.

2. **The film 'Jesus'** (CCC) has been one of the most widely shown films in history. This moving rendering of the Gospel of Luke is, on average, being shown to 300,000 people nightly in over 85 languages. Pray for:

a) **The completion of the target** of dubbing this film, into all the 271 languages spoken by over one million people, by 1990.

b) **Eternal fruit**. The interest and initial response has been outstanding; but rarely are there adequate means for counselling, discipleship and gathering into churches of those who show a desire to follow Christ.

c) **The removal of censorship** against the showing of the film in some lands hostile to the gospel. This is particularly true of some Muslim and Communist lands.

d) **The circulation of video tape and microfiche versions** of the film. In closed lands this has become a major means of communicating the gospel.

3. The whole ministry of Christian film and TV programme production is costly in time and finance but, if well done, it is a good investment. Pray for all involved in this type of work.

4. Many national TV networks are willing to show good Christian productions. Pray for this trend to increase.

Dec 4

BIBLE CORRESPONDENCE COURSES (BCCs)

Special Ministries

This ministry is only about 40 years old, but it has grown and become one of the most effective means for following up contacts from literature distribution and Christian radio programmes. The relative ease in using the post in sensitive areas of the world and the emphasis on studying the Word of God has had a great impact on **BCC** students — some being converted, and others being strengthened in their Christian life. This has proved the best single means of winning Muslims.

1. **There are reckoned to be over 300 centres sending out evangelical BCCs.** Pray for the workers involved in preparation of materials, and helping the students through the post.

2. **Pray for the publicizing of BCCs** through tracts, radio programmes or through other students, in lands where there are few believers, and doors are closed to missionaries.

3. **Pray for the effective, personal follow-up of students** by local Christians, and for their integration into Christian fellowships.

Special Ministries

BIBLE SOCIETIES

Dec 5

It is hard to overestimate the importance of the organizations that provide God's Word for the peoples of the world. Most significant are the 70 national Bible Societies, and a further 30 national Bible Society offices, in a total of 100 countries working in over 180 territories, who are grouped under the United Bible Societies (**UBS**). Pray for:

1. **The staffs** of the Bible Societies with their special skills for the many tasks. Pray for their walk with God, for guidance in what translation and printing projects to tackle, etc.

2. **Translation and revision work** — **UBS** staff workers give much encouragement and advice to missionaries and nationals in new language and modern speech translation programmes. Much wisdom is needed in the many problems that arise. The **UBS** was engaged in 562 translation projects in 1984.

3. **The UBS goal of providing common language** versions in every language spoken by more than one million speakers. Pray for the initiation of translation in all of them by 1990 which is the goal deadline.

4. **The printing of the Scriptures**. This presents many problems — in some areas it is high costs, in others it is the lack of facilities or materials. The cost of Bibles is reduced through subsidies. Pray for the provision of the large sums of money needed. The **UBS** budget for 1984 was $27,300,000.

5. **The importation of Scriptures** which is sometimes difficult because of war, political crises or hostile regimes — as with some Communist and Muslim lands. Long and difficult negotiations are needed. The bad economic climate in Latin America and Africa have greatly increased the problems of distribution and sale of Scriptures.

6. **Distribution**. Sometimes the **UBS** depot or shop is the only source of Christian literature and Bibles in a country. In others a vast network of churches, shops and local distributors move out millions of portions of the Scriptures. In 1984 worldwide distribution was 12 million Bibles, 13 million NTs, and 445 million portions of the Scriptures. What a spiritual impact this could have!

7. The work of **SGM** in distributing superbly produced Scripture portions, selections and Gospels. This has been a remarkable ministry around the world. Often an **SGM** Scripture portion is used and treasured for years. In many languages an **SGM** booklet is the first portion of the Scriptures ever published.

Special Ministries

BIBLE TRANSLATION

Dec 6

This is an essential ministry if strong, culturally relevant, Bible-reading churches are to be planted. Pray for:

1. **The unfinished task**. There are complete Bibles in 286 languages and NTs in 594. Of the 5,455 known languages in the world only 1,808 have any part of the Scriptures. The remaining 3,647 languages are spoken by only 3% of the world's population. **SIL** estimates that of the latter, 723 definitely need Bible translation work.

2. **Translators**. Pray for the calling of more missionaries, and also nationals for this ministry, and for their adequate training. This is a long and slow work — to reduce a language to writing, to learn to speak it fluently, and then to be able to translate the Scriptures both accurately and understandably.

3. **Wycliffe Bible Translators (SIL)** is a mission wholly committed to Bible translation. In 1983 there were 4,826 members and associates of this agency. **SIL** is praying for a staff of 8,000 translators and supportive workers to be able to tackle known needs. **SIL** translation teams are working in 694 languages worldwide, but at least 548 other translation projects must yet be started.

Dec 7	CHILDREN, MINISTRY TO	Special Ministries

The importance of ministry to children and young people cannot be overestimated. They will be the Church of the next generation. Consider the following:

1. **Over one-third (35%) of the world's population** is under 15. Nearly half of Africa's population (45%) is under 15.
2. **Every year 130 million babies are born**, but 112 million of these are born in less developed countries. Many of the latter will grow up malnourished and with limited expectations of a viable economic future.

Prayer points:

1. **Christian parents.** They face a difficult task in bringing up children in the fear of the Lord in today's world. The pressures of surrounding society, the impact of the media, and the yawning generation gap have never been so acute as today. Their teaching by word of mouth and example is the most formative influence on the spiritual development of their offspring.

2. **The children themselves**. Only in a few lands can it be said that a reasonably adequate range of evangelistic and teaching ministries is widely available. In many nations where there has been rapid church growth over the last decade, there has been too little done to evangelize the children, and incorporate them into the Body of Christ. A nominal conformism or an anti-Christian rebelliousness may be the result.

3. **The churches**. Most churches concentrate their ministry on the adults. All too often churches have little or no youth work, and Sunday School programmes are woefully inadequate. There are too few Christian workers trained for such ministry, and few churches see the need. Pray for the development of effective training programmes and for their local funding.

4. **Agencies ministering to children and young people.** Many of the larger denominations have well developed programmes. Interdenominational agencies such as **Youth For Christ**, **SU**, **Boys' Brigade**, **Crusaders**, **Child Evangelism Fellowship** and many others, have developed effective literature, training, teaching and evangelistic programmes; but in most countries the percentage of young people and children reached is still small.

5. **Christian children** face many pressures and even persecution in non-Christian homes, schools and, in some cases, even from the authorities. It is only by God's grace that those who are converts from out of a non-Christian environment will continue to follow the Lord.

6. **Camp ministries** have been much used of God and possibly been the single most fruitful way of evangelizing and teaching young people. Many churches and agencies run such camps, but there are rarely enough spiritual leaders for this ministry.

7. **Literature for children** is a big need in many countries. Only in a few languages is there a wide variety of good literature for this age group. The Communist-ruled nations are particularly needy in this respect.

Special Ministries	CHILDREN, Missionaries' (MKs)	Dec 8

The education of missionaries' children is one of the major causes for suspending or terminating the cross-cultural ministry of missionaries at the very time when they are at the peak of their usefulness. Prayer points:

1. **The children themselves.** MKs often live under unusual conditions; many have an identity crisis as they grow up in two worlds, and some become resentful or rebellious. Pray that both parents and children may be a united team for the spread of the gospel, and for a right balance between ministry and family.

2. **Primary education** is often provided locally or through correspondence courses with parental guidance. It is hard for mothers and fathers to play the dual role of parent and teacher, and stresses in this area can impair the ministry.

3. **Secondary education** is the major problem. In some cases MK schools on the field are possible. In other cases, the only possibility for further education is in the home country — which means either boarding school or for the whole family to return home for an extended period, or permanently. Parents need wisdom and flexibility before the Lord in the decisions they make for their children's education. All alternatives are costly, in finance and emotion, but worthwhile if it means extending the missionaries' period of service. Pray that home churches may fully understand this crucial issue as an integral part of missionary support.

4. **MK schools** are vital for the retention of more mature missionaries, but are costly in both finance and personnel. There is an ever-present need for the right number and balance of staff with the appropriate spiritual gifts and teaching skills.

Special Ministries	CHRISTIAN LITERATURE	Dec 9-10

More than half the born-again Christians in the world testify that literature played a part in their conversion. Its role in strengthening Christians is incalculable. The Communists appreciate the importance of literature and spent over $5,000 million on propaganda in one year. The astonishing impact of Mao Tse Tung's little Red Book of quotations is well known — 740 million copies were produced between 1966 and 1968. Someone made the observation: "The missionaries taught the people to read, but the Communists supplied the reading material." Here are some prayer points:

1. **Crash literacy programmes** in many parts of the world create an immense desire for *any* literature among newly literates. Pray for a greater interest among churches in this ministry. Pray for more and better Christian literature.

2. **Very few languages have an adequate range of Christian literature.** Literature translated from English can be good, but can never be a substitute for that written by nationals. Yet there is a critical lack of spiritual and mature Christian writers in nearly every language.

3. **The rapidly increasing cost of printing** and the poverty of the people most needing the literature hinder this ministry. Pray for needed funds to launch programmes. Pray that profitable areas for selling Christian literature may be used to finance production in poorer areas and where there are few Christians.

4. **There is a worldwide shortage of Christian printers.** Pray for all those engaged in printing, and also for the smooth running of expensive machinery — breakdowns in under-developed lands can be disastrous.

5. **Literature missionaries are too few.** Pray for the calling of those with the the right qualities and qualifications for this ministry — in journalism, printing, publishing, writing, distribution, etc. Few Bible schools give adequate attention to the training of literature missionaries.

6. **Distribution** — Christian bookstores, colportage, Bible vans, etc. — pray for those serving in such. Pray for opportunities for personal witnessing and counselling in this distribution work. Pray for fruit from the literature sold or handed out. One mission worthy of prayer is the **CLC** — with 150 Christian bookstores or centres in 44 countries. **CLC** urgently needs 200 more workers!

7. **Christian magazines** have had a valuable ministry in many parts of the world — both evangelistically and in helping Christians. Heavy production costs now harm sales, and threaten their viability. Pray for guidance for those who have to make difficult decisions. Pray also for spiritual fruit from this ministry.

8. **Gospel broadsheets** have had an amazing growth since God called **WEC** to this ministry. These ***SOON*** broadsheets are produced bi-monthly in English, French, Portuguese, Spanish, Arabic, Urdu, Thai, Hindi, Bengali, etc., and distributed free by hand and post. The testimonies, short articles and offers of BCCs have brought a dramatic response. Over one and a half million copies are printed every issue.

Dec 11

CHRISTIAN TENTMAKERS

Special Ministries

Since the time of tentmaker Paul it has often been expedient or essential to use a secular skill or profession as a platform for sharing the gospel (Acts 18:3). Great movements of people seeking employment or education opportunities since 1950 have enabled Christians to use the same means to evangelize nations, peoples, and strata of society otherwise closed to full-time Christian workers. There are about 60 nations in the world where this is the major means for gaining entry into a country, and in 33 of these it is the *only* way. The number of lands in this category is increasing.

1. **Hundreds of thousands of Western, Middle Eastern, Asian and African Christians** have sought education opportunities or employment as doctors, lecturers, teachers, engineers, agriculturalists, house servants, road sweepers, etc. Most have done it for personal reasons. Pray that they may be stirred to witness to non-Christians as they observe the darkness, need and misconceptions of the indigenous populations around them.

2. **Pray for the specific calling of Christians** with the necessary qualifications and spirituality to serve in "closed" lands — specifically the Muslim heartlands, Central Asia and Communist ruled lands.

3. **Adequate cultural and spiritual preparation** is hard to obtain while retaining the necessary expertise, yet it is essential. Pray for good, appropriate training and screening of this special type of worker.

4. **These tentmakers frequently go to areas where the authorities or the people are hostile to Christianity.** Fellowship and pastoral care are vital ingredients in their ability to survive spiritually and be fruitful, but are often hard to provide. Pray especially for those living in lonely pressurized situations where every action can be carefully monitored. Pray for their protection as they challenge the entrenched powers of darkness.

5. **Wisdom and tact, together with a holy boldness**, are needed where active proselytization is forbidden, so that there may be conversions and the establishing of fellowships of believers.

6. **The right use of time** is important. Appropriate employment that gives opportunity both for doing the job in a Christ-uplifting way and for friendship evangelism is not easy to procure.

7. **Pray for the conversion of prominent citizens** of these countries through the witness of tentmakers. This could totally change the attitudes of governments and open the doors for other Christian workers.

Special Ministries

CULTISTS, OUTREACH TO

Dec 12

The worldwide growth and spread of missionary cults of western and eastern origin has been a striking phenomenon in the twentieth century. Note the following:

a) **Jehovah's Witnesses** have grown worldwide from 916,000 members in 1960 to 2,842,000 in 1984. There are over 7,500,000 adherents today. Many give sacrificial hours in door-to-door work to proclaim a false message in 202 nations.

b) **The Mormons** (The Church of Jesus Christ of Latter Day Saints) have similarly grown from 1,408,000 adherents in 1960 to 5,300,000 in 1985. The short-term missionary work of the Mormons puts many Protestant churches to shame.

c) The multiplication of exotic Hindu-Buddhist cults among disillusioned young people in the West has brought many into bondage and distress.

d) The high profile activities of the Unification Church (Moonies) and Scientology are well known.

Praise God for many thousands who have left such cults and found salvation in Christ. Many more are still bound by these delusions.

2. **Pray for the work of specific Christian ministries working among these groups**, who seek to lead individuals to Christ and produce suitable literature to help cultists. Names and addresses of a number of evangelical agencies are given below:

a) **Christian Research Institute**, Box 500, San Juan Capistrano, CA 92693, USA.

b) **MacGregor Ministries**, Box 1215, Delta, BC V4M 3T3, Canada.
Box 538, Prospect East, SA 5082, Australia.

c) **Reachout**, Box 43, Twickenham TW2 7EG, UK.

d) **Bethel Ministries** (for Jehovah's Witnesses),
Drawer CP-258, Manhattan Beach, CA 90266, USA.

e) **Saints Alive in Jesus** (for Mormons), Box 1076, Issaquah, WA 98027, USA.

3. **Suitable literature** in many languages is lacking or in short supply. Pray for all seeking to meet this specific need.

Special Ministries

DEVELOPMENT MINISTRIES

Dec 13

Christian workers have gained credibility for the gospel, and economic viability for local churches, through development programmes. In many poverty-stricken areas preaching the gospel without meeting the felt needs of the community would be counterproductive. Dealing with the basic root causes of famine, disease and economic deprivation is not as glamorous as emergency aid in a major crisis or disaster, but far more effective. Pray for:

1. **Christian churches, agencies and missions** with development projects. Many agencies have been specifically set up to fund and initiate such schemes. Pray that all projects selected may be those most beneficial to local communities, and pray for a wise selection of appropriate technology that can be continued and expanded locally without foreign input.

2. **Christian workers.** Honest, humble, dedicated expatriate and national workers who have both the technical expertise and the love of Christ are in great demand. Pray for many to be called and equipped for such ministries, and that their labours may win opportunities to share the gospel. Agriculture, development of effective markets for products, provision of clean water, literacy campaigns, preventive medicine, etc., are all key areas of need in many parts of the developing world.

3. **The planting and strengthening of local churches** through these projects. The whole ministry should be geared to bring the gospel to the people helped, and to plant churches, or, where churches already exist, to enable them to raise the finances to support local and missionary work and workers.

Dec 14

INTERNATIONAL CONFERENCES

Special Ministries

The ease and speed of international travel has made possible a growing number of world and regional evangelical conferences. Some of these have been pivotal for a great mobilization of believers for world evangelization.

The first world conference, the Edinburgh World Missionary Conference (1910), was a great stimulus for world evangelization. Sadly, the original emphasis was gradually watered down and virtually lost in subsequent conferences of what, ultimately, became the World Council of Churches. Oh that this body would return to its theological and biblical roots rather than concentrating on socio-political issues!

The post World War II period has been marked by several streams of evangelical congresses and conferences, each with their distinctive emphases and constituencies, but with considerable overlap and oneness of purpose.

1. **The Lausanne Movement**, which inaugurated great conferences in Berlin (1966), Lausanne (1974), Thailand (1980), has another major conference planned for 1989 in Lausanne. The constituency being Evangelicals in all Protestant churches and agencies.

2. **The World Evangelical Fellowship**, representing national and regional Evangelical Fellowships around the world, has held a number of regional and international conferences, the last being in Wheaton USA (1983).

3. **The Explo Mission Congresses**, which were organized by **Campus Crusade** in 1972 and 1974, culminated in 1985 in a worldwide satellite link-up of 300,000 believers in 53 countries.

4. **Great Youth Congresses** emphasizing missions have involved thousands of young people and stirred them with world vision — such as the triennial Urbana Missionary Congresses in North America, IVCF(**IFES**), and the Mission '80, '83 and '87 in Europe (**TEMA**).

5. **International conferences for itinerant evangelists** (Billy Graham Evangelistic Assoc.) in Amsterdam, Netherlands, in 1983 and 1986 have once more brought to the fore the biblical basis and vital importance of evangelism worldwide.

These conferences can be expensive luxuries with little long-term impact, or they can be vital catalysts for the advancement of the cause of Christ. Future conferences need prayer for:

a) **The primacy of the goal of world evangelization to be retained**, and increasing co-operation to that end to be the result.

b) **Lasting results**. The euphora and multiplicity of words can be temporary.

c) **The organization and supply of all expenses**. The cost in time, travel and finances can be huge — but it can be a good investment for eternity.

d) **The selection of themes, speakers and delegates** — always a delicate and important matter; the guidance of the Spirit rather than ecclesiastical politics must be the decisive element.

Special Ministries

MEDICAL MISSION WORK

Dec 15

This ministry has been one of the major Christian ministries on the mission field for many years. The appalling suffering and need, and the total lack of any medical attention in many fields, impelled the pioneer missionaries to expend much labour and money in developing clinics, hospitals, leprosaria, etc. It is estimated that today there are about 10,000 missionaries who have some medical ministry worldwide. This ministry needs prayer in these days of change, for:

1. **Adaptability**. Governments demand higher standards, and in some lands, are taking over all non-government health services. Medical missionary work must constantly be assessed as to its usefulness in changing circumstances. The present trend is for fewer but better equipped and staffed mission hospitals, and an emphasis on preventive medicine.

2. **Supply of needs in funds and personnel** — that the mission boards and national churches responsible may know how best to apportion them in accordance with the spiritual benefits to be reaped. Such programmes can too often become the master rather than the servant!

3. **Usefulness in winning people to the Lord and for the churches**. The primary aim of medical missionary work can sometimes be forgotten in the busyness of a large institution. Yet many can be and are won by this means. Pray for the right balance between medical and spiritual needs.

4. **The opening of doors to the gospel**. In many lands this is the only means for entry and witness; for example in North Yemen, Afghanistan, Nepal, Bhutan, etc. Pray that the witness of these medical missionaries, albeit tactful, may lead to the conversion of some, and also the planting of churches.

5. **Leprosy work**. This will probably long remain a ministry for which Christians will have a large input, for the disease is unpleasant, the cure long, and the psychological and social problems many. There are about 15,000,000 leprosy sufferers in the world, but only 20% are receiving treatment. Pray for the work of **The Leprosy Mission**, and others, in seeking to alleviate the sufferings of these unfortunate people, and win them for the Lord, in leprosaria and specialized clinics around the world. Pray for the conversion of some, and also that they may integrate into their communities as witnessing Christians and become the means of starting new congregations.

Special Ministries

MEDICAL WORKERS

Dec 16

The evangelizing and discipling of medical workers. Because more people pass through the hospitals of the world than through its churches, the **IHCF** seeks to win for Christ and train medical personnel — doctors, dentists, nurses, para-medicals, etc. — to share their faith with those whom they serve medically. Pray for:

1. **The conversion to Christ** of many members of the healing team.

2. **The witness of Christians** in the healing team to be both wise and bold to patients and colleagues.

3. **Christian medical workers serving in harzardous circumstances.** Communist takeovers mean the closing of churches, but not of hospitals — hence the strategic value of this work.

4. **Pray for IHCF staff workers round the world.** Pray for additional staff. Pray also for the IHCF Staff Training Centre in the Netherlands, the *HEART* magazine that circulates in 100 lands, and for the radio ministry through **TWR.**

Dec 17

MISSIONARY AVIATION

Special Ministries

What an essential means for evangelism and church growth the Christian "air force" has become! In many areas access is difficult by any other means. There are about 476 aircraft in 48 lands that are used to transport Christian workers, supplies, hospital patients and aid. Without this service, ministries would be slowed or stopped. Many mission agencies have their own aircraft, but others exist solely for the purpose of serving churches and missions. Pray for:

1. **The staff.** There are about 600 missionary pilots, mechanics and support personnel serving the Body of Christ. Their exacting ministry demands high technical ability and efficiency. They also can have a vital spiritual ministry for which they have many unique opportunities. Pray for the provision of workers technically and spiritually equipped for this ministry.

2. **Missionary Aviation Fellowship**, which is unique and deserving of special prayer as the pioneer of this ministry and the largest agency, with four branches operating in over 22 countries, flying over 30,000 hours per year. JAARS (Jungle Aviation and Radio Service), is a vital component of **SIL**'s Bible translation ministry in 11 lands.

3. **The supply of all needs.** Although the overall savings in time and finance are enormous, this is high-tech ministry and costly for both the operators and users.

4. **Safety.** The record has been good, but there have been a number of tragic accidents. Pilots must often operate from primitive airstrips in wild terrain and dangerous climatic conditions. A single mistake by a mechanic or pilot can have tragic consequences.

Dec 18

MISSIONARY NAVY

Special Ministries

A number of missions use ships for a wide variety of Christian ministries. Among these are:

1. **Operation Mobilisation's MV *Doulos*** and **MV *Logos*** with up to 450 crew and personnel at any one time involved in evangelism, ministry to Christians and literature distribution in ports around the world.

2. **YWAM's MV *Anastasis*** with up to 600 serving the Lord at any one time. A wide variety of ministries are based on the ship — schools of evangelism, discipleship training, evangelism, a university, and an aid ministry in areas of disaster or need.

3. **Small boat outreach** which is vital for many small island and coastal communities in the Pacific, Caribbean and Indonesia. ***Daystar III*** based in New Zealand (**UBS**) and **YWAM** have such a ministry.

Pray for:

a) **Provision of funds** for these expensive, yet strategic ministries. Costs have risen dramatically over the past decade.

b) **Provision of technically qualified crew and staff**, without whom ships may not sail. This is a constant need.
c) **The spiritual health and growth of all involved** in this demanding ministry. People from many nations have to live and witness together.
d) **The ministry of the ships** to stimulate world vision, local evangelism and holy living in ports of call.

Special Ministries

CHRISTIAN RADIO AND TELEVISION

Dec 19-20

This is potentially one of the most useful aids for world evangelization but, as yet, is inadequately exploited. Pray for:

1. **Agencies specializing in programming and broadcasting**. There were 1,450 Christian radio and TV stations worldwide in 1980 the number is now larger. There are over 13 major Protestant interdenominational agencies with international outreach — the largest being **FEBC** in the Far East, **TWR** with 750 missionaries in five continents and broadcasting in 75 languages, **WRMF** (Voice of the Andes, and missionary radio pioneer) in Ecuador, **FEBA** in Seychelles, ELWA (**SIM**) in Liberia, **IBRA** in Europe, etc. The USSR is the major nation for international broadcasting, with 310 hours of broadcasting Communist propaganda daily, but the 893 hours transmitted daily by Christian stations exceeds it by far — though with less transmitting power.

2. **Christian radio**: the only direct means of preaching the gospel in 45 lands, reaching potentially 1,700 million people (one-third of mankind), especially Communist and Muslim lands. The message still penetrates the Iron and Bamboo Curtains despite Communist attempts to jam them. Many churches have been planted as a result of this ministry, and there are possibly one million believers in Russia converted through such broadcasts. Pray for the raising up of national believers, originally from closed lands, who may be able to prepare and broadcast programmes to them.

3. **The listeners**. There are 1,200 million radio receivers in the world and, potentially, most of the world's population could have access to a set. It is estimated that there were 960 million regular listeners to Christian broadcasts in 1980. Pray for spiritual fruit in souls saved, Christians strengthened and churches planted.

4. **Effective cooperation** between radio agencies; there has often been too much competitiveness in the past. Three of the major agencies — **WRMF**, **FEBA** and **TWR** — have committed themselves to cooperate in research and broadcasting to make the gospel available to every person on earth in a language they can understand by the year 2000. Christian programmes are now broadcast in 103 or more languages, but there are 271 languages with over one million speakers. Pray that this goal may be achieved.

5. **Missions specializing in this ministry**. Most notable are the original pioneers — the **World Radio Missionary Fellowship** in Ecuador. Other major broadcasters are: ELWA (**SIM**) in Liberia, **TWR** in Monaco, Netherlands Antilles, Swaziland and Sri Lanka, **FEBA** in Seychelles, **FEBC** in the Philippines. The latter produces about 1,000 hours of programmes every week. Christian broadcasters put out more hours of broadcasting than Communist propaganda stations.

6. **Good reception in target areas**. The wave bands are increasingly crowded. More and more powerful transmitters are needed to shout down competing stations. Much technical skill is needed to transmit effectively. Jamming by Communist states is an ever-present problem. Short programmes in minority languages of closed countries are hard to publicize.

7. **The RICE project** which has been proposed by **FEBC** (**R**adio **i**n **C**hurch planting and **E**vangelism). This project aims at a long-term strategy for using radio (and other means where possible) for evangelism and church planting among unreached peoples. Pray for research, pilot programmes, effective evaluation and a radical step forward in the strategic use of radio through the RICE project.

8. **Follow-up.** Many stations and programming agencies have a large staff to handle the four to five million letters sent in by listeners annually. Pray for the protection of letters in the post — in many Muslim and Communist countries there is heavy censorship and only a small proportion of the letters get through. Pray for personal letters, literature and **BCCs** sent out in return. Pray for the linking up of new converts with groups of other believers. There may be over two million isolated radio believers in areas where churches are few.

Dec 21

RELIEF AND AID MINISTRIES

Special Ministries

Wars, famines, natural disasters and overpopulation have brought immense suffering to millions of fellow human beings. The vivid portrayal of suffering on TV screens has stirred many to give generously. Consider the following:

a) Over 900 million people of the Third World live below the bread line in extreme poverty.
b) The average yearly death rate through malnutrition or starvation is around 15 million.
c) In 1983 it was estimated that there were 16 million refugees in the world; the number is now higher due to the Sahel famines and continuing Afghan war.
d) The Sahel famine deeply affected the lives of over 100 million people. In 1985 there were 21 million still dependent on foreign aid for survival.

The potential for calamities of ever-increasing proportions is alarmingly high. Pray:

1. **That the generous giving by Christians** to aid programmes be wisely used. Prestige projects, lack of long-term strategy, inefficient communications, self-seeking bureaucracies, etc., can gobble up vast sums of money with little material or spiritual benefit to the sufferers.

2. **For those who administer the aid** and resettlement programmes. Many agencies have sprung up to channel the giving of Evangelicals — there are over 100 such in North America. Some of the better known are: **WV**, **TEAR Fund**, MAP International. Pray for the provision of the right personnel, a balance between physical and spiritual needs, and for evangelism and church planting to be furthered. Praise the Lord that where care and tact has been exercised, and a loving Christian testimony shared, there has been a harvest of souls in a number of countries.

3. **For the right balance in giving.** Christian donors need to be guided by the Lord rather than by their emotional response to physical suffering. The famine of the Word of God is a far more serious problem than that of food in Africa today. The giving by Christians to the sufferers of famine in Ethiopia was commendable, but must be matched by a similar generosity to train spiritual leaders for the undertaught Church in Africa.

Special Ministries

SATURATION EVANGELISM

Dec 22

Saturation evangelism is the total mobilization of the active membership of a church or group of churches to cover an entire area with the gospel. This has had many titles and forms over the past 20 years.

a) **Evangelism in Depth (EiD)** pioneered in the '60s by **LAM** in Latin America.
b) **New Life For All (NLFA)** in Africa (**SIM** and others).
c) **Evangelism Explosion (EE)** in the USA and beyond.

The effects were beneficial in areas where there were strong young evangelical churches (as in parts of Latin America and central Nigeria), but less so in other areas. More recent expressions of this vision have had more lasting benefits for local churches — especially in **EE**.

1. **Pray for a continued development of the scriptural principles of SE.** The ideal is correct, but many mistakes have been made in the past — too grandiose schemes, involvement of the unconverted in trying to win the unconverted, too hasty a preparation time, lack of spiritual local leaders to mobilize the ordinary believers, etc.

2. **Many local churches are now adapting the principles** for individual congregations, accompanied by much prayer backing and careful spiritual preparation of the believers, with very beneficial results. This is the more efficient method of believer mobilization. Pray for this to become the basic life pattern of churches all over the world, and not just a once-for-all effort.

3. **Mass evangelism crusades** have been much criticized, but they have played an important role in post-war evangelical growth in not only winning individuals to the Lord (many converts of Billy Graham's crusades are pastors or missionaries today!), but also in making many non-believers aware of the claims of Christ and uniting believers of many denominations in outreach. Pray for the successful integration of both mass and local church evangelism into the programme for world evangelization.

Special Ministries

SHORT TERM WORKERS (STWs)

Dec 23

More and more young people (and some older ones too!) have been serving the Lord in a cross-cultural situation for periods of a few weeks to three years. This is a significant worldwide development. It is impossible to reckon the numbers of believers all over the world who give some or all of their time during one year to missionary work, for this may equal the world's entire full-time missionary force! Many thousands of young people in Europe, Africa and Asia move out every year with such groups as **YWAM**, **CCC**, **OM**, TEEN Missions, and Horizons as short-term literature missionaries, evangelists, etc. Others serve the Lord for special projects with missionary societies. Pray for:

1. **Usefulness** in these short spells of service. Such short-term 'blitzes' can do much to revolutionize the spiritual situation in a hard field, and also inspire local believers to get out in direct evangelism.

2. **Avoidance of blunders** — through inexperience, lack of understanding of different cultures and languages, etc.

3. **The calling of more suitable young people** into such ministries. Unsuitable short-termers can cause havoc in teams when circumstances become difficult.

4. **The training programmes and leaders** upon whom so much responsibility falls.

5. **The challenging of short-termers** to a more holy and earnest living for God when their term is ended. Pray for many to be called into full-time service, and all to become more useful members of local churches as a result.

Dec 24

STUDENT MINISTRIES

Special Ministries

This is often one of the most neglected, yet strategic, fields of Christian witness (there are about 20 million university students in the world). A number of interdenominational organizations have been raised up by God to fill this need — to mention a few worthy of much prayer:

1. **Scripture Union** has an outreach to secondary schools round the world, with remarkable fruit among the educated young people in Africa, Europe and parts of Asia. **SU** is working in 67 countries of the world.

2. **Campus Crusade for Christ** maintains a vigorous ministry in North America which also fans out to 70 other countries all over the world. **CCC** emphasizes mass evangelism by mobilization of believers and discipleship training, largely among university students.

3. **International Fellowship of Evangelical Students (IFES)** has become a worldwide fellowship of autonomous national movements in universities, with a wide variety of local names. The emphasis of this ministry is evangelism, Bible study groups, literature and missions. This vital field needs much prayer:

   a) **For the extension of the evangelical witness to universities where, to date, none exists.** Areas of need — Latin America, Muslim world, French-speaking Africa.

   b) **For the right leadership** in the rapidly changing population of the student world — for adult advisers, travelling secretaries and student leaders.

   c) **For the Christian students and their growth in the Lord**, and that from their number some may go into full-time service for the Lord.

4. **The Navigators** with their unique personal discipleship programmes have made a deep impact on many. Their work began among the military in the USA, but they now minister among university students at 298 locations in 34 countries. Their emphasis is upon multiplying spiritual labourers through disciplined study and application of God's Word. They are moving out increasingly into local church-related ministries.

5. **Agencies specializing in ministry among international students**, such as **ISI**, **IFES** and others, have developed effective outreach to some of the 450,000 international students in English-speaking nations. In other language areas the coverage is poorer — especially in Francophone universities. Many of these students come from lands closed to the gospel and, sadly, the majority are repelled by the coldness and lack of concern of "Christians", and return home disillusioned. Others have been wonderfully converted. Students converted in the West could become a decisive factor for the spread of the gospel when they return home.

Special Ministries

TAPE, RECORD AND CASSETTE MINISTRIES

Dec 25-26

The arrival of cheap cassette tape recorders has made it possible to distribute Christian tapes widely and fairly cheaply to both Christians and the unconverted. This has become a valuable tool for evangelism, teaching and the encouragement of believers. Numerous local and international agencies have been founded for the production and distribution of cassette tapes. Pray for:

1. **Skilled labourers** who can handle the expensive equipment necessary to make good recordings, maintain cassette playback machines, and effectively distribute the tapes. Few mission agencies have grasped the significance of this ministry or exploited its potential.

2. **Evangelism through tapes. Gospel Recordings (GRI)** pioneered the use of simple messages on gramaphone records for evangelizing minority people groups and more inaccessible populations. These messages are now commonly produced on tapes as well. Often these records and tapes are the *only* means available to communicate the gospel to them. Recordings can be made far more speedily than sending in a missionary to learn the language or translate portions of God's Word. This is a vital tool for evangelism among unreached peoples. Pray for:

   a) **An increase in the numbers and availability of recorded messages.** There are now recordings made in 4,300 languages and dialects, but there are probably over 4,000 other languages and dialects which could be recorded with profit. Most of these are in Africa, South Asia, China and the Pacific.

   b) **Field recordists.** Over 50 are needed to supplement those already in the work. The work is arduous and difficult, requiring much travel and hard living conditions. Pray for the right language informants, preparation of texts, recording and production of tapes. Pray for the protection of delicate equipment handled in such conditions.

   c) **The Gospel Recordings World Fellowship** is a fellowship of seven autonomous agencies. Pray for the strategic development of the vision of reaching every tongue with the gospel by means of recorded messages.

   d) **The distribution of the records and cassettes.** Importation into many lands is difficult due to import restrictions, prohibitions, high customs dues, etc. Pray for wise distribution by Christian workers.

   e) **Spiritual fruit.** The response is very good in Mexico and Brazil at present. Pray that there may also be fruit in areas closed to the proclamation of the gospel by other means.

3. **Teaching and church growth through tapes.** In many spiritually hard areas of the world, the few Christians are isolated and have little opportunity to learn new hymns and choruses, or receive adequate teaching. Messages on tape can fill that void. Pray for the provision of the equipment, batteries and relevant messages.

4. **Bible tapes.** Many new translations of the Scriptures are first circulated on tape with great blessing. This is particularly useful for illiterate people and for those who have no written Scriptures, and where there is a real threat that political events may prevent the printing and distribution of the Word of God.

Dec 27

THEOLOGICAL EDUCATION BY EXTENSION (TEE)

Special Ministries

This is one of the exciting new tools in the hands of the Church for the training of church leaders. For years the churches of the West have used seminaries and Bible colleges for the training of full-time workers, but in the rest of the world this system has its weaknesses — too few of the right candidates; lack of funds; the poverty of the students; and those trained are often not the actual leaders in the churches. The rate of multiplication of churches in many parts of the world is so great that no residential training scheme could ever provide the workers needed. TEE is a system of training the actual leaders as they lead their congregations, by helping them to study in their homes using specially prepared teaching materials (programmed instruction) and frequent contacts with travelling lecturers. TEE is cheap, practical, adaptable, and can be tailored to fit the individual student and his needs. TEE has spread to every continent. In 1980 there were at least 250 evangelical centres with over 27,000 students all over the world. Pray for:

1. **Trained workers** to prepare teaching materials and maintain contact with the students. Preparing the literature is a skilled task, needing prayer.

2. **The students** — often studying under difficult conditions in simple homes, and in the midst of a very busy life.

3. **The enrichment of the churches** through a better teaching and pastoral ministry.

Dec 28-29

URBAN EVANGELIZATION

Special Ministries

Urban Evangelization is becoming one of the key challenges for the Church and for mission agencies. In 1985 there were 309 world class cities (those with a population of over a million), but it is expected that in 15 years' time there will be 433. Of these, 79 will have over four million people, and 24 will have over 10 million. The potential for ecological, economic and political catastrophes will greatly increase as the world becomes more urbanized. The cities are strategic for the gospel, but 57% of them have a non-Christian majority and are increasingly indifferent or hostile to the gospel. Pray for:

1. **Adequate strategies** for the evangelization of the major non-Christian cities of the world. The racial, ethnic, linguistic, social and religious complexities of modern cities make an all-out effort essential to reach each cultural unit of these cities. Los Angeles, in California, for example, will soon have 300 distinct ethno-linguistic people groups, and be 60% Hispanic.

2. **Major international and regional conferences** which will increasingly focus on urban ministries over the coming decade. Pray that these may lead to effective cooperation among churches and agencies without which the task will be impossible to achieve.

3. **The mobilization of a trained and efficient work force**. Christian workers, in general, fear the cities, especially the less comfortable slums and inner cities, and do not know how to handle the high costs, complexities and tensions of city ministry. Pioneer work in concrete jungles has to be seen as just as valid as pioneering in rural areas.

4. **The essential and effective use of all modern methods of communication**. Millions need to be confronted with the claims of Christ in as short a time as possible. No one medium can achieve this, but a combination of all in a concerted effort could decisively change the spiritual climate of a city.

Special Ministries

OPERATION WORLD

Dec 30

There has been an encouraging response to earlier editions of ***Operation World*** from individuals, churches and missions. Pray for:

1. **The 1986 English edition.** Pray that it will be used of God around the world to give vision, a prayer burden and stimulus for the completion of world evangelization.

2. **Other language versions.** At the time of writing, translation is under way in French, German, Portuguese and Spanish, and is contemplated in Dutch, Korean, Indonesian, Italian, Icelandic and other languages. The task of translation and adaptation is not easy, and in some languages it is hard to translate concepts widely understood in English.

3. **Revisions.** Corrections and updatings are constantly needed and appreciated, but it is hard to find time to do it. The author would value prayer for his own ministry too!

4. **Prayer cards and prayer diaries** derived from this volume. Pray that by all means the vision of a lost but winnable world may be imparted to as many Christians as possible.

Special Ministries

THE LORD'S RETURN

Dec 31

The last prayer in the Bible is "Come, Lord Jesus" (Rev. 22:20). Peter tells us that we should be "looking for and **hastening** the coming of the day of God" (2 Pet. 3:12). How better can we do it than by praying for the fulfilment of Gen. 12:3, Rev. 7:9-10 and Matt. 24:14? Pray for:

1. **The speediest possible evangelization of the world** — of every unreached people group, area, city and nation.

2. **Your part in achieving this.** What is God's will for ***your*** life? In the coming year are you willing to do whatever He commands regarding the need of the world? Is it possible God is calling ***you*** to a specific ministry in praying, supporting, or even personally going to the ends of the earth for your Master?

3. **Your local church's part.** Pray that your fellowship may grow in missionary zeal and commitment in the coming year.

APPENDIX 1

THE LEADERS OF THE WORLD'S NATIONS

Political changes in the world today are so rapid that the names of leaders have not been included in the text for the individual countries. This would date the information too fast! In this appendix we give the leaders that are probably the **most important decision-makers**, and not necessarily the titular head of state, who often plays a more ceremonial role. The details were correct for February-March 1986. The final column is left blank for you to fill in leadership changes. See p. 39 in the section on the **WORLD** for prayer points.

State or Territory	Title	Name	
Afghanistan	President, Revolutionary Council	**Ahmadzai**, Najib	
Albania	Chairman, Presidium, People's Assembly	**Alia**, Ramiz	
Algeria	President	**Bendjedid**, Chadli	
Angola	President	**dos Santos**, José	
Antigua & Barbuda	Prime Minister	**Bird**, Vere C.	
Argentina	President	**Alfonsin**, Raúl	
Australia	Prime Minister	**Hawke**, Robert	
Austria	Chancellor	**Sinowatz**, Fred	
Bahamas	Prime Minister	**Pindling**, Lynden O.	
Bahrain	Amir	**Al Khalifa**, Isa bin Sulman	
Bangladesh	Chief Martial Law Administrator/President	**Ershad**, Hussain	
Barbados	Prime Minister	**St John**, H. Bernard	
Belgium	Prime Minister	**Martens**, Wilfried	
Belize	Prime Minister	**Esquivel**, Manuel	
Benin	President	**Kérékou**, Mathieu	
Bermuda	Premier	**Swan**, John W. D.	
Bhutan	King	**Wangchuck**, Jingme Singye	
Bolivia	President	**Siles** Zuazo, Hernán	
Botswana	President	**Masire**, Quett	
Brazil	President	**Sarney** Costa, José	
Brunei	Sultan/Prime Minister	**Hassanal** Bolkiah	
Bulgaria	Chairman, State Council	**Zhivkov**, Todor Khristov	
Burkina Faso	Chairman, CNR	**Sankara**, Thomas	
Burma	President	**San Yu**	
Burundi	President	**Bagaza**, Jean-Baptiste	
Cameroon	President	**Biya**, Paul	
Canada	Prime Minister	**Mulroney**, Brian	
Cape Verde	President	**Pereira**, Aristides	
Central African Rep.	President	**Kolingba**, André-Dieudonne	
Chad	President	**Habré**, Hissene	
Chile	President	**Pinochet** Ugarte, Augusto	
China	Premier, State Council	**Zhao** Ziyang	
China (Taiwan)	President	**Chiang**, Ching-Kuo	
Colombia	President	**Betancor** Cuartas, Belisario	
Comoros	President	**Abdallah Abderemane**, Ahmed	
Congo	President	**Sassou-Nguesso**, Denis	
Costa Rica	President	**Arias** Sánchez, Oscar	
Cuba	President of the Councils of State	**Castro** Ruz, Fidel	
Cyprus	President	**Kyprianou**, Spyros	
Czechoslovakia	President	**Husák**, Gustáv	

State or Territory	Title	Name	
Denmark	Prime Minister	**Schlûter**, Paul	
Djibouti	President	**Hassan**, Gouled	
Dominica	Prime Minister	**Charles**, Mary Eugenia	
Dominican Republic	President	**Jorge** Blanco, Salvador	
Ecuador	President	**Febres-Cordero**, Leọn	
Egypt	President	**Mubarak**, Mohammed Hosni	
El Salvador	President	**Duarte** Fuentes, José Napoleón	
Equatorial Guinea	President	**Obiang Nguema**, Teodoro	
Ethiopia	Chairman of the Provisional Military Administrative Council	**Mengistu**, Haile-Mariam	
Fiji	Prime Minister	**Mara**, Kamisese	
Finland	Prime Minister	**Sorsa**, Kalevi	
France	President	**Mitterand**, Francois	
	Prime Minister	**Chirac**, Jacques	
Gabon	President	**Bongo**, El Hadj Omar	
Gambia	President	**Jawara**, Dawda Kairaba	
Germany (East)	Chief of Party and State	**Honecker**, Erich	
Germany (West)	Chancellor	**Kohl**, Helmut	
Ghana	Chairman, Provisional National Defence Council	**Rawlings**, Jerry	
Greece	Prime Minister	**Papandreou**, Andreas	
Grenada	Prime Minister	**Blaize**, Herbert	
Guatemala	President	**Arévalo**, Vinicio Cerezo	
Guinea	President	**Conté**, Lansana	
Guinea-Bissau	President	**Vieira**, João Bernardo	
Guyana	Executive President	**Hoyte**, Desmond	
Haiti	Chairman, Military Junta	**Namphey**, Henri	
Honduras	President	**Suazo** Córdova, Roberto	
Hungary	First Sec. of Communist Party	**Kadar**, Janos	
Iceland	Prime Minister	**Hermannsson**, Vigdis	
India	Prime Minister	**Gandhi**, Rajiv	
Indonesia	President	**Suharto**, General	
Iran	Prime Minister	**Musavi-Khamenei**, Mir Hosein	
Iraq	President	**Saddam**, Husayn	
Ireland (Eire)	Prime Minister	**Fitzgerald**, Garret	
Israel	Prime Minister	**Peres**, Shimon	
Italy	Prime Minister	**Craxi**, Bettino	
Ivory Coast	President	**Houphouët-Boigny**, Félix	
Jamaica	Prime Minister	**Seaga**, Edward	
Japan	Prime Minister	**Nakasone**, Yasuhiro	
Jordan	King	**Hussein** I	
Kampuchea	Head of State	**Samrin**, Heng	
Kenya	President	**arap Moi**, Daniel	
Kiribati	President	**Tabai**, Jeremia	
Korea (N)	President	**Kim** Il-song	
Korea (S)	President	**Chun** Doo Hwan	
Kuwait	Amir	**Sabah**, Jabir al-Ahmad	
Laos	Chairman	**Kaysone**, Phomuihan	
Lebanon	President	**Gemayel**, Amine	
	Prime Minister	**Karami**, Rashid	
Lesotho	King	**Moshoeshoe** II	
	Head of Military Council	**Lekhanya**, Justin	
Liberia	President	**Doe**, Gen. Samuel	
Libya	Chief of State	**Gaddafi**, Muammar	
Liechtenstein	Prime Minister	**Brunhart**, Hans	

State or Territory	Title	Name	
Luxemburg	Prime Minister	**Santer**, Jacques	
Madagascar	President	**Ratsiraka**, Didier	
Malawi	President-for-life	**Banda**, H. Kamuzu	
Malaysia	Prime Minister	**Mahathir** bin Mohamad	
Maldives	President	**Gayoom**, Maumoon Abdul	
Mali	President	**Traoré**, Moussa	
Malta	Prime Minister	**Mifsud Bonnici**, Karmenu	
Mauritania	Head of State	**Taya**, Maaouiya Ould Sid Ahmed	
Mauritius	Prime Minister	**Jugnauth**, Aneerood	
Mexico	President	**De la Madrid**, Hurtado, Miguel	
Monaco	Chief of State	**Ranier** III (Prince)	
Mongolia	Leader	**Batmunkh**, Zhambyn	
Morocco	King	**Hassan** II	
Mozambique	President	**Machel**, Samora	
Nepal	King	**Birendra**, Bir Bikram Shah Dev	
Netherlands	Prime Minister	**Lubbers**, Ruud	
New Zealand	Prime Minister	**Lange**, David	
Nicaragua	Prime Minister	**Ortega** Saavedra, Daniel	
Niger	President, Supreme Military Council	**Kountché**, Seyni	
Nigeria	Head of State	**Babangida**, Ibrahim	
Norway	Prime Minister	**Brundtland**, Gro Harlem	
Oman	Sultan	**bin Said**, Qaboos	
Pakistan	President	**Zia-ul-Haq**, Mohammad	
Panama	President	**del Valle**, Eric	
Papua New Guinea	Prime Minister	**Somare**, Michael	
Paraguay	President	**Stroessner**, Alfredo	
Peru	President	**Garcia**, Alan Perez	
Philippines	President	**Aquino**, Corazon	
Poland	Chairman, Council of Ministers	**Jaruzelski**, Wojciech	
Portugal	President	**Soares**, Dr Mario	
Qatar	Amir	**Thani**, Khalifa bin Hamad Al	
Romania	President	**Ceauşescu**, Nicolae	
Rwanda	President	**Habyarimana**, Juvénal	
St. Christopher and Nevis	Prime Minister	**Simmonds**, Kennedy	
St. Lucia	Prime Minister	**Compton**, John	
St. Vincent	Prime Minister	**Mitchell**, James	
Sao Tomé & Principé	President	**da Costa**, Manuel Pinto	
Saudi Arabia	King	**Saud**, Fahd bin Abd al-Aziz	
Senegal	President	**Diouf**, Abdou	
Seychelles	President	**René**, France Albert	
Sierra Leone	President	**Momoh**, Joseph	
Singapore	Prime Minister	**Lee** Kuan Yew	
Solomon Islands	Prime Minister	**Kenilorea**, Peter	
Somalia	President	**Barre**, Mohamed Siad	
South Africa	State President	**Botha**, Pieter	
Spain	Prime Minister	**González** Márquez, Felipe	
Sri Lanka	President	**Jayewardene,** J. R.	
Sudan	Prime Minister	**el-Mahdi**, Sadiq	
Suriname	Chief of State	**Bouterse**, Desire	
Swaziland	Prime Minister	**Dlamini**, Bhekimpi	
Sweden	Prime Minister	**Carlsson**, Ingvar	

State or Territory	Title	Name	
Switzerland	President	**Furgler**, Kurt	
Syria	President	**Assad**, Hafiz	
Tanzania	President	**Mwinyi**, Ali Hassan	
Thailand	King	**Bhumibolh**, Adulyadej	
	Prime Minister	**Prem**, Tinsulanonda	
Togo	President	**Eyadéma**, Gnassingbé	
Tonga	King	**Tupou IV**, Taufa'ahau	
Trinidad & Tobago	Prime Minister	**Chambers**, George	
Tunisia	President	**Bourguiba**, Habib	
Turkey	Prime Minister	**Özal**, Turgut	
Tuvalu	Prime Minister	**Puapua**, Tomasi	
Uganda	Head of State	**Museveni**, Yoweri	
Union of Soviet Socialist Republics	Gen. Secretary of the Politburo	**Gorbachev**, Mikhail	
United Arab Emirates	Prime Minister	**Maktum**, Rashid bin Said	
United Kingdom of Gt. Britain & N. Ireland	Prime Minister	**Thatcher**, Margaret	
United States of America	President	**Reagan**, Ronald	
Uruguay	President	**Sanguinetti**, Julio	
Vanuatu	Prime Minister	**Lini**, Walter	
Venezuela	President	**Lusinchi**, Jaime	
Vietnam	Chairman, National Assembly	**Nguyen** Huu Tho	
Western Samoa	Prime Minister	**Eti**, Tofilau	
Yemen (North)	President	**Salih**, Ali Abdallah	
Yemen (South)	Civil War; uncertain outcome	—	
Yugoslavia	President	Rotating leadership	
Zaire	President	**Mobutu** Sese Seko	
Zambia	President	**Kaunda**, Kenneth	
Zimbabwe	Prime Minister	**Mugabe**, Robert	

APPENDIX 2

The information in ***Operation World*** is too general, but is useful to give an overview of the world. In every region and country some agencies have been indicated in **bold type abbreviations**. This is to enable you to receive regular, specific prayer information. This book goes out with the prayer that you may link up with some of these agencies and become more personally involved in the missionary task.

The names and addresses of ***three*** categories of agencies are given below. It is impossible to give more than a reasonable selection of key denominational and interdenominational agencies that will be useful to a worldwide readership. I trust that all are in sympathy with the evangelical stance of the author!

Most of the agencies mentioned below have asked to be included, and all are considered to have a unique or significant contribution to the evangelization of the world. Please do not consider that this list is an expression of approval, and that those not mentioned are unacceptable. Several agencies specifically asked not to be included here. However, many other denominational and interdenominational agencies are mentioned in the text elsewhere.

I

Publications providing worldwide prayer information in English
Here follows a brief list of publications which are wholly or partially given to the provision of such information.

	Title	Type	Address
			UNITED STATES OF AMERICA
1.	**Christianity Today**	Magazine	PO Box 354, Dover, NJ 07801.
2.	**Church Around the World**	Leaflet	Tyndale House Publishers, 336 Gundersen Dr., Wheaton, IL 60187.
3.	**Decision**	Magazine	Billy Graham Evangelistic Assoc. 1300 Harmon Place, Minneapolis Minnesota 55403.
4.	**Evangelical Missions Quarterly**	Magazine	Evangelical Missions Information Service **(EFMA/IFMA)**, PO Box 794, Wheaton, IL 60189.
5.	**Global Church Growth**	Magazine	**OC Ministries**, 25 Corning Ave., Milpitas, CA 95035.
6.	**Global Prayer Digest**	Magazine	Frontier Fellowship, PO Box 90970, Pasadena, CA 91104.
7.	**International Journal of Frontier Missions**	Magazine	**US Center for World Mission** PO Box 40638, Pasadena, CA 91104.
8.	**Missionary News Service & Pulse**	Broadsheet	Evangelical Missions Information Service **(EFMA/IFMA)**, PO Box 794, Wheaton, IL 60189.
9.	**Praise & Prayer Calendar & Information Bulletin**	Broadsheet	Lausanne Committee for World Evangelization (**LCWE**), PO Box 2308, Charlotte NC 28211.
10.	**World Christian**	Magazine	PO Box 40010, Pasadena, CA 91104.
11.	**World Vision Magazine**	Magazine	**WV**, PO Box 0, Pasadena, CA 91109.
			UNITED KINGDOM
1.	**British Church Growth**	Magazine	164 Alinora Cresc., Goring-by-Sea, Worthing, W. Sussex BN12 4HW.

Title	Type	Address
2. **EMA Bulletin/IDEA**	Broadsheet	Evangelical Missionary Alliance, Whitefield Hse, 186 Kennington Park Rd., London SE11 4BT.
3. **FFM** (Emphasis on Muslims)	Magazine	Fellowship of Faith, 2 Old Parr Rd., Banbury, Oxon OX16 8HT (**Also** 205 Yonge St., Rm 25, Toronto, Ontario, Canada M5B 1NZ.)
4. **World Prayer News/ Missionary Mandate**	Broadsheet	Lancing Tabernacle, 20 Abbots Way, Lancing, West Sussex BN15 9DH.
6. **World Vision of Britain**	Magazine	Dychurch House, 8 Abington Street, Northampton NN1 2AJ.

OTHER WESTERN NATIONS

1. **IDEA**	Broadsheet	Evangelical Missionary Alliance (AEM), Dobelstr. 14, 7000 Stuttgart 1, West Germany.
2 **LOOK**	Broadsheet	**WEC International**, 37 Aberdeen Ave., Hamilton, Ontario, Canada L8P 2N6.
3. **LOOK** (Easy English)	Broadsheet	211 Fremont Ave. E, Hutchinson, MN 55350, USA.
4. **Prayer Special & Mission**	Broadsheet/ Magazine	The Evangelical Missionary Assoc. (TEMA) CH-1032 Romanel, Switzerland.
5. **World Report**	Broadsheet	United Bible Societies (**UBS**), Box 755, 7000 Stuttgart 1, West Germany.

ASIA

1. **Asian Report**	Magazine	Asian Outreach, GPO Box 3448, Hong Kong.
2. **Asian Church Today** **Church around Asia**	Magazine Broadsheet	Evangelical Fellowship of Asia, 803/92 Deepali, Nehru Place, New Delhi, 100019, India.
3. **India Church Growth Quarterly**	Magazine	Post Bag No. 768, Kilpauk, Madras, 600100, India.
4. **Mission Outreach**	Magazine	Indian Evangelical Mission, 38 Langford Rd., Bangalore 560025, India.

II

INTERDENOMINATIONAL INTER-MISSION ASSOCIATIONS

Significant national evangelical bodies, in mainly English-speaking missionary sending countries, are given below as representative of a large number of smaller mission agencies based in these lands that are too numerous to be included here. Many produce useful prayer information.

Africa	**AEAM**	Association of Evangelicals in Africa and Madagascar, PO Box 49332, Nairobi, Kenya.
Asia	**ACCF**	Asia Christian Communications Fellowship, c/o CCL, PO Box 95364 Tsimshatsui, Kowloon, Hong Kong.
	EFA	Evangelical Fellowship of Asia. See **EFI**.

Australia	**EMA**	The Australian Evangelical Alliance, PO Box 243, Box Hill, Vic. 3128.
Brazil	**AMTB**	Associaçã de Missões Transculturais Brazileiras, c/o CP 582, 01051-S. Paulo.
Germany	**AEM**	Arbeitsgemeinschaft Evangelikaler Missionen (EMA), Dobelstr. 14, 7000 Stuttgart 1.
Hong Kong	**HKACM**	Hong Kong Association of Christian Missions, 525 Nathan Rd., Bell House, Bock A, Flat 2003, Kowloon.
India	**EFI**	Evangelical Fellowship of India, 92/803 Deepali, Nehru Place, New Delhi 110019.
Netherlands	**EZA**	Stichting Evangelische Zendings Alliantie (EMA), Vlaanderenlaan 54, 8072 CG Nunspeet.
New Zealand	**EMA**	Evangelical Missionary Alliance, PO Box 68-140, Auckland 1.
Nigeria	**NEMA**	Nigeria Evangelical Missions Assoc., U.I.PO Box 9890, Ibadan, Oyo State.
Philippines	**PCEC**	Philippine Council of Evangelical Churches, Inc., PO Box 10121, Q.C.P.O., Quezon City 3008.
Singapore	**EFS**	Evangelical Fellowship of Singapore, #04-05, Bible House, 7 Armenian St., Singapore 0617.
South Africa	**SAAWE**	Suid-Afrikaanse Aksie vir Wêrlde-vangelisasle, PO Box 709, Kempton Park 1620, South Africa.
UK	**EMA**	Evangelical Missionary Alliance, Whitefield House, 186 Kennington Park Rd., London SE11 4BT.
USA	**EFMA**	Evangelical Foreign Missions Association, Box 794, Wheaton, IL 60189-0395.
	IFMA	Interdenominational Foreign Mission Assoc., Box 395, Wheaton IL 60189-0395.
	MARC(WV)	Missions Advanced Research and Communications Center, 919 W. Huntington Drive, Monrovia, CA 91016.
	USCWM	US Center for World Mission, PO Box 40638, Pasadena, CA 91104.

III

AGENCIES AND THEIR ADDRESSES

All agencies in **bold type abbreviations** in the text are given below. The number of agencies included is 92, but nearly half of the world's Protestant missionaries serve in these agencies.

Only a selection of addresses for each agency is given, and these addresses are primarily in lands where English is commonly spoken or from where English language prayer information is sent out. Other language editions of ***Operation World*** will include mission base addresses in their own language area.

The total number of missionaries in each agency serving from each country, is the most accurate we could obtain, but inevitably some workers are omitted who should be included and vice versa. The world totals in the final column include those of other nationalities not included in the previous one. Please note the following key:

[ ] Predominantly national workers — not included in the world totals for missionaries.

(?) Statistics that are more than five years old or, in some cases, estimates.

* Total for both Canada and the USA.

† Total for both Australia and New Zealand.

§ Total includes missionaries of other nations.

Abbr.	Mission name and address	Total missionaries National	World
ABMS	See **BMS**.		
AE	**Africa Enterprise**		(?) 40
	S. Africa PO Box 647, Pietermaritzburg 3200.		
AEF	**Africa Evangelical Fellowship**		321
	UK Int.Office. 17 Westcote Rd., Reading, Berks RGA3 2DL.		
	UK Br.Office. 30 Lingfield Rd., London SW19 4PU.	44	
	USA PO Box 1679 Bloomfield, NJ 07003.	212*	
	NZ PO Box 1390, Invercargill.	5	
	S. Africa Rowland Hse, Montrose Ave., Clairmont 7700.	27	
	Aust. PO Box 292, Castle Hill, NSW 2154.	22	
AIM	**Africa Inland Mission**		650
	UK 2 Vorley Rd., Archway, London N19 5HE.	121	
	USA PO Box 178, Pearl River, New York 10965.	350*	
	Aust. 36 Hercules St., Chatswood, NSW 2067.	17	
	NZ 144 White Swan Rd., Auckland 4.	5	
AO	**Asian Outreach International Ltd**		17
	Hong Kong GPO Box 3448.		
	USA PO Box 9000, Mission Viejo, CA 92690.	4	
	UK 2 Kingswood Close, Lytham, Lancs FY8 4RE.		
	NZ PO Box 2160, Tauranga.	10	
	Singapore Maxwell Rd., PO Box 3038, Singapore 9050.		
AoG	**Assemblies of God**		(?)1,900
	USA Div. of For. Miss., 1445 Boonville Ave., Springfield, MO 65802.	1,358	
	UK 106/114 Talbot St., Nottingham NG1 5GH.	68	
	Aust. PO Box 229, Nunawading, Vic. 3131.	47	
	NZ PO Box 8023, Tauranga.	20	
APCM	**Asia Pacific Christian Mission**		180
	Aust. 345 Bell St., Preston, Vic. 3072.	115	
	NZ 427 Queen St., Auckland 1.	28	
AsEF	**Asia Evangelistic Fellowship**		[100]
	Singapore Maxwell Rd., PO Box 579, Singapore 9011.		
	Aust. PO Box 122, Epping, NSW 2121.		
BCU	**Bible Christian Union**		67
	USA PO Box 718, Lebanon, PA 17042.		
BCMS	**Bible Churchman's Missionary Society** (Anglican)		96
	UK 251 Lewisham Way, London SE4 1XF.	84	
BEM	**Belgian Evangelical Mission**		22
	UK High House, Walcote, Lutterworth, Leicester LE17 4JW.		

Abbr.	Mission name and address	Total missionaries National	World
BFM	**Bethany Fellowship Missions**		172
	USA 6820 Auto Club Rd., Minneapolis, MN 55438.	129	
BMMF	**BMMF International**		390
	UK 186 Kennington Park Rd., London SE11 4BT.	131	
	USA PO Box 418, Upper Darby, PA 19082-0418.	50	
	Can. 4028 Sheppard Ave. E., Agincourt, Ont. M1S 1S6.	25	
	Aust. 7 Ellingworth Parade, Box Hill, Victoria 3128.	60	
	NZ PO Box 10-244, Balmoral, Auckland 4.	55	
BMS	**Baptist Missionary Society**		(?)500
	UK 93 Gloucester Place, London W1H 4AA.	191	
	Aust. ABMS, PO Box 273, Hawthorn, Victoria 3122.	144	
Brethren	**UK** Echoes, 1 Widcombe Cresc., Bath, Avon BA2 6AQ.	398§	1,223
	USA CMML Inc., PO Box 13, Spring Lake, NJ 07762.	397	
	Can. Missionary Service Committee, 1562A Dunforth Ave., Toronto, Ontario M4J 1N4.	189	
	Aust. 19 Alexander Ave., Willoughby, NSW 2068.	63	
	NZ Missionary Funds (NZ) Inc., PO Box 744, Palmerston North.	176	
CAM	**Central Asian Mission**		20
	UK 166 Tonbridge Rd., Maidstone, Kent ME16 8SR.		
CAMI	**CAM International**		332
	USA 8625 La Prada Drive, Dallas, TX 75228.		
CBFMS	**Conservative Baptist Foreign Missionary Society.**		699
	USA PO Box 5, Wheaton, IL 60189-005.		
CBOMB	**Canadian Baptist Overseas Mission Board**		(?)90
	Can. 217 St. George St., Toronto, Ontario M5R 2M2.		
CCC	**Campus Crusade for Christ International**		(?)600
	USA Arrowhead Springs, San Bernardino, CA 92414.	500	
	UK 103 Friar St., Reading Berks RG1 1EP.	45	
	NZ 73 Khyber Pass Rd., Auckland 3.	2	
CLC	**Christian Literature Crusade**		630
	UK 201 Church Rd., London SE19 2PT.	118	
	USA PO Box C, Fort Washington, PA 19034.	63*	
	Aust. PO Box 91, Pennant Hills, NSW 2120.	22†	
CM	**Calvary Ministries**		50
	Nigeria PO Box 6001, Jos, Plateau State, Nigeria.		
CMA	**Christian & Missionary Alliance**		960
	USA PO Box C, Nyack, NY 10960.	940*	
	Can. PO Box 7900, Station B, Willowdale, Ontario M2K 2R6.		
	Aust. 86 The Esplanade, French's Forest, NSW 2086.	11†	

Abbr.	Mission name and address	Total missionaries National	World
CMF	**Christian Missionary Foundation**		(?)20
	Nigeria PO Box 9890, U.I.P.O., Ibadan, Nigeria.		
CoN	**Church of the Nazarene** (Holiness)		(?)650
	USA PO Box 655, Fergus Falls, MN 56537.	580	
CRWM	**Christian Reformed World Missions**		(?)280
	USA 2850 Kalamazoo SE, Grand Rapids, Michigan 49560.		
CWI	**Christian Witness to Israel**		58
	UK Seven Trees, 44 Lubbock Rd. Chislehurst, Kent BR7 5JX.	32	
	NZ 88 Jervois Rd., Herne Bay, Auckland 2.	3†	
DM	**Dorothea Mission**		85
	S. Africa PO Box 219, 0001 Pretoria.		
	UK 179 Coldharbour Rd. Bristol BS6 7SX.		
ECF	**Evangelize China Fellowship, Inc.**		[150]
	USA 1583 E. Colorado Blvd., Pasadena, CA 91106.		
ECM	**European Christian Mission**		136
	UK PO Box 180, Northampton.	32	
	W. Germany Postfach 1103, 7842 Kandern 1.	14	
	Can. Miss. to Europe's Millions, 116, 1077-56 St., Delta, BC V4L 2A2.	32*	
	Aust. PO Box 15, Croydon, NSW 2132.	16†	
EHC	**World Literature Crusade** (Every Home Crusade)		[?]
	USA PO Box 1313, Studio City, CA 91604.		
Elim	**Elim Pentecostal Churches International Missions Dept.**		70
	UK PO Box 38, Cheltenham, Gloucestershire GL50 3HN.	59	
	NZ 26 Burleigh Rd., Blenheim.		
EMS	**Evangelical Missionary Society — of Ev. Ch. of W. Africa, Nigeria**		622
	Nigeria PO Box 63, Jos, Plateau State.		
	USA c/o SIM International, PO Box C, Cedar Grove, NJ 07009.		
EUSA	**Evangelical Union of South America** (with the **Andes Evang. Mission)**		71
	UK 186 Kennington Park Rd., London SE11 4BT.	64	
FEBA	**Far East Broadcasting Association**	39	
	UK Ivy Arch Rd., Worthing, W. Sussex BN14 8BU.		
FEBC	**Far East Broadcasting Company, Inc.**		108
	USA PO Box 1, La Mirada, CA 90637.	55	
	Aust. PO Box 183, Caringbah, NSW 2229.	6	
	NZ PO Box 4140, Hamilton.	2	
Fron.	**Frontiers**		
	USA 1610 Elizabeth St., PO Box 40159, Pasadena, CA 91104.	?	?
GEM	**Greater Europe Mission**		320
	USA PO Box 668, Wheaton, IL 60189.		
GMU	**Gospel Missionary Union**		
	USA 10000 N. Oak, Kansas City, MO 64155.		489

Abbr.	Mission name and address	Total missionaries National	World
GRI	**Gospel Recordings World Fellowship**		58
	USA 122 Glendale Blvd., Los Angeles, CA 90026.	40*	
	UK PO Box 62, Gloucester GL1 5SE.	3	
	Aust. G. R. Inc., PO Box 171, Eastwood, NSW 2122.	13†	
	Can. G. R. Inc., 2 Audley St., Toronto, Ont. M8Y 2X2.		
	India G. R. Assoc., 8 Commissariat Rd., Bangalore 560025.		
	S. Africa G. R. Inc., PO Box 62, Observatory, Cape Town 7935.	2	
HCJB	See **WRMF** (World Radio Missionary Fellowship)		
IBRA	**International Broadcasting Association**		(?) 10
	Sweden S-105 36 Stockholm.		
ICF	**International Christian Fellowship**		112
	UK 20 Vicarage Farm Rd., Hounslow, Middx. TW3 4NW.	46	
	USA 213 Naperville St., Wheaton IL 60187.	31	
	Aust. PO Box 206, Box Hill, Vic. 3128.	16†	
IEM	**Indian Evangelical Mission**		192
	India Post Bag 2557, Bangalore 560025.		
IHCF	**International Hospital Christian Fellowship**		[110]
	USA PO Box 4004, San Clemente, CA 92672.	6	26
	Aust. 24 Box St., Merbein, Victoria 3505.	?	
	Holland Noordersingel 90, 3781 XK Voorthuizen.	10§	
IMI	**International Mission, Inc.**		240
	USA PO Box 323, Wayne, NJ 07470.		
IMF	**Indonesian Missionary Fellowship**		225
	Indonesia Jln Trunojoyo 2, Batu 65301, E. Java.	180	
INF	**International Nepal Fellowship**		110
	UK 2 West St., Reading, Berks RG1 1TT.	42	
	Aust. 20 Cunningham St., Matraville, NSW 2036.	8	
	NZ PO Box 144, Wellington 1.	18	
IFES	**International Fellowship of Evangelical Students**		55
	UK 55 Palmerston Rd., Wealdstone, Harrow, HA3 7RR.	10	
	USA Inter-Varsity Christian Fell., PO Box 270, Madison, WI 53701.	10	
	Aust. AFES, 129 York St., Sydney 2000.		
	NZ TSCF, PO Box 9672, Wellington.		
ISI	**International Students Inc.**		138
	USA Star Ranch, PO Box C, Colorado Springs, CO 80901.		
	UK I.S.C.S., 59 Petts Wood Rd., Orpington, Kent BR5 1JU.		
JEB	**Japan Evangelistic Band**		16
	UK 275 London Rd., North End, Portsmouth PO2 9HE.	9	
	USA 2237 Manhattan Ave., Hermosa Beach, CA 90254.	4	
	Aust. PO Box 167, Collins St., Victoria 3000.		

Abbr.	Mission name and address	Total missionaries National	World
LAM	**Latin America Mission Inc.**		159
	USA PO Box 341368, Coral Gables FL 33134.		
LM	**Leprosy Mission (International)**		71
	UK 50 Portland Place, London W1N 3DG.	37	
	Aust. 174 Collins St., Melbourne, Vic. 3000.	14	
	NZ 591 Dominion Rd., Balmoral, Auckland 4.	12	
MAF	**Mission Aviation Fellowship**		427
	USA Mission Aviation Fell., PO Box 202, Redlands, CA 92373.	252*	
	UK Ingles Manor, Castle Hill Ave., Folkestone, Kent CT20 2TN.	40	
	Aust. PO Box 211, Box Hill, Vic. 3128.	110	
	NZ PO Box 611, Manurewa, Auckland.	25	
MECO	**Middle East Christian Outreach**		60
	Cyprus PO Box 662, Larnaca.		
	UK 22 Culverden Park Rd., Tunbridge Wells, Kent TN4 9RA.	25	
	Aust. PO Box 528 Camberwell, Vic. 3124.	22*	
	USA PO Box 725, Highland Park, IL 60035.	5	
MT	**The Messianic Testimony**		43
	UK 189 Whitechapel Rd., London E1 1DN.	26	
Nav	**The Navigators**		[2,655]
	USA PO Box 6000, Colorado Springs, CO 80934.	327*	440
	UK Tregaron House, 27 High St., New Malden, Surrey KT3 4BY.	30	
	Aust. PO Box A-143, Sydney South, NSW 2000.	7	
	NZ PO Box 1951, Christchurch.	4	
NAM	**North Africa Mission**		175
	UK 2 Radmoor Rd., Loughborough, Leics. LE11 3BS.	41	
	USA 47 Long Lane, Upper Darby, PA 19082.	122*	
NGK	**Nederduits Gerefermeeerde Kerk** (Dutch Ref. Church)		294
	S. Africa Algemene Sendingsekretaris N. G. Kerk, Posbus 433, Pretoria 0001.		
NTM	**New Tribes Mission**		1,809
	USA 1000 E. First St., Sanford, FL 32771.	1,474	
	UK Derby Rd., Matlock Bath, Matlock, Derbys. DE4 3PY.	60	
	Aust. PO Box 84, Rooty Hill, NSW 2766.	49	
	NZ PO Box 2339, Christchurch.	26	
NWF	**North-West Frontiers Fellowship**		14
	UK 12 Horsebrook Park, Calne, Wilts. SN11 8EX	5	
	USA 1107 Mayette Avenue, San Jose, CA 95125	3	
	NZ 25a Haultain St., Hamilton.	6†	
OCMin	**OC Ministries**		232
	USA 25 Corning Ave., Milpitas, CA 95035	227	
OD	**Open Doors**		n/a
	Netherlands PO Box 47, 3840 AA Harderwijk.		
	UK PO Box 6, Standlake, Witney, Oxon OX8 7SP.		
	USA PO Box 2006, Orange, CA 92669.		
	S. Africa PO Box 41, Kenilworth 7745.		

Abbr.	Mission name and address	Total missionaries National	World
OM	**Operation Mobilisation** (also Send The Light).		1,700
	UK The Quinta, Weston Rhyn, Oswestry, Shropshire SY10 7LT.		
	Send The Light, PO Box 48, Bromley, Kent BRI 1BY.	275	
	USA PO Box 148, Midland Park, NJ 07432.	80	
	Aust. 62 Glengale Drive, Rochedale, Brisbane, Qld 4123.	15	
	Singapore PO Box 1063, Bedok S. PO 9146.	7	
OMF	**Overseas Missionary Fellowship**		996
	Singapore 2 Cluny Rd., Singapore 1025.	10	
	USA 404 South Church St., Robesonia, PA 19551.	317*	
	Hong Kong 108 Boundary St., G/F, Kowloon.	13	
	Philippines PO Box AC 458, Quezon City 3001.	13	
	UK Belmont, The Vine, Sevenoaks, Kent TN13 3TZ.	300	
	Aust. 14 Grange Rd., Kew, Vic. 3103.	79	
	NZ PO Box 10-159, Auckland 4.	60	
	S. Africa 5 Rippleby Rd., Claremont, 7700 Cape Town.	23	
OMS	**OMS International**		512
	USA PO Box A, Greenwood, IN 46142.	487	
	UK 1 Sandleigh Ave., Didsbury, Manchester M20 9LN.	10	
	NZ PO Box 962, Hamilton.	10†	
QIM	**Qua Iboe Fellowship**		42
	UK Room 317, 7 Donegal Square West, Belfast BT1 6JE.	39	
PAoC	**Pentecostal Assemblies of Canada, Overseas Miss. Dept.,**	(?)192	
	Can. 10 Overlea Boulevard, Toronto, Ontario M4G 1A5.		
RBMU	**RBMU International**		273
	UK Whitefield House, 186 Kennington Park Rd., London SE11 4BT.	83	
	USA 8102 Elberon Ave., Philadelphia, PA 19111	145	
	Aust. PO Box 554, Camberwell, Vic. 3124.	24	
RSMT	**Red Sea Mission Team**		88
	USA PO Box 16227, Minneapolis, MN 55416.	13*	
	UK 33/35 The Grove, Finchley, London N3 1QU.	34	
	Aust. PO Box 3302, Sydney, NSW 2001.	12	
	NZ 24 Firth Rd., Browns Bay, Auckland 10.	2	
SA	**Salvation Army**		500
	UK 101 Queen Victoria St., London EC4P 4EP.		
	Aust. PO Box 1287K, Melbourne, Victoria 3001.		
SAMS	**South American Missionary Society** (Anglican)		102
	UK Allen Gardiner House, Pembury Rd., Tunbridge Wells TN2 3QU.	93	
	Aust. 25 Alexander Parade, Roseville, NSW 2069.	9	
SAO	**Southeast Asian Outreach**		9
	UK 90 Windmill St., Gravesend, Kent DA12 ILH.		

Abbr.	Mission name and address	Total missionaries National	World
SBC	**Southern Baptist Convention**		3,200
	USA PO Box 6597, Richmond, VA 23230.		
SEND	**SEND International**		312
	USA PO Box 513, Farmington, MI 48024.	292	
SGM	**Scripture Gift Mission**		
	UK Radstock House, 3 Eccleston St., London SW1W 9LZ.		
	Aust. PO Box 163, Summer Hill, NSW 2130.		
SIL	**Summer Institute of Linguistics — see WBT.**		
SIM	**SIM International**		981
	USA PO Box C, Cedar Grove, NJ 07009.	520	
	UK Joint Missions Centre, Ullswater Cresc., Coulsdon, Surrey CR3 2HR.	112§	
	Aust. PO Box 171, Summer Hill, NSW 2130.	53	
	NZ PO Box 38-588, Howick.	46	
	Nigeria ECWA/SIM, PMB 2009, Jos, Plateau State.		
	Singapore Bras Basah, PO Box 239, Singapore 9118.	4	
SGA	**Slavic Gospel Association, Inc.**		[260]
	USA PO Box 1122, Wheaton, IL 60189.	89	(?)100
	Aust. PO Box 216, Box Hill, Vic. 3128.	8†	
	UK 37a The Goffs, Eastbourne, E. Sussex BN21 1HF.		
SSEM	**South Sea Evangelical Mission**		60
	Aust. 12a Coronation Str., Hornsby, NSW 2077.	27	
	NZ PO Box 67010, Mt. Eden 1003.	16	
SU	**Scripture Union**		[900]
	UK 130 City Road, London EC1V 2NJ.	[232]	
	Aust. 129 York St., Sydney NSW 2000.		
SUM	**The SUM Fellowship**		480
	UK 75 Granville Rd., Sidcup, Kent DA14 4BU.	89	
	Aust. PO Box 237, Baulkham Hills, NSW 2153.	27†	
	Nigeria Church of Christ in Nigeria, PMB 2127, Jos, Plateau State.		
TEAM	**The Evangelical Alliance Mission**		1,088
	USA PO Box 969, Wheaton, IL 60189.	1,076*	
	Can. PO Box 980, Regina, SK S4P 3B2.		
	Aust. 26 Homebush Rd., Homebush, NSW 2140.	12†	
TEAR Fund	**The Evangelical Alliance Relief Fund**		100
	UK 11 Station Rd., Teddington, Middx. TW11 9AA.		
	Aust. PO Box 464, Hawthorn, Vic. 3122.		
	NZ PO Box 68-140 Auckland 1.	13	
TWR	**Trans World Radio**		777
	USA PO Box 98, Chatham, New Jersey 07928.	380	
	UK 45 London Rd., Biggleswade, Beds. SG18 8ED.	15	
UBS	**United Bible Societies World Service**		
	UK First Floor, 63 Carter Lane, London EC4 5DY.		

Abbr.	Mission name and address	Total missionaries National	World
UFM	**Unevangelized Fields Mission**		56
	UK 47a, Fleet St., Swindon, Wilts. SN1 1RE.	56	
UWM	**United World Mission**		115
	USA PO Box 8000, St. Petersburg, FL 33738.	99	
WBT	**Wycliffe Bible Translators Inc.**		4,826
	USA Huntington Beach, CA 92647.	3,829	
	Aust. Graham Rd., Kangaroo Ground, Vic. 3097.	334	
	NZ PO Box 10, Featherston, Wairarapa.	71	
	UK Horsleys Green, High Wycombe, Bucks. HP14 3XL.	218	
WEC	**WEC International**		1,059
	UK Bulstrode, Gerrards Cross, Bucks. SL9 8SZ.	299	
	USA PO Box 1707, Fort Washington, Penna 19034.	170	
	Can. 37 Aberdeen Ave., Hamilton, Ontario L8P 2N6.	80	
	Aust. 48 Woodside Ave.,Strathfield, NSW 2135.	187	
	NZ PO Box 27264, Mt. Roskill, Auckland 4.	89	
	Singapore c/o PO Box 185, Colombo Court Post Office, 9117.	4§	
	Hong Kong Block D, Flat 2003, Amoy Gardens, 77 Ngau Tau Kok Rd., Kowloon.	2	
WRMF	**World Radio Missionary Fellowship, Inc.** (Radio **HCJB**)		310
	USA PO Box 3000, Opa Locka, FL 33055.	260	
	NZ PO Box 27-172, Auckland 4.	25†	
	UK 7 West Bank, Dorking, Surrey RH4 3BZ	16	
WT	**Worldteam**		272
	USA PO Box 143038, Coral Gables, FL 33114.	250	
WV	**World Vision International**		(?)80
	USA 919 W. Huntington Dr., Monrovia, CA 91016.	35*	
	Can. 6630 Turner Valley Rd., Mississauga, Ontario L5N 2S4.		
	Aust. PO Box 399 C, Melbourne, Vic. 3001.		
	NZ PO Box 1923, Auckland 1.	17†	
YWAM	**Youth With A Mission**		4,600
	USA Int. HQ, 75-5851 Kuakini Highway, Kailua-Kona, HI 96740		
	Office of the Americas, Box 4600, Tyler, TX 75712.		
	UK 13 Highfield Oval, Ambrose Lane, Harpenden Herts. AL5 4BX.	133	
	NZ PO Box 13-580, Auckland 6.	250	
	Netherlands Samaritan's Inn, Prins Hendrikkade 50, 1012 AC Amsterdam.		
	Singapore PO Box 246, 118 Fidelio St., Bras Basah, Singapore 9118.		
TOTAL Missionaries in these 94 agencies			40,112

APPENDIX 3

OTHER ABBREVIATIONS

a	affiliated Christians
ABFMS	American Baptist Foreign Mission Society (USA)
ABWE	Association of Baptists for World Evangelization
AIC	African Independent Church(es)
AME	African Methodist Episcopal Church
AMG	American Mission to Greeks
ASEAN	Assoc. of South East Asian Nations
Ang.	Anglican
BCC	Bible Correspondence Course(s)
BEM	Borneo Ev. Fellowship — see **OMF**
Bi	Bible
BMM	Baptist Mid-Missions
CAPRO	See Calvary Ministries (**CM**, Nigeria)
CCAP	Church of Central Africa, Presbyterian
Ch	Church
CIM	China Inland Mission; now **OMF**
CMJ	Church Mission to the Jews (Anglican)
CMML	Christian Missions in Many Lands, see **Brethren**
CNEC	Christian Nationals Evangelism Commission
CNI	Church of North India
CSI	Church of South India
DRC	Dutch Reformed Church (South Africa, Netherlands)
EEC	European Economic Community
EHC	Every Home Crusade — see **WLC**
EiD	Evangelism in Depth — see p. 475
EKD	Evangelische Kirche in Deutschland (Germany)
EMF	European Missionary Fellowship
Ev	Evangelical
FEBIAS	Far East Bible Institute and Seminary (Philippines)
FMPB	Friends Missionary Prayer Band (India)
GDR	German Democratic Republic (East Germany)
HCJB	Radio Voice of the Andes (**WRMF**, Ecuador) IEP
IEP	Iglesia Evangelica Peruana (**EUSA**, **SIM**, **RBMU**)
IFCG	International Church of the Foursquare Gospel
Ind.	Independent
JW	Jehovah's Witnesses
LMS	London Missionary Society (UK)
m	members
MB	Mission Biblique (France/Switzerland)
MKs	Missionaries' children
NATO	North Atlantic Treaty Organization
NGK	Nederduits Gereformeerde Kerk — (Dutch Reformed Church, S. Africa)
NLFA	New Life For All
NLM	Norwegian Lutheran Mission
NT	New Testament
PEMS	Paris Evangelical Missionary Society; now DEFAP
por	portion (of Bible)
RC	Roman Catholic
$	USA dollars
SAM	South American Mission
SDA	Seventh Day Adventist Church
SFM	Swedish Free Mission

SIB	Sidang Injil Borneo (Malaysia, BEM-OMF)
SwAM	Swedish Alliance Mission
sq.km.	square kilometres
TEE	Theological Education by Extension — see p. 478
TSPM	Three Self Patriotic Movement (China)
UCCF	Universities and Colleges Christian Fellowship (IFES)
UK	United Kingdom of Great Britain and Northern Ireland
UN	United Nations
USPG	United Society for the Propagation of the Gospel (Anglican)
UVM	Upper Volta Mission (Burkina Faso)
WCE	*World Christian Encyclopedia*
YFC	Youth For Christ
YMCA	Young Men's Christian Association
ZEM-NM	Zambesi Evangelical Mission — Nyasa Mission (Malawi)

APPENDIX 4

DEFINITIONS

Here are a few definitions of terms used throughout the book that could be otherwise misunderstood.

adherent. A follower of a particular religion, church or philosophy. This is the broadest possible category of such followers, and includes professing, affiliated adults and children (practising and non-practising) who may reside in a given area or country. As it refers to those who, if not under coercion, would take the name of a religion (i.e. nominal adherents), it is the only figure that can be used to adequately compare the relative numbers of different religions and Christian traditions.

adult members. Adult church members of over 12-18 years of age (depending on the denomination) who are communicants or full members. In the church statistics in ***Operation World*** the letter 'm' is used to signify adult members.

affiliated Christians. All who are considered as belonging to organized churches. This includes full members, their children and other occasional attenders who would see themselves as part of the Church community. These figures represent the whole Christian community or inclusive membership. In this book the letter 'a' is used to signify affiliated Christians.

Black theology. Christian theology as interpreted from the viewpoint of the oppressed Black race.

born-again believer. Those who by grace and through faith in the atoning work of Christ have been regenerated by the Holy Spirit. However, in common usage it often refers to those who testify to an evangelical conversion experience.

Church (with capital C). A particular denomination, or the universal Church at a national or worldwide level. Where a denomination's name is followed by initials in brackets, the parent mission is indicated (this is to identify the ecclesiastical origin or current affiliation for the reader, and does not mean present control!).

church (with a small c) a local fellowship of believers. The starting of such churches is termed church planting. The word is commonly used to mean a church building or church service, but here this usage has been avoided.

cross-cultural missionaries. Full-time Christian workers sent by their churches to work among peoples of a different culture, either within their own nations or abroad.

ethnolinguistic people. An ethnic or racial group speaking its own language. A people group identified by its evident ethnicity or language.

Evangelicals. The subdivision of Protestantism (including Anglicans and non-Western evangelical groups) which generally emphasize:

1. Commitment to a personal faith and emphasis on personal conversion or new birth.

2. A recognition of the inspired Word of God as the only basis for faith and Christian living.

3. Biblical preaching and evangelism.

Note: The definition of Evangelicals and the statistics relating to them are so fundamental to the contents of this book, that it is important for the reader to understand the implications. It is a helpful measure of the size and spectacular numerical growth of evangelical Christians over the last few decades.

The noun "Evangelical" is capitalized since it represents a body of Christians with a fairly clearly defined theology (as also Orthodox and Catholic bodies etc.) Evangelicals are here defined as:

1. All affiliated Christians (church members, their children, etc.) of denominations that are evangelical in theology as defined above.

2. The proportion of the affiliated Christians in other Protestant denominations and Anglican dioceses (that are not wholly evangelical in theology) who would hold evangelical views.

3. The proportion of affiliated Christians in denominations in non-Western nations (where doctrinal positions are less well defined) that would be regarded as Evangelicals by those in the above categories.

Note: This is a theological and not experiential definition. It does *not* mean:

1. That all Evangelicals as defined above are actually born-again. In many nations only 10-40% of Evangelicals so defined may have had a valid conversion and also regularly attend church services. However, it does show how many people align themselves with churches where the gospel is being proclaimed.

2. That it is impossible for Christians of other traditions to be born-again, for an increasing number of Catholics, Orthodox and others have a clear testimony to a personal meeting with the Lord and hold an evangelical position regarding the Bible.

evangelize. To spread the good news of Jesus Christ, persuading and convincing people to obey Him as Lord in the fellowship of His Church, and to serve Him responsibly in the world.

evangelized. The state of having had the gospel spread or offered in such a way that the hearer becomes aware of the claims of Christ, and the need to obey and follow Him. Possibly between one billion and 1.9 billion have been exposed to the gospel, but are not linked with any Christian church.

liberation theology. Christian theology redefined on the basis of Marxist presuppositions of society and social change.

marginal groups. A general term used in this book to describe all semi-Christian or fringe groups, sects and cults that accept certain Christian features, and parts of the Scriptures, together with supplementary divine revelations. Most claim that they alone have the 'truth'.

missionary. One who is sent with a message. This word of Latin derivation has the same basic meaning as the wider use of the term 'apostle' in the New Testament which is derived from Greek. The Christian missionary is one commissioned by a local church to evangelize, plant churches and disciple people away from his home area, and often among people of a different race, culture or language. Modern usage is rather different. We now use this term for all those who are sent across cultural barriers for Christian service of any kind, even though they may not necessarily be apostles in the biblical sense.

people group. A significantly large sociological grouping of individuals who perceive themselves to have a common affinity with one another. From the viewpoint of evangelization, this is the largest possible group within which the gospel can be spread without encountering barriers of understanding or acceptance. There are basically three types:

1. **Ethnolinguistic people group** which defines a person's identity and primary loyalty according to language and/or ethnicity. This is the category that has been emphasized in this book. **Cross-cultural** church planting teams of missionaries are needed for people groups in this category. Of the estimated 12,000 ethnolinguistic people groups, probably almost 9,000 already have at least one or two viable indigenous churches within their culture.

2. **Sociological people group** — a grouping which, to some degree, is subject to personal choice and allows for considerable mobility. Regional and generational groups, and caste and class divisions are representative of such people groups. In most cases local church outreach is required — either to plant daughter churches or to incorporate converts into multi-social congregations. There are probably hundreds of thousands of such people groups.

3. **Incidental people groups** — casual associations of individuals which may be temporary, and usually the result of circumstances rather than personal choice. Examples of such groups are high-rise flat dwellers, drug addicts, occupational groupings, commuters, etc. These groupings present unique problems and opportunities for evangelism, but only rarely will it be appropriate for specific churches to be planted for the sole benefit of such groups.

people movement. A movement of a large number of non-Christians in a particular people group into the Church. This is frequently a group decision. It presents a wonderful opportunity to win and disciple many for the Lord by leading them into a personal faith in the Lord Jesus Christ. Failure to do so can soon lead to nominalism or syncretism.

reached/unreached. A term that is widely used today to describe people groups and areas that have or have not responded to the preaching of the gospel. This wide use of the term has been continued in this book, despite the faultiness of the terminology. Strictly, it should be a measure of the **exposure** of a people group to the gospel, and not a measure of the **response**.

renewal. A quickening or enlivening in personal commitment to Christ in the churches. Charismatic renewal in the historic denominations is an example.

revival. The restoring to life of believers and churches which have previously experienced the regenerating power of the Holy Spirit, but have become cold, worldly and ineffective. The word is often wrongly used of evangelistic campaigns, but it really means a sovereign act of God in bringing about a religious awakening and outpouring of the Spirit on His people.

unreached people group: a people group among whom there is no viable indigenous community of believing Christians with adequate numbers and resources to evangelize their own people group without outside (cross-cultural) assistance. Other researchers have adopted the terms "hidden peoples" or "frontier people groups".

APPENDIX 5

CHURCH STATISTICS

Since the publication of the last edition of ***Operation World*** a large amount of new research data and denominational statistics have been gathered. The publication in 1982 of the ***World Christian Encyclopedia*** was a pivotal event in Christian research. The volume and variety of information in the WCE continues to astonish and bewilder many!

We made the decision to incorporate all the available church statistics from 1960 onwards in a large computer database in order to more accurately assess the growth of the Church in every country of the world. This proved a massive undertaking which was both frustrating and rewarding. The results are the basis of the church statistics in this volume. Our frustrations included the following:

1. The confusion in terminology of what constitutes church membership. Worldwide agreement on what constitutes adult membership, inclusive membership/affiliated members, church attendance, etc., would be of inestimable value in assessing the health of the Church in the future!
2. The failure of many churches and denominations to keep adequate statistics forced us to make many approximations.
3. The absence of the date and sources of denominational statistics in the WCE. Our own independently gathered information enabled us to modify or crosscheck many of the WCE figures.

4. Worship service attendance figures would give a far more realistic indication of the degree of commitment of Christians affiliated with the churches, but only rarely are such statistics available. In some large mainline denominations only two to three per cent of the inclusive membership go to church services regularly, and yet in others attendance figures are larger than church membership!

The size of our computer system limited the amount of interactive data that could be entered. Of the 22,189 denominations in the world (WCE 1985) we were able to enter statistics on over 3,300 of the more significant ones and make totals of the remainder. Even so, we have made over 120,000 data entries!

The purpose of the data base is:

1. To make church growth projections to June 1985.
2. To make national regional and world totals for the six ecclesiological types.
3. To analyse the strength and growth of the evangelical movement.

Modifications to the WCE approach: The sophisticated statistical analysis of the WCE has had to be greatly simplified for such a volume as this. However the WCE gave us a valuable starting point for the construction of our denominational database. We have made the following adaptations:

1. The seven ecclesiological types of the WCE have been slightly adjusted. The seven types are Anglican, Catholic (non-Roman), Non-White indigenous, Marginal Protestant, Orthodox, Protestant and Roman Catholic.
   a) Anglicans have been included with Protestants.
   b) 'Non-White indigenous' is a classification based on non-Western origin of such denominations — a useful concept to quantify the strength and variety of such movements, but not adequate for our purposes. These denominations have been redistributed among the other ecclesiological types according to church structure and doctrine, — and only more marginal or syncretic non-Western groups have been retained under this classification so that the term becomes 'non-Western indigenous marginal'.
2. We have only retained the concept of professing Christians (those known to the government or public as such) and affiliated Christians (those known to the churches). We have adjusted the statistics of professing and affiliated Christians to allow for dual membership, secret believers, etc.
3. We have not quantified the charismatic or neo-pentecostal movement within non-Pentecostal denominations.

Please refer to the WCE for more information.

The data entered:

1. The name, ecclesiastical type and denominational family of most significant denominations.
2. The adult church membership and/or inclusive (affiliated) membership for each denomination in six five-yearly periods between 1960 and 1985. Where only one of the two figures was known, a membership-affiliation ratio, unique to that denomination, was used to calculate the other. Where no statistics for a given period were available, growth curves from known data and local trends were plotted and any intermediate data gaps filled in with estimates. The date and source of every statistic was also entered into the database.
3. The percentage of Evangelicals was derived as follows:
   a) **Conservative evangelical denominations** were entered as 100% evangelical, i.e. all those affiliated with such denominations would be totalled as Evangelicals.
   b) **Pluralistic denominations** (those with a variety of theological views other than evangelical — such as sacramentalist, liberal, etc.). The estimated percentage of Evangelicals in the denomination in 1960 was entered, and then used to calculate Evangelicals affiliated with all Protestant denominations in each nation.
   c) Where there has been a known increase or decline in the percentage of Evangelicals within a particular denomination, this was allowed for by the entry of a further positive or negative incremental percentage figure.

The complete print-out of the data and derived results for every country in the world is available on microfiche.

APPENDIX 6

STATISTICAL SOURCES

A complete bibliography is impossible to provide here! Only some of the more significant sources can be given.

Primary sources

1. **Personal correspondence**. We have sent out approximately 4,000 — 5,000 letters for information or checking the manuscript.

2. **Numerous surveys, documents, interviews with individuals, magazines (secular and religious), as well as circulars and reports**. Much of the more significant information gathered has been collated in subject and date order and is available on microfiche for those who request fuller information. (70 frames per fiche; requiring a fiche reader with 24x magnification lens.) Fuller details are obtainable from the International Research Office, WEC International, Bulstrode, Gerrards Cross, Bucks. SL9 8SZ, England.

Secondary sources

The preferred source in the text is indicated by the order given:

1. **General**

The World in Figures (The Economist Newspaper 1984) ISBN 0 85058 064 1.
Countries of the World (2 Volumes) (Gale Research 1985) ISBN 0 8103 2117 3.
Area Handbook Series, US Government Printing Office.
Encyclopedia Brittanica (30 volumes) 15th edition 1981. ISBN 0 85229 378 X.

2. **Religious**

The World Christian Encyclopedia, David B. Barrett, Ed. (Oxford University Press 1982) ISBN 0 19 572435 6.
The World Christian Handbooks 1962, 1967. World Dominion Press, London, UK.
The World Christianity Series. Volumes 1-5. 1979-1985 **MARC.**

3. **Statistics for specific topics**

Area	***The World in Figures*** (see above).
Population	***World Population Data Sheet*** (1985). Population Reference Bureau, Box 35012, Washington, DC 20013, USA. World Population Prospects as assessed in 1980 (UN 1981).
Peoples	Government censuses where an ethnic or linguistic question was asked. ***World Christian Encyclopedia.*** ***Unreached Peoples Annuals*** 1979, 1980, 1981, 1982, 1983, 1984. **MARC**, USA.
Literacy	Government census where available. **UBS** Annual Report 1984. ***World Christian Encyclopedia.***
Languages	***Ethnologue*** Tenth Edition, Barbara F. Grimes, Ed. (WBT/**SIL** 1984) ISBN 0 88312 597 8.
Bible translation	***Ethnologue*** 1984. ***World Translations Progress Report*** **UBS** (1980).
Income/Person	***World Population Data Sheet*** 1985. Figures valid for 1983.
Urban statistics	United Nations. ***World Population Data Sheet*** 1985. ***Patterns of Urban and Rural Population Growth*** (UN 1980).

Religion	Denominational statistics (where obtainable). ***World Christian Encyclopedia.*** National surveys, handbooks, etc. from numerous countries. Church Growth books, Wm. Carey Libary, etc. ***World Christianity Series.***
Missions	***North American Protestant Ministries Overseas,*** Samuel Wilson, Ed., **MARC** 1980. ISBN 0 912552 1 34 4. ***UK Christian Handbook*** 1985/86, Peter Brierley, Ed. MARC Europe. ISBN 0 947697 03 9. ***The Last Age of Missions,*** Lawrence E. Keyes, William Carey Library, 1983. ISBN 0 87808 4355.